The Theft Of Art
and
The End Of Time

Michael R. Ludovici

ISBN: 978-1-4033-6864-5 (sc)
ISBN: 978-1-4033-6863-8 (e)

Print information available on the last page.

This book is printed on acid free paper.

1stBooks – rev. 05/28/03

I have been –

"Still, I must tell you the truth:
it is for your own good that I am going
because unless I go,
the Advocate will not come to you;
but if I do go,
I will send him to you.
And when he comes,
he will show the world how wrong it was,
about sin,
and about who was in the right,
and about judgment:
about sin:
proved by their refusal to believe in me;
about who was in the right:
proved by my going to the Father
and your seeing me no more;
about judgment:
proved by the prince of this world being already condemned.
I still have many things to say to you
but they would be too much for you now.
But when the Spirit of truth comes
he will lead you to the complete truth,
since he will not be speaking as from himself
but he will say only what he has learned;
and he will tell you of the things to come.
He will glorify me,
since all he tells you
will be taken from what is mine.
Everything the Father has is mine;
that is why I said:
All he tells you
will be taken from what is mine."
John 16: 7-15

Sent with this message: This is the end of time, and everybody is going to
die: soon. But that's not the worst part. The worst part, is that the vast majority of
mankind, while at this point in time, and while upon the threshold of the 21st century,
has allowed their own selves to become a victim of a con: the greatest collective con
in the entire history of mankind. Which has enabled them: the majority of mankind,
to actually become capable of selling their souls, and also incapable of even caring.
Here's why.

The beginning of the theft of art: or the con that is now capable of being defined as art, did begin with the very beginning a mankind's recording of time, and with the birth of two-dimensional art. Which was as Paleolithic man, did start to produce two-dimensional illustrations while being projected upon – and/or drawn upon, the walls of their caves. The illustrations were then communicable: while existing as a projected abstraction from within reality, to any other person who had, also, enabled themselves to become capable of forming an understanding of our truly humanistic environment, and too which was while actually occurring within their own individual uniquely humanistic mind. Within which: a human being's mind, there does actually exist no projected images of any tangible form masses, and/or any images of any things whatsoever. While these renderings, which were simply drawn upon their individual cave man walls, are testimony to mankind's ability to become capable of forming truly humanistic self-consciousness. As they became capable of communicating an acquired understanding of their deliberate earthly existence within Reality. This acknowledged understanding of Reality, and the fact that there does exist no projected images of things within our uniquely humanistic minds, does then enable us to begin to prove the scientific fact that if a picture – any picture, does not contain a projected representation of a humanistic reality: actually represented upon it and such as any asinine Cubist picture, it can, exactly, not be defined as a representation of intelligence. And as a matter of scientific fact, it can only be defined as a representation of truly humanistic brain death, and/or brainwashing.

Because, there would be made manifest countless two-dimensional plane pictures, while functioning as a simple communicative apparatus and as a representation of reality, throughout the recorded history of mankind's existence. But none was ever capable of being defined as the manifestation of a noble art, and/or intelligence, while existing as the abstracted, and reapplied, function, of science, music, or mathematics, and as was practiced by noble intellectuals such as Plato, Euclid, and Pythagoras, and too while capable of existing as the absolute truth within reality, as the word science does simply mean truth. Until the dawn of the Renaissance, and the rebirth of mankind's awareness of his deliberate earthly position within reality, while as directly relative to his formed understanding of a more complex order, which does actually enable our very humanistic existence upon this point-mass of Earth. As mankind did, then and only with the dawn of the Renaissance, begin to become capable of entering into the fourth dimension of Time. The result of which did, then, enable mankind to become capable of substantiating his possible acquired belief in a more divinely purposeful existence, while being made manifest as uniquely humanistic multidimensional effectual causes. And too, which: while capable of functioning as a concordant polyphonically structured whole, is while functioning as complex Time *made manifest*, and/or – in simple English: HARMONY.

1

While, the rebirth of mankind's awareness: of his deliberate earthly position within reality, was ushered in at the point in time when the architect Fillipo Brunelleschi introduced, to mankind, his own personal formed understanding of a single truly humanistic differential, and/or truly humanistic variable: and/or pattern in space/time, as he abstracted it from within four-dimensional reality: which was as he identified a single point located within the depth of space, to begin his formed understanding. Brunelleschi did then project his abstracted understanding upon a two-dimensional plane exactly as Paleolithic man had, and while being simply defined as a picture, and too which did occur while in the year 1413. But this was the very first picture, to every show a mathematically accurate representation of a single, completed, harmoniously proportioned volume of identifiable humanistic space, while being projected upon a two-dimensional plane: upon which there can be NO three-dimensional space. This reapplied understanding did then enable Brunelleschi to represent the depth of space while he was functioning in a truly, and uniquely, humanistic manner: as he abstracted his formed understanding from within his mind, and projected it upon a two-dimensional plane. And too while he did become capable of accurately representing an abstracted understanding of elementary "perspective," and/or elementary Time *made manifest*: and/or a single pattern in space/time, while being abstracted, and projected, as from a single point time zero, located within identifiable humanistic space. Also, of course, the Renaissance would give rise to a number of relatively intelligent human beings, who were endowed with the ability to comprehend some of the relatively complex functions of our humanistic environment, and, then, to reapply their acquired understanding of reality while as through intellectual and cultural endeavors. Such as the architect Brunelleschi, the mathematician Alhazan, and the artist Leon Baptista Alberti, who would write the world's first significant artistic treastise. Within which was contained a detailed explanation of Brunelleschi's reapplied understanding, and: while being simply defined as elementary perspective, which was while capable of functioning as elementary Time *made manifest*, and/or purposefully directed movement from point A to point B: actually within space, while beginning to make manifest Time.

This same artistic treatise was read by the scientist Leonardo da Vinci, as he was beginning to learn how to expand upon Alberti's communicated understanding of Reality. Which did, then: as he expanded upon Alberti's understanding and while actually making manifest Time, enable Leonardo da Vinci to become capable of reapplying his formed understanding of complex Time *made manifest*, as he became capable of making manifest the world's first, and only, literal visual musical equivalency, and which was while he did project it upon a two-dimensional plane. While, we can simply understand this little known, or – rather, absolutely unknown, scientific fact: the existence of a single visual musical equivalency which NO ONE knows exists, by simply reiterating our acknowledged understanding of exactly what a REAL musical symphony, and/or orchestration, "is": within identifiable scientific Reality. That is the applicable function of, and exactly as was explained by

Leonardo da Vinci; "True sciences are – the principles of mathematics, that is to say, number and measure – termed arithmetic and geometry, which deal with discontinuous and continuous quantities with the utmost truth. Here no one hazards guesses as to whether two threes makes more or less than six" – pure math, and/or the real applied function of harmoniously proportioned simultaneously relative differentials, and/or variables. Which is, simply, exactly what a concordant polyphonically structured whole is: an orchestration *of* musical sounds, and/or many patterns in space/time.

This literal visual musical equivalency, and/or patterns in space/time, is exactly what Leonardo da Vinci did project upon a two-dimensional plane, and which could – then, function as a communicated understanding, which has been abstracted from within four-dimensional reality, just as musical notation is capable of being projected upon a two-dimensional plane, and just as musical notation is capable of being communicated as a formed understanding of Reality. But, of course, just as musical notation: written on and across a two-dimensional plane, must be converted back into an actual perceivable four-dimensional function, so too this literal visual musical equivalency must be converted back into an actual perceivable and effectual function. Which is the function of visual harmoniously proportioned variables and/or patterns in space/time, while capable of functioning, and being identified, as simultaneously to/from, and within, a single point time zero, located within identifiable truly humanistic space. And, again, which is the applicable function of; "True sciences are – the principles of mathematics, that is to say, number and measure – termed arithmetic and geometry, which deal with discontinuous and continuous quantities with the utmost truth" – pure identifiable math, pure identifiable science, and the absolute truth, and while capable of being identified as mathematical formulas. The formulas, and/or universally applicable: not rhetorical, but ACTUALLY UNIVERSALLY APPLICABLE AND FROM ONE END OF THE UNIVERSE TO THE OTHER, communicable language, for which, is only capable of being accessed as individual human beings do enable themselves to become capable of forming an understanding of complex Time *made manifest,* while occurring within an individual human being's electrical potential mass of a mind, and within which there are contained no projected images of things. But, primarily, differential and geometrical equations, and/or discontinuous and continuous quantities. As they are made manifest, and actually functioning, while being projected as simultaneously relative to/from, and within, a single cognizable point time zero, and which are then capable of functioning as the basic mathematical formula for the formation of a literal visual musical equivalency: such as Leonardo da Vinci's.

In addition, Leonardo da Vinci's one, and absolutely unknown, literal visual musical equivalency, which is made manifest within the two-dimensional projected abstraction termed *The Annunciation*, is also the literal Holy Grail of Understanding, and/or The Missing piece to the puzzle that we human beings do call civilization. As it: *The Annunciation* and/or the world's only literal visual musical equivalency, is also a literal, perceivable and effectual, space/time continuum: while actually functioning as simultaneously relative harmoniously proportioned differentials, being made manifest as simultaneously relative to/from, and within, a single cognizable point time zero, or the point of The Big Bang. Which is the exact definition of Albert Einstein's explained Theory of Relativity, and/or Reality, and/or many patterns in space/time.

Exactly as Albert Einstein did begin to become capable of explaining is what Reality is, while actually functioning as an effectuated space/time continuum, and while having first occurred as a formed understanding within Albert Einstein's own mind. Within which: any human being's mind, there does exist no projected images of any things, but only simultaneously relative differential equations. But which was a formed understanding, of Reality, that Albert Einstein had introduced to mankind only while occurring at the beginning of the 20th century, and which was 400 years after Leonardo da Vinci had already defined it: Reality, and made the abstracted and projected representation of a space/time continuum manifest as a perceivable reality. But too which was: Albert Einstein's explained theory of relativity, also occurring as mankind was led to believe that it was a brand new understanding of reality, and which is while Reality does function as a space/time continuum, and while as simultaneously to/from, and within, a single cognizable point time zero, and/or the beginning of the fourth dimension of Time. Which exactly is: a human being's ability to cognize the fourth dimension of Time and a space/time continuum, some thing, of a non-thing actually functioning as intelligence, that is –

"Neither you nor I can visualize a fourth dimension..."
Phillippe Le Corbeiller – The Curvature of Space, The New Astronomy

Supposed to be impossible to do.

Which is exactly how we can now know, for a fact, that it: the absolutely unknown and identifiable non-tangible form structure of *The Annunciation*, is the actual Holy Grail of Understanding, and the missing piece to the puzzle that is called civilization. As: but only in identifiable scientific reality, this word: civilization, does mean: "an advanced state of human society, in which a high level of culture, science, industry, and government has been reached," and to; "civilize: to make civil; bring out of a primitive or uneducated state; enlighten" – bring out of a primitive or uneducated state too, but – again, only in scientific Reality, and not in the mind of any one individual person.

And, of course, they are absolutely correct: no human being can simply see it with their eyes alone, they can only understand it: within their minds alone. Just as Christopher Columbus could not simply see that the world was not flat, and/or as simple as walking across a two-dimensional plane. But Christopher Columbus did begin to become capable of believing the truth within his mind, and which: his personal belief, did then turn into a formed understanding of Reality, within his mind. Which: his own personally formed understanding of reality and within his mind alone, did – then, become a proven fact, for all the world to simply see with our eyes alone. But only because he did go in search of it: the absolute truth and the Holy Grail of Understanding, while upon his most arduous journey as he sailed off into uncharted territories. Exactly as Leonardo da Vinci had done as he sailed off into uncharted territories, and began to become capable of proving his own personally formed understanding of Reality, for all the world – now, to simply see with our eyes alone, as he formed the world's first, and only, literal visual musical equivalency, and while in the year 1480.

      The result of which did then, and only then, enable visual art, and which means anything that is capable of being seen within our minds wherein there are no projected images of things, to acquire the title of a Noble Art. And, again, which is only exactly because it is, and exactly as Leonardo da Vinci did explain; "True sciences are (the) principles of mathematics, that is to say, number and measure – termed arithmetic and geometry, which deal with discontinuous and continuous quantities with the utmost truth" – pure identifiable Math. To understand this scientific fact, and to exactly now and as Leonardo da Vinci did also explain; "True Sciences are those which have penetrated through the senses as a result of experience and thus silencing the tongues of disputants" – silence the tongues of the disputants, we can simply, again, reiterate our understanding of exactly what a symphony, and/or an orchestration and/or a concordant polyphonically structured whole, actually is in scientific reality, and which is while we do understand that the word concord does, simply, mean: harmony. Which: an orchestration, is simply a harmonizing of individually completed harmoniously proportioned differential equations, and/or a harmonizing of individually completed projections of musical sounds: made manifest as simultaneously to/from, and within, a single point time zero, and which can be received, and perceived, within our three-dimensional electrical potential mass of a mind. Within which: a human being's three-dimensional mind, there does exist, only, simultaneously effectuated differentials, and differential equations, made manifest from everything – EVERYTHING, we do visually perceive. Which does mean, for a scientific fact, that the non-tangible form projected image of every one three-dimensional thing which we can perceive: within our electrical potential mass minds and within which there are no projected images of things, is a visual equivalency sound, *the* completed non-tangible form projected image of every one three-dimensional thing that we do perceive within our minds, and in neuroscientific reality. Now, in order for us to become capable of forming a visual symphony, and/or an orchestration, what we do need to do, and exactly as Leonardo da Vinci did explain, is to; "The harmonic proportionality – is composed simultaneously from various components" – harmonize, the perceivable non-tangible form projections. As they are made manifest, and effectual, as from every single three-dimensional thing within reality, and/or purposefully direct movement between identifiable points: of things, within simultaneously relative space/time, while beginning to make patterns in space/time, and which are made manifest as simultaneously to/from, and within, a single cognizable point time zero, and/or the point of the beginning of the orchestration, and/or the point of The Big Bang and the beginning *of* Time *made manifest*. This exact formed understanding of Reality can then be abstracted from within reality, and projected upon a two-dimensional plane, and while existing as the universally applicable Omnidimensional language of Reality: as from one end of the universe to the other and simultaneously too, and which is *The Annunciation*. It is the purest of Math, it is the purest of Universal Truths, and it is also the pinnacle antithesis of personal opinion and/or entertainment, and which: entertainment, is only an; "the act of entertaining – a diversion or amusement" – exact deviation from Reality. While this: absolute truth, is exactly how it: visual art, did begin to become capable of acquiring the title of a Noble art, by being both the absolute truth and the pinnacle antithesis of entertainment, and/or a diversion from Reality.

Which: our acknowledged understanding of scientific Reality, does simply enable us to understand exactly how the con, which is now simply capable of being defined as "art," was enabled to become perpetuated, as from the point in time when Leonardo da Vinci did become capable of transforming it. Because they did, first, tell the entire world that actually becoming capable of seeing it: the fourth dimension of Time, is impossible, and too so that it did exist only as a formed understanding of Reality within Albert Einstein's mind, which nobody can see. They also told the world that, it: the formed understanding within Albert Einstein's mind, is the pinnacle of truly humanistic conscious cognizant capabilities, and/or the pinnacle of truly humanistic intelligence, while nobody can simply see it: the pinnacle of truly humanistic intelligence and/or the formed understanding within Albert Einstein's mind. So what they did simply do, to actually become capable of affecting the con and in identifiable scientific reality only of course, was to simply tell the ENTIRE WORLD a LIE, and/or that the –

"Picasso and Einstein cross paths, and offer a mirthful night –
In the program for *Picasso at the Lapin Agile*, which opened Tuesday at the Arden Theater, the director, cast and staff pose 20 questions you might ponder after viewing the play. 'What is genius?' they ask. How does genius get recognized..."
Clifford A Ridley – The Philadelphia Inquirer – Thursday March 8, 2001

Projected abstraction of one individual human being's own personally affected, and absolutely dysfunctional, three-dimensional electrical potential mass of a mind, is the very definition of intelligence. **NO IT IS NOT**: IN IDENTIFIABLE TRULY HUMANISTIC SCIENTIFIC REALITY. It is, exactly and only, a "diversion," and/or the very definition of –

"Narrowing Search on Schizophrenia -
Schizophrenia – is characterized by apathy, delusions, disorganized thinking,
and disconnected social interactions..."
    Shanker Vendantum – The Philadelphia Inquirer – Friday April 28, 2000

Schizophrenia at least, and truly humanistic brain death at worst, and/or NO
patterns in space/time. While it: Pablo Picasso's mind and any two-dimensional
Cubist picture, is exactly the very definition of schizophrenia, as there is exactly no
such thing as a two-dimensional Cubist thing in Reality, and it: any Cubist thing,
was only the projected abstraction of Pablo Picasso's; "characterized by apathy,
delusions, disorganized thinking, and disconnected social interactions" – absolutely
abstracted, delusional and fragmented, childish imagination, and in truly humanistic
identifiable scientific reality. Within which: a truly humanistic being's mind and
Reality, there can, exactly, exist no such thing as a two-dimensional Cubist thing,
unless it: a human being's mind, is schizophrenic.
    And while all truly intelligent human beings must have empathy for
schizophrenics, we sure, as hell, better not give them the Key to the Kingdom, and/or
the asylum either, because – then, everybody dies, including the schizophrenics,
and/or the ones who are providing the diversion, and/or entertainers too. And too,
but only in neuroscientific reality and within any one individual human being's mind
that has already begun to become affected, there is – exactly, no such thing as
a "fine line between intelligence and insanity." It is –

"Dr David Pickar: Dealing with the cortex of a schizophrenic is an
unbelievable thing. It's alien, yet there are these essential moments when you know
a patient well and you can peak into that world. It's an abyss – empty..."
    The 3-Pound Universe – Judith Hooper and Dick Teresi

    A huge abyss.
    Which is simple to understand, now and only exactly because of
neuroscience, by: simply, understanding this scientific fact, and which is the fact
that Leonardo da Vinci, did –

"Leonardo tended to string ideas together with chains of 'whichs,' 'ands,'
'becauses,' 'hences' and so on, often with sustained assides and sometimes without
clearly returning to the home base of discussion – some of the structures he used
became so tangled as to obscure his meaning – they do not always make for easy
reading..."
    Martin Kemp – Introduction to Leonardo on Painting

    Appear to be: almost, exactly similar to –

"Ernst Hanfstaengl, describes the shapelessness at the root of Hitler's mesmerizing oratorical power: 'His brain was a sort of primeval jelly or ectoplasm which quivered in response to every impulse from its surroundings – You could never pin him down, say that he was this thing or that thing, it was all floating, without roots, intangible and mediumistic – Momentum had driven him into an extreme position from which there was no escape – What has been so far the ultimate violence in human history can also be considered as a ghastly kind of artistic production – performance art at its largest – impressing upon an otherwise inattentive public certain feelings and ideas – He was a tremendous salesman of ideas..."

Michael Nelken M.D. – Hitler Unmasked

Adolf Hitler: but only within the mind of any one individual that has, already, allowed themselves to begin to become affected, and a victim of the con, and which is the beginning of the end of time.

Because, it is simply impossible to duplicate the extreme truly humanistic conscious cognizant capabilities, of a truly humanistic being three-dimensional electrical potential mass of a mind, and parallel functioning central nervous system, in an absolutely abstracted manner of any kind, and/or while as in a unidirectional manner of any kind. NO WORDS; NO MUSIC; NO NOTHING, can duplicate it: the possible extreme conscious cognizant capabilities of a truly humanistic being's mind, and parallel functioning central nervous system, and/or Reality. And which does mean: in identifiable scientific reality only, that words, and/or any thing besides consciously cognizing space/time continuums, are exactly a constraint for a truly intelligent humanistic being mind, while – simultaneously, they: words and/or any thing besides consciously cognizing a space/time continuum, are only exactly nothing more than "fuel for the fire," and/or a sign of truly humanistic dysfunction, and/or brain death: within an individual humanistic being mind that is beginning to become incapable of understanding Reality. And within which: a truly humanistic being's parallel functioning mind and central nervous system *and* Reality, there are contained no projected images of things, but only purposefully effectuated simultaneously relative differential equations. And, only in simultaneously relative Reality, which: the purposefully effectuated simultaneously relative differential equations, are expanded into a simultaneously relative hierarchically structured whole, while actually effectually functioning as a space/time continuum: which is purposefully effectuated while as through the universally applicable function of quantized electrodynamics, and while as simultaneously to/from, and within, a purposefully effectuated single cognizable point time zero, which is "Relativity." And which is, also, exactly why Reality is divine, and as this word: divine, does *only* mean: "relating to or being God," and/or and exactly as Leonardo da Vinci did explain while in the year 1480 –

"Think to comprehend the mind of God which embraces the whole universe."

Consciously cognizing an Omnidimensional space/time continuum, and/or patterns in space/time, that is: the absolute extreme of purposefully effectuated truly humanistic conscious cognizant capabilities. But only while actually functioning as applied simultaneously relative quantum electrodynamics, and as simultaneously to/from, and within, a single purposefully effectuated, and simultaneously relative, truly humanistic point time zero, and which exactly can not be simply seen with our eyes alone: it can only be understood, within our minds alone. And too which does mean, that we: the entire world, can now know, and for a verified scientific fact, that there is a –

"Candace Pert – I see the brain in terms of quantum mechanics – the brain is just a receiver, an amplifier, a little wet minireceiver for collective reality. We make maps, but we should never confuse the map with the territory...the ratio of frontal core (cerebral cortex) to the rest of the cortex may be one index of evolutionary advancement. Do these lobes govern some essential feature of humanness, or even godliness, as some scientists have suggested? 'If God speaks to man, if man speaks to God,' neuroscientist Candace Pert tells us, it would be through the frontal lobes..."
The 3-Pound Universe – Judith Hooper and Dick Teresi

God. Because He did "talk back." Which is exactly *The Annunciation*. But, of course, which is also, exactly, incapable of being simply seen with our eyes alone, it can only be understood: while actually occurring within our truly humanistic three-dimensional, and quantum dynamical, electrical potential mass minds. And, just like a real symphony and as was exactly explained by Wolfgang Amadeus Mozart –

"Once I have my theme, another melody comes, linking itself with the first one, in accordance with the needs of the composition as a whole – Then my soul is on fire with inspiration. The work grows; I keep expanding it, and conceiving it more and more clearly until I have the entire composition finished in my head though it may be long – It does not come to me successively, with various parts worked out in detail, as they will later on, but in its entirety."
Wolfgang Amadeus Mozart – Roger Penrose – The Emperor's New Mind

Which can only be understood within our minds alone. As simultaneously to/from, and within, a single purposefully effectuated, and cognizable, point time zero: the simultaneously relative non-tangible form synthetical structuring, while actually functioning as quantized electrodynamics, and too which: the actual simultaneously relative, and cognizable, non-tangible form structure, is, only, exactly what is capable of causing a fire in a truly humanistic being's soul, as they begin their journey throughout, and within, simultaneously relative space/time. And as was EXACTLY experienced by –

"Thomas Jefferson: Those which depend on ourselves, are the only pleasures a wise man will count on: for nothing is ours, which another may deprive us of. Hence the inestimable alum of intellectual pleasures. Ever in our power, always leading us to something new, never cloying, we ride serene and sublime above the concerns of this mortal world, contemplating truth and nature, matter and motion, the laws which bind up their existence, and that Eternal Being who made and bound them by those laws...Put into one scale the pleasures which any object may offer; but put fairly into the other, the pains which are to follow, and see which preponderates – Let this be our employ. Leave the bustle and the tumult of society to those who have not talents to occupy themselves without them..."
    Thomas Jefferson: letter to Mrs. Cosway – The Life and Selected Writings of Thomas Jefferson – Edited by Adrienne Koch and William Peden

Thomas Jefferson: as he did allow himself to become capable of traveling throughout, and within, a space/time continuum, while experiencing the Mind of God, and His laws too.
    Which does enable us now, only exactly because of 20th century neuroscientific research, to know, exactly, how we can prove the fact of the function of the structure which is *The Annunciation*. That is exactly because, and just like a real symphony, it is simply pure math, and it is simply pure truth, so we can absolutely –

"Cracking the Cosmic Code With a Little Help From Dr. Hawking –
...Dr Hawking's first book for a wide audience, 'A Brief History of Time,' took readers on a tour through black holes, the gravitational traps from which not even light can emerge, and imaginary time as he described the quest for the vaunted 'theory of everything' that would enable us to 'know the mind of God'...quantum theory and relativity have taught us, science is about what can be observed and measured or it is about nothing at all. In science, as in democracy, there is no hidden secret knowledge, all that counts is on the table, observable and falsifiable. All else is metaphysics."
    Dennis Overbye – The New York Times – Tuesday December 11, 2001

Identify it: the "non-tangible form synthetical structure," actually functioning as Omnidimensional Time *made manifest*. Which is, actually, the very definition of the function of purposefully effectuated simultaneously relative quantized electrodynamics, subservient to a hierarchically structured whole, and/or The Mind of God made manifest, and too exactly what that means: in identifiable scientific reality, and for all the world to simply see with our eyes alone. As we can now, FINALLY, reveal only the absolute scientific truth, and for the entire world to simply see with our eyes alone: AS WE CAN – NOW, "CRACK THE COSMIC CODE" WHICH IS THE "MIND OF GOD MADE MANIFEST," and exactly as was explained by Leonardo da Vinci while in the year 1480: "True sciences are those which have penetrated through the senses as a result of experience and thus silencing the tongues of disputants, not feeding investigators on dreams but always proceeding successively from primary truths and established principles, in a proper order towards the conclusion. This may be witnessed (only) in the principles of mathematics, that is to say, number and measure – termed arithmetic and geometry, which deal with discontinuous and continuous quantities with the utmost truth...Here all guesswork remains destroyed in eternal silence, and these sciences are enjoyed by their devotees in peace, which is not possible with the delusory sciences of a wholly cerebral kind."

Which does enable us to; "Leonardo tended to string ideas together with chains of 'whichs,' 'ands,' 'becauses,' 'hences' and so on, often with sustained asides and sometimes without clearly returning to the home base of discussion" – return to the home base of discussion, and come full circle to the beginning of the birth, and theft, of art, the con which is now simply defined as art, and to the beginning of Time *made manifest*. And to explain exactly why this: the revealing of the absolute truth for all the world to simply see with our eyes alone, is the beginning of the end of time, while along with revealing the greatest collective con in the entire history of mankind, and, too, which: the con, has: at this point in time while upon the threshold of the 21st century, affected the overwhelming vast majority of mankind. Which is: that we can now prove and for a scientific fact that this is the greatest collective con in the entire history of mankind and that this is the beginning of the end of time, only exactly because of our allowed access to 20th century scientific research.

To enable ourselves to fully understand this fact: which is the fact that everything, and while including truly humanistic dysfunction, can now be explained to be a fact, we can simply reiterate our understanding of Christopher Columbus' formed understanding, of simultaneously relative Reality. And the absolute scientific fact, that the entire world did actually believe: within their individual minds alone, that the world was flat, before Christopher Columbus could become capable of proving the fact: of Reality, and which did – then, enable them: the entire world, to simply see the absolute truth with their eyes alone. So, Christopher Columbus did allow himself to begin to become capable of forming a belief about Reality within his mind, but which was exactly contrary to the dogmatic human interpretations of the majority of the world, and/or all of the individuals who simply did not want to look at Reality. And/or, all of the individuals who simply did not want to risk a journey into uncharted territory, as they simply wanted to allow themselves to remain a part of the In Crowd, and/or the absolutely abstracted from Reality crowd. So: exactly what was "it" that they were so afraid of? What they were afraid of, was the absolute truth, and/or scientific Reality. Simply because, the absolute truth is, and exactly as Thomas Jefferson did explain; "Put into one scale the pleasures which any object may offer; but put fairly into the other, the pains which are to follow, and see which preponderates" – very – *very* painful. And, sometimes, it: the absolute truth, can be very difficult to find, but he: Christopher Columbus, did do it, and he did also exactly find it: the truth and/or The Holy Grail of Understanding, for himself too, because he went and found it for himself. Which was only exactly because he did, and as Leonardo da Vinci did explain –

"You can have neither a greater nor a less dominion than that over yourself."

Take control of his own self, and his own destiny too. Which did – then and as he took control of his own destiny, allow Christopher Columbus to acquire the Holy Grail of understanding for his own self: to be in possession of intelligence, and control of his own destiny, for his own self. So, what did the the Monarch get: some stuff, and some access to absolutely abstracted effectual stimulus, and/or some absolutely abstracted knowledge, and apathy too, and which was to simply feed her addiction: to worldly power, and truly humanistic brain death only. And – too, which was exactly enabled: her ability to gain access to some stuff and her truly humanistic brain death also, simply because she did have control of the money, and/or access to some simply acquired worldly power, and which she did take control of: her worldly power that is. Why? Because she was – exactly, in possession of no intelligence, and/or exactly nothing except for her own personally affected truly humanistic brain death, which did become affected exactly because of her addiction to worldly power. Because she had no control over her very own self, so she did exactly have to take it: CONTROL OVER EVERYTHING ELSE, simply because she was a coward: because she was afraid of Reality. Which is exactly why, she did simply choose the –

"Enter by the narrow gate, since the road that leads to perdition is wide and spacious, and many take it; but it is a narrow gate and a hard road that leads to life, and only a few find it."
Matthew 7: 13-14

Path of least resistance, and/or the security which is our worldly apathetic 21st century absolutely abstracted, and artificially effectuated, environment. Because, we can now know and for a scientific fact, it: Reality, is so exceedingly painful, that the overwhelming vast majority of mankind: while at this point in time and while upon the threshold of the 21st century, will simply sell their very souls, rather than to simply face-up to reality. And/or the –

"And indeed, everybody who does wrong
hates the light and avoids it,
for fear his actions should be exposed;
but the man who lives by the truth
comes out into the light
so that it may be plainly seen that what he does is done in God."
John 3: 20-21

Absolute truth, and/or the; "In science, as in democracy, there is no hidden secret knowledge" – observable facts.

Which is exactly because, the Monarch, and as this word does mean: "a heredity sovereign with more or less limited powers – a person or thing that holds a dominant position," and/or "being superior to all others," along with her affected truly humanistic brain death and control over some stuff, did get, also, only a whole lot of delusion. While this word: delude, does mean: "to mislead the mind or judgment of; to deceive – to mock or frustrate the hopes or aims of," and/or brainwashing too, and which is as this word: brainwashing, does mean: "A method for systematically changing attitudes or altering beliefs, esp. through the use of drugs, or psychological-stress techniques," from everybody. EVERYBODY, which was while including especially her; "heredity" – parents, was telling her only exactly what she wanted to hear, and which was that she was –

"Guess What Sells Cars. Guess Again –
The full-page ad, which appeared in this (The New York Times) newspaper on Oct. 12, is dominated by a head-and-shoulders photograph of three dewy teenage models, their perfect faces nestled together like roses in a vase, their expressions vacant yet laden with expectation – 'If their Daddies could buy them CLK's,' the tag line reads, 'so could yours'...In a telephone call from London, where he is shooting a Burberry campaign, Mr. Lipman (who is responsible for the campaign) said he got the inspiration for the ad from two personal experiences last year. First, his 5-year-old daughter asked him if she could have a Mercedes someday. 'It just knocked me out,' he said. Then, while he was having lunch at Cipriani's Downtown in SoHo, three young girls drove by in a CLK. 'I thought it was just terrific,' he said. 'Isn't that what life's all about, giving your kids all that you can, showering them with love, making them feel special?"
Nancy Hass – The New York Times – Sunday October 22, 2000

Special, and/or simply superior: to all others. And which was also – exactly, actually occurring, while they: EVERYBODY, was –

"Stone Cold Picnic –
WrestleMania XV ended the way it had to, the way any good populist fairy tale must: with the working man hero Stone Cold Steve Austin the new World Wrestling Federation champion, with the 20,000 fans who'd packed the First Union Center on their feet, and the WWF owner and Corporation bad guy Mr. McMahon on his knees and covered in Coors Light – along the way, there were the requisite helpings of blood and gore and bad language, Satanic symbols, broken tables, broken chairs, fireworks, men the size of SUVs and woman the shape of Barbie dolls – There were no big surprises in Sunday night's contest. In the world of 'sports entertainment,' the outcomes are scripted, the finales are choreographed, and the guiding principle is 'Give the people what they want' – And the crowd eats it up –

Last night, the traveling show that is the WWF was set to go live from the Meadowlands in New Jersey – And the fans would be right there with them. 'It makes you want more,' said fifteen-year-old Matt of Lansdale. I can't wait to see what they'll do next."
Jennifer Weiner – The Philadelphia Inquirer – March 30, 1999

Giving her only exactly what she wanted, and never what she only needed.

So, the Monarch: the special child, got a whole lot of tangible form mass stuff, a whole lot of truly humanistic brain death, a whole lot of delusion, and a whole lot of addiction too. Which was an absolute addiction only to escaping the pain of facing-up to Reality, any way she possibly could. And too which was while, and simultaneously, nobody forced her to do absolutely anything, to begin to become capable of taking back control over her very own self, and for her own self, and/or forced her to face-up to Reality, for her own self. While they: EVERYBODY, did only exactly, and simultaneously also, allow themselves to become capable of becoming a part of the In Crowd, which was being allowed exposure to the entertainment, and/or the diversion from Reality. And which was, also, while she: the Monarch and/or special child, sure; "Isn't that what life's all about, giving your kids all that you can" – AS HELL, DID NOT; "Enter by the narrow gate, since the road that leads to perdition is wide and spacious, and many take it; but is a narrow gate and a hard road that leads to life, and only a few find it" – get life. And – again and as we can remember, which was: that the child was allowed to suffer truly humanistic brain death for her own self, only exactly because they: EVERBODY, was afraid of uncharted territories, and/or the absolute truth of Reality, and/or; "it is a narrow gate and a hard road that leads to life, and only a few find it" – Life. So they did willfully choose death, for their child and for their very own selves also: the majority of the entire world that is.

And then – finally, somebody did actually –

"A Declaration by the Representatives of the United States of America:
We hold these truths to be self-evident: that all men are created equal; that they are endowed by their Creator with CERTAIN [*inherent and*] inalienable rights; that among these are life, liberty, and the pursuit of happiness; that to secure these rights, governments are instituted among men, deriving their just powers from the consent of the governed; that whenever any form of government becomes destructive of these ends, it is the right of the people to alter or to abolish it, and to institute a new government, laying its foundation on such principles, and organizing its power in such form, as to them shall seem most likely to effect their safety and happiness..."
Thomas Jefferson

Do something about it: The ignorance of the truth which is Reality that is. And they did simply place the self-evident truth before mankind: for all the world to simply see and with their eyes alone. They did simply say, and to the entire world,

that you – the "ENTIRE WORLD": HAVE NO RIGHT TO SUBJUGATE THIS
CHILD; YOU HAVE NO RIGHT TO BRAINWASH THIS CHILD; YOU HAVE
NO RIGHT TO FORCE THIS CHILD TO EXPERIENCE TRULY HUMANISTIC
BRAIN DEATH FOR THEIR OWN SELVES, AND YOU HAVE NO RIGHT TO
SIMPLY EXIST IN IGNORANCE OF REALITY.

And then, of course, they: the aristocratic elite, were not going to let
them: the truly virtuous common man masses, begin to take back control over their
very own selves, without a war being waged, for that control. Because, as we can
remember, they: the Monarchy and/or aristocratic elite and/or entertainers, were in
possession of absolutely nothing, except for their own personally affected truly
humanistic brain death, their control over other human beings, and their tangible
form mass stuff, which they got by maintaining their control over everything – all of
it. So if they were to begin to lose control over other human beings, then
they: the aristocratic elite and the entertainers who were creating the diversions,
would be forced to face-up to reality, and while experiencing extreme withdrawal for
their very own selves. While that: facing-up to Reality, is –

"A Painkiller's Double Life As an Illegal Street Drug –
In a scene of creepy voyeurism and joltingly effective reporting, a 22-year-
old named Troy S-, who looks like any middle-class college student in a red
sweatshirt and baseball cap, sits in his messy apartment in Maine and prepares to
stick a needle in his arm as the cameras watch. 'I'm ashamed of it,' he tells Harold
Dow, the CBS reporter sitting next to him as he crushes a pill, cooks it up in a spoon
and ties off his arm – Later, as Mr. S- travels to California for a rapid detox treatment
that promises to cure him in hours after four years of addiction, CBS gives him a
video camera so he can tape himself preparing his syringe in an airport bathroom –
Mr. S-'s mother pays $9,800 dollars for his detox treatment...We observe him in a
hospital bed, sedated so he will not be aware of what we see: his body twitches as it
goes through withdrawal – (The program returns) to Mr. S- two months after his
treatment. He is still clean, but does not have much of a life. He lives with his
mother, works as a laborer, avoids his old drug-using friends. We are left with the
insoluble question of how much the camera's presence affects its subject's behavior
and the thorny issue of how reporters, subjects and viewers become complicit in
shattering that subjects privacy..."
Caryn James – The New York Times – Wednesday December 12, 2001

Very painful: facing up to reality that is.
So they: the drug-dealers and/or entertainers, simply created a diversion, so
that no one would have to face-up to Reality. Unless, of course and just like
Christopher Columbus, somebody did go off into uncharted territories, and in search
of the Absolute Truth. So I did, and here it is.
It: the "camera's presence," is no longer "insoluble," it is a scientific fact,
and: HERE IS THE ABSOLUTE TRUTH, FOR ALL THE WORLD TO SIMPLY

15

SEE WITH THEIR EYES ALONE.
    The scientific fact, is that –

    "Clustered in loose knots buried deep in the brain (are) neurons that produce molecular messengers – (within) the primitive structure that is one of the brain's key pleasure centers. At a purely chemical level (just as the injection of) heroin triggers release of dopamine – every experience humans find enjoyable – embracing a lover or savoring chocolate – amounts to little more than an explosion of dopamine in the nucleus accumbens, as exhilarating and ephemeral as a firecracker – dopamine, can be elevated by a hug, a kiss, a word of praise..."
    Addicted – J. Madeleine Nash – Time – May 5, 1997

    Every "thing" *is* a "drug." Which is while including the newly perceived non-tangible form projected image, of every thing that human beings are capable of perceiving, within three-dimensional Reality.
    Which is simple to understand, while we remember exactly why Christopher Columbus did set sail into uncharted territories. And that is: neurophysiologically, because human beings are born with a need to be programmed to function in a truly humanistic manner, and/or they need to learn, how to "think" and "within" their three-dimensional electrical potential mass minds, within which there are no projected images of things. And, even simpler to understand here in the early 21st century, a human being mind is just like a computer: it must be programmed. So, the will to learn things anew comes from biochemical inductions: within a human being's electrical potential mass of a mind, within which there are contained NO projected images of things. Which is exactly where the problem begins, within the truly humanistic being minds.
    Because, the projected newly perceived image of every single thing that human beings do perceive, is capable of causing a purposefully effectuated biochemical induction, of dopamine, within a human being's mind: EVERY SINGLE NEWLY PERCEIVED NON-TANGIBLE FORM IMAGE. Which would include: "watching television" – *is* a "drug," "going to the movies" – *is* a "drug," "reading a novel" – *is* a "drug," "looking at a picture" – *is* a "drug," "patronizing spectator sporting events" – *is* a "drug," "driving a car" – *is* a "drug," "buying something" – *is* a "drug," "accessing abstracted knowledge" – *is* a "drug," "worldly power" – *is* a "drug," "the accompaniment of another human being" – *is* a "drug," EVEN SIMPLY; "a word of praise" – being told exactly "what you want to hear" and/or being enabled to merely do exactly "what you want to do," and/or: "living in ignorance of neuroscientific reality" – IS A DRUG. They all do cause a purposefully effectuated dopamine biochemical induction, within a human being's electrical potential mass of a mind, within which there are contained no projected images of things. The only "thing" that does NOT cause a purposefully effectuated biochemical induction of dopamine within a human being's mind, is –

"Princeton's (Barry) Jacobs believes that, based on experiments with cats, repetitive motor activity – walking – stimulates the release of serotonin..."
The Mood Molecule – Michael D. Lemonick Time, September 29, 1997

NOTHING. Consciously cognizing humanistic nothingness, is the only thing that does not cause a purposefully effectuated dopamine biochemical induction, within a humanistic being's mind. Which: consciously cognizing nothingness, does also – and simultaneously, enable the function of reuptake to occur within a humanistic being's mind. And which is the exact period of time, and/or purposefully effectuated amount of time, when the biochemical induction of dopamine can be purposefully reabsorbed, back into the individual neurons of the mind. And too which: consciously cognizing humanistic nothingness, is exactly what produces serotonin within a human being's mind. So, we can now know, and for a verified neuroscientific fact, that human beings were never supposed to watch television, and/or go to the movies, and/or look at a picture, and/or drive a car, and/or patronize spectator sporting events, and/or simply exist in an absolutely abstracted, and apathetic, environment. Exactly simply because, the biochemical induction of dopamine: within our minds, must –

"Dopamine, however, is more than just a feel-good molecule. It also exercises extraordinary power over learning and memory – Dopamine, like most biologically important molecules, must be kept within strict bounds – Too much causes the hallucinations, and bizarre thoughts, of schizophrenia – addicts' neurons assaulted by abnormally high levels of dopamine, have responded defensively and reduced the number of sites (or receptors) to which dopamine can bind – so while addicts begin by taking drugs to feel high, they end up taking them in order not to feel low."
Addicted – J. Madeleine Nash – Time May 5, 1997

"Be kept within strict bounds": as a matter of scientific fact. While there can be NO deliberate cognizance of nothingness, upon a two-dimensional plane: of a television screen – or a movie screen – or a computer monitor screen – or a novel, or anything except for Reality. And there can be no purposefully effectuated reuptake function either: of the biochemical dopamine, within the individually affected minds, that are being allowed exposure to these abstracted effectual stimuli: it is a neurophysiological impossibility. And too which, that these individually affected minds are producing too much dopamine, is occurring while – and simultaneously, they: the individually affected minds, are exactly not producing serotonin either. While diminished purposefully effectuated serotonin production, does –

"A Little Help From Serotonin –
Could a single brain chemical hold the key to happiness...as the 20th century

17

winds down, we humans seem increasingly convinced that serotonin is the key to a good life – and it's easy to see why. This once obscure neurotransmitter is the secret behind Prozac, the drug that revolutionized the pursuit of happiness ten years ago this winter. Prozac and its mood altering cousins all work by boosting serotonin activity in the brain – serotonin is so basic to life that even worms and sea slugs make it...When a nerve impulse reaches a branch ending, the neuron releases serotonin into a tiny space, or synapse – Microseconds later, the neuron that released the chemical takes it back in – a process known as reuptake – serotonin pacifies neurons in the limbic system, the Brain's Department of Animal Instincts. 'Serotonin puts the brakes on primitive behaviors like sex, aggression and excessive eating,' says Dr. Larry Siever of New York's Mount Sinai School of Medicine...Our serotonin systems are affected not only by what we ingest but by our genes, experiences and attitudes...Scientists may someday learn how all of these forces interact, but a good life will still take work."

Geoffrey Cowley / Anne Underwood – Newsweek – December 29, 1997

Begin to enable a humanistic being to function in an animalistic manner. Which is, exactly, as they will remain incapable of putting the breaks on their own selves, and/or incapable of controlling their own selves. And which is while – and simultaneously, their dopamine levels are being severely affected also, and, too, which is also while they: the 21st century; "Scientists may someday learn how all of these forces interact" – scientists, still don't get it: the absolute scientific truth that is. And which is – exactly, what is responsible for a good life.

Because, have you ever heard of Prozac? Of course you have, here – in the early 21st century, EVERYBODY has heard of Prozac, and that is exactly because everybody is "on " Prozac. But, did you, also, ever wonder exactly why, even only 20 years ago, NOBODY had ever heard of Prozac, and nobody was on Prozac either? And too which is while Prozac is a serotonin reuptake inhibitor, and which is while, here in their early 21st century, everybody is on it. How about "Ecstasy?" Have you ever heard of Ecstasy, and what Ecstasy is capable of doing? Well, Ecstasy does –

"Experiencing Ecstasy –
MDMA is different from all the drugs that came before it – which explains why it has become the fastest-growing illegal substance in America...Whereas Prozac-type SSRI antidepressants keep your brain from emptying reservoirs of serotonin too quickly, Ecstasy floods your brain with the stuff – you feel so connected to the continuum of your life. A subtle, purifying something descends (over you) – You're warm. You're not hungry – You have everything you need. Just breathing is really good on this stuff..."

Matthew Klam – The New York Times Magazine – January 21, 2001

Flood the brain with serotonin.

And, yet, the 21st century scientists still don't get it. So, here it is: HUMAN
BEINGS WERE NEVER SUPPOSED TO WATCH TELEVISION; HUMAN
BEINGS WERE NEVER SUPPOSED TO GO TO THE MOVIES; HUMAN
BEINGS WERE NEVER SUPPOSED TO DRIVE AUTOMOBILES; HUMAN
BEINGS WERE NEVER SUPPOSED TO USE COMPUTERS; HUMAN BEINGS
WERE NEVER SUPPOSED TO DO ABSOLUTELY NOTHING, EXCEPT SIT
INSIDE AND AFFECT TRULY HUMANISTIC BRAIN DEATH FOR
THEMSELVES. What "human beings" were supposed to do, was to actually go out
into three-dimensional reality, and learn Reality. Which would have been while
enabling themselves to affect, only, exactly proportional amounts of purposefully
affected biochemical inductions, within their own individually affected minds, and
central nervous systems. And which is –

"It should be stressed that transmitters (and their regulators) are semantically
as well as syntactically functional – As they synaptic signals, transmitters obviously
alter communication and function. Consequently, transmitters are not simply
indifferent or neutral storehouses of environmental information. Rather,
environmental alteration of long-term transmitter function *ipso facto* alters function
of the nervous system."
   Ira Black – Molecular Memory Mechanisms, Synapses Circuits and the
   Beginnings of Memory – Gary Lynch

   As a matter of scientific fact.
   So there it is – it couldn't be any simpler, and/or any more factual. And, yet,
you will not simply see this scientific fact being simply communicated, by any one
single neuroscientist, anywhere else on the entire face of this Earth, and/or in the
entire history of mankind. And – specifically, that a human being must only affect
exactly proportional amounts of purposefully affected biochemical inductions, within
their own selves: while according to Reality and while especially as through
purposefully affected serotonin production. Which: purposefully affected serotonin
production, is directly responsible for; "...serotonin pacifies neurons in the limbic
system, the Brain's Department of Animal Instincts" – letting people live in peace.
   Well, actually, that's not the absolute truth, and we are only dealing in
absolute truths here, and/or pure scientific fact, and exactly not metaphysics.
Because there was one other scientist, who did plainly explain it prior to this point in
time, and that was the scientist –

"For everyone will be salted with fire. Salt is a good thing, but if salt has
become insipid, how can you season it again? Have salt in yourselves and be at
peace with one another."
   Mark 9: 48-50

   Jesus of Nazareth: as a matter of fact.

And, too, exactly as 20th century scientific research has confirmed –

"At birth, a baby's brain contains about 100 million neurons, the brain cells that carry electrical messages through the brain. Each one can produce up to 15,000 synapses, or connections to the other cells. Those synapses are the key to healthy development and learning – At birth a baby is flooded with sensory experiences: light, sound, smells, things to touch, things to taste. These experiences cause the brain to create trillions of connections, essentially 'wiring' the brain for learning – Repeated early experiences determine how the brain is wired. Those synapses that have been activated frequently by virtue of repeated early experience tend to become permanent; the synapses that have not been used at all, or often enough, tend to become eliminated..."
Catherine Long – Seattle Times/Philadelphia Inquirer – Tuesday, May 29, 1997

And, which was also plainly explained 2000 years prior to the fact: by the scientist Jesus of Nazareth, *is* the scientific fact *that* –

"Then the disciples went up to him and asked, 'Why do you talk to them in parables?' 'Because,' he replied, the mysteries of the kingdom of heaven are revealed to you, but they are not revealed to them. For anyone who has will be given more, and he will have more than enough; but from anyone who has not, even what he has will be taken away."
Matthew 13: 10-13

Human beings must have a desire to go and seek the absolute truth. And/or, to actually begin to become capable of functioning in a truly humanistic manner, and not, simply, begin to experience truly humanistic brain death for their own selves, so they must have the will to learn: the Truth. But, as we can remember Christopher Columbus' journey into uncharted territories, finding the Absolute Truth is –

"Great crowds accompanied him on his way and he turned and spoke to them. 'If any man comes to me without hating his father, mother, wife, children, brothers, sisters, yes and his own life too, he cannot be my disciple. Anyone who does not carry his cross and come after me cannot be my disciple.
And indeed, which of you here, intending to build a tower, would not first sit down and work out the cost to see if he had enough to complete it? Otherwise, if he laid the foundation and then found himself unable to finish the work, the onlookers would all start making fun of him and saying, 'Here is a man who started to build and was unable to finish."
Luke 14: 25-31

Very painful.

While that: building a truly humanistic multidimensional foundation, within a human being's parallel functioning mind and central nervous system, is very difficult, even without any –

"He said to his disciples, 'Obstacles arc sure to come, but alas for the one who provides them! It would be better for him to be thrown into the sea with a millstone put around his neck than he should lead astray a single one of these little ones. Watch yourselves!"
Luke 17: 1-3

Obstacles: for the child.
And which is exactly why, it: the formation of the world's first –

"We hold these truths to be self-evident: that all men are created equal; that they are endowed by their Creator with CERTAIN [*inherent and*] inalienable rights; that among these are life, liberty, and the pursuit of happiness; that to secure these rights, governments are instituted among men, deriving their just powers from the consent of the governed; that whenever any form of government becomes destructive of these ends, it is the right of the people to alter or to abolish it, and to institute a new government, laying its foundation on such principles, and organizing its power in such form, as to them shall seem most likely to effect their safety and happiness..."

Truly humanistic foundation: within the Child of the Monarch, was such a uniquely unhumanistic phenomenon.
Exactly because, what they: the truly virtuous common man masses, did exactly do, and for the very first time in the entire history of mankind, was to purposefully leave them: the Monarchy, and/or the aristocratic elite, and/or the entertainers, and while including their truly humanistic brain death for themselves, which was affected as through their addiction to excessive dopamine biochemical inducing stimulus and their control over every thing, behind. They did, exactly, willfully choose to leave it: the stuff – the entertainers – the aristocratic elite – the security of the mother's breast – the addiction and the brain death too, behind, and exactly on purpose: IT WAS NO ACCIDENT – IT WAS A REVOLUTIONARY CONCEPT. Which was exactly as they went sailing off into uncharted territories, and in search of the Absolute Truth for themselves.
And, exactly as Thomas Jefferson did explain –

"...The practice of Kings marrying only in the families of Kings, has been that of Europe for some centuries. Now, take any race of animals, confine them in idleness and inaction, whether in a sty, a stable or a state-room, pamper them with high diet, gratify all their sexual appetites, immerse them in sensualities, nourish their passions, let everything bend before them, and banish whatever might lead them to think, and in a few generations they become all body and no mind; and this,

too, by a law of nature, by that very law by which we are in the constant practice of changing the characters and propensities of the animals we raise for our own purposes. Such is the regiment in raising Kings, and in this way they have gone on for centuries...In this state Bonaparte found Europe; and it was this state of its rulers which lost it without scarce a struggle. These animals had become without mind and powerless; and so will every hereditary monarch be after a few generations..."
    Thomas Jefferson (To) Governor John Langdon – Monticello, March 5, 1810

    The quickest way to begin to affect truly humanistic brain death: for an entire society and which may then become easily consumed by a disgruntled adolescent, is to begin to destroy the very foundation of a society: while causing a severe neurophysiological dysfunction within the child, and while confining them to the "idleness of a state-room." And which is exactly, what –

"Dolls, trikes and now for tots – TVs
    The parental plaint is often heard: 'My kids watch too much TV' – It would seem, then, that parents would do something about that – But explain this: A new study on children's viewing habits reported that one-quarter of children ages 2 to 5, and 40 percent of those 6 to 11, have their own television sets – And, not surprisingly, it found that children are watching more TV..."
    Kathy Boccella – The Philadelphia Inquirer – Sunday, January 4, 1998

    Allowing the child to watch television is: in scientific reality.
    It is giving the child access to; "At a purely chemical level (just as the injection of) heroin triggers release of dopamine – Every experience humans find enjoyable – amounts to little more than an explosion of dopamine in the nucleus accumbens, as exhilarating and ephemeral as a firecracker" – pure heroin, and only brain death too: FOR THE CHILD AND ONLY IN NEUROSCIENTIFIC REALITY. But not in the mind of any one individual that has already begun to become affected, and/or a victim of the con. There: within their minds alone, it is simply called an opinion, and which: an opinion, is only a; "a belief or judgment that rests on grounds insufficient to produce certainty – beliefs or judgments shared by many" – personal belief in reality. But, it: the belief, may be "shared by many" too, and/or an; "obstinate or conceded with regard to ones opinions" – ignoramus in scientific reality, and/or simply an absolute ignorance of Reality. As this word: ignorant, does mean: "lacking in knowledge or training; unlearned – lacking knowledge about a particular subject or fact – uninformed; unaware," and/or to simply ignore. And as this word: ignore, does mean: "to refrain from noticing or recognizing," and only in neuroscientific reality. It is not an opinion in scientific reality: it is only a scientific fact, in Reality. And here it: The Absolute Truth, is again.
    Everybody has heard of "The birds and the bees" in reality. And that birds and bees can't possibly consciously know anything: like a human being can in

reality, except, of course, to move their physiological bodies while as in a purposefully effectuated direction: from point A to point B within three-dimensional space. And towards the perceivable non-tangible form mass projected image of a real tangible form mass, and/or a pretty color, and as this word: pretty, does simply mean: "pleasing or attractive to the eye in – a childlike way." But, if a bird or a bee cannot consciously know anything, how can they possibly know to move while in a purposefully effectuated direction, and while in a childlike way towards a pretty color? Well, the scientific answer is –

"Candace Pert: we've measured opiate receptors in everything from fruit fly heads to human brains. Even uni-cellular organisms have peptides' – Do you think even cockroaches feel some sort of emotion we ask...'They have to, because they have chemicals that put them in the mood to mate and chemicals that make them run away when they're about to be killed. That's what emotions are about – sex and violence, pain and pleasure. Even bacteria have a little hierarchy of primitive likes and dislikes. They're programmed to migrate toward or away from a chemotactic substance; they're little robots that go for sugar at all costs and away from salt. If you were designing a robot vehicle to walk into the future and survive, as God was when he designed human beings, you'd wire it up so that behavior that ensured the survival of self or species – like sex and eating – would be naturally reinforcing. Behavior is controlled by the anticipation of pain or pleasure, punishment or reward. And that has to be coded in the brain."
The 3-Pound Universe – Judith Hooper and Dick Teresi

Dopamine – the biochemical induction: within a child's brain, and which must "be coded in the brain."
So, when a young child does consciously perceive, and/or simply see, the projected non-tangible form image of some thing that he has never seen before, there will: then and upon the perceived non-tangible form projected image of the tangible form mass, be induced: within his mind, a biochemical induction of dopamine, and which is while actually functioning as pure *pleasure*. Which will then, and exactly as Thomas Jefferson did explain; "...lead him to think" – cause him to move while in a purposefully effectuated direction, towards the perceivable tangible form mass stimulus. Then: as the child does physiologically move his body through space, and over time, while as from point A towards point B, the child will begin to make manifest time traveled, with his physiological body and while as from point A towards point B, and throughout and within three-dimensional space. And which will then – simultaneously and while as through the passage of time, enable the child's mind to perform the function of; "later, the neuron that released the chemical takes it back in – a process known as reuptake" – reuptake, and/or simply reabsorbing the biochemical induction, of dopamine, back into the individual molecular structure of the mind, and out of the synaptic area. And, too, which is: the purposefully effectuated physiological movement of the child's body, while

capable of being understood, and effectually functioning, as a relatively painful experienced humanistic phenomenon, and/or: *pain*. Now, if we were to simply, and exactly as Thomas Jefferson did explain; "Now, take any race of animals, confine them in idleness and inaction – gratify all their sexual appetites, immerse their sensualities, nourish their passions, let everything bend before them, and banish whatever might lead them to think" – take away the three-dimensional Reality, and/or purposefully effectuated physiological movement through three-dimensional space, and then leave: for the child, only the allowed exposure to the non-tangible form projected image, of the newly perceived visual effectual stimulus, what we would end up with, is; "Dolls, trikes and now for tots: TVs" – the purposefully effectuated biochemical induction of dopamine only. And exactly NO purposefully effectuated reuptake function: within the individually affected child's mind, and each and every one of them. And that purposefully effectuated allowed exposure, to excessive dopamine biochemical inducing effectual stimulus, is – again, EXACTLY EQUIVALENT TO –

"Clustered in loose knots buried deep in the brain (are) neurons that produce molecular messengers – (within) the primitive structure that is one of the brain's key pleasure centers. At a purely chemical level (just as the injection of) heroin triggers release of dopamine – every experience humans find enjoyable – amounts to little more than an explosion of dopamine in the nucleus accumbens, as exhilarating and ephemeral as a firecracker..."
Addicted – J. Madeleine Nash – Time – May 5, 1997

Giving the child heroin.
And it: each and every dopamine induction for the child, and while as through the perceived non-tangible form projected image of every thing he's never seen before, and which is while including the projected non-tangible form image of a television screen, is – also, exactly equivalent to –

"Drugs are like sledgehammers,' observes Dr. Eric Nestler of the Yale University School of Medicine. 'They profoundly alter many pathways' – the realization that dopamine may be a common endpoint of all those pathways represents a signal advance. Provocative – the dopamine hypothesis provides a basic framework for understanding (what does) create a serious behavioral disorder..."
Addicted – J. Madeleine Nash – Time – May 5, 1997

A sledgehammer: *pounding* at the child's very foundation, of his own individually affected mind. And while – simultaneously, beginning to; "They profoundly alter many pathways" – lead them in a direction towards truly humanistic brain death: for the child. Because of the parent giving them only what they want, which is a recently verified scientific fact. And, too – as we can remember, which was exactly explained, by the scientist –

24

"He said to his disciples, 'obstacles are sure to come, but alas for the one who provides them! It would be better for him to be thrown into the sea with a millstone put around his neck than he should lead astray a single one of these little ones. Watch yourselves!"

Luke 17: 1-3

Jesus of Nazareth.

And, of course, it: the allowed exposure to the television and the excessive dopamine biochemical induction affected because of that exposure, without ever performing any reuptake function, is, and as we can remember, only the very beginning of –

"Dopamine, however, is more than just a feel-good molecule. It also exercises extraordinary power over learning and memory – Dopamine, like most biologically important molecules, must be kept within strict bounds – Too much causes the hallucinations, and bizarre thoughts, of schizophrenia – addicts' neurons assaulted by abnormally high levels of dopamine, have responded defensively and reduced the number of sites (or receptors) to which dopamine can bind – so while addicts begin by taking drugs to feel high, they end up taking them in order not to feel low."

Addicted – J. Madeleine Nash – Time – May 5, 1997

An addiction, and schizophrenic behavior too, and/or truly humanistic brain death: for the individually affected child, and society too.

Exactly because, with their affected addiction, they: the children and the society too, are –

"Stone Cold Picnic –

WrestleMania XV ended the way it had to, the way any good populist fairy tale must...There were no big surprises in Sunday night's contest. In the world of 'sports entertainment,' the outcomes are scripted, the finales are choreographed, and the guiding principle is 'Give the people what they want' – And the crowd eats it up – 'It makes you want more,' said fifteen-year-old Matt..."

Jennifer Weiner – The Philadelphia Inquirer – March 30, 1999

Going to need more: more stimulus – more drugs – more stuff, and more brain death too. And which is to simply consume for their very own selves, and/or to become capable of; "In the world of – 'entertainment' – the guiding principle is 'Give the people what they want' – And the crowd eats it up – 'It makes you want more,' said 15-year-old Matt" – consuming their very own selves, and just like a; "Dr. Hawking's first book for a wide audience, 'A Brief History of Time,' took readers on a tour through black holes, the gravitational traps from which not even light can emerge" – real black hole, from which not even light can escape. And/or the beginning of the End of time, and/or a space/time singularity: actually functioning as zero Time *made manifest*.

Because, and of course, with the acquiring of the world's first Truly Idealist Democratic society, the purposefully affected brainwashing: of the individual human beings which comprise a society, and as we can remember the definition of brainwashing as "A method for systematically changing attitudes or altering beliefs, esp. through the use of drugs," did – too, begin almost immediately. And/or the applicable function of the art of the con, and by the worldly political opportunists, and/or Sophists, and/or worldly con-artists. Exactly because, as everyone knows: "Power corrupts and absolute power corrupts absolutely" – but only in identifiable scientific reality. And, with the acquisition of the world's first Truly Idealist Democrat society, and as this word: con, does mean: "to convince – to abuse the confidence of – to commit to memory – to direct the steering of," the applied art of the con, did begin almost immediately too. Because, the world's First Truly Idealist Democratic Society, was established in The Land of Plenty: plenty of stuff, and plenty of worldly opportunities for allowed access to excessive dopamine biochemical inductions: which could be simply acquired by gaining control over other individual human beings, just like the Monarch. And too which they: the formers of the world's first Truly Idealist Democratic Society, did leave behind on purpose. But, all worldly power, and/or some purposefully allowed access to an excessive; "Dopamine, however, is more than just a feel-good molecule. It also exercises extraordinary power over learning and memory" – simple mind-altering, and/or a brainwashing, dopamine biochemical induction, is extraordinarily: and/or; "beyond what is usual, ordinary, or established" – beyond the usually, and/or daily, powerful.

And so, the brainwashing did begin, and too while at the very base of the foundation which forms a Truly Idealist Democratic Society: within the individually affected minds, of the human beings which comprise a society. And it: the applied art of the con, did begin to erode the very base of that foundation, of the minds. So, it wasn't very long before the individually affected human beings, did simply begin to believe: within their individually affected minds and as they were being steered in a direction away from the function of a Truly Idealist Democratic Society, and only in scientific reality too, that "they": individual human beings, should only begin to want to; "Stone Cold Picnic – WrestleMania XV ended the way it had to, the way any good populist fairy tale must: with the working man hero Stone Cold Steve Austin the new World Wrestling Federation champion" – be in possession of absolutely nothing, except for a desire to take control over everything. And/or to simply experience affected truly humanistic brain death too: for their own selves, and just like the –

"Best friends enjoy the royal treatment, courtesy of 'A makeover Story':
They are both physical therapists, mother's of three, and married – and this season, the two best friends who describe themselves as 'twin sisters separated at

birth' are being featured in *A Makeover Story* on The Learning Channel – Those similarities were just what producers at *A Makeover Story* were looking for, said Tom Farrell, executive producer of the show...'We treat people like kings and queens for a day,' Farrell said – On June 2, the day of the Mom Prom, stylists cut and colored the women's hair and topped their looks off with make-up – For me, it was great,' O- said. We both felt like we looked like a million dollars' – When the two friends entered the prom, a camera crew was there to catch the reactions of the other partygoers, who applauded the woman as they entered the rented Kimberton hall – 'Our goal is to have those jaw-dropping reactions,' Farrell said."

Kelly Wolfe – The Philadelphia Inquirer – Thursday, December 13, 2001

Real Monarch. And/or, at least, a part of the In Crowd which is being purposefully allowed exposure to the aristocratic environment, functioning as excessive absolutely abstracted dopamine biochemical inducing effectual stimulus only. And which is as they: the individually affected members of this once Truly Idealist Democratic Society, have been exactly diverted from the Truth: IT WAS A REVOLUTIONARY CONCEPT; THEY DID CONSCIOUSLY CHOOSE TO WILLFULLY –

"When that day comes, anyone on the housetop, with his possessions in the house, must not come down to collect them, nor most anyone in the fields turn back either. Remember Lot's wife. Anyone who tries to preserve his life will lose it; and anyone who loses his life will keep it safe."

Luke 17: 31-34

Leave it: the stuff – the aristocratic environment – the allowed access to excessive dopamine biochemical inducing effectual stimulus and the truly humanistic brain death too, behind – and on purpose.

Exactly because, it: allowed access to abstracted dopamine biochemical inducing effectual stimulus of any kind actually functioning as pure *pleasure*, does, as a matter of neuroscientific fact, begin to affect –

"At a purely chemical level (just as the injection of) heroin triggers release of dopamine – every experience humans find enjoyable, amounts to little more than an explosion of dopamine in the nucleus accumbens, as exhilarating and ephemeral as a firecracker – dopamine can be elevated by a hug, a kiss, a word of praise (But) Dopamine, like most biologically important molecules, must be kept within strict bounds – Too much causes the hallucinations, and bizarre thoughts, of schizophrenia – addicts' neurons assaulted by abnormally high levels of dopamine, have responded defensively and reduced the number of sites (or receptors) to which dopamine can bind – so while addicts begin by taking drugs to feel high, they end up taking them in order not to feel low."

Addicted – J. Madeleine Nash – Time – May 5, 1997

An absolute addiction: to pure *pleasure*. And to simply enable themselves to feel alive, for their own selves: within the individually affected human being minds, of any age.

And which does enable us to exactly –

"Dolls, trikes and now for tots – TVs
The parental plaint is often heard: 'My kids watch too much TV' – It would seem, then, that parents would do something about that – But explain this: A new study on children's viewing habits reported that one-quarter of children ages 2 to 5, and 40 percent of those ages 6 to 11, have their own television sets – And, not surprisingly, found that children are watching more TV..."
Kathy Boccella – The Philadelphia Inquirer – Sunday, January 4, 1998

Explain the exact scientific reason for the children's "new viewing habits," and/or "this" simple understanding of the absolute scientific truth. And that is exactly because –

"Most of the youngsters said they had not even asked for TVs, although some were too young to speak for themselves. At 2, Carolyn M- of New Hope has had a TV for half her life – 'She can't reach it, so we only watch it when I'm with her,' said her mother, Mary – at least one of the family's eight television sets is on from 8 a.m. to 11 p.m. she said. There is a TV in each of four bedrooms, one of which they plan to make into a nursery when they have another child – Unless we go out, it's on – (Andrea) W- said she had no misgivings about giving her children TVs – 'Some of my friends say they can't believe (the children) have TVs and VCRs in their rooms, she said. I tell them to mind their own business..."
Kathy Boccella – The Philadelphia Inquirer – Sunday, January 4, 1998

And/or exactly why the parents do not; "It would seem, then, that parents would do something about that" – do absolutely anything: in reality, except ignore it: scientific Reality. Which is simply the acknowledged understanding, of the scientific fact, that the parents are addicted themselves – in denial only, and/or simply remaining ignorant of reality, and projecting their own personally affected dysfunction upon the Child too.

Which is also while they: the individuals who have already been affected, are, simply, only going to; "Stone Cold Picnic – There were no big surprises in Sunday night's contest. In the world of 'sports entertainment,' the outcomes are scripted – And the fans would be right there with them. 'It makes you want more,' said fifteen-year-old Matt" – need more, and lots of it: purposefully allowed exposure to abstracted dopamine biochemical inducing effectual stimulus, and/or entertainment, functioning as pure pleasure. And which is, of course, no; "There were no big surprises" – big surprise.

Which is exactly because, their individually affected dopamine systems, and three-dimensional electrical potential mass minds too, are –

"Drug's Effect On Brain Is Extensive, Study Finds –
Heavy users (of highly addictive stimulants) are doing more damage to their
brains than scientists had thought, according to the first study that looked inside
addicts' brains nearly a year after they stop using the drug – At least a quarter of a
class of molecules that help people feel pleasure and reward were knocked out – This
is the first study to show directly that brain damage (caused by the addiction)
produces deficits in learning and memory – In the study, Dr. (Nora) Volkow used an
imaging technique – to measure dopamine levels in the brains of 15 recovering
addicts and 18 healthy volunteers. Dopamine is a brain chemical that regulates
movement, pleasure and motivation. When the dopamine system goes seriously
awry, she said, people lose their excitement for life and can no longer move their
limbs – The addicts (started out as) occasional users but over time the drug hijacked
their natural dopamine systems..."
Sandra Blakeslee – The New York Times – Tuesday, March 6, 2001

Being hijacked: and being led on a collision course with our own destiny.
Exactly because, the damage which is beginning to occur: within all of the
individually affected minds, that are being allowed exposure to the abstracted
stimulus, is beginning to occur within the –

"PET-scan images of the brains of recovering – addicts reveal other striking
changes, including a dramatically impaired ability to process glucose, the primary
energy source for working neurons. Moreover, this impairment – which persists for
up to 100 days after withdrawal – is greatest in the prefrontal cortex..."
Addicted – J. Madeleine Nash – Time – May 5, 1997

Uniquely humanistic prefrontal cortex.
And the prefrontal cortex, is the exact area of human being's mind, which is
directly responsible for –

"The prefrontal cortex (is) a dopamine-rich area of the brain that controls
impulsive and irrational behavior. Addicts, in fact, display many of the symptoms
shown by patients who have suffered strokes or injuries to the prefrontal cortex.
Damage to this region, University of Iowa neurologist Antonio Damasio and his
colleagues have demonstrated, destroys the emotional compass that controls
behaviors that the patient (should) know are unacceptable."
Addicted – J. Madeleine Nash – Time – May 5, 1997

Controlling their own selves.
While, it is also – and simultaneously, the exact area of the human being's
mind, which is directly responsible for –

"Paul MacLean, for one, considers the frontal lobes the 'heart' of the cortex –
Clinically, there is evidence that the prefrontal cortex by looking inward, so to speak,
obtains the gut feeling for identifying with another individual. In other words:
empathy – Through its centers for vision, hearing, and bodily sensations, we traffic
with the external world."
The 3-Pound Universe – Judith Hooper and Dick Teresi

Empathy: and/or simply understanding anything.
And, too, the uniquely humanistic prefrontal cortex is – also and
simultaneously, the exact area of a human being's mind, which actually is directly
responsible for –

"Drug's Effect On Brain Is Extensive, Study Shows –
Heavy users (of highly addictive stimulants) are doing more damage to their
brains than scientists had thought, according to the first study that looked inside
addicts' brains nearly a year after they stop using the drug – At least a quarter of a
class of molecules that help people feel pleasure and reward were knocked out – But
the biggest surprise is that another brain region responsible for spatial perception and
sensation, which has never before been linked to (substance) abuse, was hyperactive
and showed signs of scarring – the study's biggest surprise was that the addicts'
parietal lobes, the parts of the brain used for feeling sensation and for recognizing
where the body is in space, were metabolically overactive, Dr Volkow said – It is the
equivalent of an inflammation or scarring response."
Sandra Blakeslee – The New York Times – Tuesday, March 6, 2001

Beginning to become capable of consciously cognizing simultaneously
relative patterns in space/time: functioning as simultaneously relative to/from, and
within, a single cognizable point time zero. While actually occurring: within a
human being's truly humanistic three-dimensional electrical potential mass of a
mind, as it is within simultaneously relative truly humanistic Reality, and while upon
this point-mass of Earth. And/or the very definition of –

"One way to think about this view is to imagine spatial relationships as a kind
of universal language that the brain uses no matter what specific language – social,
moral, engineering, poetic – we are using at the moment – (George) Lakoff believes
he can tie this mental language to the physical structure of the brain and its maps –
'When you think about dynamic structure, you begin to think there are a lot of things
that are analogous with life. Life is more pattern(s) in space/time than it is a set of
particular physical things."
Jim Jubak – In the Image of the Brain

LIFE.
And exactly as the neuroscientist Jesus of Nazareth did –

"Enter by the narrow gate, since the road that leads to perdition is wide and spacious, and many take it; but it is a narrow gate and hard road that leads to life, and only a few find it."
Matthew 7: 13-14

Explain. And as a matter of scientific fact, and for the entire world to simply see with our eyes alone: the scientific fact that is. And/or the –

"So Pilate went back into the Pretorium and called Jesus to him, 'Are you the king of the Jews? he asked. Jesus replied, 'Do you ask this of your own accord, or have others spoken to you about me?' Pilate answered, 'Am I a Jew? It is your own people and the chief priests who have handed you over to me: what have you done?' Jesus replied, 'Mine is not a kingdom of this world; if my kingdom were of this world, my men would have fought to prevent my being surrendered to the Jews. But my kingdom is not of this kind.' So you are a king then?' said Pilate. 'It is you who say it,' answered Jesus. 'Yes, I am a king. I was born for this, I came into this world for this: to bear witness to the truth; and all who are on the side of truth listen to my voice.' 'Truth?' said Pilate, 'What is that?'"
John 18: 33-38

Absolute Truth. That all of Reality, and which is the explained Theory of Relativity, "is" the purposefully effectuated formation of simultaneously relative harmoniously proportioned differential equations, actually functioning as simultaneously relative to/from, and within, a single purposefully effectuated, and cognizable, point time zero: the "point" of the Big Bang and applied function of Omnidimensional Time *made manifest*, and as a matter of fact. And too – and of course only in scientific reality, this does mean, that we can now know that Jesus of Nazareth was, also, the single greatest astrophysicist that has ever walked upon this point-mass of Earth, along with his being the single greatest neuroscientist that has ever walked upon this point-mass of Earth. Because, he did also simply explain, that this: a purposefully effectuated formed understanding of universally applicable *a priori* Reality, actually functioning as simultaneously relative Omnidimensional Time *made manifest*, and as real simultaneously relative quantum electrodynamics, can exactly not be simply seen with our eyes alone, it can only –

"Asked by the Pharisees when the Kingdom of God was to come, he gave them this answer, 'The Kingdom of God does not admit of observation and there will be no one to say, look here! Look there! For, you must know, the Kingdom of God is within you."
Luke 17: 20-21

Be understood: within an individual human being's quantum dynamically functioning three-dimensional electrical potential mass of a mind, and central nervous system, which is while actually functioning as Omnidimensional Time *made manifest*. And which *is* –

"Candance Pert – I see the brain in terms of quantum mechanics – the brain is just a receiver, an amplifier, a little wet minireceiver for collective reality. We make maps, but we should never confuse the map with the territory – the ratio of frontal core to the rest of the cortex may be one index of evolutionary advancement – What the frontal lobes 'control' is something like awareness, or self-awareness – Do these lobes govern some essential feature of humanness, or even godliness, as some scientists have suggested? 'If God speaks to man, if man speaks to God,' neuroscientist Candace Pert tells us, 'it would be through the frontal lobes, which is the part of the brain that has undergone the most evolutionary expansion' – Stephen LaBarge – 'And it's capable of what look like miraculous things, so miraculous that we're tempted to say it's divine, that it's not 'natural.' But I don't think there's any mystery about where different levels of mind come from. I see them as a result of various complex interactions of the brain."
The 3-Pound Universe – Judith Hooper and Dick Teresi

As a matter of neuroscientific fact.
And we can simply reiterate our understanding of this scientific fact, by remembering that all little children do begin to "learn" that God *is* "Omni" "potent," He *is* "Omni" "powerful," He *is* "Omni" "present," He *is* "Omni" "dimensional," and He *is* "Omni" "knowing" too: all of the above and simultaneously. And/or simultaneously relative Omnidimensional Time *made manifest* – "The Mind of God Made Manifest," and/or The –

"...As we found with quantum mechanics, the full structure of the world is richer than our language can express and our brains comprehend – it is not possible for us to visualize the geometries of dimensions higher than three. Yet it is important to recognize that the property of flatness or curviness is intrinsic to the space. No reference is needed to some putative higher-dimensional space – There are two essential yet complementary aspects of this new vision of time which are as striking in contrast as heaven and hell. Heaven is ruled by dynamical equations that are reversible and 'timeless'; their simplicity ensures stability for eternity. Hell is more akin to the real world, where fluctuations, uncertainty and chaos reign..."
The Arrow of Time – Peter Coveney and Roger Highfield

Eternal Harmony that is: of purposefully effectuated simultaneously relative harmoniously proportioned differential equations, expanded into a simultaneously relative, and hierarchically structured, whole, and/or patterns in space/time, and which is while functioning as Omnidimensional Time *made manifest*.
And: yes, it is exactly richer than any human language can express, but it is also exactly not putative: it is a scientific fact, and there must be a truly humanistic

32

reference: simultaneously relative single cognizable point time zero. And, exactly as was explained by the neuroscientist Jesus of Nazareth –

"Do not store up treasures for yourselves on earth, where moths and woodworms destroy them and thieves can break in and steal. But store up treasures for yourselves in heaven, where neither moth nor woodworms destroy them and thieves cannot break in and steal. For where your treasure is, there will your heart be also."
Matthew 6: 19-21

It is exactly not richer than our minds can: possibly, comprehend.

But, an individual human being must learn how to escape the confines of this mortal world, before they can even begin to allow their own selves to become capable of gaining access to the; "Heaven is ruled by dynamical equations that are reversible and 'timeless'; their simplicity ensures stability for eternity" – Eternal Harmony.

Which we exactly can not simply see: we can only understand. But we can also exactly experience it, just like a real symphony, and/or simultaneously relative concordant polyphonically structured whole, and identify it too. But which is, of course and also, rather –

"Thomas Chase – But the brain is much more complicated and plastic (than previously thought). If I ask you, 'Why does a board float in water?' – a question that involves some understanding of physics and a lot of cognitive skill, half your brain will light up..."
The 3-Pound Universe – Judith Hooper and Dick Teresi

Difficult. And/or painful: beginning to become capable of cognizing simultaneously relative Reality that is. And/or beginning to become capable of; "At birth, a baby's brain contains about 100 million neurons, the brain cells that carry electrical messages through the brain. Each one can produce up to 15,000 synapses, or connections to the other cells. Those synapses are the key to healthy development and learning" – acquiring the key to the Eternal Harmony. And, too, which is while we can become capable of acquiring access to the keys of –

"The Superstring theory resembles the quantum field theory because it is based on elementary units of matter. Instead of point particles, however, the superstring theory is based on strings that interact – According to this theory, the infinite variety of particles found in nature are simply different resonances of the same string, with no particle any more fundamental than any other – The symmetry of the superstring, once considered too beautiful to have any practical application, (has now become) the key to eliminating all infinities and anomalies."
Michio Kaku – Beyond Einstein

Supersymmetry and superstrings too. .

Which we can begin to do: escape the confines of this mortal world and gain access to the keys which unlock supersymmetry – superstrings, and the Eternal Harmony, by, first, reiterating our understanding of exactly what real: observable and effectual, truly humanistic quantum electrodynamics "is": actually occurring within truly humanistic simultaneously relative four-dimensional reality, and while upon this simultaneously relative point-mass of Earth. And which is while simultaneously effectually occurring, within a humanistic being's simultaneously relative: "quantum dynamically functioning," four-dimensional electrical potential mass of a mind, and within which are contained no projected images of things, but, only, cognizable simultaneously relative differential equations: while actually effectually functioning as simultaneously relative to/from, and within, a single cognizable point time zero.

And which we can do while beginning right here: point time zero, and the simultaneously relative point of this word: bird, upon this page located at an identifiable point within simultaneously relative space/time, and this word: bee, also located at another – separate and identifiable, point within simultaneously relative space/time, and while upon this page: point time zero, functioning as a single cognizable three-dimensional point projected into our minds, within which there are contained no projected images of things. Now, if we were to attempt to read this word: bird, located at that exact single identifiable point while upon this two-dimensional plane, while we do also – and simultaneously without moving our eyes from that point, attempt to read this word: bee, we can become capable of understanding that this: attempted conscious cognizant capability, is exactly a neurophysiological impossibility. And because human beings can only consciously focus upon a single ten degree point, while at any one point within simultaneously relative space/time. But, we can simultaneously consciously "see": within our peripheral vision and which does mean within our three-dimensional electrical potential mass minds within which there are contained no projected images of things, BOTH words: BIRD and BEE – SIMULTANEOUSLY. Which is while actually occurring within our three-dimensional electrical potential mass minds, and within which there are contained no projected images of things. But only simultaneously relative fundamental frequency modulations, made manifest as from the projected image of all identifiable three-dimensional masses, located within simultaneously relative space/time, and exactly as was explained by Leonardo da Vinci: "True sciences are – the principles of mathematics, that is to say, number and measure – termed arithmetic and geometry, which deal with discontinuous and continuous quantities with the utmost truth."

And which does mean, that the projected image of this word: bird, must be projected as simultaneously relative from that point – upon this page and within identifiable space, as to this single point: bee, located upon this page and within identifiable space, and while – simultaneously, the single point: of a word upon this page, must be projected as from this page AND INTO OUR MINDS. Which does mean, as we become capable of consciously cognizing each, and every, single cognizable point time zero – and/or word, upon this page, all of the remaining perceivable, and effectual, non-tangible form projected images: of all of the perceivable words upon this page, and/or things located within our peripheral vision, must have their non-tangible form projected image made manifest: within our three-dimensional electrical potential mass minds and within which there are contained no images of things, while as through the applicable function of quantized electrodynamics: actually functioning as light, and/or the universal constant of Time. And/or, that our three-dimensional electrical potential mass minds are capable of "traveling": as through the applied function of quantized electrodynamics, through the distances of space represented, and/or "time traveled," within simultaneously relative space/time, without actually "moving" through the space, and/or the time traveled: THIS IS A REAL QUANTUM LEAP FROM POINT A TO POINT B, and it is – also and simultaneously, elementary – and/or unidirectionally successive, Time *made manifest*. And too which is actually occurring: that are minds are capable of making manifest these real quantum leaps and while as from point A to point B, while our minds are also – and simultaneously, capable of being "at" both point A *and* point B: simultaneously. But which is, also, while these words, actually projected upon this two-dimensional plane, are not real three-dimensional points, they are simply an abstracted and projected representation of Reality: within which is where is contained real quantum electrodynamics – supersymmetry and superstrings too, and real Omnidimensional Time *made manifest*.

Because: within simultaneously relative Omnidimensional Reality, all of the simultaneously relative three-dimensional things: which human beings are capable of perceiving in reality, and within their electrical potential mass minds within which there are contained no images of things, must be located at a simultaneously relative point within simultaneously relative space/time: within identifiable truly humanistic three-dimensional space. And too which is while – simultaneously, all real points: in quantum electrodynamics – supersymmetry and superstrings real applicable functions, are only simultaneously relative fundamental frequency modulations, and/or "notes." AND – JUST LIKE A REAL SYMPHONY, which are expanded into harmoniously proportioned simultaneously relative differential equations, which are effectually functioning, while they are being expanded into a simultaneously relative hierarchically structured whole: truly humanistic being simultaneously relative three-dimensional quantum dynamically functioning mind, and central nervous system.

And until this: simultaneously relative function of Reality, does actually occur: within a human being's mind and while as on a regular daily basis, there can be –

"Parents Allegedly Kept Four Children In Home At All Times –
A couple allegedly shuttered their four children from the world by forbidding them from going outside the family home. Three of the children can speak only broken English and communicate with one another in their own language...The children do not seem to have been physically abused, L- said. The eldest child can easily converse with other people, but the three youngest communicate among themselves in their own primitive language, 'It's gibberish,' she said..."
James Hannah – Philadelphia Inquirer/Associated Press – April 16, 1999

Zero Time *made manifest*: within their minds and at all times too.
And, in identifiable scientific reality only, these; "A couple allegedly shuttered their four children from the world by forbidding them from going outside the family home. The children can speak only broken English and communicate with one another in their own language" – children, are actually much better off than these; "Dolls, trikes and now for tots – TVs – A new study on children's viewing habits reported that one-quarter of children ages 2 to 5, and 40 percent of those 6 to 11, have their own television sets" – children are. And, as was exactly explained by the scientist –

"Then Jesus said to his disciples, 'I tell you solemnly, it will be hard for a rich man to enter the kingdom of heaven. Yes, I tell you again, it is easier for a camel to pass through the eye of a needle than for a rich man to enter the kingdom of heaven. 'When the disciples heard this they were astonished. 'Who can be saved, then?' they said. Jesus gazed at them. 'For men, he told them, 'this is impossible; for God everything is possible."
Matthew 19: 23-26

Jesus of Nazareth.
And – again, as it: the absolute scientific truth, has been confirmed by –

"Drugs are like sledgehammers,' observes Dr. Eric Nestler of the Yale University School of Medicine. 'They profoundly alter many pathways..."
Addicted – J. Madeleine Nash – Time – May 5, 1997

Late 20th century neuroscientific research, and/or pure observable facts.
And, too, which: that it will be just about impossible for the majority of this affected generation to begin to take back control of their very own selves, is exactly because, we: society, did–

"Rat-a-tat-tat. Rat-a-tat-tat. Rat-a-tat-tat – If scientists could eavesdrop on the brain of a human embryo 10, maybe 12 weeks after conception, they would hear an astonishing racket. Inside the womb, long before light first strikes the retina of the eye or the earliest dreamy images flicker through the cortex, nerve cells in the developing brain crackle with purposeful activity – But these neurons – as the long, wiry cells that carry electrical messages through the nervous system and brain are called – are not transmitting signals in scattershot fashion. That would produce a featureless static – On the contrary, evidence is growing that the Staccato bursts of electricity that form these distinctive rat-a-tat-tats arise from coordinated waves of neural activity, and that those pulsing waves, like currents shifting sand on the ocean floor, actually change the shape of the brain – the same processes that wire the brain before birth, neuroscientists are finding, also drives the explosion of learning that occurs immediately afterward – of all the problems the growing nervous system must solve, the most daunting is posed by the wiring itself. After birth, when the number of connections explodes, each of the brain's billions of neurons will forge links to thousands of others – the developing nervous system has strung the equivalent of telephone trunk lines between the right neighborhoods in the right cities. Now it has to sort out which wires belong to which house, a problem that cannot be solved by genes alone for reasons that boil down to simple arithmetic – These axons start out as a scrambled bowl of spaghetti – what sorts out the mess, scientists have established, is neural activity – If parents and policymakers don't pay attention to the conditions under which this delicate process takes place, we will all suffer the consequences – starting around the year 2010."

Fertile Minds – Madeleine Nash – Time – February 3, 1997

Forget to pay attention: to Reality only. Exactly instead of letting ourselves become diverted by entertainment, and/or anything except for purposefully allowed exposure to only harmonious proportions of Reality, for our children's minds to be programmed by.

And which is exactly because, a truly humanistic being electrical potential mass of mind, is almost exactly "analogous to a computer," but it is also – and simultaneously, absolutely nothing "like a computer." Which is while beginning with the fact, that a human being's mind, does contain the possibility for purposefully effectuated biochemical inductions, and which may, then, enable a human being to begin to become capable of experiencing truly humanistic emotions. And, also, a human being's mind is exactly not like a computer, because it: a human being's simultaneously relative "hard-wiring," is –

"If humans are less robotlike than salamanders or ducks, it's not because we have no wired-in behaviors. In fact, we have quite a few. What makes the difference is the ratio of 'un-wired' to wired-in gray matter, because neurons that are not committed at birth to a set function – are available for learning, for modification. Virtually all the cells in an amphibian or reptile brain directly process sensory information – or control movement, but in humans a great gray area – about three-fourths of the cortex – lies between sensory input and motor output, called the association areas. These include the frontal lobes..."

The 3-Pound Universe – Judith Hooper and Dick Teresi

Pliable: the actual yet to be formed hard-wiring. And/or as it: the actual individually affected hard-wiring, is actually capable of being formed: while as through purposefully allowed exposure to all simultaneously relative stimuli. And too which is while including, and beginning with, the –

"...by virtue of its morphological identity – each spine may be regarded as a functional unit, interacting with other spine units (while) the wide range of spine shapes and sizes (may) reflect ongoing dynamic changes in spine excitability properties dependent on frequency of synaptic input. Different spine shapes (and effectuated) spine geometry – may thus reflect different stages of spine maturation."
Gordon M. Shephard – Apical Dendritic Spines of Cortical Pyramidal Cells
Gary Lynch – Synapses, Circuits and the Beginning of Memory

Individually affected neurons: are capable of being purposefully altered. Into purposefully effectuated geometrical formations, and/or individually completed harmoniously proportioned fundamental frequency modulations – and/or "notes," and which is while actually effectually functioning as subservient to a hierarchically structured whole: exactly as is simultaneously relative Omnidimensional Reality, or exactly not.
And we can reiterate our acknowledged understanding of this scientific fact by, first, reiterating our understanding of the purposefully effectuated formation of the world's first Truly Idealist Democratic Society: within the individually affected minds, of the individual human beings, who were directly responsible for that purposeful formation. Which was while actually functioning, and as was exactly explained by Thomas Paine, as –

"Society is produced by our wants, and government by our wickedness; the former promotes our happiness *positively* by uniting our affections, the latter negatively by restraining our vices. The one encourages intercourse, the other creates distinction. The first is a patron, the last a punisher...There are injuries which nature cannot forgive; she would cease to be nature if she did – The Almighty hath implanted in us these indistinguishable feelings for good and wise purposes – They are the guardians of his image in our hearts. They distinguish us from the herd of common animals – I draw my idea of the form of government from a principle in nature, which no art can overturn, viz. that the more simple anything is, the less liable it is to be disordered...Thomas Paine: *Common Sense*"
Common Sense – Thomas Paine

Common Sense. And/or the universally applicable empirical self-conscious awareness: intelligence, that all of mankind, can – possibly, have – and/or be "in possession of," "in common," while "effectuated as through their senses." And/or uniquely humanistic parallel functioning minds, and central nervous systems, and while specifically effectually functioning within a humanistic being's cerebral cortex, which is exactly what does; "They are the guardians of his image in our hearts. They distinguish us from the herd of common animals" – distinguish a human being from an animal, and/or even a; "If humans are less robotlike than salamanders or ducks, it's not because we have no wired-in behaviors. In fact, we have quite a few. What makes the difference is the ratio 'un-wired' to wired-in gray matter" – mindless automaton.

While, as applicable to the formation of the world's first Truly Idealist Democratic Society, and while, simultaneously, effectually occurring within the individually affected minds, we can reiterate our understanding of the fact, that each individual neuron: contained within an individual human being's mind, is equivalent to a house and/or point. But within which: a new society and a human being's newly born mind, there are not yet any roads, and/or connections, formed: between the individual houses, and/or neurons, and/or points. So there must be a desire, and/or a will, to purposefully effectuate the connections between the individual houses, and/or neurons and/or points, and too which is while: "uniting our affections" *by* "encouraging intercourse." Which would actually be; "At a purely chemical level (just as the injection of) heroin triggers release of dopamine – every experience humans find enjoyable – embracing a lover or savoring chocolate – amounts to little more than an explosion of dopamine in the nucleus accumbens, as exhilarating and ephemeral as a firecracker – dopamine, can be elevated by a hug, a kiss, a word of praise" – DOPAMINE.

So that, a young child who can not be in possession of very much universally applicable empirical self-consciousness, will be in possession of – only, the ability to experience a heightened dopamine biochemical induction, and/or a sense of awe, within his childishly impressionable mind. And, as we can remember, because of his allowed exposure to the non-tangible form projected image of any newly perceived tangible form mass thing, and/or "color," that he has never seen before. And which will – then and because of the purposefully effectuated dopamine biochemical induction actually functioning *as* a "sense of awe," cause the child to move, and while in a "childlike way," from point A: his house, towards point B: the apparent position of any newly perceived non-tangible form projected image, of *any* tangible form mass dopamine biochemical inducing effectual stimulus, and/or any newly perceived stimulus at all actually effectually functioning as: 1. And – again which is as we can remember and as 20th century neuroscientific research has confirmed, which: that a truly humanistic being's three-dimensional electrical potential mass of a mind, and parallel functioning central nervous system, is just beginning to become programmed, is while beginning as from a truly humanistic being's –

"Rat-a-tat-tat. Rat-a-tat-tat. Rat-a-tat-tat – If scientists could eavesdrop on the brain of a human embryo 10, maybe 12 weeks after the conception, they would hear an astonishing racket. Inside the womb, long before light first strikes the retina of the eye or the earliest dreamy images flicker through the cortex, nerve cells in the developing brain crackle with purposeful activity – But these neurons – as the long, wiry cells that carry electrical message through the nervous system and brain are called – are not transmitting signals in scattershot fashion. That would produce a featureless static..."

Fertile Minds – Madeleine Nash – Time – February 3, 1997

Simultaneously relative single cognizable point time zero: secured within her mother's womb, and while upon, and within, this simultaneously relative point-mass of Earth. And – while functioning as a simultaneously relative three-dimensional electrical potential mass within which are contain no images of things, is: that a truly humanistic being's mind is capable of being programmed, while beginning to be affected by –

"A great deal of work has been directed at long-term potentiated (LTP) effect, and while many issues remain unresolved, a number of its characteristics have been determined, among which are the following:

Cooperatively LTP is larger and more reliably elicited by high-frequency stimulation delivered to a group of axons generating overlapping synaptic fields than when small numbers of fibers are stimulated – Cumulative Nature LTP is not all-or-none effect in that, up to a point, successive episodes of high-frequency stimulation produced increasing amounts of synaptic facilitation – Regional Distribution Long-Term potentiation is not restricted to the hippocampus and can be elicited in the cortex, a variety of sites throughout the telencephalon (cerebral hemispheres), and possibly elsewhere in the central and peripheral nervous system – The wide range of spine shapes and sizes (may) reflect ongoing dynamic changes in spine excitability properties dependent on frequency of synaptic input. Different spine shapes (and effectuated) spine geometry – may thus reflect different stages of spine maturation...To summarize, physiological stimulation of hippocampal pathways causes lasting specific changes in the physiology, anatomy and chemistry of synapses, and the latter two effects are correlated with the first. These results offer a plausible substrate of memory storage and tell us that hippocampal synapses must contain a biological process that when transiently activated yields long-lasting, functionally significant modification of the synapses."

Gary Lynch – Synapses, Circuits and the Beginning of Memory

Every "simultaneously relative thing." Which is while actually effectually occurring within a human being's simultaneously relative, three-dimensional, electrical potential mass of a mind, and parallel functioning central nervous system, actually functioning within truly humanistic simultaneously relative Reality. And within: a truly humanistic being's three-dimensional quantum dynamically functioning electrical potential mass of mind and central nervous system *and* simultaneously relative Omnidimensional Reality, there are contained NO projected images of things, but only simultaneously relative differentials/differential equations. There it: the Music and Science, and/or the plain, and simple, absolute neuroscientific truth, is – in simple English, and in black and white. And, yet, they –

"Music and Science Meet on a Piano Bench –
After reverently shaking hands with the great pianists Josef Hofmann and Leopold Godowsky at a party, a fan was struck that the men's hands were so small. 'How can you great artists play the piano so magnificently with such small hands?' the women asked. Godowsky replied, 'Where in the world did you get the idea that we play the piano with our hands' –The piano is primarily an instrument of the mind – was made abundantly clear Thursday at a concert and panel discussion, titled 'Polymaths and the piano,' at Caspary Hall at Rockefeller University. Eight talented amateur pianists who happen to earn their livings as doctors, mathematicians, biologists and computer scientists presented a program of music that, surprisingly, did not contain a single piece by Bach – After the music making, the pianists took part in a panel discussion led by Michael Kimmelman, the chief art critic of The New York Times, who is himself a gifted amateur pianist. Mr. Kimmelman tried to get his panelists to explore the cognitive connection between music and science – Judging from the performances and from the panelists' experiences, the connection between music and Science is more visceral than intellectual. 'What is it about some tones that seem to generate something in the solar plexus that moves us to tears?' Dr. H- wondered – Steven H- an electrical engineer – said that acquaintances often speculated about the connection between his field and music – The only connection that Mr. H- would venture was that both engineering and music required a lot of discipline. 'A young piano student, even a prodigy, has to develop some systematic approach to practicing,' he said. So in that sense, the two fields may involve certain neural activities that are similar – Steven D- , was the only member of the panel who claimed not to spend much time thinking about the connection between music and science – not because the task does not interest him, but simply because it is too difficult. 'I'm sure there is a connection,' he added – Balancing the hours practicing the piano requires with the demands of their professional careers is a trick that the performers manage in a variety of ways. 'No TV, no videos, no useless movies, no mindless entertainment,' Dr. H- insisted – The ultimate connection between music and science was left unsettled. It became clear that to most of the performers, music, like science, was a way to grapple with mysteries of existence. The universe a composer creates in a composition is no less impenetrable than the physical universe of science. As Mr. H- summed it up, in the end, 'Music is evidence that reason is incapable of understanding everything."
Bruce Schechter – The New York Times – Tuesday February 13, 2001

Still don't get it: YOU HAVE GOT TO BE KIDDING ME – I KEEP HOPING TO WAKE UP FROM THIS NIGHTMARE.
And these are supposed to be some of the world's most intelligent human beings too: it is no wonder that they do have schizophrenic two-dimensional brain dead Cubist things hanging in their museums. And too – that they still don't get it,

41

which is even after Albert Einstein did plainly explain it, for all the world to simply see, and with our eyes alone too. And as was recently reiterated by –

"a brief history of relativity –

toward the end of the 19th century scientists believed they were close to a complete description of the universe. They imagined that space was filled with everything by a continuous medium called ether – Soon, however, discrepancies with the idea of an all-pervading ether began to appear – it was a young clerk named Albert Einstein, working in a Swiss Patent Office in Bern, who cut through the ether and solved the speed-of-light problem once and for all. In June 1905 he wrote one of three papers that would establish him as one the world's leading scientists – and in the process start two conceptual revolutions that changed our understanding of time, space and reality – In that 1905 paper, Einstein pointed out that because you could not detect whether or not you were moving through the ether, the whole situation of an ether was redundant. Instead, Einstein started from the postulate that the laws of science should appear the same to all freely moving observers. In particular, observers should all measure the same speed for light, no matter how they were moving – Einstein's postulate that the laws of nature should appear the same to all freely moving observers was the foundation of the theory of relativity, so called because it implies that only relative motion is important – Einstein's general theory of relativity transformed space and time from a passive background in which events take place to active participants in the dynamics of the cosmos – General relativity completely changed the discussion of the origin and fate of the universe. A static universe could have existed forever or could have been created in its present form at some time in the past. On the other hand, if galaxies are moving apart today, they must have been closer together in the past. About 15 billion years ago, they would all have been on top of one another and their density would have been infinite. According to the general theory, this Big Bang was the beginning of the universe and of time itself – General relativity also predicts that time comes to a stop inside black holes, regions of space/time that are so warped that light cannot escape them – The equations of general relativity are his (best) memorial. They should last as long as the universe ..."

Stephen Hawking – Time – December 31, 1999

Dr. Stephen Hawking. Being in that, all of simultaneously relative reality, is only simultaneously relative individually completed fundamental frequency modulations, and/or simultaneously relative individually completed differentials, and/or simultaneously relative individually completed velocities, and/or simultaneously relative individually completed movements, and/or simultaneously relative individually completed notes – and/or Time "made manifest." Which are effectually functioning while remaining subservient to, and having been simultaneously effectually formed as through, a hierarchically structured whole: concordant polyphonically structured orchestration, while having been formed as

42

simultaneously to/from, and within, a single cognizable point time zero: the point of the beginning of the symphony; the point the Big Bang – the point of the beginning of Omnidimensional Time *made manifest*. Yet they still don't get it, as it does –

> **"unfinished symphony -**
> Strings may do what Einstein finally failed to do: tie together the two great irreconcilable ideas of 20th century physics
>
> 'I am generally regarded as a sort of petrified object, rendered deaf and blind by the years,' Albert Einstein confided near the end of his life. He was, alas, correct. During the last three decades of his remarkable career, Einstein had become obsessed by the dream of producing a unified field theory, a series of equations that would establish an underlying link between the seemingly unrelated forces of gravity and electromagnetism – In so doing Einstein hoped also to resolve the conflict between two competing visions of the universe: the smooth continuum of space/time, where stars and planets reign, as described by his general theory of relativity, and the unseemingly jitteriness of the submicroscopic quantum world, where particles hold sway – Einstein worked hard on the problem, but success eluded him – The equations of general relativity simply can't handle such a situation, where the laws of cause and effect break down and particles jump from point A to point B without going through the space in between. In such a world, you can only calculate what will probably happen next – which is just what quantum theory is designed to do – A new generation of physicists has at last taken on the challenge of creating a complete theory – one capable of explaining, in Einstein's words, 'every element of the physical reality' – The trouble is (no one) knows how many other pieces must fall into place before scientists succeed in solving this greatest of all puzzles – In string theory, says (Brian) Greene, 'we're still trying to figure out the central nugget of truth' – In 1995, (Edward) Witten, perhaps the most brilliant theorist working in physics today, declared that all five supersymmetric string theories represented different approximations of a deeper, underlying theory. He called it M theory – The *M* in M theory stands for many things, says Witten, including matrix, mystery and magic – Which shapes represent the fundamental structures in our universe? On this point, string theorists are currently clueless. For the world conjured into existence by M theory is so exotic that scientists are being forced to work not just at the frontier of physics but at the frontier of mathematics as well. Indeed, it may be that they lack some absolutely essential tool and will have to develop it, just as Isaac Newton was pushed by his investigations of the laws of motion to develop the calculus – It might in the end take an Einstein to complete Einstein's unfinished intellectual symphony."
>
> J. Madeleine Nash – Time – December 31, 1999

Remain an unfinished symphony. So: let's finish it – the "intellectual symphony."

And, no, it does not "take an Einstein," but it does simply require a return to innocence. Which is by, first, gaining access to the absolutely essential tool which is required for consciously cognizing Omnidimensional Time *made manifest*, and as was exactly explained by –

"The Kingdom of Heaven is like treasure hidden in a field which someone has found; he hides it again, goes off happy, sells off everything he owns and buys the field. Again, the Kingdom of Heaven is like a merchant looking for fine pearls; when he finds one of great value he goes off and sells everything he owns to buy it."
Matthew 13: 44-46

Jesus of Nazareth.
And which is, only: that any individual can enable themselves to gain access to the Eternal Harmony, as any individual human being, does begin to become neurophysiologically capable of effectively forming, a purposefully effectuated, truly humanistic, three-dimensional and simultaneously relative, quantum dynamically functioning, and geometrically effectuated, "point-system," and/or "matrix." And/or, a –

"Diamond – (which is a) pure form of carbon naturally crystallized in the isometric system...(and while) through which, starting from disordered atoms, pieces of matter are derived which are tightly organized in a periodical or homogenous manner. At the moment of formation, in the course of growth, the mineral is attempting to achieve a state of equilibrium with its environment."
Rocks and Minerals – Simon and Schuster/Ed. M. Prinz, G. Harlow, J. Peters

Crystalline latticework. And/or, a truly humanistic parallel functioning, quantum dynamical, three-dimensional electrical potential mass of a mind, and central nervous system, and/or Omnidimensional refractive gem of a mind. Which may, then, become capable of cognizing Omnidimensional Time *made manifest*. And which is, and exactly as Jesus of Nazareth did explain –

"Do not imagine that I have come to abolish the law of the Prophets. I have come not to abolish but to complete them. I tell you solemnly, till heaven and earth disappear, not one dot, not one little stroke, shall disappear from the law until its purpose is achieved. Therefore, the man who infringes even one of the least of these commandments and teaches others to do the same will be considered the least in the kingdom of heaven.'
'If, then, they say to you, 'Look, he is in the desert,' do not go there; 'Look, he is in some hiding place,' do not believe it; because the coming of the Son of Man will be like lightning striking in the East and flashing far into the West. Wherever the corpse is, there the vultures will gather.'
'He put another parable before them. The kingdom of heaven is like a mustard seed which a man took and sowed in his field. It is the smallest of all the seeds, but when it has grown it is the biggest shrub of all and becomes a tree so that

the birds of the air come and shelter in its branches.'

'He told them another parable, 'the kingdom of heaven is like the yeast a woman took and mixed in with three measures of flour till it was leavened all through."

Matthew 5: 17-19, 24: 26-28, 13: 31-32, 13: 33

As all of simultaneously relative Omnidimensional Reality: while actually functioning as the universally applicable simultaneously relative Common Law of Reality, and while simultaneously effectually forming tangible form mass stimulus: 1, and non-tangible form mass nothingness: 0, is capable of effectually functioning as quantum dynamically functioning applied three parts, of: the nuclear strong/weak and electromagnetism, to form one whole: gravity – while actually functioning as simultaneously to/from, and within, a single cognizable point time zero. And too as it: applied three parts to form one whole, is also the universally applicable effectual cause, for all of simultaneously relative Reality. And which is – while actually functioning as simultaneously relative Omnidimensional Time *made manifest,* and as the universally applicable effectual cause for all of simultaneously relative Reality, and exactly as was explained by Albert Einstein; "But if every gram of material contains this tremendous energy, why did it go so long unnoticed? The answer is simple enough – it is as though a man who is fabulously rich should never spend or give away a cent; no one can tell how rich he was" – simply invisible. As was also exactly explained by –

"Do not store up treasures for yourselves on earth, where moths and woodworms destroy them and thieves can break in and steal. But store up treasures for yourselves in heaven, were neither moth nor woodworms destroy them and thieves cannot break in and steal. For where year treasure is, there will your heart be also."

Matthew 6: 19-21

Jesus of Nazareth. That an individual humanistic being cannot simply see it: the Eternal Harmony functioning as Omnidimensional Time *made manifest*, they can only understand it: within their individually affected, truly humanistic being, simultaneously relative Omnidimensional refractive gem of a mind, as it is capable of effectually functioning only within; "The ultimate connection between music and science was left unsettled. It became clear that to most of the performers, music, like science, was a way to grapple with mysteries of existence. The universe a composer creates in a composition is no less impenetrable than the physical universe of science..." – truly humanistic simultaneously relative Reality, and/or every thing in the entire universe.

So, let's Return to innocence, and –

"Tuning Up The Brain –

The 'Mozart effect' suggests that classical compositions can stimulate learning. But the jury is still out – What scientists do know is that keyboard instruction – making music, not just hearing it – seems to resonate within the brain. In one typical study, neuroscientists led by Gordon Shaw of the University of California, Irvine, tested 3- to 5-year-olds who received six months of piano lessons. The researchers found that the tiny pianists improved significantly in spatial-temporal reasoning – Such effects are even more pronounced in older kids. After a year of twice-a-week piano lessons, a recent study in California found, second graders from a poor district improved their math scores to those of fourth graders from an affluent one..."

Sharon Begley – Newsweek – Fall/Winter 2000

Practice our scales of Reality. And: as we begin to practice our scales of Reality and as young children, which is, exactly as Leonardo da Vinci did explain, while enabling ourselves to –

"Therefore O students study mathematics and do not build without foundations."

Build our truly humanistic foundations: within our individually affected truly humanistic being three-dimensional electrical potential mass minds, and parallel functioning central nervous systems.

So, let's go back to point time zero: upon our keyboard, and form the connection between the abstraction, which is termed music, and the function of Reality. And – exactly because there is no such thing as an abstraction within simultaneously relative Reality, which is the abstracted, and reapplied, function of simultaneously relative Reality, and practice our scales of Reality. And/or, purposefully effectuate a simultaneously relative gradated series, of: quantized individually completed movements, and/or notes, actually functioning as harmoniously proportioned individually completed displacements: 1, of humanistic nothingness: 0, and/or harmoniously proportioned fundamental frequency modulations, and while beginning at the low end of the scale – with a modulation of 27 cycles per second: OF Time. Which does mean, that there are made manifest 27 points displacing humanistic nothingness: while actually functioning as through the quantized wave function, for every second of Time *made manifest*, and, again, which is while beginning at the low end of the scale, and while making manifest a low simultaneously relative fundamental frequency modulation. As we begin: from point time zero and/or point A, to move up through the scale, and into higher simultaneously relative fundamental frequency modulations, out into simultaneously relative space *while* making manifest Time. Continuing all the way up to the high end of the scale, at 4096 cycles per second which is point B, and which is also, of course, an acknowledged universally applicable function which no one questions.

But, they do plainly admit, that they *do*; "The ultimate connection between music and science was left unsettled – 'Music is evidence that reason is incapable of understanding everything" – have a little trouble making the connection to Reality. So, together, let's take a walk outside, into uncharted territories, and make the connection to Reality.

And, too, which: our physiological movement and as we walk throughout simultaneously relative reality, we can begin to make manifest, while purposefully making manifest simultaneously relative largo tempoed movement: actually with our bodies, and throughout, and within, simultaneously relative space/time. While this word: largo, does mean: "slow; in a broad, dignified style," and too which: our purposefully effectuated physiological movement, we can begin to make manifest while walking upon a sidewalk. Now, as we continue to walk all throughout, and within, simultaneously relative Reality, and the way everyone would have done while as within the world's first Truly Idealist Democratic Society, let's begin to take a good look at all of simultaneously relative Reality, and which is while occurring within our simultaneously relative three-dimensional electrical potential mass minds, and parallel functioning central nervous systems, and within which there are contained no images of things. And too: that we are actually beginning to take a good look at all of simultaneously relative Reality, we should do while we do remain focused upon infinity, and/or our truly humanistic horizon line, and which was exactly as Christopher Columbus did, and not, simply, upon the ground immediately in front of us, and/or any single thing for that matter, and/or as Thomas Jefferson did explain; "Those which depend on ourselves, are the only pleasures a wise man will count on: for nothing is ours, which another may deprive us of. Hence the inestimable alum of intellectual pleasures. Ever in our power, always leading us to something new, never cloying, we ride serene and sublime above the concerns of this mortal world, contemplating truth and nature, matter and motion, the laws which bind up their existence, and that Eternal being who made and bound them by those laws" – any of the animalistic concerns of this mortal world. And, so, we can now see the absolute truth of all of simultaneously relative Reality, and which is the neuroscientific fact, that we can "see": within our peripheral vision while remaining focused upon eternity, and within our truly humanistic parallel functioning minds and central nervous systems: wherein there are contained no projected images of things, that all of the simultaneously relative individually completed movements, and/or points, of pavement, appear to be farther: from each other, where our humanistic feet are simultaneously in contact with the ground: as simultaneously relative to far away – in the simultaneously relative distance. Which does mean, that at our truly humanistic point time zero: point A where our feet are in contact with the ground and as the apparent image of the individually completed movements of points is made manifest as through the applied function of light, and/or the universal constant of Time, that the simultaneously relative fundamental frequency modulation, and/or displacements of humanistic nothingness, is low – as we are actually capable of perceiving it: as simultaneously relative to our humanistic position within simultaneously relative space/time, upon this point-mass of Earth. Just like that which is capable of being made manifest upon a keyboard, and which is an "abstracted function" *of* "simultaneously relative Reality" only, while as from one end of the universe to the other: because Time is the universal constant of Reality. And, of course, which does mean, that we can now: as we are actually capable of consciously cognizing all of simultaneously relative Reality within our minds, see: within our simultaneously relative peripheral vision, that the actual simultaneously relative fundamental frequency: of points and/or displacements of nothingness as measured by the universal constant of Time, does begin to rise, and/or increase tempo, as the simultaneously relative distance increases: as simultaneously relative to, and from, our identifiable single cognizable point time zero, and/or point A. End of mystery.

Which wasn't really that difficult either, or painful. Well, actually, it was a little more painful than simply sitting inside alone, and even a little more painful, still, than sitting inside with another human being, and – too, quite a bit more painful than being a part of a large group of people while socializing, and/or simply having fun, and it was even, still, a lot more painful than watching television. Because, as we can remember, all of those other things are capable of affecting a simple dopamine biochemical induction within a human being, which is capable of being consciously cognized as a purely pleasurable experienced humanistic phenomenon, while walking through reality is exactly not. Except, remember exactly what walking through reality is capable of inducing, and while only beginning with a relatively largo tempoed movement? Well, that would be; "Princeton's (Barry) Jacobs believes that, based on experiments with cats, repetitive motor activity – walking, stimulates the release of serotonin" – serotonin, and as a matter of neuroscientific fact. And remember exactly what an artificially effectuated elevated serotonin induction is capable of doing, while simply being induced as through the consumption of Ecstasy? Well, that would be; "Ecstasy floods your brain with serotonin, you feel so connected to the continuum of your life. A subtle, purifying something descends over you" – connecting us with the continuum of our life, and/or as it: a purposefully effectuated elevated serotonin induction, does exactly; "What is it about some tones that seem to generate something in the solar plexus that moves us to tears" – begin to move us to tears. End of mystery – again.

Which is exactly not; "Music is evidence that reason is incapable of understanding everything" – incapable of being understood, and/or, too, exactly not incapable of being explained in neuroscientific reality. Which is the fact, that the effectuated cognizance of a purposefully effectuated harmoniously proportioned largo tempoed movement: *of* harmoniously proportioned simultaneously relative fundamental frequency modulations and/or notes, can induce a purposefully effectuated serotonin induction, within a human being's parallel functioning mind, and central nervous system. And which is while beginning with a relatively slow, and largo tempoed, movement, while we are simultaneously in contact with the ground. Now, take a look at the ground: what tone and/or color is it? That, of course, would be a dark tone and/or color, and as simultaneously relative to humanistic nothingness, which is exactly no color – and/or a simultaneously relative light tone, and as it: humanistic nothingness, is simultaneously up, and away, from our simultaneously relative position upon the dark in tone point-mass of Earth. And too, which is as it: the light in tone relative distance as from our contact with the point-mass of Earth, is the exact direction in which the simultaneously relative higher frequencies are. Which: if we wanted to move in a purposefully effectuated direction towards, would require us: as humanistic beings, to expend a relative amount of humanistic energy, to enable ourselves to become capable of moving while in the purposefully effectuated direction towards, and too which would – then, enable us: as humanistic beings, to begin to become capable of experiencing a relatively happy, and/or joyful, and/or energetic, experienced humanistic phenomenon. And which actually would, become affected as through a purposefully effectuated; "Candace Pert: we've measured opiate receptors in everything from fruit fly heads to human brains" – biochemical endorphin induction. And – again and again: End of mystery.

And, too, which is as this word: mystery, does mean: "something that is secret or impossible to understand," or – perhaps, even: "ancient religions that admitted candidates by secret rites and rituals known only to initiates." Except, while functioning as a scientist who was seeking only admittance to the absolute truth, I did actually go to one of these; "Music and Science Meet on the Piano Bench – The piano is primarily an instrument of the mind – was made abundantly clear Thursday at a concert and panel discussion, titled 'Polymaths and the piano,' at Caspary Hall at Rockefeller Center" – things once. And – while I did see many peculiar paganish rituals occurring, I didn't actually see any bodies moving, except, of course, for my own self, and right for the door and out of there, simply because of the overbearing stench of truly humanistic brain death, and hypocrisy too, wafting through their aristocratic environment. While they: the so-called human beings who do make manifest these environments, are nothing more than, as was exactly explained by Leonardo da Vinci –

"Though I might not know, like them, how to cite from the authors, I will cite something far more worthy, quoting experience, mistress of their masters. These very people go about inflated and pompous, clothed and adorned not with their own labors but with those of others."

A bunch of pompous asses.

So, we can now know, when truly humanistic beings do become capable of functioning in an intelligent manner, they do only; "Tuning Up The Brain – The 'Mozart effect' suggests that classical compositions can stimulate learning. But the jury is still out – What scientists do know is that keyboard instruction – making music, not just hearing it – seems to resonate within the brain – researchers found that (young) pianists improved significantly in spatial-temporal reasoning" – move

49

within their minds alone, as they begin to become capable of making manifest Time. So I did, as I did move in a purposefully effectuated direction right out of their brain dead excessive aristocratic environment, and back outside: with my mind and body.

So, let's go back outside – into simultaneously relative Omnidimensional Reality, and go in search of the absolute truth again, and the very definition of truly humanistic intelligence, and truly humanistic brain death also. Because, we do know, exactly, that it is not in there: simply inside anywhere, and especially within their minds. Which is, actually, by their very own admission too. As they did plainly declare: in words, that they: the world's most supposedly intelligent humanistic beings, are the exact only ones who are capable of; "Where in the world did you get the idea that we play the piano with our hands' – The piano is primarily an instrument of the mind" – fully understanding the simultaneously relative abstracted function of Omnidimensional Reality, and/or exactly what musical notes are in Reality. But, then, they did actually only; "The ultimate connection between music and science was left unsettled" – contradict their own selves, and plainly admit that they do not understand Reality. And then, of course, they did only simply go on to actually prove; "Judging from the performances of the panelists' experiences, the connection between music and Science is more visceral than intellectual" – that they are neurophysiologically capable of understanding absolutely nothing. And which is as they are – only, capable of; "What is it about some tones that seems to generate something in the solar plexus that moves us to tears" – physiologically responding to a perceivable stimulus, and/or a single projected unidirectionally successive, and harmoniously proportioned, musical sound, and/or a song. Which is while actually functioning as unidirectionally successive harmoniously proportioned, and elementary, Time *made manifest*. And: in scientific reality, even a –

"Color often signifies the difference between being seen, and consequently finding a partner, and being ignored – a male frigate-bird in the Galapagos Islands inflates the red pouch beneath its bill to attract a female."
Colors for Survival – Marco Ferrari

Bird's brain can do that. While, in reality, if any one person were to, simply, inform any other one individual person, that they were – only, capable of functioning as a bird's brain is capable of functioning, that would be an insult. Because, in scientific reality, the very definition of a bird's brain, is: "a dolt or scatterbrain," and, too, which is as this word: dolt, is defined as: "a dull, stupid person; blockhead." And too, in identifiable neuroscientific reality, we do also know, that a bird's brain can make manifest an infinite amount of different songs also, and/or harmoniously proportioned unidirectionally successive tonal variations. Which are capable of actually functioning as elementary Time *made manifest*. So, that: functioning as a bird's brain is capable of functioning, while making manifest unidirectionally successive tonal variations, and/or songs, is exactly not the definition of truly humanistic intelligence: in identifiable reality only, and as a

50

matter of fact only also.

While, as we can remember, we do also now know, as a matter of neuroscientific fact, that a bird's brain can move in a purposefully effectuated direction: while as from point A towards point B, to enable itself to become capable of consuming its allowed exposure to an effectual stimulus, and/or to enable itself to become capable of experiencing a simple dopamine biochemical induction, actually functioning as pure *pleasure*. And, too, which is – only, exactly as an; "That's what emotions are about – sex and violence, pain and pleasure. Even bacteria have a little hierarchy of primitive likes and dislikes. They're programmed to migrate toward or away from a chemotactic substance; they're little robots that go for sugar at all costs and away from salt" – amoeba is capable of doing in neuroscientific reality. So, we can also know, that this: "That's what emotions are about – sex and violence, pain and pleasure. Even bacteria have a little hierarchy of primitive likes and dislikes," and which is the ability for an individual humanistic being to enable themselves to move while as in a purposefully effectuated direction: from point A towards point B, and too while as in a unidirectionally successive manner, to simply enable themselves to become capable of consuming allowed exposure to an abstracted biochemical inducing effectual stimulus, is – too, exactly not the definition of truly humanistic intelligence. And too we do also now know, and because this is the early 21st century as we do have access to computers, that a bird's brain is exactly differed from –

"Any computing machine that is to solve a complex mathematical problem must be 'programmed' for this task. Hence it is to be expected that – an efficiently organized large artificial automaton (like a large computing machine) will – do things successively – one thing at a time."
>   John VonNeumann – The Computer and the Brain – The World Treasury of Physics, Astronomy and Mathematics, Ed. Timothy Ferris

A mindless automaton. Which: a mindless automaton and/or a machine, can only function in an absolutely abstracted, and unidirectionally successive, manner, and/or access an infinite amount of abstracted information. And which: absolutely abstracted anything, is capable of actually functioning as an abstracted dopamine biochemical inducing effectual stimulus, and capable of causing an amoeba to move while in a purposefully effectuated direction, to enable itself to become capable of experiencing a purely pleasurable experienced phenomenon. So, we can now know, for a verified neuroscientific fact, that this: access to abstracted knowledge and/or absolutely abstracted anything while functioning in a unidirectionally successive manner, is, also, exactly not the definition of truly humanistic intelligence.

And we sure, as hell, know that simply creating a diversion, and/or producing entertainment, could never be the definition of truly humanistic intelligence, and too which is as this word: sure, does mean: "assured and certain beyond question." And too and of course, we can also, and sure as hell, know that simply –

51

"The little red wagon keeps flying along: imaginations can go flying on red wagons – For 80 years now, children have climbed into their Radio Flyers and hitched their little red wagons to a star without batteries or high-tech innovations, these venerable toys have allowed young minds to soar – 'A wagon unleashes a child imagination,' said Robert – ' It can be anything a child imagines it to be..."
Cliff Edwards – Philadelphia Inquirer/A.P.-Saturday, May 3, 1997

Employing the use of our childish imaginations, could not, possibly, be the definition of truly humanistic intelligence. While they are only the extreme conscious cognizant capabilities of a young child too: any and/or all of them.

While, any and/or all of them: accessing unidirectionally successive and abstracted knowledge, making manifest entertainment, making manifest escapism and while employing the use of our childish imaginations, and/or simply existing while in ignorance of neuroscientific reality, are all simply an absolute ignorance of uniquely humanistic Reality.

So, exactly what is the very definition of truly humanistic intelligence? Well, the definition of truly humanistic intelligence, is –

"intelligence: capacity for reason, understanding – the faculty of understanding..."
The Random House College Dictionary

Understanding Reality. And –

"intellect: the power or faculty of the mind by which one knows or understands, as distinguished from that by which one feels and that by which one wills..."
The Random House College Dictionary

Again: understanding Reality, as a matter of fact.
Which is exactly why –

"TIME: Person Of The Century; Albert Einstein
relativity's rebel: he combined rare genius with a deep moral sense and a total indifference to conviction
He was the pre-eminent scientist in a century dominated by science – To the world at large, relativity seemed to pull the rug out from under perceived reality...Only recently Canadian researchers probing (Einstein's preserved brain) found that he had an unusually large inferior parietal lobe – a center of mathematical thought and spatial imagery – and shorter connections between the frontal and temporal lobes – he was strongly influenced by his domineering, musically inclined mother, who encouraged his passion for the violin and such classical composers as Bach – Mozart...(Einstein) often spoke about trying to understand how the Lord (*der*

Alte, or the Old Man) shaped the universe..."
     Frederic Golden – Time – December 31, 1999

     Albert Einstein was capable of being defined as intelligent, as a matter of fact. Because he did begin to become capable, of; "Einstein – often spoke about trying to understand how the Lord – shaped the universe" – simply understanding simultaneously relative Reality. The harmoniously proportioned – universally applicable and simultaneously relative, non-tangible form mass synthetical structure that is, and/or beginning to become neurophysiologically capable of consciously cognizing Omnidimensional Time *made manifest.* And which is while effectually functioning as a concordant polyphonically structured whole: actually functioning while as a whole, and while as simultaneously relative to/from, and within, a single cognizable point time zero. Or – in simple English: syntax. And/or, beginning to become neurophysiologically capable of consciously cognizing the simultaneously relative non-tangible form synthetical structure *of* Reality: the verbs – the functions, the things we can not simply see with our eyes alone: of identifiable simultaneously relative Reality.

     Or, in even simpler English: What Albert Einstein did begin to become capable of understanding, is that all of simultaneously relative reality is governed, and which is as this word: governed, does mean; "to rule by right of authority – to exercise a directing or restraining influence over – to hold in check; control," by the universally applicable Common law of Reality, which is Harmony, and/or Time *made manifest.* And too which: Time *made manifest,* is while actually functioning as applied three parts to form one whole, and as the simultaneously relative non-tangible form synthetical structuring, of all of simultaneously relative Reality. While this word: synthesis, does mean: "The combining of the constituent elements of separate material or abstract entities into a single unified entity – a complex whole formed by combining," in Reality: *is* effectually functioning while beginning with the formation of atoms. Which are harmoniously proportioned simultaneously relative fundamental frequency modulations only, in Reality: tones and/or notes, which are effectually formed, as through the applied function of applied three parts to form one whole – while actually simultaneously functioning as a part of a larger whole: structure. Again, in simple English, imagine yourself and two friends arranged in a circle formed on the floor, at right angles to each other – a couple of feet distanced from each other, and, raise your hands up in the air above yourselves, and begin to lean in towards one another, which will then form a single point where your hands are conjoined, and too which will appear to be, only, a single point from any relative distance away. But which actually *is*: " in" simultaneously relative Reality, the real simultaneously relative applicable function of the quantum dynamically functioning nuclear strong/weak, and electromagnetism, and which is as it was exactly explained by the nuclearphysicist Jesus of Nazareth: "He told them another parable, 'the kingdom of heaven is like the yeast a women took and mixed in with three measures of flour till it was all leavened through," and, too, which is the function of atoms: within simultaneously relative Reality, actually functioning as the very foundation for all things. Which: the foundation, can then be built upon, just like in reality. Except that, in Reality, every thing is simultaneously effectually formed, but, again, we are attempting to simplify the understanding.

So, we have our foundation: the apparent single point of atoms formed by three parts leaning in towards one another at a single point in time, while actually functioning as a simple completed geometrical formation: to be built upon, and again as we are attempting to simplify the understanding. Which would be to imagine, that the formation of our selves and our two friends – standing in a vertical position upon the ground, leaning in towards one another, while having our hands conjoin at a single point above our heads, can function as a beam for a tangible form mass structure, and/or a horizontally placed second beam of the actual two-dimensional plane of the floor, which we can stand upon, and/or rest upon. And which does enable us to understand exactly what gravity is: within simultaneously relative Reality, while actually functioning as a simultaneously relative function of Omnidimensional Reality. Because is not as simple as a two-dimensional plane, it is the simultaneously relative universally applicable function, of the three projections of the nuclear strong/weak, and electromagnetism, to form one whole, made manifest as through the simultaneously relative vector function. Which is, as the word: vector, does mean: "a quantity possessing both magnitude and direction, represented by an arrow the direction of which indicates the direction of the quantity and length of which is proportional to the magnitude." Which, again, and/or in simple English, does simply mean, that the function of gravity is the effectuated formation of the projections where they overlap, and/or the points where our own selves and our two companions hands meet: is what planets are in simultaneously relative Reality, and/or perceivable tangible formed point-mass nouns. Which we can – then, build things upon: because of gravity, and which is simply a function in reality, but not a simple function, while actually functioning as pure harmony: while beginning with a single purposefully effectuated harmoniously proportioned simultaneously relative fundamental frequency modulation; atom, and/or musical tone. And – again, which is actually functioning as the foundation for all things, while remaining subservient to a hierarchically structured whole.

Which is exactly why, if we were to actually disrupt the function of a single one of those harmoniously proportion tones, and/or atoms, and/or if we were to actually; "To the world at large, relativity seemed to pull the rug out from under perceived reality" – simply pull the rug out from under one of our two friends, functioning as the foundation for all of simultaneously relative Reality, we would begin to become capable of creating –

"At Hiroshima: The common lot was random, indiscriminate and universal violence inflicting terrible pain, the physics of hydraulics and leverage and heat run riot...A junior-college girl: 'Ah, that instant! I felt as though I have been struck on the back with something like a big hammer, and thrown into boiling oil – I seem to

54

have been blown a good way to the north, and I felt as though the directions were all changed around."
    Richard Rhodes – The Making of The Atomic Bomb

    Chaos, and/or discord: and pain and death and suffering too.
    And too which was: in neuroscientific reality, only exactly because, one individual human being: just one, was exactly not –

    "When he asked, she bought him a piano. He studied for just a few months; actual playing at the piano did not interest mother or son. Adolf (Hitler) protested his isolation and entrapment with outrageous demands; his mother soothed him by granting them."
    Michael Nelken M.D. – Hitler Unmasked

    Ever encouraged to practice his scales *of* Reality, as a matter of fact. While he was, exactly and instead, simply allowed to–

    "In Hitler's youth, his schoolteachers flunked him and Kubizek found him strangely depressed and enraged. Yet Adolf and his family saw no problem with his loafing around the house for years, nursing huge aspirations. They explained his condition as an interest in the arts."
    Michael Nelken M.D. – Hitler Unmasked

    Do whatever he wanted, whenever he wanted to do it, and to whomever he wanted to do it to. Which was, also, as he did become capable of making manifest his own personally affected inarticulate cry for attention, and –

    "Adolf Hitler: Fear of obscurity –
    The greatest revolutionary changes and achievements of this earth, its greatest cultural accomplishments, the immortal deeds in the field of statesmanship, etc., are forever inseparably bound up with a name and are represented by it...Consider that six or seven men, all nameless poor devils, had joined together with the intention of forming a movement, hoping to succeed – If people had attacked us in those days – we would have been happy. For the oppressive thing was neither the one nor the other; it was the complete lack of attention we found in those days from which I suffered most...An agitator who demonstrates the ability to transmit an idea to the broad masses must always be a psychologist, even if he were only a demagogue – For leading means: being able to move masses."
    Adolf Hitler – Mein Kamph

    By his own admission. Before the fact, and for the entire world to simply see with their eyes alone too.
    But, the majority – not all but the majority, of an entire society, had begun to

enable their own selves to begin to become capable of experiencing, exactly as was explained by Jesus of Nazareth, truly humanistic –

"The disciples had forgotten to take any food and they had only one loaf with them in the boat. Then he gave them this warning, 'Keep your eyes open; be on your guard against the yeast of the Pharisees and the yeast of Herod.' And they said to one another, 'It is because we have no bread.' And Jesus knew it, and he said to them, 'Why are you talking about having no bread? Do you not yet understand? Have you no perception? Are your minds closed? Have you *eyes that do not see, ears that do not hear*? Or do you not remember? When I broke the five loaves for the four thousand, how many baskets full of scraps did you collect?' And they answered, 'Seven.' Then he said to them, 'Are you still without perception?'"
Mark 8: 14-21

Brain death: for their own selves.
As they had, simply, forgot to pay attention to Reality. Which did, then, enable Adolf Hitler an opportunity to, simply, project his own personally affected neurophysiological dysfunction upon mankind. And too, which was – all of it, exactly unlike –

"Albert Einstein (was) strongly influenced by his domineering, musically inclined mother, who encouraged his passion for the violin and such classical composers as Bach – Mozart..."
Frederic Golden – Time – December 31, 1999

Albert Einstein: who was encouraged, by his parents, to learn Reality, and not simply allowed to exist in ignorance of it. Which was also –

"His father, Leopold Mozart, was a violinist and composer, and author of an important violen tutor. Leopold encouraged Wolfgang..."
The New College Encyclopedia of Music – J.A. Westrup and F.Ll. Harrison

Exactly what Wolfgang Amadeus Mozart was encouraged to do: LEARN REALITY, and not simply escape it while as through allowed exposure to excessive amounts of romanticized escapism.
And, I'm sure, everyone has seen that particular romanticized escapism movie: *Amadeus*. And, too I'm sure, everyone probably wondered whether, or not, it was actually possible to do exactly what Antonio Salieri was supposed to be doing, in the movie and within his mind alone, and which was, that he was actually hearing the sound of the music: *in his mind*, while he was – *actually*, only looking at the abstracted, and projected, two-dimensional plane representation, of the actual three-dimensional functions: of the Reality, which *is* musical sounds. And the answer is –

"Scientists: Musicians' brains wired differently –

Neuroscientists, using brain-scanning MRI machines to peer inside the minds of professional German violinists, found they could hear the music simply by thinking about it, a skill amateurs in the study were unable to match – The research offers insight into the inner workings of the brain and shows that musician's brains are uniquely wired for sound, researchers said at the annual meeting for the Society for Neuroscience – Neuroscientists often study how we hear and play music because it is one of few activities that use many functions of the brain, including memory, learning, motor control, emotion and creativity, said Dr. Robert Zatorre of the Montreal Neurological Institute – 'It offers a window onto the highest levels of human cognition,' Zatorre said..."

AP – Bucks County Courier Times – Thursday November 15, 2001

Yes: as a matter of neuroscientific fact. But only with a tremendous amount of practice: throughout and within simultaneously relative Omnidimensional reality, while learning that function: *of* Reality. While simultaneously occurring within, their own personally affected three-dimensional electrical potential mass minds, and parallel functioning central nervous systems, and which is while – simultaneously, a human being's three-dimensional electrical potential mass of a mind, and parallel functioning central nervous system, is capable of functioning as a; "Candance Pert – I see the brain in terms of quantum mechanics – the brain is just a receiver, an amplifier, a little wet minireceiver for collective reality" – receiver for collective Reality.

Which does, also, enable us, now and only because of neuroscience, to begin to become capable of answering that other question that everybody, most probably, asked themselves while they were watching that movie, and too which was while not simply enabling themselves to be entertained. And that is, and exactly as Antonio Salieri did explain: in the movie, whether, or not, Wolfgang Amadeaus Mozart was actually: "...taking dictation from God." And the answer is –

"Candance Pert – I see the brain in terms of quantum mechanics – the brain is just a receiver, an amplifier, a little wet minireceiver for collective reality – the ratio of frontal core to the rest of the cortex may be one index of evolutionary advancement – Do these lobes govern some essential feature of humanness, or even godliness, as some scientists have suggested? 'If God speaks to man, if man speaks to God,' neuroscientist Candace Pert tells us, 'it would be through the frontal lobes."

The 3-Pound Universe – Judith Hooper and Dick Teresi

Yes: as a matter of neuroscientific fact.
And, which was exactly as Wolfgang Amadeus Mozart did –

"...in the night when I cannot sleep, thoughts crowd into my mind as easily as you could wish. Whence and how do they come? I do not know and I have nothing to do with it. Those which please me I keep in my head and hum them; at least others have told me that I do so. Once I have my theme, another melody comes, linking itself with the first one, in accordance with the needs of the composition as a whole: the counterpoint, the part of each instrument and all the melodic fragments at last produce a complete work. Then my soul is on fire with inspiration. The work grows; I keep expanding it, conceiving it more and more clearly until I have the entire composition finished in my head though it may be long. Then my mind seizes it as a glance of my eye a beautiful picture or a handsome youth. It does not come to me successively, with various parts worked out in detail, as they will later on, but in its entirety that my imagination lets me hear it."

Wolfgang Amadeus Mozart – Roger Penrose – The Emperor's New Mind

Plainly explain: in reality – not in the movie fantasy.

And too which: that Wolfgang Amadeus Mozart could actually "see" the entire structure of simultaneously relative Reality in his mind alone, was exactly as Antonio Salieri, in the movie at least, did explain: as he was looking at the two-dimensional projected abstract function *of* Reality, and actually hearing the musical sounds in his mind, and being: Antonio Salieri did explain and in the movie, in that if you were to actually: "...misplace one note – and the entire structure would begin to fall," and which is just like in Reality.

And there was one other unresolved mystery – not simply in the movie, but in the reality of Wolfgang Amadeus Mozart's life, which was exactly the unfinished symphony: not the *Requiem Mass*, but the –

"Day of wrath, that day
Will dissolve the earth in ashes
As David and the Sibyl bear witness

What dread there will be
When the Judge shall come
To judge all things strictly.

A trumpet, spreading a wondrous sound
Through the graves of all lands
Will drive mankind before the throne.

Death and Nature shall be astonished
When all creation rises again
To answer to the Judge.

A book, written in, will be brought forth
In which is contained everything that is,
Out of which the world shall be judged.

When therefore the Judge takes His seat
Whatever is hidden will reveal itself.
Nothing will remain unavenged..."

Function of it: this is that book – the book which is written in, out of
which the world shall be judged. And *The Annunciation* is that sound, and nothing
will remain unavenged: It is Time – It is *The Annunciation*.

So, exactly what is this function which is *The Annunciation*: that no one can
"see" – and/or has seen for over 500 years. And which is – also and simultaneously,
The Holy Grail of Understanding, and The; "The equations of general relativity
simply can't handle such a situation, where the laws of cause and effect break down
and particles jump from point A to point B without going through the space in
between. In such a world, you can only calculate what will probably happen next –
which is just what quantum theory is designed to do – A new generation of physicists
has at last taken on the challenge of creating a complete theory – one capable of
explaining, in Einstein's words, 'every element of the physical reality' – The trouble
is (no one) knows how many other pieces must fall into place before scientists (can)
succeed in solving this greatest of all puzzles" – missing piece to the puzzle which is
called Civilization too? It: the missing piece to the puzzle and the thing that is
contained within *The Annunciation*, is: "Omnidimensional non-tangible form
syntax," and/or Omnidimensional simultaneously relative non-tangible form
synthetical structuring. Which is, simultaneously effectually functioning, as
simultaneously relative to/from, and within, a single universally applicable, and
cognizable, point time zero: the point of the Big Bang, and the simultaneously
relative applied function of Omnidimensional Time *made manifest,* as a matter of
fact. And – again, and/or in simple English: the universally applicable verbs, and/or
the universally applicable simultaneously relative functions – the universally
applicable, and identifiable, truly humanistic non-tangible form mass things, that no
one can simply see: with their eyes alone, and which is the; "In science, as in
democracy, there is no hidden secret knowledge, all that counts is on the table,
observable and falsifiable. All else is metaphysics – quantum theory and relativity
have taught us, science is about what can be observed and measured or it is about
nothing at all" – only absolute in Reality. This: *The Annunciation*, is the only
"thing" – in the entire history of mankind, which does contain truly humanistic
syntax: and/or truly humanistic intelligence, and as a matter of fact. That is except,
of course, for –

"TIME: Person Of The Century; Albert Einstein
He was a pre-eminent scientist in a century dominated by science – To the
world at large, relativity seemed to pull the rug out from under perceived
reality...Only recently Canadian researchers probing (Einstein's preserved brain)
found that he had an unusually large inferior parietal lobe – a center of mathematical
thought and spatial imagery – and shorter connections between the frontal and

temporal lobes – he was strongly influenced by his domineering, musically inclined mother, who encouraged his passion for the violin and such classical composers as Bach – Mozart...(Einstein) often spoke about trying to understand how the Lord (*der Alte*, or the Old Man) shaped the universe..."
Frederic Golden – Time – December 31, 1999

Reality: while beginning to actually function as a formed understanding of Reality, within Albert Einstein's three-dimensional electrical potential mass of mind, and parallel functioning central nervous system. And within which: any human being's mind, would have been, and is, contained only, and exactly as was explained by Johannes Keplar –

"Geometrical non-tangible forms: God wanted us to recognize them, when He created us after His image, so that we should share in His thoughts. For what is implanted in the mind of man other than numbers and magnitudes? These alone we comprehend correctly, and if piety permits us to say so, his recognition is of the same kind as the divine, at least insofar as we in this mortal life of ours are capable of grasping part of it...Geometry is one and eternal, a reflection of the mind of God – nature loves these relationships in everything that is capable of being related. They are also loved by the intellect of man who is an image of the Creator."
Johannes Keplar – Max Casper

Simultaneously relative differential equations: actually functioning while remaining subservient to, and having been formed as through, the simultaneously relative universally applicable function of a hierarchically structured whole, and while in the year 1595 that is. That Johannes Keplar did, exactly, begin to become capable of simply communicating his own personally –

"...then he becomes aware that he walks in the light of truth; he is seized by an unbelievable rapture and, exulting, he here surveys most minutely, as though from a high watch-tower, the whole world in all the differences of its parts."
Johannes Keplar – Max Casper

Formed understanding of the Mind of God: it is not a "belief" – it is an "understanding," which is beyond belief.
Which does enable us, now, to answer that question: as to why any one individual, would ever bother to –

"Then to all he said, 'If anyone wants to be a follower of mine, let him renounce himself and take up his cross every day and follow me. For anyone who wants to save his life will lose it; but anyone who loses his life for my sake, that man will save it. What gain, then, is it for a man to have won the whole world and to have lost or ruined his very self? For if anyone is ashamed of me and of my words,

of him the Son of Man will be ashamed when he comes in his own glory and in the glory of the Father and the holy angels."
Luke 9: 23-26

Actually endure a lifetime's worth of *pain*: while practicing our scales of simultaneously relative reality only, and simultaneously building our truly humanistic multidimensional foundations. And to, not so simply, enable ourselves to begin to become neurophysiologically capable of consciously cognizing the Mind of God made manifest, and, too, which is while – and simultaneously, most others are being purposefully allowed exposure to a lifetime's worth of exposure to excessive dopamine biochemical inducing effectual stimulus only, and/or romanticized escapism, actually functioning as pure *pleasure*, and simply existing in denial of Reality too. The answer is: because it causes an effect that is beyond belief, and as a matter of fact: it is like nothing in this world could ever possibly be. And as a matter of –

"Candace Pert: I see the brain in terms of quantum mechanics – the brain is just a receiver, an amplifier, a little wet minireceiver for collective reality. We make maps, but we should never confuse the map with the territory' – the ratio of frontal core to the rest of the cortex may be one index of evolutionary advancement – What the frontal lobes 'control' is something like awareness – Do these lobes govern some essential feature of humanness, or even godliness, as some scientists have suggested? 'If God speaks to man, if man speaks to God,' neuroscientist Candace Pert tells us, it would be through the frontal lobes – Stephen LaBarge: 'And it's capable of what look like miraculous things, so miraculous that we're tempted to say it's divine, that it's not natural...'"
The 3-Pound Universe – Judith Hooper and Dick Teresi

Neuroscientific fact.
So, what exactly is actually experiencing It: The Mind of God, like: in simple English? Well, if an individual were to attempt to imagine it, and not actually experience it, it would be, kind of, like and exactly as Jesus of Nazareth did explain, to –

"Be compassionate as your Father is compassionate. Do not judge, and you will not be judged yourselves; do not condemn, and you will not be condemned yourselves; grant pardon, and you will be pardoned. Give, and there will be gifts for you: a full measure, pressed down, shaken together, and running over, will be poured into your lap; because the amount you measure out is the amount you will be given back."
Luke 6: 36-38

Take some heroin – some Ecstasy – some cocaine: all of our dopamine, serotonin and endorphins too, and/or drugs, and which is while including every experience that truly humanistic beings can ever possibly experience within reality, and while escaping it too, and then to access: harness and compound, them, to an infinite degree: while simultaneously effectually traveling at the speed of light, and from here to eternity and back again too, and which is while: simultaneously, effectually functioning as the Eternal Harmony. And – then, an individual human being, who has not yet actually experienced it, could only begin to imagine what it is like – while attempting to actually effectually experience It: the Eternal Harmony. But which is also while, and simultaneously, they: any individual human being who does actually access any of those things, while including dopamine, would – actually and in neuroscientific reality only, be moving while as in an effectuated direction away, from beginning to allow themselves to become capable of gaining access to the Eternal Harmony.

Because, and as a matter of neuroscientific fact, all of those things do only begin to cause a permanently effectuated neurophysiological dysfunction, within any individual human being who is allowed to access them, while including dopamine. And – simultaneously, gaining access to the Eternal Harmony, does require a prerequisite effectuated cognizance of humanistic nothingness: 0, while actually functioning as rest. So, any individual human being who does – only, continue to escape reality, and by any means they possibly can, will – also and simultaneously, continue to move while as in a purposefully effectuated direction, towards truly humanistic brain death: for their own selves to experience, and instead of the Eternal Harmony. Which: the Eternal Harmony actually functioning as the Mind of God and Omnidimensional Time *made manifest* too, is – also and simultaneously, like nothing that mankind can ever experience: in simple humanistic three-dimensional reality, and/or in their childish imaginations either, and which is also as it actually is beyond belief.

So, exactly how did I know that it: the syntax, and/or the simultaneously relative non-tangible form synthetical structuring, which no one can see and which is contained within *The Annunciation*, even exists. Because I've seen it: not the picture, which I did, eventually, see, but the function of the truly humanistic universally applicable, and simultaneously relative, non-tangible form synthetical structuring, which is defined as *The Annunciation*. Which is while actually functioning as Omnidimensional Time *made manifest* too: as I experienced it within simultaneously relative Reality, and I did, then, know what I saw, and/or recognize it, when I saw it being projected upon the two-dimensional plane termed *The Annunciation*. And too which is exactly only as this word: recognize, does actually mean: "to identify as something or someone previously seen, known, etc. – to identify from knowledge of appearance or characteristics – to perceive as existing or true; realize." But only in scientific reality, and exactly not in the mind of any individual person who is delusional, and – again, which is as this word: delusional, does mean: "a false belief or opinion: *delusions of grandeur* – an act or instance of deluding," and – too and again, which is also as this word: delude, does mean: "to mislead the mind or judgment of; deceive – to mock or frustrate the hopes or aims of," but only in identifiable neuroscientific reality.

So that: in identifiable scientific reality only, I was enabled to begin to become capable of forming a belief, within my mind and because of Mom and Dad and/or their worldly influence over me – I read *the* Book, which did – then, enable me to begin to become capable of forming an understanding of Reality. Which is while actually functioning as the universally applicable language, of universally applicable simultaneously relative Reality, and/or Omnidimensional Time *made manifest*, and which I can, now, communicate, while actually functioning as the universally applicable function of Omnidimensional Time *made manifest*. And/or recognize, while actually functioning as an abstracted, and projected, understanding of Reality. Which is, exactly, how I was capable of recognizing the function of *The Annunciation*: 500 years after the fact, while – simultaneously, no one else, in the entire history of mankind, except of course for Leonardo da Vinci, has even known that it exists. And/or, that it is –

"...As we found with quantum mechanics, the full structure of the world is richer than our language can express and our brains comprehend – it is not possible for us to visualize the geometries of dimensions higher than three..."
The Arrow of Time – Peter Coveney and Roger Highfield

Even capable of existing. And, of course, which is, also and simultaneously, exactly what does –

"Gory Details Cheerfully Supplied –
Trading Police Forensics For Writer's Life on 'C.S.I.'
The writers of the highly successful CBS drama 'C.S.I.: Crime Scene Investigation' sat slumped around a table one afternoon this month at a studio in this quite, mountainous region about an hour's drive north of Los Angeles. Armed with notepads and coffee cups, they threw out ideas as Andrew Lipstiz, a producer, stood at a blackboard and outlined an episode (that) like most of the shows episodes, came from actual events – Eventually everyone turned to Elizabeth D- , 41, a crime scene investigator with the Los Angeles County Sheriff's Department for fifteen years who began as an adviser on 'C.S.I.' and left her job to become a writer on the show – 'In real cases the police would bring in someone to interpret,' Ms. D- told the other writers when the subject of language came up – It's common for police shows to seek expert advice – But the need is especially acute for 'C.S.I.,' a show about a team of forensic scientists in Las Vegas who must come up with intricate explanations for mysterious crimes – 'The show is, in some ways, post- modernist,' Ms. D- said after the writers' meeting. 'It provides a definite and final answer, and people crave that – The audience loves the finality of this show. We deal with the evidence. We say who did it and how they did it. And people love that closure."
Bernard Weinraub – The New York Times – Monday December 24, 2001

Make this crime, as we do remember that the name of this story is
The Theft Of Art and The End Of Time and while this book does simply prove it for
the entire world to simply see with their eyes alone, such a compelling crime.
Because it is a real crime, while it is based on factual events, and the absolute truth,
and/or a; "story that – came from actual events" – real life story. In addition to such
a enigmatic crime, because nobody in the entire world even knows about it yet, and
it: the revealing of the absolute truth which is the greatest single crime in the entire
history of mankind, does exactly preclude the beginning of the end of time. And too
such an astronomical crime: because the majority of the entire world has been
affected, and/or become a victim of the con, and they don't even know it yet. And
what they have stolen, is –

"Do not be afraid of them therefore. For everything that is now covered will
be uncovered, and everything now hidden will be made clear. What I say to you in
the dark, tell in the daylight, what you hear in whispers, proclaim from the
housetops.

Do not be afraid of those who kill the body but cannot kill the soul; fear him
rather who can destroy both body and soul in hell. Can you not buy two sparrows
for a penny? And yet not one falls to the ground without your Father knowing.
Why, every hair on your head has been counted. So there is no need to be afraid;
you are worth more than hundreds of sparrows.

So if anyone declares himself for me in the presence of men, I will declare
myself for him in the presence of my Father in heaven. But the one who disowns me
in the presence of men, I will disown in the presence of my Father in heaven."
Matthew 10: 26-33

The collective consciousness of mankind, and/or their souls. Which, again, is
as; "Candance Pert – I see the brain in terms of quantum mechanics – the brain is just
a receiver, an amplifier, a little wet minireceiver for collective reality. We make
maps, but we should never confuse the map with the territory" – a matter of scientific
fact. And – too and of course but only in scientific reality, which is: the fact that it
is such an effective con, the –

"Anyone who wants to win the broad masses must know the key that opens
the door to their heart...propaganda tries to force a doctrine on the whole people –
The whole art consists in doing this so skillfully that everyone will be convinced that
the fact is real, the process necessary, the necessity correct, etc. But since
propaganda is not and cannot be the necessity in itself, since its function, like the
poster, consists in attracting the attention of the crowd, and not in educating those
who are already educated or who are striving after education – The progress and
culture of humanity are not a product of the majority, but rest exclusively on the
genius and energy of the personality – Some idea of genius arises in the brain of a
man who feels called upon to transmit his knowledge to the rest of humanity. He

64

preaches his view and gradually wins a certain circle of adherents. This process of the direct and personal transmittance of a man's ideas to the rest of his fellow men is the most ideal and natural...In the place of committee decisions, the principle of absolute responsibility was introduced...(To): Adolf Hitler."

    Adolf Hitler – Mein Kamph

    Primary objective of any truly great con-artist: that all of the individuals who are affected, will not even know that they are the exact ones who have been conned, until after the fact, when it is then too late. Which is: exactly, as all of the individually affected people, will, simply, have handed over their own personal power: while as to any one other individual humanistic being, and/or an; "The progress and culture of humanity are not a product of a majority, but rest exclusively on the genius and energy of the personality – He preaches his view and gradually wins a certain circle of adherents" – elitist group of individuals. Who: the elite who are in possession of the power, will be giving them: all of the victims of the con-artists, only exactly; "Stone Cold Picnic – WrestleMania XV ended the way it had to, the way any good populace fairy tale must – in the world of 'sports entertainment,' the outcomes are scripted, the finales are choreographed and the guiding principle is 'Give the people what they want" – what they want: a diversion from Reality.

    So let's go back into Reality only, and begin to uncover the scene of the crime, and/or pull back the facade, as it is capable of actually functioning as the diversion from Reality. And exactly only function as scientists are supposed to function, which will enable us to begin to reveal the absolute truth, and explain exactly what happened: in identifiable neuroscientific reality only of course, and which *does* mean within the mind of any one individual that has been affected. While, to do that, we do have to return back to point time zero, and/or return to –

    "People were bringing little children to him, for him to touch. The disciples turned them away, but when Jesus saw this he was indignant and said to them, 'Let the little children come to me; do not stop them; for it is to such as these that the kingdom of God belongs. I tell you solemnly, anyone who does not welcome the kingdom of God like a child will never enter it.' Then he put its arms around them, laid his hands on them and gave them his blessing."

    Mark 10: 13-16

    Innocence: and enter into the mind of the child.

    Because, we do now know, for an acknowledged universally applicable fact, that the very definition of intelligence is syntax, and/or the "synthetical conjoining of the primary elements to form a coherent whole," and, too, that the very definition of the ability to function in a truly humanistic manner, is the ability to process complex simultaneously relative multidimensional sensory input information. And again, which is an acknowledged understanding of reality that nobody questions, and, so, we can now simply know, for an acknowledged neuroscientific fact, that the very definition of truly humanistic intelligence: within a child's mind, *is* the beginning of the ability to form simultaneously relative multidimensional syntax. Or – again in simple English which everyone can simply understand, and nobody can refute, to simply enable us to reiterate our understanding of this universal truth, we can reiterate our understanding of the function, and/or intelligence, and/or synthetical structuring, of any sentence that mankind can ever speak, in the entire history of mankind, and such as: May I have the ball. Which: the sentence, we can dissect, and/or break down into, two primary elements: tangible form point-mass nouns/noun phrases – "things" we can "touch," and non-tangible form verbs/verb phrases – "things" we can not "touch." And – then, we can identify the universally applicable syntax, and/or intelligence, and which is, simply, the purposefully effectuated conjoining *of* the tangible form point-mass nouns *by* the purposefully effectuated directed movement *of* the non-tangible form verbs. And which is while actually functioning in an absolutely abstracted, and unidirectionally successive, manner: while as from point A – the point *of* point time zero, projected in purposefully effectuated direction towards point B – the identifiable position of the second tangible form point-mass noun. While that is another revealed absolute truth, which no individual human being on the entire face of this Earth, can question. And, I don't know what planet they: any supposedly humanistic beings who could actually stand in front of any two-dimensional Cubist thing, are from, but here – on Planet Earth and any other planet in this universe for that matter, there is only one way to get from point A to point B, and that is while as through the universally applicable vector function: actually functioning as unidirectionally successive Time *made manifest*. Now, take a good look at three-dimensional Reality, and/or any abstracted and projected representation of three-dimensional reality, and/or any two-dimensional picture of truly humanistic three-dimensional reality: DO YOU SEE ANY VERBS IN REALITY, AND/OR WITHIN ANY TWO-DIMENSIONAL ABSTRACTED AND PROJECTED PICTURE OF THREE-DIMENSIONAL REALITY? Of course not, they exist only –

"a brief history of relativity
... Einstein started from the postulate that the laws of science should appear the same to all freely moving observers. In particular, observers should all measure the same speed for light, no matter how they were moving – Einstein's postulate that the laws of nature should appear the same to all freely moving observers was the foundation of the theory of relativity, so called because it implies that only relative motion is important – Einstein's general theory of relativity transformed space and time from a passive background in which events take place to active participants in the dynamics of the cosmos – General relativity completely changed the discussion of the origin and fate of the universe. A static universe could have existed forever or could have been created in its present form at some time in the past. On the other hand, if galaxies are moving apart today, they would have all been on top of one

another and their density would have been infinite. According to the general theory, this Big Bang was the beginning of the universe and of time itself..."
Stephen Hawking – Time – December 31, 1999

Within the mind of any individual human being, who does begin to enable their own selves: truly humanistic three-dimensional electrical potential mass of a mind, and parallel functioning central nervous system, to become intelligent. And, while –

'Rat-a-tat-tat. Rat-a-tat-tat. Rat-a-tat-tat – If scientists could eavesdrop on the brain of a human embryo 10, maybe 12 weeks after conception, they would hear an astonishing racket. Inside the womb, long before light first strikes the retina of the eye or the earliest dreamy images flicker through the cortex, nerve cells in the developing brain crackle with purposeful activity...After birth, when the number of connections explodes, each of the brain's billions of neurons will forge links to thousands of others – the developing nervous system has strung the equivalent of telephone trunk lines between the right neighborhoods in the right cities. Now it has to sort out which wires belong to which house, a problem that cannot be solved by genes alone for reasons that boil down to simple arithmetic – These axons start out as a scrambled bowl of spaghetti – what sorts out the mess, scientists have established, is neural activity..."
Fertile Minds – Madeleine Nash – Time – February 3, 1997

Beginning at point time zero.
That is what the exact definition of truly humanistic intelligence "is," in truly humanistic identifiable neuroscientific reality. Which is, exactly; "Einstein's postulate that the laws of nature should appear the same to all freely moving observers was the foundation of the theory of relativity, so called because it implies that only relative motion is important – Einstein's general theory of relativity transformed space and time from a passive background in which events take place to active participants in the dynamics of the cosmos – According to the general theory, (the) Big Bang was the beginning of the universe and of time itself" – PUTTING SPACE, and/or purposefully effectuated, and directed, simultaneously relative movement: actually effectually functioning as syntax – and/or time made manifest, BETWEEN THE; "After birth, when the number of connections explodes, each of the brain's billions of neurons will forge links to thousands of others – the developing nervous system has strung the equivalent of telephone trunk lines between the right neighborhoods in the right cities. Now it has to sort out which wires belong to which house – These axons start out as a scrambled bowl of spaghetti – what sorts out the mess, scientists have established, is neural activity" – already existing tangible form point-mass nouns. Which is while actually functioning as Time *made manifest*: actually functioning as simultaneously relative to/from, and within, a; "According to the general theory, this Big Bang was the beginning of the universe and of time

itself" – single cognizable, and universally applicable, point time zero. And which is the very definition of a truly humanistic being's; "Einstein's postulate that the laws of nature should appear the same to all freely moving observers was the foundation of the theory of relativity, so called because it implies that only relative motion is important" – own purposefully effectuated foundation: within their truly humanistic, simultaneously relative, three-dimensional electrical potential mass of a mind, and parallel functioning central nervous system, while effectually functioning as Omnidimensional Time *made manifest*, and Reality too. But: in Reality, there were not – yet, any tangible form point-mass nouns existing: before the applied function of Omnidimensional Time *made manifest* was actually made manifest, which is what makes Reality so complex, and while – simultaneously, all of the individual neurons: within an individual human being's three-dimensional electrical potential mass of a mind, are, themselves, actually capable of being simultaneously effectually altered: while as through the applied function of Omnidimensional Time *made manifest*, which is exactly what makes a human being, a "human" being.

While, to enable ourselves to reiterate our understanding of the fact that Time does – exactly, not function in a unidirectionally successive manner, we can, simply, perform a simple experiment for own selves: which we can see with our eyes alone, while remaining secured within the comfort of our own homes. And too as we access universally applicable Time and/or a light bulb placed inside a lamp, and centered within the parametered boundaries of a room, and/or a formed cubic volume of space: just like the cubic volume of space which is called Reality, but which would not yet exist in Reality, until the applied function of Time is *made manifest*. And if we were to switch on the light bulb: actually functioning as quantized electrodynamic radiant energy and/or the universal constant of Time, and while as from point time zero, and/or the identified point of the light bulb positioned within the parametered boundaries of the room, we could allow ourselves to become capable of simply seeing: with our eyes alone, that the projected vector function, and/or the beam of light, would be projected to a far wall: point B, opposite of the light and our position within the room, while it is – simultaneously, projected to the near wall: point A, as relative to our position in the room. And, which is as exactly as the amount of Time, and/or function of Time, will be squared as relative to the position of point time zero and the two walls, as capable of being observed by our own selves, while actually occurring within our quantum dynamically functioning electrical potential mass minds, and central nervous systems. Again – in simple English, meaning that the amount of Time "made manifest," for the light beam to travel to the far wall: as from point time zero, will be exactly equivalent to the amount of time it does take for the light beam to travel to the near wall: as from point time zero, and which: the amount of time traveled, will also – and simultaneously, be exactly "doubled" as simultaneously relative to point A *and* point B *and* point time zero: as we are capable of consciously cognizing it within our minds, and/or as it is capable of functioning within Reality.

Except, in Omnidimensional Reality, there are no walls formed yet, until the function of Reality is applied, and/or any tangible form mass walls at all for that matter: IN identifiable simultaneously relative Reality, but there is identifiable simultaneously relative non-tangible form structure in Reality, while actually functioning as real multidimensional syntax. And – again in simple English, which is the formation of identifiable simultaneously relative patterns in space/time, and, too and of course, which is exactly what we can NOT simply see with our eyes alone, and JUST LIKE THERE IS IN "MUSIC."

But we also do now know, for a verified scientific fact, that if do simply stay inside, and remain shuttered from Reality, we will, never, become capable of learning about Reality for own selves. So, let's: together, take a quantum leap into –

"From One Quantum State to Another, It's Shades of 'Star Trek'

It's not 'Star Trek,' but physicists in Denmark have demonstrated a step that could lead to a primitive form of instantaneous teleportation – Even if follow-up experiments succeed, all that will be teleported is a magnetic field from one bunch of atoms to another. But that advance could eventually be used for encryption techniques that are fundamentally impossible to break and for building computers that employ quantum mechanical principles to dash through their calculations – Imagine that we want to transmit this quantum state of an object, from one place to another,' said Dr. Eugene S. Polzik, a professor of physics at the University of Aarhus in Denmark. 'We can't do it, because we're not to look at it. We're not allowed to write its parameters and send it over the phone. We have to do tricks' – The trick is an odd phenomenon of quantum mechanics known as entanglement. Under carefully constructed situations, two particles can become 'entangled,' where changes to one instantly alter the other – For example, scientists can create two entangled photons, or particles of light, such that the oscillating electrical fields of each must point in the same direction. Thus, measuring the orientation of the electric field of one photon tells the orientation of the other – What confounds common sense is that it is not a matter of the fields always being aligned in a certain direction and simply not knowing what that direction is until the measurement is made. Rather, the theory of quantum mechanics states that all possibilities exist simultaneously, and the act of looking causes the possibilities to collapse into a single reality. 'That's what makes the quantum world weird,' Dr. Polzik said..."
Kenneth Chang – The New York Times – Tuesday, October 9, 2001

Another state of mind, a higher state of mind.

Which is as we do: and; "the theory of quantum mechanics states that all possibilities exist simultaneously" – simultaneously, break free from the parameters of the room, and/or our simple mortal existence upon this point-mass of Earth, and –

"Back to Basics: how did space get its dimensions?

In the beginning, there was little need for physicists. The universe, poised at the moment of creation, was ruled not by the four different forces observed in latter times, but by just a single superforce. Instead of a smattering of different particles, there was only the tiny primordial mass – the grandmother of all particles – ready to explode in the Big Bang – Then came the detonation, giving scientists some messiness to study. As the newborn universe cooled, the single force splintered into four forces, radiating through the four dimensions of space and time, and various classes of particles sprang forth one by one – This scientific creation story, embraced by physicists and cosmologists alike, seems to account for just about everything – with one glaring exception: Where did the dimensions come from? – Now some physicists are adding a touch to the Edenic tale. A paper published last month in Physical Review Letters suggests that the dimensions, like the forces and particles, may have popped into being as the universe cooled. Though the idea is still in a very preliminary form, physicists are intrigued by the implication that reality may have started with just a single dimension: time. As temperatures dropped in the moments after the primordial explosion, the spatial dimensions – height, length and breadth – crystallized into existence. Creation was not just a matter of 'let there be light,' but 'let there be space' as well – From a unifier's point of view, one of the most interesting things about the new theory is the way it conflates these seemingly very different notions of dimensions and forces. A dimension arises when a force is generated that allows movement into a new domain – Dr. Arkani-Hamed said that the hypothetical particles behind these forces would be similar to the gluons that carry the strong nuclear force. Like gluons, the dimension-creating particles might be very weak at high energies and stronger at lower energies (and) said what particularly attracted him was the notion that space might have emerged from a universe that started with just time..."

George Johnson – The New York Times – Tuesday, June 26, 2001

Allow our selves to enter into a whole new dimension: Time *made manifest*. And – *no*, it: entering into a whole new dimension and in this Edenic tale too, is, exactly, not as; "A paper published last month in Physical Review Letters suggests that the dimensions, like the forces and particles, may have popped into being as the universe cooled" – simple as turning a page, and/or accessing some newly published abstracted knowledge, and/or popping into being either. It is more like –

"Computing One Atom At a Time
The only hint that anything extraordinary is happening inside the brown stucco building at Los Alamos National Laboratory is a small metal sign posted in front: 'Warning! Magnetic Field in Use. Remain on Sidewalk.' Come much closer and you may risk having the magnetic strips on your credit cards erased – The powerful field is emanating from the supercooled superconducting magnets inside a tanklike machine called a nuclear resonance spectrometer – The machine at Los Alamos has been enlisted on a recent morning for a (grand) purpose: to carry out an experiment in quantum computing. By using radio waves to manipulate atoms like so many quantum abacus beads, the Los Alamos scientists will coax a molecule

(into) executing a simple computer program – Each atom can be thought of as a little switch, a register that holds a 1 or a 0 (But) the paradoxical laws of quantum mechanics confer a powerful advantage: a single atom can do two calculations at once. Two atoms can do four, three atoms can do eight...The goal, still but a distant glimmer, is to harness thousands of atoms, resulting in a machine so powerful that it would easily break codes now considered impenetrable and solve other problems that are impossible for even the fastest supercomputer – 'We are at the border of a new territory,' said Dr. Raymond Laflamme, one of the leaders of the Los Alamos project – 'The big question,' he added, 'is whether we can make the transition from theory to practice'...At its root, computation is just a matter of shuffling bits, the 1's and 0's of binary arithmetic. So suppose an atom pointing up means 1 and an atom pointing down means 0. Flip around these bits by zapping the atoms with laser beams or radio waves and the result is an extremely tiny computer – But that would be just the beginning of its power. Quantum mechanics, the rules governing subatomic particles, dictates that these quantum bits, called qubits, can also be in a 'super-position,' indicating 1 and 0 at the same time – Put together a few dozen atoms, it seemed, and they could perform vast numbers of calculations simultaneously...After the machine is calibrated the experiment can begin. At first, the nuclei in the molecules are pointing every which way, creating a predominantly random soup. But the strong magnetic field causes a fraction of the molecules (to) line up so that all their nuclei are pointing up: 11111 – Using pulses of radio waves, an operator sitting at the controls of an N.M.R. machine can choose an individual nucleus (and) strike it like a bell. Throughout the flask, trillions of (nuclei) will chime in synchrony...What has been described so far is just the quantum version of a light switch. The reason a molecule can be used to calculate is that its nuclei, like the tiny switches inside a computer chip, interact with one another: a radio pulse will cause a certain nucleus to change from 1 to 0 – but only if the nucleus to its left is 1. In an ordinary computer these kinds of arrangements are called logic gates, the building blocks of computation. String enough of them together and any calculation can be performed..."

George Johnson – The New York Times – Tuesday, March 27, 2001

Beginning: as we do take a quantum leap into a whole new dimension, to allow our very own selves to become capable of doing, exactly, what is supposed to be impossible to do, for even the world's fastest supercomputers. Which is as we do allow our selves to take a quantum leap into Omnidimensional Reality, and begin to become capable of doing some real time quantum computing. And too, which is while actually occurring within our own personal, and personally effectuated, truly humanistic nuclear resonance spectrometer, and/or –

"Of Nanotubes and Buckyballs: Atomic-Scale Building Blocks –
Once, scientists knew of only two forms of pure carbon: diamonds and graphite. Then in 1985 came the discovery of soccer-ball-shaped molecules known

as buckyballs, followed a few years later by nanotubes, cylinder-shaped molecules that look like rolled-up chicken wire – Scientists are now assembling and arranging these carbon building blocks like a Tinker Toys set on an atomic scale...At this point, these feats remain just laboratory tricks. But one day, scientists say, they may be able to use them to make molecule-size electronic devices. Already, they have made simple components – 'We believe there is a revolution going on the nanoscale,' said Dr. David Tomanek, a professor of physics at Michigan State..."

Kenneth Chang – The New York Times – Tuesday, March 27, 2001

Carbon based mass: truly humanistic quantum dynamically functioning, simultaneously relative, three-dimensional electrical potential mass of a mind, and parallel functioning central nervous. Which: a humanistic mind, is the only single machine, on the face of this point-mass of Earth, which is actually capable of doing some real time quantum computing: in identifiable neuroscientific reality only of course. But – only, which: that a truly humanistic being can begin to become neurophysiologically capable of doing some real time quantum computing, is while functioning, as –

"Again, you have learned how it was said to our ancestors: *You must not break your oath, but must fulfill your oaths to the Lord.* But I say this to you: do not swear at all, either by *heaven*, since that is God's throne; or by the *earth*, since that is *his footstool*; or by Jerusalem, since that is *the city of the great king.* Do not swear by your own head either, since you cannot turn a single hair white or black. All you need to say is 'Yes' if you mean yes, 'No' if you mean no; anything more than this comes from the evil one."

Matthew 5: 33-37

Simultaneously relative to/from, and within, a truly humanistic, simultaneously relative, and universally applicable, single cognizable point time zero. The point time zero for the beginning of the orchestration, of the simultaneously relative harmoniously proportioned differential equations, and/or individually completed harmoniously proportioned movements, which comprises a symphony. Exactly because, if –

"The stability of muscular performance is yet another example of all-pervading influence of negative feedback – (while) in the Second World War, the (human central nervous) system was freely compared with mechanical devices which exemplified the engineering device known as servo-loop – By elucidating the mathematical principles of such error-activated performance, the military Physiologists found that they were printing out the engineering specifications for a human nervous system. By treating a man as if he were part of a mechanical setup, they began to discover the extent to which he as a whole actually was one – The sensations which arise from muscle, joint and tendon, are conveniently grouped under one heading not because of their anatomical source, but because they collaborate to provide the brain with a distinctive form of information – None of this information could be put to use unless it was firmly located against a fixed horizon; it would float weightlessly in a vacuum. If you regard the body as an aircraft flying in a thick cloud, the proprioceptive system re-creates a scale-model of a machine on the instrument board..."

The Body in Question – Jonathan Miller

There was NO single simultaneously relative – and cognizable, truly humanistic point time zero: the point of the beginning of the purposeful orchestration, of the individually completed harmoniously proportioned movements, and/or the simultaneously relative harmoniously proportioned differential equations, and/or the point of the purposefully effectuated function of; "Einstein's general theory of relativity transforms space and time from a passive background in which events take place to active participants in the dynamics of the cosmos – General relativity completely changed the discussion of the origin and fate of the universe. A static universe could have existed forever or could have been created in its present form at some time in the past. On the other hand, if galaxies are moving apart, they must have been closer together in the past. About 15 billion years ago, they would all have been on top of one another and their density would have been infinite. According to the general theory, this Big Bang was the beginning of the universe and of time itself" – the Big Bang: while actually functioning as Omnidimensional Time *made manifest*, there could "be" nothing. Except –

"At Hiroshima: The common lot was random, indiscriminate and universal violence inflicting terrible pain, the physics of hydraulics and leverage and heat run riot...A junior-college girl: 'Ah, that instant! I felt as though I have been struck on the back with something like a big hammer, and thrown into boiling oil – I seem to have been blown a good way to the north and I felt as though the directions were all changed around."

Richard Rhodes – The Making of The Atomic Bomb

Chaos, and confusion too. And, only also, terrible pain and death and suffering, while it: the chaos and the pain and death and suffering, will be universally applicable: at the end of time. And too at the beginning of the end of time, there will be no cognizance of simultaneously relative patterns in space/time, and/or truly humanistic intelligence, left, anywhere, and by anyone either, on the entire face of this Earth: exactly preceding the beginning of the end of time.

But, we are beginning to get a little ahead of our selves: as we move in the direction towards the end of time, and we do not want to do that yet, in this Edenic story. So we will continue in the direction back through time, to begin to enable our selves to understand exactly what happened, within this greatest con in the entire history of mankind. And exactly only because this is the 21st century, we could,

73

perhaps and while moving in a direction back towards point time zero and/or our childhood innocence, take a –

"One thing has become clear to scientists: memory is absolutely crucial to our consciousness. Says Javellen Huttenlocher, a professor of psychology at the University of Chicago: 'There's almost nothing you do, from perception to thinking, that doesn't draw continuously on your memory. (And) It can't be otherwise, since there is really no such thing as a present (while) memory provides a personal context, a sense of self and a sense of (the) past and present and a frame for the future.' (But) Memory is not a single phenomenon. 'We don't have a memory system in the brain,' says James McGaugh, director of the Center for Neurobiology of Learning and Memory at the University of California, Irvine. 'We have memory systems, each playing a different role – Within explicit, or declarative, memory – there are specific subsystems that handle shapes, textures, sounds, faces, names – even distinct systems to remember nouns vs. verbs. All of these different types of memory are ultimately stored in the brain's cortex – what's happening when the brain forms memory (is that) it's the connections between nerve cells – and particularly the strength of those connections – that are altered by experience (as) nerve cells are firing simultaneously and coordinating different sets of information (And) Experts in brain imaging are only beginning to understand how the parts are reassembled into a coherent whole – When everything is going right, these different systems work together seamlessly. If you're taking a bicycle ride, for example, the memory of how to operate the bike comes from one set of neurons; the memory of how to get from here to the other side of town comes from another; the nervous feeling you have left over from taking a bad spill last time out comes from still another. Yet you are never aware that your mental experience has been assembled, bit by bit, like some invisible edifice inside your brain."

Michael D. Lemonick – Smart Genes? – Time – Sept. 13, 1999

Ride upon a bicycle.

And – too and as we are beginning to return back to innocence and while moving back through time, which will, exactly, begin to enable our own selves to become capable of beginning to; "One thing has become clear to scientists: memory is absolutely crucial to our consciousness – 'There's almost nothing you do, from perception to thinking, that doesn't draw continuously on your memory. (And) It can't be otherwise, since there really is no such thing as a present (while) memory provides a personal context, a sense of self – (But) memory is not a single phenomenon – 'We have memory systems, each playing a different role" – actually effectually form our own personally effectuated, and universally applicable: and simultaneously relative, truly humanistic self-consciousness.

And: again as we are beginning to return back to innocence and while riding upon a bicycle built for one, which will be while – and *simultaneously*, enabling our very own selves to effectually employ the use of, and/or harness the use of, and as was exactly explained by Thomas Jefferson –

"Walking is the best possible exercise. Habituate yourself to walk very far. The Europeans value themselves on having subdued the horse to the uses of man; but I doubt whether we have not lost more than we have gained, by the use of this animal. No one has occasioned so much the degeneracy of the human body...While this gives a moderate exercise to the body, it gives boldness, enterprise, and independence to the mind. Games played with the ball, and others of that nature – stamp no character on the mind. Let your gun, therefore, be the constant companion of your walks – A strong body makes the mind strong – Time now begins to be precious to you – A little walk of half an hour, in the morning, when you first rise, is also advisable. It takes off sleep, and produces other good effects in the animal economy. Rise at a fixed and an early hour, and go to bed at a fixed and early hour also. Sitting up late at night is injurious to the health, and not useful to the mind...If ever you find yourself environed with difficulties and perplexing circumstances, out of which you are at a loss how to extricate yourself, do what is right, and be assured that that will extricate you the best of the worst situations. Though you cannot see, when you take one step, what will be the next, yet follow truth, justice, and plain dealing, and never fear their leading you out of the labyrinth, in the easiest manner possible...When your mind shall be well improved with science, nothing will be necessary to place you in the highest points of view, but to pursue the interests of your country, the interest of your friends, and your own interests also, with the purest integrity, the most chaste honor. The defect of these virtues can never be made up by all the other acquirements of body and mind. Make these, then, your first object. Give up money, give up fame, give up science, give up the earth itself and all it contains, rather than do an immoral act. And never suppose, that in any possible situation, or under any circumstances, it is best for you to do a dishonorable thing, however slightly so it may appear to you. Whenever you are to do with a thing, though it can never be known but to yourself, ask yourself how you would act were all the world looking at you, and act accordingly..."
Thomas Jefferson (To) Peter Carr – Paris, August 19, 1785

ZERO "HORSEPOWER": NOT A SINGLE ONE.
Which: the diversion of the harnessed worldly power of a single horse, and/or any games, and/or entertainment of any kind either, would be – only, for our very own selves to simply consume, and/or be affected by, while functioning as a diversion from reality. And too which: that it would be only a diversion from Reality and that we do only purposefully avoid it, is while we do begin to enable our very own selves to continue while on our journey back to find our Innocence lost, and/or to –

"...Read – Milton's 'Paradise Lost' – Plato's Socratic dialogues...never suppose, that in any possible situation, or under any circumstances, it is best for you to do a dishonorable thing, however slightly so it may appear to you – Encourage all your virtuous dispositions, and exercise them whenever an opportunity arises; being assured that they will gain strength by exercise, as a limb of the body does, and that exercise will make them habitual...From the practice of the purest virtue, you may be assured you will derive the most sublime comforts in every moment of life, and in the moment of death...Thomas Jefferson"

Thomas Jefferson (To) Peter Carr – Paris, August 19, 1785

Find our Paradise Lost: the truly virtuous Child, while actually functioning as the formation of the world's first Truly Idealist Democratic Society. Which is while beginning with the individually affected minds: of the people, and while beginning with the formation of the truly virtuous child, who: the original truly virtuous, and truly innocent, Child, would sooner give up everything: than do an immoral act. And – while beginning with the individually affected child's mind and while in an attempt to find our Innocence Lost, which is as they: all of the individually affected child's minds, do, exactly, unleash the bridal to worldly power, and let it go too. As they: everyone who has been affected, do instead –

"...He proves also, that man, once surrendering his reason, has no remaining guard against absurdities the most monstrous, and like a ship without rudder, is the sport of every wind. With such persons, gullibility which they call faith, takes the helm from the hand of reason, and the mind becomes a wreck...Thomas Jefferson"

Thomas Jefferson (To) James Smith – Monticello, December 8, 1822

Begin to become capable of taking back control over their own selves.

And too, as we do begin to let it: the bridal and/or persuasion of worldly power, go, and while on our journey back to find our innocence lost, which will be exactly as –

"The young Newton was as sensitive to the rhythms of nature as he was indifferent to those of men. As a child he built clocks and sundials and was known for his ability to tell time by the sun, but he habitually forgot to show up for meals, a trait that persisted throughout his life – Sent to gather in livestock, he was found an hour later standing on the bridge leading to the pasture, gazing fixedly into a flowing stream. On another occasion he came home trailing a leader and bridle, not having noticed that the horse he had been leading had slipped away...At college he filled his lonely life with books. '*Amicus Plato amicus Aristoteles magis amica veritas,*' he wrote in his student notebook – 'Plato is my friend, Aristotle is my friend, but my greatest friend is truth...'"

Timothy Ferris – Coming Of Age In The Milky Way

Isaac Newton did do. While as in his own personal attempt to find Paradise Lost, and the Absolute truth also. And which: while as in our attempt to find the lost innocence of the child, is while we do continue in a direction back towards point time zero, and pass through –

"When you're 5 years old, and just about three feet tall, this is what you do in kindergarten class: 'I learn how to draw 5-2-1-6. I learn about 7. I learn e-k-g-s-k-c-w-x-y-z. I play with the dollhouse and the kitchen table. I can draw a 5. It's like this: up and down'...that's just the beginning. By June, Miah and her kindergarten classmates will be expected to know – thirty-two reading words. Phonic sounds. How to read simple sentences. How to write numbers (and) recognize number patterns. The basics of telling time and measurements, as well as the concepts of addition and subtraction..."
Monica Rhor – The Philadelphia Inquirer – October 30, 1997

Our worldly childish existence: while *actually* functioning upon this simultaneously relative point-mass of earth. And – while actually functioning upon this simultaneously relative point-mass, which is, and in our childhood innocence, that all young children must begin to learn how to effectually cognize, and within their minds alone, the very foundation, and/or basics, of childish: universally applicable – simultaneously relative and unidirectionally successive, Time *made manifest*, and/or simple universally applicable syntax, functioning as the verbs. And/or how to move: within our minds alone, and while: within our minds alone, the child does begin to learn how to effectually move while in a purposefully effectuated direction, while as from point A towards point B and while making manifest elementary; "The basics of telling time" – Time *made manifest* that is, that a young child does begin to learn truly humanistic empirical self-consciousness. Within his individually affected, and truly humanistic being, mind, and too and of course, while there is some time, for the young children, which is purposefully designated to allow them; "I play with the dollhouse and the kitchen table" – to escape Reality, while playing house, and consuming some abstracted effectual stimulus also. And which: that young children can begin to learn about Reality and escape it too, is, only, neurophysiologically capable of occurring after –

"At birth a baby's language of the senses is primitive...he sees vague shapes, or flashes of light, but without meaning. His eyes can neither focus on nor follow a moving object. He is even farsighted since his eyeballs are foreshortened at birth. And what he sees is flat. He uses only one eye at a time, his eyes not yet working together to sight an object three-dimensionally..."
The Senses of Man – Joan Steen Wilentz

A child is born into this world, as pure innocence. After having begun: the effectuated formation of a child's mind, at –

"Rat-a-tat-tat. Rat-a-tat-tat. Rat-a-tat-tat – If scientists could eavesdrop on the brain of a human embryo 10, maybe 12 weeks after conception, they would hear an astonishing racket. Inside the womb, long before light first strikes the retina of the eye or the earliest dreamy images flicker through the cortex, nerve cells in the developing brain crackle with purposeful activity..."
Fertile Minds – Madeleine Nash – Time – February 3, 1997

Point time zero: actually secured within his mother's womb.

Then, a child is born: into simultaneously relative truly humanistic Reality, and begins –

"A baby passes her first amazing milestone before the typical mother has even wiped off the sweat of labor. Full-term newborns, scientist established in 1996, recognize and prefer their mother's face to all others – In the ingenious experiment, the scientists had babies suck a special pacifier that controlled a video screen. Depending on how the infant sucked, fast or slow, the image of Mom or another woman appeared; babies sucked so they'd see Mom...(And) Some motor-skill delays may be easily explained by, for instance, the fact that 'children need the opportunity to do things on their own,' says (Dr. Chris) Johnson. When one set of parents brought their son in because he wasn't rolling over, Johnson asked if they ever put the child on the floor. The answer was no. The child was always being held. Within a few days of being placed on the floor so he could see the world from a different perspective, he rolled over, and went on to develop just fine. 'We all want (to) do for our kids,' says Johnson. 'A child needs to do for himself...'"
Joan Raymond – Newsweek – Fall/Winter 2000

His, or her, own personal journey into uncharted territories, and begins to learn how to "do" not only for their own selves too: while as in our attempt to find Paradise Lost. And/or, begin to learn how to become neurophysiologically capable of experiencing –

"Be compassionate as your Father is compassionate. Do not judge, and you will not be judged yourselves; do not condemn, and you will not be condemned yourselves; grant pardon, and you will be pardoned. Give, and there will be gifts for you: a full measure, pressed down, shaken together, and running over, will be poured into your lap; because the amount you measure out is the amount you will be given back."
Luke 6: 36-38

Truly humanistic love: unbridled compassion, and the Eternal Harmony too.
So: let's do that. Let us return the innocence back to the child, and do, and/or measure out, for our own selves, and –

"If one day we awoke and truly saw the world this way (effectually functioning as a continuum), the ramifications would shake our psyche to its foundations. Assuming we remained sane, the relationship of I to thou, of individual to planet, of my action to yours, would be revolutionized..."
Arthur Zajonc – Catching the Light

For the entire world too: let us start a brand new revolution. Let us see things from a whole new perspective: as they have never been seen before, and while as through the eyes of a child. And which is –

"...Descartes's emphasis on depicting motion algebraically encouraged Newton to develop a dynamics written in terms of algebra's alternative, geometry; as this was not yet mathematically feasible, Newton found it necessary to invent a brand new branch of mathematics, the calculus. Infinitesimal calculus set geometry in motion: The parabolas and hyperbolas Newton drew on the page could be analyzed as the product of a moving point – As Newton put it, 'Lines are described, and thereby generated, not by the opposition of parts, but by the continued motion of points' – Newton is said to have recalled, near the end of his life, that this inspiration came to him when he saw an apple fall from the tree in front of his mother's house. This story may be true – Newton's desk in his bedroom looked out (a) window (and onto) an orchard – (While) Hally and Hooke – felt certain that the inverse-square law could explain Keplar's discovery that the planets move in elliptical orbits, each sweeping out an equal area within its orbit and an equal time – (only) Newton had realized that the earth's gravitational force can be treated as if it were concentrated at a point at the center of the earth – Whenever an immobile object is set into motion, or a moving object changes its velocity or direction of motion, Newton infers that a *force* is responsible. Such a change may be expressed as *acceleration*, the rate of change of velocity with time..."
Timothy Ferris – Coming Of Age In The Milky Way

While gaining access to the exact same key which was obtained by Isaac Newton. Which: the key that Isaac Newton did take hold of, was simply his formed understanding of simultaneously relative Reality, and/or the perception of a single simultaneously relative differential equation. Isaac Newton did, simply, begin to enable his very own self to become neurophysiologically capable of seeing not just point A: the tree and attached apple – extended to the moon, or point B: the ground – extended to the very center of the earth, but the actual cause: within his mind, which was responsible for the perceivable effect: effectually functioning as a simultaneously relative gradient, and/or differential. While this was only possible, the formed understanding within his mind, because, as we can remember, Isaac Newton did allow himself to; "The young Newton was as sensitive to the rhythms of nature as he was indifferent to those of men– On (an) occasion he came home trailing a leader and bridle, not having noticed that the horse he had been leading had

79

slipped away" – let it go. He did – exactly, allow his very own self to break free of the attractive force, which is our simple mortal existence while upon this point-mass of Earth, and, then –

"Do not be afraid of them therefore. For everything that is now covered will be uncovered, and everything now hidden will be made clear. What I say to you in the dark, tell in the daylight, what you hear in whispers, proclaim from the housetops.
Matthew 10: 26-27

Leading individual human beings towards the absolute truth, for their very own selves to simply see, with their eyes alone too.
So, let's make clear another absolute, and absolutely unknown, universally applicable truth: for our own selves and the entire world to simply see, with our eyes alone. Which we can enable our own selves to do, again, while employing the use of the exact same key which Isaac Newton did employ the use of: to enable him to see Reality, and which was his; "Newton's desk in his bedroom looked out (a) window (and onto) an orchard" – two-dimensional plane of a window, while actually perceiving all of simultaneously relative four-dimensional Reality, beyond the two-dimensional plane, of the window: actually occurring within his mind, while as through his function of sight, and/or his eyes. Which: our eyes, truly are the "windows to our souls." And – too and as we can remember, which we can do: look past the two-dimensional plane and see the function of four-dimensional reality, while functioning in a manner similar to Fillippo Brunelleschi, and while in the year 1413. Which, if we can remember, was simply while Brunelleschi did – simply, designate a single point, located within the depth of simultaneously relative three-dimensional reality, and did – then, draw a mathematically accurate representation of a single volume of space: projected upon the two-dimensional plane of a window, and which was while occurring at the dawn of the Renaissance. While enabling individual human beings to move into the depth of three-dimensional space, within their minds alone, while in a harmoniously proportioned manner and for the very first time in history of mankind, and while in the year 1413 too. So: let's actually do it, for our very own selves and the entire world too: let's go find the absolute truth, which is beyond the two-dimensional plane.
To actually do it, we will need a piece of glass, which we can draw upon, and which we can carry too, and a simultaneously relative three-dimensional Reality, beyond the two-dimensional piece of glass: to see within our three-dimensional minds. Which: the actual projections made manifest from within simultaneously relative three-dimensional Reality, we can trace: being projected from within Reality, and because of the function of quantized electromagnetism *and/or* light *and/or* the universal constant of Time *made manifest*, upon the two-dimensional plane of a window. And too as we can remember, which will be: that we are beginning to move into three-dimensional reality while moving our bodies, a bit

more painful than simply sitting inside and looking at a two-dimensional plane: of any kind, and, too, it: looking at scientific reality, will be a lot more painful than simply existing in ignorance of reality. And too: as we do actually begin to coordinate our journey into uncharted territories, we will be functioning in a manner similar to Christopher Columbus, as he did; "The sensations which arise from muscle, joint and tendon are conveniently grouped under one heading not because of their anatomical source, but because they collaborate to provide the brain with a distinctive form of information – None of this information could be put to use unless it was firmly located against a fixed horizon; it would float about weightlessly in a vacuum" – designate a single point on the horizon, within simultaneously relative Reality while upon this point-mass of Earth. Which he did, then, go sailing off towards, while in a purposefully effectuated direction: to find the truth only.

Which is while beginning at point time zero: within the comfort of our artificially effectuated mother's womb environment of our homes, and which is also while actually looking through our two-dimensional plane of a window, while beginning to coordinate our purposefully directed movement throughout, and within, truly humanistic simultaneously relative space/time: while tracing the projections made manifest upon the two-dimensional plane of a window. Which will: be made manifest and while we remember which is as in an attempt to find our Paradise lost, as from the tangible form mass Tree: at the edge of the Garden, some more tangible form mass Trees: deeper in the Garden and actually comprising the Garden, another tangible form mass of a humanistic being: standing by the edge of the Garden holding the Apple and/or guarding the entrance to the Garden, and our identified simultaneously relative worldly existence while upon this point-mass of earth, and/or our worldly paths, and/or sidewalk, leading towards, and/or away from, The Garden. Now – at point time zero within our minds while the remainder of the projections made manifest from simultaneously relative reality are actually being projected upon the two-dimensional plane, we can begin to effect our coordinate point-system, and/or identify the simultaneously relative position of all of the remaining identifible three-dimensional tangible form point-mass nouns: within our parametered simultaneously relative visual field, of humanistic three-dimensional space. So, we can identify point A: as within our minds, point B: the humanistic being holding the Apple and/or guarding the entrance to the Garden, point C: the Apple, point D: the Tree, point E: another Tree, point F: the left visual parameter, point G: the right visual parameter, point H: the top visual parameter, point I: the bottom visual parameter, and the remaining points of the individual formations of the completed movements of the sidewalk, and/or path, leading in a direction towards the entrance to The Garden. Now – after we have designated the points of the simultaneously relative positioning of the three-dimensional tangible form point-mass nouns, within humanistic space, we can begin to trace the outlines: as to point time zero, made manifest as from the projections of the tangible form point-mass nouns, while actually functioning as quantized electromagnetism, and which we should actually do: trace them upon the window. And which means to actually draw a line: upon the two-dimensional plane of the window, from the single point of the humanistic being's eyes: point B, out towards the left and right side visual parameters: points F and G, now draw another line: upon the two-dimensional plane, from the point of the Apple: point C, out towards the left and right visual parameters. And now draw another line, out towards the top, and bottom, visual parameters, from all of the trees, and also draw lines out to the left and right visual parameters, from the top and bottom of the humanistic being's head and feet: where they are in contact with the ground, at the edge of the path leading towards the Garden. Now, use a compass, and measure the distance from the humanistic being's eyes and the point of the position of the Apple, and draw a circle: with the compass and double the distance as from the Apple to the humanistic being's eyes; upon the two-dimensional plane of glass, and do the same with the distance from the humanistic being to the tree. And now, draw a line from the humanistic being's eyes out towards the corners where the parametered visual scene intersects: all four of them, and draw the parameter too.

And – now, what we are capable of seeing: with our eyes alone, is the real projected representation *of* many real: perceivable and effectual, truly humanistic non-tangible form projections, *of* : squares – circles – rectangles and triangles, and which actually are no less real than the sound of a human being's voice. And –

"...Many of the provinces of the brain (are) topographical maps of projections of the sensory fields which they represent – the same geometrical decorum applies to all projections – physical events impinging on the sensory surface are transformed into the characteristic digital language of the brain – Unfortunately, the word 'projection' has misleading connotations of pictorial display, which tempt one to assume that the human mind hovers over the dimly lit screen of its own brain like a phantom spectator watching the projected images of the passing scene – Once a pattern of light has struck the retina, as soon as a train of sound-waves has traveled up the spiral of the cochlea, the events are translated into sequences of nervous information so that the transmission no more resembles what it represents than the currents in a television circuit resemble the pictures which they carry – when a television picture is transmitted, there are no ghostly images flying through the air: the picture is converted into a series of visual unrecognizable radio pulses, and when these are picked up – (they) reconstitute the picture – a linear code dictates the construction of the visible object."
Jonathan Miller – The Body in Question

As a matter of neuroscientific fact.
And they: non-tangible form geometrical projections made manifest while actually effectually functioning as quantized electrodynamics, are – also and as a matter of neuroscientific fact, the –

"The equivalent of the machine language of the brain, in (Alan) Gevin's view, is very complex electromagnetic field configurations, with very fine modulation in amplitude, frequency, wave shape and spatial distribution...(And) After several years of painstaking mapping of these psychic never-never lands, discovered an extraordinary thing: The mind of man contains only so many visions – four basic, recurrent geometrical forms..."
The 3-Pound Universe – Judith Hooper and Dick Teresi

Only "thing" within our minds.
And as was exactly explained by –

"Geometrical non-tangible forms: God wanted us to recognize them, when He created us after His image, so that we should share in His thoughts. For what is implanted in the mind of man other than numbers and magnitudes? These alone we comprehend correctly, and if piety permits us to say so, his recognition is of the same kind as the divine, at least insofar as we in this mortal life of ours are capable of grasping part of it...Geometry is one and eternal, a reflection of the mind of God – nature loves these relationships in everything that is capable of being related. They are also loved by the intellect of man who is an image of the Creator."
Johannes Keplar – Max Casper

Johannes Keplar. And while in the year 1595, and as a matter of fact too.
And, of course, as was also plainly explained: in the year 1480, by –

"Therefore O students – think to comprehend the mind of God: study mathematics and do not build without foundations – True sciences are those which have penetrated through the senses as a result of experience and thus silencing the tongues of disputants, not feeding investigators on dreams but always proceeding successively from primary truths and established principles, in a proper order towards the conclusion. This may be witnessed in the principles of mathematics, that is to say, number and measure – termed arithmetic and geometry, which deal with discontinuous and continuous quantities with the utmost truth – Here all guesswork remains destroyed in eternal silence..."

Leonardo da Vinci. And while in the year 1480, and as a matter fact too.
And they: all of the individually completed non-tangible form mass geometrical projections, which we did trace upon the two-dimensional piece of glass, are also – as we can remember: collectively as a whole, the function of; "There are two essential yet complementary aspects of this new vision of time which are as striking in contrast as heaven and hell. Heaven is ruled by dynamical equations that are reversible and 'timeless'; their simplicity ensures stability for eternity. Hell is more akin to the real world, where fluctuations, uncertainty and chaos reign" – hell on earth. Which is – exactly, because there is no syntax anywhere within simple

three-dimensional reality: except within *The Annunciation,* or the mind of any individual who has enabled themselves to learn the language of Omnidimensional Time *made manifest*.

So: Let's silence the tongues of the disputants – FOREVER, and for our own selves too. Pick up the two-dimensional plane of glass, and begin to move your body, and/or begin walking, and exactly as; "Walking is the best possible exercise. Habituate yourself to walk very far – Time now becomes precious to you" – Thomas Jefferson did do, while upon a path to find Paradise Lost. Which is exactly what we have begun to do: while moving in a purposefully effectuated direction towards the Garden, and – too, as we begin to move in a purposefully effectuated largo: slow, tempoed movement, and while as from point A: secured within our homes, towards point B: the Garden, and while making manifest Time too: while moving in a purposefully effectuated direction as from point A towards point B. Now – while carrying the two-dimensional plane of the window in our hands, and remaining focused upon the single vanishing point/horizon line: point B, continue to move: your body, while in a purposefully effectuated direction, and – now while beginning to increase tempo, continue to move while in the purposefully effectuated direction, while as from point A towards point B. And – too, which will be as we continue to move through space, and over time, while as through an adagio: leisurely, manner, and continue as through allegro: brisk or rapid, tempoed movement, and then all the way up to presto: quick or rapid, tempoed physiological movement. And, which does mean, that – now that we actually are moving at Presto tempoed movement, we should be running, and – too, just about approaching the Garden Wall, and, now, we should stop: our movement, just outside the Garden Wall. And – now, pick up the two-dimensional plane of the window, and hold it up to look through it, and actually see the reality, of: the Trees – which comprises the Garden, the humanistic being: guarding the entrance to the Garden, and the Apple too, and too which is while now actually seeing things from a whole new perspective: while actually seeing the absolute truth for own selves, and while as through the eyes of a child also.

So, hold it: the two-dimensional plane of the window, up: to the Reality of the Garden: the trees – the humanistic being guarding the entrance, and the Apple too. What we can now simply see, is the absolute truth. And/or, the fact that every thing has now changed: the coordinates, upon the two-dimensional plane, and all of the simultaneously relative differential equations, which were represented upon the two-dimensional plane *and* within our truly humanistic three-dimensional electrical potential mass minds too, as simultaneously relative to/from, and within, a single cognizable point time zero, and/or as capable of being measured as from the identified point time zero. Except: in identifiable simultaneously relative reality, what did *actually* change? The answer is, of course, absolutely nothing, *except* for our own identifiable position within truly humanistic simultaneously relative space/time, and while upon this simultaneously relative point-mass of Earth. And, now, let's turn around – and look behind us, and which will now simply enable us to see: and with our eyes alone, the entire structure of the actual tangible form mass

House which we did begin our journey into uncharted territories from, and/or the artificially effectuated mother's womb environment which we begin each new day, and/or daily completed symphony, from. And, too, we can now also plainly see, the entire tangible form mass House, as it is located at the very beginning of our journey into uncharted territories. Which: our journey into uncharted territories, we did begin while located upon the path, and/or sidewalk, leading to the Garden.

Except – wait a minute, let's hold up that two-dimensional plane window again, and look at the path which we did begin our journey on, and/or the sidewalk which is capable of actually functioning as our truly humanistic constant. And we can now actually see, with our eyes alone, that the points: of the individually completed movements of the sidewalk, that we are actually standing upon: while positioned at point B, appear to be: upon the two-dimensional plane and within our minds also, exactly the same: as they were at point A, and/or point time zero. But, we do know, for a fact and within our minds alone, that we did move our bodies, and while moving in a purposefully effectuated direction while as from point A towards point B. And which we do know: within our own personal minds, only exactly because we did see: not *just* "with" our eyes but "within" our minds, the apparent simultaneously relative size, of all of the tangible form masses, become progressively larger – and smaller, as we did move our bodies all throughout, and within, truly humanistic space/time. And – too, which we can know is a scientific fact, because we do know that we are not delusional, and/or simply misled. And/or, exactly not –

"...Joyce Kovelman and Arnold Scheibel of UCLA's Brain Research Institute spotted a weird cellular 'disarray' in the schizophrenic brains (and not in the matched controls). The pyramid-shaped cells of the hippocampus, normally arranged in an orderly manner, were grossly misaligned...A schizophrenic's dopamine neurons would start to fire in two different rhythms and rapidly become uncoupled – 'I think that in schizophrenia the brain fragments into active and inactive clusters of neurons and different parts of the brain become dissociated,' says (Roy) King. 'You might get an asymmetry between the left and the right side, say. Schizophrenics often feel that their minds and bodies are split apart'..."
The 3-Pound Universe – Judith Hooper and Dick Teresi

Schizophrenic: we do know that we are not.
Because: we do know that we are not schizophrenics, we are capable of understanding the absolute truth. And actually –

"Space, Mach argued, is not a thing, but an expression of interrelationships among events. '*All* masses and *all* velocities, and consequently *all* forces, are relative,' he wrote. Einstein agreed, and was encouraged to attempt to write a theory that built space and time out of events alone, as Mach prescribed. He never entirely succeeded in satisfying Mach's criteria – it may be that no workable theory can – but the effort helped impel him toward relativity – With the special theory of relativity, Einstein had at last resolved the paradox that occurred to him at age sixteen, that Maxwell's equations failed if one could chase a beam of light at the velocity of light. He did so by concluding that one *cannot* accelerate to the velocity of light – 'To the concept of absolute rest there correspond no properties of the phenomena, neither in mechanics, nor in electrodynamics.' What matters are observable events, and no event can be observed until the light (that) brings news of it reaches the observer. Einstein had replaced Newton's space with a network of light beams; *theirs* was the absolute grid, within which space itself became – Observers in motion experience a slowing in the passage of time – Mass, too, is rendered plastic within the framework of light beams; objects approaching the speed of light increase in mass – If the earth could be accelerated to the velocity of light (a feat that would require infinite energy to achieve) it would contract into a two-dimensional wafer of infinite mass, on which time would come to a stop – which is one way of saying the acceleration to light speed is impossible – Nor are these effects illusory – They are as real as the stone that Dr. Johnson kicked in his famous refutation of Bishop Berkeley, and have been confirmed in scores of experiments – 'On the Electrodynamics of Moving Bodies,' his aim was to redeem the laws of electrodynamics so that they could be shown to work in every imaginable situation – Einstein reasoned that if the effects of gravitation are mimicked by acceleration, gravitation itself might be regarded as a kind of acceleration. But acceleration through what reference frame? It could not be ordinary three-dimensional space – The search for an answer required, brought Einstein to consider the concept of a four-dimensional space/time continuum. Within its framework, gravitation *is* acceleration, the acceleration of objects as they glide along 'world lines'– the special theory of relativity has been viewed in terms of 'space/time continuum' ever since – (In which) The force of gravitation disappears, and is replaced by the geometry of space itself – Einstein struggled through the complexities of curved space, seeking to assign the fourth dimension to time and make the whole, infernally complicated affair come out right – doing important work in quantum mechanics and a half-dozen other fields – But he kept returning to the riddle of gravitation, trying to find patterns of beauty and simplicity among thick stacks of papers black with equations. Like a lost explorer discarding his belongings on a trek across the desert, he found it necessary to part company with some of the most cherished of his possessions – 'In all my life I have never before labored so hard,' he wrote to a friend.'...Compared with this problem, the original theory of relativity is child's play..."

    Timothy Ferris – Coming Of Age In the Milky way

    Neurophysiologically capable of moving: within our truly humanistic quantum dynamically functioning three-dimensional electrical potential mass minds, and parallel functioning central nervous systems, alone, into all of truly humanistic simultaneously relative space/time. Which is while actually functioning: within our truly humanistic minds alone, as: Omnidimensional Time *made manifest*.

Which is: in identifiable neuroscientific reality only, exactly how we: all individual human beings, can know that we are; "in schizophrenia the brain fragments into active and inactive clusters of neurons and different parts of the brain become dissociated" – not schizophrenic: as a matter of scientific fact. And – again, which is: here at this point in time and while upon the threshold of the 21st century, some thing: of a truly humanistic non-thing, that is supposed to impossible to do.

But which: consciously cognizing Omnidimensional Time *made manifest*, was some thing: of a truly humanistic non-thing, that –

" ...I hold, (without appeal to revelation) that when we take a view of the universe, in its parts, general or particular, it is impossible for the human mind not to perceive and feel a conviction of design, consummate skill, and indefinite power in every atom of its composition. The movements of the heavenly bodies, so exactly held in their course by the balance of centrifugal and centripetal forces; the structure of our earth itself, with its distribution of lands, waters and atmosphere; animal and vegetable bodies, examined in all their minutest particles; insects, mere atoms of life, yet as perfectly organized as man or mammoth; the mineral substances, their generation and uses; it is impossible, I say, for the human mind not to believe, that there is in all this, design, cause and effect, up to an ultimate cause, a Fabricator of all things from matter and motion, their Preserver and Regulator while permitted to exist in their present forms, and their regeneration into new and other forms. We see, too, evident proofs of the necessity for a superintending power, to maintain the universe in its course and order. Stars, well known, have disappeared, new ones have come into view; comets, in their incalculable course, may run foul of suns and planets, and require renovation under other laws; certain races and animals are become extinct; and were there no restoring power, all existences might extinguish successively, one by one, until all should be reduced to shapeless chaos. So irresistible are these evidences of an intelligent and powerful Agent, that, of the infinite numbers of men who have existed through all time, they have believed, in the proportion of a million at least to unit, in the hypothesis of an eternal pre-existence of a Creator, rather than in that of a self-existent universe...Thomas Jefferson."

Thomas Jefferson (To) John Adams

Every "body," or – rather, beings, who are –

"...We have indeed an innate sense of what we call beautiful – nature hath implanted in our breasts a love of others, a sense of duty to them, a moral instinct, in short, which prompts us irresistibly to feel and to succor their distresses – I sincerely, then, believe – in the general existence of a moral instinct. I think it the brightest gem with which the human character is studded, and the want of it is more degrading than the most hideous of bodily deformities...Thomas Jefferson "

Thomas Jefferson (To) Thomas Law

In possession of a uniquely humanistic refractive gem of a mind, are capable of doing: consciously cognizing the Mind of God made manifest that is.

And – again and again, which: consciously cognizing Omnidimensional Time *made manifest*, is some thing: of a uniquely humanistic non-thing, that is supposed to be impossible to do: here on the threshold of the 21st century, and: again and again, only exactly within individually affected humanistic being minds alone of course, that it is supposed to be impossible.

And which is exactly why – now, we can begin to move while in a direction towards –

"A Brief Walk Through Time –
My old sauntering buddy Danny got an offer he couldn't refuse, if he had been given the chance – Somehow this thwarted adventure precipitated the recent arrival of Danny and me at the front steps of the American Museum of Natural History – We were walking through the universe, traipsing back to time's beginning and exploring the edges of cosmic knowledge (while) our undertaking was the decidedly humble one of seeing what the place was like from the viewpoint of the average Joe – We decided to begin at the Rose Center for Earth and Space – We made our way to the Hayden Sphere. Its 429 seats are arranged circularly – The voice of Tom Hanks narrated as the view morphed magically from two to three dimensions, and we zoomed through supergalaxies (at) the speed of light. 'Wow,' Danny said – 'It's almost like coming out of church,' – 'You can't think to describe what you've seen'...We found ourselves on a 400-foot-long walkway intended to show the vastness of the cosmos – It was almost lunchtime, and Danny was reflective – The signs on exhibits are hopelessly stilted,' he said – 'You've got to remember this is a very pompous institution,' he continued. 'It's funded by millionaires who constantly remind you they're doing you a service...' – In the Hall of Meteorites it is easy to be awestruck by the Cape York meteorite. It is 4.5 billion years old and weighs 34 tons, making it the heaviest meteorite on display anywhere. Its supports go to the bedrock below the building. It is believed to come from the center of a planet...By this time we generously calculated that we had walked four miles. We approach the popular 'Pearls' exhibition. Our first sight was an eerily realistic video of pearl divers slithering up and down a screen, which fills a whole wall. The crowd, largely female, was riveted, and why not...'Ooh la la!' exclaimed a woman – Danny was swaying back and forth, which he said made the jewelry wink like Christmas lights: 'If they wink for me, imagine how much they would wink for a lady' – But his final conclusion was that the fabulous collection of pearls 'is sort of like stealing from Mother Nature' – 'If they were supposed to be harvested,' he reasoned, 'they'd be easier to harvest...''
Douglas Martin – The New York Times – Friday, January 4, 2002

The beginning of the End of time.
And exactly because, this –

"The Kingdom of Heaven is like treasure hidden in a field which someone has found; he hides it again, goes off happy, sells off everything he owns and buys the field.

Again, the Kingdom of Heaven is like a merchant looking for fine pearls; when he finds one of great value he goes off and sells everything he owns to buy it."
Matthew 13: 44-46

Is *exactly* –

"Colors Are Truly Brilliant In Trek Up Mount Metaphor –
Hovering above the ghoulish terrain, a visitor might feel transported to a distant planet – But the territory exists only in the realm of the abstraction, as arrangements of data in two experiments that have nothing to do with outer space. One involves genetics, the other quantum physics...But the practice of bringing substance to abstractions with pictures and analogies is as old as science itself...In Jonathan Franzen's new novel, 'The Corrections,' Arthur Lambert, a retired engineer, sits in his basement gloomily testing Christmas lights, only to discover in the depths of the tangle a blacked-out string of bulbs. A 'substantia nigra,' Mr. Frazen calles it – The metaphor, if a little obscure, is pitch perfect. The substantia nigra ('black substance') is a region deep in the brain that produces the neurotransmitter dopamine...in literature, as well as science, illuminating the intangible with a good metaphor is a powerful art."
George Johnson – The New York Times – Tuesday December 25, 2001

Not a simple metaphor, while: "bringing substance to abstractions," and too while: "illuminating the intangible with a good metaphor," also.
And as was exactly explained by –

"Then the disciples went up to him and asked, 'Why do you talk to them in parables?' 'Because,' he replied, 'the mysteries of the kingdom of heaven are revealed to you, but they are not revealed to them. For anyone who has will be given more, and he will have more than enough; but from anyone who has not, even what he has will be taken away. The reason I talk to them in parables is that they look without seeing and listen without hearing or understanding. So in their case this prophecy of Isaiah is being fulfilled:
You will listen and listen again, but not understand,
see and see again, but not perceive.
For the heart of this nation has grown course,
their ears are dull of hearing, and they have shut their eyes,
for fear they should see with their eyes,
hear with their ears,
understand with their heart,
and be converted

and be healed by me.
   But happy are your eyes because they see, your ears because they hear! I tell you solemnly, many prophets and holy men longed to see what you see, and never saw it; to hear what you hear, and never heard it."
   Matthew 13: 10-17

   The scientist Jesus of Nazareth: people can, actually, begin to experience truly humanistic – and uniquely humanistic, brain death, and –

   "...Psychopaths seem to know the dictionary meanings of words but fail(ed) to comprehend or appreciate their *emotional* value or significance (while functioning as if) 'He knows the words but not the music' – Recent laboratory research provides convincing support for these clinical observations. This research is based on evidence that, for normal people, neutral words generally convey less information than do emotional words: A word such as PAPER has dictionary meaning, whereas a word such as DEATH has dictionary meaning *plus* emotional meaning and unpleasant connotations. Emotional words have more 'punch' than do other words – Picture yourself sitting before a computer screen on which groups of letters are flashed for a fraction of a second. Electrodes for recording brain responses have been attached to your scalp and connected to an EEG machine, which draws a graph of the electrical activity of the brain. Some of the groups of letters flashed up on the screen form common words found in the dictionary; other strings form no words, only nonsense syllables. For example, TREE forms a word but RETE does not. Your task is to push a button as quickly as possible whenever you have decided that a true word appeared on the screen. The computer measures the time it takes you to make your decisions; it also analyzes your brain responses during the task – You will probably respond more quickly to an emotional word than to a neutral one. For example, you – and most other people – would push the button more quickly at the word DEATH than the word PAPER. The emotional content of a word seems to give a sort of 'turbo-boost' to the decision-making process. At the same time, the emotional words evoke *larger* brain responses than do neutral words, a reflection of the relatively large amount of information contained in the emotional words – When we used this laboratory test with prison inmates, the non-psychopaths showed the normal pattern of response – but the psychopaths did not: *They responded to emotional words as if they were neutral words* – to a psychopath, a word is just a word."
   Dr. Robert D. Hare – Without Conscience

   As a matter of neuroscientific fact.
   While they: any, and/or all, individuals, who have begun to become affected by the con, and who have begun to enable their very own selves to become capable of functioning only in a psychopathic manner, while experiencing truly humanistic brain death for their own selves, will also – and simultaneously, only simply –

"Psychopaths are notorious for not answering the question posed them or for answering in a way that seems unresponsive to the question – It is *how* they string words and sentences together, not *what* they actually say, that suggests abnormality – part of a general tendency to 'Go off track.' That is, they frequently change topics, go off on irrelevant tangents, (and do) fail to connect phrases and sentences in a straightforward manner – Jack was a mile-a-minute talker, with the psychopath's characteristic ability to contradict himself from one second to the next – One other point about the way in which psychopaths use language: Their 'Mental packages' are not only small but (they are also) two-dimensional, devoid of emotional meaning – Lying, deceiving, and manipulation are natural talents for psychopaths. With their powers of imagination in gear and focused on themselves, psychopaths appear amazingly unfazed by the possibility – or even the certainty, of being found out. When caught in a lie or challenged with the truth, they are seldom perplexed or embarrassed – they simply change their stories or attempt to rework the facts so that they appear to be consistent with the lie. "

> Dr. Robert D. Hare – Without Conscience

Continue to ignore the scientific evidence: which we can simply see with our eyes alone. And/or attempt to simply create a diversion: and/or attempt to rework the facts, so that they appear to be consistent with the lie.

Because, we can now know: for verified scientific fact, that –

"Psychopaths seem to suffer a kind of emotional poverty that limits the range and depth of their feelings. While at times they appear cold and unemotional, they are prone to dramatic, shallow, and short-lived displays of feeling. Careful observers are left with the impression that they are play-acting and that little is going on below the surface – Sometimes they claim to experience strong emotions but are unable to describe the subtleties of various affective states. For example, they equate love with sexual arousal, sadness with frustration and anger with irritability – In some respects they're like the emotionless androids depicted in science fiction, unable to imagine what real humans experience."

> Dr. Robert D. Hare – Without Conscience

The only "thing": in the entire history of mankind, which is capable of inducing a truly humanistic emotional response: within a truly humanistic being, is *The Annunciation*, and/or Reality of course. While the only, so-called, human beings, who will remain neurophysiologically incapable of understanding this fact, are impostors – unable to imagine what real humans experience, and could only, possibly, be like some thing transported to our truly humanistic point-mass of Earth, from some kind of foreign point-mass. And/or, some kind of –

"What is a black hole? For astronomical purposes it behaves as a small highly condensed dark 'body.' But it is not really a material body in the ordinary sense. It possesses no ponderable surface. A black hole is a region of empty space (albeit a strangely distorted one) which acts as a center of gravitational attraction..."

Roger Penrose – Black Holes – The World Treasury of Physics, Astronomy and Mathematics – Ed. Timothy Ferris

Black hole.

And which: our acknowledged understanding of Reality, does exactly enable us: the entire world and now and forever too, to –

"Myths About Genius –
Does genius exist?

The idea generally seems highly exaggerated. Great reputations grow regardless of talent. Acclaim is assigned by luck or wealth. Superior perches are reached through sycophantism or exploitation...The urge to reduce the idea of genius may even arise because of the immensity of its claim."

Edward Weinstein – The New York Times – Saturday, January 5 2002

Eliminate all of the myths about intelligence.

Which: the acquiring of uniquely and truly humanistic, intelligence, is the –

"Many Heavens, Many Ways To Gain an Entrance There –
In a new book, 'The Quest for Paradise: Visions of Heaven and Eternity in the World's Myths and Religions,' John Ashton, the Bible scholar, and Tom Whyte, a former BBC journalist, include as an illustration a beautiful 17th century Iranian painting of a woman standing in a garden...Paradise, like righteousness, is a concept about which opinions clearly differ (but) paradise has been widely considered to entail as an entrance requirement some kind of physical renunciation – We take for granted that paradise should entail sacrifice, if not martyrdom – otherwise, what would be the point of guilt, suffering and penance..."

Michael Kimmelman – The New York Times – Saturday, January 5, 2002

Only single key which unlocks the door to gain entrance into the Eternal Harmony.

And, again, as was exactly explained by –

"Do not store up treasures for yourselves on earth, where moths and woodworms destroy them and thieves can break in and steal. But store up treasures for yourselves in heaven, were neither moth nor woodworms destroy them and thieves cannot break in and steal. For where your treasurer is, there will your heart be also."

Matthew 6: 19-21

Jesus of Nazareth.

While it: the key to the Eternal Harmony and/or a truly humanistic being's mind, is the only single thing: anywhere, that can not not be simply touched, it: a truly humanistic being's mind, can not be simply seen, it: a truly humanistic being's mind, can not be simply acquired, it: a truly humanistic being's mind, can not be bought by any humanistic being, and it: a truly humanistic being's mind, can not be forcibly taken from another humanistic being. But, it: any one individual humanistic being's mind, can exactly be conned out of them.

And – too, as was exactly explain by –

"Many are those who trade in tricks and simulated miracles, duping the foolish multitude; and if nobody unmasked their subterfuges, they would impose them on everyone."

Leonardo da Vinci.

So – again, let's: together, unmask their subterfuges some more, let's actually pull back their: all of the worldly psychopathic con-artists, facade: of the two-dimensional plane – the simple spoken word, and all of the lies, some more, let's reveal some more universally applicable, while as from one end of the universe to the other, absolute truths, and let's do it while functioning in a manner exactly as Leonardo da Vinci did. And which was while –

"Therefore O students study mathematics and do not build without foundations – No man has a capacity for virtue who sacrifices honour for gain. Fortune is powerless to help one who does not exert himself – There is no perfect gift without great suffering. Our triumphs and our pomps pass away; gluttony and sloth and enervating luxury have banished every virtue from the world; so that as it were wandering from its course our nature is subdued by habit – Whoso curbs not lustful desires puts himself on the level with the beasts. If your excuse is that the struggle against poverty has left you no time to study and truly ennoble yourself, blame no one but yourself, because it is the study of virtue that is food for both body and soul. If your excuse is that you have children to feed, a little will suffice for them: see to it that their sustenance be the virtues, which are the true riches, for they never leave us, departing only with life itself...That man becomes happy who follows Christ..."

Following his guide, on his most arduous journey: throughout and within the Mind of God, functioning as Omnidimensional Time *made manifest*. And which was while; "Therefore O students study mathematics and do not build without foundations" – enabling his own self to begin to become capable of forming a truly humanistic foundation: within his uniquely humanistic quantum dynamically functioning mind. Which does – then, begin to enable any individual humanistic being, to begin to become neurophysiologically capable of gaining access to the key which will enable them: any individual, to gain admittance to the Eternal Harmony: The Kingdom of Heaven actually functioning as the Mind of God made manifest, and as a matter of fact. And which is while beginning at –

"...a point. A center of symmetry is the midpoint common to the lines which connect equivalent points in a crystal: it thus coincides with the center of gravity of a perfect crystal (A) Diamond (which is a) pure form of carbon naturally crystallized in the isometric system (and while) through which, starting with disordered atoms, pieces of matter are derived which are tightly organized in a periodical or homogenous manner. At the moment of formation, and in the course of growth, the mineral is attempting to achieve a state of equilibrium with its environment..."
Rocks & Minerals – Simon & Schuster – Ed. M. Prinz, G. Harlow, J. Peters

Point time zero: a single cognizable point located within simultaneously relative space/time, and/or its; "At the moment of formation, and in the course of growth, the mineral is attempting to achieve a state of equilibrium with its environment" – truly humanistic simultaneously relative three-dimensional environment. From which we can, then, begin to build our formation, of our –

"Do not store up treasures for yourselves on earth, were moths and woodworms destroy them and thieves can break in and steal. But store up treasures for yourselves in heaven, were neither moth nor woodworms destroy them and thieves cannot break in and steal. For where year treasure is, there will your heart be also.
Matthew 6: 19-21

Uniquely humanistic Omnidimensional refractive gem of a mind. And/or our own personally effectuated quantum dynamically functioning carbon based mass, of a crystalline latticework: matrix, refractive gem of mind.
Again, in simple English to eliminate any confusion. Being in that, in order for anyone to communicate anything – anything, there must be a purposefully affected single cognizable point time zero: preceding the affected communication, which has been abstracted from – and effectually formed, within simultaneously relative three-dimensional reality. And, for example: "May I have the ball?" actually functioning as a simple: two-dimensional and unidirectionally successive, abstracted understanding *of* simultaneously relative four-dimensional Reality. And too, as we can remember, which is: any sentence and in the entire history of mankind, simply the purposefully effectuated directed movement, from the first tangible form point-mass noun: located within point A – the Child – "May I," towards the second identifiable tangible point-mass noun: located at point B – "the ball." While actually functioning as through the universally applicable: and absolutely identifiable, non-tangible form mass verb function, and which is while actually functioning as the identifiable vector function, and as syntax too: and/or

94

unidirectionally successive, and universally applicable, intelligence, from one end of the universe to the other. So that, there must be a purposeful effectuated single cognizable point time zero: preceding the abstracted and projected communication, and/or formation within an individual's mind, and of any kind.

Except, truly humanistic four-dimensional Reality is a bit more complex than simply walking across a two-dimensional plane. If a human being – any human being, did not – first, actually learn the function of unidirectionally successive simultaneously relative three-dimensional Reality: actually functioning as harmoniously proportioned three-dimensional tonal variations, and which is exactly what words are in scientific reality, they would be able to communicate nothing, and/or understand nothing also. And again – remember, our four-dimensional reality is a bit more complex than simply walking: in a unidirectionally successive manner, across a two-dimensional plane. So: go outside and look at something – any single three-dimensional thing, in simultaneously relative four-dimensional Reality. Is "it" bigger than your eye? The answer is, of course and only in scientific reality, yes it is: much bigger. But yet – and simultaneously, its projected non-tangible form image, is actually capable of entering into our three-dimensional electrical potential mass minds, and wherein: our truly humanistic three-dimensional electrical potential mass minds, there are no projected images of things, but only simultaneously relative differential equations. And, too, remember the birds and the bees, and how we are capable of seeing the word bird: located at point A, within our simultaneously relative three-dimensional peripheral vision, while remaining focused upon the single simultaneously relative ten degree point of bee: located at point B. And, which is while being made manifest as through the applied simultaneously relative quantized electrodynamic radiant vector function, and/or applied quantized electromagnetism actually functioning as Time *made manifest,* while projecting the non-tangible form mass image of point A towards point B, located at an identifiable position within simultaneously relative space/time: as it is within our simultaneously relative three-dimensional electrical potential mass minds, while being reduced to a single point too: as it is projected throughout, and within, simultaneously relative space/time. And – again, remember how actually cognizing simultaneously relative Reality, is a bit more complex than simply walking across a two-dimensional plane, and how: within truly humanistic simultaneously relative four-dimensional reality and within our minds too, every single three-dimensional thing we do actually perceive: within simultaneously relative space/time as it is within our electrical potential mass minds, is simultaneously effectually occurring, within a parametered visual field: within our quantum dynamical electrical potential mass minds, as it is within simultaneously relative space/time. Which is actually effectually functioning while – simultaneously, the projected non-tangible form image, of every single three-dimensional tangible form mass: located at all identifiable points, must have its entire non-tangible form image projected, as simultaneously relative from its position within the parametered visual field: at all identifiable points and while actually functioning as truly humanistic real cognizable quantum electrodynamics, to the simultaneously relative single cognizable point time zero: point A, located within our quantum dynamically functioning electrical potential mass minds, as it is within simultaneously relative space/time: projected to any identifiable single simultaneously relative point B, also – simultaneously, located within our quantum dynamically functioning minds. Which: all simultaneously relative non-tangible form projections actually functioning as quantized electrodynamics, are being made manifest: while actually functioning and as quantized electrodynamics within a truly humanistic parametered visual field and as it is simultaneously within our minds, while moving at the actual speed of light, and/or quantized electrodynamics actually functioning as truly humanistic unidirectionally successive, and universally applicable, Time *made manifest*. And – again, which is while – and simultaneously, all of the individually completed simultaneously relative non-tangible form projections, which are made manifest: from every single simultaneously relative three-dimensional thing within simultaneously relative reality, must have its simultaneously relative non-tangible form image projected as from its identifiable position within simultaneously relative space/time, to our simultaneously relative projected to, and from, single cognizable point time zero: POINTS A AND B. As it: every single, and identifiable, simultaneously relative three-dimensional projected image, is being reduced to a single point, and which is while actually functioning as projected non-tangible form simultaneously relative tetrahedrally arranged, octahedrally formed, dihedral angles: which are effectually functioning in a simultaneously relative isosymmetric system, and/or –

"...a point. A center of symmetry is the midpoint common to the lines which connect equivalent points in a crystal: it thus coincides with the center of gravity of a perfect crystal (A) Diamond (which is a) pure form of carbon naturally crystallized in the isometric system (and while) through which, starting with disordered atoms, pieces of matter are derived which are tightly organized in a periodical or homogenous manner..."
    Rocks & Minerals – Simon & Schuster – Ed. M. Prinz, G. Harlow, J. Peters

    Individually completed non-tangible form refractive gem diamonds: in simple English. And, again, as was exactly explained by –

"Do not store up treasures for yourselves on earth, where moths and woodworms destroy them and thieves can break in and steal. But store up treasures for yourselves in heaven, where neither moth nor woodworms destroy them and thieves cannot break in and steal. For where your treasure is, there will your heart be also."
    Matthew 6: 19-21

    Jesus of Nazareth.

Because, remember how we did proceed to walk towards, and away from, the Garden. While actually moving our bodies all throughout, and within, simultaneously relative truly humanistic space/time, and while upon this point-mass of Earth: as capable of being consciously cognized within our truly humanistic simultaneously relative three-dimensional electrical potential mass minds, and parallel functioning central nervous systems. And how, the individually completed movements: of the sidewalk actually functioning as visual equivalency notes, did, always, remain the same: while we did actually move our bodies, and while making manifest unidirectionally successive Time. But how – also and simultaneously, every thing else did change: all of the simultaneously relative coordinates, and/or positioning of the simultaneously relative tangible form point-mass nouns, while actually functioning as simultaneously relative to/from, and within, a single cognizable point time zero, located within our minds: which is located within simultaneously relative truly humanistic space/time. And which is while, and simultaneously, we are capable of cognizing these simultaneously relative changes as differential equations, only and within our minds. Well, this purposely effectuated cognizance: of truly humanistic simultaneously relative Reality, is the –

"Tuning Up The Brain –
The 'Mozart effect' suggests that classical compositions can stimulate learning. But the jury is still out – What scientists do know is that keyboard instruction – making music, not just hearing it – seems to resonate within the brain. In one typical study, neuroscientists led by Gordon Shaw of the University of California, Irvine, tested 3- to 5-year-olds who received six months of piano lessons. The researchers found that the tiny pianists improve significantly in spatial-temporal reasoning – Such effects are even more pronounced in older kids.
Sharon Begley – Newsweek – Fall/Winter 2000

Visual equivalency of Practicing our scales: as a matter of fact.
While actually functioning –

"Cooperatively LTP is larger and more reliably elicited by high-frequency stimulation delivered to a group of axons generating overlapping synaptic fields than when small numbers of fibers are stimulated – successive episodes of high-frequency stimulation produce increasing amounts of synaptic facilitation – Regional Distribution Long-Term potentiation – can be elicited in the cortex, a variety of sites throughout the telencephalon (cerebral cortex), and possibly elsewhere in the central and peripheral nervous system...To summarize, physiological stimulation – causes lasting specific changes in physiology, anatomy, and chemistry of synapses, and the latter two effects are correlated with the first."
Gary Lynch – Synapses, Circuits and the Beginning of Memory

All throughout, and within, the entire central nervous system. And which is while including the peripheral nervous system: as simultaneously relative to/from, and within, a single cognizable point time zero, and: while functioning as a foundation, which is while – and simultaneously, beginning to cause permanently effectuated changes all the way down to the foundation a of humanistic being's central nervous system, and/or the base of their spine, while beginning at the base of the neck. And: while beginning to effect permanently effectuated changes within a human being's entire central nervous system, which: allowed exposure to all effectual stimuli, is – and again, while beginning to effect –

"...(a single) quantum can produce (an effect) that is anything but 'miniature'; with different estimates of quintal inductance – the reason, of course, is that the spine head, because of its very small size and narrow stem, has a very high impedance – by virtue of its morphological identity – each spine may be regarded as a functional unit, interacting with other spine units (while) the wide range of spine shapes and sizes (may) reflect ongoing dynamic changes in spine excitability (with) properties dependent on frequency of synaptic input. Different spine shapes (and effectuated) spine geometry – may thus reflect different stages of spine maturation."
        Gordon M. Shepard – Apical Dendritic Spines of Cortical Pyramidal Cells

        All individually affected neurons: while actually functioning simultaneously within, and throughout, the entire central nervous system. Which: while actually occurring all throughout and within the central nervous system, is while, and simultaneously, actually functioning as simultaneously relative to/from, and within, a single cognizable point time zero: and/or a single quantum of applied quantized radiant electromagnetism. And/or the –

        "In the late 1980's, John Larson, a postdoctoral student in (Gary) Lynch's Lab, added another piece to this picture – He found that the timing of the electrical bursts that traveled through the neurons was crucial for producing long term potentiation. The electrical signals could be very small, but if they arrived in a fixed, repeated rhythm (then) long-term potentiation resulted – Even John Larson's puzzle solving created new problems for understanding long-term potentiation and how it generates memories. Time suddenly seemed to be a crucial ingredient, and once they looked, Lynch and his colleagues began to discover time everywhere in the system."
        Jim Jubak – In the Image of the Brain

        Very beginning of Time *made manifest*: while capable of causing permanently affected neurophysiological changes, within all individually affected human beings.
        Again: in simple English, which: the purposefully effectuated simultaneously relative truly humanistic foundation, within any human being's quantum dynamically functioning simultaneously relative central nervous system, is capable of being understood while we remember how we did, with the help of our

two friends, become capable of forming the function of a single atom: of quantized electrodynamics. Which was while we: the three points of people effectually functioning as a wave, did lean in towards a single point while at a single point in time, and which was while actually functioning, as: applied three parts to form one whole. And – too, which is while this simultaneously relative applied function, is capable of functioning as dynamic symmetry: between three points while actually functioning as a wave of quantized electromagnetism, and/or an atom: and/or as a single harmoniously proportioned simultaneously relative fundamental frequency modulation, actually functioning as a note, and/or a single basic completed geometrical formation. Which: the completed simultaneously relative geometrical formation, was actually functioning as simultaneously relative to/from, and within, a single cognizable point time zero. And, too, remember how: within simultaneously relative reality and exactly as Thomas Jefferson did explain: "The movements of heavenly bodies, so exactly held in their course by the balance of centrifugal and centripetal forces," everything within simultaneously relative reality, is balanced by these: centrifugal – out *and* centripetal – in, forces. But, also how: with our two friends and ourselves leaning in towards a single point, we did have to say: now – at a single point in time, to enable our selves, and our two friends, to lean in: towards point time zero, and while simultaneously being pushed out: away from point time zero. As this does, then, create a wave of dynamic symmetry between the three points, and which is while actually functioning as a harmoniously proportioned whole: quantized fundamental frequency modulation – atom – note, and too which is while actually functioning within a hierarchically structured whole: Reality. And too how: within truly humanistic simultaneously relative Reality, all atoms are, simply, different harmoniously proportioned variations of this exact same function: while remaining subservient to a hierarchically structured whole, and while being effectually conjoined as through the universally applicable vector function, which is simply a directed projection of energy in Reality: while as from point A towards point B. And remember, too, how we are capable of perceiving things within simultaneously relative Reality. Which is as they: all simultaneously relative positions and/or completed differential equations, must be reduced to a single point, and while actually functioning as through tetrahedrally arranged, octahedrally formed, dihedral angles, and/or a projected pyramid of rays, and as simultaneously to/from, and within, a single cognizable point time zero. And – too, remember exactly how Mach did begin to explain Reality to Albert Einstein: "Space, Mach argued, is not a thing, but an expression of interrelationships among events. '*All* masses and *all* velocities, and consequently *all* forces, are relative,' he wrote. Einstein agreed," but remember exactly how Einstein did begin to become capable of understanding Reality. And which was only while actually; "Einstein – was strongly influenced by his domineering, musically inclined mother, who encouraged his passion for the violin and such classical composers as Bach – Mozart" – practicing his scales of simultaneously relative Reality.

Which means: in Reality, the function of scales: which is capable of being replicated upon a keyboard, and which is exactly an abstracted function of simultaneously relative Reality, is: exactly, equivalent to our perceiving: within our minds, each harmoniously proportioned individually completed movement, of: the sidewalk. And which is – exactly, the actual relative width: of the base of the pyramid, which comprises the completed geometrical formation, of a single harmoniously proportioned fundamental frequency modulation, and/or note, and/or atom, and which is the only "thing" which is capable of being altered, while actually functioning as a completed geometrical formation. In Reality: REPLICATED UPON A KEYBOARD, each note is – exactly and simply, a harmoniously proportioned variation of this function: the formation of a non-tangible form pyramid. While, the simultaneously relative width of the base of the pyramid, determines the function of the applied fundamental frequency modulation, and/or note, and/or atom: within simultaneously relative Reality. Wherein: simultaneously relative Reality, there is exactly only; "Space Mach argued , is not a thing, but an expression of interrelationships among events. '*All* masses *all* velocities, and consequently *all* forces are relative, he wrote. Einstein agreed, and was encouraged to write a theory that built space and time out of events alone: a space/time continuum, (wherein) Einstein had replaced Newton's space with a network of light beams; *theirs* was the absolute grid" – the universally applicable function of quantized electrodynamics, and/or harmoniously proportioned simultaneously relative velocities, and/or harmoniously proportioned simultaneously relative fundamental frequency modulations, and/or harmoniously proportioned simultaneously relative notes, and/or harmoniously proportioned simultaneously relative atoms/superstrings. Which actually are: simultaneously, expanded into harmoniously proportioned simultaneously relative differential equations, and/or the Symphony which comprises Reality: The Eternal Harmony – The Mind of God made manifest – The Kingdom of Heaven. And, remember how when we were walking: all throughout and within simultaneously relative reality, while moving our bodies in a harmonious manner, how we were capable of perceiving all of simultaneously relative Reality: within our minds and while every thing was being made manifest as a non-tangible form projection of a pyramid of rays, and how the perceivable image of all things appeared to become larger, and smaller, as we moved all throughout and within simultaneously relative Reality. And how too, the individually completed sections of sidewalk, seemed to become larger and smaller also: as we do now know which is while functioning as visual equivalency scales, while as through the effectuated formation of individually completed non-tangible form geometrical formations: and/or a pyramid of rays. And – too, remember how we do form truly humanistic universally applicable empirical self-consciousness, and/or truly humanistic memory; "One thing has become clear to scientists: memory is absolutely crucial to our consciousness – 'There's almost nothing you do, from perception to thinking, that doesn't draw continuously on your memory. (And) It can't be otherwise, since there really is no such thing as a present – memory provides a personal context, a sense of self and a sense of familiarity – past and present and a frame for the future (But) memory is not a single phenomenon – We have memory systems – All of these different types of memory are ultimately stored in the brain's cortex (what's) happening when the brain forms memory (is that) it's the connections between the cells, and particularly the strength of those connections, that are altered by experience – When everything is going right these systems work together seamlessly" – in simultaneously relative Reality. And too, remember how when we are practicing our scales of simultaneously relative Reality, and/or beginning to form truly humanistic universally applicable empirical self-consciousness, how it: the simultaneously relative formation, does – exactly, begin to occur on a; "Yet you are never aware that your mental experience has been assembled, bit by bit, like some invisible edifice inside your brain" – subconscious level. And how this: scientific fact, was also explained by –

"He also said, 'This is what the kingdom of God is like. A man throws seed on the land. Night and day, while he sleeps, when he is awake, the seed is sprouting and growing; how, he does not know. Of its own accord the land produces first the shoot, then the ear, then the full grain in the ear. And when the crop is ready, he loses no time: he starts to reap because the harvest has come."
Mark 4: 26-29

Jesus of Nazareth.
And too as it: the formed understanding of Reality actually functioning as a space/time continuum, was beginning to occur within –

"Wolfgang Amadeaus Mozart:
...in the night when I cannot sleep, thoughts crowd into my mind as easily as you could wish. Whence and how do they come? I do not know and I have nothing to do with it. Those which please me I keep in my head and hum them; at least others have told me that I do so. Once I have my theme, another melody comes, linking itself with the first one, in accordance with the needs of the composition as a whole: the counterpoint, the part of each instrument and all of the melodic fragments at last produce the complete work. Then my soul is on fire with inspiration. The work grows; I keep expanding it, conceiving it more and more clearly until I have the entire composition finished in my head though it may be long. Then my mind seizes it as a glance of my eye a beautiful picture or a handsome youth. It does not come to me successively, with various parts worked out in detail, as they will later on, but in its entirety that my imagination lets me here it."
Roger Penrose – The Emperor's New Mind

Wolfgang Amadeaus Mozart.
And, as we can remember, which was only exactly because –

"...His father, Leopold Mozart, was a violinist and composer, and author of an important violin tutor. Leopold encouraged Wolfgang, who gave clavier recitals in Munich and Vienna at the age of six...Music flowed from Mozart unceasingly..."
The New College Encyclopedia of Music – J. A. Westrup and F. Ll. Harrison

He: Wolfgang Amadeaus Mozart, was encouraged to practice his scales: of truly humanistic universally applicable Reality, and by his father.

Which did then: as Wolfgang Amadeus Mozart was actually encouraged to practice his scales by his father and on a daily basis, enable him: Wolfgang Amadeus Mozart, to become capable of functioning in a –

"Candace Pert: 'the more advanced the animal, the more the sensory input is processed, and the more type one receptors it has – I see the brain in terms of quantum mechanics – the brain is just a receiver, an amplifier, a little wet minireceiver for collective reality. We make maps, but we should never confuse the map with the territory' – If humans are less robotlike than salamanders or ducks, it's not because we have no wired-in behaviors. In fact, we have quite a few. What makes the difference is the ratio of 'unwired' to wired-in gray matter, because neurons that are not committed at birth to a set function – are available for learning, for modification – in humans a great gray area – about three-fourths of the cortex – lies between sensory input and motor output, called the association areas. These include the frontal lobes – What the frontal lobes 'control' is something like awareness, or self-awareness – the ratio of frontal core to the rest of the cortex may may be one index of evolutionary advancement. Do these lobes govern some essential feature of humanness, or even godliness, as some scientists have suggested? 'If God speaks to man, if man speaks to God,' neuroscientist Candace Pert tells us, 'it would be through the frontal lobes' – Stephen Labarge: 'And it's capable of what look like miraculous things, so miraculous that we're tempted to say it's devine, that it's not natural."
The 3-Pound Universe – Judith Hooper and Dick Teresi

Truly, and uniquely, humanistic manner: as a matter of neuroscientific fact.

As he: Wolfgang Amadeus Mozart, did begin to become capable of; "the more advanced the animal, the more the sensory input is processed" – processing complex simultaneously relative multidimensional information: and/or uniquely humanistic simultaneously relative Omnidimensional Reality, and/or simultaneously relative Omnidimensional Time *made manifest*, and – again, which is only as a matter of neuroscientific fact, and – exactly, not an opinion.

Which: an opinion and remember, can only be a belief in scientific Reality, and/or a complete and utter ignorance of scientific Reality, and – too, only within the mind of any one individual that has already begun to become affected – a victim of the con, and actually: neurophysiologically, incapable of understanding scientific Reality.

Which: truly humanistic scientific Reality, is exactly what Wolfgang Amadeus Mozart, was encouraged to learn, by his father and/or worldly authoritative god figure, and while not simply allowed to remain ignorant of it: Reality. And too only – *if* Wolfgang Amadeus Mozart was never encouraged by his father to learn Reality, capable of forming a personal opinion: within his mind, and exactly instead of being encouraged to practice his scales of truly humanistic simultaneously relative Omnidimensional Reality, as Wolfgang Amadeus Mozart was: by his father.

Which: coming to an understanding of identifiable scientific Reality, and/or actually facing-up to Reality, is – as we can remember and as was exactly explained by Jesus of Nazareth, rather –

"I tell you most solemnly,
you will be weeping and wailing
while the world will rejoice;
you will be sorrowful,
but your sorrow will turn to joy.
A woman in childbirth suffers
because her time has come;
but when she has given birth to the child she forgets the suffering
in her joy that a man has been born into the world."
John 16: 20-21

Painful: learning and/or coming to an understanding of, Reality, that is. As was exactly explained by Jesus of Nazareth: in plain English too.

Except, of course, Jesus of Nazareth did not speak English, He spoke –

"If God were your father, you would love me
since I have come from God; yes, I have come from him;
not that I came because I chose,
no, I was sent, and by him.
Do you know why you cannot take in what I say?
It is because you are unable to understand my language."
John 8: 42-43

The Universal Language: of Omnidimensional Time *made manifest*, actually functioning as the Mind of God made manifest, as simultaneously relative to/from, and within, the entire universe: simultaneously. Which does mean, that we can now know, for a verified scientific fact, that Jesus of Nazareth was a Translator, a Messenger: sent by God.

But, of course, which we can only know: for our very own selves, while we do begin to enable our very own selves to gain access to The Universal Language, of Omnidimensional Time *made manifest*, actually functioning as the Mind of God made manifest. As was exactly explained by –

"True sciences are those which have penetrated through the senses as a result of experience and thus silencing the tongues of disputants, not feeding investigators on dreams but always proceeding successively from primary truths and established principles, in a proper order towards the conclusion. This may be witnessed in the principles of mathematics, that is to say, number and measure, termed arithmetic and geometry, which deal with discontinuous and continuous quantities with the utmost truth. Here no one hazards guesses as to whether two threes makes more or less than six, or whether the angles of a triangle are less than two right angles: All the instances of perspective are expounded through the five terms of the mathematicians, namely point, line, angle, surface and body – Nothing can be found in nature that is not a part science, like continuous quantity, that is to say geometry, which, commencing with the surface of bodies is found to have its origins in lines – The point is the first principle of geometry, and no other thing can be found either in nature or in the human mind that can give rise to the point – Point is said to be that which cannot be divided into any part. Line is said to be made by moving the point along. Therefore line will be divisible in its length, but its breadth will be completely indivisible. Surface is said to be like extending the line into breadth – From the visual rays, the science of perspective has arisen, since it consists of radiant visual lines and intersected pyramids – The eye is the true intermediary between objects and the imprensiva, which immediately transmits with the highest fidelity the true surfaces and shapes of whatever is in front of it. And from these is born the proportionality called harmony, which delights the sense with sweet concord, no differently from the proportionality made by different musical notes to the sense of hearing (and as they are) born of continuous and discrete quantities (while effectuating a composition which) simultaneously conveys the proportional harmony of which the parts of the whole are composed (and which is while) composing the proportional harmonies that are produced by divine proportions (and as it) can generate a proportional harmony in the time equivalent to a single glance – The harmonic proportionality (of the whole) is composed simultaneously from various components, the sweetness of which may be judged instantaneously, both in its general and particular affects – in general according to the dictates of the composition; in particular according to the dictates of the component parts from which the totality is composed – amid the greatest things around us the existence of nothingness hold the first place, and its function extends among the things which have no existence, and its essence dwells as regards time..."

Leonardo da Vinci, and while in the year 1480 too.
Which is, also, exactly why Leonardo da Vinci did plainly explain, that –

"Let no man who is not a mathematician read the elements of my work."

All human beings must – first, learn the language: of universally applicable Omnidimensional Time *made manifest*, before they can – then, begin to be affected by it: Omnidimensional Reality.

Which: that all individual human beings can actually begin to become capable of functioning as truly humanistic beings, is while – as we can remember, beginning to become capable of understanding Reality: while actually practicing their scales of Reality, and becoming capable of causing permanently affected neurophysiological changes, within their minds. And too, which is: the permanently affected changes within individual's minds, while capable of causing –

"In 1984 (Gary) Lynch and Michael Baudry postulated that memory – is created when messenger calcium sets of permanent changes in the structure of the synapse. Lynch and Baudry theorized that certain kinds of activity patterns, such as bursts of high activity at the synapse, change the electrical voltage of the target cell enough to allow the opening of NMDA receptors. These receptors, just one among many kinds on either side of the synapses, allow the passage of calcium into the postsynaptic dendrite spine. 'That calcium goes in and does some mysterious thing,' (Richard) Granger says – changing the surface membrane of the spine so that it is then more effective."

Jim Jubak – In The Image Of The Brain

Calcium induction: within the individually affected synaptic areas, and which is an electropositive element.

This purposefully allowed exposure to Reality, and/or actually practicing our scales of Omnidimensional Reality, does then – and simultaneously, begin to enable any individual human being, such as Wolfgang Amadeus Mozart and/or Leonardo da Vinci, to become capable of gaining access to –

"Spin' Could Be Quantum Boost for Computers –

Electronic devices, like radios and computers, work by shuttling around the electric charges of electrons. Hence, the 'electron' in 'electronics' – But besides their electric charge, electrons also have a less exploited property: 'spin,' an angular momentum that makes electrons act like tiny bar magnets. Researchers are beginning to tap into electrons' magnetic side as part of an emerging field known as spintronics. Already, spintronics has yielded a couple of uses and may eventually provide the underpinning for computers that employ quantum mechanical efforts to perform calculations – Electrons can be thought of as tops that spin clockwise or counter-clockwise but always at one fixed speed, and the spinning generates an intrinsic magnetic field. Electron spins are in many ways ideal for representing 0's and 1's, the binary on-off language that computers use in their calculations – because the spins exist in both states (up and down) at once, a spin-based quantum computer using the spins would, in theory, compute all possible answers in one pass – While quantum computers are probably decades away, recent experiments have begun to fill in some pieces of the puzzle – 'All of us have in mind the holy grail of memory,' said Dr. (Randall) Isaac of IBM. We've shown that magnetic memory works. The physics of it works..."

Kenneth Chang – The New York Times – Tuesday, August 21, 2001

The Holy Grail of understanding, and the missing piece to the puzzle that is called civilization too.

So, let's actually do that: find the Holy Grail of understanding, for our very own selves, and the Lost Child too. Which: beginning our journey to find the Holy Grail of understanding: our Paradise Lost – The Entrance to the Garden, and The Eternal Harmony, we can do while actually envisioning a young child walking down the path, and while beginning to move in a relatively largo tempoed movement, and/or while moving slowly, and while actually occurring within our minds also. Now, as we are actually envisioning it within our minds, we can begin to imagine that the child has spent quite some time actually functioning as a navigator, and/or actually practicing his, or her, scales, of Reality. So that: now and as we are continuing to envision it within our minds, we can know that the young child is growing through adolescence, and is beginning to become capable of functioning in a much more complex manner, and, too, while beginning to become capable of moving at a relatively accelerated velocity, and/or while beginning to move as through adagio and allegro tempoed movement, while all throughout, and within, simultaneously relative space/time. And which we should actually continue to envision within our minds: the movement of the Lost Child becoming progressively quicker, and more frantic too.

Which: that we are beginning to become more frantic, with the passing of time, is exactly because, as Albert Einstein did plainly explain: as we are beginning to move faster and faster through space and time, our relative mass is beginning to increase, as is the gravitational pull of our daily mortal existence. So, as we continue on our journey to find our Paradise Lost: The Entrance to The Garden and The Eternal Harmony, we do know that we are going to need to employ the use of more energy, as we move faster and faster still, and too which we should be continuing to envision within our minds, and – too, just as; "With the special theory of relativity, Einstein had at last resolved the paradox that occurred to him at age sixteen, that Maxwell's equations failed if one could chase a beam of light at the velocity of light. He did so by concluding that one cannot accelerate to the velocity of light" – Albert Einstein did begin to do: within his mind alone, as he did fail. So: let's go faster still in Reality, and which is as this word: still, does mean: "remaining in place or at rest; motionless; stationary: to stand still," and as we do continue to envision it within our minds. So that, now: as we are actually moving faster and faster, all things are beginning to fly by us: as we continue to move with our bodies, while in a unidirectionally successive manner, and as we continue to move in a direction towards faster still, and too while we do know that we; "He did so by concluding that one cannot accelerate to the velocity of light" – do need to go faster still. Which is, also, as our relative mass is increasing tremendously, and we are – also and simultaneously, beginning to; "If the earth could be accelerated to the velocity of light, a feat that would require infinite energy to achieve, it would contract into a two-dimensional wafer of infinite mass, on which time will come to a stop – which is one way of saying that acceleration to light speed is impossible" – expend, just about, an infinite amount of energy, while needing to go faster still. So, we need to let "it": the "mass," go, and – then, allow our selves to become capable of; "At its root, computation is just a matter of shuffling bits, the 1's and 0's of binary arithmetic. So suppose an atom pointing up means 1 and an atom pointing down means 0. Flip around these bits by zapping the atoms with laser beams, and the result is an extremely tiny computer – What has been described so far is just the quantum version of a light switch" – hitting the switch, and go faster still. As we become capable of making the quantum leap, to the speed of light: within our minds, while remaining: with our bodies, still. Which: as we do actually travel at the speed of light, will be as we do begin to become capable of actually traveling: quantum electrodynamically Omnidimensionally, and simultaneously: as simultaneously relative to/from, and within, a single cognizable point time zero, while actually traveling at the speed of light. Which will – then and simultaneously, enable us: any individual who has spent a lifetime practicing our scales of Reality, to go –

"Wending Through Time, a Cosmic Web –

If the story of the universe were made into a summer movie, starting with the biggest, baddest explosion ever and building up to the glorious development of stars, galaxies and human life, what sort of flick would it be? – Whatever its genre, it would more than satisfy Samuel Goldwyn's famous demand for a story that 'starts with an earthquake and works its way up to a climax,' because an earthquake looks like a mosquito's hiccup next to the big bang explosion in which the universe was born – what would put the movie over the top are its stunning visuals and the subtle but unbroken thread that connects virtually every important event in the story. Those advantages are the result of a gorgeous feature of the universe that determines its density and permeates space like a vast, three-dimensional system of rivers, tributaries, creeks and rivulets: the cosmic web...Though it is little known outside the circle of cosmologists who study it, it is a central part of explanations of how the force of gravity has created all the structure in the cosmos – from swarms of galaxies to the building blocks of life – 'It's like the cartography of the universe,' said Dr. Wayne Hu, a cosmologist at the University of Chicago – 'It's pretty clear that if you could see the cosmic web in its full glory, it would be quite visually stunning,' said Dr. Craig Hogan, an astrophysicist at the University of Washington – And it is the thematic tapestry that links a whole series of recent astronomical discoveries involving various epochs of cosmic history – 'It's the largest scale on which structures exist today,' said Dr. Adrian Melott, an astrophysicist at the University of Kansas, adding that the pattern was simply 'a reflection of the laws of gravity."
James Glanz – The New York Times – Tuesday August 14, 2001

Sailing, and/or traveling, all throughout, and within, simultaneously relative

Reality, and/or The Entire Universe: The Eternal Harmony – The Mind of God and The Kingdom of Heaven too. And while – also and of course, actually effectually traveling at the speed of light: actually functioning as Omnidimensional Time *made manifest*, and/or universally applicable quantized radiant electrodynamics, while –

"A great advance in neuroscience took place in an Italian kitchen in 1872. Camillio Golgi, a young medical graduate at Pavia University, was so fascinated by the brain that he set up a makeshift laboratory. The problem plaguing Golgi concerned the very essence of the physical brain: the matter of which it was composed. At that time, although the brain could be sliced into small slivers and placed under the microscope, only a homogenous pale mass could be detected. Until its basic building blocks could be identified, it would prove impossible to discover how the brain worked. Then one day, so the story goes, Golgi knocked a block of brain into a dish containing a solution of silver nitrate, where it remained lost for several weeks. It turned out that Golgi had discovered a critical reaction. When he retrieved the brain block, a transformation had taken place. Under the microscope there appeared to be a complex pattern of dark blobs suspended within netlike tangles..."
The Human Brain – Susan A. Greenfield

Actually effectually functioning as simultaneously relative to/from, and within, a single cognizable point time zero: located within truly humanistic simultaneously relative Omnidimensional space/time, and while actually effectually functioning as quantized radiant electrodynamics, as it: the applied quantized radiant electrodynamic function, is: ACTUALLY EFFECTUALLY FUNCTIONING, as simultaneously relative to/from, and within, a single cognizable point time zero. Located within a –

"Candace Pert – I see the brain in terms of quantum mechanics – the brain is just a receiver, an amplifier, a little wet minireceiver for collective reality. We make maps, but we should never confuse the map with the territory' (while) the ratio of frontal core – to the rest of the cortex, may be one index of evolutionary advancement – what the frontal lobes 'control' is something like awareness, or self-awareness – Do these lobes govern some essential feature of humanness or even godliness, as some scientists have suggested? 'If God speaks to man, if man speaks to God,' neuroscientist Candace Pert tells us, it would be through the frontal lobes – Stephen LaBarge: 'And it's capable of what look like miraculous things, so miraculous that we're tempted to say it's divine, that it's not natural...'"
The 3-Pound Universe – Judith Hooper and Dick Teresi

Truly humanistic being's own personally effectuated, quantum electrodynamically functioning, and simultaneously relative, Omnidimensional refractive gem of a mind, and parallel functioning central nervous system. And as was –

"Asked by the Pharisees when the kingdom of God was to come, he gave them this answer, 'The coming of the kingdom of God does not admit of observation and there will be no one to say, 'Look here! Look there! For, you must know, the kingdom of God is within you."
Luke 17: 20-21

Exactly explained by the Son of God
And – again, in simple English, or – rather, to actually simplify this understanding, which is Omnidimensional simultaneously relative space/time actually functioning as Reality, but which is – also, exactly not a simple metaphorical analogy, we can simply remember Wolfgang Amadeaus Mozart, and how he did simply explain that he did –

"...in the night when I cannot sleep, thoughts crowd into my mind as easily as you could wish – Once I have my theme, another melody comes, linking itself with the first one, in accordance with the needs of the composition as a whole: the counterpoint, the part of each instrument and the melodic fragments at last produce a complete work. Then my soul is on fire with inspiration. The work grows; I keep expanding it, conceiving it more and more clearly until I have the entire composition finished in my head though it may be long. Then my mind seizes it as a glance of my eye a beautiful picture or a handsome youth. It does not come to me successively, with various parts worked out in detail, as they will later on, but in its entirety that my imagination lets me hear it."
Wolfgang Amadeus Mozart – Roger Penrose – The Emperor's New Mind

Actually see: within his mind, the whole of the simultaneously relative non-tangible form synthetical structure: which actually is the "orchestration." Of harmoniously proportioned, and individually completed, simultaneously relative differentials/notes, expanded into harmoniously proportioned, and individually completed, differential equations/melodic movements, while "functioning as," and "remaining subservient to," a hierarchically structured whole: orchestration. And which he: Wolfgang Amadeus Mozart, could actually see, within his mind, while actually functioning as quantized radiant electrodynamics, and/or Time *made manifest*, and as simultaneously relative to/from, and within, a single cognizable point time zero: the single point located within space/time, for the beginning of the orchestration. And/or the harmonizing of individually completed, and harmoniously proportioned, differentials/notes, expanded into harmoniously proportioned, simultaneously relative and individually completed, differential equations, and while effectually functioning as, and remaining subservient to, A single hierarchically structured whole: ORCHESTRATION. AND AS WAS EXACTLY EXPLAINED BY –

"Do you not know that our soul is composed of harmony, and that harmony cannot be generated other than when the proportions of the (non-tangible) form are seen and heard instantaneously...The eye is the true intermediary between the objects and the imprensiva, which immediately transmits with the highest fidelity the true surfaces and shapes of whatever is in front of it. And from these is born the proportionality called harmony, which delights the sense with sweet concord, no differently from the proportionality made by different musical notes to the sense of hearing (and as they are) born of continuous and discrete quantities (while effecting a composition which) simultaneously conveys the proportional harmony of which the parts of the whole are composed (and which is while) composing the proportional harmonies that are produced by divine proportions – The harmonic proportionality (of the whole) is composed simultaneously from various components, the sweetness of which may be judged instantaneously, both in its general and particular affects – in general according to the dictates of the composition; in particular according to the dictates of the component parts from which the totality is composed (and as it) can generate a proportional harmony in the time equivalent to a single glance...amid the greatest things among us the existence of nothingness holds the first place, and its function extends among the things which have no existence, and its essence dwells as regards time ..."

Leonardo da Vinci.
While occurring within his mind too: while actually functioning as universally applicable Omnidimensional Time *made manifest*. And as "visual" harmoniously proportioned simultaneously relative, and individually completed, differentials/notes, expanded into harmoniously proportioned simultaneously relative, and individually completed, differential equations/melodic movements, and as simultaneously relative to/from and within a single cognizable point time zero: the beginning of the orchestration, and of simultaneously relative non-tangible form, and projected, geometrical equations. And/or, the only truly humanistic –

"The equivalent of the machine language of the brain, in (Alan) Gevin's view, is very complex electromagnetic field configurations, with very fine modulation in amplitude, frequency, wave shape and spatial distribution...(And) After several years of painstaking mapping of the psychic never-never lands, discovered an extraordinary thing: The mind of man contains only so many visions – four basic, recurrent geometrical forms..."
The 3-Pound Universe – Judith Hooper and Dick Teresi

Universally applicable language, of Reality.
And – again, while simplifying the understanding, in addition to being exactly not a metaphorical analogy, and while remembering Wolfgang Amadeus Mozarts' ability to "see" the entire non-tangible form synthetical structuring, we can exactly understand, our –

"On hearing this, one of those gathered around the table said to him, 'Happy the man who will be at the feast in the kingdom of God!' But he said to him, 'There was a man who gave a great banquet, and he invited a large number of people. When the time for the banquet came, he sent his servant to say to those who had been invited, 'Come along: everything is ready now.' But all alike started to make excuses. The first said, 'I have bought a piece of land and must go and see it. Please accept my apologies.' Another said, 'I have bought five yoke of oxen and am on my way to try them out. Please accept my apologies.' Yet another said, 'I have just got married and so am unable to come.'

The servant returned and reported this to the master. Then the householder, in a rage, said to his servant, 'Go out quickly into the streets and alleys of the town and bring in here the poor, the crippled, the blind and the lame.' 'Sir,' said the servant, 'your orders have been carried out and there is still room.' Then the master said to his servant, 'Go to the open roads and the hedgerows and force people to come in to make sure my house is full; because, I tell you, not one of those who were invited shall have a taste of my banquet."
Luke 14: 15-24

Simple humanistic, and/or animalistic, ability, to see the whole of a tangible form mass structured House. Which all human beings are actually capable of simply, and neurophysiologically, "seeing": within their minds as a whole, and while there are no images of things within our minds.

And – again, while simplifying the understanding and while being exactly NOT a metaphorical analogy too, we can reiterate our recently acknowledged neuroscientific understanding of fact, that –

"Scientist: Musicians' brains wired differently –
Neuroscientests, using brain-scanning MRI machines to peer inside the minds of professional German violinists, found they could hear the music simply by thinking about it, a skill amateurs in the study were unable to match – The research offers insight into the inner workings of the brain and shows that musicians' brains are uniquely wired for sound, researchers said at the annual meeting of the Society for Neuroscience – Neuroscientests often study how we hear and play music because it is one of a few activities that use many functions of the brain, including memory, learning, motor control, emotion and creativity, said Dr. Robert Zatorre of the Montreal Neurological Institute – 'It offers a window onto the highest levels of human cognition,' Zatorre said..."
AP – Bucks County Courier Times – Thursday November 15, 2001

When a human being does practice their scales of simultaneously relative Reality, while as on a daily basis, they do begin to become capable of causing permanently effectuated neurophysiological changes, within their individually affected quantum electrodynamical minds, and parallel functioning central nervous

111

systems. Which: the individually affected minds and parallel functioning central nervous systems, can actually become capable of "hearing" the "sounds" of the harmoniously proportioned differentials/notes/equations/movements, by "seeing" the two-dimensional plane abstracted and projected representation, of the actual simultaneously relative Omnidimensional function: of Reality – within their minds, and within which: A humanistic being's mind, there are NO "images of things." And – while being exactly NOT a metaphorical analogy, we can also remember the Movie *Amadaeus* Mozart too. And how, in the movie, Antonio Salieri did explain, that –

"...On the page, it looked: nothing, the beginning simple, almost comic. Just a pulse, bassoons – basset horns, like a rusty squeeze-box. And then: suddenly, high above it, an oboe: A single note – hanging there, unwavering, *until* a clarinet takes it over, and sweetens it into a phrase of such delight...He had simply written down music already finished in his head: As if he was taking dictation. And music finished as no music is ever finished. Misplace one note, and the (entire) structure would fall. Here again, was the very voice of God. I was staring through the cage of those meticulous strokes at an absolute beauty...This was a music I had never heard (before), filled with such longing, such unfulfillable longing..."

He was capable of beginning to "see," the entire simultaneously relative non-tangible form synthetical structuring, of the "House": within his mind, and as simultaneously relative to/from, and within, a single cognizable point time zero, located within truly humanistic simultaneously relative space/time. And of the "structure": "of" individually completed, and simultaneously relative, harmoniously proportioned differential equations, effectually functioning as, and remaining subservient to, A "hierarchically structured whole" – orchestration, **THE**: "Here again, was the very voice of God," actual Mind of God, and/or The Eternal Harmony too.

And – again, while being exactly NOT a metaphorical analogy, we can go back outside: into Reality out of our tangible form mass Houses and onto the beginning of the path leading up to The Garden, and while bringing our portable CD-player too, and Wolfgang Amadeus Mozart's *Serenade for Winds, K. 361; 3rd movement*, and exactly as Antonio Salieri did see it, and begin to exactly understand the Absolute Truth of Reality.

Now, while actually standing upon the Path: Leading up towards the Garden, and/or sidewalk, we can plainly see that the actual width of the individually completed movement: of the section of sidewalk, which we are actually standing upon, while at point time zero, is actually a little wider than the exact nest individually completed movement: of "A" section of the sidewalk. And, we can remember, that each completed section of the sidewalk, and/or individually completed movement, must have its entire image projected into our minds, while being reduced to a single point, and while actually functioning as a simultaneously

112

relative non-tangible form projection of a pyramid of rays: actually functioning as quantized electrodynamics, and as the cognizable function of a simultaneously relative note, and/or harmoniously proportioned fundamental frequency modulation. And which is while: only, as simultaneously relative to our actual truly humanistic identifiable point within truly humanistic space/time, while upon this point-mass of Earth. And – too and as we can remember, which: that we are actually standing upon the simultaneously relative point-mass of Earth and while at point time zero, "is": beginning to actually effectually occur, while our actual simultaneously relative, and truly humanistic, point time zero: on The Earth at point time zero and as we do actually begin our simultaneously relative movement, is a simultaneously relative dark: in tone, and a heavy: in mass, and a low: fundamental frequency modulation, too, and Wolfgang Amadeus Mozart's; "On the page, it looked: nothing, the beginning simple, almost comic. Just a pulse, bassoons, basset horns, like a rusty squeeze-box" – beginning of the pulse too: as we do begin our purposefully effectuated directed movement, within simultaneously relative space/time. While as from point A, and in a purposefully effectuated direction towards point B: The Garden, and which we are, exactly and within our minds alone, actually beginning to do: move while in a purposefully effectuated direction, from point A towards point B and The Garden too, while actually moving while as through space, and over Time, and while making manifest A largo tempoed movement, and Time too. And which we are only capable of doing, while actually beginning to move: within our minds alone of course, while we do – exactly and neurophysiologically, become capable of cognizing: and/or seeing, the individually completed harmoniously proportioned movements of the sidewalk, and/or notes, and within our minds: as we actually begin to move through space while actually making manifest Time. And, too, while continuing to move while as in a largo tempoed movement, and while as from point A towards point B: "...like a rusty squeeze-box." And then; "...suddenly, high above it, an oboe: A single note" – the simultaneously relative function of a relatively small individually completed, and harmoniously proportioned, movement, and/or note: high above the relatively largo tempoed movement, and which is The Apple, and actually; " – hanging there, unwavering" – hanging there: "in" identifiable simultaneously relative space/time, above the relatively largo tempoed movement, and relatively dark: in tone, and heavy: in mass, simultaneously relative point-mass of Earth, and point time zero: A, too. And which is actually: "hanging there," until a; "...*until* a clarinet takes it over" – clarinet: and/or relatively bigger individually completed, and simultaneously relative, harmoniously proportioned movement, and/or note, does actually take it over: and actually bring it back down towards the simultaneously relative point-mass of Earth, and while in a; "...and sweetens it into a phrase of such delight" – direction back towards point time zero: point A, while upon the Path which leads to The Garden. And too where we can retire at night for restful sleep, while actually being secured within the artificially effectuated restful mother's womb of our Houses. EXCEPT, remember –

"Color often signifies the difference between being seen, and consequently finding a partner, and being ignored – a male frigate-bird in the Galapagos Islands inflates the red pouch beneath its bill to attract a female."
Colors for Survival – Marco Ferrari

Even a bird's brain can do that.
And, THAT IS EXACTLY **NOT**, what –

"...The work grows; I keep expanding it, conceiving it more and more clearly until I have the entire composition finished in my head though it may be long. Then my mind seizes it as a glance of my eye a beautiful picture or a handsome youth. It does not come to me successively, with various parts worked out in detail, as they will later on, but in its entirety that my imagination lets me hear it."

Wolfgang Amadeus Mozart did actually do: within his mind alone.
And/or –

"Do you not know that our soul is composed of harmony, and that harmony cannot be generated other than when the proportions of the (non-tangible) form are seen and heard instantaneously – The harmonic proportionality (of the whole) is composed simultaneously from various components, the sweetness of which may be judged instantaneously, both in its general and particular affects – in general according to the dictates of the composition; in particular according to the dictates of the component parts from which the totality is composed (and as it) can generate a proportional harmony in the time equivalent to a single glance."

Leonardo da Vinci did do too: within his mind alone, too.
And too we can remember, how, in the movie: *Amadeus*, Antonio Salieri had only –

"...Here again was the very voice of God. I was staring through the cage of those meticulous strokes at an absolute beauty...This was a music I had never heard (before), filled with such longing, such unfulfillable longing..."

Begun to become capable of actually doing: seeing the entire simultaneously relative non-tangible form synthetical structuring. While remaining a –

"Each of us lives within the universe – the prison – of his own brain. Projecting from it are millions of fragile sensory nerve fibers, in groups, uniquely adapted to sample the energetic states of the world around us: heat, light, force, and chemical compositions. That is all we ever know directly; all else is logical inference..."
The 3-Pound Universe – Judith Hooper and Dick Teresi

114

Prisoner of his mind: and; "I was staring through the cage of those meticulous strokes, at an absolute beauty" – trapped behind the two-dimensional plane.

And – too, we can remember, that –

"Back to Basics: how did space get its dimensions?

In the beginning – The universe, poised at the moment of creation, was ruled – by just a single superforce. Instead of a smattering of different particles, there was only the tiny primordial mass – the grandmother of all particles – ready to explode in the Big Bang – Then came the detonation – This scientific creation story, embraced by physicists and cosmologists alike, seems to account for just about everything – with one glaring exception: Where did the dimensions come from? – Now some physicists are adding a touch to the Edenic tale – Though the idea is still in a very preliminary form, physicists are intrigued by the implication that reality may have started with just a single dimension: time. As temperatures dropped in the moments after the primordial explosion, the spatial dimensions – height, length and breadth – crystallized into existence. Creation was not just a matter of let 'there be light,' but 'let there be space' as well – A dimension arises when a force is generated that allows movement into a new domain – Dr. Arkani-Hamed said that, what particularly attracted him was the notion that space might have emerged from a universe that started with just time..."

George Johnson – The New York Times – Tuesday June 26, 2001

At Point time zero, there was no space, and no tangible form point-mass nouns either: THERE WAS ONLY "TIME."

Which we can simply reiterate our understanding of, now and forever too, while we remember, how we did hit the switch in the dark room: to turn on the light while at point time zero. And how: while actually functioning as the universally applicable constant of quantized radiant electrodynamics and/or Time, we did become capable of observing that the light beams projected out in all directions, and simultaneously: as simultaneously relative to/from and within point time zero. "To" being: as from the point in time when we hit the switch, and as relative to each volume of space opposite of the point of the light bulb, and as simultaneously relative to each other too. "From" being: as relative out from the position of the bulb, and while effectually functioning as: and being the simultaneously relative positioning of, point time zero. "Within" being: as relative to the effectuated, and/or formed, parametered volume of space: actually formed within the walls, and/or the room. Which: In simultaneously relative Reality, are the Planetary Orbits, and/or the manifolds: of simultaneously relative space/time, and which: in Reality, did not exist yet: at point time zero – until the simultaneously relative applied function of Omnidimensional Reality was actually "applied," to "form" all of simultaneously relative: non-tangible, and synthetically structured, Reality.

This function we can simply reiterate our understanding of, and now and forever too, by taking two narrow beamed flashlights and going out into the darkness, and then turning them: both of them, on at a single point time zero, and which is while the beams: of quantized radiant electrodynamics and/or light, can be identified as Time. Now, after the beams are turned on, simply point them: the beams, in a direction parallel to each other: while actually functioning in a unidirectionally successive manner, out into space. Which would form absolutely nothing, in reality, and – so, there would have been no Reality. Now, you: actually functioning as a being who is causing an effect at a single point in time, do this on purpose: take both of the beams of quantized electrodynamics and/or light and/or Time, and: at point time zero, cross them over: to actually intersect with one another, and to cause an effect. Which does – then, enable us to plainly see: with our eyes alone, the simple fact, that at the single simultaneously relative point where the two beams intersect, there is – now, a greater amount of energy: built-up, at that single simultaneously relative point: of Time. This actual purposefully effectuated simultaneously relative function: of Time, is what does – then, form the actual simultaneously relative tangible form mass point-mass nouns: and/or the planets. And – then and simultaneously, form gravity: and/or simultaneously relative space, between the Planets, and which is the simultaneously relative synthetical structuring of space/time, and/or The Mind of God made manifest. And of which: these purposefully effectuated simultaneously relative functions, and/or purposefully effectuated; "A dimension arises when a force is generated that allows movement into a new domain" – dimensions, there are an infinite amount: not simply four. Which is exactly why, it: Reality, is an Omnidimensional space/time continuum, and too exactly why, it: Reality, could have – only, been a "caused affect," as we did just simply prove, for our very own selves.

And – again, which we can simply understand: that all of simultaneously relative Reality is actually an Omnidimensional space/time continuum, by explaining exactly what "it" was that both Wolfgang Amadeus Mozart, and Leonardo da Vinci, did become capable of actually "seeing": within their quantum electrodynamically functioning minds, and parallel functioning central nervous systems, alone. While actually seeing the entire simultaneously relative non-tangible form synthetical structuring, of the –

"The servant returned and reported this to his master. Then the householder, in a rage, said to his servant, 'Go out quickly into the streets and alleys of the town and bring in here the poor, the crippled, the blind and the lame.' 'Sir,' said the servant, 'your orders have been carried out and there is still room.' Then the master said to his servant, 'Go to the open roads and hedgerows and force people to come in to make sure my house is full; because, I tell you, not one of those who were invited shall have a taste of my banquet."
Luke 14: 21-24

HOUSE: The Mind of God made manifest – The Kingdom of Heaven – The

116

Garden – Our Paradise Lost and The Eternal Harmony too.

Which we can do: reiterate our understanding of the simultaneously relative quantized radiant electrodynamic function, which does; "With the special theory of relativity – Einstein had replaced Newton's space with a network of light beams; *theirs* was the absolute grid, within which space itself became – the special theory of relativity has been viewed in terms of a 'space/time continuum' ever since (In which) The force of gravitation disappears, and is replaced by the geometry of space itself" – actually form all of simultaneously relative Reality, while we remember the birds and the bees. And our real elementary quantum dynamic functioning capabilities: only beginning to become effectuated within a child's electrical potential mass of a mind, and parallel functioning central nervous system. And how we are actually capable of seeing the word BIRD within our peripheral vision: within our quantum dynamically functioning minds, within which there are no images of things, while remaining focused upon the single ten degree point of BEE, and which we can now do again to reaffirm our understanding of, for our own selves too. While we did come to understand, that this real simultaneously relative applied quantum dynamic function, is – exactly, capable of occurring, because: as we remain focused upon the single ten degree point of bee, the non-tangible form projected image of the word bird, must be: simultaneously, projected to that single identifiable point of bee located within simultaneously relative space/time. And too, how this ability: to cognize this simultaneously relative differential, is our ability to consciously cognize an individually completed visual effectual note: while functioning as a pyramid of rays made manifest between two simultaneously relative points, and while being reduced to a single point: within our minds. And how: now we can begin to understand, as we did begin to move: within our minds alone, while upon our journey to find the entrance to The Garden, and while beginning to experience Wolfgang Amadeus Mozart's communicated understanding too: and/or his orchestration of a space/time continuum, we did actually begin at a simultaneously relative point time zero: BOTH POINTS A AND B, and while remaining focused upon a; "None of this information could be put to use unless it was firmly located against a fixed horizon; it would float about weightlessly in a vacuum" – single simultaneously relative, and truly humanistic, point time zero: of a single point positioned within truly humanistic simultaneously relative space/time. And we can remember, how we did enable ourselves to actually purposefully form a single point of quantized radiant electrodynamics for our own selves, by purposefully crossing the beams of light: made manifest from the flashlights, and how – now, we can understand, that while we do actually purposefully maintain both points A: our simultaneously relative position upon the path, and point B: the point of the beginning of the orchestration, we can become capable of applying the simultaneously relative vector function, and which is – simply, a purposefully directed projection, while as from point A towards B. And then, how this: actual purposefully affected simultaneously relative applied function, does – then and simultaneously, form a point within the orchestration of the space/time continuum.

And how: within Wolfgang Amadeus Mozart's orchestration, he did, simply, explain that he does; "Once I have my theme" – actually begin at this simultaneously relative point time zero, and which is his identified central keynote theme: located, and functioning, within truly humanistic space/time. And remember how we did begin to demonstrate, for ourselves, the simultaneously relative positioning of the humanistic being while at the entrance to The Garden, and how we did actually draw a line: upon the two-dimensional plane of glass, while as from her positioning within simultaneously relative space/time: being projected out towards our identified parametered visual field and horizontally too, and how – now, we can understand, that this simultaneously relative applied function, does – then and simultaneously, begin to enable us to effectually form another simultaneously relative point within space/time: where these two simultaneously relative applied vector functions do intersect. And too remember how we did draw another line: upon the two-dimensional plane of glass and vertically, while as from the identified positioning of the trees: within the Garden, and while out to the top and bottom parameters, and how – now and simultaneously too, we are beginning to become capable of forming many more simultaneously relative points made manifest, and while as from the projected vector functions within simultaneously relative space/time, and – too, which are only capable of being effectually formed while we do actually maintain the simultaneously relative positioning of the individually completed movements, within our minds, and/or; "Newton – develop(ed) a dynamics written in terms of algebra's alternative, geometry – Infinitesimal calculus set geometry in motion – As Newton put it, 'Lines are described, and thereby generated not by the opposition of parts, but by the continued motion of points – Einstein reasoned that – gravitation itself might be regarded as a kind of acceleration – the special theory of relativity has been viewed in terms of a space/time continuum ever since – (In which) The force of gravity disappears, and is replaced by the geometry of space itself" – simultaneously relative, and individually completed, harmoniously proportioned velocities: and/or simultaneously relative, and individually completed, differentials, expanded into simultaneously relative, and individually completed, differential equations.

Because, we can remember: in a real orchestration, there are no actual tangible form point-mass nouns. So the identifiable major points: to begin to form structure within Wolfgang Amadeus Mozart's orchestration, and Leonardo da Vinci's too, are – actually, the point where a velocity changes direction, and does – then and simultaneously, continue to purposefully intersect: while being effectuated as a purposefully directed movement, with the truly humanistic central keynote theme, and/or parametered visual field of simultaneously relative space/time, and while all of the points, too, must be maintained within our minds. But: too remember – how we did cross over the beams of the flashlights to form a point, and in the Reality, of a space/time continuum, there are no points yet formed, and which are while actually functioning as simultaneously relative to/from, and within, the single simultaneously relative, and purposefully effectuated, point time zero, and which can – then and simultaneously, begin – and simultaneously, to actually effectually function as an integral part of The Orchestration. And which is while functioning as a purposefully effectuated Omnidimensional space/time continuum, and/or as; "From One Quantum State to Another – What confounds common sense is that it is not a matter of the fields always being aligned in a certain direction and simply not knowing what that direction is until the measurement is made. Rather, the theory of quantum mechanics states that all possibilities exist simultaneously, and the act of looking causes the possibilities to collapse into a single reality. 'That's what makes the quantum world weird" – real quantum mechanics.

To simplify this understanding again, and while being not a simple metaphorical analogy again too, we can remember how we did actually walk down the path, while as in a purposefully effectuated direction towards The Garden, and while as from point A towards point B. And how – then and after we did move through space and over Time, The Garden did appear to become much larger: within our minds, and too and after we did turn around, we were capable of seeing: within our minds, that the entire tangible form mass House: where we did begin our journey from, had become much smaller, and within our minds alone too. And – too we were capable of seeing and within our minds alone, the whole of the House and while; "Then my mind seizes it as a glance of my eye – It does not come to me successively, with various parts worked out in detail, as they will later on, but in its entirety – The harmonic proportionality (of the whole) is composed simultaneously from various components, the sweetness of which may be judged instantaneously, both in its general and particular affects – in general according to the dictates of the composition; in particular according to the dictates of the component parts from which the totality is composed (and as it) can generate a proportional harmony in the time equivalent to a single glance" – in a single glance: as simultaneously relative to/from, and within, a single cognizable point time zero. And – again, remember how when we did move down the path: after we did turn around and then within our minds alone, we did become capable of practicing our scales of simultaneously relative Reality, and – too, which is as the definition of scales is: "a succession or a progression of steps or degrees; a gradated series," but only while effectually functioning within truly humanistic simultaneously relative space/time: as simultaneously relative to, and from, point time zero, and within our minds. And how then too, we are capable of identifying each simultaneously relative individually completed movement of the sidewalk: and/or note, and/or individually completed differential/velocity, as a simultaneously relative point within truly humanistic space/time: as to and from point time zero. And remember how Isaac Newton did define how line is formed, and that is only exactly while; "Infinitesimal calculus set geometry in motion – As Newton put it, 'Lines are described, and thereby generated not by the opposition of parts, but by the continued motion of points" – purposefully conjoining the simultaneously relative points within space/time, and, remember too, how this exact same function was exactly explained by Leonardo da Vinci: "The point is the first principal of geometry, and no other thing can be found either in nature or in the human mind that can give rise to the point – Point is said to be that which cannot be divided into any part. Line is said to be made by moving the point along." Which does exactly enable us to simply understand, that as we do begin to move: within our minds alone, through space while making manifest Time, and while as simultaneously relative to and from point time zero, we can begin to form a projected line: as from point A towards point B and within our minds alone, while functioning as the projected vector function. And – too as we can remember, which is while actually beginning with a simultaneously relative largo tempoed movement, as we begin to move through space over time, and while making manifest Time. Which does then, as we begin to move through space over time and while as through the function of scales and/or steps, enable us to understand what exactly it is that we are doing, and while making manifest space/time. And that is, simply, beginning to move up to another height: as we do also and simultaneously move farther away, as simultaneously relative to and from point time zero: while upon this point-mass of Earth, and while beginning to build – and/or form, a non-tangible form wall. Which does also – then and simultaneously, enable us to understand: within our minds and while actually feeling the effect, that we are – also and simultaneously, being effectually pulled in a direction back down towards the ground: as we do move up through space, and as we begin to make manifest Time: within our minds alone.

Which does – then and simultaneously, enable us to understand: within our minds and parallel functioning central nervous systems while actually feeling the effect, that after we do affect a completed first movement: and/or completed gradated series actually functioning as steps, we will have risen to the point of a completed simultaneously relative major velocity: and/or completed melodic movement, and which can – then and simultaneously, actually effectually function as a major point of rest, and as a plateau: upon which we can build, and/or begin a second movement, but only while we do maintain the completed first movement within our minds. And which we can simply understand, while we remember The House. So that, we can understand and within our minds alone, we can actually see the completed first movement: affected through the function of individually completed differentials, and/or steps, and/or scales, progressing through a gradated series, actually rising to the point of what would actually be a common denominator point: of a 1st floor ceiling/2nd floor floor, but – too, which is only actually capable of being supported: within a space/time continuum, by a simultaneously relative projected function. Which we can simply understand, for ourselves, while we remember how we did form the function of an atom, with our own selves and our two friends leaning in while at a single point in time. And how – then as we did balance the centrifugal and centripetal forces, we did – then, become capable of placing a beam upon the formed center point: of individually completed Time *made manifest*. But how – in reality, the beam, and/or major point of rest actually functioning as a 1st floor ceiling/2nd floor floor, would have to be supported by some "thing." Which can only be, as we can remember, a; "A dimension arises when a force is generated that allows movement into a new domain" – purposefully effectuated: and/or directed, simultaneously relative vector function, and while actually functioning as a quantity possessing both magnitude and direction: through space/time. And which does – also and simultaneously, purposefully intersect with our established vertical parameters: of and within our simultaneously relative coordinate point system of space/time, and which can – then and simultaneously, actually function as a common denominator point of a 1st floor ceiling/2nd floor floor, and as a major point of rest, and which can – then, be built upon. But, only while we do actually maintain the first individually completed movement within our minds: as simultaneously relative to/from and within point time zero – and while actually functioning as an individually completed, and harmoniously proportioned, simultaneously relative differential equation, and as Time *made manifest*. Which, as we can also remember, we can actually only do: form the entire first simultaneously relative and completed harmoniously proportioned differential equation and/or first movement, while we actually do – also and simultaneously, maintain all of the individually completed harmoniously proportioned velocities – and/or differentials – and/or notes – and/or points – and/or Time *made manifest*, within our minds also, and as simultaneously relative to/from, and within, point time zero also. Which: the simultaneously relative points within a space/time continuum, **DO NOT YET EXIST: WITHIN A SPACE/TIME CONTINUUM**, until we do apply the function of simultaneously relative Reality: which is actually effectually functioning as simultaneously relative quantum electrodynamics, and as simultaneously relative Omnidimensional Time *made manifest*, **AND AS THE** –

"There are two essential yet complementary aspects of this new vision of time which are as striking in contrast as heaven and hell. Heaven is ruled by dynamical equations that are reversible and 'timeless'; their simplicity ensures stability for eternity. Hell is more akin to the real world, where fluctuations, uncertainty and chaos reign..."
The Arrow of Time – Peter Coveney and Roger Highfield

Eternal Harmony: The Mind of God made manifest – The Kingdom of Heaven and Our innocence lost too. And The Entrance to –

"One way to think about this view is to imagine spatial relationships as a kind of universal language that the brain uses no matter what specific language – social, moral, engineering – we are using at the moment – (George) Lakoff believes he can tie this mental language to the physical structure of the brain and its maps – 'When you think about dynamic structure, you begin to think there are a lot of things that are analogous with life. Life is more pattern(s) in space/time than it is a set of particular physical things."
Jim Jubak – In the Image of the Brain

The Garden that is. And as was exactly explained by –

"Enter by the narrow gate, since the road that leads to perdition is wide and spacious, and many take it; but it is a narrow gate and a hard road that leads to life, and only a few find it."
Matthew 7: 13-14

The Son of God: again. And –

"Asked by the Pharisees when the kingdom of God was to come, he gave them this answer, 'The kingdom of God does not admit of observation and there will be no one to say, look here! Look there! For, you must know, the kingdom of God is within you."
Luke 17: 20-21

Again.
And as was exactly –

"Candace Pert – I see the brain in terms of quantum mechanics – the brain is just a receiver, an amplifier, a little wet minireceiver for collective reality'...the ratio of frontal core to the rest of the cortex may be one index of evolutionary advancement – What the frontal lobes 'control' is something like awareness, or self-awareness – Do these lobes govern some essential feature of humanness, or even godliness, as some scientists have suggested? 'If God speaks to man, if man speaks to God,' neuroscientist Candace Pert tells us, it would through the frontal lobes..."
The 3-Pound Universe – Judith Hooper and Dick Teresi

Verified by 20th century neuroscientific research: again. And –

"The equivalent of the machine language of the brain, in (Alan) Gevin's view, is very complex electromagnetic field configurations, with very fine modulation in amplitude, frequency, wave shape and spatial distribution...(And) After several years of painstaking mapping of these psychic never-never lands, discovered an extraordinary thing: The mind of man contains only so many visions – four basic, recurrent geometrical forms..."
The 3-Pound Universe – Judith Hooper and Dick Teresi

Again.
Which enables us to understand: now and for a scientific fact, that it: The Mind of God made manifest – The Kingdom of Heaven and Our Paradise Lost too: actually functioning as The Eternal Harmony, is – exactly, not a belief: it is a formed understanding of Reality. And which: the formed ability to come to an understanding of all of simultaneously relative *a priori* Reality, and which is while actually functioning as Omnidimensional Time *made manifest*, does –

122

"Johannes Keplar: then he becomes aware that he walks in the light of truth; he is seized by an unbelievable rapture and, exulting, he here surveys most minutely, as though from a high watch-tower, the whole world and all the differences of its parts."

Cause an effect: which is beyond belief.
And – too and simultaneously, this purposefully caused effect does –

"If one day we awoke and truly saw the world this way (effectually functioning as a continuum), the ramifications would shake our psyche to its foundations. Assuming we remained sane, the relationship of I to thou, of individual to planet, of my action to yours, would be revolutionized..."
Arthur Zajonc – Catching the Light

Strike an individual down to their very foundation.
Which: forming a truly humanistic foundation within a truly humanistic being, any one individual could only have done, while going out each and every day, and actually practicing their scales of simultaneously relative Reality, and while –

"At birth, a baby's brain contains about 100 million neurons, the brain cells that carry electrical messages through the brain. Each one can produce up to 15,000 synapses, or connections to the other cells. Those synapses are the key to healthy development and learning – Repeated early experiences determine how the brain is wired. Those synapses that have been activated frequently by virtue of repeated early experience tend to become permanent; the synapses that have not been used at all, or often enough, tend to become eliminated..."
Catherine Long – Seattle Times/Philadelphia Inquirer – Tuesday, May 29, 1997

Causing permanently effectuated multidimensional synaptic capabilities: while actually functioning as a foundation, within any one individually affected truly humanistic being's quantum electrodynamically functioning mind, and parallel functioning central nervous system. And: again –

"Then the disciples went up to him and asked, 'Why do you talk to them in parables?' 'Because,' he replied, the mysteries of the kingdom of heaven are revealed to you, but they are not revealed to them. For anyone who has will be given more, and he will have more than enough; but from anyone who has not, even what he has will be taken away."
Matthew 13: 10-13

As was exactly explained by the Son of God.
And which can – then, be –

"If God were your Father, you would love me
since I have come from God; yes, I have come from him;
not that I came because I chose,
no, I was sent, and by him.
Do you know why you cannot take in what I say?
It is because you are unable to understand my language."
John 8: 42-43

Communicated as a formed understanding of Reality.

Which may be harnessed within truly humanistic reality – abstracted from within Reality, and – then, communicated as a formed understanding of Reality.

Which is simple to understand, while we remember the function of any language in the entire history of mankind. And the neuroscientific fact, that a child must, first, become capable of –

"Parents Allegedly Kept Four Children In Home At All Times –

A couple allegedly shuttered their four children from the world by forbidding them from going outside the family home. Three of the children can speak only broken English and communicate with one another in their own language – The eldest child can converse easily with other people, but the three youngest communicate with themselves in their own primitive language – 'It's gibberish...'"

James Hannah – Philadelphia Inquirer/Associated Press – April 16, 1999

Learning the function of simultaneously relative – universally applicable and harmoniously proportioned, Reality: within their individually affected quantum dynamically functioning minds, and parallel functioning central nervous systems. Before they can become capable of abstracting the formed understanding from within reality: of reality, and – then, communicating an understanding of truly humanistic *a priori* Reality: abstractly.

THIS: formed understanding of universally applicable, and simultaneously relative, *a priori* truly humanistic Reality, actually effectually functioning as Omnidimensional Time *made manifest*: The Mind of God – Our paradise Lost and The Eternal Harmony too, is the language which is contained within *The Annunciation*, and only *The Annunciation*.

THIS: formed understanding of the Mind of God made manifest and while actually effectually functioning as Omnidimensional Time *made manifest*, is exactly what did – then and with Leonardo da Vinci's communicated understanding of *a priori* Reality only, enable "art" to acquire the title of a Noble Art.

And this: acquired title of a Noble Art and/or a virtuous human being, can only become acquired, by any one individual humanistic being, and/or any truly humanistic "thing," by existing as –

124

"True sciences are those which have penetrated through the senses as a result of experience and thus silencing the tongues of disputants, not feeding investigators on dreams but always proceeding successively from primary truths and established principles, in a proper order towards the conclusion. This may be witnessed in the principles of mathematics, that is to say, number and measure – termed arithmetic and geometry, which deal with discontinuous and continuous quantities with the utmost truth – Here all guesswork remains destroyed in eternal silence...Leonardo da Vinci."

The absolute: identifiable and universally applicable, truth.
Which is, how we can: now and forever, and while actually; "silencing the tongues of disputants" – shutting up their mouths forever too, simply prove the fact of the function which is *The Annunciation*: actually functioning as Omnidimensional Time *made manifest*. And which: proving the function of *The Annunciation*, we can actually do by –

"Candace Pert – I see the brain in terms of quantum mechanics – the brain is just a receiver, an amplifier, a little wet minireceiver for collective reality. We make maps, but we should never confuse the map with the territory..."
The 3-Pound Universe – Judith Hooper and Dick Teresi

Simply mapping out the coordinates: throughout, and within, simultaneously relative space/time, while as simultaneously relative to/from, and within, a single universally applicable, and cognizable, point time zero. Which is while actually functioning as universally applicable, and simultaneously relative, Omnidimensional Time *made manifest*: The Mind of God made manifest – The Kingdom of Heaven – The Entrance to the Garden and The Eternal Harmony too, while functioning as simultaneously relative quantized electrodynamics.
Except, of course, it: doing some real time quantum computing, is not simple at all. It is, and as Albert Einstein did plainly explain –

"...Einstein struggled through the complexities of curved space, seeking to assign the fourth dimension to time and make the whole, infernally complicated affair come out right – doing important work in quantum mechanics and a half-dozen other fields – But he kept returning to the riddle of gravitation, trying to find patterns of beauty and simplicity among thick stacks of papers black with equations. Like a lost explorer discarding his belongings on a trek across the desert, he found it necessary to part company with some of his most cherished possessions – among them were the central precepts of the special theory itself, which to his joy was ultimately to return as a local case within a broader scheme of the general theory. 'In all my life I have never before labored so hard,' he wrote to a friend'...'Compared with this problem, the original theory of relativity is child's play...'"
Timothy Ferris – Coming Of Age In The Milky Way

The single most difficult thing any one could ever do.

And, yes, it: doing some real time quantum computing, is even more difficult than they could ever possibly imagine, and for many reasons. The least of which is not that, as all scientists do plainly know, the total power of the universe: and/or the total amount of Time *made manifest*, is a constant. While all of simultaneously relative Reality, and/or the explained theory of relativity, is an absolute invariant under time translations, and which is exactly why Albert Einstein did actually prefer the term "invariance theory." So that, we can know and while doing some real time quantum computing, the total numerical quantity: of the individually completed harmoniously proportioned differential equations effectually functioning as, and while remaining subservient to, a whole, must remain constant: while doing the real time quantum computing, and which must be done simultaneously: while affecting the individually completed movements, which are subservient to a hierarchically structured whole, and which is while – and simultaneously, the total numerical quantity must remain infinite: and/or the applied function of an Eternal Harmony – and/or "timeless."

And – again and in simple English, we could imagine building a real tangible form mass House for our own selves, while not being allowed to use, and/or even simply see, any blueprints: for the House. And/or, being not allowed to simply see the actual lumber to be used to construct the tangible form mass House, to function as an artificially effectuated mother's womb for our own selves: to enable our own selves to retire to restful sleep at night, and/or to simply find a point of rest for our own selves. And: while actually being not allowed to see any blueprints and/or any building materials at all before beginning to build, which is while – also and simultaneously, being allowed to use only that exact amount of lumber: which we exactly are not allowed to see before we begin, and/or while during the construction either, and, too and simultaneously, while we are only allowed a certain amount of time to complete the construction and we are not allowed to know when to begin, and/or when to finish, the construction, or the amount of time we are allowed to complete the construction either. And as was exactly explained by –

"Great crowds accompanied him on his way and he turned and spoke to them. If any man comes to me without hating his father, mother, wife, children, brothers, sisters, yes and his own life too, he cannot be my disciple. Anyone who does not carry his cross and come after me cannot be my disciple.

And indeed, which of you here, intending to build a tower, would not first sit down and work out the cost to see if he had enough to complete it? Otherwise, if he laid the foundation and then found himself unable to finish the work, the onlookers would all start making fun of him and saying, 'Here is a man who started to build and was unable to finish."

Luke 14: 25-31

The Son of God.

And of course also, actually performing a demonstration of the function which *is The Annunciation* for the entire world to simply see with their own eyes, and while doing some real time quantum computing for our own selves, will not be capable of causing an effect within any individual, who has not spent a lifetime learning the language: of Omnidimensional Time *made manifest*.

Which is simple to understand, while we can reiterate our understanding of the real applicable function of any language, and in the entire history of mankind. Which: all humanistic languages, are, simply, an abstracted application of the same exact function, which is capable of being replicated upon a keyboard. Which is, simply, the universally applicable function, of harmoniously proportioned simultaneously relative differentials, and/or harmoniously proportioned unidirectionally successive tones, expanded into harmoniously proportioned, and unidirectionally successive, tonal variations: and/or words expanded into sentences. And, as we can remember, while as through the universally applicable function of unidirectionally successive syntax: to function as elementary universally applicable intelligence. While, in neuroscientific reality, each – and every, language, and in the entire history of mankind, employs the use of the exact same tones, which are simply conjoined differently, to form words, and/or tonal variations, and while expanded into sentences. Any humanistic language, must be learned in reality first, before it can be communicated to any other human being, and which does mean while actually occurring within an individual human being's electrical potential mass of a mind, while actually functioning as the universally applicable function of Reality. The function: of universally applicable, and unidirectionally successive, Reality, can, then, be abstracted from within Reality, and projected upon a two-dimensional plane, to simply function as a communicated understanding of Reality. And – again, in simple English, if you are an individual human being who has learned English, and you do walk into a room where everyone else is speaking a foreign language, you will not be capable of understanding exactly what it is that they are saying, and not even –

"Whoever believes in me
believes not in me
but in the one who sent me,
and whoever sees me,
sees the one who sent me.
I, the light, have come into the world,
so that whoever believes in me
need not stay in the dark any more.
If anyone hears my words and does not keep them faithfully,
it is not I who shall condemn him,
since I have come not to condemn the world,
but to save the world:
he who rejects me and refuses my words

127

has his judge already:
the word itself that I have spoken
will be his judge on the last day.
For what I have spoken does not come from myself;
no, what I was to say, what I had to speak,
was commanded by the Father who sent me,
and I know that his commands mean eternal life.
And therefore what the father has told me
is what I speak."
John 12: 44-50

To save your very own self.

And, too of course, before any one individual could ever even begin to perform a demonstration of the function: which is *The Annunciation*, they must, first, become capable of learning the language: of Omnidimensional Time *made manifest*, and which is while including, and simultaneously, the prerequisite function of the identifiable coordinates – the coordinators, and the simultaneously relative function: which *is* Omnidimensional Time *made manifest*. And there is only one human being who can do that, on the entire face of this point-mass of Earth, and that is this human being.

But, it does allow us to prove the fact of the function: which is of universally applicable Omnidimensional Time *made manifest,* and for all the world to simply see with our eyes alone. Which is, as we can remember and as any true scientist, and/or truly humanistic being, does plainly understand, the –

"Cracking The Cosmic Code With a Little Help From Dr. Hawking –
...Dr. Hawking's first book for a wide audience, 'A Brief History of Time,' took readers on a tour through black holes, the gravitational traps from which not even light can emerge, and – time as he described the quest for the vaunted 'theory of everything' that would enable us to 'know the mind of God'...quantum theory and relativity have taught us, science is about what can be observed and measured or it is about nothing at all. In science, as in democracy, there is no hidden secret knowledge, all that counts is on the table, observable and falsifiable. All else is metaphysics."
Dennis Overbye – The New York Times – Tuesday December 11, 2001

Only thing which matters, and/or all that counts: in science and in democracy too.
All that matters: In Reality – Science and Democracy too, is the –

"And indeed, everybody who does wrong
hates the light and avoids it,
for fear his actions should be exposed;

128

but the man who lives by the truth
comes out into the light
so that it may be plainly seen that what he does is done in God."
John 3: 20-21

Absolute truth.

So, here is some more: absolute and universally applicable scientific truth. Which is the fact that it: the function which is *The Annunciation* and which is the function of consciously cognizing Omnidimensional Time *made manifest,* while functioning as truly humanistic simultaneously relative patterns in space/time, is the definition of –

"Do not be afraid of them therefore. For everything that is now covered will be uncovered, and everything now hidden will be made clear. What I say to you in the dark, tell in the daylight, what you hear in whispers, proclaim from the housetops.

Do not be afraid of those who kill the body but cannot kill the soul; fear him rather who can destroy both body and soul in hell. Can you not buy two sparrows for a penny? And yet not one falls to the ground without your Father knowing. Why, every hair on your head has been counted. So there is no need to be afraid; you are worth more than hundreds of sparrows.

So if anyone declares himself for me in the presence of men, I will declare myself for him in the presence of my Father in heaven. But the one who disowns me in the presence of men, I will disown in the presence of my Father in heaven."
Matthew 10: 26-33

A human being's "soul."

Which is, while the exact definition of a human being's soul is: "The principle of life, feeling, thought, and action in man, regarded as a distinct entity separate from the body – the spiritual part of man regarded in its moral aspect, or as capable of surviving death and subject to happiness or misery in a life to come – the emotional part of man's nature; the seat of the feelings or sentiments – a human being; person," simply one more thing which the Son of God did plainly explain, and while being the function which is *The Annunciation*, which does exist as –

"If humans are less robotlike than salamanders or ducks, it's not because we have no wired-in behaviors. In fact, we have quite a few. What makes the difference is the ratio of 'un-wired' to wired-in gray matter, because neurons that are not committed at birth to a set function – are available for learning, for modification – in humans a great gray area – about three-fourths of the cortex, lies between sensory input and motor output, called the association areas. These include the frontal lobes – The equivalent of the machine language of the brain, is very complex electromagnetic field configurations, with very fine modulation in amplitude, wave

129

shape and spatial distribution...The mind of man contains only so many visions – four basic, recurrent geometrical forms – Candace Pert: I see the brain in terms of quantum mechanics – the brain is just a receiver, an amplifier, a little wet minireceiver for collective reality – the ratio of frontal core to the rest of the cortex may be one index of evolutionary advancement – What the frontal lobes 'control' is something like awareness, or self-awareness – Do these lobes govern some essential feature of humanness, or even godliness, as some scientists have suggested? 'If God speaks to man, if man speaks to God,' neuroscientist Candace Pert tells us, 'it would be through the frontal lobes' – Stephen Labarge: 'And it's capable of what look like miraculous things, so miraculous that we're tempted to say it's divine, that it's not natural..."

The 3-Pound Universe – Judith Hooper and Dick Teresi

A matter of neuroscientific fact: for all the world to simply see with our eyes alone.

While this: absolute neuroscientific truth, is simple to understand, because we do know that it: a truly humanistic being's soul, can not: possibly, be simply that which –

"Candace Pert: we've measured opiate receptors in everything from fruit fly heads to human brains. Even uni-cellular organisms have peptides' – Do you think even cockroaches feel some sort of emotion we ask – 'They have to, because they have chemicals that put them in the mood to mate and chemicals that make them run away when they're about to be killed. That's what emotions are about – Behavior is controlled by the anticipation of pain or pleasure, punishment or reward. And that has to be coded in the brain."

The 3-Pound Universe – Judith Hooper and Dick Teresi

An amoeba, and/or an animal, is capable of experiencing: within Reality.

And too, we can now know and for an absolute scientific fact, that it: a truly humanistic being's soul, can not possibly be simply accessing abstract knowledge, and/or simply functioning while as in an absolutely abstracted, and unidirectionally successive, manner, of any kind. Because –

"Any computing machine that is to solve a complex mathematical problem must be 'programmed' for this task. Hence it is to be expected that – an efficiently organized large artificial automaton (like a large computing machine) will – do things successively – one thing at a time."

John VonNewman – The Computer and The Brain – The World Treasury of Physics, Astronomy and Mathematics, Ed. Timothy Ferris

Even a mindless automaton can do *that*.

And too which: consciously cognizing truly humanistic simultaneously relative patterns in space/time, "as" simultaneously relative to/from, and within, a single cognizable point time zero, is, simply, the exact definition of a truly humanistic being's universally applicable empirical self-consciousness, and/or the exact definition of –

"One thing has become clear to scientists: memory is absolutely crucial to our consciousness – 'There's almost nothing you do, from perception to thinking, that doesn't draw continuously on your memory – It can't be otherwise, since there is really no such thing as a present (while) memory provides a personal context, a sense of self and a sense of familiarity – past and present and a frame for the future.' (But) Memory is not a single phenomenon. 'We don't have a memory system in the brain' – 'We have memory systems, each playing a different role – All of these different types of memory are ultimately stored in the brain's cortex – what's happening when the brain forms memory (is that) it's the connections between nerve cells – and particularly the strength of those connections – that are altered by experience (as) nerve cells are firing simultaneously and coordinating different sets of information – When everything is going right, these different systems work together seamlessly. If you're taking a bicycle ride, for example, the memory of how to operate the bike comes from one set of neurons; the memory of how to get from here to the other side of town comes from another; the nervous feeling you have left over from taking a bad spill last time out comes from still another. Yet you are never aware that your mental experience has been assembled, bit by bit, like some invisible edifice inside your brain..."
Michael D. Lemonick – Smart Genes? – Time – Sept. 13, 1999

Truly humanistic universally applicable memory: simultaneously effectually functioning, as universally applicable empirical self-consciousness.
Again, which: the function of empirical self-consciousness, is: actually functioning, while –

"...Many of the provinces of the brain (are) topographical maps of projections of the sensory fields which they represent – the same geometrical decorum applies to all projections – physical events impinging on the sensory surface are transformed into the characteristic digital language of the brain – Once a pattern of light has struck the retina, as soon as a train of sound-waves has traveled up the spiral of the cochlea, the events are translated into sequences of nervous information so that the transmission no more resembles what it represents than the currents in a television circuit resemble the pictures which they carry – a linear code dictates the construction of the visible object."
Jonathan Miller – The Body in Question

The same geometrical decorum does apply to all projections.
And again in simple English, which does simply mean that, and as was

exactly explained by Johannes Keplar and while in the year 1595 too –

"Geometrical non-tangible forms: God wanted us to recognize them, when He created us after His image, so that we should share in His thoughts. For what is implanted in the mind of man other than numbers and magnitudes? These alone we comprehend correctly, and if piety permits us to say so, his recognition is of the same kind as the devine, at least insofar as we in this mortal life of ours are capable of grasping part of it...Geometry is one and eternal, a reflection of the mind of God – nature loves these relationships in everything that is capable of being related. They are also loved by the intellect of man who is an image of the Creator."

The only things which exist within our minds, are individually completed geometrical formations. Which is simple to understand, by simply looking at any "thing" around us, while remembering that our minds are a quantum dynamically functioning three-dimensional electrical potential mass, within which are contained no images of things. So that, we can simply understand and as we do look at all things, that all things: in Reality, are simply the tangible formation of conjoined basic geometrical tangible form masses: which are projected into our minds, and wherein there are no images of things, but – simply, a linear code of all perceivable tangible form masses. In addition, we can plainly understand, that each, and every, thing, that human beings do: within our entire lives and while upon this point-mass of Earth, is – simply, to make manifest simultaneously relative journeys throughout, and within, all of simultaneously relative space/time, and while as simultaneously relative to, and from, our daily truly humanistic point time zero: our artificially effectuated mother's womb of our houses. Where we do retire at night, for nighttime restful sleep, and – then after rising from nighttime restful sleep, do – only, begin to make manifest many patterns in truly humanistic space/time: while actually moving our bodies all throughout, and within, simultaneously relative space/time, and while forming truly humanistic memories within our truly humanistic electrical potential mass minds, and parallel functioning central nervous systems. Wherein, there does exist only a projected linear code, of simultaneously relative Reality, and/or truly humanistic universally applicable empirical self-consciousness, actually functioning as –

"Space Mach argued, is not a thing, but an expression of interrelationships among events. '*All* masses and *all* velocities, and consequently *all* forces, are relative,' he wrote. Einstein agreed, and was encouraged to attempt to write a theory that built space and time out of events alone – He never entirely succeeded in satisfying Mach's criteria – but the effort helped impel him toward relativity – Einstein had replaced Newton's space with a network of light beams; *theirs* was the absolute grid, within which space itself became..."
Timothy Ferris – Coming of Age in the Milky Way

Individually completed simultaneously relative patterns in space/time, and within which space itself "becomes": within any one individual, and truly humanistic being's, quantum electrodynamically functioning mind, and parallel functioning central nervous system. And –

"Candace Pert: we've measured opiate receptors in everything from fruit fly heads to human brains. Even uni-cellular organisms have peptides' – Do you think even cockroaches feel some sort of emotion we ask – 'They have to, because they have chemicals that put them in the mood to mate and chemicals that make them run away when they're about to be killed. That's what emotions are about – pain and pleasure – Behavior is controlled by the anticipation of pain or pleasure, punishment or reward. And that has to be coded in the brain."
The 3-Pound Universe – Judith Hooper and Dick Teresi

Purposefully effectuated biochemical inductions. Such as endorphin: to enable us to experience joy and/or exultation, and serotonin: to enable us to experience melancholy and/or sadness.
And do you remember how all human beings do actually become capable of producing serotonin, within their own personally affected, and truly humanistic, electrical potential minds, and parallel functioning central nervous systems, while –

"Princeton's (Barry) Jacobs believes that, based on experiments with cats, repetitive motor activity – walking – stimulates the release of serotonin..."
The Mood Molecule – Time, September 29, 1997 – Michael D. Lemonick

Actually physiologically moving their bodies all throughout, and within, truly humanistic simultaneously relative space/time.
And do you remember what serotonin is capable of doing: within any human being's quantum electrodynamically functioning electrical potential mass of a mind, and parallel functioning central nervous system, and that is –

"Experiencing Ecstasy –
...Whereas Prozac-type SSRI antidepressants keep your brain from emptying reservoirs of serotonin too quickly, Ecstasy floods your brain with the stuff – you feel so connected to the continuum of your life. A subtle, purifying something descends (over you) – You're warm. You're not hungry – You have everything you need. Just breathing is readily good on this stuff..."
Matthew Klam – The New York Times Magazine – January 21, 2001

Connecting us with the continuum of our lives: while actually practicing our scales of truly humanistic simultaneously relative Reality, actually functioning as Omnidimensional Time *made manifest* while on a daily basis too, and for 2-to3 hours daily, and for a minimum of 10-to-15 years also: while actually beginning to form a truly humanistic foundation, within any individual's own personally effectuated, quantum electrodynamically functioning, mind, and parallel functioning central nervous system. While allowing us to –

"Tuning Up The Brain –
The 'Mozart effect' suggests that classical compositions can stimulate learning. But the jury is still out – What scientists do know is that keyboard instruction – making music, not just hearing it – seems to resonate within the brain..."
Sharon Begley – Newsweek – Fall/Winter 2000

Cause permanently effectuated multidimensional, and truly humanistic, long term potentiated synaptic capabilities, within our –

"Do not store up treasures for yourselves on earth, where moths and woodworms destroy them and thieves can break in and steal. But store up treasures for yourselves in heaven, where neither moth nor woodworms destroy them and thieves cannot break in and steal. For where your treasure is, there will your heart be also."
Matthew 6: 19-21

Personally affected quantum electrodynamically functioning Omnidimensional refractive gem of the mind, and parallel functioning central nervous system.
And which: a truly humanistic Omnidimensional refractive gem of a mind and parallel functioning central nervous system, may, then, become capable of –

"Wolfgang Amadeus Mozart: When I feel well and in good humour, or when I am – walking after a meal, or in the night when I cannot sleep, thoughts crowd into my mind as easily as you could wish. Whence and how do they come? I do not know and I have nothing to do with it. Those which please me I keep in my head and hum them; at least others have told me that I do so. Once I have my theme, another melody comes, linking itself with the first one, in accordance with the needs of the composition as a whole: the counterpoint, the part of each instrument and all the melodic fragments at last produce the complete work. Then my soul is on fire with inspiration (as) my mind seizes it as a glance of my eye – It does not come to me successively – but in its entirety..."
Wolfgang Amadeus Mozart – Timothy Ferris – The Emperor's New Mind

Experiencing truly humanistic simultaneously relative multidimensional emotions, and a Fire in their soul too: just as Wolfgang Amadeus Mozart did. And too which is just as only –

"Psychopaths seem to know the dictionary meanings of words but fail(ed) to comprehend or appreciate their *emotional* value or significance (while functioning as if) 'He knows the words but not the music' – Recent laboratory research provides convincing support for these clinical observations – Psychopaths seem to suffer a kind of emotional poverty that limits the range and depth of their feelings. While at times they appear cold and unemotional, they are prone to dramatic, shallow, and short-lived displays of feeling. Careful observers are left with the impression that they are play-acting and that little is going on below the surface – Sometimes they claim to experience strong emotions but are unable to describe the subtleties of various affective states. For example, they equate love with sexual arousal, sadness with frustration and anger with irritability – psychopaths sometimes verbalize remorse but then contradict themselves in words or actions – In some respects they are like the emotionless androids depicted in science fiction, unable to imagine what real humans experience."

Dr. Robert D. Hare – Without Conscience

Truly humanistic beings can do: experience truly humanistic simultaneously relative multidimensional emotions, and/or have a soul.

And – too, which does – now, enable us to reiterate our understanding of simultaneously relative proportional equivalences: actually functioning as within truly humanistic simultaneously relative Omnidimensional space/time. Which are, only, while capable of functioning as simultaneously relative to/from, and within, a single cognizable point time zero, and – too, which is while actually effectually functioning as simultaneously relative complex Omnidimensional Time *made manifest*, and/or as a concordant polyphonically structured whole. And too, as individually completed harmoniously proportioned differential equations, which are subservient to, and actually effectually functioning as, a hierarchically structured whole: concordant orchestration of many individually completed harmoniously proportioned differential equations, and/or: "many voices." Which is – as we did reiterate our understanding of while at the beginning of this Edenic tale, capable of actually functioning as the substantiating of a truly humanistic being's – possible, formed understanding of a more divinely purposeful existence: beyond this point-mass of Earth, and an excessively simplistic, and animalistic, tangible form mass of a body: for their own selves to be in possession of only. While along with their truly humanistic Omnidimensional refractive gem of a mind, and parallel functioning central nervous system, to have actually become capable of forming for their own selves. And, as we can remember, which is only capable of becoming effectually formed, as an individual human being does, actually, begin to become capable of purposefully affecting truly humanistic simultaneously relative multidimensional synaptic capabilities: within their own individually affected truly humanistic being simultaneously relative quantum electrodynamically functioning mind, and parallel functioning central nervous system. As they will have spent a lifetime, actually practicing their scales of truly humanistic simultaneously relative

Omnidimensional Reality, and which was while capable of causing permanently affected changes, within an individual's own personal three-dimensional electrical potential mass of a mind, and parallel functioning central nervous system, and within which there are contained no projected images of any things, and/or any things whatsoever. But – only, individually completed differential equations, and while effectually functioning as simultaneously relative to/from, and within, a single cognizable point time zero. But also, remember, which: all of the individually completed differential equations, are – most usually, only –

"There are two essential yet complementary aspects of this new vision of time which are as striking in contrast as heaven and hell. Heaven is ruled by dynamical equations that are reversible and 'timeless'; their simplicity ensures stability for eternity. Hell is more akin to the real world, where fluctuations, uncertainty and chaos reign..."
The Arrow of Time – Peter Coveney and Roger Highfield

Hell made manifest.
But not while they are capable of functioning as Omnidimensional Time *made manifest*, and as a simultaneously relative concordant polyphonically structured whole also: while actually functioning as simultaneously relative to/from, and within, a single truly humanistic, and simultaneously relative, cognizable point time zero. Which is located within simultaneously relative Omnidimensional space/time: as it is within a truly humanistic being's simultaneously relative quantum electrodynamically functioning mind, and parallel functioning central nervous system: while actually functioning as truly humanistic quantized electrodynamics, and as "simultaneously relative to" and "effectually functioning as" a "hierarchically structured whole." While, in the entire history of mankind, there is only the one of *The Annunciation*, or Wolfgang Amadeus Mozart's *Requim Mass*.
Which is also exactly why, the simultaneously relative Omnidimensional function *of* Wolfgang Amadeus Mozart's *Requiem Mass*, is exactly paralleled by the unidirectionally successive three-dimensional function:

"Day of wrath, that day
Will dissolve the earth in ashes
As David and the Sibyl bear witness.

What dread there will be
When the Judge shall come
To judge all things strictly.

A trumpet, spreading a wondrous sound
Through the graves of all the lands,
Will drive mankind before the throne.

Death and nature shall be astonished
When all creation rises again
To answer to the Judge.

A book, written in, will be brought forth
In which is contained everything that is,
Out of which the world shall be judged.

When therefore the Judge takes His seat
Whatever is hidden will reveal itself.
Nothing will remain unavenged.

What then shall I say, wretch that I am,
What advocate entreat to speak for me,
When even the righteous may hardly be secure?

King of awful majesty,
Who freely savest the redeemed,
Save me, O fount of goodness.

Remember, blessed Jesu,
That I am the cause of Thy pilgrimage,
Do not forsake me on that day.

Seeking me Thou didst sit down weary,
Thou didst redeem me, suffering death on the cross.
Let not such toil be in vain.

Just and avenging Judge.
Grant remission
Before the day of reckoning.

I groan like a guilty man.
Guilt reddens my face.
Spare a suppliant, O God.

My prayers are not worthy,
But Thou in Thy merciful goodness grant
That I burn not in everlasting fire.

Place me among Thy sheep
And separate me from the goats,
Setting me on Thy right hand.

When the accursed have been confounded
And given over to bitter flames,
Call me with the blessed.

I pray in supplication on my knees.
My heart contrite as the dust,
Safeguard my fate.

Mournful that day
When from the dust shall rise
Guilty man to be judged.
Therefore spare him, O God.
Merciful Jesu, Lord
Grant them rest."

Which is exactly something else that any one individual actually does begin
to become capable of doing, while they do become neurophysiologically capable of
consciously cognizing the Mind of God made manifest. That is, to beg forgiveness
for the ineptitudes of our excessively simplistic mortal existence: while upon this
point-mass of Earth, and which is God's footstool. So I do also: Beg forgiveness for
the ineptitudes of my excessively simplistic mortal existence, upon this point-mass
of Earth.

But which: the things that I do beg forgiveness for, are, most probably, none
of which what a mere mortal would think. And too which: that I have come to a
complete understanding of the ineptitudes of my excessively simplistic mortal
existence, is simply because, I was the one responsible for communicating this
understanding: The understanding of the function of The Law – the Letter of which I
read as a young child, and which: the Function, I can: now, begin to communicate
my learned complete understanding of, and too which is while being contained
within this book: The book which is written in, now brought forth, and from which
mankind will be judged. And: no, it was not something that I did particularly want
to do, I was –

"Still, I must tell you the truth
it is for your own good that I am going
because unless I go
the Advocate will not come to you;
but if I do go,
I will send him to you.
And when he comes,
he will show the world how wrong it was,
about sin,
and about who was in the right,

and about judgment:
about sin:
proved by their refusal to believe in me;
about who was in the right:
proved by my going to the Father
and your seeing me no more;
about judgment:
proved by the prince of this world being already condemned.
I still have many things to say to you
but they would be too much for you now.
But when the Spirit of truth comes
he will lead you to the complete truth,
since he will not be speaking as from himself
but he will say only what he has learned;
and he will tell you of the things to come.
He will glorify me,
since all he tells you
will be taken from what is mine.
Everything the Father has is mine;
that is why I said:
All he tells you
will be taken from what is mine."
John 16: 5-15

Not so simply (told) to do it: communicate my learned understanding of the Function of The Law, and/or *a priori* Reality. And – too, which is while proving the scientific fact that Jesus of Nazareth is, most probably, *the* Son of God. Which is while remembering the fact that the word science does, simply, mean "Truth," and that true scientists deal, only, in mathematical probabilities: before they can become capable of proving anything, and –

"Cracking The Cosmic Code With a Little Help From Dr. Hawking –
...Dr. Hawking's first book for a wide audience – took readers on a tour through black holes, the gravitational traps from which not even light can emerge, and – time as he described the quest for the vaunted 'theory of everything,' that would enable us to 'know the mind of God'...quantum theory and realativity have taught us, science is about what can be observed and measured or it is about nothing at all..."
Dennis Overbye – The New York Times – Tuesday – December 11, 2001

For the entire world to simply see with our eyes alone of course.
But too which: our understanding of science, is exactly what makes doing some real time quantum computing: while actually functioning as the real

139

experiencing *of* an Omnidimensional space/time continuum, so weird, and, seem to, actually contradict common sense. Because, experiencing an Omnidimensional space/time continuum is, literally, beginning to become capable of experiencing every experience human beings can ever possibly experience, and which is while actually functioning as Omnidimensional Time *made manifest*. Which is simple to understand, by simply remembering that every experience human beings can experience: within truly humanistic Reality, is, simply, the simultaneously effectuated function of individually completed patterns in space/time, and while actually effectually occurring within truly humanistic simultaneously relative Reality. Which truly humanistic beings do become capable of experiencing: within truly humanistic simultaneously relative space/time, and/or Reality, while beginning to become capable of experiencing truly humanistic emotions. Which are: truly humanistic emotions, and such as melancholy and/or sadness, through the range of truly humanistic emotions to joy and/or exultation, capable of being experienced while as through the effectuated function of biochemical inductions. Such as serotonin, being induced while as through the experiencing of a largo tempoed movement: to enable a truly humanistic being to experience a relatively sad, and/or melancholy, experience, and while actually occurring within their parallel functioning minds, and central nervous systems. And the induction of endorphin, being induced while as through the experiencing of a presto tempoed movement: to enable a truly humanistic being to experience a relatively joyful, and/or exultant, experience. But which: experiencing truly humanistic emotions and while actually effectually functioning as gradients – while actually experiencing an orchestration, and/or Reality, is, and as we can remember, contingent upon the function of reuptake occurring: within a human being's quantum dynamically functioning mind, and parallel functioning central nervous system. Which is, as Leonardo da Vinci did explain –

"...amid the greatest of things around us the existence of nothingness holds the first place, and its function extends among the things which have no existence, and its essence dwells as regards time..."

The period of time when an individual human being, does become capable of cognizing humanistic nothingness: functioning as truly humanistic "rest." So that, while an individual human being does become capable of being affected by truly humanistic emotions: which are capable of becoming effectuated while as through the function of an orchestration, and as the orchestration is capable of replicating the function of truly humanistic Reality, they: any one truly humanistic being who is capable of experiencing truly humanistic emotions, must: also and simultaneously, become neurophysiologically capable of consciously cognizing an amount of humanistic nothingness: affected after each, and every, note. And while they must also become capable of consciously cognizing the exact function of each and every note. And too, which does mean actually cognizing its: the exact note, simultaneously relative position "within" identifiable simultaneously relative space/time. So that we can understand, during an actual orchestration, a human being can, simply, perform the function of reuptake while the orchestration is – only, capable of functioning while as in a unidirectionally successive manner.

But which is exactly not so while experiencing an Omnidimensional space/time continuum. Which: experiencing an Omnidimensional space/time continuum, while actually functioning as the Mind of God made manifest and the Eternal Harmony too, does enable a human being, to experience every truly humanistic emotion that mankind can ever experience, and/or every truly humanistic experience, that mankind can ever experience: SIMULTANEOUSLY. Which is while actually effectually functioning, and/or traveling, while as at the speed of light: simultaneously squared – harnessed and unleashed, and while traveling on a journey from one end of the universe to the other, and simultaneously too. Which is exactly what makes it so weird, and seem to confound common sense too. Because: it does not function simultaneously, but it can only function simultaneously, and which is while capable of causing a fire in a human being's soul. And/or causing an effect that is, again and as Johanes Keplar did plainly explain –

"...then he becomes aware that he walks in the light of truth; he seized by an unbelievable rapture..."

Beyond belief: It is not a belief – it is an understanding, which is beyond belief.

And – again, it is impossible to describe, and/or to explain: the actual experience that is. But it would be, kind of, as if any one individual human being, who has never experienced it, were to actually take some heroin – some Ecstasy and some cocaine, all of our worldly drugs: dopamine – serotonin and endorphins too, and, then, to mix them all up and consume them simultaneously, and while compounding them to an infinite degree too. But – again, it actually is, and simultaneously too, nothing, at all, like anything that human beings can ever simply experience, for their own selves. And, again too, any individual human being, who does continue to access any forms of artificially inducing stimulus, will continue, only, to move while in the purposefully effectuated direction away from The Mind of God made manifest: Our Innocence Lost – The Entrance to the Garden, and The Eternal Harmony too.

To enable our own selves to understand exactly why this: abstracted communicated understanding of Reality, is the beginning of the end of time, we can simply understand Reality. And/or exactly what has actually happened in humanistic reality, and while simply taking a walk back through unidirectionally successive time. Beginning with the function of 21st century reality, and the proliferation of computers, within our humanistic society and while affecting the so-called communication age, and which is, simply, allowed access to an even greater amount of absolutely abstracted effectual stimulus, and some abstracted humanistic knowledge too. Which: 21st century computers, can function within reality, and as allowed access to absolutely abstracted biochemical inducing effectual stimulus, along with the proliferation of television sets: within all American households, and/or our artificially effectuated mother's womb environments, of our homes, and while – simultaneously, capable of effectually functioning: television sets, as an absolutely abstracted, and artificially effectuated, biochemical inducing effectual stimulus. Which: television sets, were introduced to mankind as society did begin to become an absolutely segregated, and/or abstracted, society, with the proliferation of segregated communities: suburban mass produced housing developments, and shopping malls. Within which: suburban mass produced housing developments and shopping malls, were located some movie theater parks, and allowed access to, some more, absolutely abstracted, and artificially effectuated, biochemical inducing effectual stimulus. Which: the proliferation of suburban mass produced housing developments and shopping malls, required the proliferation of relatively accelerated transportation methods, and/or mass produced automobiles, and allowed access to even more absolutely abstracted, and artificially effectuated, biochemical inducing effectual stimulus. Which: mass produced relatively accelerated transportation methods, and/or automobiles, were capable of being produced, only because of the advent of the industrial revolution. Which: the industrial revolution, did allow access to even greater amounts of absolutely abstracted, and artificially effectuated, biochemical inducing effectual stimulus, and too which: our arrival at the industrial revolution, is as we continue our walk back through time, and all the way to –

"A Declaration by the Representatives of the United States of America:
We hold these truths to be self-evident: that all men are created equal; that they are endowed by their Creator with CERTAIN [*inherent and*] inalienable rights; that among these are life, liberty, and the pursuit of happiness; that to secure these rights, governments are instituted among men, deriving their just powers from the consent of the governed; that whenever any form of government becomes destructive of these ends, it is the right of the people to alter or to abolish it, and to institute a new government, laying its foundation on such principles, and organizing its power in such form, as to them shall seem most likely to effect their safety and happiness..."

The formation of the world's first Truly Idealist Democratic Society
Wherein: the formation of the world's first Truly Idealist Democratic Society, the truly virtuous child: of the Monarch, did enable their own selves to become virtuous, by having everybody walking around, and practicing their scales of Reality, and on a daily basis too. Wherein: the individually affected minds of the people which constituted the world's first Truly Idealist Democratic Society, was the purposeful formation of a truly humanistic foundation: within the individually affected quantum electrodynamically functioning minds, and parallel functioning central nervous systems, and which were – then and simultaneously, capable of cognizing the universally applicable *a priori* self-evident truths of truly humanistic

Reality, and while as in their pursuit of happiness – liberty, and life too. While also affecting a government to secure these rights: for the people, and laying it's: The Government's, foundation, in those self-evident truths: of universally applicable *a priori* Reality, exactly while as in an attempt to affect our: the once truly virtuous Child, safety and happiness. And too which they: the truly virtuous Child which constituted the world's first Truly Idealist Democratic Society, were capable of communicating an understanding of: The actual *a priori* FUNCTION of the letter *of* The Law, as through their public declaration.

Which: the individually affected truly humanistic foundations, as we can remember, did begin to become degraded almost immediately, and – too of course, which was not simply occurring within the once Truly Idealist Democratic Society, but globally as well, and simultaneously of course. As less and less individually affected human beings, were enabling their own selves to practice their scales of simultaneously relative Reality, and while on a daily basis too. Which was: also and simultaneously, as more and more individuals, were beginning to allow their own selves, to become capable of being reprogrammed: within their individually affected minds and parallel functioning central nervous systems, as through allowed exposure to absolutely abstracted: two-dimensional and unidirectionally successive, and artificially effectuated, biochemical inducing effectual stimulus. While beginning to become capable of regressing all the way back, to –

"A baby passes her first amazing milestone before the typical mother has even wiped off the sweat of labor. Full-time newborns, scientist established in 1996, recognize and prefer their mother's face to all others – In the ingenious experiment, the scientists had babies suck a special pacifier that controlled a video screen. Depending on how the infant sucked, fast or slow, the image of Mom or another woman appeared; babies sucked so they'd see Mom..."
Joan Raymond – Newsweek – Fall/Winter 2000

Point time zero: within the individually affected three-dimensional minds, and parallel functioning central nervous systems.
Which does mean: literally, that all of these individually affected human beings, did, actually, begin to become –

"The psychopath is like an infant, absorbed in his own needs, vehemently demanding satiation,' – Psychopaths are very good at giving their undivided attention to things that interest them most and at ignoring other things. Some clinicians have likened this process to a narrow-beam search-light that focuses on only one thing at a time..."
Dr. Robert D. Hare – Without Conscience

Neurophysiologically incapable of seeing: and/or consciously cognizing, past a single point of simultaneously relative space/time, while at any one point within simultaneously relative space/time, and only, and simultaneously too, capable of functioning in a purely psychopathic manner – at best, and as a matter of fact.

And what they have done: to their very own selves and neurophysiologically, is to allow their very own selves, to affect their very own –

"What is a black hole? For astronomical purposes it behaves as a small, highly condensed dark 'body.' But is not really a material body in the ordinary sense. It possesses no ponderable surface. A black hole is the region of empty space (albeit a strangely distorted one) which acts as a center of gravitational attraction. At *one* time a material body *was* there. But the body collapsed inwards under its own gravitational pull. The more the body concentrated itself towards the center the stronger became its gravitational field and the less was the body able to stop itself from yet further collapse. At a certain stage a point of no return was reached..."
Roger Penrose – Black Holes – The World Treasury of Physics,
Astronomy and Mathematics – Ed. Timothy Ferris

Black Hole: and/or a space/time singularity, and within their own, individually affected, three-dimensional electrical potential mass mind, and parallel functioning central nervous system. Which: their own individually affected truly humanistic brain dead minds, will remain neurophysiologically incapable of cognizing any Time *made manifest*: of any kind, and too they will remain neurophysiologically incapable of experiencing any truly humanistic emotions, and/or any truly humanistic things whatsoever: it is a neurophysiological impossibility. They will – exactly and instead, remain only capable of physiologically responding to some form of excessive, and absolutely abstracted, purely –

"Candace Pert: We've measured opiate receptors in everything from fruit fly heads to human brains. Even uni-cellular organisms have peptides' – Do you think even cockroaches feel some sort of emotion we ask – 'They have to, because they have chemicals that put them in the mood to mate and chemicals that make them run away when they're about to be killed. That's what emotions are about – pain and pleasure. Even bacteria have a little hierarchy of primitive likes and dislikes. They're programmed to migrate toward or away from a chemotactic substance; they're little robots that go for sugar at all costs and away from salt. If you were designing a robot vehicle to walk into the future and survive, as God was when he designed human beings, you'd wired it up so that behavior that ensures survival of self or species – would be naturally reenforcing. Behavior is controlled by the anticipation of pain or pleasure, punishment or reward. And that has to be coded in the brain."
The 3-Pound Universe – Judith Hooper and Dick Teresi

Animalistic biochemical inducing effectual stimulus: of some and/or any kind, while actually functioning as "1."

And too, as they: all of the individually affected electrical potential mass minds, will remain –

"Hawking's Breakthrough Is Still an Enigma –

In the fall of 1973 Dr. Stephen W. Hawking – discovered to his disbelief that they (black holes) could leak energy and particles into space, and even explode in a fountain of high-energy sparks – Dr Hawking's celebrated breakthrough resulted partly from a fight. He was hoping to disprove the contention of Jacob Bekenstein – that the area of a black hole's boundary, the point of no return in space, was a measure of the entropy of a black hole. In thermodynamics, the study of heat and gases, entropy is a measure of wasted energy or disorder, which might seem like a funny concept to crop up in black holes. But in physics and computer science, entropy is also a measure of the information capacity of a system – the number of bits that it would take to describe its internal state. In effect, a black hole or any other system was like a box of Scrabble letters – the more the letters in the box the more words you could make, and the more chances of gibberish – Black holes, he said in his papers and talks in the late 1970's, were ravengers of information, spewing indeterminacy and undermining law and order in the universe...(And) Weird as it may be, quantum theory is nonetheless the foundation on which (the) world is built – and it is the language in which all of the fundamental laws of physics (are) expressed...'What happens when you squeeze too much information into an object is that you pack more more energy in,' Dr. Bousso said. But if it gets too heavy for its size, it becomes a black hole, and then 'the game is over,' as he put it. 'Like a piano with lots of keys but you can't press more than five of them at once or the piano will collapse."

Dennis Overbye – The New York Times – Tuesday January 22, 2002

Only capable of experiencing pure gibberish: within their individually affected minds, and parallel functioning central nervous systems. And/or, only neurophysiologically capable of functioning while as in an absolutely abstracted, and unidirectionally successive, manner, and not while as in a truly humanistic, and simultaneously relative quantum electrodynamical, manner. And exactly because they have no; "Weird as it may be, quantum theory is nonetheless the foundation on which (the) world is built – and is the language in which all the fundamental laws of physics (are) expressed" – truly humanistic simultaneously relative quantum electrodynamical functioning foundation, for their own selves to be in possession of. So they can not speak the language: of real time quantum electrodynamics, and/or Omnidimensional Time *made manifest* either, and; "Like a piano with lots of keys but you can't press more than five of them at once or the piano will collapse" – will never experience the Eternal Harmony.

And no, this: truly humanistic brain death for individual human beings to experience for their own selves, is not a brand new 21st century phenomenon, it is merely a brand new phenomenon, to be experienced by the overwhelming vast majority of mankind. As the aristocratic elite have always enabled their own selves to experience truly humanistic brain death, for themselves to be in possession of: absolutely nothing, except for their own personally affected truly humanistic brain death. And as was exactly explained by –

"Then Jesus said to his disciples, 'I tell you solemnly, it will be hard for a rich man to enter the kingdom of heaven. Yes, I tell you again, it is easier for a camel to pass through the eye of a needle than for a rich man to enter the kingdom of heaven.' When the disciples heard this they were astonished. 'Who can be saved, then?' they said. Jesus gazed at them. 'For men, he told them, 'this is impossible; for God everything is possible."
Matthew 19: 23-26

The Son of God.
Simply exactly because, the aristocratic elite have never practiced their scales, of truly humanistic Reality on a daily basis. Which is while actually functioning as all relatively painful experienced humanistic phenomena, and/or *pain*, while they have – and simultaneously, only – always, allowed themselves to excessively indulge in all relatively pleasurable experienced humanistic phenomena, and/or *pleasure*, exactly and instead. So that they did – always, simply enable themselves to effectually regress back to point time zero, of their own personally affected existence within truly humanistic simultaneously relative space/time, and while – then, enabling their own selves to experience truly humanistic brain death for themselves, and while remaining neurophysiologically incapable of experiencing any truly humanistic multidimensional emotions, and/or simply neurophysiologically incapable of consciously cognizing any truly humanistic Time *made manifest*. And only capable of –

"Cezanne...tried to make the ultimate journey back through time – Cezanne claimed – to believe in his own sensations – moreover, he said himself, quite categorically; 'what counts is only mass'...this is an imaginary world which Cezanne could not have seen in his dreams – it is impossible to tell – I could not decide – I do not know – we do not know (Cezanne created) a kind of space where the distance seems near – one technique to create depth is canceled out by the other – in other words Cezanne is the painter of distance that seems near – this was obviously against the classical rule of the constant observation point."
Cezanne – Yvon Taillainder

Consciously cognizing zero Time *made manifest*: and/or an; "one technique to create depth is canceled out by the other" – actual space/time singularity, for their truly humanistic brain dead selves to consume, and/or be affected by, *the*; "what counts is only mass" – pure drug functioning as stimulus, and/or "1." And/or –

"At a purely chemical level (just as the injection of) heroin triggers release of dopamine – every experience humans find enjoyable, amounts to little more than an explosion of dopamine in the nucleus accumbens, as exhilarating and ephemeral as a firecracker. (But) Dopamine, like most biologically important molecules, must be kept within strict bounds. Too much causes the hallucinations, and bizarre thoughts, of schizophrenia – addicts' neurons assaulted by abnormally high levels of dopamine, have responded defensively and reduced the number of sites (or receptors) to which dopamine can bind – so while addicts begin by taking drugs to feel high, they end up taking them in order not to feel low."
    Addicted – J. Madeleine Nash – Time – May 5, 1997

    Heroin: for their own selves to consume. And: as they have regressed all the way back to point time zero, while experiencing truly humanistic brain death for their own selves: while continuing to be affected and while actually passing the point of no return, they can – NOW, begin to –

"Pablo Picaso: Cubism is neither the seed of a new art nor its germination: it represents a stage in the development of original pictorial forms. Once realized these forms have a right to an independent existence."

    Experience schizophrenia for their own selves: to be exposed to.
    And which: any two-dimensional schizophrenic Cubist thing, is – only and of course, the pictorial representation of –

"At Hiroshima: The common lot was random, indiscriminate and universal violence inflicting terrible pain, the physics of hydraulics and leverage and heat run riot...A junior college girl: 'Ah, that instant! I felt as though I have been struck on the back with something like a big hammer, and thrown into boiling oil – I seem to have been blown a good way to the north and I felt as though the directions were all changed around...a six-year-old boy: 'If you think of Brother's body divided into left and right halves, he was burned on the right side, and on the inside of the left side...''
    Richard Rhodes – The Making of The Atomic Bomb

    A nuclear Holocaust. And/or, the –

"The blast wave, rocketing several hundred yards from the hypocenter at 2 mi. per second and then slowing to the speed of sound 1,100 feet per second, threw up a vat cloud of smoke and dust. 'My body seemed all black,' a Hiroshima physicist (said), everything seemed dark, dark all over – then I thought, 'the world is ending."
    Richard Rhodes – The Making of The Atomic Bomb

    End of time.
    And –

"A six-year-old boy: 'Near the bridge there were a whole lot of dead people. There were some who were burned black and died, and there were others with huge burns who died with their skin bursting, and some others who died all stuck full of broken glass. There were all kinds. Sometimes there were ones who came to us asking for a drink of water. They were bleeding from their faces and from their mouths and had glass sticking from their bodies. And the bridge itself was burning furiously – the details and the scenes were just like Hell."
    Richard Rhodes – The Making of The Atomic Bomb

    Hell made manifest: for everyone to plainly see, with their eyes alone.
    Which is exactly what any two-dimensional brain dead Cubist thing is in Reality. And too, as is any "thing" in the entire history of mankind, which does not contain truly humanistic, and identifiable, simultaneously relative multidimensional, and/or Omnidimensional, syntax: while actually functioning as simultaneously relative to/from, and within, a single cognizable – and universally applicable, point time zero, and as truly humanistic Omnidimensional Time *made manifest*.
    And there is only the one of *The Annunciation*, and/or Wolfgang Amadeus Mozart's Requiem Mass. Everything else is, only and neurophysiologically, the function of truly humanistic brain death, and as a matter of –

    "Psychopaths seem to know the dictionary meaning of words but fail(ed) to comprehend or appreciate their emotional value or significance (while functioning as if) 'He knows the words but not the music' – Recent laboratory research provides convincing support for these clinical observations – Picture yourself sitting before a computer screen on which groups of letters are flashed for a fraction of a second. Electrodes for recording brain responses have been attached to your scalp and connected to an EEG machine, which draws a graph of the electrical activity of the brain – You will probably respond more quickly to an emotional word than to a neutral one. For example, you – and most other people – would push the button more quickly at the word DEATH than the word PAPER. Emotional content of a word seems to give a sort of 'turbo-boost' to the decision-making process. At the same time, emotional words evoke larger brain responses than do neutral words, a reflection of the relatively large amount of information contained in the emotional words – When we used this laboratory test with prison inmates, the non-psychopaths showed the normal pattern of response – but the psychopaths did not: *They responded to emotional words as if they were neutral words* – to a psychopath, a word is just a word."
    Dr. Robert D. Hare – Without Conscience

    Neuroscientific fact.
    Because: remember, there are –

"Many of the provinces of the brain (are) topographical maps of projections of the sensory fields which they represent – the same geometrical decorum applies to all projections – physical events impinging on the sensory surface are transformed into the characteristic digital language of the brain – Once a pattern of light has struck the retina, as soon as a train of sound-waves has traveled up the spiral of the cochlea, the events are translated into sequences of nervous information so that the transmission no more resembles what it represents than the currents in a television screen resemble the pictures which they carry – a linear code dictates the construction of a visible object."

Jonathan Miller – The Body in Question

No images of things in our minds: but only simultaneously relative fundamental, and individually completed, frequency modulations, expanded into simultaneously relative, and individually completed, differential equations. While actually functioning as truly humanistic elementary, and universally applicable, unidirectionally successive Time *made manifest*: as simultaneously relative to/from, and within, a single cognizable point time zero, and while actually occurring within our truly humanistic three-dimensional electrical potential mass minds, and parallel functioning central nervous systems.

And, remember, the definition of intellect is; "The power or faculty of the mind by which one knows or understands, as distinguished from that by which one feels and that by which one wills; the faculty of thinking and acquiring knowledge" – simply beginning to become capable of understanding Reality.

And – remember, the exact definition of a "humanistic" being, is –

"Candace Pert: I see the brain in terms of quantum mechanics – the brain is just a receiver, an amplifier, a little wet minireceiver for collective reality. We make maps, but we should never confuse the map with the territory' (while) the ratio of frontal core – to the rest of the cortex may be one index of evolutionary advancement – what the frontal lobes 'control' is something like awareness, or self-awareness – Do these lobes govern some essential feature of humanness or even godliness, as some scientists have suggested? 'If God speaks to man, if man speaks to God,' neuroscientist Candace Pert tells us, it would be through the frontal lobes."

The 3-Pound Universe – Judith Hooper and Dick Teresi

The ability to function quantum electrodynamically: simultaneously and in real time, while processing complex simultaneously relative multidimensional sensory input information, and/or Time *made manifest,* while actually functioning as Omnidimensional Reality.

And – remember, if there is no "syntax," and/or "synthetical structuring," contained within any "thing": in the entire universe, then "it": any and/or every thing and in the entire universe, is –

149

"There are two essential yet complementary aspects of this new vision of time which are as striking in contrast as heaven and hell. Heaven is ruled by dynamical equations that are reversible and 'timeless'; their simplicity ensures stability for eternity. Hell is more akin to the real world, where fluctuations, uncertainty and chaos reign..."

The Arrow of Time – Peter Coveney and Roger Highfield

The "reign of chaos," and/or hell made manifest: within their minds, and for eternity too.

Because – REMEMBER, we are –

"There are two essential yet complementary aspects of this new vision of time which are as striking in contrast as heaven and hell. Heaven is ruled by dynamical equations that are reversible and 'timeless'; their simplicity ensures stability for eternity. Hell is more akin to the real world, where fluctuations, uncertainty and chaos reign..."

The Arrow of Time – Peter Coveney and Roger Highfield

Surrounded by chaos.

So, why would any one individual ever move in any purposely effectuated direction, to simply allow themselves to "see" any two-dimensional representation of it: chaos and/or hell made manifest, when they could simply open their eyes, and see it: chaos and/or hell made manifest, functioning right in front of their brain dead aristocratic elite faces. The answer is, of course, because of their –

"At a purely chemical level (just as the injection of) heroin triggers release of dopamine – every experience humans find enjoyable – embracing a lover or savoring chocolate, amounts to little more than an explosion of dopamine in the nucleus accumbens, as exhilarating and ephemeral as a firecracker – dopamine, can be elevated by a hug, a kiss, a word of praise – Dopamine, like most biologically important molecules, must be kept within strict bounds – Too much causes the hallucinations, and bizarre thoughts, of schizophrenia – addicts' neurons assaulted by abnormally high levels of dopamine, have responded defensively and reduced the number of sites (or receptors) to which dopamine can bind – so while addicts begin by taking drugs to feel high, they end up taking them in order not to feel low."

Addicted – J. Madeleine Nash – Time – May 5, 1997

Truly humanistic brain dead aristocratic elite addiction: to abstracted dopamine biochemical inducing effectual stimulus of any, and/or all, kinds, while functioning as pure *pleasure*, and to simply enable their own selves to feel alive.

Which is as they: all individuals who have experienced truly humanistic brain death for their own selves, do continue to allow their very own selves to simply move, and/or be; "What is a black hole – A black hole is a region of empty space which acts as a center (of) attraction – The interior region – is defined by the fact that no matter, light, or signal of any kind can escape" – purposefully drawn into pure chaos, and death too, is simply because they have –

"The prefrontal cortex (is) a dopamine-rich area of the brain that controls impulsive and irrational behavior. Addicts, in fact, display many of the symptoms shown by patients who have suffered strokes or injuries to the prefrontal cortex. Damage to this region – destroys the emotional compass that controls behaviors that the patient (should) know are unacceptable."
Addicted – J. Madeleine Nash – Time – May 5, 1997

Lost control of their very own selves. Which is exactly why they would allow their very own selves: and/or souls, to be –

"Drug's Effect on Brain Is Extensive, Study Finds –
Heavy users (of highly addictive stimulants) are doing more damage to their brains than scientists had thought – This is the first study to show directly that brain damage (caused by addiction) produces deficits in learning and memory – In the study, Dr. (Nora) Volkow used an imaging technique (to) measure dopamine levels in the brains of 15 recovering addicts – The addicts (started out as) occasional users but over time the drug hijacked their natural dopamine systems..."
Sandra Blakeslee – The New York Times – Tuesday March 6, 2001

Hijacked: and led on a collision course with their very own destiny too.
Because – remember, all truly humanistic "languages" are, simply, the individually varied, and unidirectionally successive, abstracted function of the exact same harmoniously proportioned three-dimensional tones, expanded into, simple, harmoniously proportioned three-dimensional tonal variations: which are capable of being replicated upon a keyboard, and when conjoined, to form a language, can be identified as by their synthetical structuring, and/or intelligence. Which: universally applicable and elementary intelligence, as we can remember, must be –

"When you're 5 years old, and just about three feet tall, this is what you do in kindergarten class: 'I learn how to draw 5-2-1-6. I learn about 7. I learn e-k-g-s-k-c-w-x-y-z – It's like this: up and down'...that's just the beginning. By June, Miah and her kindergarten classmates will be expected to know – thirty-two reading words. Phonic sounds. How to read simple sentences. How to write numbers up to 20 and recognize number patterns. The basics of telling time and measurements...."
Monica Rhor – Philadelphia Inquirer – October 30, 1997

Learned by any one individual human being: within their individually affected mind, and parallel functioning central nervous system, while actually functioning as universally applicable Reality. Before it: universally applicable

Reality, can be communicated to any other human being.

So, if one individual human being, has never learned how to communicate their formed understanding of Reality, and/or if they simply have never actually even been enabled to form an understanding of Reality, then they will have no choice, but to make manifest "a" –

"Pablo Picaso: Cubism is neither the seed of a new art nor its germination: it represents a stage of development of original pictorial forms. Once realized these forms have a right to an independent existence."

Schizophrenic inarticulate cry for attention.

Which: the schizophrenic inarticulate cry for attention made by any one child, will – then, enable the child to receive –

"A baby passes her first amazing milestone before the typical mother has even wiped off the sweat of labor. Full-term newborns, scientists established in 1996, recognize and prefer their mother's face to all others – In the ingenious experiment, the scientists had babies suck a special pacifier that controlled a video monitor. Depending on how the infant sucked, fast or slow, the image of Mom or another woman appeared; babies sucked so they'd see Mom..."

Joan Raymond – Newsweek – Fall/Winter 2000

Their mother's breast to suckle. And/or –

"The psychopath is like an infant, absorbed in his own needs, vehemently demanding satiation' – One other point about the way in which psychopaths use language: Their 'Mental packages' are not only small but two-dimensional, devoid of emotional meaning..."

"Clustered in loose knots buried deep in the brain (are) neurons that produce molecular messengers – (within) the primitive structure that is one of the brain's key pleasure centers. At a purely chemical level (just as the injection of) heroin triggers release of dopamine – every experience humans find enjoyable – embracing a lover or savoring chocolate – amounts to little more than an explosion of dopamine in the nucleus accumbens, as exhilarating and ephemeral as a firecracker – dopamine, can be elevated by a hug, a kiss, a word a of praise..."

Dr. Robert D. Hare – Without Conscience

Addicted – J. Madeleine Nash – Time – May 5, 1997

An extreme dose of dopamine biochemical induction for their own selves to consume, actually functioning as pure *pleasure* only. Which is while allowing their own selves to remain the In Crowd, of the brain dead aristocratic elite. That is being allowed exposure to, and/or admittance into, the excessive brain dead aristocratic elite environment: wherein is located all of the excessive abstracted biochemical dopamine inducing stimulus, and/or drugs. And, of course, wherein: their brain dead excessive aristocratic elite environment of the In Crowd, everybody is speaking the exact same brain dead aristocratic elite language. Which is –

"I think that in schizophrenia the brain fragments into active and inactive clusters of neurons and different parts of the brain become disassociated,' says (Roy) King. 'You might get an asymmetry between the left and the right side, say. Schizophrenics often feel that their minds and bodies are split apart' – The litany of schizophrenic symptoms reads like a guidebook to the underworld. Most patients suffer from hallucinations, delusions, and 'thought disorders,' a category that includes impaired logic, jumbled thinking, bizarre ideas, and 'loose' associations. They may sound like beat poets out of control, employing skewed semantics, neologisms, stream-of-consciousness ramblings..."
The 3-Pound Universe – Judith Hooper and Dick Teresi

The language of schizophrenia.
Within which: all of their individually affected minds, there can be no single universally applicable, and cognizable, point time zero maintained. And no individually completed, and harmoniously proportioned, differential equations, actually functioning as individually completed, and harmoniously proportioned, geometrical equations, either: maintained, and/or functioning, within their minds. Which: individually completed, and harmoniously proportioned, non-tangible form geometrical equations, actually functioning as simultaneously relative to/from, and within, a single cognizable point time zero, is – remember, the –

"One way to think about this view is to imagine spatial relationships as a kind of universal language that the brain uses no matter what specific language – social, moral, engineering – we are using at the moment – (George) LaKoff believes he can tie this mental language to the physical structure of the brain and its maps – 'When you think about dynamic structure, you begin to think there are a lot of things that are analogous with life. Life is more pattern(s) in space/time than it is a set of particular physical things."
Jim Jubak – In the Image of the Brain

Universally applicable language of Reality: and/or Life.
So, if they: simultaneously relative individually completed, and harmoniously proportioned, non-tangible form geometrical equations, actually functioning while as simultaneously relative to/from, and within, a single cognizable point time zero, are not there: within their minds, then they: all of the individually affected human beings, are: as a matter of neuroscientific fact, truly humanistic brain dead. And too they: all of the individually affected human being minds, sure, as hell, can not –

"Candace Pert: I see the brain in terms of quantum mechanics – the brain is just a receiver, an amplifier, a little wet minireceiver for collective reality. We make maps, but we should never confuse the map with the territory (While) the ratio of frontal core may be one index of evolutionary advancement – 'If God speaks to man, if man speaks to God,' neuroscientist Candace Pert tells us, it would be through the frontal lobes ..."
The 3-Pound Universe – Judith Hooper and Dick Teresi

Function simultaneously, and quantum electrodynamically, in Reality: while attempting to cognize any Time *made manifest*.
And too remember, exactly what else, besides enabling any one individual to maintain control over their very own selves, and/or beginning to become capable of coming to an understanding of a more divinely purposeful existence for their own selves, the prefrontal cortex is directly responsible for –

"Paul MacLean, for one, considers the frontal lobes the 'heart' of the cortex – Clinically, there is evidence that the prefrontal cortex by looking inward, so to speak, obtains the gut feeling for identifying with another individual. In other words: empathy – Through its centers for vision, hearing, and bodily sensations, we traffic with the external world."
The 3-Pound Universe – Judith Hooper and Dick Teresi

Trafficking with the external world: and/or simply understanding Reality, while beginning to become capable of seeing past a single cognizable point time zero, at any one point within simultaneously relative space/time. And/or –

"Drugs Effect On Brain Is Extensive, Study Finds –
Heavy users (of highly addictive stimulants) are doing more damage to their brains than scientists had thought – At least a quarter of a class of molecules that help people feel pleasure and reward were knocked out – Some of the addict's brains resembled those of people with early and mild Parkinson's disease. But the biggest surprise is that another brain region responsible for spatial perception and sensation, which has never before been linked to (substance) abuse, was hyperactive and showed signs of scarring – the study's biggest surprise was that the addicts' parietal lobes, the parts of the brain used for feeling sensation and for recognizing where the body is in space, were metabolically overactive, Dr. (Nora) Volkow said – It is the equivalent of an inflammation or scarring response."
Sandra Blakeslee – The New York Times – Tuesday March 6, 2001

Beginning to become neurophysiologically capable of consciously cognizing simultaneously relative patterns in space/time: as simultaneously relative to/from, and within, a single cognizable point time zero.
And again remember, exactly how the prefrontal cortex does become

154

destroyed, while as through –

"The prefrontal cortex (is) a dopamine-rich area of the brain that controls impulsive and irrational behavior. Addicts, in fact, display many of the symptoms shown by patients who have suffered strokes or injuries to the prefrontal cortex. Damage to this region – destroys the emotional compass that controls behaviors that the patient (should) know are unacceptable..."
Addicted – J. Madeleine Nash – Time – May 5, 1997

Purposefully allowed exposure to all abstracted dopamine biochemical inducing effectual stimulus: which is every "thing," except Reality.
And – too, it: allowed exposure to all abstracted dopamine biochemical inducing effectual stimulus functioning as pure *pleasure,* and while never performing proportional amounts of purposefully affected reuptake function, and/or serotonin production, does enable an individual, to –

"Joyce Kovelman and Arnold Scheibel of UCLA's Brain Research Institute spotted a weird cellular 'disarray' in the schizophrenic brains – The pyramid-shaped cells of the hippocampus, normally arranged in an orderly manner, were grossly misaligned – A schizophrenic's dopamine neurons would start to fire in two different rhythms and rapidly become uncoupled – 'I think that in schizophrenia the brain fragments into active and inactive clusters of neurons and different parts of the brain become dissociated,' says (Roy) King. 'You might get an asymmetry between the left and right side, say' – Fortunately King had a Ph.D. in math from Cornell under his belt. He went to his computer, plugged in the variables for dopamine synthesis and released, in 1981, 'Catastrophe Theory of Dopaminergic Transmission: A Revised Dopamine Hypothesis of Schizophrenia' was published – The gist of the theory is that the key to schizophrenia is chaotic fluctuations in dopamine production..."
The 3-Pound Universe – Judith Hooper and Dick Teresi

Cause their own selves: all of the individual human beings who have allowed their own selves to become affected; by the con and as they have become victims themselves – because of their purposefully allowed exposure to excessive amounts of abstracted dopamine biochemical inducing effectual stimulus, actually functioning as pure *pleasure* only, to become neurophysiologically capable of only functioning while as in a purely schizophrenic manner, for their very own selves. Each and every one of them, and –

"Remember, blessed Jesu,
That I am the cause of Thy pilgrimage,
Do not forsake me on that day.

Seeking me Thou didst sit down weary,
Thou didst redeem me, suffering death on the cross.
Let not such toil be in vain.

Just and avenging Judge.
Grant remission
Before the day of reckoning.

I groan like a guilty man.
Guilt reddens my face.
Spare a suppliant, O God.

My prayers are not worthy,
But Thou in Thy merciful goodness grant
That I burn not in everlasting fire.

Place me among Thy sheep
And separate me from the goats,
Setting me on Thy right hand.

When the accursed have been confounded
And given over to the bitter flames,
Call me with the blessed.

I pray in supplication on my knees.
My heart contrite as the dust,
Safeguard my fate.

Mournful that day
When from the dust shall rise
Guilty man to be judged.
Therefore spare him, O God.
Merciful Jesu, Lord
Grant them rest."

Accursed and confused: by all of the psychopathic con-artists. And –

"Candace Pert – I see the brain in terms of quantum mechanics – the brain is
just a receiver, an amplifier, a little wet minireceiver for collective reality. We make
maps, but we should never confuse the map with the territory..."
The 3-Pound Universe – Judith Hooper and Dick Teresi

As a matter of neuroscientific fact.

And remember, as was exactly explained by the Son of God –

"Do not be afraid of those who kill the body but cannot kill the soul; fear him rather who can destroy both body and soul in hell. Can you not buy two sparrows for a penny? And yet not one falls to the ground without your Father knowing. Why, every hair on your head has been counted. So there is no need to be afraid; you are worth more than hundreds of sparrows."
Matthew 10: 28-31

Again. And –

"No servant can be the slave of two masters: he will either hate the first and love the second, or treat the first with respect, and the second with scorn. You cannot be the slave of both God and money."
Luke 16: 13

Again.
And remember too, as was exactly verified by 20th century neuroscientific research –

"PET-scan images of the brains of recovering – addicts reveal other striking changes, including a dramatically impaired ability to process glucose, the primary energy source for working neurons. Moreover, this impairment – is greatest in the prefrontal cortex..."
Addicted – J Madeleine Nash – Time – May 5, 1997

Again. And –

"Heavy users (of highly addictive stimulants) are doing more damage to their brains than scientists had thought – This is the first study to show directly that brain damage (caused by addiction) produces deficits in learning and memory – The addicts (started out as) occasional users but over time the drug hijacked their natural dopamine systems..."
Sandra Blakeslee – The New York Times – Tuesday March 6, 2001

Again.
Because: that those who have become confused by all of the worldly psychopathic con-artists are the accursed, is exactly because: in neuroscientific reality only of course, remember how a young child is only neurophysiologically capable of –

"At birth a baby's language of the senses is primitive: he sees vague shapes, or flashes of light, but without meaning. His eyes can neither focus nor follow a moving object. He is even farsighted since his eyeballs are foreshortened at birth. And what he sees is flat. He uses only one eye at a time, his eyes not yet working together to sight an object three-dimensionally..."
The Senses of Man – Joan Steen Wilentz

Understanding absolutely nothing: and/or being in possession of absolutely nothing, while including zero universally applicable empirical self-consciousness, for the young child to be in possession of. So all they can have: for their own selves, is the innocence of the child, while being in possession of zero truly humanistic universally applicable empirical self-consciousness too: they are actually capable of knowing, and/or understanding, absolutely nothing, for their own selves. And remember how their innocence does begin to become capable of becoming lost, and/or how a young child does begin to become capable of acquiring truly humanistic, universally applicable, empirical self-consciousness, and/or capable of understanding, and knowing, anything for their own selves, and which is while as through –

"Candace Pert: We've measured opiate receptors in everything from fruit fly heads to human brains. Even uni-cellular organisms have peptides' – Do you think even cockroaches feel some sort of emotion we ask – 'They have to, because they have chemicals that put them in the mood to mate and chemicals that make them run away when they're about to be killed. That's what emotions are about – pain and pleasure – punishment and reward. Even bacteria have a little hierarchy of primitive likes and dislikes. They're programmed to migrate toward or away from a chemotactic substance; they're little robots that go for sugar at all costs and away from salt. If you were designing a robot vehicle to walk into the future and survive, as God was when he designed human beings, you'd wire it up so that behavior that ensures survival of the species – would be naturally reinforcing. Behavior is controlled by the anticipation of pain or pleasure, punishment or reward. And that has to be coded in the brain."
The 3-Pound Universe – Judith Hooper and Dick Teresi

Universally applicable biochemical inductions: actually functioning as the absolute extreme of basic biological functioning capabilities within all living creatures, while as from one end of the universe to the other, and as *pleasure* and *pain*. And/or as dopamine and serotonin, and with a dopamine biochemical induction, being induced within any human being's parallel functioning mind, and central nervous system, while as through allowed exposure to all newly perceived effectual stimulus: while functioning as pure *pleasure*, and serotonin being induced, within any human being's parallel functioning mind and central nervous system, while as through –

158

"Princeton's (Barry) Jacobs believes that, based on experiments with cats, repetitive motor activity – walking, stimulates the release of serotonin..."
The Mood Molecule – Time – September 29, 1997 – Michael D. Lemonick

Allowed exposure to harmoniously proportioned amounts of truly humanistic nothingness only: functioning as *pain*, and while in exact proportional amount to the amount of biochemical dopamine effectual stimulus, functioning as *pleasure*. And which is only universally applicable Reality: and/or absolutely no allowed exposure to any amounts of abstracted biochemical dopamine inducing effectual stimulus, functioning as pure *pleasure* only.

So: Have you ever heard of "primary suggestibility," most people have, but they may not be familiar with the term. Well, primary suggestibility is –

"Two simple experiments reveal the power of suggestion in different contexts. The first looks at an individual's response to someone who is in a position of authority. An experimenter repeatedly gives the subject the same suggestion: for example, she tells the subject that his body is swaying. Soon his body will begin to sway. Not everyone is susceptible to this form of suggestibility – sometimes known as primary suggestibility, and neurotic people succumb more easily than 'well-balanced' individuals. In another famous experiment in the 1950's, the social psychologist Solomon Asch looked at group dynamics. He presented a group of seven to nine subjects with a card showing three lines of different lengths: the subjects were asked in turn to identify the one line that was the same length as a reference line shown on another card. The correct answer to the question was obvious – one line clearly matched the length of the reference line, but all the members of the group, except one, were experimental 'plants': they had been briefed by Asch to give an incorrect answer. The point of the experiment was to determine how far the true subject, the one 'innocent' member of the group, would go along with the others. The researchers found that only one in four individuals held out consistently against the view of the group, proving that the power of suggestion can sometimes override the evidence of our own senses."
David Cohen – The Secret Language of The Mind

The point in time when any one individual human being will – exactly, contradict whatever is exactly right if front of their very own eyes: and/or very own selves too, and even if it: the thing right in front of their very own eyes, is the simplest of perceivable absolute truths in reality: and/or universally applicable Reality itself, and/or pure science. And/or: primary suggestibility is, the point in time when any one individual human being, allows their very own selves to become confused, and/or afraid of being; "The researchers found that only one in four individuals held out consistently against the view of the group, proving that the power of suggestion can sometimes override the evidence of our own senses" – left out, and of the –

"Anyone who wants to win the broad masses must know the key that opens the door to their heart: propaganda tries to force a doctrine on the whole people – The whole art consists in doing this so skillfully that everyone will be convinced that the fact is real, the process necessary, the necessity correct, etc. But propaganda is not and cannot be the necessity in itself, since its function, like the poster, consists in attracting the attention of the crowd, and not in educating those who are already educated or who are striving after education – The progress and culture of humanity are not a product of the majority, but rest exclusively on the genius and energy of the personality – Some idea of genius arises in the brain of a man who feels called upon to transmit his knowledge to the rest of humanity. He preaches his view and gradually wins a certain circle of adherents. This process of the direct and personal transmittance of a man's ideas to the rest of his fellow men is the most ideal and natural: In the place of committee decisions, the principle of absolute responsibility was introduced (To):   Adolf Hitler."

Adolf Hitler – Mein Kamph

In Crowd that is. Which comprises all of the individuals, who are being allowed exposure to the excessive amounts of abstracted dopamine biochemical inducing effectual stimulus, actually functioning as pure *pleasure* only, and/or drugs. And/or truly humanistic brain death, or apathy that is also: that they remain confined to, and while only remaining ignorant of scientific Reality also. And/or everything, except for –

"The psychopath is like an infant, absorbed in his needs, vehemently demanding satiation' – Lying, deceiving, and manipulation are natural talents for psychopaths. With their powers of imagination in gear and focused on themselves, psychopaths appear amazingly unfazed by the possibility – or even the certainty, of being found out. When caught in a lie or challenged with the truth, they are seldom perplexed or embarrassed, they simply change their stories or attempt to rework the facts so that they appear to be consistent with the lie – One other point about the way in which psychopaths use language: Their 'Mental packages' are not only small but two-dimensional, devoid of emotional meaning – In some respects they are like emotionless androids depicted in science fiction, unable to imagine what real humans experience."

Dr. Robert D. Hare – Without Conscience

Their own personal physiological self-indulgences functioning as pure *pleasure,* and/or their drugs that is: they will remain only neurophysiologically capable of caring about. And/or their purposefully allowed exposure to abstracted dopamine biochemical inducing effectual stimulus, and any one individual who has allowed their very own selves to become a victim of the con.

And, here's why: in neuroscientific reality only of course, because –

"Dopamine, however, is more than just a feel-good molecule. It also exercises extraordinary power over learning and memory – Dopamine, like most biologically important molecules, must be kept within strict bounds – addicts' neurons assaulted by abnormally high levels of dopamine, have responded defensively and reduced the number of sites (or receptors) to which dopamine can bind – so while addicts begin by taking drugs to feel high, they end up taking them in order not to feel low."

Addicted – J. Madeleine Nash – Time – May 5, 1997

It is a neurophysiological impossibility for them: any one individual who has become affected, and a victim of the con, to care about anything, except for their "drugs."

Again, in the simplest English in the entire history of mankind, and to enable our: the entire world, own selves to simply understand: the absolute neuroscientific fact, for our own selves. Take a "plastic bag" and "wrap it around your head," and "tape it around your neck" too, and – now, begin to –

"Drugs are like sledgehammers' – 'They profoundly alter many pathways' – the realization that dopamine may be a common endpoint of all those pathways represents a signal advance. Provocative – the dopamine hypothesis provides a basic framework for understanding (what does) create a serious behavioral disorder..."

Addicted – J. Madeleine Nash – Time May 5, 1997

Understand exactly what an addiction "is": in neuroscientific Reality.

And: that they have actually allowed their very own selves to experience truly humanistic brain death and while actually becoming addicted, which is to –

"Clustered in loose knots buried deep in the brain (are) neurons that produce molecular messengers – (within) the primitive structure that is one of the brain's key pleasure centers. At a purely chemical level (just as the injection of) heroin triggers release of dopamine – every experience humans find enjoyable – embracing a lover or savoring chocolate – amounts to little more than an explosion of dopamine in the nucleus accumbens, as exhilarating and ephemeral as a firecracker – dopamine, can be elevated by a hug, a kiss, a word of praise – Dopamine, however, is more than just a feel-good molecule. It also exercises extraordinary power over learning and memory – Dopamine, like most biologically important molecules, must be kept within strict bounds – Too much causes the hallucinations, and bizarre thoughts, of schizophrenia – addicts' neurons assaulted by abnormally high levels of dopamine, have responded defensively and reduced the number of sites (or receptors) to which dopamine can bind – so while addicts begin by taking drugs to feel high, they end up taking them in order not to feel low."

Addicted – J. Madeleine Nash – Time – May 5, 1997

Everything: all abstracted biochemical dopamine inducing effectual stimulus that is, while actually functioning as pure *pleasure* only, and while including apathy too: and/or simply existing in ignorance of Reality. And to simply enable their very own selves, to; "so while addicts begin by taking drugs to feel high, they end up taking them in order not to feel low" – feel alive, and/or to simply enable their very own selves to become capable of breathing again. And/or, to simply enable their very own selves an opportunity to remain a part of the In Crowd: which *is* being allowed exposure to the purely pleasurable dopamine biochemical inducing stimulus, they *will* do –

"The chief priests and elders, however, had persuaded the crowd to demand the release of Barabbas and the execution of Jesus. So when the governor spoke and asked them, 'Which of the two do you want me to release for you?' they said, 'Barabbas.' 'But in that case,' Pilate said to them, 'what am I to do with Jesus who is called Christ?' They all said, 'Let him be crucified!' 'Why?' he asked. 'What harm has he done?'"
Matthew 27: 20-23

Absolutely anything: to enable their very own selves to remain a part of the In Crowd. Which is being allowed exposure to the abstracted dopamine biochemical inducing stimulus, actually functioning as pure *pleasure* that is: they will do absolutely anything – first: for their very own selves only. And to, simply, enable their very own selves to remain a part of the In Crowd, of the aristocratic elite. And they will *then* –

"The passers-by jeered at him; they shook their heads and said, 'So you would destroy the Temple and rebuild it in three days! Then save yourself! If you are God's son, come down from the cross! The chief priests and scribes and elders mocked him in the same way. 'He saved others,' they said, 'he cannot save himself. He is the king of Israel; let him come down from the cross now, and we will believe in him. For he did say, 'I am the son of God."
Matthew 27: 39-34

Justify it, and/or rationalize it: any way they possibly can. Which is as this word: rationalize, does mean: "To ascribe (one's acts, opinions, etc.) to causes that seem valid but actually are not true, possibly unconscious causes – to invent plausible explanations for acts, opinions, etc., that actually have other causes," in scientific reality only of course. But not within their: any one individual who has already become affected by the con, minds, and because it is a neurophysiological impossibility.

Because – remember, when any one individual human being does become addicted, they do begin to feel as though they simply cannot breathe: and/or as though they do have a plastic bag wrapped around their head, when they are not being allowed access to their drugs. Which is allowed access to all abstracted dopamine biochemical inducing effectual stimulus, actually functioning as pure *pleasure* only, and while including truly humanistic apathy too, and/or simply being told exactly what you want to hear, by any other human being. And – too, the feeling: of being simply incapable of feeling alive unless you are allowed access to the drug, does only become worse, and worse, with each passing day. Which: as any one individual does become continuously affected and grow worse with each passing day, does simply enable any one: who has become affected by the con, to begin to: neurophysiologically, actually become capable of effectually regressing back towards point time zero: of their own personally affected existence within simultaneously relative truly humanistic space/time, and for their own selves too. And, too remember, which is while – and simultaneously, moving in a direction back towards truly humanistic brain death, for their very own selves to experience: for their own selves to be in possession of, and for their very own selves only also. And/or towards the actual point of no return: they will be moving in a direction towards, and while in a purposefully effectuated direction towards the point of the event horizon line also, and of the black hole: while actually functioning as any space/time singularities, and/or pure chaos – discord and pain and death and suffering too, but which: the black hole, is capable of functioning as pure stimulus and/or "1": for themselves to consume, and for their own selves to be consumed by also.

Because – remember, they will have begun to become neurophysiologically incapable of consciously seeing: and/or consciously cognizing, past a single point, while at any one point within simultaneously relative space/time, and which can only be: neurophysiologically, the single point of their very own selves, and as they will, simultaneously, remain neurophysiologically incapable of experiencing any truly humanistic emotions, and/or truly humanistic empathy either: for any thing besides their very own selves, they will remain incapable of caring about. And which: that they have actually effectually regressed back towards point time zero, while beginning to experience truly humanistic brain death for their own selves, is as they have –

"The prefrontal cortex (is) a dopamine-rich area of the brain that controls impulsive and irrational behavior. Addicts, in fact, display many of the symptoms shown by patients who have suffered strokes or injuries to the prefrontal cortex. Damage to this region – destroys the emotional compass that controls behaviors that the patient (should) know are unacceptable."
Addicted – J. Madeleine Nash – Time – May, 5, 1997

Begun to lose control over their very own selves: remember? And they still need –

"Stone Cold Picnic –

WrestleMania XV ended the way it had to, the way any good populist fairy tale must: with the working man hero Stone Cold Steve Austin the new World Wrestling Federation champion, with the 20,000 fans who'd packed the First Union Center on their feet, and the WWF owner and Corporation bad guy Mr. McMahon on his knees and covered in Coors Light – along the way, there were the requisite helpings of blood and gore and bad language, Satanic symbols, broken tables, broken chairs, fireworks, men the size of SUV's and woman the shape of Barbie dolls – In the world of 'sports entertainment,' the outcomes are scripted, the finales are choreographed, and the guiding principle is 'Give the people what they want' – And the crowd eats it up – 'It makes you want more,' said fifteen-year-old Matt of Lansdale. I can't wait to see what they'll do next."

Jennifer Weiner – The Philadelphia Inquirer – March 30, 1999

More: and lots of it too. And to, simply, enable their very own selves, to become capable of feeling alive also.

So, somebody is –

"If the world hates you
remember that it hated me before you.
If you belonged to the world,
the world would love you as its own;
but because you do not belong to the world,
because my choice withdrew you from the world,
therefore the world hates you.
Remember the words I said to you:
A servant is not greater than his master.
If they persecuted me,
they will persecute you too;
if they kept my word,
they will keep yours as well.
But it will be on my account that they do all this,
because they do not know the one who sent me."

John 16: 18-21

Going to have to die: first, and before everybody dies too.

Because: everybody is going to die, soon. And too remember, which is as the function of this book, is to simply communicate an understanding: of Reality. And which is: in neuroscientific reality, no different than communicating an understanding of the fact that $2 + 2$ does equal 4: always and as an Absolute Truth also, and/or that all of simultaneously relative Reality is an absolute invariant under time translations, while actually functioning as Omnidimensional Time *made manifest,* and/or the explained theory of relativity. And/or –

"Jesus left the Temple, and as he was going away his disciples came up to him to draw his attention to the Temple buildings. He said to them in reply, 'You see all these things? I tell you solemnly, not a single stone here will be left on another: everything will be destroyed.' And when he was sitting at the Mount of Olives the disciples came and asked him privately, 'Tell us, when is this going to happen, and what will be the sign of your coming and the end of the world?'

And Jesus answered them, 'Take care that no one deceives you; because many will come using my name and saying, 'I am the Christ,' and they will deceive many. You will hear of wars and rumors of wars; do not be alarmed, for this is something that must happen, but the end will not be yet. For nation will fight against nation, and kingdom against kingdom. There will be famines and earthquakes here and there. All this is only the beginning of the birth pangs.

Then they will hand you over to be tortured and put to death; and you will be hated by all nations on account of my name. And then many will fall away; men will betray one another and hate one another. Many false profits will arise; they will deceive many, and with the increase of lawlessness, love in most men will grow cold; but the man who stands firm to the end will be saved.

This Good News of the kingdom will be proclaimed to the whole world as a witness to all the nations. And then the end will come."
Matthew 24: 1-14

The proof of The Eternal Harmony – The Kingdom of Heaven – The Mind of God made manifest, and the fact that Jesus of Nazareth is the Son of God too. Which is the function of this book: for all the world to simply see, and with their eyes alone also. Then the end will come, and which is the exact function of *The Annunciation.*

But too remember, which is not simply because of the function of this book that the end will come, but because of the real global dysfunction, of the majority of the world's global population. And/or the –

"What is a black hole? For astronomical purposes it behaves as a small, highly condensed dark 'body.' But it is not really a material body in the ordinary sense. It possesses no ponderable surface. A black hole is a region of empty space – which acts as a center of gravitational attraction – Since the black hole acts as a center of attraction it can draw new material towards it, which once inside can never escape..."
Roger Penrose – Black Holes – The World Treasury of Physics, Astronomy and Mathematics – Ed. Timothy Ferris

Black hole: of the dysfunction which is simply called unbridled truly humanistic conspicuous consumption. And/or self-lust only: that the overwhelming vast majority of mankind is now only capable of neurophysiologically experiencing, for their own selves. And which is, now, capable of; "The material thus swallowed

165

contributes to the effective mass of the black hole – Its attractive power likewise increases, so the alarming picture presents itself of an ever-increasing celestial vacuum cleaner" – simply consuming us: the entire world.

So, this is what they did: to allow themselves to become capable of affecting the greatest collective con in the history of mankind. Remember how a newly born child, is capable of being in possession of zero universally applicable empirical self-consciousness. Which is as they are: neurophysiologically, incapable of consciously knowing anything whatsoever, and – simultaneously, incapable of speaking the language: of universally applicable Reality, and/or any language for their own selves: to attempt to communicate anything – to enable their own selves to receive anything, and which: anything, they can not possibly get for their own selves, to be in possession of: any things, and/or abilities whatsoever. Except for the ability to make manifest –

"A baby passes her first amazing milestone before the typical mother has even wiped off the sweat of labor. Full-term newborns, scientists established in 1986, recognize and prefer their mother's face to all others – In the ingenious experiment, the scientists had babies suck a special pacifier that controlled a video screen. Depending on how the infant sucked, fast or slow, the image of Mom or another woman appeared; babies sucked so they'd see Mom..."
Joan Raymond – Newsweek – Fall/Winter

An inarticulate cry for attention: to enable their own selves to become capable of receiving what they do need from Mom or Dad, and/or their worldly authoritative god figures. Who: Mom and Dad functioning as a young child's worldly authoritative god figure, must explain the meaning of everything to a young child: who can consciously know nothing for their own selves. But who: a young child and in his innocence, can only experience truly humanistic Reality for their own selves, and as they cannot form an abstracted associated cognition of anything. Which: an abstracted associated cognition, and/or absolutely abstracted, and unidirectionally successive, knowledge, is the only thing that a parent, and/or worldly authoritative god figure, can simply give to a child, and/or truly humanistic brain death too. Because – remember, a young child is –

"Candace Pert: We've measured opiate receptors in everything from fruit fly heads to human brains. Even uni-cellular organisms have peptides' – Do you think even cockroaches feel some sort of emotion we ask – 'They have to, because they have chemicals that put them in the mood to mate and chemicals that make them run away when they're about to be killed. That's what emotions are about – pain and pleasure – punishment and reward – Behavior is controlled by the anticipation of pain or pleasure, punishment or reward. And that has to be coded in the brain."
The 3-Pound Universe – Judith Hooper and Dick Teresi

Only capable of physiologically reacting to the two extremes of basic biological, and physiological, reactionary capabilities, of: *pleasure* and *pain*. Which: the ability to respond to the two extremes of physiological reactionary capabilities and of *pleasure* and *pain*, is an ability which is encoded within the DNA of all living cells. And which: the ability to experience a simple dopamine biochemical induction actually functioning as pure *pleasure* and as we can remember, is the thing which does cause a young child to want to begin to become capable of gaining access to the key, which enables them to become capable of acquiring truly humanistic intelligence, and/or truly humanistic empirical self-consciousness: for their own selves to be in possession of. And – then, for themselves to: eventually, begin to become capable of gaining access to the key which is responsible for enabling their own selves, to become capable of being in possession of –

"Asked by the Pharisees when the kingdom of God was to come, he gave them this answer, 'The kingdom of God does not admit of observation and there will be no one to say, look here! Look there! For, you must know, the kingdom of God is within you."
Luke 17: 20-21

A truly humanistic Omnidimensional refractive gem of a mind, and parallel functioning central nervous system: for their own selves to be in possession of only. And the keys to The Eternal harmony – The Mind of God made manifest, and The Garden too: for their own selves to be in possession of also.

And remember, they: the aristocratic elite, can, and most usually, be in possession of –

"Then Jesus said to his disciples, 'I tell you solemnly, it will be hard for a rich man to enter the kingdom of heaven. Yes, I tell you again, it is easier for a camel to pass through the eye of a needle than it is for a rich man to enter the kingdom of heaven.' When the disciples heard this they were astonished. 'Who can be saved, then? they said. Jesus gazed at them. 'For men, he told them, this is impossible; for God everything is possible."
Matthew 19: 23-26

The key to absolutely nothing. Except for their own personally affected brain death, their addiction to tangible form mass stuff, and their control over other human beings. Which is exactly why they are so miserable.

So, have you ever heard the expression: "Misery loves company." Well, this is what they: all of the worldly psychopathic con-artists, did simply do: to enable their very own selves to become capable of affecting the greatest collective con in the entire history of mankind, so that they would not have to suffer all alone. They did simply take hold of –

"Adolf Hitler: Anyone who wants to win the broad masses must know the key that opens the door to their heart – propaganda tries to force a doctrine on the whole people – The whole art consists in doing this so skillfully that everyone will be convinced that (it) is real..."

Adolf Hitler's key: and/or his applied formula for enabling individual worldly psychopathic con-artists, to become capable of gaining control over any other individual human beings. Who: any one individual human being, may allow their own selves to become a; "The whole art consists in doing this so skillfully that everyone will be convinced" – victim of the con. And – again, which is exactly as this word: con, does mean: "to convince – to abuse the confidence of – to commit to memory – to direct the steering of," in neuroscientific reality only of course. And which: that they did simply employ the use of Adolf Hitler's applied formula for worldly political empowerment, was as they would simply enable all of their brain dead aristocratic elite friends, to move while as in a purposefully effectuated direction: towards the excessive psychopathic visual effectual stimulus of any and/or all kinds, and then enable them to begin to experience the orgy for their own selves to consume, while functioning as pure dopamine biochemical inducing effectual stimulus, and/or *pleasure*. And too which is as this word: orgy, does mean: "any proceedings marked by unbridled indulgence of passions," in Reality. And – then, to enable them: any one individual who is being allowed access to the abstracted dopamine biochemical inducing effectual stimulus, and while actually functioning as pure *pleasure*, to become capable of –

"After being released into the synapses (the gap between nerve endings and receiver cells), dopamine binds to receptors on the next neuron – the dopamine is either quickly reabsorbed or broken down by the enzyme monoamine oxidase."
Addicted – J. Madeleine Nash – Time – May 5, 1997

Having an orgasm, and/or reaching climax, for their own selves. And – too, which is as this word: orgasm, does mean: "intense or unrestrained excitement," and this word: climax, does mean: "the highest or most intense point in the development of something," in scientific reality, and which can be simply defined as a human being experiencing an: OHH. And – then after the climax, enabling all of the individuals: who have been allowed access to the spectacle of excessive dopamine biochemical inducing stimulus functioning as pure *pleasure*, to become capable of simply disassociating themselves from the reality before them: and/or a possible formed understanding of it, and then to –

"The little red wagon keeps flying along; imaginations can go flying on red wagons – 'A wagon unleashes a child's imagination – It can be anything a child imagines it to be..."
Cliff Edwards – Philadelphia Inquirer/A. P.-Saturday May 3, 1997

Reapply your childish imagination: while as in an attempt to define the experience which you were just allowed exposure to. And by the worldly psychopathic con-artists, who are functioning as any one individual's worldly authoritative god figures, and, too, which can be simply defined as a human being experiencing an: AHH.

Because – remember, any one individual human being who has begun to experience truly humanistic brain death for their own selves, and/or any newly born human being child who can be in possession of zero universally applicable empirical self-consciousness, will remain: neurophysiologically, capable of understanding absolutely nothing, for their own selves. So – too and simultaneously, they will become: neurophysiologically, capable of believing absolutely anything that they are told, and by any other individual human being too. And – too, we can remember, which is – and simultaneously, as any one individual human being, may begin to become capable of –

"Brainwashing: intense psychological indoctrination, usually political, for the purpose of displacing the individual's previous thoughts and attitudes with those selected by the regime or person inflicting the indoctrination."
Taber's Medical Dictionary

Becoming brainwashed: for their own selves, and by all worldly psychopathic con-artists.

And too and of course, while they have enabled their own selves to regress back to point time zero: of their own personally experienced existence within truly humanistic simultaneously relative space/time, and become capable of understanding absolutely nothing for their own selves, they can begin to become capable of –

"GLITZ BLITZ –
Contrary to the wisdom of socialites, you can be too rich and too thin. But you cannot be too honored – which is why there is as many awards shows as there are entertainers – Oscars, Grammys, Golden Globes. People's Choice, Soap Opera Digest. NAACP Image, Tejano Music, VH1 Fashion. They are proliferating so fast that statuette season has permanently replaced winter..."
Carrie Ricky – Philadelphia Inquirer – Saturday March 3, 2001

Worshiping their worldly gods: who are supplying them with allowed access to all of the abstracted psychopathic dopamine biochemical inducing stimulus, while functioning as pure *pleasure* only, and/or drugs.

And – too and of course, while they are – also and simultaneously, only neurophysiologically capable of functioning as young children, and while remaining dependent upon their worldly gods, to supply them with allowed access to all excessive dopamine biochemical inducing stimulus, actually functioning as pure *pleasure*, they will also and simultaneously and as we can remember, become capable of only experiencing the two extremes of basic biological reactionary capabilities for themselves, and which is *pleasure* and *pain*. Which: while actually functioning as pure *pleasure*, will be only a sense of awe that they are capable of experiencing: for their own selves, and – exactly, while as through their allowed exposure to the purely pleasurable dopamine biochemical inducing stimulus. And so, they will begin to become capable of –

"Rose Rage: An Interview Stirs A Storm –
It was supposed to be a night to stand in awe of the greatest baseball players of our lifetimes – but the minute the baseball pooh-bahs decided to allow Rose into the ballpark Sunday night for the hallowed All-Century team ceremonies, they should have known that this journey back in baseball time was going to careen off into a whole different neighborhood..."
Jayson Stark – The Philadelphia Inquirer – Tuesday October 26, 1999

Standing in awe in front of their worldly gods: who are supplying them with allowed access to all of their excessive dopamine biochemical inducing stimulus, functioning as pure *pleasure* only, and the beginning of their own personally affected truly humanistic brainwashing too.
And of course also, as they: all of the individually affected victims of the psychopathic con-artists, do begin to become capable of allowing their very own selves to become brainwashed: by the psychopathic con-artists who are allowing them exposure to all of the dopamine biochemical inducing stimulus only and which is while functioning as pure *pleasure*, which will be: that all of the individually affected human beings are actually allowing themselves to become victims of the con, while – and simultaneously as they are becoming brainwashed, the psychopathic con-artists will be telling them: all of the individually affected victims of the con, that they are –

"Stars to party with Clintons –
Tapping his long list of famous friends, President Clinton is throwing a new year's celebration so glitzy and large it might be easier to guess who's *not* coming to dinner – Roughly 1,000 people – ranging from Muhammad Ali to Elizabeth Taylor – will descend upon the White House on New Year's Eve – 'It's meant to reflect all of that's best about America,' said Marsha Berry, first lady's spokeswoman. These people have been invited because they've achieved greatness..."
Sanyo Ross – AP – The Philadelphia Inquirer – Friday December 17, 1999

A very small part of truly humanistic greatness, and/or that they are beginning to become capable of functioning as truly virtuous humanistic beings.
And too of course, because no humanistic society would ever publicly admit, that they are –

"Ads Suggest the Pitfalls Of Losing Art Education –

At the beginning of a television commercial that will be broadcast tomorrow, a boy, about 10 years old, walks past a street musician playing a violin, looks toward him, and blurts, 'Get a job' – The commercial, for Americans for the Arts, a national arts advocacy organization, is part of a large public service campaign to support financing for arts education..."

The New York Times – Saturday January 26, 2002

Only capable of functioning as psychopaths are capable of functioning. Which is while being concerned, only, with their own: excessive, personal physiological self-indulgences: functioning as unbridled conspicuous consumption, of psychopathic dopamine biochemical inducing stimulus, actually only functioning as pure *pleasure*: only.

So, what the psychopathic con-artists did simply do: to enable their own selves to become capable of simply affecting the con, was to begin to become capable of only brainwashing all of their individually affected victims, into believing that it: gaining access to truly humanistic intelligence, and/or a truly virtuous humanistic existence for our own selves, and/or a formed understanding of a more divinely purposeful existence for our own selves to be in possession of, and, too, which is while beyond that which an animal is *only* capable of experiencing for their own selves, is: "Just that easy." **NO IT IS EXACTLY NOT**: within identifiable neuroscientific Reality. That is only the exact definition of –

"The psychopath is like an infant, absorbed in his own needs, vehemently demanding satiation' – Psychopaths (do also) display a general lack of empathy. Psychopaths are very good at giving their undivided attention to things that interest them most and at ignoring other things. Some clinicians have likened this process to a narrow-beam search-light that focuses on only one thing at a (point in) time (While) Their 'Mental packages' are not only small but two-dimensional, devoid of emotional meaning – Psychopaths seem to suffer a kind of emotional poverty that limits the range and depth of their feelings. While at times they appear cold and unemotional, they are prone to dramatic, shallow, and short-lived displays of feeling. Careful observers are left with the impression that they are play-acting and that little is going on below the surface – Sometimes they claim to experience strong emotions but are unable to describe the subtleties of various affective states. For example, they equate love with sexual arousal, sadness with frustration and anger with irritability (There are) similarities between EEG's (record brain waves) of adult psychopaths – and those of children (while displaying symptoms) including egocentricity, impulsivity, selfishness, and unwillingness to delay gratification – To some investigators, this suggests little more than a developmental delay. Harvard psychologist Robert Kegan, for example, has argued that behind (the psychopath's) 'Mask of sanity' lies not insanity but a young child of nine or ten – Psychopaths are easily bored (and they) have an ongoing and excessive need for excitement – In

171

some respects they are like the emotionless androids depicted in science fiction, unable to imagine what real humans experience."

Dr. Robert D. Hare – Without Conscience

Individually affected truly humanistic brain death at best: for all of the individually affected victims of the psychopathic con-artists to be in possession of only, and for their own selves. And/or –

"Schizophrenics don't do well at cocktail parties,' says (E. Fuller) Torrey (who himself has a schizophrenic sister). 'They simply can't process all the incoming stimuli. So they withdraw. The limbic sensory-processing equipment isn't doing a good job. In order to communicate at all, the schizophrenic has to use the simplest mechanisms in the brain – the reptilian brain: It's like having you're leg crippled from polio and trying to walk as best you can' – 'From early on,' says Alan F. Mirsky – 'schizophrenics find it difficult to distinguish between signal and noise and to assign levels of importance to various classes of stimuli. Everything becomes important; nothing is trivial' – Add to this a distorted sense of self, a feeling of personal unreality, often coupled with a distorted body image' – The litany of schizophrenic symptoms reads like a guidebook to the underworld. Most patients suffer from hallucinations, delusions, and 'thought disorders,' a category that includes impaired logic, jumbled thinking, bizarre ideas, and 'loose' associations. They may sound like beat poets out of control, employing skewed semantics, neologisms, stream-of-consciousness ramblings, punning, echolalia (parroting), and 'word salads.' E. Fuller Torrey – once quizzed a hundred schizophrenic patients on the meaning of the proverb 'People who live in glass houses shouldn't throw stones.' Only a third were able to supply the standard explanation; all the others gave extravagant, overly literal, or highly personalized translations – Joyce Kovelman and Arnold Scheibel of UCLA's Brain Research Institute spotted a weird cellular 'disarray' in the schizophrenic brains (and not in the matched controls). The pyramid-shaped cells of the hippocampus, normally arranged in an orderly manner, were grossly misaligned – A schizophrenic's dopamine neurons would start to fire in two different rhythms and rapidly become uncoupled – 'I think in schizophrenia the brain fragments into active and inactive clusters of neurons and different parts of the brain become disassociated,' says (Roy) King. 'You might get an asymmetry between the left and right side, say. Schizophrenics often feel that their minds and bodies are split apart – What I saw was that people were fluctuating between opposite states,' he tells us. 'And a light bulb went off in my head. I saw that the key to psychotic behavior was not too much or too little of a specific neurotransmitter. It was the unstable fluctuations in a chemical system' (The theory is that) the key to schizophrenia is chaotic fluctuations in dopamine production – Robert G. Heath: 'The primary symptom of schizophrenia isn't hallucinations or delusions,' he tells us. 'It's a defect in the pleasure response. Schizophrenics have a predominant of painful emotions. They function in an almost continuous state of fear or rage, fight or flight, because they don't have the pleasure to neutralize it – schizophrenics are extremely insensitive to pain – and (are) unreactive to other sensory stimuli, as well' – psychiatrist Monte Buchsbaum – measured patient's brain-wave responses to electrical shocks and auditory signals and found these EEG's to be abnormally flat, specifically at higher levels of intensity. He concluded that – schizophrenics were 'reducers' (as opposed to augmenters), that their brains naturally reduced, or dampened, stimuli..."

The 3-Pound Universe – Judith Hooper and Dick Teresi

The absolute end of Time *made manifest,* and/or complete and absolute death for our entire global society.

Because remember, the absolute last thing a society is supposed to do, is simply –

"Ernst Hanfstaengl, describes the shapelessness at the root of Hitler's mesmerizing oratorical power: 'His brain was a sort of primeval jelly or ectoplasm which quivered in response to every impulse from its surroundings – You could never pin him down, say that he was this thing or that thing, it was all floating, without roots, intangible and mediumistic – Momentum had driven him into an extreme position from which there was no escape – What has been so far the ultimate violence in human history can also be considered as a ghastly kind of artistic production – performance art at its largest, impressing upon an otherwise inattentive public certain feelings and ideas – He was a tremendous salesman of ideas..."

Michael Nelken M. D. – Hitler Unmasked

Give the keys to the kingdom to the schizophrenics, and because – then, everybody dies.

And too remember, as this self-evident universally applicable truth, was exactly explained by Thomas Jefferson –

"...I hold, (without appeal to revelation) that when we take a view of the universe, in its parts, general or particular, it is impossible for the human mind not to perceive and feel a conviction of design, consummate skill, and indefinite power in every atom of its composition. The movements of the heavenly bodies, so exactly held in their course by the balance of centrifugal and centripetal forces; the structure of our earth itself...We see, too, evident proofs of the necessity for a superintending power, to maintain the universe in its course and order. Stars, well known, have disappeared, new ones have come into view; comets, in their incalculable course, may run foul of suns and become extinct; and require renovation under other laws; certain races and animals are become extinct; and were there no restoring power, all existences might extinguish successively, one by one, until all should be reduced to shapeless chaos. So irresistible are these evidences of an intelligent and powerful Agent, that, of the infinite numbers of men who have existed through all time, they have believed, in the proportion of a million at least to unit, in the hypothesis of an eternal pre-existence of a Creator, rather than in that of a self-existent universe..."

Also.

And remember, which: that the individuals which comprise a society can begin to become capable of forming a truly humanistic foundation for their own selves, is only capable of becoming effectuated: within their individually affected truly humanistic parallel functioning minds and central nervous systems, as they: all individual human beings, do begin to become capable of acquiring truly humanistic universally applicable empirical self-consciousness, for their own selves to be in possession of.

And, too – remember, Thomas Paine, in his explanation of the function of the universally applicable Common Sense of mankind, did –

"The wise, and the worthy, need not the triumph of a pamphlet: The cause of America is in a great measure the cause of all mankind. Many circumstances hath, and will arise, which are not local, but universal, and through which the principles of all lovers of mankind are affected, and in the event of which, their affections are interested – There are injuries which nature cannot forgive; she would cease to be nature if she did – The Almighty hath implanted in us these inextinguishable feelings for good and wise purposes – They are the guardians of his image in our hearts. They distinguish us from the herd of common animals – I draw my idea of a form of government from a principle in nature, which no art can overturn, viz. that the more simple anything is, the less liable it is to be disordered…And when a man seriously reflects on the idolatrous homage which is paid to the persons of Kings, he need not wonder, that the Almighty, ever jealous of his honor, should disapprove of a form of government which so impiously invades the prerogative of heaven – O ye that love mankind! Ye that dare oppose, not only the tyranny, but the tyrant, stand forth! Every spot of the world is over-run with oppression – O! Receive the fugitive, and prepare in time an asylum for mankind: But where says some is the King of America? I'll tell you Friend, he reigns above, and doth not make havock of mankind like the Royal – of Britain. Yet that we may not appear to be defective even in earthly honors, let a day be solemnly set apart for proclaiming the charter; let it be brought forth on the Divine law, the word of God; let a crown be placed thereon, by which the world may know, that so far as we approve of monarchy, that in America THE LAW IS KING."

Also plainly communicate his formed understanding of this self-evident universally applicable truth.

It: the formation of the world's first Truly Idealist Democratic Society which did pay homage to NO man, WAS A REVOLUTIONARY CONCEPT.

It was a revolutionary concept: That the overwhelming vast majority, of a society, did not enable their very own selves to become enveloped by the vortex, which is truly humanistic dysfunction, and did not, simply, enable their very own selves to become capable of experiencing truly humanistic brain death for their own selves. And which would be: then and as any society becomes enveloped by the vortex of truly humanistic dysfunction, and while enabling their own selves to become capable of experiencing truly humanistic brain death also, to enable their own selves to become victims of the con, and as miserable as the Monarch was, and Adolf Hitler too.

And it: truly humanistic brain death and becoming a victim of the con too, is the only thing: in the entire history of mankind and within the entire universe also, which is: Just that easy.

Because – remember, we do now know: for an absolute neuroscientific fact, that the very definition of humanistic intelligence, is –

"Candace Pert: I see the brain in terms of quantum mechanics – the brain is just a receiver, an amplifier, a little wet minireceiver for collective reality. We make maps, but we should never confuse the map with the territory' (while) the ratio of frontal core may be one index of evolutionary advancement – What the frontal lobes 'control' is something like awareness, or self-awareness – Do these lobes govern some essential feature of humanness, or even godliness, as some scientists have suggested? 'If God speaks to man, if man speaks to God,' neuroscientist Candace Pert tells us, 'it would be through the frontal lobes' – Stephen LaBarge: 'And it's capable of what look like miraculous things, so miraculous that we're tempted to say it's divine, that it's not natural."

The 3-Pound Universe – Judith Hooper and Dick Teresi

The uniquely humanistic ability, to purposefully consciously cognize simultaneously relative patterns in space/time: while actually functioning quantum electrodynamically, and as simultaneously relative to/from, and within, a single cognizable point time zero. And which: the uniquely humanistic simultaneously relative patterns in space/time, is while actually functioning as the universally applicable function of Omnidimensional Time *made manifest* – The Mind of God made manifest – The Eternal Harmony, and our Innocence Lost too. And too remember, which is: only and in the entire history of mankind, the function of *The Annunciation* and/or *a prioi* Omnidimensional Reality, and/or Wolfgang Amadeus Mozart's Requiem Mass.

Which: actually beginning to become capable of purposefully consciously cognizing Omnidimensional Time *made manifest*, any one individual can begin to become capable of doing: only for their very own selves, as they do, actually, begin to become capable of forming uniquely humanistic universally applicable empirical self-consciousness, and for their very own selves to be in possession of. And/or, remember, "truly humanistic" –

"One thing has become clear to scientists: memory is absolutely crucial to our consciousness – 'There's almost nothing you do, from perception to thinking, that doesn't draw continuously on your memory. (And) It can't be otherwise, since there really is no such thing as a present (while) memory provides a personal context, a sense of self and a sense of familiarity – past and present and a frame for the future' – But memory is not a single phenomenon. 'We don't have a memory system in the brain' – 'We have memory systems, each playing a different role' – All of these different systems of memory are ultimately stored in the brain's cortex – what's happening when the brain forms memory (is that) it's the connections between nerve cells – and particularly the strength of those connections, that are altered by experience (as) the cells are firing simultaneously (and) coordinating different sets of information – When everything is going right, these different systems work together seamlessly. If you're taking a bicycle ride, for example, the memory of how to operate the bike comes from one set of neurons; the memory of how to get from here to the other side of town comes from another; the nervous feeling you have left over from taking a bad spill last time out comes from still another. Yet you are never aware that your mental experience has been assembled, bit by bit, like some invisible edifice inside your brain..."

Michael D. Lemonick – Smart Genes? – Time – September 13, 1999

Memory.

So we can now know, for a verified and absolute neuroscientific fact, exactly what they: all of the worldly psychopathic con-artists and in the entire history of mankind, did actually steal, was mankind's universally applicable empirical self-consciousness, and/or their souls. And too which: as individual human beings did allow their own selves to become victims *of* the worldly psychopathic con-artists, was while actually functioning as mankind's collective consciousness, that they became capable of betraying. And for the psychopathic con-artists to become capable of –

"Do not be afraid of them therefore. For everything that is now covered will be uncovered, and everything now hidden will be made clear. What I say to you in the dark, tell in the daylight, what you hear in whispers, proclaim from the housetops.

Do not be afraid of those who kill the body but cannot kill the soul; fear him rather who can destroy both body and soul in hell. Can you not buy two sparrows for a penny? And yet not one falls to the ground without your Father knowing. Why, every hair on your head has been counted. So there is no need to be afraid; you are worth more than hundreds of sparrows.

So if anyone declares himself for me in the presence of men, I will declare myself for him in the presence of my Father in heaven. But the one who disowns me in the presence of men, I will disown in the presence of my Father in heaven."

Matthew 10: 26-33

Consuming: and while enabling their very own selves to become capable of becoming consumed also.

Which is exactly why, the Son of God is also defined as –

"And he began to teach them that the Son of Man was destined to suffer grievously, to be rejected by the elders and the chief priests and scribes, and to be put to death, and after three days to rise again; and said all this quite openly. Then, taking him aside, Peter started to remonstrate with him. But, turning and seeing his disciples, he rebuked Peter and said to him, 'Get behind me Satan! Because the way you think is not God's but man's."
Mark 27: 20-23

The Son of Man: Because He is the Collective Consciousness of Mankind.

Which is exactly why, the Son of God did have to make manifest the perceivable proof, of the function that is worldly primary suggestibility. Simply because: as individuals do begin to become victims of the con, and begin to experience truly humanistic brain death for their own selves, they: all of the individual victims of the con, will begin to become neurophysiologically incapable of understanding anything for their own selves, and – simultaneously, begin to become capable of believing *only* exactly what they are being told to believe: by their worldly gods, who are controlling them.

Because – remember, once an individual has –

"Alas for you, scribes and Pharisees, you hypocrites! You who shut up the kingdom of heaven in men's faces, neither going in yourselves nor allowing others to go in who want to."
Matthew 23: 13

Begun to enable their own selves to become capable of experiencing truly humanistic brain death, for their own selves to be in possession of *only*, words can –

"Alas for you, scribes and Pharisees, you hypocrites! You who pay your tithe of mint and dill and cumin and have neglected the weightier matters of the Law – justice, mercy, good faith! These you should have practiced, without neglecting the others. You blind guides! Straining out gnats and swallowing camels!

Alas for you, scribes and Pharisees, you hypocrites! You who clean the outside of the cup and dish and leave the inside full of extortion and intemperance. Blind Pharisee! Clean the inside of the cup and dish first so that the outside may become clean as well.

Alas for you, scribes and Pharisees, you hypocrites! You who are like white-washed tombs that look handsome on the outside, but inside are full of dead men's bones and every kind of corruption. In the same way you appear to people from the

outside like good honest men, but inside are full of hypocrisy and lawlessness."
Matthew 23: 23-28

Have no effect.

Except, of course, to enable them to begin to become capable of understanding, that somebody may begin to become capable of exposing the absolute truth. And so that they: the psychopathic con-artists, may – then, begin to become capable of losing control over that which enables them to feed their addiction: to all worldly stuff, while including worldly power. Which: worldly power, does – and simultaneously, enable them to continue to feed their addiction: to every thing, and while including worldly power. Which they cannot possibly live without: worldly power, and their control over other human beings. Because: remember, they are in possession of absolutely nothing for their own selves, except for their personally experienced truly humanistic brain death, and their addiction: to all their worldly stuff.

So, as somebody does begin to become capable of exposing the absolute truth, they: all of the worldly psychopathic con-artists, will simply –

"The Pharisees, who loved money, heard all this and laughed at him. He said to them, 'You are the very ones who pass yourselves off as virtuous in people's sight, but God knows your hearts. For what is thought highly of by men is loathsome in the sight of God."
Luke 16: 14-15

Create a diversion: from Reality.

And too, they: the worldly psychopathic con-artists, did – always, continue to laugh all the way to their worldly banks, and to their worldly graves also. But, now, we can know and for a verified scientific fact, that this, is when the –

"But alas for you who are rich: you are having your consolation now. Alas for you who have your fill now: you shall go hungry. Alas for you who laugh now: you shall mourn and weep. Alas for you when the world speaks well of you! This was the way their ancestors treated the false prophets."
Luke 6: 24-26

Laughter does stop.

And, of course, as the absolute scientific truth is being exposed: that they have actually experienced truly humanistic brain death for their own selves, and allowed themselves to become capable of only functioning while as in a purely psychopathic, and/or schizophrenic, manner, they: all of individual worldly psychopathic con-artists, will –

"Besides being impulsive – doing things on the spur of the moment – psychopaths are highly reactive to perceived insults or slights. Most of us have powerful inhibitory controls over our behavior – In psychopaths, these inhibitory controls are weak, and the slightest provocation is sufficient to overcome them. As a result, psychopaths are short-tempered or hot-headed, and tend to respond to frustration, failure, discipline, and criticism with sudden violence, threats, and verbal abuse. They take offense easily and become angry and aggressive over trivialities, and often in a context that seems inappropriate to others."
Dr. Robert D. Hare – Without Conscience

Simply perceive it: the fact of their own personally affected dysfunction, as an insult.

And simple to understand now: because of verified 20th century neuroscientific research, and while simply understanding exactly what; "You blind guides! Straining out gnats and swallowing camels" – straining out gnats and swallowing camels, does mean in scientific reality, and while actually functioning as blind guides also. Because, who exactly do you think was –

"Pablo Picaso: Cubism is neither the seed of a new art nor its germination: it represents a stage of development of original pictorial forms. Once realized these forms have a right to an independent existence."

Standing in front of all of those two-dimensional brain dead Cubist things. And while with their –

"The Penis as Text for Serious Thinkers –
Lyndon B. Johnson once answered reporters badgering him about why the United States was in Vietnam with a simple, unmistakable off-the-record gesture: he unzipped, pulled out his penis and said, 'This is why!'"
Emily Nussbaum – The New York Times – Saturday December 22, 2001

Hands on their penises: masturbating upon the collective consciousness of mankind, and while –

"The Barnes vs. Reality –
Latches Lane is a quiet place these days. No buses block the streets. There are no protesters, no police, no yellow hazard tape. After a rancorous decade of lawsuit and countersuit, the Barnes Foundation is bruised, but gamely carrying on. Its endowment is gone. Its daily finances are teetering. But the Merion institution still houses one of the great art collections in the world, and it still cleaves to its mission of using art to teach the world how to think and see..."
Stephen Salisbury – The Philadelphia Inquirer – Sunday October 28, 2001

Conning the entire world into believing, that they: the psychopathic con-artists and who were actually functioning as blind guides, were teaching them: all of the individually affected victims of the con, how to think: understand universally applicable *a priori* Reality, and see: not begin to become capable of experiencing truly humanistic brain death, for their own selves. And which, of course, does simply mean: in scientific reality only of course and within all of the individually affected victims too, that the function was –

"Lying, deceiving, and manipulation are natural talents for psychopaths. With their powers of imagination in gear and focused on themselves, psychopaths appear amazingly unfazed by the possibility – or even the certainty – of being found out. When caught in a lie or challenged with the truth, they are seldom perplexed or embarrassed – they simply change their stories or attempt to rework the facts so that they appear to be consistent with the lie – Psychopaths have what it takes to defraud and bilk others: They are fast-talking, charming, self-assured, at ease in social situations, cool under pressure, unfazed by the possibility of being found out, and totally ruthless. And even when exposed, they can carry on as if nothing has happened, often leaving their accusers bewildered and uncertain about their own positions – Given their personality, it comes as no surprise that psychopaths make good impostors...."
Dr. Robert D. Hare – Without Conscience

Exactly backwards: as is everything, and it is a scientific fact.
So that, because of 20th century neuroscientific research, we can now know, that everything – every thing, that they: all of the worldly psychopathic con-artists and in the entire history of mankind too, taught, is exactly backwards, and – too and simultaneously, all they ever did actually do: in the entire history of mankind too, was to simply create truly humanistic dysfunction: truly humanistic brain death, and truly humanistic physiological death also. Which was while actually functioning as blind guides, and –

"Alas for you, scribes and Pharisees, you hypocrites! You who shut up the kingdom of heaven in men's faces, neither going in yourselves nor allowing others to go in who want to."
Matthew 23: 13

Beginning to become capable of causing other individual human beings, to begin to become capable of experiencing truly humanistic brain death, for their own selves. Which was while actually regressing back towards point time zero, of their effectuated existence within truly humanistic simultaneously relative space/time, and beyond, and which is while – then, beginning to lose control over their very own selves.
Which: the fact of the function that actually is the con, is simple to

understand, for all the world to simply see, with our eyes alone too. Exactly simply because, they: all of the worldly psychopathic con-artists in the entire history of mankind, were the exact same ones: individually affected human beings, who were standing in front of all of those two-dimensional brain dead Cubist things, and/or any two-dimensional thing in the entire history of mankind that does not contain a representation of syntax, and there is only the one of *The Annunciation*. Which was actually occurring, while – and simultaneously, they: all of the individually affected victims who were in possession of a three-dimensional electrical potential mass of a mind, within which there are contained no images of things, did simply allow their very own selves, to –

"At birth a baby's language of the senses is primitive: he sees vague shapes, or flashes of light, but without meaning. His eyes can neither focus nor follow a moving object. He is even farsighted since his eyeballs are foreshortened at birth. And what he sees is flat. He uses only one eye at a time, his eyes not yet working together to sight an object three-dimensionally..."
The Senses of Man – Joan Steen Wilentz

Effectually regress back to point time zero: within their individually affected three-dimensional electrical potential mass minds, and parallel functioning central nervous systems, and as a matter of scientific fact. They did, actually, simply allow their very own selves, to become capable of experiencing truly humanistic brain death, for their own selves: because they never practiced their scales of truly humanistic simultaneously relative *a priori* Reality. And they never performed a proportional amount of purposefully effectuated reuptake function, calcium induction/production, and/or serotonin induction/production, within their own individually affected minds, and parallel functioning central nervous systems. Which did – then and simultaneously, begin to become incapable of functioning quantum electrodynamically: simultaneously and in parallel, and while cognizing Time *made manifest* and/or beyond a two-dimensional plane, and/or a single point while at any one point within simultaneously relative space/time. And which was, as they: all of the individually affected victims and while as in the entire history of mankind, did allow their very own selves to become –

"Each of us lives within the universe – the prison – of his own brain. Projecting from it are millions of fragile sensory nerve fibers, in groups, uniquely adapted to sample the energetic states of the world about us: heat, light, force, and chemical compositions. That is all we ever know directly; all else is logical inference..."
The 3-Pound Universe – Judith Hooper and Dick Teresi

An absolute prisoner of: and/or confined to, their own personal, and biochemically affected: dysfunctional – fragmented – paranoid delusional –

obsessive compulsive – psychopathic and schizophrenic, random and chaotic
agglomeration of individual nerve cells. Wherein: their own personal, and
absolutely dysfunctional, random agglomeration of individual nerve cells, there can
be no simultaneously relative single cognizable point time zero maintained, it is –

"Ernst Hanfstaengl, describes the shapelessness at the root of Hitler's
mesmerizing oratorical power: 'His brain was a sort of primeval jelly or ectoplasm
which quivered in response to every impulse from its surroundings – You could
never pin him down, say that he was this thing or that thing, it was all floating,
without roots, intangible and mediumistic – Momentum had driven him into an
extreme position from which there was no escape – What has been so far the ultimate
violence in history can also be described as a ghastly kind of artistic production –
performance art at its largest, impressing upon an otherwise inattentive public certain
feelings and ideas – He was a tremendous salesman of ideas..."
Michael Nelken M. D. – Hitler Unmasked

A neurophysiological impossibility.
But which: that they had experienced truly humanistic brain death for their
own selves, and while functioning as blind guides and as psychopathic con-artists
too, was while actually beginning to become capable of conning the world, into
believing that –

"Picasso And Einstein cross paths, and offer a mirthful night –
In the program for *Picasso at the Lapin Agile*, which opened Tuesday at the
Arden Theater, the director, cast and staff pose 20 questions you might ponder after
viewing the play. 'What is genius? they ask. How does genius get recognized..."
Clifford A. Ridley – The Philadelphia Inquirer – Thursday March 8, 2001

They: all of the psychopathic con-artists, and in the entire history of mankind
too, were simply functioning as truly intelligent, and/or virtuous, human beings.
And which: in neuroscientific reality only of course, is simply –

"Psychopaths are notorious for not answering the question posed them or for
answering in a way that seems unresponsive to the question – It is *how* they string
words and sentences together, not *what* they actually say, that suggests abnormality
– It now appears that the communications of psychopaths sometimes are subtly odd
and part of a general tendency to 'Go off track.' That is, they frequently change
topics, go off on irrelevant tangents, and fail to connect phrases and sentences in a
straightforward manner...Jack was a mile-a-minute talker, with the psychopath's
characteristic ability to contradict himself from one sentence to the next..."
Dr. Robert D. Hare – Without Conscience

A contradiction: their minds that is. And to –

"...As we found with quantum mechanics, the full structure of the world is richer than our language can express...There or two essential yet complementary aspects of this new vision of time which are as striking in contrast as heaven and hell. Heaven is ruled by dynamical equations that are reversible and 'timeless'; their simplicity ensures stability for eternity. Hell is more akin to the real world, where fluctuations, uncertainty and chaos reign..."

The Arrow of Time – Peter Coveny and Roger Highfield

Reality.

So that, the only thing that can possibly exist: within their individually affected three-dimensional electrical potential mass minds, and parallel functioning central nervous systems, is; "Hell is more akin to the real world, where fluctuations, uncertainty and chaos reign" – individually fragmented tones, expanded into individually fragmented tonal variations, and/or: "fluctuations" – "uncertainty" and "chaos" too.

Which is exactly why, they would ever begin to believe, that they: all of the worldly psychopathic con-artists, could –

"Cezanne...tried to make the ultimate journey back through time – Cezanne claimed – to believe in his own sensations – moreover, he said himself, quite categorically; 'what counts is only mass' – this is an imaginary world which Cezanne could not have seen in his dreams – it is impossible to tell – I could not decide – I do not know – we do not know...(Cezanne created) a kind of space where the distance seems near – one technique to create depth is canceled out by the other – in other words Cezanne is the painter of distance that seems near – this was obviously against the classical rule of the constant observation point. Cezanne was a lion in Nietzche's sense and rules mattered little to him..."

Cezanne – Yvon Taillainder

Simply make up their own rules. And/or that they could simply contradict the universally applicable *a priori* rules of Reality, functioning as Omnidimensional Time *made manifest*, while as in an attempt to simply make manifest a schizophrenic inarticulate cry for attention. And too, for their own selves to become capable of receiving, the simple –

"At a purely chemical level (just as the injection of) heroin triggers release of dopamine – every experience humans finding enjoyable – amounts to little more than an explosion of dopamine in the nucleus accumbens, as exhilarating and ephemeral as a firecracker – dopamine, can be elevated by a hug, a kiss, a word of praise..."

Addicted – J. Madeleine Nash – Time – May 5, 1997

Dose of biochemical dopamine induction that they have become dependent upon, and for their own selves to become capable of consuming of course. And while simply claiming: in words, that they: all of the worldly psychopathic con-artists and in the entire history of mankind, are: simply, becoming capable of proving how intelligent they are, and capable of; "But the Merion institution still houses one of the great art collections in the world, and it still cleaves to its mission of using art to teach the world how to think and see" – teaching mankind exactly how to think, and see: for their very own selves, and to become capable of empowering their very own selves too. And which is – of course, only exactly backwards: all of it.

So that, we can now know and for a verified scientific fact, that all of the worldly psychopathic con-artists, and in the entire history of mankind too, did, always, only simply begin to allow themselves to become capable of creating truly humanistic dysfunction: and/or truly humanistic brain death, while – and *exactly* simultaneously, simply claiming, and in simple spoken words, that they were attempting to help mankind. And which is –

"Lying, deceiving, and manipulation are natural talents for psychopaths. With their powers of imagination in gear and focused on themselves, psychopaths appear amazingly unfazed by the possibility – or even the certainty – of being found out. When caught in a lie or challenged with the truth, they are seldom perplexed or embarrassed – they simply change their stories or attempt to rework the facts so that they appear to be consistent with the lie."
Dr. Robert D. Hare – Without Conscience

A lie: and/or exactly backwards in Reality.
And too, remember how there is only the one single two-dimensional abstracted, and projected, representation of universally applicable truly humanistic Omnidimensional intelligence, while as in the entire history of mankind too: which is *The Annunciation*. And remember how that one single abstracted, and projected, two-dimensional representation: of truly humanistic universally applicable intelligence, was made manifest by Leonardo da Vinci, and remember how Leonardo da Vinci used to speak:

"Leonardo tended to string ideas together with chains of 'whichs,' 'ands,' 'becauses,''hences,' and so on, often with sustained asides and sometimes without clearly returning to the home base of discussion – some of the structures he used became so tangled as to obscure his meaning – they do not always make for easy reading...'
Martin Kemp – Introduction to Leonardo on Painting

And too, remember how they: all of the worldly psychopathic con-artists, did simply tell mankind that there is: "a fine line between intelligence and insanity," and, too I'm sure, we've all heard the expression: "Using different parts of our minds," and which we can now know, is simply –

184

"Joyce Kovelman and Arnold Scheibel of UCLA's Brain Research Institute spotted a weird cellular 'disarray' in the schizophrenic brains (and not in the matched controls). The pyramid-shaped cells of the hippocampus, normally arranged in an orderly manner, were grossly misaligned – A schizophrenic's dopamine neurons would start to fire in two different rhythms and rapidly become uncoupled – 'I think in schizophrenia the brain fragments into active and inactive clusters of neurons and different parts of the brain become disassociated,' says (Roy) King. 'You might get an asymmetry between the left and the right side, say."

The 3-Pound Universe – Judith Hooper and Dick Teresi

The literal definition of schizophrenia.
And remember what "primary suggestibility" is:

"Two simple experiments reveal the power of suggestion in different contexts. The first looks at an individual's response to someone who is in a position of authority. An experimenter repeatedly gives the subject the same suggestion: for example, she tells the subject that his body is swaying. Soon his body will begin to sway. Not everyone is susceptible to this form of suggestibility – sometimes known as primary suggestibility, and neurotic people succumb more easily then 'well-balanced' individuals. In another famous experiment in the 1950's, the social psychologist Solomon Asch looked at group dynamics. He presented a group of seven to nine subjects with a card showing three lines of different lengths: the subjects were asked in turn to identify the one line that was the same length as a reference line shown on another card. The correct answer to the question was obvious – one line clearly matched the length of the reference line, but all the members of the group, except one, were experimental 'plants': they had been briefed by Asch to give an incorrect answer. The point of the experiment was to determine how far the true subject, the one 'innocent' member of the group, would go along with the others. The researchers found that only one in four individuals held out consistently against the view of the group, proving that the power of suggestion can sometimes override the evidence of our senses."

David Cohen – The Secret Language of The Mind

So that we can now know, and for a scientific fact, that what they: all of the worldly psychopathic con-artists and again, did actually do, was to begin to become capable of simply creating extreme neurophysiological dysfunctions: for individuals to become capable of experiencing for their own selves, and while becoming victims of the con too, and while simply informing them: all of the victims of the worldly psychopathic con-artists, that they might: just possibly, begin to become capable of functioning as a genius is capable of functioning. And – then, begin to become capable of –

"Cracking the Cosmic Code With a Little Help From Dr. Hawking –

...Dr. Hawking's first book for a wide audience, 'A Brief History of Time,' took readers on a tour through black holes, the gravitational traps from which not even light can emerge, and imaginary time as he described the quest for the vaunted 'theory of everything' that would enable us to 'know the mind of God."

Dennis Overbye – The New York Times – Tuesday December 11, 2001

Going on the ultimate journey and while gaining access to The Mind of God made manifest – The Eternal Harmony: Omnidimensional Time *made manifest*, The Kingdom of Heaven, and finding the entrance to The Garden too.

But, instead and in identifiable scientific reality only, they: all of the worldly psychopathic con-artists and again, did – only, enable their victims: of primary suggestibility, an opportunity to –

" The chief priest and elders, however, had persuaded the crowd to demand the release of Barabbas and the execution of Jesus. So when the governor spoke and asked them, 'Which of the two do you want me to release for you?' they said, 'Barabbas.' 'But in that case,' Pilate said to them, 'what am I to do with Jesus who is called Christ?' They all said, 'Let him be crucified!' 'Why?' he asked. 'What harm has he done?"

Matthew 27: 20-23

Become a part of the In Crowd: of individuals who were being allowed exposure to the purely pleasurable biochemical dopamine inducing spectacle, and while experiencing pure *pleasure* for their own selves to consume only, and too while exactly betraying the Collective Consciousness of Mankind.

And too of course, as the psychopathic con-artists did begin to experience truly humanistic brain death for their own selves, they did – also and simultaneously, begin to become capable of only functioning while as in an –

"One other point about the way in which psychopaths use language: Their 'Mental packages' are not only small but two-dimensional, devoid of emotional meaning."

Dr. Robert D. Hare – Without Conscience

Absolutely abstracted, and unidirectionally successive, manner. But, quite often, very efficiently, because –

"...towards the middle of the fifth century B. C. – So it was that there arose in Greece a class that devoted itself to the teaching of rhetoric, or the art of persuasion, upon which worldly success so largely depended. The ministers of this new gospel of utility and 'Business first' were known as Sophists – They had themselves to be thoroughly conversant, not only with rhetoric and all its branches, such as grammar, diction, logical argument, an appeal to the emotions, but also with constitutional, civil, and criminal law, and parliamentary procedure. Furthermore, they must keep their ear to the ground and know everything that was going on behind the scenes, if they were to get expert advice to their clients – Moreover, as his opinions change, so each man's truth will change. What appeared true yesterday looks false today. Very well, what *was* true for the individual *is* asserting that one man's truth is truer than another's, so in the same individual there is no possible means of measuring the truth of one moment against that of the next. Whatever it is that seems true is true so long as it seems so and no longer. All of my shifting opinions are equally true for me during the time that I hold them and equally false after I have discarded them – There is no 'Reality' that reason can know...Unscrupulousness of the Sophists – Again, this habit turned the Sophists into servants of the rich, and allied them with the classes against the masses, since naturally they put themselves at the disposition of the highest bidder."

B. A. G. Fuller – The History of Philosophy

They can make a lot of money doing *that*.

And, of course, I have personally experienced this an innumerable amount of times, and each, and every, time, it becomes more and more bizarre. So that, I've heard and right from their very mouths and to my very face: "Well, you have employed the use of a dangling participle here," and after they did simply claim: in simple spoken words, that they are the exact only ones capable of understanding the language: of universally applicable Omnidimensional Reality. And/or, that they are the exact only ones, capable of –

"Picasso and Einstein cross paths, and offer a mirthful night –
In the program for *Picasso at the Lapin Agile*, which opened Tuesday night at the Arden Theater, the director, cast and staff pose 20 questions you might ponder after viewing the play. 'What is genius? they ask. How does genius get recognized..."

Clifford A Ridely – The Philadelphia Inquirer – Thursday March 8, 2001

Simply recognizing it: let alone actually capable of harnessing and reapplying it too, they did simply claim, and in simple spoken words.

So: Dangle this –

"The Penis as Text for serious Thinkers –
Lyndon B. Johnson once answered reporters badgering him about why the United States was in Vietnam with a simple, off-the-record gesture: he unzipped, pulled out his penis and said, 'This is why!'"

Emily Nussbaum – The New York Times – Saturday, December 22, 2001

Sophist: People are dying here – what is *your* concern?

And, eventually, I did simply also learn, that: they are lying, and right through their lying psychopathic mouths. Because: I did simply place it right in front of their very faces; time, after time, after time, again, and, too, only after they did – first, simply claim that they were fully capable of understanding, and – then, watch them deviate exactly from their own personally affected neurophysiological dysfunctions.

And now we: the entire world, can watch them begin to –

"The police went back to the chief priests and Pharisees who said to them, 'Why haven't you brought him?' The policed replied, 'There has never been anybody who has spoken like him.' 'So,' the Pharisees answered, 'you have been led astray as well? Have any of the authorities believed in him? Any of the Pharisees? This rabble knows nothing about the Law – they are damned.' One of them, Nicodemus – the same man who had come to Jesus earlier – said to them, 'But surely the Law does not allow us to pass judgment on a man without giving him a hearing and discovering what he is about?' To this they answered, 'Are you a Galilean too? Go into the matter, and see for yourself: prophets do not come out of Galilee."
John 7: 45-52

Deviate exactly from the facts: and/or begin to create a diversion, and which is while – and simultaneously, beginning to become capable of interpreting the Law to suit their own personal predilections only.

And of course, Leonardo da Vinci did simply explain, exactly why they: the Sophists, are always the very first ones to begin to enable their own selves to become capable of –

"Anyone who argues on the basis of authority does not exploit his insight but his memory. Good writing is born of good and natural understanding, and since the cause is to be praised rather than the effect, you should praise natural understanding without bookish learning rather than bookish learning without understanding...People who are little reliant upon nature are dressed in borrowed cloths, without which I would rank them with the herds of beasts."

Experiencing truly humanistic brain death for their own selves: to enable their own selves to become, only, capable of functioning as an animal is capable of functioning. And/or, only as –

"Any computing machine that is to solve a complex mathematical problem must be 'programmed' for this task. Hence it is to be expected that – an efficiently organized large artificial automaton (like a large computing machine) will – do things successively – one thing at a time."
John VonNeumann – The Computer and the Brain – The World Treasury of Physics, Astronomy and Mathematics, Ed. Timothy Ferris

A mindless automaton is capable of functioning, and/or machine. Which is while beginning to become, only, capable of functioning while as in an absolutely abstracted, and unidirectionally successive, manner. And/or simply as –

"If humans are less robotlike than salamanders or ducks, it's not because we have no wired-in behaviors. In fact, we have quite a few. What makes the difference is the ratio of 'un-wired' to wired-in gray matter, because neurons that are not committed at birth to a set function – are available for learning, for modification. Virtually all the cells in amphibian or reptile brain directly process sensory information – or control movement, but in humans a great gray area – about three-fourths of the cortex, lies between sensory input and motor output, called the association areas. These include the frontal lobes..."
The 3-Pound Universe – Judith Hooper and Dick Teresi

Some kind of cross breed between an animal and a robot.
Which is exactly simply because, they: the Sophists, never purposefully enabled their very own selves to practice their scales of simultaneously relative Reality. And which would be, while beginning to enable their own selves to become capable of effectually forming simultaneously relative multidimensional synaptic capabilities, within their individually affected three-dimensional electrical potential mass minds, and parallel functioning central nervous systems. And too which is, and again as we can remember, exactly because an individual human being, can, exactly, simply not make any money while practicing our scales, of Reality.
But the truly astounding thing is, that they are so brain dead that they do actually continue to employ the use of the name of Leonardo da Vinci: as a reference for their own selves, to validate their function, while – and simultaneously, Leonardo da Vinci was actually –

"There is among the number of fools a certain sect, called hypocrites, who constantly strive to deceive themselves and others but more the others than themselves. In truth, they deceive themselves more than the others – these men possess a desire only for material wealth and are entirely devoid of the desire for wisdom, which is the sustenance and truly dependable wealth of the mind – for in truth great love is born of thorough knowledge of the beloved and if you do not know it, you can love it if little at all. If you love knowledge for the returns you expect of it, and not for its great virtue, you are like the dog who wags its tail and makes a fuss and jumps up on whoever might give it a bone. But if it could understand the man's goodness it would love him even more – if the concept of such goodness were within his understanding..."

Addressing them: the brain dead hypocritical Sophists, who are only capable of functioning as animals are capable of functioning, and/or mindless automatons.
And too, which was as they did continue to –

189

"The abbreviators of works do injury to knowledge and to love, for love of anything is the offspring of knowledge, love being more fervent in proportion as knowledge is more certain; and this certainty springs from a thorough knowledge of all those parts which united compose the whole of that which ought to be loved – Of what use, pray, is he who in order to abridge the part of the things of which he professes to give complete information leaves out the greater part of the matters of which the whole is composed...And it seems to you that you have performed miracles when you have spoiled the work of some ingenious mind, and you do not perceive that you are falling into the same error as does he who strips a tree of its adornment of branches laden with leaves intermingled with fragrant flowers or fruits, in order to demonstrate the suitability of the tree for making planks."

Abridge his: Leonardo da Vinci's, mind: to suit their own personal predilections, in an attempt to empower their own selves: while exactly hijacking, and/or stealing, his name, and his function as a Noble intellect too. And which is while in addition to putting a constraint upon that mind: the communicated understanding of Reality, and the function of it: *The Annunciation,* functioning as The Eternal Harmony – Omnidimensional Time *made manifest*, and The Mind of God made manifest.

And too exactly because of 20th century neuroscientific research, we can now simply understand exactly why placing a three-dimensional constraint, upon an Omnidimensional refractive gem of a mind, is so exceedingly painful, and exactly why –

"The Pharisees, who loved money, heard all this and laughed at him. He said to them, 'You are the very ones who pass yourselves off as virtuous in people's sight, but God knows your hearts. For what is thought highly of by men is loathsome in the sight of God."
Luke 16: 14-15

The mere perception of all things worldly, will cause a severe neurophysiological disturbance within the mind, and parallel functioning central nervous system, of any one individual human being, who has allowed their own selves to become capable of forming an Omnidimensional refractive gem of a mind, for their own selves to be in possession of. Which: an individual human being's Omnidimensional refractive gem of a mind, is capable of consciously cognizing The Mind of God made manifest, and The Eternal Harmony too, and while, beginning, to become capable of functioning as The mind of God is capable of functioning. And which is exactly because of –

"In 1984 (Gary) Lynch and Michael Baudry postulated that memory – is created when messenger calcium sets off permanent changes in the structure of the synapse. Lynch and Baudry theorized that certain kinds of activity patterns, such as

190

bursts of high activity at the synapse, change the electrical voltage of the target cell enough to allow the opening of NMDA receptors. These receptors, just one among many kinds on either side of the synapses, allow the passage of calcium into the postsynaptic dendrite spine. 'That calcium goes in and does some mysterious thing,' (Richard) Granger says – changing the surface membrane of the spine so that it is then more effective."

Jim Jubak – In The Image Of The Brain

Calcium induction: within the individually affected synaptic areas, of an individual human being's quantum electrodynamically functioning electrical potential mass of a mind, and parallel functioning central nervous system, and within which there are contained no images of things, but only simultaneously relative fundamental frequency modulations. And – again, which is –

"It should be stressed that transmitters (and their regulators) are semantically as well as syntactically functional – As they synaptic singles, transmitters obviously alter communication and function. Consequently, transmitters are not simply indifferent or neutral storehouses of environmental information. Rather, environmental alteration of long-term transmitter function *ipso facto* alters function of the central nervous system."

Ira Black – Molecular Memory Systems, Synapses Circuits and the Beginnings of Memory – Gary Lynch

While capable of causing permanently affected neurophysiological changes, within any one individual's own quantum electrodynamically functioning mind, and central nervous system: while beginning to allow an individually affected human being to become more, and more, and more, sensitive, to everything. And which is while functioning as –

"Candace Pert: I see the brain terms of quantum mechanics – the brain is just a receiver, an amplifier, a little wet minireceiver for collective reality..."

The 3-Pound Universe – Judith Hooper and Dick Teresi

A receiver: an amplifier, to every thing. While including all other –

"Paul MacLean, for one, considers the frontal lobes the 'heart' of the cortex – Clinically, there is evidence that the prefrontal cortex by looking inward, so to speak, obtains the gut feeling for identifying with another individual. In other words: empathy. Through its centers for vision, hearing, and bodily sensations, we traffic with the external world."

The 3-Pound Universe – Judith Hooper and Dick Teresi

Individually affected human beings: and/or The Entire World too.

To the degree: that an individual's mind can become affected, and which is while functioning as a quantum electrodynamically functioning amplifier and while becoming more, and more, and more, sensitive, with each passing day, that an individually affected human being, can actually begin to become capable of feeling other human being's emotions – and/or their feelings, and as they are actually feeling them for their own selves. And which is, of course, simply another way of saying, that an individual human being can begin to become capable of reading minds, and/or capable of –

"An intelligence knowing, at a given instance of time, all forces acting in nature, as well as the momentary positioning of all things of which the universe consists, would be able to comprehend the motions of the largest bodies of the world and those of the lightest atoms in one single formula – to him nothing would be uncertain, both past and future would be present in his eyes..."
Pierre-Simon de Laplace, Timothy Ferris, Coming of Age in The Milky Way

Predicting the future.
Which is yet another reason exactly why all things worldly do begin to become so loathsome to simply even see, and – too, which is as this word: loathing, does actually mean: "strong dislike mingled with disgust; intense aversion," and as this word: aversion, does mean: "a strong desire to avoid because of dislike; repugnance."
Which: "a strong desire to avoid," is to all things worldly, and while the mere existence of all things worldly: all things worldly, does actually cause a severe neurophysiological disturbance within any one individual human being, who has allowed their very own selves to become capable of forming an Omnidimensional refractive gem of a mind, and parallel functioning central nervous system, for themselves to be in possession of only, and no things worldly.
And the strong desire to avoid, while being as to all things worldly, would be to all worldly psychopathic – and/or schizophrenic, dopamine biochemical inducing effectual stimulus: and/or all things worldly, while including – especially, worldly apathy, and/or simply existing while in ignorance of Reality. But none, is as vile and disgusting, as –

"He said to his disciples, 'Obstacles are sure to come, but alas for the one who provides them! It would be better for him to be thrown into the sea with a millstone put around his neck than he should lead astray a single one of these little ones. Watch yourselves!"
Luke 17: 1-3

Watching so-called adult human beings, simply handing over their children's souls, to the worldly psychopathic con-artists: to be simply consumed by them, and simply because the so-called adult humanistic beings are afraid of their very own

192

selves.

But too which: the ability to become capable of experiencing all things to such an extreme degree, is exactly what does begin to enable an individual to become capable of experiencing things which are beyond belief, and – yes, even to the point where –

"Experiencing Ecstasy –
...Wheras Prozac-type SSRI antidepressants keep your brain from emptying reservoirs of serotonin too quickly, Ecstasy floods your brain with the stuff – you feel so connected to continuum of your life. A subtle, purifying something descends (over you) – You're warm. You're not hungry – You have everything you need. Just breathing is really good on this stuff..."
Matthew Klam – The New York Times Magazine – January 21, 2001

Simply breathing can be an incomprehensibly beautiful experience. And, not to mention, beginning to become capable of experiencing truly humanistic emotions to such a degree, and as Wolfgang Amadeus Mozart did explain, that –

"...Once I have my theme, another melody comes, linking itself with the first one, in accordance with the needs of the composition as a whole: the counterpoint, the part of each instrument and all the melodic fragments at last produce a complete work. Then my soul is on fire with inspiration..."

You do actually begin to feel as though your soul: and/or truly humanistic quantum electrodynamically functioning mind and parallel functioning central nervous system, is on fire. And/or that everything is magnified within your soul, while beginning to become capable of experiencing The Mind of God made manifest, and The Eternal Harmony too. And – again, which is impossible to describe and/or explain, but would be, kind of, like taking some heroin, some Ecstasy and some cocaine, all of our worldly drugs: dopamine – serotonin and endorphins too, and then to mix them all up and consume them simultaneously, and while compounding them to an infinite degree also. But – again too, any individual who does continue to simply consume any artificially effectuated biochemical inducing stimulus, will only – and simultaneously, continue to move while in a purposefully effectuated direction away from beginning to become capable of consciously cognizing The Mind of God made manifest, and The Eternal Harmony too, and/or any truly humanistic emotions at all for that matter.

Which is exactly why, the same exact degradation, that was actually occurring within all things worldly, was beginning to occur in music, and while immediately after Wolfgang Amadeus Mozart's death. And too, which was while beginning with –

"Ludwig van Beethoven –

...Ludwig Van Beethoven was born in Bonn, the son of a tempestuous father who raised Beethoven to succeed Mozart and then drank himself to death – The music, bridging the catastrophic finale of the old century of his birth and the febrile promise of a new era, had the whiff of revolution, destroyed the classical symphonic molds and established a new era of Romanticism...'

Time – December 31, 1999

The Romantic period: In music and the world too.

And what the beginning of the Romantic period was, was simply the beginning of the absolute elimination of the Central Keynote Theme: and/or any complex simultaneously relative synthetical structuring at all, while actually functioning as Time *made manifest,* as simultaneously relative to/from, and within, a single cognizable point time zero. And – again and in simple English, what they did begin to do, was to simply begin to eliminate any complex structure at all, and rest too effectually functioning as: "0," and too then – and simultaneously, begin to put in a whole lot more stuff, and/or stimulus effectually functioning as "1." And too remember, which was because all of the individual patrons: of classical music, were simply all of the exact same individual human beings, who had begun to experience truly humanistic brain death for their own selves, and who could not maintain a single cognizable point time zero: within their individually affected minds. So, too, they could not possibly cognize any truly humanistic complex simultaneously relative Time *made manifest*: and/or any complex simultaneously relative non-tangible form synthetical structuring, at all. So the individually completed movements: and/or individually completed musical sounds, had to become much more easily accessible, so that they could be affected by them: the individually completed musical sounds, and/or tonal gradients. Which is exactly why –

"...not until Beethoven establishd himself in Viena did the risk of being a freelance begin to diminish."

The New College Encyclopedia of Music – J. A. Westrup and Fl. Harrison

Ludwig Van Beethoven did become the world's first Audio pop icon.

And too remember, simply because they had allowed their own selves to become capable of experiencing truly humanistic being brain death: for their own selves, they did begin to become capable of believing: within their individually affected minds, that they: the brain dead aristocratic elite, could simply –

"Cezanne...tried to make the ultimate journey back through time – Cezanne claimed – to believe in his own sensations – moreover, he said himself, quite categorically; 'what counts is only mass' (while) one technique to create depth is canceled by the other – in other words Cezanne is the painter of distance that seems near – this was obviously against the classical rule of the constant observation point.

Cezanne was a lion in Nietzche's sense and rules mattered little to him..."
Cezanne – Yvon Taillainder

Rewrite the rules of *a priori* Reality: to conform to their own personally affected brain death. Which is as this word: *a priori*, does actually mean: "from cause to effect; from a general law to a particular instance – valid independent of observation," that It: universally applicable harmoniously proportioned *a priori* Omnidimensional Reality, exists independent of human beings: human beings can only learn the universally applicable laws of nature. And – then, truly humanistic beings, can learn how to harness them: the universally applicable *a priori* laws of nature, abstract them from within Reality, and – *then*, learn how to reapply them: the universally applicable laws of Reality.

So that, we can actually know, what they: the brain dead aristocratic elite, did begin to become capable of believing: within their individually affected brain dead minds, was exactly backwards: as is everything.

And – remember, Wolfgang Amadeus Mozart simply explaining –

"...Once I have my theme, another melody comes, linking itself with the first one, in accordance with the needs of the composition as a whole: the counterpoint, the part of each instrument and all the melodic fragments at last produce the completed work. Then my soul is on fire with inspiration. The work grows; I keep expanding it, conceiving it more and more clearly until I have the entire composition finished in my head though it may be long. Then my mind seizes it as a glance of my eye – It does not come to me successively, with various parts worked out in detail, as they will later on, but in its entirety that my imagination lets me here it."
Wolfgang Amadeus Mozart – Roger Penrose – The Emperor's New Mind

There must be a Central Keynote Theme – or there can be no complex simultaneously relative non-tangible form synthetical structuring.

So that, we can also know, what they: The Romantic Period, did simply begin to do, was to begin to create many little individually completed movements, and/or rooms, simply stack them one on top of another, and enable individual human beings to, simply, respond to the individually completed melodic movements, and while enabling them to experience a simple biochemically induced affect, to the harmoniously proportioned intervals, and/or songs.

And too remember, even a –

"Color often signifies the difference between being seen, and consequently finding a partner, and being ignored – a male frigate-bird in the Galapagos Islands inflates the red pouch beneath its bill to attract a female."
Marco Ferrari – Colors For Survival

Bird's brain can do that.

And too and of course, the degradation did continue. Because – remember, individually affected human beings, were spending less and less time practicing their scales of Reality, and forming less, and less, truly humanistic simultaneously relative multidimensional synaptic capabilities: within their individually affected minds. And beginning to become neurophysiologically capable of, only, functioning while as in an absolutely abstracted, and unidirectionally successive, manner, and while actually regressing back towards –

"Rat-a-tat-tat. Rat-a-tat-tat. Rat-a-tat-tat – If scientists could eavesdrop on the brain of a human embryo 10, maybe 12 weeks after conception, they would hear an astonishing racket. Inside the womb, long before light first strikes the retina of the eye or the earliest dreamy images flicker through the cortex, nerve cells in the developing brain crackle with purposeful activity – But these neurons – as the long, wiry cells that carry electrical messages through the nervous system and brain are called – are not transmitting signals in scattershot fashion. That would produce a featureless static – On the contrary, evidence is growing that the Staccato bursts of electricity that form these distinctive rat-a-tat-tats arise from coordinated waves of neural activity, and that those pulsing waves, like currents shifting sand on the ocean floor, actually change the shape of the brain..."
Fertile Minds – J. Madeleine Nash – Time – February 3, 1997

Point time zero: of their own personally affected existence within truly humanistic simultaneously relative – universally applicable and harmoniously proportioned, *a priori* Reality: actually functioning as Omnidimensional space/time. And which is as this word: staccato, does actually mean: "Music – composed of notes played as a series of completely separate sounds," the applied function of elementary *a priori* Reality: and/or unidirectionally successive Time *made manifest*.
And then, of course, they: all of the individually affected human beings, did continue to regress back towards point time zero: of their purposefully affected existence within simultaneously relative *a priori* Reality, while continuing in a direction past the –

"What is a black hole? For astronomical purposes it behaves as a small, highly condensed dark 'body.' But it is not really a material body in the ordinary sense. It possesses no ponderable surface. A black hole is a region of empty space – What is known as a space/time singularity – a place where physical laws, as presently understood, must cease to apply..."
Roger Penrose – Black Holes – The world Treasury of Physics, Astronomy and Mathematics – Ed. Timothy Ferris

Point of no return, and past the point of the event horizon line, while in a direction towards truly humanistic brain death for themselves to experience. Which is exactly why, they would ever begin to purposefully make manifest –

"91 Years After Dying, Mahler Hits His Stride –

Classical musicians sometimes apply what they call the hundred-year rule to composers. Only a century after music is composed, they say, can its quality and value truly be appraised – By that standard, the works of Gustav Mahler, who died in 1911, should now be reaching their largest audience – Today, after the 20th century's world wars and mass slaughters, Mahler's music touches many more souls than it did when it was written..."

Stephen Kinzer – The New York Times – Thursday January 17, 2002

"Atonality" – "polytonality" – "dissonance" and "discord": for their own selves to be purposefully exposed to, and while occurring within the confines of their absolutely abstracted, and purposefully effectuated, excessive brain dead aristocratic elite environments. And too which: atonality – polytonality – dissonance and discord, is – of course, simply another name for –

"At Hiroshima: The common lot was random, indiscriminate and universal violence inflicting terrible pain, the physics of hydraulics and leverage and heat run riot...A junior-college Girl: 'Ah, that instant! I felt as though I have been struck on the back with something like a big hammer, and thrown into boiling oil – I seem to have been blown a good way to the north and I felt as though the directions were all changed around."

Richard Rhodes – The Making of The Atomic Bomb

Chaos: and/or absolutely excessively fragmented every "thing." And/or what was only capable of occurring, within –

"Ernst Hafstaengl, describes the shapelessness at the root of Hitler's mesmerizing oratorical power: 'His brain was a sort of primeval jelly or ectoplasm which quivered in response to every impulse from its surroundings – You could never pin him down, say that he was this thing or that thing, it was all floating, without roots, intangible and mediumistic – Momentum had driven him into an extreme position from which there was no escape..."

Michael Nelken M. D. – Hitler Unmasked

Adolf Hitler's mind: prior to it occurring within reality.
And, which is exactly why –

"We know that Adolf Hitler was easily influenced as a youth, avidly soaking up the ideas of those – Wagner and Nietzche, for instance – who impressed him..."

The Occult Connection – Frank Smyth – Ed. Peter Brookesmith

Adolf Hitler loved It: chaos – atonality – polytonality – dissonance and discord, and pain and death and suffering too of course: it is all the same thing

neuroscientific reality: HE LOVED IT.
   And too, Adolf Hitler did love –

   "Anyone who wants to win the broad masses must know the key that opens
the door to their heart (while) propaganda tries to force a doctrine on the whole
people – The whole art consists in doing this so skillfully that everyone will be
convinced that the fact is real, the necessity correct – we must avoid excessive
intellectual demands on our public, and too much effort cannot be exerted in this
direction – the receptivity of the great masses is very limited, their intelligence is
small (while) their power of forgetting is enormous – The progress and culture of
humanity are not a product of the majority, but rest exclusively on the genius and
energy of the personality – Some idea of genius arises in the brain of a man who
feels called upon to transmit his knowledge to the rest of humanity. He preaches his
view and gradually wins a certain circle of adherents. This process of the direct and
personal transmittance of a man's ideas to the rest of his fellow men is the most ideal
and natural – In the place of committee decisions, the principle of absolute
responsibility was introduced (to): Adolf Hitler."

   Beginning to become capable of believing that he was special: and that the
truly humanistic universally applicable rules of *a priori* Reality, simply did not apply
to him. And/or, to –

   "Adolf Hitler: The Aristocratic Principle: The realization that peoples are
not equal transfers itself to the individual man within a national community, in the
sense that men's minds cannot be equal, since here, too, the blood components,
though equal in their broad outlines, are, in particular cases, subject to thousands of
the finest differentiations – A philosophy of life which endeavors to reject the
democratic mass..."

   All of his individually affected aristocratic elite friends either: who did
become capable of comprising the In Crowd. Which was being purposefully allowed
exposure to the spectacle, of the purely pleasurable excessive dopamine biochemical
inducing stimulus, actually functioning as –

   "Adolf Hitler: They are always on the lookout for new stimulation. These
people are quick to weary of everything; they want variety, and they are never able
to feel or understand the needs of their fellow man (While) the red color of our
posters itself drew them into our meeting halls – By 'us' I mean all the hundreds of
thousands who fundamentally long for the same thing without as individuals finding
the words to describe outwardly what they inwardly visualize..."

   Pure *pleasure* only. And/or any –

"Adolf Hitler: And this is not complicated, but very simple and all of a piece. It does not have multiple shadings; it has a positive and a negative; love or hate, right or wrong, truth or lie, never half this way or half that way, never partially or that kind of thing."

Excessively high contrasted: absolutely abstracted – unidirectionally successive, and elementary, simple –

"Clustered in loose knots buried deep in the brain (are) neurons that produce molecular messengers – (within) the primitive structure that is one the brain's key pleasure centers. At a purely chemical level (just as the injection of) heroin triggers release of dopamine – every experience humans find enjoyable – amounts to little more than an explosion of dopamine in the nucleus accumbens, as exhilarating and ephemeral as a firecracker – dopamine, can be elevated by a hug, a kiss, a word of praise..."
Addicted – J. Madeleine Nash – Time – May 5, 1997

Psychopathic dopamine biochemical inducing effectual stimulus, actually functioning as pure *pleasure*: of any and/or all kinds. Which they: everyone who became a victim of a con, did –

"The German people, groaning from the agonies of a ghastly war, a bad peace and a deep economic depression, stumble into the arms of an angry young politician – Rash and ruthless, Hitler invented quick, radical solutions to what he saw as social problems, then he lied, seduced, shamed and terrorized until he got his way – Erik Erickson emphasized Hitler's power not merely to lie but to create myths – He was a tremendous salesman of ideas, an extraordinary orator who could pivot with the mood of an audience and mold it – He tried to bury his confusion under shouts of ultra-nationalism, but this only led to more rage – along the way, he became a monster who devoured German and non-German alike."
Michael Nelken M. D. – Hitler Unmasked

Allow themselves to become capable of constructing their entire socioeconomic system upon: the facade of *all* psychopathic dopamine biochemical inducing stimulus, functioning as pure *pleasure* only, and to consume for their own selves. While only capable of functioning as an escape from Reality, or simply a reluctance to face-up to it.

And then – of course which we do now know after the fact and while at that point in time before anybody could even understand what had happened in reality, it was too late, and it: *all* of the dysfunction, did simply consume them.

And remember, all of which: the discord and chaos and pain and death and suffering too, was made manifest as a –

"Adolf Hitler: Fear of obscurity – The greatest revolutionary changes and achievements of this earth, its greatest cultural accomplishments, the immortal deeds in the field of statesmanship, etc., are forever inseparably bound up with a name and are represented by it – consider that six or seven men, all nameless poor devils, had joined together with the intention of forming a movement, hoping to succeed – If people had attacked us in those days – we would have been happy. For the oppressive thing was neither the one nor the other; it was the complete lack of attention we found in those days from which I suffered most – An agitator who demonstrates the ability to transmit an idea to the broad masses must always be a psychologist, even if he were only a demagogue – For leading means: being able to move masses."

Schizophrenic inarticulate cry for attention.
And too remember, which: all of the chaos and discord and pain and death and suffering too, was made manifest: as a personally affected schizophrenic inarticulate cry for attention, exactly simply because one: just one, individual human being, was never –

"When he asked, she bought him a piano. He studied for just a few months; actual playing at the piano did not interest mother or son. The purchase showed their attitudes: Adolf protested his isolation and entrapment with outrageous demands; his mother soothed him by granting them."
Michael Nelken M. D. – Without Conscience

Encouraged to practice his scales.
And – instead, he: Adolf Hitler, was simply enabled –

"In Hitler's youth, his schoolteachers flunked him and Kubizek found him strangely depressed and enraged. Yet Adolf and his family saw no problem with his loafing around the house for years, nursing huge aspirations. They explained his condition as an interest in the arts."
Michael Nelken M. D. – Hitler Unmasked

To do whatever he wanted, whenever he wanted to do it, and to whomever he wanted to do it to: while simply existing in ignorance of Reality, and/or absolutely abstracted from it. While beginning to become capable of, only, functioning while as in a –

"Joyce Kovelman and Arnold Scheibel of UCLA's Brain Research Institute spotted a weird cellular disarray in the schizophrenic brains (and not in the matched controls). The pyramid-shaped cells of the hippocampus, normally arranged in an orderly manner, were grossly misaligned – A schizophrenic's dopamine neurons would start to fire in two different rhythms and rapidly become uncoupled – 'I think that in schizophrenia the brain fragments into active and inactive clusters of neurons and different parts of the brain become disassociated,' says (Roy) King. You might get an asymmetry between the left and right side, say. Schizophrenics often feel that their minds and bodies are split apart."

The 3-Pound Universe – Judith Hooper and Dick Teresi

Schizophrenic manner.

And which was as he: Adolf Hitler, did begin to become capable of making manifest real –

"91 Years After Dying, Mahler Hits His Stride –

Classical musicians sometimes apply what they call the hundred-year rule to composers. Only a century after music is composed, they say, can its quality and value truly be appraised – By that standard, the works of Gustav Mahler, who died in 1911, should now be reaching their largest audience – Today, after the 20th century's world wars and mass slaughters, Mahler's music touches many more souls than it did when it was written..."

Stephen Kinzer – The New York Times – Thursday January 17, 2002

Schizophrenic discord, and atonality – polytonality, and dissonance too. Which was simply to enable all of the individual members of the brain dead aristocratic elite, to be affected by it: the absolutely abstracted – excessively high contrasted – unidirectionally successive, and monochromatic, dopamine biochemical inducing schizophrenic effectual stimulus, actually functioning as pure *pleasure*, and within their brain dead aristocratic elite minds only.

Because – remember, as an individual human being does begin to practice their scales of *a priori* Omnidimensional Reality less and less, they will actually begin to become capable of –

"It should be stressed that the transmitters (and their regulators) are semantically as well as syntactically functional – As they synaptic singles, transmitters obviously alter communication and function. Consequently, transmitters are not simply indifferent or neutral storehouses of environmental information. Rather, environmental alteration of long-term transmitter function *ipso facto* alters function of the central nervous system."

Ira Black – Molecular Memory Mechanisms, Synapses Circuits the Beginnings of Memory – Gary Lynch

Causing permanently affected neurophysiological damage, to their own personally affected three-dimensional electrical potential mass of a mind, and parallel functioning central nervous system. And which will – then and simultaneously, begin to become capable of: effectually, actually regressing back towards –

"Cezanne – tried to make the ultimate journey back through time – Cezanne claimed – to believe in his own sensations – moreover, he set himself, quite categorically; 'what counts is only mass' – Cezanne (created) a kind of space where the distance seems near – one technique to create depth is canceled out by the other – in other words Cezanne is the painter of distance that seems near...'
Cezanne Yvon – Taillainder

Point time zero: of an individual human being's own purposefully effectuated existence within –

"At birth a baby's language of the senses is primitive: he sees vague shapes, or flashes of light, but without meaning. His eyes can neither focus upon nor follow a moving object. He is even farsighted since his eyeballs are foreshortened at birth. And what he sees is flat. He uses only one eye at a time, his eyes not yet working together to sight an object three-dimensionally..."
The Senses of Man – Joan Steen Wilentz

Truly humanistic simultaneously relative Omnidimensional space/time. And which is while beginning to become capable of actually experiencing –

"Brain death: cessation of brain function. Criteria for conclusion that the brain has died include lack of response to stimuli; absence of all reflexes; absent respirations."
Taber's Cyclopedic Medical

Absolute: truly humanistic, brain death, for their own very selves to be in possession of only. Only a –

"Ernst Hafstaengl, describes the shapelessness at the root of Hitler's mesmerizing oratorical power: 'His brain was a sort of primeval jelly or ectoplasm which quivered in response to every impulse from its surroundings – You could never pin him down, say that he was this thing or that thing, it was all floating, without roots, intangible and mediumistic – The chaos at the head of affairs is becoming greater every moment' – Warlimont at first takes a mild view: 'Hitler did not want unity; he preferred diversity.' But Warlimont gains intensity: 'Hitler's flow of speech however must have been the worst, well-nigh physically intolerable burden – The urgent questions and proposals under discussion would be drowned in a ceaseless repetitive torrent of words in which matters old and new, important and unimportant were jumbled up together' – 'Hitler simply insists: *I am in command and everybody must obey me without question*' – Hafstaengle paints a forlorn Hitler drunk with power: 'Momentum had driven him into an extreme position from which there was no escape – His limited provincial mind had finally swallowed his twisted Nordic Nazi myth (that) provided him with the one (firm) mental buttress in a dream world of infinite proportions – He was like an airman in a fog, who loses all contact with earth."

Michael Nelken M. D. – Hitler Unmasked

Worthless and chaotic agglomeration of individual nerve cells. Within which there can be no –

"The sensations which arise from muscle, joint and tendon are conveniently grouped under one heading not because of their anatomical source, but because they collaborate to provide the brain with a distinctive form of information – None of this information could be put to use unless it was firmly located against a fixed horizon; it would float about weightlessly in a vacuum. If you regard the body as an aircraft flying in a thick cloud, the proprioceptive system re-creates a scale-model of a machine on the instrument board..."

The Body in Question – Jonathan Miller

Truly humanistic – simultaneously relative, and universally applicable, single cognizable point time zero maintained: it is a neurophysiological impossibility. And which is an absolute –

"It should be stressed that transmitters (and their regulators) are semantically as well as syntactically functional – As they synaptic signals, transmitters obviously alter communication and function. Consequently, transmitters are not simply indifferent or neutral storehouses of environmental information. Rather, environmental alteration of long-term transmitter function *ipso facto* alters function of the central nervous system."

Ira Black – Molecular Memory Systems, Synapses Circuits and the Beginnings of Memory

Neuroscientific fact: again. And –

"Joyce Kovelmam and Arnold Scheibel of UCLA's Brain Research Institute spotted a weird cellular 'disarray' in the schizophrenic brains (and not in the matched controls). The pyramid-shaped cells of the hippocampus, normally arranged in an orderly manner, were grossly misaligned – A schizophrenic's dopamine neurons would start to fire in two different rhythms and rapidly become uncoupled – 'I think that in schizophrenia the brain fragments into active and inactive clusters of neurons and different parts of the brain become disassociated,' says (Roy) King. 'You might get an asymmetry between the left and right side, say. Schizophrenics often feel that their minds and bodies are split apart."

The 3-Pound Universe – Judith Hooper and Dick Teresi

Again.

And if there can be no truly humanistic – simultaneously relative, and universally applicable, single cognizable point time zero: maintained, within their three-dimensional electrical potential mass minds, and parallel functioning central nervous systems, there can also – and simultaneously, be exactly no –

"Candace Pert: I see the brain in terms of quantum mechanics – the brain is just a receiver, an amplifier, a little wet minireceiver for collective reality. We make maps, but we should never confuse the map with the territory' (While) the ratio of frontal core may be one index of evolutionary advancement – What the frontal lobes 'control' is something like awareness, or self-awareness – Do these lobes govern some essential feature of humanness or even godliness, as some scientists have suggested? If God speaks to man, if man speaks to God,' neuroscientist Candace Pert tells us, 'it would be through the frontal lobes' – Stephen LaBarge: 'And it's capable of what look like miraculous things, so miraculous that we're tempted to say it's divine, that it's not natural."
The 3-Pound Universe – Judith Hooper and Dick Teresi

Purposefully effectuated truly humanistic simultaneously relative quantum electrodynamical functioning capabilities: within all of their individually affected minds, and parallel functioning central nervous systems. It actually simply is a neurophysiological impossibility.
And if there can be no purposefully effectuated simultaneously relative quantum electrodynamical functioning capabilities: within their minds and as simultaneously relative to/from, and within, a single universally applicable, and cognizable, point time zero, there can – also and simultaneously, be no –

"The equivalent of the machine language of the brain, in (Alan) Gevin's view, is very complex electromagnetic field configurations, with very fine modulation in amplitude, frequency, wave shape and spatial distribution – And after several years of painstaking mapping of these psychic never-never lands, discovered an extraordinary thing: The mind of man contains only so many visions – four basic, recurrent geometrical forms..."
The 3-Pound Universe – Judith Hooper and Dick Teresi

Purposefully effectuated cognizance of simultaneously relative patterns in space/time: Time *made manifest*, and/or –

"One way to think about this view is to imagine spatial relationships as a kind of universal language that the brain uses no matter what specific language – social, moral, engineering – we are using at the moment – (George) Lakoff believes he can tie this mental language to the physical structure of the brain and its maps – 'When you think about dynamic structure, you begin to think there are a lot of things that are analogous with life. Life is more pattern(s) in space/time than it is a set of

particular physical things."
Jim Jubak – In the Image of the Brain

Life: Our Innocence Lost – The Kingdom of Heaven – The Mind of God made manifest – The Eternal Harmony and The Entrance to The Garden too. And as was exactly explained by –

"Enter by the narrow gate, since the road that leads to perdition is wide and spacious, and many take it; but it is a narrow gate and a hard road that leads to life, and only a few find it."
Matthew 7: 13-14

The Son of God – again.
And – again, which is exactly how we can now know: for a verified scientific fact, that –

"Remember, blessed Jesu,
That I am the cause of Thy pilgrimage,
Do not forsake me on that day.

Seeking me Thou didst sit down weary,
Thou didst redeem me, suffering death on the cross.
Let not such toil be in vain.

Just and avenging Judge.
Grant remission
before the day of reckoning.

I groan like a guilty man.
Guilt reddens my face.
Spare a suppliant, O God.

My prayers are not worthy,
But Thou in Thy merciful goodness grant
That I burn not in everlasting fire.

Place me among Thy sheep
And separate me from the goats,
Setting me on Thy right hand.

When the accursed have been confounded
And given over to the bitter flames,
Call me with the blessed.

205

I pray in supplication on my knees.
My heart contrite as the dust,
Safeguard my fate.

Mournful that day
When from the dust shall rise
Guilty man to be judged.
Therefore spare him, O God.
Merciful Jesu, Lord
Grant them rest."

The confounded have become the accursed.

Because, when an individually affected human being does not practice their truly humanistic scales of simultaneously relative Omnidimensional Reality, and while as on a daily basis too: and/or perform no proportional amounts of purposefully effectuated biochemical reuptake function – no proportional amounts of purposefully effectuated calcium production/induction, and no proportional amounts of purposefully effectuated serotonin production/induction, for their own selves, they will only – and simultaneously, allow their very own selves to begin to become capable of effectually regressing back towards point time zero: of their own personally effectuated existence within truly humanistic simultaneously relative Omnidimensional space/time. And they will then, and simultaneously, allow their very own selves, to begin to become capable of experiencing truly humanistic brain death for their own selves, and to be in possession of only too. And they will – then and simultaneously, become neurophysiologically incapable of simply seeing: and/or purposefully consciously cognizing, past a single point: of truly humanistic space/time, while at any one point within truly humanistic universally applicable, and simultaneously relative, Omnidimensional space/time: they will remain neurophysiologically incapable of consciously cognizing any Time *made manifest* whatsoever. And so they will –

"Each of us lives within the universe – the prison – of his own brain. Projecting from it are millions of fragile sensory nerve fibers, in groups, uniquely adapted to sample the energetic states of the world about us: heat, light, force, and chemical compositions. That is all we ever know directly; all else is logical inference..."
The 3-Pound Universe – Judith Hooper and Dick Teresi

Become a prisoner of their own personal biochemically affected, and absolutely dysfunctional: chaotic – discordant and amorphous, random agglomeration of individual nerve cells, of a brain. And while remaining confined only to their own –

"What is a black hole? For astronomical purposes it behaves as a small, highly condensed dark 'body.' But it is not really a material body in the ordinary sense. It possesses no ponderable surface. A black hole is a region of empty space – which acts as a center of gravitational attraction – Since the black hole acts as a center of attraction it can draw new material towards it, which once inside can never escape – What is known as a 'space/time singularity' – a place where physical laws, as presently understood, must cease to apply."

Roger Penrose – Black Holes – The World Treasury of Physics, Astronomy and Mathematics – Ed. Timothy Ferris

Black hole: of a brain, and for their own selves to be in possession of only.

Which will then: as any one individually affected human being does begin to become capable of experiencing truly humanistic brain death for their own selves, begin to become capable of enabling them: the individually affected human being's three-dimensional electrical potential of a mind, within which there are contained no images of things, to remain neurophysiologically incapable of maintaining a single cognizable: simultaneously relative and truly humanistic, point time zero: within their minds, and too remain neurophysiologically incapable of consciously cognizing any simultaneously relative patterns in space/time. And/or, simply incapable of –

"Wending Through Time, a Cosmic Web –
If the story of the universe were made into a summer movie, starting with the biggest, baddest explosion ever and building up to the glorious development of stars, galaxies and human life, what sort of flick would it be? – Whatever its genre, it would more than satisfy Samuel Goldwyn's famous demand for a story that 'starts with an earthquake and works its way up to a climax,' because an earthquake looks like a mosquito's hiccup next to the big bang explosion in which the universe was born – what would put the movie over the top are its stunning visuals and the subtle but unbroken thread that connects virtually every important event in the story. Those advantages are the result of a glorious feature of the universe that determines its density and permeates space like a vast, three-dimensional system of rivers, tributaries, creeks and rivulets: the cosmic web – 'It's like the cartography of the universe...'"

James Glanz – The New York Times – Tuesday August 14, 2001

Traveling on a journey all throughout, and within, simultaneously relative Omnidimensional Time *made manifest*: The Eternal Harmony – The Mind of God – The Kingdom of Heaven and while finding our Our Innocence Lost, and The Entrance to The Garden also. And – again, which is –

"Johannes Keplar...then he becomes aware that he walks in the light of truth; he is seized by an unbelievable rapture and, exulting, he here surveys most minutely, as though from a high watch-tower, the whole world and all the differences of its parts."

An experience which is beyond belief. And which is while actually neurophysiologically "moving" all throughout, and within, simultaneously relative Omnidimensional space/time, and actually neurophysiologically experiencing The Mind of God made manifest: The Eternal Harmony, and The Kingdom of Heaven too.

But – instead, as an individual does allow their very own selves to become capable of experiencing truly humanistic being brain death for their very own selves, they will begin to become incapable of consciously cognizing past a single point, while at any one point within simultaneously relative space/time: and/or incapable of mapping out a simultaneously relative journey all throughout, and within, truly humanistic simultaneously relative Omnidimensional space/time, and they will actually begin to become incapable of differentiating between the map and the territory. And/or –

"Candace Pert: I see the brain in terms of quantum mechanics – the brain is just a receiver, an amplifier a little wet minireceiver for collective reality. We make maps, but we should never confuse the map with the territory..."
The 3-Pound Universe – Judith Hooper and Dick Teresi

Capable of "confusing the map with the territory." And/or simply –

"To say that prediction is the purpose of scientific theory is to confuse means with ends. It is like saying that the purpose of a spaceship is to burn fuel..."
David Deutsch – The Fabric Of Reality

Begin to become capable of experiencing truly humanistic brain death for their own selves to be in possession of only. And/or begin to become capable of functioning as, only, a mindless automaton is capable functioning, and/or as an animal is capable of functioning. Who: a mindless automaton and/or an animal and/or an amoeba even, can have no greater purpose than to simply exist in a vacuum, and/or while moving in a unidirectionally successive, and purposefully effectuated, direction, and while as with their bodies alone. While only anticipating their next allowed exposure, to –

"Clustered in loose knots buried deep in the brain (are) neurons that produce molecular messengers – (within) the primitive structure that is one of the brain's key pleasure centers. At a purely chemical level (just as the injection of) heroin triggers release of dopamine – every experience humans find enjoyable – amounts to little more than an explosion of dopamine in the nucleus accumbens, as exhilarating and ephemeral as a firecracker – dopamine, can be elevated by a hug, a kiss, a word of praise – Dopamine, like most biologically important molecules, must be kept within strict bounds – Too much causes the hallucinations, and bizarre thoughts, of schizophrenia – addicts' neurons assaulted by abnormally high levels of dopamine, have responded defensively and reduced the number of sites (or receptors) to which dopamine can bind – so while addicts begin by taking drugs to feel high, they end up taking them in order not to feel low."

Addicted – J. Madeleine Nash – Time – May 5, 1997

An absolutely abstracted: unidirectionally successive – elementary and excessively high contrasted, simple: absolutely animalistic – and/or psychopathic – and/or schizophrenic, dopamine biochemical inducing effectual stimulus of some kind, to become capable of allowing themselves to simply consume it, and which is while actually functioning as pure *pleasure* only also, and too as: "1" – only. And which *is* –

"91 Years After Dying, Mahler Hits His Stride –
Classical musicians sometimes apply what they call the hundred-year rule to composers. Only a century after music is composed, they say, can its quality and value truly be appraised – By that standard, the works of Gustav Mahler, who died in 1911, should now be reaching their largest audience – Today, after the 20th century's world wars and mass slaughters, Mahler's music touches many more souls than it did when it was written..."

Stephen Kinzer – The New York Times – Thursday January 17, 2002

The truly humanistic brain dead sound, of: atonality – polytonality – dissonance and discord, and/or chaos, and pain and death and suffering too. Because it's all the same thing: in truly humanistic neuroscientific Reality only of course, and within their individually affected minds too of course. And which is while only capable of functioning as a simple dopamine biochemical inducing effectual stimulus too of course, and while to simply enable them to feel alive for their own selves: to feed their addiction.

And – too remember, they did already plainly admit, that –

"Music and Science Meet on the Piano Bench –
After reverently shaking hands with the great pianists Josef Hofmann and Leopold Godowsky at a party, a fan was struck that the man's hands were so small. 'How can you great artists play the piano so magnificently with such small hands?' the woman asked. Godowsky replied, 'Where in the world did you get the idea that we play the piano with our hands' – The piano is primarily an instrument of the mind – was made abundantly clear Thursday at a concert and panel discussion, titled 'Polymaths and the piano,' at Caspary Hall at Rockefeller University – Steven D-, was the only member of the panel who claimed not to spend too much time thinking about the connection between music and science – not because the task does not interest him, but simply because it is too difficult. 'I'm sure there is a connection,' he

added – The ultimate connection between music and science was left unsettled..."
Bruce Schechter – The New York Times – Tuesday February 13, 2001

They did not have even a clue, that there even existed such a thing as truly humanistic universally applicable non-tangible form simultaneously relative Omnidimensional synthetical structuring: of harmoniously proportioned universally applicable, and truly humanistic, simultaneously relative *a priori* Omnidimensional Reality, and while actually functioning as Omnidimensional Time *made manifest*.

So that we can now know, if they so much as even open their brain dead aristocratic elite mouths, except to admit that they did not know that such a thing existed, and exists *a priori*, they will become only capable of proving, that they –

"Psychopaths are notorious for not answering the question posed them or for answering in a way that seems unresponsive to the question – It now appears that the communications of psychopaths sometimes are subtly odd and part of a general tendency to 'Go off track.' That is, they frequently change topics, go off on irrelevant tangents, and fail to connect phrases and sentences in a straightforward manner – Jack was a mile-a-minute talker, with the psychopath's characteristic ability to contradict himself from one sentence to the next...With their powers of imagination in gear and focused on themselves psychopaths appear amazingly unfazed by the possibility – or even the certainty, of being found out. When caught in a lie or challenged with the truth, they are seldom perplexed or embarrassed – they simply change their stories or attempt to rework the facts so that they appear to be consistent with the lie."
Dr. Robert D. Hare – Without Conscience

Are only capable of functioning as lying psychopathic con-artists.

Unless, of course, they do plainly admit that they did make a mistake. And begin to become capable of experiencing, truly humanistic –

"What is your opinion? A man had two sons. He went and said to the first, 'My boy, you go and work in the vineyard today.' He answered, 'I will not go,' but afterward thought better of it and went. The man then went and said the same thing to the second who answered, 'Certainly, sir,' but did not go. 'Which of the two did the father's will?' 'The first,' they said. Jesus said to them, 'I tell you solemnly, tax collectors and prostitutes are making their way into the kingdom of God before you. For John came to you, a pattern of true righteousness, but you did not believe him, and yet the tax collectors and prostitutes did. Even after seeing that, you refused to think better of it and believe in him."
Matthew 21: 28-32

Humility: for their own selves.

Because, everybody makes mistakes, and because also, that is exactly what makes us, nothing more than, human beings. But, the difference between a truly virtuous human being, and an individual who has begun to experience truly humanistic brain death for their own selves, is – exactly, the ability to simply understand, and/or recognize, The Absolute Truth: and/or pure science. And, we can remember, we *can* –

"...Many of the provinces of the brain (are) topographical maps of projections of the sensory fields which they represent – the same geometrical decorum applies to all projections – physical events impinging upon the sensory surface are transformed into the characteristic digital language of the brain – a linear code dictates the construction of the visible object."
Jonathan Miller – The Body in Question

Simply see the Truth: of universally applicable – simultaneously relative and harmoniously proportioned, *a priori* Reality: actually functioning as Time *made manifest,* with our very own eyes. And/or the function of atonality, polytonality, dissonance and discord: and/or chaos, and pain, and death, and suffering also.
So, let's go back outside into universally applicable: harmoniously proportioned, simultaneously relative *a priori* Reality, again, while upon – and within, the universal constant of Time *made manifest*: and/or upon the pavement, and take a good look at it again. And too while we can remember, that it: the pavement, is the function of visual equivalency scales, and the universal constant of Time *made manifest*, and – as we can remember, which is as the varied universally applicable function, is simply a different variation of the width: of the base of the pyramid, which comprises the simultaneously relative function, of the actual note/differential/velocity/atom. So, go ahead and take a very good look at it: all of simultaneously relative *a priori* Reality, and while as simultaneously relative to, and from, our single cognizable point time zero: within our minds located at an identifiable point upon the pavement, and – too as we can remember, which is while functioning as a scale, and/or quantized gradient. And we can now plainly see: with our very own eyes alone too, that each preceding individually completed section of the sidewalk: as simultaneously relative to our single cognizable point time zero, is just a little more wide, than each succeeding individually completed section of the sidewalk, and so the universally applicable simultaneously relative function does extend to infinity, and too which is while actually functioning as the universal constant of Time *made manifest*. And so, we can simply see, that atonality, polytonality, dissonance, and discord, is –

"At Hiroshima: The common lot was random, indiscriminate and universal violence inflicting terrible pain, the physics of hydraulics and leverage and heat run riot...A junior-college girl: 'Ah that instant! I felt as though I have been struck on the back with something like a big hammer, and thrown into boiling oil – I seem to have been blown a good way to the north and I felt as though the directions were all

211

changed around."
Richard Rhodes – The making of The Atomic Bomb

Chaos made manifest. And/or the simultaneously relative: monochromatic and excessively fragmented, function of: "extremely big pyramid" – "extremely big pyramid" – "extremely big pyramid" – "tiny pyramid" – "tiny pyramid" – "extremely big pyramid" – "tiny pyramid" – "extremely big pyramid" – "tiny pyramid," and too with no "rest" actually effectually functioning as "0" whatsoever, and for –

"There are two essential yet complementary aspects of this new vision of time which are as striking in contrast as heaven and hell. Heaven is ruled by dynamical equations that are reversible and 'timeless'; their simplicity ensures stability for eternity. Hell is more akin to the real world, where fluctuations, uncertainty and chaos reign..."
The Arrow of Time – Peter Coveney and Roger Highfield

Eternity too.
And which was while actually functioning as pure abstracted dopamine biochemical inducing effectual stimulus also, and/or as tangible form mass stimulus, and/or "1" only, while actually functioning as pure *pleasure* only also.
Which was as they: the aristocratic elite and within the once Truly Idealist Democratic Society, did actually continue to move while as in a purposefully effectuated direction, to allow themselves to become capable of consuming it. And/or being affected by it: discord and/or chaos made manifest, simply because they had actually, and as Thomas Jefferson did explain –

"...The practice of Kings marrying only in the families of Kings, has been that of Europe for some centuries. Now, take any race of animals, confine them in idleness and inaction, whether in a sty, a stable or a state-room, pamper them with high diet, gratify all their sexual appetites, immerse them in sensualities, nourish their passions, let everything bend before them, and banish what might ever lead them to think, and in a few generations they become all body and no mind; and this to, by a law of nature, by that very law by which we are in constant practice of changing the characters and propensities of the animals we raise for own purposes. Such is the regiment in raising Kings, and in this way they have gone on for centuries...In this state Bonaparte found Europe; and it was this state of its rulers which lost it without scarce a struggle. These animals had become without mind and powerless; and so will every hereditary monarch be after a few generations..."
Thomas Jefferson (To) Governor John Langdon – Monticello, March 5, 1810

Begun to become capable of effectually regressing all the way back towards point time zero: of their own personally effectuated existence within truly humanistic simultaneously relative Omnidimensional space/time. And so – then, they: all of the individually affected victims of the psychopathic con-artists and/or entertainers, and which is, as we can remember, as this word: entertain, does actually mean: "to create a diversion," in neuroscientific reality, could begin to become capable of experiencing truly humanistic brain death for their own selves, and to be in possession of only. And – remember, which is just like the child: upon the pavement, and searching for the Entrance to Garden, and/or their Innocence Lost too, or –

"If an alien answered...what would you say?
Imagine that our radio antennas picked up a signal from aliens in a galaxy far away. What would we want to say to them? Would we want to make them like us? Would we want to be honest about our human failings – We're woefully unprepared to reply to a message from the stars, said psychologist Douglas V-, whose job is to think about just that: What should we say to aliens that would reflect something universal about all six billion of us on Earth – It would be much more difficult than we could possibly imagine,' said V-, 40, the first social scientist to be employed full time by the Search for Extraterrestrial Intelligence (SETI), in Mountain View, Calif...V- doesn't worry that aliens are likely to be hostile. His main concern is that they would have no way to relate to us. 'The difficulty is that we don't share a common language,' he said..."
Faye Flam – The Philadelphia Inquirer – Tuesday February 5, 2002

Their mother's breast: and/or the Apple too.
What they: any one individual human being who can not simply see past a single point while at any one point within simultaneously relative space/time, and/or who is looking for a more intelligent life in outer space, is simply searching for, is proof that there is, a –

"The Mystery of The Universe –
...Could it be that God was needed to set the dials?"
Faye Flam – The Philadelphia Inquirer – Monday May 3, 1999

God: a "programmer," and/or for their Mothers to tell them that everything is "going to be all right," and for eternity too. And/or – again, the –

"A baby passes her first amazing milestone before the typical mother has even wiped off the sweat of labor. Full-term newborns, scientists established in 1996, recognize and prefer their mothers face to all others – In the ingenious experiment, the scientists had babies suck a special pacifier that controlled a video screen. Depending on how the infant sucked, fast or slow, the image of Mom or another woman appeared; babies sucked so they'd see Mom..."
Joan Raymond – Newsweek – Fall/Winter

Security of their mother's breast: their artificially effectuated mother's womb environment – the dopamine biochemical inducing effectual stimulus of the shiny red Apple, and/or a simple perceivable proof that there does exist A God: They are all the same thing in neuroscientific reality.

Because – remember, the human being mind is –

"Candace Pert: I see the brain in terms of quantum mechanics – the brain is just a receiver, an amplifier, a little wet minireceiver for collective reality..."
The 3-Pound Universe – Judith Hooper and Dick Teresi

A receiver – an amplifier: for collective *a priori* universally applicable, and simultaneously relative, Omnidimensional Reality. Which may, possibly, actually begin to become neurophysiologically capable of speaking the universally applicable *a priori* language: of simultaneously relative Omnidimensional Time *made manifest*, and/or capable of recognizing it. And, as we can remember, as did Johannes Keplar:

"Geometrical non-tangible forms: God wanted us to recognize them, when he created us after His image, so that we should share in His thoughts. For what is implanted in the mind of man other than numbers and magnitudes? These alone we comprehend correctly, and if piety permits us to say so, his recognition is of the same kind as the Divine, at least insofar as we in this mortal life of ours are capable of grasping part of it – Geometry is one and eternal, a reflection of the mind of God – nature loves these relationships in everything that is capable of being related. They are also loved by the intellect of man who is an image of the Creator."
Johannes Keplar – Max Casper

So that, we can know, that the only thing that they: any one individual human being who can not neurophysiologically see past a single point, while at any one point within simultaneously relative space/time, can only – possibly, be looking for, is a programmer: as the human mind is capable functioning as a receiver.

And too remember how the Son of God did plainly explain, that –

"If God were your father, you would love me,
since I have come from God; yes, I have come from him;
not that I came because I chose,
no, I was sent, and by him.
Do you know why you cannot take in what I say?
It is because you are unable to understand my language."
John 8: 42-43

When an individual human being does begin to become capable of speaking the language: of *a priori* universally applicable Omnidimensional Time *made manifest*, they can then – and simultaneously, begin to become capable of consciously cognizing The Mind of God made manifest, and/or capable of "seeing" God, and which is while beginning to understand that it is beyond belief: and that it can only be understood. So that, as an individual does begin to become capable of cognizing The Mind of God made manifest, while experiencing The Eternal Harmony and while finding their Innocence Lost too, and/or The Entrance to The Garden, they do also – and simultaneously, begin to allow themselves, to become capable of coming to an understanding of a more divinely purposeful existence: for their own selves to be in possession of only too, while along with their Omnidimensional refractive gem of a mind. Which: an individual human being's personally affected Omnidimensional refractive gem of a mind, may become capable of traveling all throughout, and within, simultaneously relative Omnidimensional Time *made manifest,* and/or begin to become capable of coming to an understanding of a more divinely purposeful existence for their own selves to be in possession of. Or, and exactly as Thomas Jefferson did explain, exactly –

"...He proves also, that man, once surrendering his reason, has no remaining guard against absurdities the most monstrous, and like a ship without rudder, is the sport of every wind. With such persons, gullibility which they call faith, takes the helm from the hand of reason, and the mind becomes a wreck..."
Thomas Jefferson (To) James Smith – Monticello, December 8, 1822

Not, and become capable of losing control over your very own self. And which is while, and simultaneously, beginning to become neurophysiologically capable of understanding absolutely nothing: for your own self, and being in possession of absolutely nothing: for your own self. Except, of course, for truly humanistic brain death: for your own self, and – then, begin to become capable of believing absolutely anything, that you may be told, by all of the worldly psychopathic con-artists, who are simply creating the diversions, and/or entertainers too. Which was as the degradation, of the once Truly Idealist Democratic Society, did continue, as did: simultaneously, all of the individually affected human beings, and within which: the majority of individual human beings which comprised the original Truly Idealist Democratic Society, there was, once, a truly virtuous human being foundation. Which: the individual truly virtuous human beings, did purposefully effect the Revolution: against the tyranny of the Monarch and their forcibly acquired control over everything, and which is while including all of the individually affected –

"In concert Spears is a slave 4 fashion –
Brittany Spears paid a visit to the First Union Center on Monday night, and the runway show did not disappoint – the pop princess opened with a beguiling little number in sequined black, reminiscent of an Elvis jumpsuit, but showing more skin than the King would have dared. Sequens were the theme of the concert, delicately balanced by an abundance of midriff and cleavage – Halfway through the collection,

Spears paraded around in a hat that easily could have doubled as a dark-chocolate cake topped with strawberry frosting. Meanwhile, apparently hungry dancers clad in '80s-retro, puffy-painted spandex, circled the fashion-forward chanteuse. Gasps were audible as the encore outfit, a shimmering cowboy ensamble, and wearer rose skyward on a lighted platform – Plus there was music – If it seems as if Spears' career has swelled at a faster rate than even her cup size, the succession of hits performed Monday proves her worthiness to fill the major venue...you would have been hard-pressed to find a fan who didn't enjoy the spectacle."
    Bethany Klein – The Philadelphia Inquirer – Wednesday December 12, 2001

    Victims of the con: as the transformation is now complete.
    What was, once, the world's first Truly Idealist Democratic Society, has now become the world's single most dysfunctional aristocracy: as they have simply handed control, of their very selves, over to their worldly gods, and it is nothing but an absolute scientific fact, which no human being can deny, they can only remain ignorant of it: the absolute scientific fact that is. Which is the fact, of their own personally affected truly humanistic brain death: to be in possession of only, and for the majority of our entire society also.
    Because – remember, it was –

"A Declaration by the Representatives of the United States of America:
    We hold these truths to be self-evident: that all men are created equal; that they are endowed by their Creator with CERTAIN [*inherent and*] inalienable rights; that among these are life, liberty, and the pursuit of happiness; that to secure these rights, governments are instituted among men, deriving their just powers from the consent of the governed; that whenever any form of government becomes destructive of these ends, it is the right of the people to alter or to abolish it; and to institute a new government, laying its foundation on such principles, and organizing its power in such form, as to them shall seem most likely to effect their safety and happiness..."

    A revolutionary concept. To leave it: the Monarchy – the aristocratic elite – the stuff – the excessive dopamine biochemical inducing stimulus of any, and/or all, kinds – the entertainers, and the truly humanistic brain death too, behind, and on purpose, it was no accident: it was a revolutionary concept.
    They did, willfully, choose to break free of the attractive force, which is our excessively simplistic mortal existence while upon this point-mass of Earth, and, too, which was as they did go sailing off into uncharted territories. While on a journey to find the Lost Innocence of the child – The Entrance to The Garden, and our Paradise Lost, and exactly not to remain a slave to The Apple. And/or, begin to allow their own selves to become capable of becoming addicted, to absolutely abstracted, dopamine biochemical inducing stimulus, functioning as pure *pleasure* only, and/or begin to become capable of experiencing truly humanistic brain death, for their own selves only also.

And which: as individually affected human beings do actually begin to become capable of experiencing truly humanistic brain death for their own selves, is as they: all of the individually affected victims of the con, will begin to become capable of neurophysiologically understanding absolutely nothing for their own selves, and – simultaneously, begin to become, only, capable of simply believing, anything they are being told to believe: by all of the worldly psychopathic con-artists. Who are supplying them with allowed access to all of their simple dopamine biochemical inducing stimulus, actually functioning as pure *pleasure* only. And/or their –

"Clustered in loose knots buried deep in the brain (are) neurons that produce molecular messengers – (within) the primitive structure that is one of the brain's key pleasure centers. At a purely chemical level (just as the injection of) heroin triggers release of dopamine – every experience humans find enjoyable – amounts to little more than an explosion of dopamine in the nucleus accumbens, as exhilarating and ephemeral as a firecracker – dopamine, can be elevated by a hug, a kiss, a word of praise – Dopamine, however, is more than just a feel-good molecule. It also exercises extraordinary power over learning and memory – Dopamine, like most biologically important molecules, must be kept within strict bounds – Too much causes the hallucinations, and bizarre thoughts, of schizophrenia – addicts' neurons assaulted by abnormally high levels of dopamine, have responded defensively and reduced the number of sites (or receptors) to which dopamine can bind – so while addicts begin by taking drugs to feel high, they end up taking them in order not to feel low."
Addicted – J. Madeleine Nash – Time – May 5, 1997

Drugs. And which was as they were, and simultaneously, becoming –

"Brainwashing – intense psychological indoctrination, usually political, for the purpose of displacing the individual's previous thoughts and attitudes with those selected by the regime or person inflicting the indoctrination."
Taber's Cyclopedic Medical Dictionary

Brainwashed: by all of the wordily psychopathic con-artists, and/or entertainers. Who were all of the exact same master manipulators, who were beginning to become capable of supplying their victims, with allowed access to all of their excessive dopamine biochemical inducing stimulus, functioning as pure *pleasure*, and/or their drugs too: *as* they were becoming brainwashed, and remaining neurophysiologically incapable of understanding anything, and only capable of believing exactly what they were being told, by the psychopathic con-artists: who were supplying them with allowed access to all of their drugs, and too which is as everything is now, exactly, backwards. Which is exactly why, they would ever begin to believe, that –

"Ribbon is cut, accolades flow as Kimmel Center opens to the public –
The hoi polloi replaced *haut monde* yesterday at the Kimmel Center for the Performing Arts, and feel-good Philadelphia fever reached new heights – For the first time in the $265 million center's three-day history, the public was invited to share the spot-light during a day long ceremony that included a variety of performances. Thousands eagerly responded, looking skyward in awe as they streamed through the doors into the grand atrium..."
Kathleen Brady Shea – The Philadelphia Inquirer – Monday December 17, 2001

They: any individual who could actually move their bodies, in a direction towards this truly humanistic brain dead aristocratic elite spectacle, are actually functioning as truly virtuous human beings, while instead of simply understanding the neuroscientific fact, that they are beginning to become capable of experiencing truly humanistic brain death, for their own selves. And too, which was as they did become capable of believing, that –

"...'We just had to be here,' said S- , 40, of Northeast Philadelphia – As Day-Glo members of Pink Inc., a New-York based performance-art group, whirled past her husband, K- , and their children – S- waxed enthusiastic about the new centerpiece for the Avenue of the Arts – 'It's just great for the city,' she said. 'It warms my soul to see such a beautiful place in Philadelphia...I am just so into this."
Kathleen Brady Shea – The Philadelphia Inquirer – Monday December 17, 2001

They were actually experiencing a "fire in their souls," just like Wolfgang Amadeus Mozart. Which is, of course, only exactly backwards: in neuroscientific reality only of course, and their individually affected minds too. As they are, actually and as a matter of fact, simply allowing themselves an opportunity to participate in an orgy: of excessive amounts of dopamine biochemical inducing stimulus, actually functioning as pure *pleasure* only, and while actually experiencing truly humanistic brain death for their very own selves to be in possession of only also. And, which is also while actually –

"Making Shopping An Olympic Event –
Where the spectators are: the souvenir store. On a sun-baked afternoon, when the temperature reached into the 80's and the sky was a cloudless blue, the lines at these Olympic Games' most popular venue coiled back and forth across a wide plaza – A public-address announcer entertained the perspiring thousands – They were waiting to shop at the Olympic Superstore, an 11,000-square foot, licensed-merchandise department store in a building that typically houses sheep at Sydney's annual Easter show – 'Kind of humorous that they normally keep sheep here, isn't it?' said Reg H-, a bearded, bemused Olympic security guard who had

218

come here on his break to, in his words, 'laugh at these blokes – 'They're just like lambs being led to the slaughter."
Frank Fitzpatrick – The Philadelphia Inquirer – Monday September 18, 2000

Allowing their very own selves to be led to the slaughter. And/or, to actually, and simply, enable their very own souls to be consumed, by all of the worldly psychopathic con-artists, and while actually experiencing truly humanistic brain death, for their own selves to be in possession of only. And again, which is, exactly, only as a matter of –

"Drugs are like sledgehammers,' observes Dr. Eric Nestler of the Yale University School of Medicine. 'They profoundly alter many pathways' – the realization that dopamine may be a common endpoint of all those pathways represents a signal advance. Provocative – the dopamine hypothesis provides a basic framework for understanding (what does) create a serious behavioral disorder..."
Addicted – J. Madeleine Nash – Time – May 5, 1997

Neuroscientific fact.
And – remember, as was exactly explained by –

"Great crowds accompanied him on his way and he turned and spoke to them. 'If any man comes to me without hating his father, mother, wife, children, brothers, sisters, yes and his own life too, he cannot be my disciple. Anyone who does not carry his cross and come after me cannot be my disciple.
And indeed, which of you here, intending to build a tower, would not first sit down and work out the cost to see if he had enough to complete it? Otherwise, if he laid the foundation and then found himself unable to finish the work, the onlookers would all start making fun of him and saying, 'Here is a man who started to build and was unable to finish."
Luke 14: 25-31

The Son of God, and –

"Adolf Hitler: But the power which has always started the greatest religious and political avalanches in history rolling has time immortal been the magic power of the spoken word, and that alone...Particularly the broad masses of the people can be moved only by the power of speech – Only a storm of hot passion can turn the destinies of peoples, and he alone can arouse passion who bears it within himself – It alone gives its chosen one the words which like hammer blows can open the gates to the heart of a people – But the man whom passion fails and whose lips are sealed – he has not been chosen by Heaven to proclaim its will..."

The master manipulating psychopathic con-artist Adolf Hitler also.

Which is, of course, only exactly backwards, and the function of truly humanistic brain death only, of course, and only in scientific reality too of course. And/or within the mind of any one individual, who could allow their own selves to become a victim of a con, and while being in possession of absolutely nothing for their own selves, except for their own personally affected truly humanistic brain death. Who are, now, capable of understanding absolutely nothing for their own selves, and only capable of believing exactly what they have been programmed to believe, by all of the worldly psychopathic con-artists, who have stolen their very souls. And too which is exactly why, anyone would ever become capable of believing, that –

"As shock of Sept. 11 fades, subtle changes linger in U. S. –
Slightly more than a hundred days after terrorism shocked a complacent America, fear has given way to quiet resolve and to reflection about community, country and life – Americans are turning back to the security of the familiar – the comforts of home, family and tradition. If declining prescriptions for sleeping pills and tranquilizers are any measure, anxiety is fading – Popular culture reflects the country's changing mood – At 84 radio stations owned by Texas-based Clear Channel Communications, program managers decided the country needed a lift and struck gold by playing Christmas music every day, starting in November – 'If anything, Sept. 11 made people even more receptive to Christmas music early,' said Pam T- a Clear Channel spokeswoman – 'It's like a big hug coming out of the radio – At the same time, the American temper remains inflamed against the terrorists (And) On a deeper level, the tragedy has stirred thoughts about the fragility of life (While) The events of Sept. 11 left many turning to worship – On the day of the attacks, Mary – was driving through (a) Chicago suburb when she passed a church and decided to stop – 'I went in there to touch God,' she said..."
Stephen Thomma – The Philadelphia Inquirer –Wednesday, December 26, 2001

IT: gaining access to The Mind of God made manifest – The Eternal Harmony actually functioning as Omnidimensional Time *made manifest*: Finding our Innocence Lost and The Entrance to The Garden too, is: Just that easy – as only simply making manifest a public proclamation, that you do sincerely believe that it is just that easy. Where the hell: **WHERE THE HELL**, would any one individually affected human being ever get that idea: programmed into their minds that is, and except, of course, while as from Adolf Hitler. Well, that would be –

"Under pressure from Pope Julius II, Michelangelo finished the Sistine ceiling in tremendous haste. The vault was unveiled officially on 31 October 1512, the eve of All Saints, and was the subject of widespread admiration. Michelangelo was left exhausted by this titanic work: 'A great inconvenience of the project was that it forced him to paint with his head lifted, he ruined his eyesight to the extent

220

that he could not read letters or look at drawings unless they were in the air and this lasted for several months' (Vasari). The Sistine became, according to Vasari, a form of 'academy of drawing' for artists visiting Rome who saw it as a mandatory point of reference – 'At the unveiling, people came running from all the corners of the earth; this great work stopped them in amazement, left them wondering and lost for words. The Pope, his greatness fed by this success which encouraged him to further initiatives, rewarded Michelangelo with money and splendid presents.' (Vasari)"

Michelangelo – Pierluigi de Vecchi

Pope Julius II.
You remember Pope Julius, Pope Julius was the –

"Lying, deceiving, and manipulation are natural talents for psychopaths. With their powers of imagination in gear and focused on themselves, psychopaths appear amazingly unfazed by the possibility – or even the certainty – of being found out. When caught in a lie or challenged with the truth, they are seldom perplexed or embarrassed – they simply change their stories or attempt to rework the facts so that they appear to be consistent with the lie – Psychopaths have what it takes to defraud and bilk others: They are fast-talking, charming, self-assured, at ease in social situations, cool under pressure, unfazed by the possibility of being found out, and totally ruthless. And even when exposed, they can carry on as if nothing has happened – Given their personality, it comes as no surprise that psychopaths make good impostures. They have no hesitation in forging and brazenly using impressive credentials to adopt, chameleonlike, professions that give them prestige and power – If the profession also places a high premium on the ability to persuade or manipulate others, or to 'lay on hand,' so much the better. Thus, psychopaths find it easy to pose as financial consultants, ministers, counselors, and psychologists – The psychopath is like an infant, absorbed in his own needs, vehemently demanding satiation – Psychopaths (do also) display a general lack of empathy. They are indifferent to the rights and suffering of family members and strangers alike – Psychopaths are very good at giving their undivided attention to things that interest them most and at ignoring other things. Some clinicians have likened this process to a narrow-beamed searchlight that focuses on only one thing at a (point in) time (While) Their 'Mental packages' are not only small but two-dimensional, devoid of emotional meaning – Psychopaths seem to suffer a kind of emotional poverty that limits the depth and range of their feelings – Psychopaths are easily bored (and they) have an ongoing and excessive need for excitement – In some respects they are like the emotionless androids depicted in science fiction, unable to imagine what real humans experience."

Dr. Robert D. Hare – Without Conscience

Lying psychopathic con-artist who did simply hijack the name of God – The Son of God – Christianity – The Collective Consciousness of Mankind – The

Function of The Law: The Mind of God Made Manifest – The Eternal Harmony –
Our Innocence Lost: The Entrance to The Garden – The Kingdom of Heaven –
Virtue – Intelligence and Leonardo da Vinci too. And all to simply allow himself to
feed his own personally affected addiction: to worldly power only of course, and
truly humanistic being brain death only too of course.

And – remember, everything is exactly backwards, and exactly as was –

"Take care not to be deceived,' he said, 'because many will come using my
name and saying,' 'I am he'; and 'the time is near at hand.' Refuse to join them."
Luke 21: 8

Explained by the Son of God – again.
And, too, which was as He did simply explain: Don't do that! And –

"If, then, they say to you, 'Look, he is in the desert,' do not go there; 'Look, he
is in some hiding place,' do not believe it; because the coming of the Son of Man will
be like lightning striking in the East and flashing far into the West. Wherever the
corpse is, there the vultures will gather."
Matthew 24: 26-28

Again: DON'T DO THAT!   And –

"Do not imagine that I have come to abolish the law of the Prophets. I have
come not to abolish but to complete them. I tell you solemnly, tell heaven and earth
disappear, not one dot, not one little stroke, shall disappear from the law until its
purpose is achieved. Therefore, the man who infringes even one of the least of these
commandments and teaches others to do the same will be considered the least in the
kingdom of heaven."
Matthew 5: 17-19

Again: **DON'T DO THAT!**
But remember too, that all worldly psychopathic con-artists, do, always, only
exactly –

"Cezanne...tried to make the ultimate journey back through time – Cezanne
claimed, to believe in his own sensations. Cezanne was a lion in Nietzche's sense
and rules mattered little to him..."
Cezanne – Yvon Taillainder

Make up their own rules: and/or simply interpret them to conform to their
own personal predictions, and/or own personally affected truly humanistic brain
death. And too and of course, which is only exactly because, it will remain a
neurophysiological impossibility for them: any one individual who has already been

affected by the con, to understand any of the universally applicable *a priori* laws of Reality: it is a neurophysiological impossibility. While, they: any one individual who has already been affected by the con, will actually remain, only, capable of believing, exactly what they have been programmed to believe: by all of the worldly psychopathic con-artists, and/or their own personally affected, and absolutely dysfunctional, random agglomeration of individual nerve cells: of a brain.

Which will actually remain neurophysiologically incapable of understanding anything, and only neurophysiologically capable of believing, exactly only what they have been programmed to believe: by all of the worldly psychopathic con-artists. And/or their own personally affected: dysfunctional – fragmented – paranoid delusional – obsessive compulsive – psychopathic, and schizophrenic, random and chaotic agglomeration of individual nerve cells. And nobody is –

"Each of us lives within the universe – the prison – of his own brain. Projecting from it are millions of fragile sensory nerve fibers, in groups, uniquely adapted to sample the energetic states of the world about us: heat, light, force, and chemical compositions. That is all we ever know directly; all else is logical inference.."
The 3-Pound Universe – Judith Hooper and Dick Teresi

Going to explain Reality to them.
And/or too, nobody is –

"The psychopath is like an infant, absorbed in his needs, vehemently demanding satiation' – Psychopaths seem to suffer a kind of emotional poverty that limits the range and depth of their feelings – Sometimes they claim to experience strong emotions but are unable to describe the subtleties of various affective states. For example, they equate love with sexual arousal, sadness with frustration and anger with irritability – Psychopaths view people as little more than objects to be used for their own gratification – psychopaths sometimes verbalize remorse but then contradict themselves in words or actions – Besides being impulsive – doing things on the spur of the moment – psychopaths are highly reactive to perceived insults or slights – psychopaths are short-tempered or hot-headed and tend to respond to frustration, failure, discipline, and criticism with sudden violence, threats, and verbal abuse. They take offense easily and become angry and aggressive over trivialities, and often in a context that seems inappropriate to others."
Dr. Robert D. Hare – Without Conscience

Going to "Tell them what to do."
And/or begin to take away their allowed access to all of their excessive dopamine biochemical inducing effectual stimulus, functioning as pure *pleasure*. Which would be, while simultaneously explaining to them: all of the individually affected victims of the con and of the psychopathic con-artists, the absolute

neuroscientific truth. And which is the fact, that they would be only capable of functioning as an animal is capable functioning: if they do simply remain incapable of understanding, that this –

"Under pressure from Pope Julius II, Michelangelo finished the Sistine ceiling in tremendous haste. The vault was unveiled officially on 31 October 1512, the eve of All Saints, and was the subject of widespread admiration. Michelangelo was left exhausted by this titanic work: 'A great inconvenience of the project was that it forced him to paint with his head lifted, he ruined his eyesight to the extent that he could not read letters or look at drawings unless they were in the air and this lasted for several months' (Vasari). The Sistine became, according to Vasari, a form of 'academy of drawing' for artists visiting Rome who saw it as a mandatory point of reference – 'At the unveiling, people came running from all the corners of the earth; this great work stopped them in amazement, left them wondering and lost for words. The Pope, his greatness fed by this success which encouraged him to further initiatives, rewarded Michelangelo with money and splendid presents.' (Vasari)."
Michelangelo – Pierluigi de Vecchi

Excessive worldly thing, can not possibly be the very definition of The Function of The Law: The Mind of God made manifest – The Eternal Harmony – Our Innocence Lost: The Entrance to The Garden – The Kingdom of Heaven – Virtue, and Civilization too: it is a neurophysiological impossibility. And too which is – remember, as was exactly explained by –

"For I tell you, if your virtue goes no deeper than that of the scribes and Pharisees, you will never get into the kingdom of heaven."
Matthew 5: 20

The Son of God. And –

"No servant can be the slave of two masters: he will either hate the first and love the second, or treat the first with respect, and the second with scorn. You cannot be the slave of both God and money."
Luke 16: 13

Again. And –

"The Pharisees, who loved money, heard all this and laughed at him. He said to them, 'You are the very ones who pass yourselves off as virtuous in people's sight, but God knows your hearts. For what is thought highly of by men is loathsome in the sight of God."
Luke 16: 14-11

Again. And –

"But alas for you who are rich: you are having your consolation now. Alas for you who have your fill now: you shall go hungry. Alas for you when the world speaks well of you! This was the way their ancestors treated the false prophets."
Luke 6: 24-26

Again. And –

"One of the scribes who had listened to them debating and had observed how well Jesus answered them, now came up and put a question to him, 'Which is the first of all the commandments?' Jesus replied, 'This is the first: *Listen, Israel, the Lord our God is the one Lord, and you must love the Lord your God with all your heart, with all your soul, with all your mind and with all your strength.* The second is this: You must love your neighbor as yourself. There is no greater commandment than these."
Mark 12: 28-32

Again. And –

"Through towns and villages he went teaching, making his way to Jerusalem. Someone said to him, 'Sir, will there be only a few saved?' He said to them, 'Try your best to enter by the narrow door, because, I tell you, many will try to enter and will not succeed.'

'Once the master of the House has got up and locked the door, you may find yourself knocking on the door, saying, 'Lord, open to us,' but he will answer, 'I do not know where you come from.' Then you will find yourself saying, 'We once ate and drank in your company; you taught in our streets,' but he will reply, 'I do not know where you come from. *Away from me all you wicked men!*'

'Then there will be weeping and grinding of teeth, when you see Abraham and Isaac and Jacob and all the Prophets in the kingdom of God, and yourselves turned outside. And men from East and West, from the North and South will come to take their places at the feast in the kingdom of God.

'Yes, there are those now last who will be first, and those now first who will be last."
Luke 13: 22-30

Again.
And too remember, as was exactly –

"At birth a baby's language of the senses is primitive: he sees vague shapes, or flashes of light, but without meaning. His eyes can neither focus nor follow a moving object. He is even farsighted since his eyeballs are foreshortened at birth.

And what he sees is flat. He uses only one eye at a time, his eyes not yet working together to sight an object three-dimensionally..."

The Senses of Man – Joan Steen Wilentz

Verified by 20th century neuroscientific research: again. And –

"If humans are less robotlike than salamanders or ducks, it's not because we have no wired-in behaviors. In fact, we have quite a few. What makes the difference is the ratio of 'unwired' to wired-in gray matter, because neurons that are not committed at birth to a set function – are available for learning, for modification. Virtually all the cells in the amphibian or reptile brain directly process sensory information – or control movement, but in humans a great gray area – about three-fourths of the cortex, lies between sensory input and motor output, called the association areas. These include the frontal lobes..."

The 3-Pound universe – Judith Hooper and Dick Teresi

Again. And –

"Drugs are like sledgehammers,' observes Dr. Eric Nestler of the Yale University School of Medicine. 'They profoundly alter many pathways' – the realization that dopamine may be a common endpoint of all those pathways represents a signal advance. Provocative – the dopamine hypothesis provides a basic framework for understanding (what does) create a serious behavioral disorder..."

Addicted – J. Madeleine Nash – Time – May 5, 1997

Again. And –

"Candace Pert: I see the brain in terms of quantum mechanics – the brain is just a receiver, an amplifier, a little wet minireceiver for collective reality. We make maps, but we should never confuse the map with the territory' (while) the ratio of frontal core may be one index of evolutionary advancement – What the frontal lobes 'control' is something like awareness, or self-awareness – Do these lobes govern some essential feature of humanness, or even godliness, as some scientists have suggested? 'If God speaks to man, if man speaks to God,' neuroscientist Candace Pert tells us, 'it would be through the frontal lobes, which is the part of the brain that has undergone the most evolutionary expansion' – Stephen LaBarge: 'And it's capable of what look like miraculous things, so miraculous that we're tempted to say it's divine, that it's not natural."

The 3-Pound Universe – Judith Hooper and Dick Teresi

Again. And –

"...As we found with quantum mechanics, the full structure of the world is richer than our language can express – There are two essential yet complementary aspects of this new vision of time which are as striking in contrast as heaven and hell. Heaven is ruled by dynamical equations that are reversible and 'timeless'; their simplicity ensures stability for eternity. Hell is more akin to the real world, where fluctuations, uncertainty and chaos reign..."

The Arrow of Time – Peter Coveny and Roger Highfield

Again.

But too remember, we will listen to no words: while actually allowing our own selves to function as scientists within this Edenic tale, and we will employ, only, the use of our personally acquired truly humanistic empirical self-consciousness, to enable our very own selves to plainly understand the absolute truth, and for now and forever too. Which is while simply allowing our very own selves, to become capable of coming to a complete understanding, that this –

"Under pressure from Pope Julius II, Michelangelo finished the Sistine ceiling in tremendous haste. The vault was finally unveiled officially on 31 October 1512, the eve of All Saints, and was the subject of widespread admiration – The Sistine became, according to Vasari, a form of 'academy of drawing' for artists visiting Rome who saw it as a mandatory point of reference – 'At the unveiling, people came running from all the corners of the earth; this great work stopped them in amazement, left them wondering and lost for words. The Pope, his greatness fed by this success which encouraged him to further initiatives, rewarded Michelangelo with money and splendid presents.' (Vasari)"

Michelangelo – Pierluigi de Vecchi

Excessive aristocratic tangible form mass stimulus: and/or excessively worldly thing, cannot possibly be the definition of civilization. And which is – as we can remember, while the very definition of the word civilization is: "an advanced state of human society, in which a high level of culture, science, industry, and government has been reached," and to; "to make civil; bring out of a primitive or uneducated state; enlighten" – civilize too, and while within this Edenic tale also. Because: remember where we began this Edenic tale, which is of the greatest collective con in the entire history of mankind, and which was while with Paleolithic cave men, and while within the confines of their cave man caves. And – too, which was as they: Paleolithic cave men, did begin to become capable of forming truly humanistic self-consciousness, while simply communicating their formed understanding of Reality, and while simply abstractly projecting it: their personally formed understanding of elementary Reality, upon their Paleolithic cave man walls. Which was while functioning as simple two-dimensional graphic illustrations and/or pictures, and as unidirectionally successive, and elementary, Time *made manifest* also. And how – now, we can simply fully understand: for our own selves, that *this* thing –

227

"Under pressure from Pope Julius II, Michelangelo finished the Sistine ceiling in tremendous haste. The vault was unveiled officially on 31 October 1512, the eve of All Saints, and was the subject of widespread admiration – The Sistine became, according to Vasari, a form of 'academy of drawing' for artists visiting Rome who saw it as a mandatory point of reference.' (Vasari)"
Michelangelo – Pierluigi de Vecchi

Is nothing more than a fancy cave, and/or an excessive aristocratic elitist environment, actually effectually functioning as a simple dopamine biochemical inducing stimulus. And – also and simultaneously, absolutely nothing more than that which –

"Candace Pert: We've measured opiate receptors in everything from fruit fly heads to human brains. Even uni-cellular organisms have peptides' – Do you think even cockroaches feel some sort of emotion we ask – 'They have to, because they have chemicals that put them in the mood to mate and chemicals that make them run away when they're about to be killed. That's what emotions are about – pain and pleasure – punishment and reward – Behavior is controlled by the anticipation of pain or pleasure, punishment or reward. And that has to be coded in the brain."
The 3-Pound Universe – Judith Hooper and Dick Teresi

An animal is only capable of experiencing.
And – too, it is –

"...As we found with quantum mechanics, the full structure of the world is richer than our language can express – There are two essential yet complementary aspects of this new vision of time which are as striking in contrast as heaven and hell. Heaven is ruled by dynamical equations that are reversible and 'timeless'; their simplicity ensures stability for eternity. Hell is more akin to the real world, where fluctuations, uncertainty and chaos reign..."
The Arrow of Time – Peter Coveny and Roger Highfield

Only hell made manifest: within the mind of any one individual, who has, actually, allowed their own selves to become capable of forming a truly humanistic Omnidimensional refractive gem of a mind, and parallel functioning central nervous system, for their own selves, and to be in possession of only. And exactly because there is – *exactly*, no simultaneously relative Omnidimensional syntax represented there. And – too, there is less truly humanistic intelligence represented there, than there is upon the Paleolithic cave man walls. Simply because, there is *no* truly humanistic, and simultaneously relative, single cognizable point time zero, represented there: upon *any* "ceiling" of *any* kind. And *any* "thing" that is represented "projected upon a ceiling," is nothing more than that which could *only* exist, within –

"Ernst Hanfstaengl, describes the shapelessness at the root of Hitler's mesmerizing oratorical power: 'His brain was a sort of primeval jelly or ectoplasm which quivered in response to every impulse from its surroundings – You could never pin him down, say that he was this thing or that thing, it was all floating, without roots...'"

Michael Nelken M. D. – Hitler Unmasked

Adolf Hitler's mind, as a matter of fact.

And there certainly is no truly humanistic simultaneously relative Omnidimensional syntax represented there: and/or simultaneously relative Omnidimensional Time *made manifest*.

And which: simultaneously relative Omnidimensional syntax, and/or simultaneously relative Omnidimensional Time *made manifest*, is the very definition of the Mind of God made manifest – The Eternal Harmony – The Kingdom of Heaven – Our Innocence Lost and The Entrance to The Garden also, and which is the function of *The Annunciation* – and only *The Annunciation* also, while actually functioning as truly humanistic Omnidimensional Time *made manifest*.

So we can also, now, simply understand exactly what Pope Julius II did actually do: for his own self. To enable himself to become capable of receiving some worldly power for his own self, while actually functioning as a worldly psychopathic con-artist, and which was to simply employ the use of Adolf Hitler's applied basic formula for worldly political empowerment. As he: Pope Julius II, did simply enable them: his personally affected victims of primary suggestibility, and truly humanistic brainwashing too, an opportunity to move their bodies while as in a purposefully effectuated direction, to enable their own selves to become capable of consuming some excessive abstracted dopamine biochemical inducing stimulus, actually functioning as pure *pleasure* only. And which was as the individually affected human beings, were actually participating in an orgy: of excessive dopamine biochemical inducing stimulus, while becoming the In Crowd of the aristocratic elite, which was actually being purposefully allowed exposure to the dopamine biochemical inducing effectual stimulus, functioning as pure *pleasure* only: for their own selves to consume. And – then, to simply begin to increase the tempo of the party, while beginning to enable everybody to –

"After being released into the synapses (the gap between nerve endings and receiver cells), dopamine binds to receptors on the next neuron – the dopamine is either quickly reabsorbed or broken down by the enzyme monoamine oxidase (MOA)."

Addicted – J. Madeleine Nash – Time – May 5, 1997

Reach climax: and/or have an orgasm.

And – then and after reaching climax, to allow them: all of the individually affected human beings, who were actually being allowed exposure to the excessive

229

dopamine biochemical inducing effectual stimulus, functioning as pure *pleasure* only, to simply: "Dissociate yourself from the function of the Reality before you," and –

"The little red wagon keeps flying along; imaginations can go flying on red wagons – 'A wagon unleashes a child's imagination – It can be anything a child imagines it to be..."
> Cliff Edwards – Philadelphia Inquirer/Associated Press- Saturday May 3, 1997

Reapply your childish imagination: to go flying off in a direction towards heaven.

Which was, also, while actually informing them: all of his personally affected victims of primary suggestibility, and/or truly humanistic brainwashing, that it is simply: Just that easy. Actually –

"Spreading a science spark –
He rose early, left his Delaware County home, and headed over the Ben Franklin Bridge shortly after 9 a.m., arriving in a once-proud South Camden neighborhood with brimming boxes and stuffed cases – But G-'s journey was years in the making – On most days (he is) a biology professor at (a) University. Last week, however, he made his annual pilgrimage to (a) middle school to lead a group of eighth graders in a class on art and neuronanatomy, the study of the structure of the brain – They (the students) gazed up at the intense man in the long white lap coat – eight boys hungry for far more than just lunch – G- asked two boys (to) hold up a print of Michelangelo's *Creation of Adam* – The fresco, from the ceiling of the Sistine Chapel, shows God reaching out to Adam. For nearly 500 years, scholars almost uniformly interpreted the painting as showing God giving life to man – But in 1990, G- explained, a doctor pointed out that God was portrayed in front of an image that resembles an anatomically accurate human brain and hypothesized that God was giving knowledge, not just life – G- told the students about a beneficent force giving knowledge to all people – then he showed them – After engaging the boys in a lively discussion about zombies, anatomy and Descartes, he presented them with dissection equipment and eight sheep brains..."
> Kristen A. Graham – The Philadelphia Inquirer – Friday December 28, 2001

Gaining access to universally applicable Omnidimensional Time *made manifest*: The Mind of God made manifest – The Eternal Harmony – The Kingdom of Heaven – Our Innocence Lost, and The Entrance to The Garden also, and while according to the worldly psychopathic con-artist that was Pope Julius II.

Except: in scientific reality, and exactly as the scientist Leonardo da Vinci did explain –

"And you think to comprehend the mind of God which embraces the whole universe, weighing and dissecting it as though you were making an anatomy. O human stupidity! Do you not perceive that you have spent your whole life with yourself and yet are not aware of that which you have most in evidence, and that is your own foolishness?"

NO IT IS NOT: Just that easy.

Because – remember, in this real Edenic tale, there is only one thing that is exactly not just that easy, to actually become capable of acquiring for your own self to be in possession of, and/or to maintain a hold of. Which is the acquisition of truly humanistic, universally applicable, empirical self-consciousness, and/or a truly humanistic soul, and/or control over your very own self. And while – and simultaneously and while in this real Edenic tale also, there is, exactly, only one thing that is just that easy to be in possession of for your own self, and/or to become capable of experiencing for your own self, and that is – only, truly humanistic brain death, and/or the ability to actually lose control over your very own self, and/or to become capable of simply selling your soul: to a master manipulating worldly psychopathic con-artist. And too – remember and in the real Edenic tale, exactly how the worldly master manipulating psychopathic con-artist, did become capable of conning his victims into selling their souls; and/or simply beginning to become capable of actually experiencing truly humanistic brain death for their very own selves; and/or simply relinquishing control over their very own selves to the worldly psychopathic con-artist, and which was while conning them into becoming capable of understanding absolutely nothing for their own selves, and while being in possession of absolutely nothing for their own selves: except for their personally affected truly humanistic brain death. And to then – and simultaneously, become capable of believing anything that they were being told, by the worldly psychopathic con-artist, and that they could simply acquire anything they simply wanted, and/or have it simply given to them. And – too remember and while in the real Edenic tale also, exactly that the worldly master manipulating psychopathic con-artist, did become capable of conning his victims into believing: as they were beginning to become victims of the con, that if they did simply obey the exact Letter of The Law, then they: the individual victims who he was attempting to con, were – simply, allowing their very own selves to be controlled: by somebody else who was taking control over them, but how – in neuroscientific reality, that was only exactly backwards. And that they: the victims of the worldly psychopathic con-artist, did actually become capable of relinquishing control of their very own selves, and/or actually capable of selling their souls, and/or capable of exactly contradicting the letter of The Law, so that they could become capable of becoming a part of the In Crowd: which was consuming the absolutely abstracted dopamine biochemical inducing stimulus, actually functioning as pure *pleasure* only, and/or The Apple. And – too remember and again while in the real Edenic tale, that there were two separate, and individually affected, victims of the con: The Man and The Woman,

231

and while each did simply sell their souls. And how the Woman enabled herself to become the first victim, by becoming conned into believing that she could simply acquire anything she ever wanted, by allowing herself to –

"The Penis as Text for serious Thinkers –
Lyndon B. Johnson once answered reporters badgering him about why the United States was in Vietnam with a simple, off-the-record gesture: he unzipped, pulled out his penis and said, 'This is why!"
Emily Nussbaum – The New York Times – Saturday, December 22, 2001

Simply become capable of taking control over one other individually affected human being: A Man. And – too, which is to simply enable her: A Woman, own self to –

"Alas for you, scribes and Pharisees, you hypocrites! You who shut up the kingdom of heaven in men's faces, neither going in yourselves nor allowing others to go in who want to.
Alas for you, scribes and Pharisees, you hypocrites! You who travel over sea and land to make a single proselyte, and when you have him you make him twice as fit for hell as you are."
Matthew 23: 13-15

Effect one single individually affected victim of the con. Who: The Man, will simply continue to allow his very own self to be controlled, and/or simply sell his soul, so that he can continue to receive only exactly what it is that he does –

"A baby passes her first amazing milestone before the typical mother has even wiped off the sweat of labor. Full-term newborns, scientist established in 1986, recognize and prefer their mother's face to all others – In the ingenious experiment, the scientists had babies suck a special pacifier that controlled a video screen. Depending on how the infant sucked, fast or slow, the image of Mom or another woman appeared; babies sucked so they'd see Mom..."
Joan Raymond – Newsweek – Fall/Winter 2000

Need: his mother's breast, and/or allowed access to any amounts of absolutely abstracted dopamine biochemical inducing effectual stimulus, actually functioning as pure *pleasure* only. And/or –

"The Penis as Text for serious Thinkers –
Lyndon B. Johnson once answered reporters badgering him about why the United States was in Vietnam with a simple, off-the-record gesture: he unzipped, pulled out his penis and said, 'This is why!"
Emily Nussbaum – The New York Times – Saturday December 22, 2001

Sex: An orgasm – A climax – An orgy – The Apple – allowed access to any amounts of dopamine biochemical inducing effectual stimulus, actually functioning as pure *pleasure* only, it is all the exact same thing in neuroscientific Reality. And which is: that an individually affected Man is getting only exactly what he does want, while – and of course, an individually affected Woman will be also – and simultaneously, getting only exactly what she wants: while as through her ability to control a Man, and/or a single individually affected victim of the con. Which is also, while neither of which: The Man nor The Woman, will be getting only exactly what it is that they do need, and which is the ability to take back control over their very own selves, and/or the courage to face-up to our 21st century Reality. And to – then, become capable of enabling their own selves an opportunity to find their Innocence Lost: The Entrance to The Garden – The Eternal Harmony – The Kingdom of Heaven, and The Mind of God made manifest. And too which would be while, exactly while taking back control over their very own selves, enabling there own selves an opportunity to become capable of breaking free of the attractive force, which is our excessively simplistic mortal existence while upon this point-mass of Earth.

Except, remember, beginning to become capable of taking back control over your very own self, and facing-up to Reality, is extremely painful. And it is too late, for the overwhelming vast majority of mankind, at this point in time while upon the threshold of the 21st century and in this real Edenic tale too. We have exactly passed the point of no return: The cast is set, and the damage done. This is the very beginning of the end of time, and everybody is going to die: soon.

Because – remember, there is only one thing that cannot be forcibly taken from individual human beings, and that is their truly humanistic universally applicable empirical self-consciousness, and/or their truly humanistic universally applicable simultaneously relative Omnidimensional memory, and/or their truly humanistic soul. But they: any individually affected victim of the con, can also, and simultaneously, be simply conned, and/or tricked, and/or brainwashed, into simply, and "willfully," relinquishing it: control over their very own selves, to any worldly psychopathic con-artist, and/or any one other individually affected human being, who may be simply afraid of facing-up to Reality, and of being alone, just like in the real Edenic tale, and which is this one also. And the majority of our entire global society, while at this point in time while upon the threshold of the 21st century, has already lost control over their very own selves. So they will, simply and exactly, sell their souls – and/or allow their very own selves to remain controlled by all of the worldly psychopathic con-artists, who are supplying them with allowed access to all of their dopamine biochemical inducing stimulus, actually functioning as pure *pleasure* and/or The Apple. And/or they: any one individually affected victim of the con, will sell their soul, to simply appease any other one individually affected victim of the con, and all of which is to simply allow their very own selves: all of the individually affected the victims of the con and well as in this real Edenic tale too, an opportunity to –

"The chief priests and elders, however, had persuaded the crowd to demand the release of Barabbas and the execution of Jesus. So when the governor spoke and asked them, 'Which of the two do you want me to release for you?' they said, 'Barabbas.' 'But in that case,' Pilate said to them, 'what am I to do with Jesus who is called Christ?' They all said, 'let him be crucified!' 'Why?' he asked. 'What harm has he done?'"
Matthew 27: 20-23

Betray the Collective Consciousness of Mankind: Sell their souls, and/or allow their very own selves to become victims of primary suggestibility, exactly brainwashed, and while allowing their very own selves to remain controlled by their fear of facing-up to Reality. Which is as they will continue to allow their own selves to be controlled by, either, even one other individually affected human being, and/or all of the worldly psychopathic con-artists, who are supplying them with allowed access to all of their 21st century, absolutely abstracted, dopamine biochemical inducing stimulus, actually functioning as pure *pleasure* only, and/or The Apple. And too which is as they allow their own selves, an opportunity to remain a part of the In Crowd: which is being allowed exposure to –

"It was now about the sixth hour and, with the sun eclipsed, a darkness came over the whole land until the ninth hour. The veil of the Temple was torn right down the middle; and when Jesus had cried out in a loud voice, he said, 'Father, *into your hands I commit my spirit*.' With these words he breathed his last.
When the centurion saw what had taken place, he gave praise to God and said, 'This was a great and good man.' And when all the people who had gathered for the spectacle saw what had happened, they went home beating their breasts.
All his friends stood at a distance; so also did the women who had accompanied him from Galilee, and they saw all this happen."
Luke 23: 44-49

The spectacle of the two-dimensional plane: and the facade of the psychopathic aristocratic environment which it was built upon, and which is now torn in half. It is Time: This is *The Annunciation* – it is Time, and the absolute truth has now been exposed: for all the world to simply see with our eyes alone. And any one individually affected human being, who can not take back control over their very own self: has sold their soul. The two-dimensional plane has now been torn in half, and the lie which was the supposed global socioeconomic structure which was placed upon it, is –

"Therefore, everyone who listens to these words of mine and acts on them will be like a sensible man who built his house on rock. Rain came down, floods rose, gales blew and hurled themselves against that house and it did not fall: It was founded on rock. But everyone who listens to these words of mine and does not act

on them will be like a stupid man who built his house on sand. Rain came down, floods rose, gales blew and struck that house, and it fell; and what a fall it had."
Matthew 7: 24-27

Beginning to collapse.
And which is exactly why, it is –

"Do not suppose that I have come to bring peace to the earth: it is not peace I have come to bring, but a sword. For I have come to set *a man against his father, a daughter against her mother, a daughter-in-law against her mother-in-law. A man's enemies will be those of his own household.*"
Matthew 10: 34-36

Going to get really ugly – really fast.
Exactly because, it: allowed access to all worldly psychopathic dopamine biochemical inducing stimulus, actually functioning as pure *pleasure* only, is exactly what did, first, cause all of the affected truly humanistic dysfunction, and while it must be stopped: immediately. Which is exactly because –

"A Declaration by the Representatives of the United States of America:
We hold these truths to be self-evident: that all men are created equal; that they are endowed by their Creator with CERTAIN [*inherent and*] inalienable rights; that among these are life, liberty, and the pursuit of happiness; that to secure these rights, governments are instituted among men, deriving their just powers from the consent of the governed; that whenever any form of government becomes destructive of these ends, it is the right of the people to alter or to abolish it, and to institute a new government, laying its foundation on such principles, and organizing its power in such form, as to them shall seem most likely to effect their safety and happiness..."

It: all worldly purely psychopathic dopamine biochemical inducing stimulus actually functioning as pure *pleasure* only, does have no foundation in Reality, and it does too – *exactly*, have absolutely no function, in truly humanistic self-evident Reality. Except to –

"Drugs are like sledgehammers,' observes Dr. Eric Nestler of the Yale University School of Medicine. 'They profoundly alter many pathways' – the realization that dopamine may be a common endpoint of all those pathways represents a signal advance. Provocative – the dopamine hypothesis provides a basic framework for understanding (what does) create a serious behavioral disorder..."
Addicted – J. Madeleine Nash – Time – May 5, 1997

Begin to become capable of destroying the foundation, and the framework too. Of an individual human being's own personally affected mind, and parallel functioning central nervous system, and begin to become capable of actually causing a serious behavioral disorder – an extreme neurophysiological dysfunction, and personally affected truly humanistic brain death too: for all of the individually affected victims of the con. Who: all of the individually affected victims of the con, and while at this point in time while upon the threshold of the 21st century, will actually remain incapable of functioning as truly humanistic beings are capable of functioning. And which: actually functioning as a truly humanistic being, is quantum electrodynamically, simultaneously, and in parallel, and while beginning to become capable of processing truly humanistic, complex, simultaneously relative multidimensional sensory input information, and/or simply understanding truly humanistic universally applicable *a priori* Reality. And/or, beginning to become capable of actually getting on the side of truth, and/or simply beginning to become capable of understanding it. And/or – too, simply beginning to become capable of taking back control over your very own self, and while as from all the worldly psychopathic con-artists.

But, remember, all of the worldly psychopathic con-artists: who are supplying allowed access to all the worldly psychopathic dopamine biochemical inducing stimulus, actually functioning as pure *pleasure* only and/or The Apple, are not going to let that happen, without a war actually being waged for that control. And too remember, because without that: control over other human beings, they will have nothing, because they have absolutely nothing for their own selves to be in possession of, except for their own personally affected truly humanistic brain death, and their addiction to all of their worldly stuff, while including their addiction to worldly power. And without that: their control over other human beings, their –

"Therefore, everyone who listens to these words of mine and acts on them will be like a sensible man who built his house on rock. Rain came down, floods rose, gales blew and hurled themselves against that house and it did not fall: It was founded on rock. But everyone who listens to these words of mine and does not act on them will be like a stupid man who built his house on sand. Rain came down, floods rose, gales blew and struck that house, and it fell; and what a fall it had."
Matthew 7: 24-27

Entire worlds *will* come crumbling down.
So all of the worldly psychopathic con-artists, are going to be – now, beginning to create –

"Which Wizard Beats 'Em All –
There can't be many people left who haven't read a Harry Potter book or seen the movie, who don't find the name Dumbledore at least vaguely familiar. And Gandalf, the great wizard of 'The Lord Of The Rings,' has long been almost as ensconced in the popular imagination as Merlin – It also seems a strange coincidence that fantasy is having a popular surge in troubled time. But in fact all movies are

fantasies – Having more than one wizard in the multiplex does, however, raise one tremendously important question – the big question is: Who is your favorite wizard? Gandalf? Dumbledore? Merlin? The Wizard of Oz..."
James Gorman – The New York Times – Friday January 11, 2002

An even greater diversion from Reality. And while – simultaneously, telling all of their individually affected victims: of the con, to: "Pay no attention" – to the Reality beyond the facade of two-dimensional plane, or to the reality of our own personally affected 21st century absolutely dysfunctional aristocracy. And to only continue to escape it: Reality, while remaining absolutely ignorant of it, and a part of the special In Crowd, which is being allowed access into the absolutely abstracted, dopamine biochemical inducing effectual stimulus, actually functioning as pure *pleasure* only: and/or the absolute diversion from *a priori* Reality. Which is the Reality beyond the facade of the two-dimensional plane, and which has just been torn in half, and too which is while actually functioning as the function of *The Annunciation*.

Which is exactly what is, now, actually beginning to occur: the actual function of *The Annunciation*. And the very beginning of the collapse of the entire global socioeconomic system, which was simply placed upon the façade, of the psychopathic dopamine biochemical inducing stimulus, actually functioning as pure *pleasure* only and/or The Apple, and too which they did actually con the majority of the entire world, to simply not look beyond. Because: remember, human beings were simply never supposed to consume vast amounts of any of them, let alone all of them: simultaneously. And while including: all worldly political empowerment and worldly political opportunism – money, all worldly spectacle events, television, movies and the theater. All absolutely abstracted, and excessively histrionic, musical performances, while including all of the Romantic period, and atonality, polytonality, dissonance and discord, and too all excessively simplistic, and monochromatic, riffs and chords. All of "pop" any thing. All excessively, and deliberately, styled, tangible form mass buildings: art museum parks; theme parks; amusement parks; spectacle event parks, and spectator sporting event parks. All segregated shopping malls; lushly landscaped gardens; gold; silver; diamonds and fine fabrics. All alcoholic laced beverages; caffeine laced beverages; fatty tasting foods and excessively sweet foods. All deliberately styled, and relatively accelerated, transportation methods: automobiles; trains and airplanes. All grandiosely, and deliberately, styled, humanistic beings: movie stars, and television stars, and sports stars, and boy band stars, and girl band stars, and pop icon stars – all worldly god stars. All computers, and video recorders, and cell phones, and the Internet, and virtual reality, and dot-coms. All worldly things, they are all the Apple only, and –

"The Pharisees, who loved money, heard all this and laughed at him. He said to them, 'You are the very ones who pass yourselves off as virtuous in people's sight,

237

but God knows your hearts. For what is thought highly of by men is loathsome in the sight of God."
Luke 16: 14-15

Exactly loathsome in the sight of God.

While no human being society was ever supposed to actually enable their own selves, to become capable of being conned into believing that you could attempt to construct some kind of a socioeconomic structure upon it: because it has no foundation in Reality, so it is simply impossible. And the purposefully affected function, of absolute abstract consumerism, did simply mean, that the very small percentage of the –

"Grounded by an Income Gap –
For 30 years the gap between the richest Americans and everyone else has been growing so much that the level of inequality is higher than in any other industrialized nation – What no one can quit figure out, though, is why, or even whether anything should be done about it – Why there has been increasing inequality in this country has been one of the big puzzles in our field and has absorbed a lot of intellectual effort,' said M- , a professor of economics – 'But if you ask me whether we should worry about the fact that some people on Wall Street and basketball players are making a lot of money, I say no – With inequality growing throughout the industrialized world, M- like many economists, has come to see inequality as a basic feature of the new high-tech economic scene, the natural consequence of an economy that has begun to reward talent, skills, education and and entrepreneurial risk with increasing efficiency – 'There is no doubt that market forces have spoken in favor of more inequality,' said R-, a professor of economics – Just look at the figures. Most of the incredible wealth generated during the 1990's boom went to the richest of the rich. 'Fourty-seven percent of the total real income gain between 1983 and 1998 accrued to the top 1 percent of income recipients, 42 percent went to the next 19 percent, and 12 percent accrued to the bottom 80 percent'..."
Alexander Stille – The New York Times – Saturday December 15, 2001

Worldly psychopathic con-artists: corporation CEO's – Sophists – artists – novelists – entertainers – professional athletes – sports stars – pop icon stars – boy band stars – girl band stars – spin-doctors – religious political opportunists: TV evangelists – fanatics and zealots, did enable their own selves to become much richer, only while at –

"In plastic we spend, dizzyingly –
As the number of personal bankruptcies soared during the 1980's and '90s, something less obvious but more far-reaching was happening in the relationship between creditors and debtors: a dramatic shift in how Americans borrowed and spent money – The main instrument of change was the bank credit card (and) easy

access to credit they allowed – Credit cards helped fuel the 1990's boom, the longest uninterrupted economic expansion on record. They sped the latest high-tech products – CD players, Web-linked computers, wireless telephones – into people's hands much faster than hot new inventions spread in earlier eras. They helped many people, even those near the bottom of the economic ladder, share in the sense of prosperity – But there are researchers and consumer advocates who see a darker side to the changes that credit cards have fostered, especially as the economy slows down and fears of recession increase. For all the benefits the cards offered to most people, they have enabled others to get so deeply into debt that they can't see a way out. Sometimes, they can't tell what hit them until it's too late... "

Jeff Geles – The Philadelphia Inquirer – Sunday April 8, 2000

The expense of the common man masses. Which was as they: the common man masses, did simply allow their very own selves, to become consumed by truly humanistic dysfunction – addiction to excessive amounts of abstracted dopamine biochemical inducing stimulus, and truly humanistic brain death: *and* victims of the con, of their truly humanistic universally applicable empirical self-consciousness, and/or their souls.

And – remember, exactly because that: the purely humanistic ability to regress back to point time zero, while experiencing truly humanistic brain death and personally affected addictions to absolutely abstracted conspicuous consumption, and/or beginning to become neurophysiologically incapable of seeing past the single point of The Apple, was exactly the function of the con: while in this real Edenic tale. Which is the facade of the two-dimensional plane, and/or all allowed exposure to absolutely abstracted: psychopathic, dopamine biochemical inducing stimulus, actually functioning as pure *pleasure* only, and/or The Apple. And human beings were never supposed to do that: simply allow their own selves to become capable of neurophysiologically regressing back to point time zero, and *only* capable of remaining focused upon the single point of The Apple, and while actually becoming capable of experiencing truly humanistic brain death for their own selves, to be in possession of and only. And too exactly because, absolute abstracted consumerism, does have no function in truly humanistic Reality: except only to cause truly humanistic dysfunction, and while actually functioning as the applied function of *the* con. And – too remember, while it: absolutely abstracted consumerism, was simply an inversely affected part of the con, as it was proportionately applicable – as it was inversely affected by appreciated stock holdings in absolute abstract companies. While these absolutely abstracted companies, did simply begin to create a New World Order, and/or the facade of their so-called 21st century communication-age economy, while implementing the facade of their "special purpose vehicles," "credit derivatives," "gain-on-sale treatment" and "off-balance-sheet financing. " And/or their –

239

"The Financial Wizard Tied to Enron's Fall –

Before the financial shell games; before Chewco, Raptor and LJM; before the partnerships that earned him $30 million, Andrew S. Fastow had his first setback at the Enron Corporation – The setback came in 1996, when Mr. Fastow (was) nearly fired for the poor job he did running a retail unit that aimed to put Enron into competition with local utilities around the country – Mr. Fastow – was simply out of his element among the intricacies of the retail market – 'What the guy knew was numbers and finance,' a longtime colleague said – Today, investigators think Mr. Fastow's wizardry, his ability to run the company's assets and depts into complicated off-balance-sheet deals, was a central cause of Enron's undoing. What Mr. Fastow presented as an arrangement intended to benefit Enron – became, over time, a means of enriching himself personally, and facilitating manipulation of Enron's financial statements...It was not as if he needed the money, his friends say; his wife, the former Lea Weingarten, is the heiress to a Houston real estate fortune. But Mr. Fastow was adamant, friends say, in his belief that the amount of money a person made was the only meaningful measure of success in business (Even) after Mr. Fastow retreated into seclusion last fall, to continue building an 11,500 square foot house in Houston's wealthy River Oaks neighborhood – The Fastows also maintain an art collection, some of which has been displayed at the Contemporary Arts Museum and at the Menil Collection, both in Houston..."

D. Barboza/J. Schwartz – The New York Times, Wed. February 6, 2002

Financial wizardry: and/or the applied art of the con – it is all the same thing.

And, of course, which: that the worldly psychopathic con-artists did become capable of empowering only their own selves, was while they: all of the worldly psychopathic con-artists, did always only –

"Whiz Kids Living Caviar Dreams –

Rolling in dot-com riches, they're going to extremes with a devil-may-care twist on traditional travel extravagance – Luxury travel is the new domain of the young, newly rich and extremely restless – freshly minted millionaires are speed-dialing their cell phones to say: 'Book the best, and book it now' ' It's the youth and money (of new luxury-travel clients) that's absolutely staggering,' says 30-year travel agent Joyce S- ,'They want to be kept moving, they want to be entertained or pampered,' says Kelly M- (and) Price is no object for members of the mile-high-spending club – T- hosted a couple in their 20's who lunched on hamburgers washed down with (a) $1,500 bottle of Petrus bordeaux from France. 'High-end wine is big,' he says. 'It's nothing for them to spend $600 to $1,000 on a bottle for dinner'...The got-bucks young are different: they laugh louder than those at the next table...'

Kitty Bean Yancey – USA TODAY

Laugh all the way to their worldly banks.

And again, but this: *The Annunciation,* is –

240

"But alas for you who are rich: you are having your consolation now. Alas for you who have your fill now: you shall go hungry. Alas for you who laugh now: you shall mourn and weep. Alas for you when the world speaks well of you! This was the way their ancestors treated the false prophets."
Luke 6: 24-26

When the laughter does stop.
And too and of course, beginning to become capable of making large amounts of money is the single easiest thing, for any one individual person, to become capable of doing: while as in the entire history of mankind and for their own selves. And, as was exactly explained by Thomas Jefferson, which is, as –

"...Self-love, therefore, is no part of morality. Indeed it is exactly its counterpart. It is the sole antagonist of virtue, leading us constantly by our propensities to self-gratification in violation of our moral duties to others..."
Thomas Jefferson (To) Thomas Law – Poplar Forest – June 13, 1814

All an individual needs to do: to actually allow their own selves to become capable of making large amounts of money, is to enable their very own selves to become so exceedingly brain dead, that it does simply become a neurophysiological impossibility, for them to care about anything else: Except for their own brain dead Pig selves – their addiction to all things worldly, and –

"Adolf Hitler: The greatest revolutionary changes and achievements of this earth, its greatest cultural accomplishments (are) forever inseparably bound up with a name and are represented by it – The progress and culture of humanity are not a product of the majority, but rest exclusively on the genius and energy of the personality – Some idea of genius arises in the brain of a man who feels called upon to transmit his knowledge to the rest of humanity. He preaches his view and gradually wins a certain circle of adherents. This process of the direct and personal transmittance of a man's ideas to the rest of his fellow men is the most ideal and natural – They (the individual) are always on the lookout for new stimulation. These people are quick to weary of everything; they want variety, and they are never able to feel or understand the needs of their fellow man – By 'us' I mean all the hundreds of thousands who fundamentally long for the same thing without as individuals finding the words to describe outwardly what they inwardly visualize..."

All of the other individually affected so-called human beings, who are accompanying them in their misery. To simply give their worldly gods control over their own selves, while as in exchange for being allowed access to the spectacle of the excessive dopamine biochemical inducing stimulus, functioning as pure *pleasure* only.
And – again, which is as they: the worldly psychopathic con-artists who are

241

actually supplying allowed access to the spectacle, of all of our worldly psychopathic dopamine biochemical inducing stimulus functioning as pure *pleasure* only, will be continuing to tell, and/or convince, all of their individually affected victims, that they *should* only –

"Celebrities eclipse NBA court action –
All-Star Game becomes a made-for-Hollywood event.
Gazing at the celebrities gracing the sidelines for the 2002 NBA All-Star Game, you couldn't help but ask the question: What in the world do you do with a two-way pager – 'I use it to keep in touch with my daughter,' said R&B singer Angie Stone, who sang a soulful medley of 'America the Beautiful' and 'Lift Every Voice and Sing' with Grammy-nominated songstress Alicia Keys – 'It's very good to use in noisy arenas' – It must be. Because during almost every break in the action, the celebs broke out their little hand-held computers to retrieve their instant messages – And the 19,581 fans who jammed into the First Union Center watched them do it, watched their every move, watched the celebrities more than they watched the game that drew tens of thousands of fans to Philadelphia this weekend – This is what All-Star Weekend has been about – stargazing – The All-Star Game is the NBA's Super Bowl, and the marketed-minded league transformed the game into a made-for-Hollywood event – The weekend didn't come and go without much criticism. Much has been made of the excess and narcissism of players this weekend and the glorification by their fans – 'Everybody should just focus on the positive,' said Star Jones, a host of ABC's *The View* and a die-hard basketball fan who says she has attended all-Star games for the last five years. 'Overall, I think it's wonderful...'"
Annette John-Hall – The Philadelphia Inquirer – Monday February 11, 2002

Pay no attention to the reality beyond the facade of the two-dimensional plane, and/or the spectacle of excessive dopamine biochemical inducing stimulus, functioning as pure *pleasure* only, which is being supplied to you by your worldly gods. And too even as –

"What did boom years of the '90s add up to? Lots of ads –
Today's quiz features a classic SAT-test-type analogy problem. Complete the following: The boom of the 1980's was to real estate, as the boom of the 1990's was to...Time's up. Your answer? – How about advertising – Well, all right. It's not the only candidate. You could have said the Internet, computers, or technology in general, and received at least partial credit – but a more compelling case can be made that the '90s trail of irrational exuberance led ultimately to Madison Avenue. Advertising may be the single simplest answer to the question that more than a few broken hearted investors are currently asking themselves, namely: Where did all the money go? – Propelled by faith in the 'new economy' – in which the of the power of microchips, networks and innovation would triumph over all the old laws of economics – investors almost literally flung money at entrepreneurs – But where did

it all end up? Aside from computer hardware and software – there was advertising –
'A lot of money that came out of the stock market went into advertising,' (Michael)
Burt said the other day. 'That's money that's gone, not actual investment in
something productive..."

Andrew Cassel – The Philadelphia Inquirer – Monday May 14, 2001

The absolute truth is beginning to reveal itself, for all the world to simply see
with our eyes alone: **IT WAS A CON**.

The truly humanistic universally applicable *a priori* laws of nature, the laws
of economics, "say," that humanistic beings were never supposed to spend any
money – ANY MONEY, on allowed access to any amounts – ANY AMOUNTS, of
absolutely abstracted dopamine biochemical inducing effectual stimulus functioning
as pure *pleasure* only, and/or The Apple. And/or – especially, all truly humanistic
beings, were never – NEVER, supposed to enable their own selves, to simply exist
while in ignorance of, and/or absolutely abstracted from, truly humanistic universally
applicable *a priori* Omnidimensional Reality, and which is while actually effectually
functioning as the Mind of God made manifest – The Eternal Harmony – Our
Innocence Lost, and The Entrance to The Garden too. And as was exactly explained
by –

"It is like a man on his way abroad who summoned his servants and entrusted
his property to them. To one he gave five talents, to another two, to a third one; each
in proportion to his ability. Then he set out. The man who had received the five
talents promptly went and traded with them and made five more. The man who had
received two made two more in the same way. But the man who had received one
went off and dug a hole in the ground and hid his master's money. Now a long time
after, the master of those servants came back and went through his accounts with
them. The man who had received the five talents came forward bringing five more.
'Sir,' he said, 'you entrusted me with five talents; here are five more that I have
made.' His master said to him, 'Well done, good and faithful servant; come and join
in your master's happiness.' Next the man with the two talents came forward. 'Sir,'
he said, 'you entrusted me with two talents; here are two more that I have made.' His
master said to him, 'Well done, good and faithful servant; you have shown you can
be faithful in small things, I will trust you with greater; come and join in your
master's happiness.' Last came forward the man who had the one talent. 'Sir,' he
said, 'I heard you were a hard man, reaping where you have not sown and gathering
where you have not scattered; so I was afraid, and I went off and hid your talent in
the ground. Here it is; it is yours, you have it back.' But his master answered him,
'You wicked and lazy servant! So you knew that I reap where I have not sown and
gathered where I have not scattered? Well then, you should have deposited my
money with the bankers, and on my return I would have recovered my capital with
interest. So now, take the talent from him and give it to the man who has the ten
talents. For to everyone who has will be given more, and he will have more than

243

enough; but from a man who has not, even what he has will be taken away. As for this good-for-nothing servant, throw him out into the dark, where there will be weeping and grinding of teeth."

Matthew 25: 14-30

The Son of God – again.
And –

"That is why I am telling you not to worry about your life and what you are to eat, nor about your body and how you are to clothe it. Surely life means more than food, and the body more than clothing! Look at the birds in the sky. They do not sow or reap or gather into barns; yet your heavenly Father feeds them. Are you not worth much more than they are? Can any of you, for all your worrying, add one single cubit to his life span? And why worry about clothing? Think of the flowers growing in the fields: they never have to work or spin; yet I assure you that not even Solomon in all his regalia was robed like one of these. Now if that is how God clothes the grass in the field which is here today and thrown into the furnace tomorrow, will he not much more look after you, you men of little faith? So do not worry; do not say, 'What are we to eat? What are we to drink? How are we to be clothed? It is the pagans who set their hearts on all these things. Your heavenly Father knows you need them all. Set your hearts on his kingdom first, and on his righteousness, and all these other things will be given you as well. So do not worry about tomorrow: tomorrow will take care of itself. Each day has enough trouble of its own."

Matthew 6: 25-34

Again. And –

"Then he said to his host, 'When you give a lunch or a dinner, do not ask your friends, brothers, relations or rich neighbors, for fear they repay your courtesy by inviting you in return. No; when you have a party, invite the poor, the crippled, the lame, the blind; that they cannot pay you back means that you are fortunate, because repayment will be made to you when the virtuous rise again.'

On hearing this, one of those gathered around the table said to him, 'Happy the man who will be at the feast in the kingdom of God!' But he said to him, 'There was a man who gave a great banquet, and he invited a large number of people. When the time for the banquet came, he sent his servant to say to those who had been invited, 'Come along: everything is ready now.' But all alike started to make excuses. The first said, 'I have bought a piece of land and must go and see it. Please accept my apologies.' Another said, 'I have bought five yoke of oxen and am on my way to try them out. Please accept my apologies.' Yet another said, 'I have just got married and so am unable to come.'

The servant returned and reported this to his master. Then the householder, in a rage, said to his servant, 'Go out quickly into the streets and alleys of the town and bring in here the poor, the crippled, the blind and the lame.' 'Sir,' said the servant, 'your orders have been carried out and there still is room.' Then the master said to his servant, 'Go to the open roads and hedgerows and force people to come in to make sure my house is full; because, I tell you, not one of those who were invited shall have a taste of my banquet."

Luke 14: 12-24

Again.

And, too remember, which is only exactly because, it: allowed access to any amounts of absolutely abstracted dopamine biochemical inducing effectual stimulus, actually functioning as pure *pleasure* only and/or The Apple, does begin to become capable of –

"Drug's effect On Brain Is Extensive, study Finds –

Heavy users (of highly addictive stimulants) are doing more damage to their brains than scientists had thought, according to the first study that looked inside addicts' brains nearly a year after they stop using the drug – At least a quarter of a class of molecules that help people feel pleasure and reward were knocked out – This is the first study to show directly that brain damage (caused by the addiction) produces deficits in learning and memory – When the dopamine system goes seriously awry – people lose their excitement for life and can no longer move their limbs – The addicts (started out as) occasional users but over time the drug hijacked their natural dopamine systems..."

Sandra Blakeslee – The New York Times – Tuesday March 6, 2001

Causing permanently affected neurophysiological damage, within any one individually affected human being's own personal electrical potential mass of a mind, and parallel functioning central nervous system, and/or actually hijacking that individually affected human being's mind. Which is, exactly, as all of those individually affected human beings, do actually begin to become capable of experiencing truly humanistic brain death, for their very own selves to be in possession of only, and to – simultaneously, begin to become capable of effactually regressing back to point time zero, of their own personally affected existence within truly humanistic simultaneously relative Omnidimensional Reality, and begin to become capable of actually functioning while as in a purely schizophrenic manner. And to also – and simultaneously, actually begin to become neurophysiologically incapable of seeing, and/or consciously cognizing, past a single point of truly humanistic simultaneously relative space/time, while at any one point within simultaneously relative space/time, and which is the single point of their very own truly humanistic brain dead selves. And remember, which is exactly why they would ever –

"The Financial Wizard Tied to Enron's Fall –

...'What the guy knew was numbers and finance,' a long time colleague said – Today, investigators think Mr. Fastow's wizardry, his ability to run the company's assets and debts into complicated off-balance-sheet deals, was a central cause of Enron's undoing...(and) Mr Fastow was adamant, friends say, in his belief that the amount of money a person made was the only measure of success in business (Even) after Mr. Fastow retreated into seclusion last fall, to continue building an 11,500 square foot house in Houston's wealthy River Oaks neighborhood – The Fastows also maintain an art collection, some of which has been displayed at the Contemporary Arts Museum and at the Menil Collection, both in Houston..."

D. Barboza/J. Schwartz – The New York Times, Wed. February 6, 2002

Actually allow their own selves to become capable of becoming so exceedingly brain dead, that they would actually begin to become capable of simply standing in front of a two-dimensional brain dead Cubist thing, and/or any single two-dimensional thing of any kind: *and* while as in the entire history of mankind, which does not contain a representation of Omnidimensional syntax, and there is only the one of *The Annunciation*. Which is while actually beginning to become capable of understanding absolutely nothing, as they do actually sincerely believe, that they are simply "proving" how intelligent they are, instead of exactly understanding that there are only simply proving that they have experienced truly humanistic brain death, for their own selves to be in possession of only. And too and simultaneously, that have actually allowed their very own selves to become victims of the con, and of their truly humanistic simultaneously relative, and universally applicable, empirical self-consciousness, and/or their souls. And too remember, how the absolute last thing that a truly humanistic being society is ever supposed to do, is to actually simply give the keys to the kingdom to the schizophrenics. Which is because: remember, then –

"Gunshots, Blood and Chaos –

A bomb went off. The shooting began. What followed at Columbine High School was like a real-life horror movie – Chris D-, 15, a ninth grader at Columbine High School, was in the cafeteria when he saw the bomb going off in the parking lot – He crouched down in fear, and started crawling toward the staircase. He heard gunshots, he began to run – D- said of the chaos inside the yellow brick building: 'It was just a mass of confusion' – And of horror: one teacher looked around a schoolroom and saw bodies everywhere. From inside the school, other terrified students called their parents on cellular phones; one asked his mother to pray for him. Still others said the gunmen giggled as they fired – For students, teachers and parents, the shootings at Columbine High were a horror movie brought to life..."

Gwen Florio – The Philadelphia Inquirer – Wednesday April 21, 1999

EVERYBODY DIES: in Reality.

And which is exactly simply because, if that: "represented" truly humanistic brain death, and/or truly humanistic schizophrenia: chaos – discord, and pain and suffering too, is what they do actually have hanging in their art museum parks, and which is exactly where the; "the quality, production, expression, or realm of what is beautiful – or of more than ordinary significance" – what is beautiful, and/or more than ordinary, is supposed to be, then this: real chaos – real discord – real pain – real death, and real suffering too, is – EXACTLY, all that there is left outside of the museums, and –

"U. S. ATTACKED –
Hijacked Planes Destroy Trade Towers, Hit Pentagon; Thousands Feared Dead:
A series of near-precision assaults shattered two symbols of America's military and financial power yesterday, killing untold numbers of people, halting Americans' daily routine, and forever destroying a nation's feeling that it can't happen here – Within minutes after the start of the workday, unidentified terrorists hijacked two commercial jets and plunged them into the twin towers of new York's World Trade Center – reducing the 110-story landmarks to rubble and sending some workers leaping out windows – When the New York towers crumbled, clouds of dust and ash blew hundreds of feet into the air in a scene that many witnesses likened to an exploding volcano – 'At first, everyone thought the first one was a bomb,' said Dean S-, who owns a financial company on Wall Street – 'There were probably thousands of us. We all went to the South Street Seaport, and we were just standing there. These planes were flying by overhead, and everyone was just staring up because we didn't know what they were. Everybody was sort of running all sorts of ways, trying to get away, but they didn't even know what they were trying to get away from'...Near the Pentagon, Michael Walter, a television correspondent for *USA Today Live*, was stuck in traffic. He got out of his car to see what the problem was, he said, and looked up to see a plane perhaps only 20 feet over his head. When I saw it, I said, 'Oh my God! Oh my God! Oh my God! I can't believe this. I was going into a state of shock,' he said – About 10 a.m., just before the last plane went down in Pennsylvania, an emergency dispatcher received a cell-phone call from a man who said he was a passenger locked in a bathroom aboard United Flight 93 from Newark to San Francisco. The man repeatedly said the call was not a hoax, said dispatch Supervisor Glenn Cramer in neighboring Westmoreland County – 'We are being hijacked!' the man said, according to a transcript of the call – the man told dispatchers that the plane 'was going down...'"
Ralph Vigado – The Philadelphia Inquirer – Wednesday September 12, 2001

They are "dying to get in": the art museum parks that is. And/or, they are dying to –

"Teen's Lust For Killing Emerged In Prose –

Eric Harris thought about war, fantasized about war and wrote about war. He was thrilled when he heard, one morning in philosophy class, that the United States was on the verge of bombing Yugoslavia. Rebecca H- , who sat next to him, remembers Harris saying: 'I hope we do go to war. I'll be the first one there.' He wanted to be in the front lines, he said. He wanted, as he put it, to 'shoot everyone,' H- recalls – In hindsight there were many clues, many peculiar signs – Harris and Klebold (projected)...fooled, apparently, were their parents – There is now a trail of evidence that the two telegraphed their actions – In a childhood memoir he composed for creative writing class one day in early April, Harris created a world in which he and his older brother, Kevin, were young boys, sons of an Air Force pilot, playing a war game in his back yard in small-town Plattsburg, N. Y. – But the war game wasn't just a game. In a memoir, the boys were Rambo-like heroes, caught in a genuine battle for survival. Armed with M-16s, the Harris brothers were fending off an entire army of assailants – 'It sounded like they were in Vietnam,' says classmate Dominic D-, 'It was shocking because it was so good' – So good, in fact, that when it was read aloud to the class by a friend – Harris declined the honor – the students snapped their fingers vigorously, the class sign of approval...on Web pages – Under 'Philosophy' (Harris) wrote: 'My belief is if I say something, it goes. I am the law, and if you don't like it, you die. If I don't like you or I don't like what you want me to do, you die – I'll just go to some downtown area in some big ass city and blow up and shoot everything I can...Feel no remorse, no sense of shame' – District Attorney Dave Thomas said he had reviewed some of the pages of the journal found in Harris' house – detailing the year long plans for the killings, which the teenagers hoped would result in 500 people dead and with them hijacking a plane and crashing it into New York City (He said) 'What I found was disjointed. I found it rambling' – What's clear is that they liked war, war was a game, war was entertainment..."

Joel Achenbach, Dale Russakoff – Philadelphia Inquirer – April 29, 1999

Become capable of making manifest their own personally affected schizophrenic inarticulate cries for attention, while actually effectually functioning as real chaos, and real discord, and real pain and death and suffering too, and – too, which is as they DO; "Teen's Lust For Killing Emerged In Prose" – LOVE IT. They do actually love it: real chaos, and discord, and pain and death and suffering too, they simply love it: THEY LOVE IT – LOVE IT – LOVE IT, and they do love it all the way to death too.

Which is exactly why, everybody is going to die: soon.

Because, they: the overwhelming vast majority of individually affected human being's cerebral cortices, have been affected, and they have been –

"Drug's Effect On Brain Is Extensive, Study Finds –

Heavy users (of highly addictive stimulants) are doing more damage to their brains than scientists had thought, according to the first study that looked inside

addicts' brains nearly a year after they stop using the drug – At least a quarter of a class of molecules that help people feel pleasure and reward were knocked out – The addicts (started out as) occasional users but over time the drug hijacked their natural dopamine systems..."
Sandra Blakeslee – The New York Times – Tuesday March 6, 2001

Hijacked, and as we: the entire world, have been led on a collision course with our very own destiny. And which is –

"The prefrontal cortex (is) a dopamine-rich area of the brain that controls impulsive and irrational behavior. Addicts, in fact, display many of the symptoms shown by patients who have suffered strokes or injuries to the prefrontal cortex. Damage to this region, University of Iowa neurologist Antonio Damasio and his colleagues have demonstrated, destroys the emotional compass that controls behaviors that the patient (should) know are unacceptable."
Addicted – J. Madeleine Nash – Time – May 5, 1997

Beyond *our* control: because it is beyond *their* control, and as a matter of scientific fact: that everybody is going to die, and soon too.
And here is the exact "scientific" reason why, because this –

"Media Fill Up Children's Hours –
They aren't building tree houses. They aren't playing hopscotch. They aren't stringing tin cans together. So what are today's 2-to-18-year-olds doing ? – If a study released yesterday by the Henry J. Kaiser Family Foundation holds true, there's a good chance Jane and Junior are holed up alone in their bedrooms watching t.v. for hours at a time – The study, found that children are consuming vast amounts of media – almost 40 hours a week..."
Jennifer Weiner – The Philadelphia Inquirer – Thursday November 18, 1999

Purposefully allowed access: for the children, to any amounts of absolutely abstracted, and purely psychopathic, dopamine biochemical inducing stimulus, actually functioning as pure *pleasure* only, and/or –

"Clustered in loose knots buried deep in the brain (are) neurons that produce molecular messengers – (within) the primitive structure that is one of the brain's key pleasure centers. At a purely chemical level (just as the injection of) heroin triggers release of dopamine – every experience humans find enjoyable – amounts to little more than an explosion of dopamine in the nucleus accumbens, as exhilarating and ephemeral as a firecracker..."
Addicted – J. Madeleine Nash – Time – May 5, 1997

Drugs: dopamine – heroin, and/or consumable tangible form mass stimulus actually functioning as: "1," is what does actually cause truly humanistic brain death, and/or death itself: Because of absolutely abstracted and purely psychopathic dopamine biochemical inducing stimulus, actually functioning as pure *pleasure* only, and/or the Apple.

And which is, as purposefully allowed exposure to it: ANY absolutely abstracted dopamine biochemical inducing effectual stimulus at all, and let alone all of it: television – movies – computers – the Internet – virtual reality – video recorders – cell phones – novels – magazines – paintings – pictures – excessively histrionic, and monochromatic, and romanticized, riffs and cords – girl bands – boy bands – pop icon bands – spectator sporting events – spectacle events, and any aristocratic events while including parties – automobiles – trains and airplanes, mass produced and segregated suburban housing developments – mass produced and segregated suburban shopping malls – worldly political empowerment, and even large amounts of money: SIMULTANEOUSLY, and while actually functioning as The Apple only, and their Innocence Lost too, IS EXACTLY "WHAT" DOES CAUSE THIS –

"Gunshots, Blood and Chaos –
A bomb went off. The shooting began. What followed at Columbine High School was like a real-life horror movie...'It was just a mass of confusion' – And of horror..."
Gwen Florio – The Philadelphia Inquirer – Wednesday April 21, 1999

In scientific Reality. But: remember too, which is –

"Drugs are like sledgehammers,' observes Dr. Eric Nestler of the Yale University School of Medicine. 'They profoundly alter many pathways' – the realization that dopamine may be a common endpoint of all those pathways represents a signal advance. Provocative – the dopamine hypothesis provides a basic framework for understanding (what does) create a serious behavioral disorder..."
Addicted – J. Madeleine Nash – Time – May 5, 1997

Only in neuroscientific Reality. And, exactly, not within the mind of any one individual that has already become affected, and/or allowed their very own selves to become a victim of the con: of their truly humanistic universally applicable empirical self-consciousness, and/or their purely humanistic ability to consciously cognize any Time *made manifest*. And they can, only, physiologically respond to some kind of absolutely abstracted, and purely psychopathic, dopamine biochemical inducing effectual stimulus, functioning as pure *pleasure* only, and/or 1. While they have – also and simultaneously, actually allowed their very own selves to become addicted: to any, and/or all, forms of psychopathic, and/or schizophrenic, dopamine biochemical inducing stimulus, functioning as pure *pleasure* only, and/or "1." Which is as it: allowed access to any forms of absolutely abstracted dopamine biochemical

250

inducing stimulus, actually functioning as pure *pleasure* only, must be absolutely eliminated: all of it and immediately, and in order for us to simply preserve our mere mortal existence. But – remember, we: the entire world, did simply place our entire global socioeconomic structure upon it: allowed access to all forms of absolutely abstracted dopamine biochemical inducing stimulus, functioning as pure *pleasure* only. And – now, it: the facade of the so-called global socioeconomic structure, is actually beginning to collapse, right before our very eyes, which is as we can simply see it with our eyes alone, and be "affected" by it: the actual collapse of our entire global socioeconomic system, with our "bodies" alone. And too and of course, which is –

"Slump throws lives akilter –
Layoffs spread pain in region, often suddenly:
Gregory W-, 46, transferred from Atlanta to the Philadelphia area Sept. 10 so he could take his 'dream job' with Lockheed Martin in King of Prussia – The terrorist attacks the next day did not daunt the hopes he and his wife, Cindy, have for setting down in the area...But W-, director of business development for Lockheed Martin Global Telecommunications, was laid off on new Year's Eve – one of thousands in the region who lost their jobs last year as the economy soured into recession..."
Amie Parnes – The Philadelphia Inquirer – Friday January 11, 2002

Extremely painful.
And so, the absolute last thing in the world that we should be doing: to become capable of even simply saving our very own selves, is, exactly, what we are going to be doing. And that is –

"In Little Time, Pop Culture Is Almost Back To Normal –
As the country moves past its initial period of shock over last month's terrorist attacks, and movie releases and the opening of the television seasons return to their normal rhythm, what's most striking is how unchanged the appetite for popular culture seems to be – With a new television season underway and new movie releases returning in force to the multiplexes, the first indications are (that) people are embracing old favorites in the same numbers as they did before Sept. 11 (And) Television viewing is, if anything, more popular than ever..."
Rick Lyman/Bill Carter – The New York Times – Thursday October 4, 2001

Simply allow it: The black hole of truly humanistic dysfunction – the addiction to purely psychopathic dopamine biochemical inducing stimulus, actually functioning as pure *pleasure* only, and/or The Apple – the chaos and discord and pain and death and suffering too, to become capable of actually consuming us, the entire world that is, and which is exactly why everybody is going to die: soon.
And, of course, before the beginning of the end of time can actually begin to become made manifest, and while as in this real Edenic tale too, the world is going

to need some kind of –

"Gory details Cheerfully Supplied –
The writers of the highly successful CBS drama 'C. S. I.: Crime Scene Investigation' sat slumped around a table one afternoon this month at a studio in this quiet, mountainous region about an hour's drive north of Los Angeles – Eventually everyone turned to Elizabeth D-, 41, a crime scene investigator with the Los Angeles County Sheriff's Department for fifteen years who began as an adviser on 'C. S. I.' and left her job to become a writer on the show...'The show is, in some ways, post-modernist,' Ms D- said after the writers' meeting. 'It provides a definite and final answer, and people crave that – The audience loves the finality of this show. We deal with the evidence. We say who did it and how they did it. And people love that closure."

Bernard Weinraub – The New York Times – Monday December 24, 2001

Final closure. And/or, at least, a more detailed explanation of just exactly how this was actually enabled to have happened: that this real Edenic tale has come to be, while actually functioning as the greatest collective con in the entire history of mankind. And which is, as –

"Day of wrath, that day
Will dissolve the earth in ashes
As David and the Sibyl bear witness.

What dread there will be
When the Judge shall come
To judge all things strictly.

A trumpet, spreading a wondrous sound
Through the graves of all lands
Will drive mankind before the throne.

Death and Nature shall be astonished
When all creation rises again
To answer to the Judge.

A book, written in, will be brought forth
In which is contained everything that is,
Out of which the world shall be judged.

When therefore the Judge takes His seat
Whatever is hidden will reveal itself.
Nothing will remain unavenged..."

Nothing will remain unavenged: at the beginning of the end of time.

And so here *that* is, the; "It provides a definite and final answer, and people crave that – The audience loves the finality of the show. We deal with the evidence. We say who did it and how they did it. And people love that closure" – definite and final answer: the closure, and exactly who did it, and how they actually became capable of affecting the greatest collective con while as in the entire history of mankind.

Remember Albert Einstein, and how, while at the beginning of the 20th century, Albert Einstein did introduce, to mankind, a brand new explanation for communicating his formed understanding, of simultaneously relative Reality, and which is while actually effectually functioning as a space/time continuum. And remember how that communicated understanding: of simultaneously relative Reality, is actually capable of being communicated as the *a priori,* universally applicable, simultaneously relative Omnidimensional applied function: of all of simultaneously relative Reality, and which is while; "Einstein had replaced Newton's space with a network of light beams; *theirs* was the absolute grid, within which space itself became" – functioning as the "becoming" of truly humanistic simultaneously relative three-dimensional cubic space: at least. And/or, the beginning of the moving into the depth *of* simultaneously relative truly humanistic unidirectionally successive Time *made manifest*: as simultaneously relative to/from, and within, a single cognizable point time zero, actually functioning as the fourth dimension of "time." And too, how this function can be understood as: Shaping the invisible, and because that is exactly what it is: "forming the cubic volume of space." And – too remember, how nobody is really supposed to become capable of fully understanding that function: "of" *a priori* Omnidimensional Time *made manifest*, but how – too and simultaneously, which was as it: the beginning of the formed understanding, and while occurring within Albert Einstein's mind, was capable of –

"Cracking the Cosmic Code With a Little Help From Dr. Hawking –
...Dr. Hawking's first book for a wide audience, 'A Brief History of Time,' took readers on a tour through black holes – and imaginary time as he described the quest for the vaunted 'theory of everything' that would enable us to 'know the mind of God'...quantum theory and relativity have taught us, science is about what can be observed and measured or it is about nothing at all. In science, as in democracy, there is no hidden secret knowledge, all that counts is on the table, observable and falsifiable. All else is metaphysics."
Dennis Overbye – The New York Times – Tuesday December 11, 2001

Being verified: to be the absolute truth, and of pure math, pure science, and pure universally applicable facts also, and – too, which: the "verification," can actually be "simply seen" with our: the entire world, eyes alone. And remember how with this, supposed, brand new formed understanding: of simultaneously relative *a priori* Reality, Albert Einstein did become capable of –

Being recognized: for his own personally formed understanding of
universally applicable *a priori* Omnidimensional Reality, and while functioning as a
scientist too. But too remember, that the entire world was being told, that nobody
could actually see what Albert Einstein was communicating an understanding of, but
which was only capable of being "mathematically verified": for all the world to
simply see, with their eyes alone: THE "MATH."

And remember when Gutenberg invented the printing press, that was about
1460. Which enables us to simply understand, that up until this point in time: 1460
and until the invention of the printing press, the vast majority of the common man
masses, did not yet have access to the two-dimensional planes of books, so they
could not articulate the written word: they could not read and they could not write.
And so we can simply understand that, up until this point in time: 1460, the
absolutely abstracted, and projected, two-dimensional plane of pictures, was, only, a
simple communicative process: exactly as was capable of being projected upon a
Paleolithic cave man wall. Within which, of course, there was no syntax, and no
intelligence either, and there was only tangible form point-mass nouns represented,
within every picture and in the entire history of mankind. And – then and while in
the year 1480, Leonardo da Vinci: the scientist, did become capable of
communicating his own personally formed understanding: of universally applicable
simultaneously relative *a priori* Reality, actually functioning as an Omnidimensional
space/time continuum. Which was while actually forming, purposefully effectuated
harmoniously proportioned cubic volumes, *of* synthetically structured truly
humanistic three-dimensional space, functioning as subservient to, and as through
the purposeful effectuation of, a hierarchically structured whole: Omnidimensional
space/time continuum. And as Omnidimensional Time *made manifest*: actually
functioning as simultaneously relative, and individually completed, harmoniously
proportioned differential equations, having been formed as through, and while
remaining subservient to, a hierarchically structured whole: orchestration of truly
humanistic harmoniously proportioned differential equations, and as simultaneously
relative to/from, and within, a single cognizable point time zero: central keynote
theme, and which was titled *The Annunciation*, and – exactly as Leardo da Vinci did
define it, while –

"...*figurazione delle cose invisible.*"

Actually shaping the invisible: exactly as Leonardo da Vinci did define it.

And too which: *The Annunciation* as a space/time continuum, was also capable of functioning, as Plato's explained Platonic philosophy of understanding, which was as he: Plato, did communicate his explained theory of simultaneously relative Omnidimensional Reality, within his book titled *The Timeus*. And – then, after Leonardo da Vinci did actually communicate his formed understanding of simultaneously relative Omnidimensional *a priori* Reality, while contained within his two-dimensional abstracted and projected representation titled *The Annunciation*, and which was while actually functioning as Plato's explained Platonic philosophy of understanding and as Omnidimensional Time *made manifest,* and while actually becoming capable of shaping the invisible too: for all the world to simply "see" "with" their eyes alone also – while capable of being mathematically verified, Leonardo da Vinci was –

"Following the custom of the day Raphael peopled *The School of Athens* with contemporary figures. Raphael paid greatest homage to Leonardo da Vinci, choosing him to represent the man: Plato, then thought to be the greatest thinker of all time."
Leonardo – Serge Bromley

Recognized for his communicated formed understanding: "of" simultaneously relative *a priori* Omnidimensional Reality, *and* while actually functioning as an Omnidimensional space/time continuum, and/or the "shaping of the visible": The Mind of God made manifest – The Eternal Harmony – The Kingdom of Heaven – Our Innocence Lost, and The Entrance to The Garden too. And which was, of course, exactly the 16th century equivalent of –

"TIME Person Of The Century; Albert Einstein –
relativity's rebel: he combined rare genius with a deep moral sense and a total indifference to conviction
He was the pre-eminent scientist in a century dominated by science – To the world at large, relativity seemed to pull the rug out from under perceived reality..."
Frederic Golden – Time – December 31, 1999

Informing the entire world that Leonardo da Vinci had become capable of forming an understanding of all of simultaneously relative *a priori* Omnidimensional Reality, and while actually functioning as Omnidimensional Time *made manifest*: The Mind of God made manifest – The Eternal Harmony – Our Innocence Lost – The Entrance to the Garden, and Platonic philosophy of understanding. And, of course, while it: the understanding of simultaneously relative Omnidimensional Reality, cannot be simply seen with our eyes of alone, it can only be understood, within our truly humanistic simultaneously relative quantum electrodynamically functioning electrical potential mass minds, and parallel functioning central nervous systems. And too, of course, only if an individually affected human being does actually spend a lifetime practicing their scales, of simultaneously relative truly humanistic Omnidimensional Reality. And while beginning to become capable of actually forming a –

"Do not store up treasures for yourselves on earth, where moths and woodworms destroy them and thieves can break in and steal. But store up treasures for yourselves in heaven, where neither moth nor woodworms destroy them and thieves cannot break in and steal. For where your treasure is, there will your heart be also."
Matthew 6: 19-21

Truly humanistic simultaneously relative Omnidimensional refractive gem of a mind, and parallel functioning central nervous system, for their own selves to be in possession of only. Which, we do know, Pope Julius II did exactly –

"Under pressure from Pope Julius II, Michelangelo finished the Sistine ceiling in tremendous haste. The vault was unveiled officially on 31 October 1512, the eve of All Saints, and was the subject of widespread admiration – The Sistine became, according to Vasari, a form of 'academy of drawing' for artists visiting Rome who saw it as a mandatory point of reference – 'At the unveiling, people came running from all the corners of the earth; this great work stopped them in amazement, left them wondering and loss for words. The Pope, his greatness fed by the success which encouraged him to further initiatives, rewarded Michelangelo with money and splendid presents.' (Vasari)."
Michelangelo – Pierluigi de Vecchi

Not do: for his own self. And Pope Julius did become capable of, only, regressing back towards point time zero for his own self, and while beginning to become capable of experiencing truly humanistic being brain death for his own self to be in possession of only, and his addiction to all things worldly too of course. While including his addiction to worldly power, and his need to take control over other individually affected human beings: so that he could become capable of gaining access to all his worldly stuff, and –

"At a purely chemical level (just as the injection of) heroin triggers release of dopamine – every experience humans find enjoyable – amounts to little more than an explosion of dopamine in the nucleus accumbens, as exhilarating and ephemeral as a firecracker..."
Addicted – J. Madeleine Nash – Time – May, 5, 1997

The Apple only: all worldly absolutely abstracted psychopathic dopamine biochemical inducing effectual stimulus functioning as pure *pleasure* only, and for his own self to be in possession of only, and his own personally affected truly humanistic brain death, and simultaneously affected addiction to all things worldly. Which he did need to maintain: his control over other human beings, to feed his addiction to all things worldly, and which was while actually functioning as a worldly psychopathic con-artist.

So, Pope Julius II did begin; "The Sistine became (a) form of 'academy of drawing' for artists visiting Rome who saw it as a mandatory point of reference" – to create a diversion: from truly humanistic simultaneously relative Omnidimensional Time *made manifest* – The Mind of God made manifest – The Eternal Harmony – The Entrance to The Garden, and Our Innocence lost too: while actually functioning as simultaneously relative to/from and within a truly humanistic, and simultaneously relative, single cognizable point time zero – the point of The Big Bang, and the beginning of Time *made manifest*. And too, it: the diversion, was made manifest simply to; "The Pope, his greatness fed by the success which encouraged him to further initiatives, rewarded Michelangelo with money and splendid presents" – feed to Pope Julius' addiction to all things worldly. And – too, which was: that he actually did begin to become capable of creating a diversion from universally applicable *a priori* Reality, while employing the use of Michelangelo, and GeorgioVasari: to function as his co-conspirators.

Which Giorgio Vasari did simply become capable of doing: actually becoming a co-conspirator while as in the greatest collective con in the entire history of mankind, and while in this real Edenic tale too, exactly because of the invention of the printing press, and its: a book, ability to function as a –

"Adolf Hitler: A book that is destined for the broad masses must, therefore, attempt from the very beginning to have an effect both in style and in elevation..."

Political motivational tool, and/or as –

"Adolf Hitler: The context of propaganda is not science – The function of propaganda does not lie in the scientific training of the individual, but in the calling of the masses' attention to certain facts, processes, necessities, etc., whose significance is thus for the first time placed within their field of vision."

Worldly propaganda. And which is while placing it: the propaganda, within their: all of the victims of the con, affected field of vision, and/or simply letting them see "it," instead of –

"Alas for you, scribes and Pharisees, you hypocrites! You who shut up the kingdom of heaven in men's faces, neither going in yourselves nor allowing others to go in who want to."
Matthew 23: 13

Allowing them to begin to become capable of forming an understanding of truly humanistic universally applicable simultaneously relative Omnidimensional *a priori* Reality, which is while actually effectually functioning as The Mind of God made manifest: The Kingdom of Heaven – The Eternal Harmony – Our Innocence Lost, and The Entrance to The Garden also. And which is exactly while it: the propaganda, does actually begin to become capable of; "Adolf Hitler: The context of propaganda is not science – The function of propaganda does not lie in the scientific training of the individual, but in the calling of the masses' attention to certain processes, necessities, etc., whose significance is thus for the first time placed within their field of vision" – functioning as the beginning of –

"Brainwashing: intense psychological indoctrination, usually political, for the purpose of displacing the individuals previous thoughts and attitudes with those selected by the regime or person inflicting the indoctrination."
Taber's Medical Dictionary

Individually affected truly humanistic being brainwashing, and/or individually affected truly humanistic being brain death. Which is as the individual human being, is actually beginning to regress back towards point time zero: of their own personally affected existence within truly humanistic simultaneously relative space/time, and beginning to become neurophysiologically incapable of understanding anything, and – too and simultaneously, only neurophysiologically capable of believing anything: that they are being programmed to believe, by all of the worldly psychopathic con-artists. Who are beginning to become capable of controlling everything, while including an individually affected human being's allowed exposure to all purely psychopathic, and absolutely abstracted, dopamine biochemical inducing effectual stimulus, actually functioning as pure *pleasure* only, and/or drugs. And too, remember how else truly humanistic brainwashing is capable of being affected, while as through; "a method for systematically changing attitudes or altering beliefs, especially through the use of drugs" – allowed exposure to all purely psychopathic dopamine biochemical inducing effectual stimulus, actually functioning as pure *pleasure* only also: and/or drugs. And remember what consciously cognizing The Mind of God made manifest is actually capable of doing. How it is, kind of, like taking some heroin – some Ecstasy and some cocaine, all of our worldly drugs: dopamine – serotonin and endorphins too, and then to mix them all up and consume them simultaneously, while compounding them to infinite degree also, and while experiencing an experience that is like no experience mankind can ever experience for their own selves, and: simultaneously, which is like every experience mankind can ever experience, simultaneously harnessed – squared and unleashed, and which is while actually functioning at the speed, and power, of pure universally applicable energy: and/or light – and/or real Omnidimensional Time *made manifest*. And too which is while actually "shaping the invisible": as simultaneously relative to/from, and within, a single truly humanistic – universally applicable, and cognizable, point time zero: the point of the Big Bang, and

258

Omnidimensional Time becoming *made manifest,* while actually effectually functioning as quantized radiant electrodynamics, and as The Mind of God made manifest too: The Eternal Harmony – Our Innocence Lost, and The Entrance to The Garden also. And remember exactly what the newly perceived image of some thing that no one has ever seen before, is capable of causing –

"At a purely chemical level (just as the injection of) heroin triggers release of dopamine – every experience humans find enjoyable – amounts to little more than an explosion of dopamine in the nucleus accumbens, as exhilarating and ephemeral as a firecracker..."
Addicted – J. Madeleine Nash – Time – May 5, 1997

An induction of dopamine: within any individual human being's personally affected, three-dimensional electrical potential mass of a mind, and parallel functioning central nervous system, and while actually functioning as pure *pleasure* only: and within which there are contained no images of things. And too which: a purposefully affected dopamine biochemical induction, within any one individual human being's own personally affected three-dimensional electrical potential mass of a mind, and parallel functioning central nervous system: and exactly because of their purposefully allowed exposure to some thing they have never simply "seen" before, is simply –

"…Vision is the art of seeing things invisible: Oscar Wilde"

"Invisible": a "simple dopamine biochemical induction" effectually functioning as pure *pleasure* only, and/or The Apple that "is": actually occurring within a human being, every time a human being sees some thing – and/or any thing, that they have never simply seen before.
And again, so we: for our own selves, can now simply know that this is what they: Pope Julius – Michelangelo, and Giorgio Vasari, did actually do: to become capable of forming the foundation for the greatest collective con in the entire history of mankind, and/or to actually enable mankind to become capable of simply placing their entire global socioeconomic system upon the facade of the two-dimensional plane: and personally affected truly humanistic brain death. Which was, after Leonardo da Vinci did actually become capable of "shaping the invisible" – while actually functioning as The Mind of God made manifest, and The Eternal Harmony too and while actually effectually functioning as *The Annunciation* also, he was simply recognized for his accomplishment, while being communicated to the world as through Raphael's representation of *The School of Athens.* Which was, simply, a two-dimensional pictorial representation, which did glorify Leonardo da Vinci's accomplishment, and while represented within a school. Which was comprised of the greatest thinkers of all time, and who where represented while being positioned within a building too, and which any body can simply walk "into" – and become

capable of experiencing a simple dopamine biochemical induction within their individually affected mind, and while actually functioning as pure *pleasure* only. And which can not be "simply seen": truly humanistic universally applicable intelligence, actually functioning as the collective consciousness of mankind – The Mind of God made manifest actually functioning as Omnidimensional Time *made manifest*: and/or a simple dopamine biochemical induction actually functioning as pure *pleasure* only, and/or The Apple, and truly humanistic brain death too. And which: personally affected truly humanistic brain death, if you are in possession of only, you will not simply accept for your own self to be in possession of only, just as Pope Julius II, Michelangelo and Giorgio Vasari, did not. And – too remember, when *The School of Athens* was actually made manifest, it was the 16th century equivalent of Albert Einstein being "on the cover" of *Time* magazine's millennium issue: while recognizing him as a truly intelligent humanistic being, because of his communicated formed understanding, of universally applicable *a priori* Reality. And – remember, which was a formed understanding that no one individual human being, was actually supposed to be capable of seeing: while actually functioning as Time *made manifest* and as "shaping the invisible" too. And as the pinnacle of truly humanistic conscious cognizant capabilities also: which Albert Einstein did become capable of actually doing, while actually functioning as a "scientist," and while dealing with the absolute truth only, and as did Leonardo da Vinci. But – too remember, in order for Leonardo da Vinci to become capable of communicating his formed understanding: of Reality, he had to become capable of harnessing the function of Reality, abstracting the function from within simultaneously relative Omnidimensional *a priori* Reality, and then actually "communicating" his own personally formed understanding: of identifiable Omnidimensional *a priori* Reality, while actually functioning as Omnidimensional Time *made manifest* – The Mind of God made manifest, and The Eternal Harmony too. And remember, which: real Omnidimensional Time *made manifest* – The Mind of God made manifest and The Eternal Harmony, does actually function as the universal language: of truly humanistic simultaneously relative Omnidimensional Time *made manifest* – The Mind of God made manifest and The Eternal Harmony too, and which is exactly invisible. But – too, which Leonardo da Vinci did have to become capable of communicating an understanding of, while actually becoming capable of abstracting it from within simultaneously relative Omnidimensional *a priori* Reality, and projecting it upon a two-dimensional plane, and while simply being defined as a painter, and/or an "artist" too, and while actually shaping the invisible: while functioning as a scientist only that is. And too which was while they: all of the worldly psychopathic con-artists, were simply telling the world that it: actually consciously cognizing Omnidimensional Time *made manifest* – The Mind of God made manifest – The Eternal Harmony and while actually finding our Innocence Lost and The Entrance to The Garden too, is supposed to be impossible to do, and while – of course, no true scientist would ever –

"So Pilate went back into the Praetorium and called Jesus to him, 'Are you the king of the Jews?' he asked. Jesus replied,' Do you ask this of your own accord, or have others spoken to you about me?' Pilate answered, 'Am I a Jew? It is your own people and chief priests who have handed you over to me: what have you done?' Jesus replied, 'Mine is not a kingdom of this world; if my kingdom were of this world, my men would have fought to prevent my being surrendered to the Jews. But my kingdom is not of this kind.' So you are a king then?' said Pilate. 'It is you who say it,' answered Jesus. 'Yes, I am a king. I was born for this, I came into this world for this: to bear witness to the truth; and all who are on the side of truth listen to my voice.' 'Truth?' said Pilate, 'What is that?"
John 18: 33-30

Simply deviate from the absolute truth, and/or simply create a diversion, while as in an attempt to become capable of simply empowering their very own selves only, and while beginning to; "Jesus replied, 'Do you ask this of your own accord, or have others spoken to you about me" – become capable of simply brainwashing any individually affected human being. As they: all of the individually affected victims of the con, will remain incapable of understanding anything for their own selves, and only capable of believing exactly what they have been programmed to believe: by all of the worldly psychopathic con-artists, and while as within the entire history of mankind too.

So what Pope Julius II – Michelangelo, and Giorgio Vasari, did actually simply do, and again to enable their own selves to become capable of affecting the con, was to actually steal: and/or hijack, the name of Leonardo da Vinci – and his image as a Noble intellect functioning as a scientist/artist, and his ability to become capable of actually "shaping the invisible": while functioning as Omnidimensional Time *made manifest,* and as The Mind of God made manifest also. While enabling their own selves, to become –

"Gory Details Cheerfully Supplied –
The writers of the highly successful CBS drama 'C. S. I.: Crime Scene Investigation' sat slumped around a table one afternoon this month at a studio in this quiet, mountainous region – Eventually everyone turned to Elizabeth D-, 41, a crime scene investigator with the Los Angeles County Sheriff's Department for fifteen years who began as an adviser on 'C. S. I.' and left her job to become a writer on the show – 'In real cases the police would bring in someone to interpret,' Ms. D- said..."
Bernard Weinraub – The New York Times – Monday December 24, 2001

Interpreters: of Leonardo da Vinci's ability to actually shape the invisible, and while actually functioning as Omnidimensional Time *made manifest*: The Mind of God made manifest – The Eternal Harmony – Our Innocence Lost, and The Entrance to the Garden also. And too remember, as was exactly explained by Leonardo da Vinci:

"The abbreviators of works do injury to knowledge and to love, for love of anything is the offspring of knowledge, love being more fervent in proportion as knowledge is more certain; and this certainty springs from a thorough knowledge of all those parts which united compose the whole of that which ought to be loved – Of what use, pray, is he who in order to abridge the part of the things of which he professes to give complete information leaves out the greater part of the matters of which the whole is composed – And it seems to you that you have performed miracles when you have spoiled the work of some ingenious mind..."

And too remember, which: the greatest collective con in the entire history of mankind and while functioning as the real Edenic tale too, was actually beginning to occur while it: Omnidimensional Time *made manifest* – The Mind of God made manifest – The Eternal Harmony – Our Innocence Lost, and The Entrance to The Garden too, was actually being made manifest "within" the function of *The Annunciation* and while actually effectually functioning "as" *The Annunciation* also. And too, which was as Leonardo da Vinci was actually beginning to become capable of –

"There are two essential yet complementary aspects of this new vision of time which are as striking in contrast as heaven and hell. Heaven is ruled by dynamical equations that are reversible and 'timeless'; their simplicity ensures stability for eternity. Hell is more akin to the real world, where fluctuations, uncertainty and chaos reign..."
The Arrow of Time – Peter Coveney and Roger Highfield

Making manifest the actual function of *The Annunciation*: while actually transforming chaos into The Eternal Harmony, and/or Hell into Heaven, and while actually functioning as Omnidimensional Time *made manifest,* and The Mind of God made manifest also. And too, which was also occurring: that Leonardo da Vinci had become capable of transforming chaos into The Eternal Harmony, just as the printing press was being invented, but just prior to Leonardo da Vinci's ability to gain access to it: the printing press, and which prevented him: Leonardo da Vinci, from printing a detailed explanation of the actual simultaneously relative applied function: of Omnidimensional Time *made manifest*. And too which was occurring: the actual transformation and while actually functioning as the function of *The Annunciation*, just as Pope Julius was beginning to become capable of actually empowering himself, while along with Michelangelo and Giorgio Vasari, and as they: Pope Julius II, Michelangelo and Giorgio Vasari, were enabled to simply steal, and/or hijack, the name – and image, of Leonardo da Vinci. To begin to enable their own selves, to become capable of effectually forming the foundation for the greatest collective con in the entire history of mankind, and which was while actually hijacking the function of *The Annunciation*, while beginning to create chaos out of harmony, and while beginning to empower only their own selves, and while causing

262

truly humanistic brain death too: for everyone to be in possession of only and instead of the exact opposite, and which is, of course, exactly backwards – all of it, as is everything. And which is also, of course –

"He was still speaking when Judas, one of the Twelve, appeared, and with him a large number of men armed with swords and clubs, sent by the chief priests and elders of the people. Now the traitor had arranged a sign with them. 'The one I kiss,' he had said, 'he is the man. Take him in charge.' So he went straight up to Jesus and said, 'Greetings, Rabbi,' and kissed him. Jesus said to him, 'My friend, do what you are here for.' Then they came forward, seized Jesus and took him in charge. At that, one of the followers of Jesus grasped his sword and drew it; he struck out at the high priest's servant, and cut off his ear. Jesus then said, 'Put your sword back, for all who draw the sword will die by the sword. Or do you think that I cannot appeal to my Father who would promptly send more than twelve legions of angels to my defense? But then, how would the scriptures be fulfilled that say this is the way it must be?' It was at this time that Jesus said to the crowds, 'Am I a brigand, that you had to set out to capture me with swords and clubs? I sat teaching in the Temple day after day and you never laid hands on me.' Now all this happened to fulfill the prophecies in scripture."
Matthew 26: 47-56

Not a coincidence at all.
And, again and of course, we can now simply reiterate our understanding of the fact, that Pope Julius II – Michelangelo, and Giorgio Vasari, did, simply, begin to become capable of employing the use Adolf Hitler's basic applied formula, for gaining political empowerment for his own self, as they did simply take hold of the key to the basic mathematical formula for worldly political empowerment. Which was, as they: Pope Julius II, Michelangelo and Giorgio Vasari, did simply allow them: all of the individually affected victims of the con, an opportunity to become a part of the In Crowd: which was being purposefully allowed exposure to the spectacle of the excessive absolutely abstracted, and psychopathic, dopamine biochemical inducing effectual stimulus, actually functioning as pure *pleasure* only, and/or the orgy. And then to allow them to experience a climax for their own selves, while reaching orgasm, and an effectuated: OHH, and while simply experiencing something invisible. And – then and as all of the individually affected human beings will have effectually regressed back to point time zero: of their effectuated existence within truly humanistic simultaneously relative Omnidimensional Reality, and become capable of employing the use of; "At the unveiling – of the Sistine ceiling, people came running from all four corners of the earth; this great work stopped them in amazement, left them wondering and loss for words" – zero universally applicable empirical self-consciousness, and/or truly humanistic intelligence and while experiencing the function of reuptake effectually functioning as an: AHH, to enable the individually affected human beings, to become capable of employing the use,

only, of their "childish imaginations," while as in an attempt to explain the phenomenon which they had just effectually consumed. And – too, while being simply informed, by their worldly authoritative god figures, that they had just experienced the actual function of The Mind of God made manifest: applied real Omnidimensional Time *made manifest* – The Eternal Harmony – Our Innocence Lost, and The Entrance to The Garden, and/or that they are intelligent: because they did allow themselves to become a part of the In Crowd, and while programming them to believe that it is: Just that easy.

And – remember, now the printing press had been invented, and books were easily accessible, and remember too, Adolf Hitler's first phase of his two-part applied basic mathematical formula for worldly political empowerment, while as through the universally applicable function of his –

"Adolf Hitler: A book that is destined for the broad masses must, therefore, attempt from the very beginning to have an effect both in style and in elevation – The context of propaganda is not science – The function of propaganda does not lie in the scientific training of the individual, but in the calling of the masses attention to certain processes, necessities, etc., whose significance is thus for the first time placed within their field of vision."

Book: while actually functioning as propaganda only. And too while: all simple spoken words and while as in the entire history of mankind, are only capable of functioning as an exact deviation from truly humanistic universally applicable *a priori* Omnidimensional Reality: or an exact explanation of it, and only while being not so simple.

And how, now, the printing press had been invented, and so –

"Toward the middle of the sixteenth century, the prolific Giorgio Vasari, a mediocre painter but a respectable architect, began to document the lives of the Italian artists: He was inventing art history…"
Leonardo – Serge Bramley

Giorgio Vasari "wrote a book": and the mass brainwashing did begin.
And all because –

"Your: Giorgio Vasari, paintings won't last,' Biovio said to him with brutal frankness..."
Leonardo – Serge Bramley

Misery loves company.
And so, the mass brainwashing did begin to take effect, and which was while actually –

"When therefore the Judge takes His seat
Whatever is hidden will reveal itself.
Nothing will remain unavenged.

What then shall I say, wretch that I am,
What advocate entreat to speak for me,
When even the righteous may hardly be secure?

King of awful majesty,
Who freely savest the redeemed,
Save me, O fount of goodness.

Remember, blessed Jesu,
That I am the cause of Thy pilgrimage,
Do not forsake me on that day.

Seeking me Thou didst sit down weary,
Thou didst redeem me, suffering death on the cross.
Let not such toil be in vain.

Just and avenging Judge,
Grant remission
Before the day of reckoning.

I groan like a guilty man.
Guilt reddens my face.
Spare a suppliant, O God.

Thou who didst absolve Mary Magdalene
And didst harken to the thief,
To me also hast Thou given hope.

My prayers are not worthy,
But Thou in Thy merciful goodness grant
That I burn not in everlasting fire.

Place me among Thy sheep
And separate me from the goats,
Setting me on Thy right hand.

When the accursed have been confounded
And given over to the bitter flames,
Call me with the blessed.

I pray in supplication on my knees.
My heart contrite as the dust,
Safeguard my fate.

Mournful that day
When from the dust shall rise
Guilty man to be judged.
Therefore spare him, O God.
Merciful Jesu, Lord
Grant them rest."

Beginning to confuse the accursed.

And so they: all worldly psychopathic con-artists and while as in the entire history of mankind, did begin the mass brainwashing: the applied art of the con – the theft of mankind's universally applicable empirical self-consciousness, and/or their souls, and the confusing of the accursed, and too while simply stealing the name, and image as a noble intellect, of Leonardo da Vinci. And his ability to make manifest Omnidimensional Time *made manifest,* while actually functioning as simultaneously relative to/from, and within, a single cognizable point time zero, and/or central keynote theme, and too which: an actual truly humanistic simultaneously relative Omnidimensional space/time continuum, can only be simultaneously effectually understood: within an individual human being's own personally affected, and truly humanistic, quantum electrodynamically functioning Omnidimensional refractive gem of a mind, and parallel functioning central nervous system, and for their own selves to be in possession of only.

And again, which was actually occurring as the mass brainwashing was becoming affected, as they: all of the worldly psychopathic con-artists and in the entire history of mankind too, were beginning to become capable of programming them: all of the individually affected victims of the worldly psychopathic con-artists and in the entire history of mankind also, into believing that gaining access to: The Mind of God made manifest – The Eternal Harmony – The Kingdom of Heaven – The Entrance to The Garden – Truly humanistic universally applicable empirical self-consciousness and/or a human being soul – Truly humanistic universally applicable intelligence, and/or even Virtue – Integrity – Honor – Self-respect – Courage – Compassion – Law – Justice – Good faith – Mercy – Life, and all things Noble, was: Just that easy. And – too, which was: the actual brainwashing, beginning to actually occur, as more and more individually affected human beings, were spending less and less time actually practicing their scales, of truly humanistic simultaneously relative Omnidimensional Reality, and – simultaneously, beginning to effectually regress back towards point time zero: of their own personally affected existence within truly humanistic simultaneously relative Omnidimensional space/time. And beginning to become more, and more, confused, also.

And so it: the individually affected degradation, of any truly humanistic

266

simultaneously relative multidimensional synaptic capabilities, within the individually affected human beings, did continue, and as the individually affected human beings, did continue to regress back towards point time zero. And actually begin to become neurophysiologically incapable of maintaining "a" single simultaneously relative, and cognizable, point time zero: within their individually affected three-dimensional electrical potential mass minds, and parallel functioning central nervous systems. And they did begin to become neurophysiologically incapable of consciously cognizing any simultaneously relative patterns in space/time also, and/or any truly humanistic Omnidimensional Time *made manifest*, and/or any –

"In concert Spears is a slave 4 fashion –
Brittany Spears paid a visit to the First Union Center on Monday night, and the runway show did not disappoint – the pop princess opened with a beguiling little number in sequined black, reminiscent of an Elvis jumpsuit, but showing more skin than the King would have dared. Sequins were the theme of the concert, delicately balanced by an abundance of midriff and cleavage – Halfway through the collection, Spears paraded around in a hat that easily could have doubled as a dark-chocolate cake topped with strawberry frosting. Meanwhile, apparently hungry dancers clad in '80s-retro, puffy-painted spandex, circled the fashion-forward chanteuse. Gasps were audible as the encore outfit, a shimmering cowboy ensemble, and wearer rose skyward on a lighted platform – Plus there was music – it seems as if Spears' career has swelled at a faster rate than even her cup size – And you would have been hard-pressed to find a fan who didn't enjoy the spectacle."
Bethany Klein – The Philadelphia Inquirer – Wednesday December 12, 2001

Time *made manifest* at all. As The Central Keynote Theme, has been simply replaced by; "Sequins were the theme of the concert" – sequins. And/or simple allowed exposure to –

"Clustered in loose knots buried deep in the brain (are) neurons that produce molecular messengers – (within) the primitive structure that is one the brain's key pleasure centers. At a purely chemical level (just as the injection of) heroin triggers release of dopamine – every experience humans find enjoyable – amounts to little more than an explosion of dopamine in the nucleus accumbens, as exhilarating and ephemeral as a firecracker..."
Addicted – J. Madeleine Nash – Time – May 5, 1997

The spectacle: heroin – drugs – absolutely abstracted: and psychopathic, dopamine biochemical inducing effectual stimulus actually functioning as pure *pleasure* only, and/or The Apple. And/or The Woman's; "it seems as if Spears' career has swelled at a faster rate than even her cup size" – breast, and which is exactly because the entire world is suckling them, even the man who would be king of the world too.

And – too remember, all effectual humanistic phenomena, is inversely affected, and so that the affected truly humanistic brainwashing, and simultaneously affected truly humanistic brain death, is effectually occurring while actually taking quantum leaps: BACKWARDS, and which is exactly as the number of individually affected human beings: of the con *and* of their own truly humanistic universally applicable empirical self-consciousness, and/or their souls, has actually been taking quantum leaps FORWARDS. And which is, as the overwhelming vast majority of individually affected human beings has become so severely affected, and so severely confused, to the extreme degree, that they: all of the individually affected victims of the con, would –

"In year of patriotism, the stars were bright and the stripes earned –
It was a year like no other and so we will be glad, in five more days, to be rid of it – As a nation, we demonstrated the very qualities that we are always celebrating in sports – resiliency and resolve, persistence and perseverance...Sports earned its stripes in the year 2001 – it showed the good sense and compassion and taste to step respectfully aside for a week – And then it resumed its role as refuge from reality, safe harbor from all the madness – a place to stand together, hands over hearts, and sing our unsingable anthem, and belt out, straight from the heart, 'God bless America."
Bill Lyon – The Philadelphia Inquirer – Thursday December 27, 2001

Actually become capable of believing that *The* God, and/or *any* God, would actually "bless" this 21st century aristocracy: This "21st century America."
And which is – of course, and too exactly as The Son of God did plainly explain –

"Pharisees and scribes from Jerusalem then came to Jesus and said, 'Why do your disciples break away from the tradition of the elders? They do not wash their hands when they eat food.' 'And why do you,' he answered, 'break away from the commandment of God for the sake of your own tradition? For God said: *Do your duty to your father and mother* and: *Anyone who curses father or mother must be put to death.* But you say, 'If anyone says to his father or mother: Anything I have that I might have used to help you is dedicated to God,' he is rid of his duty to father or mother. In this way you have made God's word null and void by means of your tradition. Hypocrites! It was you Isaiah meant when he so rightly prophesied:
'This people honors me only with lip service,
while their hearts are far from me.
The worship they offer me is worthless;
the doctrines they teach are only human regulations.'
He called the people to him and said, 'Listen, and understand. What goes into the mouth does not make a man unclean; it is what comes out of the mouth that

makes him unclean.'

Then the disciples came to him and said, 'Do you know that the Pharisees were shocked when they heard what you said?' He replied, 'Any plant my heavenly Father has not planted will be pulled up by the roots. Leave them alone. They are blind men leading blind men; and if one blind man leads another, both will fall into a pit.'

At this, Peter said to him, 'Explain the parable for us.' Jesus replied, 'Do even you not yet understand? Can you not see that whatever goes into the mouth passes through the stomach and is discharged into the sewer? But the things that come out of the mouth come from the heart, and it is these that make a man unclean. For from the heart come evil intentions: murder, adultery, fornication, theft, perjury, slander. These are the things that make the man unclean. But to eat with unwashed hands does not make a man unclean."

Matthew 15: 1-20

Exactly impossible – exactly backwards, and exactly only a self-evident truth also.

Simply because, there has never been anything more impossible in the entire history of mankind: THERE HAS NEVER BEEN A MORE CONTEMPTUOUS SOCIETY IN THE ENTIRE HISTORY OF MANKIND.

And this is why. Because this "21st century America," is the exact same society, which did do this –

"A Shock Grows in Brooklyn –

A fiery controversy over a museum's new show brings New York's Mayor out slugging: The mayor blew up three weeks ago over the controversial exhibition, 'Sensation: Young British Artists from the Saatchi Collection.' Giuliani threatened to cut all city funding to the museum, about one third of its operating budget, unless the show was canceled. The mayor was especially outraged by 'The Holy Virgin Mary,' a painting by Chris Ofili, who used, among other materials, elephant dung. 'This is sick stuff,' Giuliani said – (Arnold) Lehman had been hoping to make a splash with this exhibition, but the uproar was much more than he'd bargained for. Negotiations between them and the city quickly broke down, and the museum filed a suit in Federal Court on First Amendment grounds – Giuliani blasted the show. 'You don't have a right to government subsidy for desecrating somebody else's religion,' he said. A Roman Catholic, the mayor says he has no problem making enemies in the art world (though it most have hurt when he was booed at the Metropolitan Opera last week, since opera is one art form he adores). 'I represent a lot of people other than the elite of the city.' He told Newsweek...polls showed that both New York residents and a nationwide sample were against shutting down the exhibit – Are Ad Mogul (Charles) Saatchi – and auctioneers Christie's – the real winners?"

C. McGuigan, M. Malone, R. Sawhill, G. Beals, Newsweek October 11, 1999

They: THIS; "polls showed that both New York (and) a nationwide sample were against shutting down the exhibit – the museum filed a suit in Federal Court on First Amendment grounds" – brain dead aristocracy, did actually defecate upon the Mother of God, and while; "And then it resumed its role as refuge from reality – a place to stand together, hands over hearts, and sing our unsingable anthem, and belt out, straight from the heart, 'God bless America'" – remaining so exceedingly brain dead, and/or removed from neuroscientific Reality, and/or brainwashed, and/or deluded: and neurophysiologically incapable of understanding anything, that they would actually continue to believe: within all of their individually affected minds, that God – The God, would bless them: as they were actually defecating upon The Mother of God. But which was, also, only after they did first –

"Piss Christ 1987 Cibachrome – 60 by 40 Inches – Andres Serrano"

Urinate upon the crucified Son of God too.
And which was: that they did simply defecate upon the Mother of God and urinate upon the crucified Son of God too, as they were simply making manifest –

"The litany of schizophrenic symptoms reads like a guidebook to the underworld. Most patients suffer from hallucinations, delusions, and 'thought disorders,' a category that includes impaired logic, jumbled thinking, bizarre ideas, and 'loose' associations. They may sound like beat poets out of control – Robert G. Heath: 'The primary symptom of schizophrenia isn't hallucinations or delusions,' he tells us. 'It's a defect in the pleasure response. Schizophrenics have a predominant of painful emotions – schizophrenics are extremely insensitive to pain – and (are) unreactive to other sensory stimuli, as well..."
The 3-Pound Universe – Judith Hooper and Dick Teresi

Their own personally affected schizophrenic inarticulate cries for attention. And which is, as they did plainly admit, only exactly because –

"...Serrano is an urban artist of considerable political sophistication...in high art the word 'moral' is usually considered laughable – juxtapositioning is Serrano's genius – he understands that there are certain factions that will always try to ensure that audiences don't think for themselves – his work shows that the conventional notion of good taste with which we are raised, and educated, is based on an illusion of social order that is no longer possible (nor desirable) to believe in..."
Andres Serrano – The spirit and the Letter – Lucy Lippard, Art in America

Misery loves company.
And, of course, which was: that they were making manifest their schizophrenic inarticulate cries for attention, and while becoming capable of appropriating the use of public funds, as they were simply functioning as –

270

"Lying, deceiving and manipulation are natural talents for psychopaths. With their powers of imagination in gear and focused on themselves, psychopaths appear amazingly unfazed by the possibility – or even the certainty – of being found out. When caught in a lie or challenged with the truth, they are seldom perplexed or embarrassed – they simply change their stories or attempt to rework the facts so that they appear to be consistent with the lie – Psychopaths have what it takes to defraud and bilk others. They are fast-talking, charming, self-assured, at ease in social situations, cool under pressure, unfazed by the possibility of being found out, and totally ruthless. And even when exposed, they can carry on as if nothing has happened, often leaving their accusers bewildered and uncertain about their own positions..."
Dr. Robert D. Hare – Without Conscience

The absolute most extreme of worldly brain dead psychopathic con-artists. But, of course and exactly as The Son of God did explain, not as –

"Pilate said, 'Take him yourselves and crucify him: I can find no case against him.' 'We have a law,' the Jews replied, 'and according to that law he ought to die, because he has claimed to be the Son of God.'
When Pilate heard them say this his fears increased. Re-entering the Praetorium, he said to Jesus, 'Where do you come from?' but Jesus made no answer. Pilate then said to him, 'Are you refusing to speak to me? Surely you know I have power to release you and I have power to crucify you?' 'You would have no power over me,' replied Jesus, 'if it had not been given to you from above; that is why the one who handed me over to you has the greater guilt."
John 19: 6-11

Brain dead as the victims are: of all of the worldly psychopathic con-artists, and while as in the entire history of mankind, who have acquired the greater guilt for their very own selves to be in possession of too, while in addition to their truly humanistic brain death, and their addiction to all things worldly. And which is as all of the individually affected victims: of the con, have simply handed over control of their very own selves, and their truly humanistic universally applicable empirical self-consciousness, and/or their souls: to all of the worldly psychopathic con-artists, to consume.
And remember, that was the exact reason for:

"A Declaration by the Representatives of the United States of America.–
We hold these truths to be self-evident: that all men are created equal; that they are endowed by their Creator with CERTAIN [*inherent and*] inalienable rights; that among these are life, liberty, and the pursuit of happiness; that to secure these rights, governments are instituted among men, deriving their just powers from the consent of the governed; that whenever any form of government becomes destructive

of these ends, it is the right of the people to alter or to abolish it, and to institute a new government, laying its foundation on such principles, and organizing its power in such form, as to them shall seem most likely to effect their safety and happiness..."

And remember too, as this: the function of the self-evident universally applicable *a priori* laws of nature, actually functioning as universally applicable Common Sense and as Harmony too, was exactly explained by –

"The wise, and the worthy, need not the triumph of a pamphlet: The cause of America is in a great measure the cause of all mankind. Many circumstances hath, and will arise, which are not local, but universal, and through which the principles of all lovers of mankind are affected, and in the event of which, their affections are interested – There are injuries which nature cannot forgive; she would cease to be nature if she did – the Almighty hath implanted in us these indistinguishable feelings for good and wise purposes – They are guardians of his image in our hearts. They distinguish us from the herd of common animals – I draw my idea of a form of government from a principle in nature, which no art can overturn, viz. that the more simple anything is, the less liable it is to be disordered…And when a man seriously reflects on the idolatrous homage which is paid to the person of Kings, he need not wonder, that the Almighty, ever jealous of his honor, should disapprove of a form of government which so impiously invades the prerogative of heaven – O ye that love mankind! Ye that dare oppose, not only the tyranny, but the tyrant, stand forth! Every spot of the world is over-run with oppression – O! Receive the fugitive, and prepare in time an asylum for mankind: But where says some is the King of America? I'll tell you Friend, he reigns above, and doth not make havock of mankind like the Royal – of Britain. Yet that we may not appear to be defective even in earthly honors, let a day be solemnly set apart for proclaiming the charter; let it be brought forth placed on the Divine law, the word of God; let a crown be placed thereon, by which the world may know, that so far as we approve of monarchy, that in America THE LAW IS KING."

Thomas Paine: while actually functioning as the universally applicable common sense, and harmoniously proportioned, *a priori* laws of Reality, and as the "prerogative of heaven" too.
And if they: The Entire World, still didn't get it, Thomas Jefferson did –

"...this was the object of the Declaration of Independence. Not to find out new principles, or new arguments never before thought of, not merely to say things which had never been said before; but to place before mankind the common sense of the subject in terms so plain and so firm as to command their assent...it was intended to be an expression of the American mind..."
Thomas Jefferson (To) Henry Lee, Monticello – May 8, 1825

Simply explain, that you – the ENTIRE WORLD: HAVE NO RIGHT TO SUBJUGATE **THIS** CHILD; YOU HAVE NO RIGHT TO BRAINWASH **THIS** CHILD; YOU HAVE NO RIGHT TO FORCE **THIS** CHILD TO EXPERIENCE TRULY HUMANISTIC BRAIN DEATH FOR THEIR OWN SELVES, AND YOU HAVE NO RIGHT TO SIMPLY EXIST IN IGNORANCE OF REALITY, and which is exactly because everything is exactly backwards.

And: remember, exactly because –

"The equivalent of the machine language of the brain, in (Alan) Gevin's view, is very complex electromagnetic field configurations, with very fine modulation in amplitude, frequency, wave shape and spatial distribution – (And) after several years of painstaking mapping of these psychic never-never lands, discovered an extraordinary thing: The mind of man contains only so many visions – four basic, recurrent geometrical forms..."

The 3-Pound Universe – Judith Hooper and Dick Teresi

There are no images of things within our truly humanistic simultaneously relative, and parallel functioning: and quantum electrodynamically functioning, three-dimensional electrical potential mass minds, and parallel functioning central nervous systems. Which are capable of beginning to become programmed only while as through, and while obeying, the two extremes of basic biological functioning capabilities: of *pleasure* and *pain*. And/or –

"One way to think about this new view is to imagine spatial relationships as a kind of universal language that the brain uses no matter what specific language – social, moral, engineering, poetic – we are using at the moment – (George) Lakoff believes he can tie this mental language to the physical structure of the brain and its maps – 'When you think about dynamic structure, you begin to think there are a lot of things that are analogous with life. Life is more pattern(s) in space/time than it is a set of particular physical things."

Jim Jubak – In the Image of the Brain

Life: simultaneously relative harmoniously proportioned patterns in space/time, and while actually functioning as simultaneously relative to/from, and within, a truly humanistic universally applicable, and single simultaneously relative, and cognizable, point time zero: while actually functioning as simultaneously relative quantum electrodynamics, and as Time *made manifest* and Life. Or –

"At Hiroshima: The common lot was random, indiscriminate and universal violence inflicting terrible pain, the physics of hydraulics and leverage and heat run riot...A junior-college girl: 'Ah, that instant! I felt as though I have been struck on the back with something like a big hammer, and thrown into boiling oil – I seem to have been blown a good way to the north and I felt as though the directions were all

273

changed around."

Richard Rhodes – The Making of The Atomic Bomb

Death.

And the American Constitution, does plainly state, that; "WE the People of the United States, in Order to form a more perfect Union, establish Justice, insure domestic tranquility, provide for the common defense, promote the general welfare, and secure the blessings of Liberty to ourselves and our posterity, do ordain and establish this Constitution for the United states of America" – the purpose of the written laws of the Constitution, was to communicate the abstracted, and projected, FUNCTION OF the universally applicable harmoniously proportioned *a priori* Laws of Reality, and while to maintain the "perfect union" of the world's first Truly Idealist Democratic Society. And while actually functioning as pure HARMONY, within the individually affected truly humanistic three-dimensional electrical potential mass minds, and parallel functioning central nervous systems: to preclude the perfect union of the society, and while securing the people's; "the blessings of Liberty to ourselves and our posterity" – Liberty. And while not brainwashing the child, and/or subjugating the child, and/or forcing the child to experience truly humanistic being brain death for their own selves, and/or allowing ANY MEMBER OF **THIS** SOCIETY, TO SIMPLY EXIST WHILE IN IGNORANCE OF NEUROSCIENTIFIC REALITY. And the American Constitution, does plainly state, within Section 8, that; "The Congress shall have Power To Lay and collect Taxes, Duties, Imposts and Excises, to pay the Depts and provide for the common defense and general Welfare of the United States; To promote the Progress of Science and useful Arts" – IT IS ABSOLUTELY ILLEGAL: IN THE UNITED STATES OF AMERICA AND WHILE ACCORDING TO THE CONSTITUTION, to employ the use of public funds for any "thing" which does *not* "provide for the common defense and general Welfare" of the people, and while as promoting the progress of; "Science and useful Arts" – *only* any "useful Arts." And so, we can now know: and for a verified "scientific fact," that the conspired collaboration: to become capable of appropriating the use of "public funds," for this –

"A Shock Grows in Brooklyn –
A fiery controversy over a museum's new show brings New York's Mayor out slugging: The mayor blew up three weeks ago over the controversial exhibition, 'Sensation: Young British Artists from the Saatchi Collection' – The mayor was especially outraged by 'The Holy Virgin Mary,' a painting by Chris Ofili, who used, among other materials, elephant dung..."

C. McGuigan, M. Malone, R. Sawhill, G. Beals – Newsweek October 11, 1999

Schizophrenic inarticulate cry for attention, IS – WAS, and always will be, ABSOLUTELY ILLEGAL. And it was, and still is, "conspiracy": against The

United States of America, to have actually financed it. And/or –

"Drugs are like sledgehammers,' observes Dr Eric Nestler of the Yale University School of Medicine. 'They profoundly alter many pathways' – the realization that dopamine may be a common endpoint of all those pathways represents a signal advance. Provocative – the dopamine hypothesis provides a basic framework for understanding (what does) cause a serious behavioral disorder..."
Addicted – J. Madeleine Nash – Time – May 5, 1997

Allowed exposure to any amounts of absolutely abstracted, and purely psychopathic, dopamine biochemical inducing effectual stimulus, functioning as pure *pleasure* only, and/or The Apple. And the government "of" – "by," and "for," The People, was supposed to have been responsible for supplying allowed access "to" ONLY –

"Candace Pert: I see the brain in terms of quantum mechanics – the brain is just a receiver, an amplifier, a little wet minireceiver for collective reality. We make maps, but we should never confuse the map with the territory' (while) the ratio of frontal core may be one index of evolutionary advancement – What the frontal lobes 'control' is something like awareness, or self-awareness – Do these lobes govern some essential feature of humanness, or even godliness, as some scientists have suggested? If God speaks to man, if man speaks to God,' neuroscientist Candace Pert tells us, 'it would be through the frontal lobes....'"
The 3-Pound Universe – Judith Hooper and Dick Teresi

Truly humanistic simultaneously relative Omnidimensional Time *made manifest,* and while functioning as The Divine Law, and/or simultaneously relative quantized electrodynamics. And/or, and as was exactly explained by Thomas Paine, the truly, and uniquely, humanistic effectual: capable of being learned, function of –

"Society is produced by our wants, and government by our wickedness; the former promotes our happiness *positively* by uniting our affections, the latter negatively by restraining our vices. The one encourages intercourse, the other creates distinction. The first is a patron, the last a punisher...There are injuries which nature cannot forgive; she would cease to be nature if she did – The Almighty hath implanted in us these indistinguishable feelings for good and wise purposes – They are the guardians of his image in our hearts. They distinguish us from the herd of common animals – I draw my idea of the form of government from a principle in nature, which no art can overturn, viz. that the more simple anything is, the less liable it is to be disordered – And when a man seriously reflects on the idolatrous homage which is paid to the persons of Kings, he need not wonder, that the Almighty, ever jealous of his honor, should disapprove of the form of government which so impiously invades the prerogative of heaven – O ye that love mankind! Ye that dare oppose, not only the tyranny, but the tyrant, stand forth! Every spot of the world is over-run with oppression – O! Receive the fugitive, and prepare in time an asylum for mankind; But where says some is the King of America? I'll tell you Friend, he reigns above, and doth not make havock of mankind like the Royal – of Britain. But that we may not appear to be defective even in earthly honors, let a day be solemnly set apart for proclaiming the charter; let it be brought forth on the Divine law, the word of God; let a crown be placed thereon, by which the world may know, that so far as we approve of monarchy, that in America THE LAW IS KING."

The Common Law of truly humanistic universally applicable simultaneously relative Omnidimensional Reality, and/or: HARMONY. While functioning as the Common Sense universally applicable empirical self-consciousness awareness all of mankind can have in common, and as gathered through their personally affected senses only: of truly humanistic universally applicable simultaneously relative Reality. And/or the –

"A Declaration by the Representatives of the United States of America:
We hold these truths to be self-evident: that all men are created equal; that they are endowed by their Creator with CERTAIN [*inherent and*] inalienable rights; that among these are life, liberty, and the pursuit of happiness; that to secure these rights, governments are instituted among men, deriving their just powers from the consent of the governed; that whenever any form of government becomes destructive of these ends, it is the right of the people to alter or to abolish it, and to institute a new government, laying its foundation on such principles, and organizing its power in such form, as to them shall seem most likely to effect their safety and happiness..."

Universally applicable self-evident *a priori* Truths of truly humanistic simultaneously relative Omnidimensional Reality. And which is every thing we did just reiterate our possible formed understanding of, within this book. And too, which NO; "I draw my idea of the form of government from a principle in nature, which no art can overturn, viz. that the more simple anything is, the less liable it is to be disordered" – worldly psychopathic con-artists, and/or their own personal opinions, can "overturn": IT IS IMPOSSIBLE – **"FUNCTION" TRUMPS "LETTER,"** and they can wager their very souls on it too: which they will.

And remember, everything is backwards, and – remember too, the human being mind is just a receiver, and remember calcium induction also: actually occurring within any one truly humanistic being's own personally affected, and simultaneously relative, quantum electrodynamically functioning three-dimensional electrical potential mass mind, and parallel functioning central nervous system. And how: as through that purposefully affected calcium induction, and while in addition to only practicing our scales of Reality: on a daily basis and while affecting only exactly harmoniously proportioned amounts of purposefully affected biochemical inductions, and reuptake function, any one individually affected humanistic being's

276

mind, does actually begin to become more and more powerful: while functioning as a "receiver," each and every day: each and every minute of each and every day. And too and of course, which does mean exactly: EXACTLY AND AS A MATTER OF NEUROSCIENTIFIC FACT, that as an individual human being does exactly follow The Letter *of* the Function of The Law, they will – also and simultaneously, begin to become MORE, and MORE, and MORE, sensitive: TO EVERYTHING, and as a matter of neurocientific fact. And which is while functioning as a truly humanistic being too, and not only as an animal is capable of functioning. And which does mean – as everything is exactly backwards, we can now know: for an absolute and unequivocal neuroscientific fact, that if any truly humanistic being were to even simply "read" these words –

"A Shock Grows in Brooklyn –
A fiery controversy over a museum's new show brings New York's Mayor out slugging: The mayor blew up three weeks ago over the controversial exhibition, 'Sensation: Young British artists from the Saatchi Collection' – The mayor was especially outraged by 'The Holy Virgin Mary,' a painting by Chris Ofili, who used, among other materials, elephant dung..."
C. McGuigan, M. Malone, R. Sawhill, Gregory Beals, Newsweek

They should actually "feel" the pain equivalent to being hit in the face with a baseball bat: REPEATEDLY, and –

"Psychopaths seem to know the dictionary meaning of words but fail(ed) to comprehend or appreciate their emotional value or significance (while functioning as if) 'He knows the words but not the music' – Recent laboratory research provides convincing support for these clinical observations. This research is based on evidence that, for normal people, neutral words generally convey less information than do emotional words: A word such as PAPER has dictionary meaning, whereas a word such as DEATH has dictionary meaning *plus* emotional meaning and unpleasant connotations. Emotional words have more 'punch' than do other words – Picture yourself sitting before a computer screen on which groups of letters are flashed for a fraction of the second. Electrodes for recording brain responses have been attached to your scalp and connected to an EEG machine, which draws a graph of the electrical activity of the brain – Emotional content of the word seems to give a sort of 'turbo-boost' to the decision-making process. At the same time, emotional words evoke larger brain responses than do neutral words – When we used this laboratory test with prison inmates, the non-psychopaths showed the normal pattern of response – but the psychopaths did not: *They responded to emotional words as if they were neutral words* – to a psychopath, a word is just a word."
Dr. Robert D. Hare – Without Conscience

ONLY IF THEY ARE NOT BRAIN DEAD: as a matter of neuroscientific fact.

And if they: any human being who has not experienced truly humanistic being brain death for their own selves to be in possession of only, were to even simply read these words –

"Piss Christ 1987 – 60 by 40 Inches – Andres Serrano"

Then they: any individual human being who is not brain dead, should actually feel like this:

"At Hiroshima: The common lot was random, indiscriminate and universal violence inflicting terrible pain, the physics of hydraulics and leverage and heat run riot...A junior-college girl: 'Ah, that instant! I felt as though I have been struck on the back with something like a big hammer, and thrown into boiling oil – I seem to have been blown a good way to the north and I felt as though the directions were all changed around."
    Richard Rhodes – The Making of The Atomic Bomb

And/or they: any individual human being who has not experienced truly humanistic brain death for their own selves to be in possession of only, should actually feel: within their own truly humanistic non-brain dead parallel functioning electrical potential mass of a mind, and parallel functioning central nervous system, AS THOUGH THEIR ENTIRE BODIES ARE SPONTANEOUSLY EXPLODING. And too they: any individual who has not allowed their own selves to become a victim of the con and who has not simply sold their souls too, should – exactly, not be able to sleep at night. And/or it should be – exactly, a neurophysiological impossibility for them to even simply "breathe," and – too, any one individual truly humanistic being SHOULD BE WILLING TO DIE SOONER THAN TO LIVE IN A SOCIETY THAT WOULD ACTUALLY DO THIS, AND WHICH **IS** –

"...and for the support of this declaration, with a firm reliance on the protection of divine providence, we mutually pledge to each other our lives, our fortunes, and our sacred honor."
    Thomas Jefferson: The Declaration of Independence

Exactly "why" they affected the "revolution."
    And remember too, there is only one thing worse than not actually reading the words, and/or simply enabling your own self to be exposed to that schizophrenic environment. And that is simply existing while in ignorance of Reality, and/or not knowing what it: "Piss Christ," actually "is": functioning as a simple schizophrenic inarticulate cry for attention, and while within the once Truly Idealist Democratic Society.
    Because it: "Piss Christ" and "The Holy Virgin Mary" with "elephant dung,"

were both "publicly financed" schizophrenic inarticulate cries for attention, and remember, there simply are –

"...Many of the provinces of the brain (are) topographical maps of projections of the sensory fields which they represent – the same geometrical decorum applies to all projections – physical events impinging on the sensory surface are transformed into the characteristic digital language of the brain..."
Jonathan Miller – The Body in Question

No "images of things" being projected throughout, and within, our truly humanistic minds, and parallel functioning central nervous systems.
And remember too, The Son of God: Jesus of Nazareth, is – also and simultaneously, The –

"And he began to teach them that the Son of Man was destined to suffer grievously, to be rejected by the elders and the chief priests and scribes, and to be put to death, and after three days to rise again; and said all this quite openly. Then, taking him aside, Peter started to remonstrate with him. But, turning and seeing his disciples, he rebuked Peter and said to him, 'Get behind me Satan! Because the way you think is not God's but man's."
Mark 8: 31-33

"Son of Man," and/or The Collective Conciseness of mankind made manifest. And remember too, the –

"Candace Pert: We've measured opiate receptors in everything from fruit fly heads to human brains. Even uni-cellular organisms have peptides' – Do you think even cockroaches feel some sort of emotion we ask – 'They have to, because they have chemicals that put them in the mood to mate and chemicals that make them run away when they're about to be killed. That's what emotions are about – pain and pleasure. Even bacteria have a little hierarchy of primitive likes and dislikes. They're programmed to migrate toward or away from a chemotactic substance; they're little robots that go for sugar at all costs and away from salt. If you were designing a robot vehicle to walk into the future and survive, as God was when he designed human beings, you'd wire it up so that behavior that ensured the survival of self or species – would be naturally reinforcing. Behavior is controlled by the anticipation of pain or pleasure, punishment or reward. And that has to be coded in the brain."
The 3-Pound Universe – Judith Hooper and Dick Teresi

Basic biological functioning capabilities, of: "*pleasure*" – dopamine – sugar, and "*pain*" – serotonin – salt, are encoded within the DNA of all living cells, and as from one end of the universe to the other, and too which is a universally applicable truth of universally applicable *a priori* Reality. And which is as *pleasure* – and/or a simple dopamine biochemical induction, is capable of functioning as "HARMONY," and while *pain* – and/or a simple serotonin induction, is capable of functioning as "CHAOS."

And what *Piss Christ* was, was a two-dimensional abstracted and projected photograph, of the crucified, and previously: betrayed – abandoned – belittled – tortured – manacled – beaten – spat upon – stabbed, and *then* hung upon a cross to die, Son of God/Son of Man/Collective Consciousness of Mankind, represented while immersed within a pool of "human urine," and which, of course, would be a saline solution, and/or salt. And too which, of course, is the absolute pinnacle of pure chaos, and discord and pain and death and suffering too, and which was publicly financed: by The Government *of* The United States of America, and which is "of" – "by," and "for," The People. And, of course, which was while along with the manifestation of: "The Holy Virgin Mary' with elephant dung." As that, too, is capable of functioning only as the absolute pinnacle of pure chaos, and discord and pain and death and suffering too, and while being financed by The Government also: "OF" – "BY," and "FOR," the "taxed" people of the United States of America.

So, we can now know, and for a verified scientific fact, that the Government of the United States of America, and/or the actual "governed common man masses," did simply allow their own selves, to become conned into allowing the aristocratic elite to actually "urinate upon their exposed raw flesh" and "defecate upon their faces" too. Which was also – and simultaneously, while they: the actual governed and taxed common man masses, did simply give them: the worldly aristocratic elite psychopathic con-artists, some of their "earned income," and/or "taxed dollars," so that they: the worldly aristocratic elite psychopathic con-artists, could actually urinate upon The Son of God's, and their: "Son of Man"/"Collective Consciousness of Mankind," exposed raw flesh, and actually defecate upon The "Mother of God's," and their, face. And as it also, and simultaneously, was so that they: the taxed common man masses, could allow them: the worldly aristocratic elite psychopathic con-artists and with the common man masses' taxed dollars, an opportunity to –

"At a purely chemical level (just as the injection of) heroin triggers release of dopamine – every experience humans find enjoyable – amounts to little more than an explosion of dopamine in the nucleus accumbens, as exhilarating and ephemeral as a firecracker – Dopamine, like most biologically important molecules, must be kept within strict bounds – Too much causes the hallucinations, and bizarre thoughts, of schizophrenia..."
Addicted – J. Madeleine Nash – Time – May 5, 1997

Buy some heroin: and/or have an orgy. And/or simply access excessive amounts of absolutely abstracted purely psychopathic, and/or schizophrenic, dopamine biochemical inducing effectual stimulus actually functioning as pure *pleasure* only, and/or The Apple. And too, which was exactly while they: the

280

worldly psychopathic con-artists and while consuming the common man masses taxed dollars and their very souls also, did simply –

"...Serrano is an urban artist of considerable political sophistication...in high art the word 'moral' is usually considered laughable – juxtapositioning is Serrano's genius – he understands that there are certain factions that will always try to ensure that audiences don't think for themselves – his work shows that the conventional notion of good taste with which we are raised, and educated, is based on an illusion of social order that is no longer possible (nor desirable) to believe in..."
Andres Serrano – The Spirit and the Letter – Lucy Lippard, Art in America

Laugh in their: the common man masses', face. As they: all of the worldly psychopathic con-artists, did simply urinate upon their exposed raw flesh, and defecate upon their faces, and use their money to buy some drugs, and/or have an orgy. And too and simultaneously, while –

"Adolf Hitler: Fear of obscurity – The greatest revolutionary changes and achievements of this earth, its greatest cultural accomplishments (and) immortal deeds – are forever inseparably bound up with a name and are represented by it – consider that six or seven men, all nameless poor devils, had joined together with the intention of forming a movement, hoping to succeed – If people had attacked us in those days – we would have been happy. For the oppressive thing was neither the one nor the other; it was the complete lack of attention we found in those days from which I suffered most – An aggitator who demonstrates the ability to transmit an idea to the broad masses must always be a psychologist, even if he were only a demagogue – For leading means: being able to move masses."

Making manifest a schizophrenic inarticulate cry for attention, and while actually functioning as the purest of chaos, and discord, and pain and death and suffering too. And too remember, which is exactly "why" they do it: allow themselves to become worldly provocateurs, while making manifest chaos, and discord, and pain and death and suffering too. And which is: remember, to simply enable their very own selves to become capable of taking control over everything, and – remember, which is because of their own personally affected truly humanistic brain death, and their inability to control their very own selves: remember, so they do – then and simultaneously, need to become capable of taking control over every thing else: remember? And – too remember, which was –

"O ye that love mankind! Ye that dare oppose, not only the tyranny, but the tyrant, stand forth! Every spot of the world is over-run with oppression – O! Receive the fugitive, and prepare in time an asylum for mankind: But where says some is the King of America? I'll tell you Friend, he reigns above, and doth not make havock of mankind like the Royal – of Britain. Yet that we may not appear to be defective in earthly honors, let a day be solemnly set apart for proclaiming the charter; let it be brought forth on the Divine law, the word of God; let a crown be placed thereon, by which the world may know, that so far as we approve of monarchy, that in America THE LAW IS KING."

Exactly what the Monarch did do in Reality: make manifest chaos – "a havock of mankind," and pain and death and suffering too: so that he could take control over everything else, to feed his addiction: to all things worldly, and while including his need to control everything: to become capable of getting money from the common man masses, to feed his addiction: to all things worldly. And which is exactly why –

"A Declaration by the Representatives of the United States of America:
We hold these truths to be self-evident: that all men are created equal; that they are endowed by their Creator with CERTAIN [*inherent and*] inalienable rights; that among these are life, liberty, and the pursuit of happiness; that to secure these rights, governments are instituted among men, deriving their just powers from the consent of the governed; that whenever any form of government becomes destructive of these ends, it is the right of the people to alter or to abolish it, and to institute a new government, laying its foundation on such principles, and organizing its power in such form, as to them shall seem most likely to effect their safety and happiness..."

They affected the "revolution": TO TAKE BACK CONTROL OF THEIR VERY OWN SELVES, and while as from the brain dead Pig worldly psychopathic con-artists. And/or the –

"Thomas Jefferson: I am convinced that those societies (as the Indians) which live without government, enjoy in general mass an infinitely greater degree of happiness than those who live under the European governments. Among the former, public opinion is in place of the law, and restrains morals as powerfully as laws ever did anywhere. Among the latter, under pretense of governing, they have divided their nations into two classes, wolves and sheep. I do not exaggerate. This is a true picture of Europe. Cherish, therefore, the spirit of our people, and keep alive their attention. Do not be too severe upon their errors, but reclaim them by enlightening them. If once they become inattentive to the public affairs, you and I, and Congress and Assemblies, Judges and Governors, shall become wolves. It seems to be the law of our general nature, in spite of individual exceptions; and experience declares that man is the only animal which devours his own kind; for I can apply no milder term to the governments of Europe, and to the general prey of the rich on the poor..."
Thomas Jefferson (To) General Edward Carrington, Paris January 16, 1687

Ravenous wolves: the aristocratic elite – remember?
And too and of course, this self-evident universally applicable truth: of truly

humanistic Reality, was exactly explained by the Son of God:

"Beware of false prophets who come to you disguised as sheep but underneath are ravenous wolves. You will be able to tell them by their fruits. Can people pick grapes from thorns, or figs from thistles? In the same way, a sound tree produces good fruit but a rotten tree bad fruit. A sound tree cannot bear bad fruit, nor a rotten tree bear good fruit. Any tree that does not produce good fruit is cut down and thrown into the fire. I repeat, you will be able to tell them by their fruits."
Matthew 7: 15-20

But – remember, nobody –

"Adolf Hitler: The Aristocratic principle – The realization that peoples are not equal transfers itself to the individual man within a national community, in the sense that men's minds cannot be equal, since here, too, the blood components, though equal in their broad outlines, are, in particular cases, subject to thousands of the finest differentiations – A philosophy of life which endeavors to reject the democratic mass..."

Is going to tell any of them: The aristocratic elite – The Monarchy – The entertainers, and all of the worldly psychopathic con-artists, "what to do." And/or simply explain the absolute truth: of self-evident truly humanistic universally applicable, and harmoniously proportioned, *a priori* Omnidimensional Reality, to them: all of the worldly psychopathic con-artists, and while including the function of their own personally affected truly humanistic being brain death too: to be in possession of only. Which is only an absolute neurophysiological impossibility for them to actually understand: their own personally affected truly humanistic brain death. And which is exactly "why" –

"A Declaration by the Representatives of the United States of America:
We hold these truths to be self-evident: that all men are created equal; that they are endowed by their Creator with CERTAIN [*inherent and*] inalienable rights; that among these are life, liberty, and the pursuit of happiness; that to secure these rights, governments are instituted among men, deriving their just powers from the consent of the governed; that whenever any form of government becomes destructive of these ends, it is the right of the people to alter or to abolish it, and to institute a new government, laying its foundation on such principles, and organizing its power in such form, as to them shall seem most likely to effect their safety and happiness..."

It: the formed and communicated understanding of the self-evident, and truly humanistic, function of universally applicable – simultaneously relative, and harmoniously proportioned, *a priori* Reality, was illegal. And so that the First

283

Amendment: of the Constitution, was affected, simply because they: the aristocratic elite, and/or the worldly psychopathic con-artists, and/or the entertainers – and who were all creating only a diversion from *a priori* Reality, did not want them: all of the individually affected victims of the con, to become neurophysiologically capable of "forming an understanding of Reality" for their own selves, and/or to become capable of forming an Omnidimensional refractive gem of a mind: for their own selves to be in possession of, and while not experiencing truly humanistic brain death for their own selves to be in possession of only. Simply because, then they: all of the worldly aristocratic elite – the psychopathic con-artists, and the entertainers, would lose control over them: all of the individually affected victims of the con, and then they: the aristocratic elite – the psychopathic con-artists and the entertainers, *would* have to –

"A Painkiller's Double Life As an Illegal Street Drug –
In a scene of creepy voyeurism – Troy S-, prepares to stick a needle in his arm as the cameras watch…Later – Mr S. travels to California for a rapid detox treatment that promises to cure him after four years of addiction…We observe him in a hospital bed, sedated so he will not be aware of what we see: his body twitches as it goes through withdrawal – (The program returns) to Mr S. two months after his treatment, he is still clean (but) he lives with his mother, works as a laborer… "
Caryn James – The New York Times – Wednesday – December 12, 2001

Go get a real job, and/or face-up to Reality, and/or their very own –

"…While in Europe, I often amused myself with contemplating the characters of the then reigning sovereigns of Europe. Louis the XVI, was a fool, of my own knowledge, and in despite of the answers made for him at his trial. The King of Spain was a fool, and of Naples the same. They passed their lives in hunting, and dispatched two couriers a week, one thousand miles, to let each other know what game they had killed the preceding days. They King of Sardina was a fool. The Queen of Portugal, a Braganza, was an idiot by nature. And so was the King of Denmark. Their sons, as regents, exercised the powers of government. The King of Prussia, successor to the great Frederick, was a mere hog in body as well in mind. Gustavus of Sweden, and Joseph of Austria, were really crazy, and George of England, you know, was in a straight waistcoat. There remained then, none but Catherine, who had been too lately picked up to have lost her common sense. In this state Bonaparte found Europe; and it was this state of its rulers which lost it without scarce a struggle. These animals had become without mind and powerless; and so will every hereditary monarch be after a few generations…"
Thomas Jefferson (To) Governor John Langdon, Monticello, March 5, 1810

Human stupidity: and a complete and utter lack of uniquely humanistic common sense empirical self-consciousness, for the worldly brain dead Pig aristocratic elite to be in possession of only. And remember, as was exactly explained by –

"And they think to comprehend the mind of God which embraces the whole universe, weighing and dissecting it as though you were making an anatomy. O human stupidity! Do you not perceive that you have spent your whole life with yourself and yet are not aware of that which you have most in evidence, and that is your own foolishness?"

Leonardo da Vinci also: that all of the individually affected victims of the con, will have experienced truly humanistic brain death for their own selves to be in possession of only. While they will remain neurophysiologically incapable of understanding anything for their own selves, and only neurophysiologically capable of believing exactly what they have been programmed to believe: by all of the Pig worldly psychopathic con-artists. And too, which is as they: all of individually affected victims of the con, will have begun to become only capable of functioning as animals themselves, as they do actually experience truly humanistic brain death for their own selves to be in possession of only: and have become capable of functioning only as the most stupid human beings in the entire history of mankind could have ever possibly have functioned. And exactly simply because, not even Adolf Hitler – NOT EVEN ADOLF HITLER, would have been stupid enough, and/or confused enough, and/or foolish enough, to have actually –

"A Shock Grows in Brooklyn –
A fiery controversy over a museum's new show brings New York's Mayor out slugging: The mayor blew up three weeks ago over the controversial exhibition, 'Sensation: Young British artists from the Saatchi Collection' – The mayor was especially outraged by 'The Holy Virgin Mary,' a painting by Chris Ofili, who used, among other materials, elephant dung. 'This is sick stuff,' Giuliani said – Giuliani blasted the show. ' You don't have a right to government subsidy for desecrating somebody else's religion, he said. A Roman Catholic, the Mayor says he has no problem making enemies in the art world (though it must have hurt when he was booed at the Metropolitan Opera last week, since opera is one art form he adores)...polls showed that both New York residents and a nationwide sample were against shutting down the exhibit ..."
C. McGuigan, M. Malone, R. Sawhill, G. Beals, Newsweek October 11, 1999

Defecated upon the mother of God, and while continuing to "believe" –

"In year of patriotism, the stars were bright and the stripes earned –
It was a year like no other and so we will be glad, in five more days, to be rid of it – As a nation, we demonstrated the very qualities that we are always celebrating in sports – resiliency and resolve, persistence and perseverance...Sports earned its

stripes in the year 2001 – it showed the good sense and compassion and taste to step respectfully aside for a week – And then it resumed its role as refuge from reality, safe harbor from all the madness – a place to stand together, hands over hearts, and sing our unsingable anthem, and belt out, straight from the heart, 'God bless America'..."

Bill Lyon – The Philadelphia Inquirer – Thursday December 27, 2001

That God – The God, any "God," would actually "bless" them: all of the individually affected victims of the con. And which is – of course, exactly the single most impossible thing in the entire history of mankind, and, also, the single simplest thing to understand in the entire history of mankind. Because, would *you* "bless" anyone – ANY ONE, who had actually defecated upon your mother's face, and while enabling their own selves to become capable of making manifest a schizophrenic inarticulate cry for attention: and/or simply enabling their own selves to become capable of creating an absolutely abstracted, and purely psychopathic, dopamine biochemical inducing environment for themselves to be exposed to: effectually functioning as pure *pleasure* only, and/or The Apple to consume, and capable of experiencing an orgy only: of excessive absolutely abstracted, and purely psychopathic, dopamine biochemical inducing effectual stimulus actually functioning as pure *pleasure* only, *and* while; "And then it resumed its role as refuge from reality" – on a daily basis too? Of course you would not – it is impossible, and any individual who says differently, is lying, and right through their lying psychopathic mouths too.

Unless, of course, you: the majority of individually affected human beings which do comprise a society, had enabled your own selves to become capable of only functioning while as in a purely schizophrenic manner. And had also, and simultaneously, allowed your own selves to begin to become neurophysiologically incapable of understanding anything, and also – and simultaneously, only capable of believing exactly what you have been programmed to believe: by all of the Pig worldly psychopathic con-artists, who are supplying you: all of the individually affected victims of the con, with all of your allowed exposure to absolutely abstracted, and purely psychopathic, dopamine biochemical inducing effectual stimulus, actually functioning as pure *pleasure* only and/or The Apple, and/or your drugs, and will have – then and simultaneously, actually simply given the keys to the kingdom to the schizophrenics. Which is exactly how we can now know: for a fact, and exactly as the Son of God did explain, that –

"Do not give dogs what is holy; and do not throw your pearls in front of pigs, or they may trample them and turn on you and tear you to pieces."
Matthew 7: 6

Everybody is going to die: soon.
And – remember too, the Son of God did plainly explain that the end of time

286

will come at the point in time when –

"Jesus left the Temple, and as he was going away his disciples came up to draw his attention to the Temple buildings. He said to them in reply, 'You see all these things? I tell you solemnly, not a single stone here will be left on another: everything will be destroyed.' And when he was sitting on the Mount of Olives the disciples came and asked him privately, 'Tell us, when is this going to happen, and what will be the sign of your coming and the end of the world?'

And Jesus answered them, 'Take care that no one deceives you; because many will come using my name and saying, 'I am the Christ,' and they will deceive many. You will hear of wars and rumors of wars; do not be alarmed, for this is something that must happen, but the end will not be yet. For nation will fight against nation, and kingdom against kingdom. There will be famines and earthquakes here and there. All this is only the beginning of the birth pangs.

Then they will hand you over to be tortured and put to death; and you will be hated by all nations on account of my name. And then many will fall away; men will betray one another and hate one another. Many false prophets will arise; they will deceive many, and with the increase of lawlessness, love in most men will grow cold; but the man who stands firm to the end will be saved.

This Good News of the kingdom will be proclaimed to the whole world as a witness to all the nations. And then the end will come."
Matthew 24: 1-14

It does become capable of proving the function of Omnidimensional Time *made manifest*: The Mind of God made manifest – The Eternal Harmony made manifest, and while actually functioning as the function of *The Annunciation* too. Which is while proving the fact that Jesus of Nazareth is the Son of God, and as the exposure of the absolute truth: of universally applicable, and truly humanistic, simultaneously relative Omnidimensional *a priori* Reality, actually functioning as The Mind of God made manifest, does become capable of pulling back the facade of the worldly psychopathic con-artists, and as it is torn in half: while revealing the absolute truth beyond the facade of all the worldly psychopathic con-artists, and as it: The Absolute Truth, does become revealed for the entire world to simply see with their eyes alone too. And too, the Son of God did explain, that it: the end of time, will come at the point time when we can become capable of proving the function of finding Our Innocence Lost, and/or The Entrance to the Garden and The Kingdom of Heaven actually effectually functioning as the Eternal Harmony too. As this too is capable of actually functioning as the real applicable function of *The Annunciation,* and as Omnidimensional Time *made manifest*, and as the function of the real Edenic tale. As it begins to become made manifest, while as through the increase of lawlessness in most men, and/or as they have become capable of functioning only while as in a purely psychopathic manner. And while experiencing truly humanistic being brain death for their selves to be in possession of only, as they will remain neurophysiologically incapable of understanding anything: and/or capable of being affected by the function of the Law, and – remember, simultaneously only capable of becoming brainwashed by the worldly psychopathic con-artists, to simply contradict the letter of the Law. And too which is while: simultaneously, actually becoming capable of becoming brainwashed by all of the worldly psychopathic con-artists, into believing that if they were to actually follow the letter of the Law, and/or actually understand its function, then they: all of the individually affected victims of the con, were – then, becoming brainwashed: by Reality, and too instead of understanding it, and which is, of course, only exactly backwards. Also: as they were becoming brainwashed by the worldly psychopathic con-artists, which was as they were becoming conned into believing that they could simply gain access to every "thing" they ever desired: Power – Truly humanistic intelligence – Truly humanistic universally applicable empirical self-consciousness – The Collective Consciousness of Mankind – The functioning of the letter of the Law: The Mind of God made manifest – Our Innocence Lost: The Entrance to The Garden – The Kingdom of Heaven: The Eternal Harmony functioning as Omnidimensional Time *made manifest* – A Truly humanistic simultaneously relative Omnidimensional refractive gem of the mind: A Truly humanistic simultaneously relative, and quantum electrodynamically functioning, three-dimensional electrical potential mass of a mind, and parallel functioning central nervous system: Virtue – Justice – Integrity – Truly humanistic love – Honor – Self-respect – Compassion – Good faith – Mercy – Courage – Truth – Life, all things Noble, by simply consuming The Apple: allowed access to all absolutely abstracted, and purely psychopathic, excessive dopamine biochemical inducing effectual stimulus, actually functioning as pure *pleasure* only. Which is, again and of course, only exactly backwards, and – too, only the willful relinquishing of any one individual human being's own personally affected, truly humanistic, and universally applicable, empirical self-consciousness: memory, and/or their –

"Then to all he said, 'If anyone wants to be a follower of mine, let him renounce himself and take up his cross every day and follow me. For anyone who wants to save his life will lose it; but anyone who loses his life for my sake, that man will save it. What gain, then, is it for a man to have won the whole world and to have lost or ruined his very self? For if anyone is ashamed of me and my words, of him the Son of Man will be ashamed when he comes in his own glory and in the glory of the Father and the holy angels."
Luke 9: 23-26

Very own "selves."
And which is exactly what has happened, at this point time while actually occurring in this real Edenic tale – all of it, and as a matter of scientific fact.
Because, remember, the –

"Candace Pert: we've measured opiate receptors in everything from fruit fly heads to human brains. Even uni-cellular organisms have peptides – They're little robots that go for sugar at all costs and away from salt. If you were designing a robot vehicle to walk into the future and survive, as God was when he designed human beings, you'd wire it up so that behavior that ensured the survival of self or species – would be naturally reinforcing. Behavior is controlled by the anticipation of pain or pleasure, punishment or reward. And that has to be coded in the brain..."
The 3-Pound Universe – Judith Hopper and Dick Teresi

Absolute extreme basic biological functioning capabilities, of: *pleasure* – dopamine – sugar – harmony, and *pain* – serotonin – salt – chaos, are encoded within the DNA of all living cells, and: "coded within the brain," and to "ensure the survival of self and species" also. And – remember too, the –

"A Shock Grows in Brooklyn -
A fiery controversy over a museum's new show brings New York's Mayor out slugging: The mayor blew up three weeks ago over the controversial exhibition, 'Sensation: Young British artists from the Saatchi Collection' – The mayor was especially outraged by 'The Holy Virgin Mary,' a painting by Chris Ofili, who used, among other materials, elephant dung...polls showed that both New York residents and a nationwide sample were against shutting down the exhibit..."
C. McGuigan, M. Malone, R. Sawhill, Gregory Beals – Newsweek

Overwhelming majority of mankind has been conned into selling their souls, and/or relinquishing all of their truly humanistic universally applicable, and simultaneously relative, conscious cognizant capabilities, and while actually functioning as truly humanistic universally applicable empirical self-consciousness: THEY HAVE EXPERIENCED TRULY HUMANISTIC BEING BRAIN DEATH, for their own selves to be in possession of only. Which is as they have – exactly, enabled their own selves to become capable of "contradicting" the extreme basic biological functioning capabilities which are exactly encoded within the DNA of all living cells, and while as from one end of the universe to the other, of: *pleasure* – harmony, and *pain* – chaos. And they have – simultaneously, enabled their own selves to become –

"...Serrano is an urban artist of considerable political sophistication...in high art the word 'moral' is usually considered laughable – he understands that there are certain factions that will always try to ensure that audiences don't think for themselves – his work shows that the conventional notion of good taste with which we are raised, and educated, is based on an illusion of social order that is no longer possible (nor desirable) to believe in..."
Andres Serrano – The Spirit and the Letter – Lucy Lippard, Art in America

Brainwashed into believing, that if they have not experienced truly humanistic brain death for their own selves to be in possession of only, and have not sold their souls, to enable their own selves an opportunity to remain a part of the In Crowd, which is being allowed exposure to the purely schizophrenic: pure chaos, excessive dopamine biochemical inducing stimulus functioning as pure *pleasure* only: within their random and amorphous agglomeration of individual nerve cells of a brain, then they: all of the individually affected victims of the con, are capable of understanding the function of the letter of the Law: and/or are neurophysiologically capable of employing the use of truly humanistic universally applicable empirical self-consciousness, and/or truly humanistic intelligence, and while coming to an understanding of universally applicable *a priori* Reality: and/or the universally applicable function of the letter of the Law. Which is, of course, only exactly backwards. And only the function of –

"Warlimont: he tampered with (his advisory staff) to make it a completely pliable tool his will (and) spread chaos in this field as in all others: Hitler mocked Germany's moral qualms – and his own: 'To find internal peace – rid the race of the consciousness of its guilt' – Hitler insisted: 'Freeing men from the dirty and degrading (ideas of) conscience and morality (is) my work."
Michael Nelken M. D. – Hitler Unmasked

All of the worldly psychopathic con-artists: while as in the entire history of mankind, and while as in this real Edenic tale too.
And remember, the function of the letter of the Law says, that it should be a neurophysiological impossibility for you: an entire humanistic being society, to allow this to happen, within the majority of individually affected truly humanistic being three-dimensional electrical potential minds. And – too, so – the function of the universally applicable *a priori* letter of the Law says, that "if" you: an entire human being society, do simply begin to allow your own selves to actually degrade, while as through a lifetime's worth of purposefully allowed exposure to, only, absolutely unbridled conspicuous consumption, of purely psychopathic, and absolutely abstracted, dopamine biochemical inducing effectual stimulus: actually functioning as pure *pleasure* only, and while functioning as the actual "increase of lawlessness," then –

"Candace Pert: 'If you were designing a robot vehicle to walk into the future and survive, as God was when he designed human beings, you'd wire it up so that behavior that ensured the survival of self or species – would be naturally reinforcing. Behavior is controlled by the anticipation of pain or pleasure, punishment or reward. And that has to be coded in the brain...''
The 3-Pound Universe – Judith Hooper and Dick Teresi

Everybody dies: in this real Edenic tale. And – too, which is as they: all of the individually affected victims of the con, and who have simply relinquished their truly humanistic universally applicable empirical self-consciousness: and/or their souls, to all of the worldly psychopathic con-artists, and as they have allowed their very own selves to become capable of experiencing truly humanistic brain death for their own selves to be in possession of only: their tangible form mass stuff and/or allowed exposure to purely psychopathic dopamine biochemical inducing stimulus functioning as pure *pleasure* only, have "done" absolutely nothing, but only spent a lifetime simply choosing pure *pleasure* only: for their very own selves to consume. And – now, they are going to –

"Again, the kingdom of heaven is like a dragnet cast into the sea that brings in a haul of all kinds. When it is full, the fishermen haul it ashore; then, sitting down, they collect the good ones in a basket and throw away those that are of no use. This is how it will be at the end of time: the angels will appear and separate the wicked from the just to throw them into the blazing furnace where there will be weeping and grinding of teeth."
Matthew 13: 47-50

Suffer *pain*.
Unless, of course, they do decide to –

"They began their accusation by saying, 'We found this man inciting our people to revolt, opposing payment of the tribute to Caesar, and claiming to be Christ, a king.' Pilate put to him this question, 'Are you the king of the Jews?' 'It is you who say it,' he replied. Pilate then said to the chief priests and the crowd, 'I find no case against this man.' But they persisted, 'He is inflaming the people with his teaching all over Judea; it has come all the way from Galilee, where he started, down to here.' When Pilate heard this, he asked if the man were a Galilean; and finding that he came under Herod's jurisdiction he passed him over to Herod who was also in Jerusalem at that time."
Luke 23: 2-7

Join the revolution.
And which we can simply understand for our own selves, the absolute and unequivocal fact that everybody is going to die soon, by exactly understanding the fact that the human being mind does function as a receiver, and an "amplifier," and while as to all effective stimuli, and/or every "thing." And the explicit function of "receptors," located within an individually affected human being's mind. And again, how there is exactly –

"...Many of the provinces of the brain (are) topographical maps of projections of the sensory fields which they represent – the same geometrical decorum applies to all projections – physical events impinging on the sensory surface are transformed

into the characteristic digital language of the brain – Once a pattern of light has struck the retina, as soon as a train of sound-waves has traveled up the spiral of the cochlea, the events are translated into sequences of nervous information: a linear code..."
Jonathan Miller – The Body in Question

No images of things being projected all throughout, and within, our electrical potential mass minds, and parallel functioning central nervous systems, but only a linear code of information: as simultaneously relative to/from, and within, a single cognizable point time zero. Which: the actual truly humanistic, universally applicable, and cognizable; "the events are translated into sequences of nervous information – a linear code" – linear code of identifiable *a priori* information, of any kind, is only capable of being –

"Candace Pert: 'I see the brain in terms of quantum mechanics – the brain is just a receiver, an amplifier, a little wet minireceiver for collective reality…'"
The 3-Pound Universe – Judith Hooper and Dick Teresi

"Received" – "perceived" and "understood," only. While actually occurring within an individual human being's own personally affected: truly humanistic, electrical potential mass of a mind, and parallel functioning central nervous system, and within which there is contained only a linear code: of information. Which: the actual *a priori,* and identifiable, linear code of information, may then – then *and* while upon *its* identifiable perception, be simultaneously interpreted: while actually occurring within any one human being's mind, and parallel functioning central nervous system. And which: the "identifiable *a priori* information," may then: upon the *a priori* information's perceived transmittance and simultaneously, become capable "of" –

"Candace Pert: 'Even uni-cellular organisms have peptides' – Do you think even cockroaches feel some sort of emotion we ask – 'They have to, because they have chemicals that put them in the mood to mate and chemicals that make them run away when they're about to be killed. That's what emotions are about – pain and pleasure – punishment and reward – Behavior is controlled by the anticipation of pain or pleasure, punishment or reward. And that has to be coded in the brain."
The 3- Pound Universe – Judith Hooper and Dick Teresi

Inducing the appropriate response: of a biochemical induction, while according to the perceived stimulus. Which: all identifiable stimuli and/or every "thing," is only capable of functioning as, either: *pleasure* – dopamine – sugar – harmony, OR: *pain* – serotonin – salt – chaos, and which: all perceivable stimuli, and/or every thing, is capable of being received – perceived, and interpreted, by "receptors." While receptors, are the "things" which are responsible for; "an end

292

organ or a group of end organs of sensory or afferent neurons, specialized to be sensitive to stimulating agents" – "receiving" – "perceiving" and "interpreting," and/or being "sensitive" to, all perceivable stimuli: and/or every thing in Reality. And – remember, everything – every "thing," in "simultaneously relative Reality," and/or within an individual human being's truly humanistic simultaneously relative Omnidimensional refractive gem of a mind, and parallel functioning central nervous system, and as simultaneously relative to/from, and within, a single cognizable point time is zero, is –

"...As we found with quantum mechanics, the full structure of the world is richer than our language can express – There are two essential yet complementary aspects of this new vision of time which are as striking in contrast as heaven and hell. Heaven is ruled by dynamical equations that are reversible and 'timeless'; their simplicity ensures stability for eternity. Hell is more akin to the real world, where fluctuations, uncertainty and chaos reign..."
The Arrow of Time – Peter Coveny and Roger Highfield

Hell made manifest: "chaos" – noise and uncertainty, of any kind, and/or discord and pain and death and suffering too. Except, of course, for: Time *made manifest*, and/or –

"Wolfgang Amadeus Mozart: Once I have my theme, another melody comes, linking itself with the needs of the composition as a whole – Then my soul is on fire with inspiration. The work grows; I keep expanding it, conceiving it more and more clearly, until I have the entire composition finished in my head though it may be long. Then my mind seizes it as a glance of my eye a beautiful picture or a handsome youth. It does not come to me successively, with various parts worked out in detail, as they will later on, but in its entirety that my imagination lets me hear it."
Wolfgang Amadeus Mozart – Roger Penrose – The Emperor's New Mind

Music: harmoniously proportioned, and individually completed, simultaneously relative differential equations: of Reality. And which is while located within truly humanistic simultaneously relative multidimensional space/time, as it is within a humanistic mind, and parallel functioning central nervous system. Within which, can be induced purposefully affected simultaneously relative biochemical inductions: to enable a human being to begin to experience truly humanistic emotions. Such as "serotonin," capable of being induced as through the effectuated cognizance of a simultaneously relative largo tempoed movement, and capable of affecting a relatively "melancholy," and/or "sad," truly humanistic emotion within a human being, and "endorphin," capable of being induced as through the effectuated cognizance of a simultaneously relative presto tempoed movement, and capable of affecting a relatively "joyful," and/or "happy," emotion within a human being. But too remember, which is while –

"Color often signifies the difference between being seen, and consequently finding a partner, and being ignored – a male frigate-bird in the Galapagos Islands inflates the red pouch beneath its bill to attract a female."
Colors for Survival – Marco Ferrari

Even a bird's brain can do that.

But a bird's brain cannot own a CD-player, and/or any recording device of any kind, as just about anyone could here in the early 21st century. To enable them to become capable of gaining access to absolutely abstracted, and reapplied, harmoniously proportioned musical sounds. Except, take away the recording devices, of any kind, and while including CD-players, and/or record players, and/or tape machines, and then where can a human being go to hear, and/or perceive, within their truly humanistic electrical potential mass of a mind wherein there are contained no images of things, anything besides "hell made manifest." And/or, a random, and chaotic, agglomeration of individually completed differential equations, which is everything "in" our daily simultaneously relative three-dimensional Reality. Well, that would be –

"Ribbon is cut, accolades flow as Kimmel Center opens to the public –
The hoi polloi replaced *haut monde* yesterday at the Kimmel Center for the Performing Arts, and feel-good Philadelphia fever reached new heights – For the first time in the $265 million center's three-day history, the public was invited to share the spot-light during a day long ceremony that included a variety of performances..."
Kathleen Brady Shea – The Philadelphia Inquirer – Monday December 17, 2001

A "music hall," of some kind.
Except: remember, exactly how else that aristocratic environment is capable of functioning, while –

"...Thousands eagerly responded, looking skyward in awe as they streamed through the doors into the grand atrium..."

Inducing a "sense of awe," within a childishly impressionable mind, and/or, within a brain dead adult human being's mind. While capable of functioning, as an absolutely abstracted, and purely psychopathic, dopamine biochemical inducing stimulus, functioning as pure *pleasure* only.
And remember what the aristocratic elite have, almost, never – never and in the entire history of mankind, done for their own selves, as was exactly explained by the Son of God, which is –

"Then Jesus said to his disciples, 'I tell you solemnly, it will be hard for a rich man to enter the kingdom of heaven. Yes, I tell you again, it is easier for a camel to pass through the eye of a needle than for a rich man to enter that kingdom of heaven.' When the disciples heard this they were astonished. 'Who can be saved, then?' they said. Jesus gazed at them. 'For men,' he told them, 'this is impossible; for God everything is possible."
Matthew 19: 23-26

To enable their own selves to begin to become capable of purposefully affecting a truly humanistic, and simultaneously relative, Omnidimensional refractive gem of a mind, and parallel functioning central nervous system, for their own selves to be in possession of, and only. Exactly because, the aristocratic elite have never enabled their own selves to purposefully practice their scales, of truly humanistic simultaneously relative Reality. And which would have been, while actually going out into truly humanistic simultaneously relative Omnidimensional Reality, and –

"If humans are less robotlike than salamanders or ducks, it's not because we have no wired-in behaviors. In fact, we have quite a few. What makes the difference is the ratio of 'un-wired' to wired-in gray matter, because neurons that are not committed at birth to a set function are available for learning, for modification."
The 3-Pound Universe – Judith Hooper and Dick Teresi

Beginning to cause purposefully affected, truly humanistic: simultaneously relative, multidimensional changes, within any one individual human being's own personally affected mind, and parallel functioning central nervous system.
Which is exactly: that the aristocratic elite have never actually practiced their scales of Reality and again, simply because –

"I tell you solemnly,
you will be weeping and wailing
while the world will rejoice;
you will be sorrowful,
but your sorrow will turn to joy.
A woman in childbirth sufferers
because her time has come;
but when she has given birth to the child she forgets the suffering
in her joy that a man has been born into the world."
John 16: 20-21

It's painful. And you can't make any money doing that: practicing our scales of Reality, and while on a daily basis too, and while alone also.
And which actually is while: simultaneously, functioning as all relative

painful experienced humanistic phenomena, and/or *pain*.

So, the aristocratic elite have: always, simply –

"The Pharisees, who loved money, heard all this and laughed at him. He said to them, 'You are the very ones who pass yourselves off as virtuous in people's sight, but God knows your hearts. For what is thought highly of by men is loathsome in the sight of God."

Luke 16: 14-15

Chosen pure *pleasure*: allowed access to only absolutely abstracted, and purely psychopathic, dopamine biochemical inducing stimulus, functioning as pure *pleasure* only. And while never – NEVER, affecting any proportional amounts of purposefully affected reuptake function, of the single affected biochemical induction, and after each, and every, newly perceived thing, and/or calcium induction: within the individually affected synaptic areas – while functioning as an electropositive element, and while: simultaneously, only affecting truly humanistic simultaneously relative multidimensional synaptic capabilities. And/or, purposefully affected serotonin induction, within the individually affected synaptic areas, and while actually functioning as all relatively painful experienced humanistic phenomena, and/or *pain*. Which would have been while beginning to cause truly humanistic brain death, within their individually affected three-dimensional electrical potential mass minds, and parallel functioning central nervous systems. And remember, exactly because of the function of; "addicts' neurons assaulted by abnormally high levels of dopamine, have responded defensively and reduced the number of sites – or receptors, to which dopamine can bind" – receptors.

So the receptors, and/or the entire mind: receiver, would have begun to become worn-out, and/or less sensitive, after – and exactly because of, each, and every, disproportioned purposefully affected dopamine biochemical inducing phenomenon: functioning as pure *pleasure* only. And/or, each, and every, allowed exposure to any amounts of absolutely abstracted, and psychopathic, dopamine biochemical inducing stimulus. Which was also – and simultaneously and remember, while they: the aristocratic elite, were exactly not practicing their scales of Reality either, and while as on a daily basis also. And so they did also: and simultaneously and remember too, actually become capable of –

"At birth a baby's language of the senses is primitive: he sees vague shapes, or flashes of light, but without meaning. His eyes can neither focus nor follow a moving object. He is even farsighted since his eyeballs are foreshortened at birth. And what he sees is flat. He uses only one eye at a time, his eyes not yet working together to sight an object three-dimensionally..."

The Senses of Man – Joan Steen Wilentz

Neurophysiologically regressing back to point time zero: of their own personally affected existence within truly humanistic simultaneously relative space/time, and while actually occurring within their own personally affected minds. And – simultaneously, they: all of individually affected human beings, did begin to become capable of experiencing truly humanistic brain death for their own selves, and actually incapable of consciously "seeing," and/or consciously cognizing, past a single point of space/time, while at any one point within space/time. And/or, incapable of even simply maintaining a single truly humanistic, and simultaneously relative, point, within their own personal, and individually affected, minds: as they were actually regressing back to point time zero, "of" their individually affected existence within "Reality." And, also and simultaneously, they did actually begin to become capable of only functioning as –

"The psychopath is like an infant, absorbed in his own needs, vehemently demanding satiation' – Psychopaths are very good at giving their undivided attention to things that interest them most and at ignoring other things. Some clinicians have likened this process to a narrow-beam search-light that focuses on only one thing at (point in) time (While) Their 'Mental packages' are not only small but two-dimensional, devoid of emotional meaning (There are) similarities between EEG's (record brain waves) of adult psychopaths – and those of children…In some respects they're like the emotionless androids depicted in science fiction, unable to imagine what real humans experience."
Dr. Robert D. Hare – Without Conscience

Truly humanistic brain dead psychopaths: "androids" transported to our truly humanistic simultaneously relative point-mass of Earth – God's footstool, from some kind of foreign planet. And/or, some kind of –

"What is a black hole? For astronomical purposes it behaves as a small, highly condensed dark 'body.' But it is not really a material body in the ordinary sense. It possesses no ponderable surface. A black hole is a region of empty space – which acts as a center of gravitational attraction – Since the black hole acts as a center of attraction it can draw new material towards it, which once inside can never escape…What is known as a 'space/time singularity,' a place where physical laws, as presently understood, must cease to apply."
Roger Penrose – Black Holes – The World Treasury of Physics, Astronomy and Mathematics – Ed. Timothy Ferris

Black hole. Wherein: all of their individually affected minds, there can be no purposefully effectuated cognizance of any "Time *made manifest*," it is simply a neurophysiological impossibility. Which is while it: all of their individually affected minds, is: "a place where physical laws, as presently understood, must cease to apply," the very definition of truly humanistic brain death: the inability to cognize any Time *made manifest*, and/or the inability to understand any of the universally applicable *a priori* laws Reality, and/or be affected by them also. And which was, exactly, because they were actually not practicing their scales of Reality, at all. And/or, using any of their –

"Last came forward the man who had the one talent. 'Sir,' he said, 'I heard you were a hard man, reaping where you have not sown and gathering where you have not scattered; so I was afraid, and I went off and hid your talent in the ground. Here it is; it is yours, you have it back.' But his master answered him, 'You wicked and lazy servant! So you knew I reap where I have not sown and gathered where I have not scattered? Well then, you should have deposited my money with the bankers, and on my return I would have recovered my capital with interest. So now, take the talent from him and give it to the man who has ten talents. For to everyone who has will be given more, and he will have more than enough; but from a man who has not, even what he has will be taken away. As for this good-for-nothing servant, throw him out into the dark, where there will be weeping and grinding of teeth."
Matthew 25: 24-30

Omnidimensional talents. So they were "taken away": from them, to enable them to experience truly humanistic brain death for their own selves. And simply thrown into a black hole of misery, too. And/or, too, the ability to experience: *only*, chaos, and/or atonality, polytonality, dissonance and discord. And – remember, which is exactly why, they: the worldly psychopathic con-artists, did actually begin to make manifest absolutely abstracted, and purely psychopathic: unidirectionally successive – excessively histrionic – monochromatic, and high-contrasted, and/or romanticized, "musical sounds," because everybody had begun to experience brain death. And it: the absolutely abstracted, and purely psychopathic, dopamine biochemical inducing stimulus functioning as pure *pleasure* only, and/or "1," was the only thing that could affect the individually affected victims. And also, of course, the –

"Ribbon is cut, accolades flow as Kimmel Center opens to the public –
The hoi polloi replaced *haut monde* yesterday at the Kimmel Center for the Performing Arts, and feel-good Philadelphia fever reached new heights – For the first time in the $265 million center's three-day history, the public was invited to share the spot-light during a day long ceremony that included a variety of performances. Thousands eagerly responded, looking skyward in awe as they streamed through the doors into the grand atrium..."
Kathleen Brady Shea – The Philadelphia Inquirer – December 17, 2001

Music halls. And/or the entire spectacle, actually functioning as purely psychopathic dopamine biochemical inducing stimulus, actually functioning as pure *pleasure* only: The Apple, and/or an orgy.

And – remember, which was also simultaneously occurring: within all of their individually affected minds, and parallel functioning central nervous systems, as they: all of the individually affected victims of the con, were actually beginning to become –

"Remember, blessed Jesu
That I am the cause of Thy pilgrimage,
Do not forsake me on that day.

Seeking me Thou didst sit down weary,
Thou didst redeem me, suffering death on the cross.
Let not such toil be in vain.

Just and avenging Judge.
Grant remission
Before the day of reckoning.

I groan like a guilty man.
Guilt reddens my face.
Spare a suppliant, O God.

My prayers are not worthy,
But Thou in Thy merciful goodness grant
That I burn not in everlasting fire.

Place me among Thy sheep
And separate me from the goats,
Setting me on Thy right hand.

When the accursed have been confounded
And given over to the bitter flames,
Call me with the blessed.

I pray in supplication on my knees.
My heart contrite as the dust,
Safeguard my fate.

Mournful that day
When from the dust shall rise
Guilty man to be judged.

Therefore spare him, O God.
Merciful Jesu, Lord
Grant them rest."

The accursed. And confused and confounded too.

And: as they were beginning to become confused, which was as they were actually beginning to become capable of "confusing" the "map": absolutely abstracted, and purely psychopathic, dopamine biochemical inducing stimulus, functioning as pure *pleasure* only, and/or The Apple: the music halls – all of the musical sounds functioning as stimulus: "1" – the musicians/entertainers functioning as worldly gods – the aristocratic environment, and/or the large masses of people – the associative cognition of worldly power – the grandiosely and deliberately styled human beings: the fine fabrics – gold – silver and diamonds too, the lushly landscaped gardens – the alcoholic laced beverages – the fatty tasting foods and the sweet tasting foods – the money – the entire orgy of the spectacle, and while actually functioning as pure *pleasure* only, and/or The Apple – THEY **DID** BEGIN TO BECOME CAPABLE OF CONFUSING "IT," with the "territory": The Eternal Harmony – The Mind of God made manifest – Finding our Innocence Lost – The Entrance to The Garden, and The Kingdom of Heaven too.

And remember too, this was the aristocratic elite: who was experiencing truly humanistic brain death for their own selves primarily, and – primarily, because the aristocratic elite have always subjugated the common masses. And/or preyed upon the poor, while consuming them, and which is exactly how they did always manage to maintain control: over everything, except for their own selves. So the aristocratic elite, were the only ones who could possibly afford to experience truly humanistic brain death, for their own selves to be in possession of. Exactly because of their allowed exposure to expendable extreme amounts of leisure time, to *exactly* escape Reality, and/or not be forced to face-up to it either, their miserable mortal existence that is. And remember what else the aristocratic elite would have been doing only too: besides experiencing truly humanistic brain death for their own selves, *and* subjugating the common man masses – *and* simply existing while in ignorance of Reality – *and* moving their bodies while as in a purposefully effectuated direction: into their grandiosely and deliberately styled elitist music halls, well, that would have been –

"Toward the middle of the sixteenth century, the prolific Giorgio Vasari, a mediocre painter but a respectable architect, began to document the lives of the Italian artists: He was inventing art history."
Leonardo – Serge Bramley

Buying, and reading, Giorgio Vasari's book, and his –

"Brainwashing: intense psychological indoctrination, usually political, for the purpose of displacing the individual's previous thoughts and attitudes with those selected by the regime or person inflicting the indoctrination."
Taber's Cyclopedic Medical Dictionary

Worldly psychopathic philosophy, and/or the applied art of the con. And while actually functioning, as –

"They are always on the lookout for new stimulation. These people are quick to weary of everything; they want variety, and they are never able to feel or understand the needs of their fellow man – Anyone who wants to win the broad masses must know the key that opens the door to their heart: propaganda tries to force a doctrine on the whole people – The whole art consists in doing this so skillfully that everyone will be convinced...we must avoid excessive intellectual demands on our public, and too much effort cannot be exerted in this direction – the receptivity of the great masses is very limited, their intelligence is small (while) their power of forgetting is enormous – The progress and culture of humanity are not a product of the majority, but rest exclusively on the genius and energy of the personality – Some idea of genius arises in the brain of a man who feels called upon to transmit his knowledge to the rest of humanity. He preaches his view and gradually wins a certain circle of adherents. This process of the direct and personal transmittance of a man's ideas to the rest of his fellow men is the most ideal and natural – In the place of committee decisions, the principle of absolute responsibility was introduced (to): Adolf Hitler."

Adolf Hitler's basic applied mathematical formula: and/or The Art of the con, for worldly political empowerment. Actually functioning as; "The whole art consists in doing this so skillfully that everyone will be convinced – the receptivity of the great masses is very limited, their intelligence is small (while) their power of forgetting is enormous" – the "power of forgetting." And/or, an actual: individually affected, "regression back to point time zero": of an individually affected human being's existence within truly humanistic simultaneously relative space/time. While beginning to experience truly humanistic brain death for their own selves, to be in possession of only: and an absolute relinquishing of their own truly humanistic, and personally affected, universally applicable empirical self-consciousness, and/or their truly humanistic universally applicable memory, and/or their souls, and while as to all of their worldly gods.

Who: all of their worldly gods, would have been supplying them, with allowed access to all of their absolutely abstracted, and purely psychopathic, dopamine biochemical inducing stimulus, functioning as pure *pleasure* only, and while allowing them to become a part of the In Crowd. Which actually was being purposefully allowed exposure to the spectacle of any kind: while actually functioning as pure *pleasure* only, and an artificially effectuated mother's womb environment: simultaneously. So that, all of the individually affected victims of the con, who were allowed to become a part of the In Crowd, were being purposefully allowed to become capable of consuming the absolutely abstracted, and purely psychopathic, dopamine biochemical inducing stimulus, functioning as pure *pleasure* only, while they did – also and simultaneously, remain secured within their worldly absolutely abstracted, and artificially effectuated, mother's womb environments. And, of course, which was also while: simultaneously, never being forced to learn about universally applicable *a priori* Reality, and/or experience any relatively painful experienced humanistic phenomena, and/or *pain*, for their own selves. Which is exactly why, they would have enabled their own selves to begin to become capable of experiencing truly humanistic brain death for their own selves, while beginning to regress back towards point time zero, of their own individually affected existence within truly humanistic simultaneously relative space/time. And remember, exactly because they would not have been practicing their scales: of truly humanistic Reality and while on a daily basis too, then they would have – and simultaneously, begun to enable their own selves to become capable of becoming brainwashed: by all worldly psychopathic con-artists, and Giorgio Vasari too: while actually become capable of "buying his book." And remember, which was as he: Giorgio Vasari, had – already, simply hijacked the name of Leonardo da Vinci, and his ability to make manifest an Omnidimensional space/time continuum, while actually functioning as the real "shaping of the invisible." And – remember, which is while capable of causing an effect that is beyond belief, and which cannot be simply seen with our eyes alone. And – remember, exactly as a dopamine biochemical induction functioning as pure *pleasure* cannot: be simply seen, and with our eyes alone too. And – remember, which would have been occurring: the actual applied art of the con and while actually affecting all of the individually affected victims of the con, as they were actually beginning to experience truly humanistic brain death for their own selves, and beginning to become capable of "regressing back towards point time zero." And – remember, who would have been – *then and simultaneously*, beginning to become capable of –

"The Barnes vs. Reality –
Latches Lane is a quiet place these days. No buses block the streets. There are no protesters, no police, no yellow hazard tape. After a rancorous decade of lawsuit and countersuit, the Barnes foundation is bruised, but gamely carrying on. Its endowment is gone – But the Merion institution still houses one of the great art collections in the world, and it still cleaves to its mission of using art to teach the world how to think and see...When Barnes died in 1951, he left his foundation with an endowment of $10 million – It protected canvases by – Cezanne... "
Stephen Salisbury – The Philadelphia Inquirer – Sunday October 28, 2001

Confusing the; "The Barnes vs. Reality" – map with the territory, and/or the two-dimensional plane: and/or *their* minds, with Reality

302

And remember too, we deal only in self-evident perceivable truths here, and, so, we can actually reveal another simple truth, for the entire world to see with our eyes alone. As we remember exactly what year Leonardo da Vinci did actually become capable of making manifest a real Omnidimensional space/time continuum. And which is while actually functioning, as the purposefully effectuated cognizing, of: truly humanistic simultaneously relative harmoniously proportioned differential equations; subservient to a hierarchically structured whole, and as simultaneously relative patterns in space/time too: while actually functioning as simultaneously relative to/from, and within, a single identifiable, and cognizable, point time zero. Which is an actual single "point": *of* truly humanistic simultaneously relative space/time; located "within" identifiable truly humanistic simultaneously relative space/time. And which *is* an actual single point of truly humanistic simultaneously relative space/time, which is approximately the size of an Apple – and located approximately 20 feet into the "depth" of truly humanistic simultaneously relative space. While – and "simultaneously," capable of beginning to become capable of functioning as truly humanistic simultaneously relative point time zero: *the* beginning of truly humanistic Time *made manifest,* and while actually occurring "within" a truly humanistic simultaneously relative three-dimensional: quantum electrodynamically functioning, mind, and parallel functioning central nervous system. Which is the single simultaneously relative point: *of* truly humanistic simultaneously relative space/time, that is actually projected "into" a human being's three-dimensional electrical potential mass of a mind, and parallel functioning central nervous system: while *simultaneously* a human being's "eyes" must be projected to that single point, located within truly humanistic, and identifiable, simultaneously relative space/time: from which a human being's eyes can NOT move. And which is while beginning to become capable of functioning quantum electrodynamically, and –

"Space, Mach argued, is not a thing, but an expression of interrelationships among events. '*All* masses and *all* velocities, and consequently *all* forces, are relative,' he wrote. Einstein agreed, and was encouraged to attempt to write a theory that built space and time out of events alone…Einstein had replaced Newton's space with a network of light beams; *theirs* was the absolute grid, within which space itself became – Einstein reasoned that if the effects of gravitation are mimicked by acceleration, gravitation itself might be regarded as a kind of acceleration – The search for an answer required brought Einstein to consider the concept of (a) space/time continuum…"
Timothy Ferris – Coming Of Age In The Milky Way

Within which "space" becomes: made manifest, as simultaneously to/from, and within, a single cognizable point time zero, and too while actually functioning as Omnidimensional Time made manifest, and as the function of *The Annunciation* too, and which was while "in" the year 1480 also.

Now: watch this and with your eyes alone, and while beginning in the year 1480 – as Leonardo da Vinci did become capable of making manifest a real, truly humanistic, simultaneously relative Omnidimensional space/time continuum. As the individually affected human beings, were required to actually "project" their minds into the depth of simultaneously relative space/time, and then while – and simultaneously, individually affected human beings, did begin to practice their scales of truly humanistic, simultaneously relative, Omnidimensional space/time, less, and less. Who did then – and simultaneously, begin to become affected more, and more, too: within their own individually affected three-dimensional electrical potential mass minds, and parallel functioning central nervous systems, and, remember, which was while beginning with Michelangelo, and Titian. And – then and simultaneously, progressing as "through" Caravaggio – Poussin – Rubins – Rembrandt – Goya – Manet – Monet – Renoir, and all the way to –

"Cezanne – tried to make the ultimate journey back through time – Cezanne claimed – to believe in his own sensations – moreover, he said himself, quite categorically; 'what counts is only mass' – Cezanne (created) a kind of space where the distance seems near – one technique to create depth is canceled out by the other, in other words Cezanne is the painter of distance that seems near..."
Cezanne – Yvon Taillainder

Paul Cezanne's own personally affected truly humanistic brain death.
And too, his own personally affected –

"What is a black hole? A black hole is a region of empty space – which acts as a center of gravitational attraction. At one time a material body was there. But the body collapsed inwards under its own gravitational pull –The interior region, is defined by the fact that no matter, light, or signal of any kind can escape from it – What is known as a 'space/time singularity' – a place where physical laws, as presently understood, must cease to apply..."
Roger Penrose – Black Holes – The World Treasury of Physics– Ed. T. Ferris

Black hole of truly humanistic dysfunction, and truly humanistic brain death too. And while –

"At birth a baby's language of the senses is primitive: he sees vague shapes, or flashes of light, but without meaning. His eyes can neither focus upon nor follow a moving object. He is even farsighted since his eyeballs are foreshortened at birth. And what he sees is flat. He uses only one eye at a time, his eyes not yet working together to sight an object three-dimensionally..."
The Senses of Man – Joan Steen Wilentz

Actually effectually regressing back all the way to point time zero: of an individual human being's own personally effectuated existence within truly humanistic simultaneously relative space/time. Which is as it did become a neurophysiological impossibility for them: all of the individually affected victims of the con, and while functioning as the aristocratic elite, to simply see, and/or consciously cognize, "past" a single point of simultaneously relative space/time, while at any one point within simultaneously relative space/time. And which was the single point of the two-dimensional plane: "upon" which was projected the representation of tangible form point-mass nouns, functioning as "1," and/or a simple absolutely abstracted, and purely psychopathic, dopamine biochemical inducing effectual stimulus, actually functioning as pure *pleasure* only. And too and again, which was as the individually affected victims of the con, had become capable of, only, functioning as a newly born child is capable of functioning, and while in the year 1880 too.

And remember, which is as a newly born child is – only, capable of responding to the two extremes of basic biological functioning capabilities, of: *pleasure* – sugar – dopamine – harmony, and *pain* – salt – serotonin – chaos, and which is also while, and simultaneously, a newly born child can be in possession of zero universally applicable empirical self-consciousness, and/or universally applicable truly humanistic intelligence, and/or capable of forming an associated cognition to any, and/or every, newly perceived "thing" that they do "see." And which: any and/or all "newly perceived" things that a young child does actually see, and as they are capable of being in possession of zero universally applicable empirical self-consciousness: and/or incapable of knowing anything, will "be": all "newly perceived things" of any and/or all kinds, capable of causing a purposefully effectuated dopamine biochemical induction, within their minds, and while only capable of functioning as pure *pleasure* only. And which will – remember, cause the young child to "move," and while in a child like way, in a purposefully effectuated direction towards the newly perceived visual effectual stimulus, and to enable the child to experience a purposefully effectuated sense of awe, within his individually affected electrical potential mass of a mind, and parallel functioning central nervous system, and to which the child will respond with an: OHH!

So along comes Paul Cezanne with his space/time singularities, and he hangs them up in their brain dead aristocratic elite art museum parks, and the aristocratic elite had never simply seen "these": space/time singularities, hanging in their art museum parks before, so they responded with an: OHH – as they did become capable of having an orgasm, and because of their ability to simply see some newly perceived thing, that they had never seen before. And: exactly because they had experienced truly humanistic brain death for their own selves, as they had actually regressed back to point time zero: of their own personal existence within space/time, they did – and simultaneously, become capable of understanding absolutely nothing for their own selves, and capable of knowing absolutely nothing for their own selves also. So they did – then and simultaneously, simply ask their worldly authoritative god figures, and/or all of the worldly psychopathic con-artists, exactly "what" the abstracted, and projected, two-dimensional plane picture was a "representation of." While they did then – and simultaneously, experience the function of "reuptake," as the biochemical induction of dopamine was reabsorbed back into the individual molecular structure of their minds, and an: AHH – as they were informed by their worldly god figures, what "it" was that they had just experienced. And, of course, which was as they allowed their very own selves to become victims of the con: as they did simply relinquish all of their truly humanistic universally applicable empirical self-consciousness, to all of their worldly authoritative god figures, and/or worldly psychopathic con-artists, who were supplying them with allowed access to all of their purely psychopathic, dopamine biochemical inducing effectual stimulus, actually functioning as pure *pleasure* only, and/or The Apple.

And – remember too, which: the fact that all of the worldly psychopathic con-artists were actually capable of affecting the con, was because they: Pope Julius II and Giorgio Vasari, had already hijacked the name Leonardo da Vinci, and his ability to shape the invisible, and which was while employing the use of the exact same method for worldly political empowerment that Pope Julius II had employed, while beginning to become capable of "selling indulgences." And which, of course, was only exactly backwards in Reality, and too and of course, simply the empowerment of Pope Julius II, and the continued brain death of his individually affected victims. But – remember, as individually affected human beings do actually begin to become capable of experiencing truly humanistic brain death for their own selves, they will, only, begin to become capable of neurophysiologically understanding absolutely nothing, and too and simultaneously, only capable of believing exactly what they are being programmed to believe, and/or brainwashed to believe, by all of the worldly psychopathic con-artists, who are supplying them with allowed access to all of their purely psychopathic dopamine biochemical inducing effectual stimulus. And so: as they were actually beginning to become victims of a con, they: all of the individually affected victims of the con, did actually become capable of believing: within their own aristocratic elite brain dead selves, that they could simply spend a lifetime's worth of time "doing" absolutely nothing, but simply obsessively indulging in excessive Pig physiological self-indulgences, and while only: simultaneously, actually beginning to become capable of experiencing truly humanistic brain death, for their own selves to be in possession of, and only too. And so – then, they: all of the individually affected victims of the con and while attempting to "prove" their intelligence, were actually conned into believing, that they could simply walk into their brain dead aristocratic elite environments, and consume The Apple: and/or experience an orgy and have an orgasm, and – then, "buy a picture": WITH SOME MONEY and "abstracted from within the orgy." And – *then*, to simply "TAKE IT HOME" – "HANG IT ON YOUR WALL," and invite all of your brain dead Pig aristocratic elite friends over: TO HAVE ANOTHER ORGY – AND SAY: "LOOK AT ME – WITH MY 'THING,' THAT YOU DONT HAVE," and –

"At a purely chemical level (just as the injection of) heroin triggers release of dopamine – every experience humans find enjoyable – amounts to little more than an explosion of dopamine in the nucleus accumbens, as exhilarating and ephemeral as a firecracker – dopamine, can be elevated by a hug, a kiss, a word of praise..."
Addicted – J Madeleine Nash – Time – May 5, 1997

Have another orgasm, by becoming the "center of attention." And "of" all of their brain dead aristocratic elite friends, who have moved their bodies while as in a purposefully effectuated direction, to simply enable their own selves to become a part of the In Crowd.
Which: the scientific fact that we can now know that any individually affected victim of the con, who does actually continue to move while as in a purposefully effectuated direction: to enable their own selves to become a part of the In Crowd which is being purposefully allowed exposure to the spectacle of any kind, has experienced truly humanistic brain death for their own selves only, and that everybody is going to die soon, is exactly only because of are allowed exposure to verified 20th century neuroscientific research. And which is while along with our acknowledged understanding of the fact, that –

"...As we found with quantum mechanics, the full structure of the world is richer than our language can express – There are two essential yet complementary aspects of this new vision of time which are as striking in contrast as heaven and hell. Heaven is ruled by dynamical equations that are reversible and 'timeless'; their simplicity ensures stability for eternity. Hell is more akin to the real world, where fluctuations, uncertainty and chaos reign..."
The Arrow of Time – Peter Coveny and Roger Highfield

Everything – every "thing," except for Time *made manifest,* is "chaos." And a human being's mind *is* –

"Candace Pert: 'I see the brain in terms of quantum mechanics – the brain is just a receiver, an amplifier, a little wet minireceiver for collective reality..."
The 3-Pound Universe – Judith Hooper and Dick Teresi

A receiver only. And –

"...Many of the provinces of the brain (are) topographical maps of projections of this sensory fields which they represent – the same geometrical decorum applies to all projections – physical events impinging on the sensory surface are transformed into the characteristic digital language of the brain – a linear code dictates the construction of the visible object..."
Jonathan Miller – The Body in Question

There simply are no images of things being projected throughout, and within, our minds, and parallel functioning central nervous systems. But only a universally applicable "linear code": of the same exact *a priori* information, which all of the individually affected minds, are being "purposefully allowed exposure to." And which: purposefully allowed exposure to every "thing," is – remember, while becoming capable of "affecting" –

"The conduction of an excitatory state (the nerve impulse) is the sole function of a nerve fiber: nerve impulse – a wave of electricity, respond to a variety of stimuli: man is equipped with *receptors* for receiving a great variety of stimuli – each receptor must be stimulated with a minimal amount of energy..."
Elbert Tokay – Fundamentals of Physiology

The "receptors," located within all of the individually affected minds, and parallel functioning central nervous systems. And which can –

"Dopamine, like most biologically important molecules, must be kept within strict bounds – addicts' neurons assaulted by abnormally high levels of dopamine, have responded defensively and reduced the number of sites – or receptors, to which dopamine can bind – so while addicts begin by taking drugs to feel high, they end up taking them in order not to feel low."
Addicted – J. Madeleine Nash – Time May 5, 1997

Exactly become "worn-out" – and "less sensitive": to every "thing," and while as through the passing of time, and slowly, and as it is exactly inversely affected: the truly humanistic brain death.
So that – slowly and gradually, as any one individually affected human being does begin to spend less, and less, and less, time, being purposefully allowed exposure to only harmoniously proportioned amounts of truly humanistic, and simultaneously relative, *a priori* Omnidimensional Reality, and which does mean any "television" AT ALL, and any "going to the movies" AT ALL, and any "riding in an automobile" AT ALL, and any "reading of a novel" AT All, and any "accessing of abstracted musical sounds" AT ALL, and any "looking at a picture" AT ALL, and any "looking at any 'thing" AT ALL, and any "accessing abstracted knowledge" AT ALL, and any "becoming a part of the In Crowd allowed exposure to any spectacle event" AT ALL, and any "using a computer – the Internet – a cell phone – a video recorder" AT ALL, and any simply existing while in ignorance of, and absolutely abstracted from, truly humanistic *a priori* Reality AT ALL, they will only continue to affect disproportionate amounts of purposely affected dopamine biochemical inductions, within their own individually affected mind, and parallel functioning central nervous system, and while capable of functioning as pure *pleasure* only. And remember, which will be while – and simultaneously, capable of beginning to cause permanently affected damage "within" –

308

"PET-scan images of the brains of recovering – addicts reveal other striking changes, including a dramatically impaired ability to process glucose, the primary energy source for working neurons. Moreover, this impairment – which persists for up to 100 days after withdrawal, is greatest in the prefrontal cortex..."
Addicted – J. Madeleine Nash – Time – May 5, 1997

The uniquely humanistic prefrontal cortex.
And remember too, the prefrontal cortex is the exact area of the human being electrical potential mass of a mind, and parallel functioning central nervous system, which is directly responsible for –

"What the frontal lobes 'control' is something like awareness, or self-awareness – Do these lobes govern some essential feature of humanness, or even godliness, as some scientists have suggested? 'If God speaks to man, if man speaks to God,' neuroscientist Candace Pert tells us, 'it would be through the frontal lobes, which is the part of the brain that has undergone the most evolutionary expansion' – Stephen LaBarge: 'And it's capable of what look like miraculous things, so miraculous that we're tempted to say it's devine, that it's not natural."
The 3-Pound Universe – Judith Hooper and Dick Teresi

Consciously cognizing Omnidimensional Time *made manifest*: The Mind of God made manifest – at its best. And –

"Drug's Effect On Brain Is Extensive, Study Shows –
Heavy users (of highly addictive stimulants) are doing more damage to their brains than scientists had thought, according to the first study that looked inside addicts' brains nearly a year after they stop using the drug – the biggest surprise is that another brain region responsible for spatial perception and sensation, which has never before been linked to (substance) abuse, was hyperactive and showed signs of scarring – the addicts' parietal lobes, the parts of the brain used for feeling sensation and for recognizing where the body is in space, were metabolically overactive – It is the equivalent of an inflammation or scarring response..."
Sandra Blakeslee – The New York Times – Tuesday March 6, 2001

Consciously cognizing any Time *made manifest* at all: at least. And/or, beginning to become neurophysiologically capable of functioning, as a human being is capable functioning: which is while beginning to become capable of consciously cognizing past a single point of simultaneously relative space/time, while at any one point within simultaneously relative space/time. Which they: any one individually affected victim of the con, exactly cannot possibly do: because their cerebral cortices have become destroyed. And so – now, they cannot possibly consciously cognize *any* Time *made manifest* at all. Exactly simply because, it is a neurophysiological impossibility for them to maintain even a single cognizable point time zero, within their individually affected minds, and parallel functioning central nervous systems: it is a neurophysiological impossibility. So they are – now, only capable of functioning, while as in a –

"Joyce Kovelman and Arnold Scheibel of UCLA's Brain Research Institute spotted a weird cellular 'disarray' in the schizophrenic brains (and not in the matched controls). The pyramid-shaped cells of the hippocampus, normally arranged in an orderly manner, were grossly misaligned – A schizophrenic's dopamine neurons would start to fire in two different rhythms and rapidly become uncoupled – 'I think that in schizophrenia the brain fragments into active and inactive clusters of neurons and different parts of the brain become disassociated,' says (Roy) King. You might get an asymmetry between the left and right side, say. Schizophrenics often feel that their minds and bodies are split apart – the key to psychotic behavior (is) the unstable fluctuations in a chemical system – the key to schizophrenia is chaotic fluctuations in dopamine production – The litany of schizophrenic symptoms reads like a guidebook to the underworld. Most patients suffer from hallucinations, delusions, and 'thought disorders,' a category that includes impaired logic, jumbled thinking, bizarre ideas, and 'loose' associations. They may sound like beat poets out of control, employing skewed semantics, nelogisms, stream-of-consciousness ramblings, punning, echolalia (parroting), and 'word salads' – 'schizophrenics find it difficult to distinguish between signal and noise and to assign levels of importance to various classes of stimuli. Everything becomes important; nothing is trivial' – Add to this a distorted sense of self, a feeling of personal unreality, often coupled with a distorted body image – Robert G. Heath: 'The primary symptom of schizophrenia isn't hallucinations or delusions,' he tells us. 'It's a defect in the pleasure response. Schizophrenics have a predominant of painful emotions. They function in an almost continuous state of fear or rage, fight or flight, because they don't have the pleasure to neutralize it – schizophrenics are extremely insensitive to pain and (are) unreactive to other sensory stimuli, as well' – a psychiatrist Monte Buchsbaum – measured patient's brain-wave responses to electrical shocks and auditory signals and found these EEG's to be abnormally flat, specifically at higher levels of intensity. He concluded that – schizophrenics were 'reducers' (as opposed to augmenters), that their brains naturally reduced, or dampened, stimuli..."
The 3-Pound Universe – Judith Hooper and Dick Teresi

Purely schizophrenic manner. As they have enabled their own selves to become capable of experiencing truly humanistic brain death for their own selves. Which is simply because, of their own personally allowed; "the key to psychotic behavior (is) the unstable fluctuations in a chemical system – the key to schizophrenia is chaotic fluctuations in dopamine production" – exposure to excessive amounts of absolutely abstracted, and purely psychopathic and/or schizophrenic, dopamine biochemical inducing effectual stimulus, actually functioning as pure *pleasure* only, and/or tangible form mass stimulus actually effectually functioning as "1" only. And which is exactly why –

"A Shock Grows in Brooklyn –
A fiery controversy over a museum's new show brings New York's Mayor out slugging: The mayor blew up three weeks ago over the controversial exhibition, 'Sensation: Young British artists from the Saatchi Collection' – The mayor was especially outraged by the 'Holy Virgin Mary,' a painting by Chris Ofili, who used, among other materials, elephant dung...polls showed that both New York residents and a nationwide sample were against shutting down the exhibit..."
Cathleen McGuigan, Maggie Malone, Ray Sawhill, Gregory Beals – Newsweek October 11, 1999

They can only make manifest personally affected schizophrenic inarticulate cries for attention: while simultaneously projecting their own personally affected neurophysiological dysfunctions upon mankind. Which is, of course, only exactly why they do it: make manifest schizophrenic inarticulate cries for attention, because of their own personally affected truly humanistic brain death, and their addictions to all things worldly. While including the need to receive a much larger induction of dopamine biochemical inducing stimulus, for their own selves to become capable of consuming, while enabling themselves to become worldly provocateurs, and then capable of becoming the "center of attention."
And remember, this is *The Annunciation*. And *The Annunciation* is –

"The Annunciation: is the moment when the archangel Gabriel informs Mary that she is to be the mother of Christ (Luke 1: 28-31). The Annunciation takes place either in an enclosed garden or loggia or in Mary's house. The time is spring – an allusion to St. Bernard's description, 'The flower willed in the time of flowers to be born of a flower.' The enclosed garden, a reference to Mary's virginity, comes from the Song of Solomon (4: 12). A rose – or a lily – also refers to the Song of Solomon (2: 1-2). Other accessories relating to cleanliness may appear in indoor settings – a water jar, a towel, a glass, a washbasin. The virgin is generally Kneeling in prayer, or reading a devotional book. Sometimes she is weaving the Veil of the Temple, a reference to the apocryphal Gospel of James. Gabriel appears on the left. He holds a scepter, symbol of power as a herald of God, or white Madonna lily, the Virgin's flower..."
Gertrude Grace Sill – a handbook of Symbols in Christian Art

The point in Time when the facade of the two-dimensional plane is torn in half: the revealing of the absolute truth, and the beginning of the end of time.
And – remember, there simply are –

"...Many of the provinces of the brain (are) topographical maps of projections of the sensory fields which they represent – the same geometrical decorum applies to

311

all projections – physical events impinging on the sensory surface are transformed into the characteristic digital language of the brain – a linear code dictates the construction of the visible object..."
Jonathan Miller – The Body in Question

No images of things being projected throughout, and within, our electrical potential mass minds, and parallel functioning central nervous systems: while as to/from, and within, any single, and identifiable, cognizable point time zero. But only the function of a linear code: of the exact information our minds are capable of receiving, and –

"The conduction of an excitatory state (the nerve impulse) is the sole function of a nerve fiber: nerve impulse – a wave of electricity, respond to a variety of stimuli: man is equipped with receptors for receiving a great variety of stimuli – each receptor must be stimulated with a minimal amount of energy. Each receptor is especially sensitive to a particular form of energy and has a lower threshold for it than any other kind. When activated, the receptor responds by initiating a volley of nerve impulses in the afferent nerve fiber that lead from it..."
Elbert Tokay – Fundamentals of Physiology

Being "affected by" the perceived linear code, of "communicated information."
And remember how all individually affected human beings do begin to become affected, by their purposefully allowed exposure to absolutely abstracted, and purely psychopathic, dopamine biochemical inducing stimulus, and while simultaneously exactly not practicing their scales of truly humanistic simultaneously relative Reality too. Which is as they do – exactly, begin to become capable of experiencing truly humanistic brain death for their own selves, and do, and simultaneously, actually begin to become capable of regressing all the way back towards point time zero: of their own personally affected existence within truly humanistic simultaneously relative Omnidimensional space/time. And while, then, actually beginning to become only capable of functioning while as in a purely psychopathic manner. And while, then – also, actually beginning to become neurophysiologically incapable of –

"The psychopath is like an infant, absorbed in his own needs, vehemently demanding satiation – Psychopaths (do also) display a general lack of empathy. They are indifferent to the rights and suffering of family members and strangers alike – Psychopaths are very good at giving their undivided attention to things that interest them most and at ignoring other things. Some clinicians have likened this process to a narrow-beam search-light that focuses on only one thing at (a point) in time..."
Dr. Robert D. Hare – Without Conscience

Simply "seeing," and/or "consciously cognizing," past a single point of truly humanistic simultaneously relative space/time, while at any one point within truly humanistic simultaneously relative space/time: it is simply a neurophysiological impossibility. Which is as they: any one single individually affected human being, will have begun to become capable of functioning as a young child is only capable of functioning. And which is as an adult human being, does actually allow their very own selves to become capable of effectually regressing back to point time zero, of their own personally affected existence within simultaneously relative space/time. And while – and simultaneously, actually beginning to become capable of only functioning as in a purely psychopathic manner for their own selves, and within their own individually affected three-dimensional electrical potential mass minds, and parallel functioning central nervous systems. Which will actually remain incapable of simply seeing past a single point of simultaneously relative space/time, while at any one single point within simultaneously relative space/time, and which is the "single point" of the two-dimensional plane, and/or the picture, and as they: any one individually affected human being, are only capable of functioning in the purely psychopathic: and truly humanistic brain dead, manner. And remember again, there simply are NO IMAGES OF THINGS within our minds, but only a linear code: of the simultaneously projected information, which is actually being made manifest, and actually capable of being interpreted, within an individually affected human being's electrical potential mass of a mind, and parallel functioning central nervous system.

And – remember too, the –

"Candace Pert: Even uni-cellular organisms have peptides' – They're programmed to migrate toward or away from a chemotactic substance. They're little robots that go for sugar at all costs and away from salt...Behavior is controlled by the anticipation of pain or pleasure, punishment or reward. And that has to be coded in the brain..."
The 3-Pound Universe – Judith Hooper and Dick Teresi

Basic biological functioning capabilities, of: *pleasure* – dopamine – sugar – harmony – Flower – Lily – Peace – Respect – Love – Virtue, and *pain* – serotonin – salt – chaos, and –

"A Shock Grows in Brooklyn –
A fiery controversy over a museum's new show brings New York's Mayor out slugging: The mayor blew up three weeks ago over the controversial exhibition, 'Sensation: Young British artists from the Saatchi Collection' – The mayor was especially outraged by 'The Holy Virgin Mary,' a painting by Chris Ofili, who used, among other materials, elephant dung..."
C. McGuigan, M. Malone, R. Sawhill, G. Beals – Newsweek

"Elephant dung": disrespect – contempt – insolence – complacency – indifference – discord – pain – death – suffering – lawlessness – truly humanistic brain death – complete and utter death for everyone, are encoded within the DNA of all living cells, while as from one end of the universe to the other, and a; "Behavior is controlled by the anticipation of pain or pleasure, punishment or reward. And that has to be coded within the brain" – human being's mind too.

So, and again to simplify, let's say the linear code for *pleasure*: dopamine – sugar – harmony – Flower/Lily, is "11111," and – simultaneously, the linear code for *pain*: serotonin – salt – chaos – elephant dung, is "10010," and – again remember, there simply are NO images of things being projected all throughout, and within, our truly humanistic electrical potential mass minds and parallel functioning central nervous systems, but only the exact replication of this exact same universally applicable function: the linear code of the information. And so, if an individual human being, who has not yet learned how to speak, and/or write, and/or become capable of communicating anything "abstractly," and unidirectionally successively, and remember exactly as Paleolithic cave men had not, wanted to simply communicate: "harmony" – and/or "peace" – and/or "respect" – and/or "love" – and/or "virtue," to any other 5-year-old human being child, and/or, any absolutely truly humanistic brain dead psychopath: who cannot possibly consciously cognize "past" a single point of truly humanistic simultaneously relative space/time, while at any one point within truly humanistic simultaneously relative space/time, how would you do THAT: communicate peace – TO THE CHILD, and/or enable them to understand "it?" The answer is, of course, by simply abstractly representing, and/or "drawing," a three-dimensional projected representation of: dopamine – sugar – harmony – peace – virtue – flower/lilly – life: "11111," not: serotonin – salt – chaos – disrespect – contempt – elephant dung – death: "10010." And too and of course, which actually would: the actual cognized perceivable appearance of serotonin – chaos – elephant dung – death – 10010, cause even an –

"Our withdrawal reflex, which causes us to pull a hand away from a hot stove, involves only the spinal cord and is similar both anatomically and in behavior to that found in earthworms."
Dana H. Zohar – The Quantum Self

Amoeba to move in a purposefully effectuated direction away from it: the actual universally applicable linear code of information. And remember too, which is exactly because, if you get to this point –

"Brain death: cessation of brain function. Criteria for conclusion that the brain has died include lack of response to stimuli; absence of all reflexes; absent respirations."
Taber's Cyclopedic Medical Dictionary

Of truly humanistic dysfunction, for the majority of our entire society to experience for their own selves, and while becoming affected as through a lifetime's worth of exposure to only absolutely abstracted, and purely psychopathic, dopamine biochemical inducing stimulus, actually functioning as pure *pleasure* only, and with the *actual* "increase of lawlessness," then –

"Candace Pert: Even uni-cellular organisms have peptides' – Even bacteria have a little hierarchy of primitive likes and dislikes. They're programmed to migrate toward or away from a chemotactic substance. They're little robots that go for sugar at all costs and away from salt. If you were designing a robot vehicle to walk into the future and survive, as God was when he designed human beings, you'd wire it up so that behavior that ensured the survival of self or species – would be naturally reinforcing. Behavior is controlled by the anticipation of pain or pleasure, punishment or reward. And that has to be coded in the brain..."
The 3-Pound Universe – Judith Hooper and Dick Teresi

Everbody dies.
Which is exactly because: remember, all of that time evolutive dopamine induced damage: of individually affected human being minds, has been occurring within the prefrontal cortex. And remember, the uniquely humanistic prefrontal cortex, is the exact area of a human being's mind, which is responsible for cognizing any Time *made manifest,* and/or any patterns in space/time, or Life, and/or actually simply functioning as a truly humanistic being is capable of functioning, and not as an animal is only capable of functioning. And – remember, which is exactly because, all of the individually affected human beings have been practicing their scales of truly humanistic simultaneously relative Omnidimensional Reality less, and less, and less, and while on a daily basis too, while – and simultaneously, actually beginning to become only capable of functioning while as in a purely schizophrenic manner. Which was also – and simultaneously, actually beginning to become capable of affecting all of the individually affected receptors: and too as they were becoming less, and less, and less, sensitive, to every thing. Which was also while, remember – as all humanistic phenomena is inversely affected, all of the individually affected human beings were beginning to become MORE, and MORE, and MORE, addicted: to excessive amounts of absolutely abstracted, and purely psychopathic, dopamine biochemical inducing stimulus actually functioning as pure *pleasure* only. And as all of the stimulus was actually becoming more and more schizophrenic: more "abstracted" – more "effectual" – more "grandiose" – more "fragmented" – more "spectacular" – more "simplistic" – more "childish" – more "colorful" – more "loud" – more "big" – more "stuff" – more "more" – more "monochromatic" – more "high-contrasted" – more "sensational" – more "discordant" – more "chaotic" – more "orgy," and more "heroin" too. And – too and again, which was actually occurring, that more and more people were beginning to become affected and victims of the con, as all of the individually affected human beings, were beginning to become

315

capable of causing permanently affected, and severe, neurophysiological damage, within their uniquely humanistic prefrontal cortices. And – remember, the uniquely humanistic prefrontal cortex, is –

"The prefrontal cortex (is) a dopamine-rich area of the brain that controls impulsive and irrational behavior. Addicts, in fact, display many of the symptoms shown by patients who have suffered strokes or injuries to the prefrontal cortex. Damage to this region, University of Iowa neurologist Antonio Damasio and his colleagues have demonstrated, destroys the emotional compass that controls behaviors that the patient (should) know are unacceptable."
Addicted – J. Madeleine Nash – Time – May 5, 1997

The exact area of a human being's mind, which is directly responsible for controlling his, or her, own self: or not as it does begin to become destroyed. And too, which is as the individually affected human beings: who are actually practicing their scales of truly humanistic simultaneously relative Reality less, and less, and less, and actually beginning to become capable of functioning while as in a purely schizophrenic manner, are beginning to become more and more "obsessive compulsive" also, and "paranoid delusional" also. And –

"We're All Suffering From Anxiety, But Why –
Our nation has developed an anxiety disorder. This anxiety affects the way we care for ourselves and our loved ones. It effects how we vote, shop, eat, sleep and even – how we think. Most of all, it affects how much we enjoy our lives – I don't know about you, but almost everyone I know suffers from anxiety. We have anxiety about our children, our future, our neighbors, and our intimate relationships – How pervasive is this anxiety? Doctors report that the majority of visits to their offices are anxiety related. More than half of all Americans report some symptoms of sleep disorder, and the age of heart attacks, has been getting lower over the last two decades. The incidence of depression and eating disorders continues to increase, and more symptoms of emotional disturbance are showing up in our children at younger ages – Most children I speak with as young as ten years old complain about too much stress in their lives...Road rage, domestic violence, workaholism, relentless striving for more, and racial and ethic discrimination are all misguided efforts to pursue security – anxiety and possessions go hand in hand..."
Dan Gottlieb – The Philadelphia Inquirer – Tuesday December 12, 2000

Extremely "anxious," and/or "disgruntled," and/or "neurotic," and/or "unbalanced," and/or just about to lose control of their very own selves, and –

"Stone Cold Picnic –
WrestleMania XV ended the way it had to, the way any good populist fairy tale must: with the working man hero Stone Cold Austin the new World Wrestling

316

Federation champion, with the 20,000 fans who'd packed the First Union Center on their feet, and the WWF owner Corporation bad guy Mr. McMahon on his knees and covered in Coors Light – along the way, there were the requisite helpings of blood and gore and bad language, Satanic symbols, broken tables, broken chairs, fireworks, men the size SUVs and woman the shape of Barbie dolls – And the crowd eats it up, 'It makes you want more,' said fifteen-year-old Matt of Lansdale. I can't wait to see what they'll do next."
Jennifer Weiner – The Philadelphia Inquirer – March 30, 1999

They need more: schizophrenic discord – CHAOS – PAIN – DEATH – SUFFERING – LAWLESSNESS – STIMULUS – SPECTACLE – SPORTS – POP SOCIETY – STUFF – COMPUTERS – NOVELS – TELEVISION – MOVIES – SEX – DOPAMINE – DRUGS – HERION, every "thing" functioning as "1." And to simply –

"Dopamine, like most biologically important molecules, must be kept within strict bounds – addicts' neurons assaulted by abnormally high levels of dopamine, have responded defensively and reduced the number of sites – or receptors, to which dopamine can bind – so while addicts begin by taking drugs to feel high, they end up taking them in order not to feel low."
Addicted – J. Madeleine Nash – Time – May 5, 1997

Enable them to feel alive. And/or – remember, to simply enable them: all of the individually affected victims of the con, who have actually regressed back to point time zero: of their own personally affected existence within truly humanistic space/time, and who are now only capable of functioning in a purely schizophrenic manner, to NOT feel as though they DO have a plastic bag placed upon their heads. And remember, this is permanently affected damage, actually having occurred within their individually affected cerebral cortices, because of their purposefully allowed exposure to excessive amounts of absolutely abstracted, and purely psychopathic, dopamine biochemical inducing stimulus, functioning as pure *pleasure* only. And remember too, which is while having never performed any proportional amounts of purposefully affected reuptake function, after each, and every, purposefully affected dopamine biochemical induction, and which is impossible while as through allowed exposure to: a television screen, and/or a computer monitor screen, and/or a movie screen, and/or a novel, and/or while riding in an automobile – train or airplane, and/or any "thing" except walking. And – too remember, they have never purposefully affected any –

"Princeton's (Barry) Jacobs (says) that, based on experiments – walking – stimulates the release of serotonin..."
Michael D. Lemonick – The Mood Molecule – Time – September 29, 1997

317

Proportional amounts of serotonin production/induction: within their individually affected minds, and parallel functioning central nervous systems. And remember exactly what, serotonin is directly responsible for –

"A Little Help From Serotonin –
Could a single brain chemical hold the key to happiness – as the 20th century winds down, we humans seem increasingly convinced that serotonin is the key to a good life – and it's easy to see why. This once obscure neurotransmitter is the secret behind Prozac, the drug that revolutionized the pursuit of happiness – serotonin pacifies neurons in the limbic system, the Brain's Department of Animal Instincts. 'Serotonin puts the brakes on primitive behaviors like sex, aggression...'"
Geoffrey Cowley/Anne Underwood – Newsweek – December 29, 1997

Controlling animalistic behaviors, and/or simply enabling people to live in peace. And, remember, as was exactly explained by –

"For everyone will be salted with fire. Salt is a good thing, but if salt has become insipid, how can you season it again? Have salt in yourselves and be at peace with one another."
Mark 9: 48-50

The Son of God.
And, of course, this is some of the easiest math in the entire history of mankind. Because, if they: the overwhelming vast majority of individually affected human beings, within our entire global society, have, already, regressed all the way back to point time zero: of their individually affected existence within Reality – and they have, *and* exactly because of their allowed exposure to excessive amounts of absolutely psychopathic – and schizophrenic, dopamine biochemical inducing stimulus, functioning as pure *pleasure* only, and too while functioning as the; "In the world of 'sports entertainment' – the guiding principle is 'Give the people what they want' – blood and gore and bad language, Satanic symbols, broken tables, broken chairs, fireworks, men the size of SUVs and women the size of Barbie dolls" – actual lawlessness: discord – chaos – pain and suffering too, *and they still need more*, what is there left to allow them to consume, and/or be affected by, and/or to allow them to actually do, except to –

"Gunshots, Blood and Chaos –
A bomb went off. The shooting began. What followed at Columbine High School was like a real-life horror movie...'It was just a mass of confusion' – And of horror..a horror movie brought to life..."
Gwen Florio – The Philadelphia Inquirer – Wednesday April 21, 1999

Make manifest death: to go along with the discord, and chaos, and pain, and suffering, and lawlessness too. And – remember, which is as –

"Teen's Lust For Killing Emerged In Prose –
Eric Harris thought about war, fantasized about war and wrote about war. He was thrilled when he heard, one morning in philosophy class, that the United States was on the verge of bombing Yugoslavia...on Web pages – Under 'Philosophy' (Harris) wrote: 'My belief is if I say something, it goes. I am the law, and if you don't like it, you die. If I don't like you or I don't like what you want me to do, you die – I'll just go to some downtown area in some big ass city and blow up and shoot everything I can...Feel no remorse, no sense of shame' – What's clear is that they liked war, war was a game, war was entertainment..."
Joel Achenbach, Dale Russakoff – Philadelphia Inquirer – April 29, 1999

They "love" it: THE LAWLESSNESS – THE SCHIZOPHRENIA – THE SPECTACLE – THE CHAOS – THE DISCORD – THE PAIN – THE SUFFERING – THE DEATH – THE HEROIN – THE ORGY: the truly humanistic brain death, they do –

"Portrait of madness –
Now that we can dissect DNA to identify a murderer or nail down fatherhood, now that we can tiptoe through the human genome to predict who will be a candidate for colon cancer or Alzheimer's disease, probing (the) tortured psyche of Vincent Van Gogh is a notion too tantalizing to resist – When you look at his work – the intensity with which he put paint on canvas – you feel so excited, stimulated and sometimes frightened. You not only see, but feel the mania – the loud color, the noise – you should relate to it from your own experiences..."
Gloria Hochman – Philadelphia Inquirer – October 22, 2000

Simply LOVE IT. They –

"The Sopranos': Brutally Honest –
At the start of the season Tony Soprano, America's favorite mob boss, was becoming a little too lovable – Season 3 fixed all that. In the last few weeks as the show's season approached its end, Tony almost strangled his girlfriend when she threatened to reveal their affair. As he flung her body in the air, slammed it to the floor, then put his hands around her neck with rage, it was entirely plausible that he was going to kill her. And his violent reaction was not an isolated event...For the first time this season's 'Sopranos' relied heavily on violence directed against innocents, especially women – The 'Sopranos,' with its superb level of accomplishment, has used extreme violence to a profound artistic end..."
Caryn James – The New York Times – Tuesday May 22, 2001

LOVE IT. They –

"Sorry spectacle –

How low can television go – Call it extreme television or even spectacle TV – shows that push the envelope until it is in shreds. In terms of graphic, shocking, explicit programs, television is breaking – maybe *plumbing* is a better word – new ground every day..."

Jennifer Weiner – The Philadelphia Inquirer – June 6, 1999

LOVE IT. They –

"Looking Like a Million Bucks –

Who wants to be a Millionaire? It's more than just a question. It's even more than just a quiz show – It's what everybody's talking about the morning after...Night after night, Americans are gathering around the tube at 8:30, captivated by the glass-and-metal gladiator's music, to Germany-disco-in-1989 lights, and the high, hard-edged contestant chairs that seem designed to provoke anxiety...ABC suits are rejoicing..."

Jennifer Weiner – The Philadelphia Inquirer – June 6, 1999

LOVE IT. They –

"Thou shalt not wallow in adultery –

We love to watch; always have. That impulse explains everything from the National Enquirer to its tamer stepchildren such as People and Us to the gossip columns in most newspapers...Sometimes, we're even a little jealous. We might tsk-tsk about Meg Ryan's running off with Russell Crow and leaving crooked-grinned Dennis Quaid and their 8-year-old son, Jack. But when the kids are crying and the house is a mess, a grin can lose its charm – at which point, you find yourself envying Meg and her rugged new guy – Because the affair nearly always has the pull of overwhelming romance – or at least, the best sex ever..."

Gwen Florio – The Philadelphia Inquirer – Sunday January 20, 2001

LOVE IT. They –

"No Jordan? No Gretzky? Now we've got Woods –

When Sinatra settled onto a stool and took a mic, all the other singers sat down and shut up. When Mark McGwire takes BP, even the strongest of the bombardiers put down their lumber and watch – And when Tiger Woods plunges a tee into manicured greensward, coils and cocks – well, this is how you know it's a moment for the ages: Michael Jordan gets goose bumps...Tiger Woods has a knack for the moment, an instinct for the theatrical..."

Bill Lyon – The Philadelphia Inquirer

LOVE IT. They –

"A Force To Be Reckoned With –
The premier of the Star Wars Prequel Lured Crowds – Neither critical darts
nor torrents of rain could keep the masses from the multiplexes yesterday, the first
full day of what could be the most anticipated movie ever. In Los Angeles, scalpers
got five times face value for tickets to midnight screenings...Companies bought their
employees tickets to yesterday's moonlight showing just to keep them at their desk
during the day...And they loved everything about Menance. The special effects. The
good-vs.-evil mythology. The pod race. The Jedi Knights and Masters...Between
the movies and related merchandising, the Force is responsible for more than $7
billion in sales..."
Daniel Rubin – Philadelphia Inquirer

LOVE IT. They –

"The House Getty Oil Built –
The Making of a Legacy – No one walks in L. A., ground zero of car culture.
Without wheels, you're just not going anywhere, you're no one – It is fitting, then,
that the new Getty Center – the city's $1 billion bid for art world respectability – is
perched above one of the nation's most congested freeways and is impossible to
reach by foot. No one walks in Los Angeles. No one walks to the Getty – Instead,
visitors ascend to the Getty's world-class Art Museum aboard driverless electric
trains..."
Janet Weeks – USA TODAY – Friday December 12, 1997

LOVE IT. They –

"As Tourists Jam Yosemite, the Warnings Go Unheeded –
It's hard to be a wilderness in the long, hot days of summer – when people
drive in by the thousands, bringing their big-city ways. Each date in high season
here, cars crash on the narrow park roads. Car alarms blare. Traffic comes to a
standstill. In crowded parking lots in Yosemite Valley, drivers circle, searching for
spaces..."
Nita Lelyveld – The Philadelphia Inquirer – Sunday July 4, 1997

LOVE IT. They –

"The Horror, The Spectacle, Then Lunch –
Ground Zero, three months later: A visit last week was unsettling, at least to
this New Yorker – The site of the terrorist attack has many identies. It is hallowed
ground, a relentless work site, an international crime scene, a backdrop for memorial
services, a destination for celebrities and tourists – It has become a magnet, drawing
people who want to see for themselves –The air is almost festive. Tour buses
promise to get customers within a few blocks of the sight, so they can walk to the

barricades, then catch the next bus..."

Marian Uhlman – The Philadelphia Inquirer – Friday June 11, 1999

LOVE IT. They –

"At this show, people cruise as cars just sit and gleam –

A bit of a queue was in the making at the new Subaru Outback, but you just have to forgive Ian S- . He was loving his time behind the wheel, snuggling down into that cushy driver's seat at the Philadelphia International Auto Show – 'It feels nice,' he said. 'Its design is cool' – He also complemented the built-in cup holder and wondered whether the rooftop rack would take all three of his bikes – Ian S- , of Stratford, Camden County, you see, is 7 – 'He loves cars,' his mother explained – Yesterday, the little guy had plenty of company. The United States is a car-and-driver nation..."

Rita Giordano – The Philadelphia Inquirer – Monday February 5, 2001

LOVE IT. They –

"Selling America on Soccer, Viagra –

At this moment in history, everything, from drugs to doughnuts to those quasi-real people called celebrities, is a product to be shaped and spun, refined and repackaged, and eventually sold to the highest bidder – And, when everything has a price, it only makes sense that everything has an ad campaign – Yesterday afternoon, 100 of the best branders in the business, as chosen by Advertising Age Magazine, gathered here to celebrate their achievements – Comedy Central hosted the event, a luncheon at the tres posh Pierre Hotel, where the elite of the ad world met, schmoozed, sucked down wine and shrimp and molten-chocolate cake, and congratulated each other on selling more people more stuff than ever before...at the luncheon were the people who last year sold America what it ate, drank, read, watched, drove, danced to, played with, or voted for – Amid this sea of sincerity, it fell to Jon Stewart of Comedy Central to remind the assembled guests and honorees of what it was really all about: money..."

Jennifer Weiner – The Philadelphia Inquirer

Love it.

They simply love it: the lawlessness; the discord; the chaos; the pain; the death; the suffering; the spectacle; the orgy, they love all of it. All of the truly humanistic brain death: purposefully allowed exposure to absolutely abstracted, and purely psychopathic, and/or schizophrenic, dopamine biochemical inducing stimulus, functioning as pure *pleasure* only. And they are going to love it all the way to death too: because they cannot live without it. And, too, they even, or rather they especially, loved this –

"U.S. ATTACKED –

Hijacked Planes Destroy Trade Towers, Hit Pentagon; Thousands Feared Dead: A series of near-precision assaults shattered two symbols of America's military and financial power yesterday, killing untold numbers of people, halting Americans' daily routine, and forever destroying a nation's feeling that it can't happen here..."

Ralph Vigado – The Philadelphia Inquirer – Wednesday September 12, 2001

They could not get enough of that: ultimate spectacle. Which is exactly why, they did simply consume it 24/7, and for weeks on end too. Simply because, it was the ultimate dose, and/or the "overdose," of discord, and/or 10010, nothing can top that. Which is exactly why, it is the ultimate –

"It will be the same as it was in Lot's day: people were eating and drinking, buying and selling, planting and building, but the day Lot left Sodom, God rained fire and brimstone from heaven and it destroyed them all. It will be the same when the day comes for the Son of Man to be revealed.

When that day comes, anyone on the housetop, with his possessions in the house, must not come down to collect them, nor must anyone in the fields turn back either. Remember Lot's wife. Anyone who tries to preserve his life will lose it; and anyone who loses it will keep it safe. I tell you, on that night two will be in one bed: one will be taken, the other left.' The disciples interrupted. 'Where, Lord?' they asked. He said, 'Where the body is, there too will the vultures gather."

Luke 17: 28-37

Schizophrenic inarticulate cry for attention.

But they still won't get it, because they are brain dead. And which is exactly why –

"Many Come to Bear Witness at Ground zero –

They came yesterday in streams of thousands, from far away places like South Carolina, England and Italy and nearby ones like Wall Street, Long Island and the Upper West Side. They carry the cameras and video equipment (and) They are directed like a funeral procession down Nassau Street south of City Hall and toward Liberty Street, where they stopped briefly before continuing south. Two speakers, mounted on a balcony of the Federal Reserve Bank on Nassau Street, blasted marching tunes...Janet E-, a flight attendant for British Airways, made the trip on foot from the Canal Street subway – She walked behind her friends, embarrassed to be seen with them when they stopped to ask for directions. She kept her camera hidden. She was thinking: Maybe I should not have come – 'I thought it was ghoulish and holidaying on other people's misery,' she said. 'But it was a compulsion..."

Dean E. Murphy – The New York Times – Tuesday September 18, 2001

They do continue to move while in a purposefully effectuated direction, towards the spectacle, to allow them to become capable of seeing it, and/or being affected by it. And – again, which is exactly simply because, they do love it: the lawlessness; the discord; the chaos; the spectacle; the television; the movies and the novels. The spectator sporting events; the amusement parks; the art museum parks; the theme parks, and spectacle event parks. The grandiosely, and deliberately, styled, automobiles, trains and airplanes. The excessively simplistic, and histrionic, and monochromatic, and romanticized, musical sounds: the boy bands – the girl bands, and pop icon bands. The grandiosely, and deliberately, styled, tangible form masses of all kinds, and/or all new things – the fine fabrics, and diamonds, and gold, and silver. The fatty tasting foods, and sweet tasting foods. The alcoholic, and caffeine, laced beverages. The computers; the Internet; the Virtual reality; the dot-coms; the cell phones, and video recorders. The aristocratic environments: the money; the worldly power; the apathy; the complacency; the truly humanistic brain death; the living in ignorance of Reality; the orgy; the heroin – The Apple: all of the allowed exposure to absolutely abstracted, and purely psychopathic – and/or schizophrenic, dopamine biochemical inducing stimulus, functioning as pure *pleasure* only: they love all of it. Just about the only thing they do *not* love, is –

"Reality' reigns –
Get real – That's with the TV networks think they're doing, unleashing a flood of 'reality' shows for this winter and spring, and, they seem to hope forevermore – Tonight on ABC, one mystery person starts sabotaging nine others. Tomorrow, Fox – who else – begins an experiment in romantic relationships that seems to promise almost-adultery and maybe even a little group sex. It delivers a more mundane package that's closer to soap opera – and seems almost eerie in its consistently second-rate imitation of so many aspects of *Survivor*, the show that set the reality hook in every TV programmer's rosy cheeks – Most important, even if they do not generate *Survivors'* response – these shows can attract young viewers – 'Young members of the audience are finding it harder and harder to suspend disbelief in the traditional story-form of programming,' (Dean) Valentine said. 'They need a greater sense of reality in what they're watching' – UPN has found success with wrestling, the overblown granddaddy of the 'reality' shows – 'We can leave aside the question of how much reality there is in reality,' Valentine said. 'But clearly young viewers feel it's a more authentic thing than watching another sitcom...' – If these 'reality' shows were *really* real, of course, nobody would watch..."
Jonathan Storm – The Philadelphia Inquirer – Tuesday January 9 to 2001

Reality.
Which is exactly why, they have actually allowed their very own selves to become only capable of functioning while as in a purely –

"Joyce Kovelman and Arnold Scheibel of UCLA's Brain Research Institute spotted a weird cellular 'disarray' in the schizophrenic brains (and not in the matched controls). The pyramid-shaped cells of the hippocampus, normally arranged in an orderly manner, were grossly misaligned – A schizophrenic's dopamine neurons would start to fire in two different rhythms and rapidly become uncoupled – 'I think that in schizophrenia the brain fragments into active and inactive clusters of neurons and different parts of the brain become disassociated,' says (Roy) King. You might get an asymmetry between the left and right side, say. Schizophrenics often feel that their minds and bodies are split apart – the key to schizophrenia is chaotic fluctuations in dopamine production – Robert G. Heath: 'The primary symptom of schizophrenia isn't hallucinations or delusions,' he tells us. It's a defect in the pleasure response – schizophrenics are extremely insensitive to pain and (are) unreactive to other sensory stimuli, as well' – a psychiatrist, Monte Buchsbaum, measured patient's brain-wave responses to electrical shocks and auditory signals and found these EEG's to be abnormally flat, specifically at higher levels of intensity. He concluded that – schizophrenics were 'reducers' (as opposed to augmenters), that their brains naturally reduced, or dampened, stimuli..."
The 3-Pound Universe – Judith Hooper and Dick Teresi

Schizophrenic manner.
And which is as they: all of the individually affected victims of the con, actually have allowed their very own selves, to become capable of experiencing truly humanistic brain death, for their very own selves. Because – again remember, which is exactly as there are no images of things within our minds, and the human being mind is –

"Candace Pert: 'I see the brain in terms of quantum mechanics – the brain is just a receiver, an amplifier, a little wet minireceiver for collective reality...'"
The 3-Pound Universe – Judith Hooper and Dick Teresi

A receiver – an "amplifier": for collective Reality.
And – too remember, exactly what the "key" to everything: to every "thing," is –

"Dopamine, like most biologically important molecules, must be kept within strict bounds – Too much causes the hallucinations, and bizarre thoughts, of schizophrenia – addicts' neurons assaulted by abnormally high levels of dopamine, have responded defensively and reduced the number of sites – or receptors, to which dopamine can bind – so while addicts begin by taking drugs to feel high, they end up taking them in order not to feel low."
Addicted – J. Madeleine Nash – Time – May 5, 1997

The receptors.

And remember too, exactly as Thomas Jefferson; "Encourage all your virtuous dispositions, and exercise them whenever an opportunity arises; being assured that they will gain strength by exercise, as a limb of the body does – We have indeed an innate sense of what we call beautiful – nature hath implanted in our breasts a love of others, a sense of duty to them, a moral instinct, in short, which prompts us irresistibly to feel and to succor their distresses – I sincerely, then, believe – in the general existence of a moral instinct. I think it the brightest gem with which the human character is studded, and the want of it is more degrading than the most hideous of bodily deformities" – did simply communicate an understanding of, and which is exactly as 20th century neuroscientific research has confirmed. Which is, the, possible, purposefully affected formation of a truly humanistic: simultaneously relative, Omnidimensional refractive gem of a mind, and parallel functioning central nervous system, for an individual human being to be in possession of only, and no things worldly, while including: only, truly humanistic brain death. And too which is as that the "deformity": of affected truly humanistic brain death, does begin to become capable of becoming a reality. Because of purposefully allowed exposure to excessive amounts of absolutely abstracted, and purely psychopathic, dopamine biochemical inducing stimulus, functioning as pure *pleasure* only: while *never* performing any proportional amounts of purposely affected "reuptake function" – of the purposefully affected dopamine biochemical inductions, and/or any proportional amounts of purposefully affected calcium induction/production, while within the purposefully affected truly humanistic simultaneously relative multidimensional synaptic capabilities, and/or any proportional amounts of purposefully affected serotonin production/induction. And how – then while as through the passing of time and gradually, as all humanistic phenomena is inversely affected, the individually affected human being minds, do actually begin to become LESS, and LESS, and LESS, sensitive: TO EVERY THING. And actually begin to become capable of functioning while as in a; "a psychiatrist, Monte Buchsbaum – measured patient's brain-wave responses to electrical shocks and auditory signals and found these EEG's to be abnormally flat, specifically at higher levels of intensity. He concluded that – schizophrenics were 'reducers' (as opposed to augmenters), that their brains naturally reduced, or dampened, stimuli" – purely schizophrenic manner. To the point, where you could actually be exposed to this –

"Beer, Football, And a Glut Of Patriotism –
...The Super Bowl is always a festival of wretched excess, but this year's tributes to patriotism and Sept. 11 were particularly excruciating...Athletes and coaches recited the Declaration of Independence and lines from presidential speeches; a president helped with the coin toss on the field. Barry Manilow sang 'Let Freedom Ring' as children in Army fatigues and firefighters' gear wheeled in a float of the Liberty Bell. Phalanxes of women dressed as the Statue of Liberty crisscrossed in rows of red, white and blue – As Mariah Carey sang the national

326

anthem, we were treated, first, to a scene on the field of Marines recreating the flag-raising at Iwo Jima, and then to a tableau of the ground zero flag-raising by firefighters...The Super Bowl, like the Olympics, is always an uncomfortable mixture of sports, commerce and nationalism. Previous societies forged bonds through public celebrations of war and religion; now we get together to watch athletes simulate battles and advertisers promise of salvation...but it was hard to discern the connection between Thomas Jefferson and the National Football League."
        John Tierney – The New York Times – Tuesday February 5, 2002

        Brain dead aristocratic elite spectacle event: it should be a neurophysiological impossibility for any human being, to actually purposefully expose their own selves to that spectacle, and it is. No truly humanistic non-brain dead being, could actually move their physiological bodies, while along with their parallel functioning minds and central nervous systems, into an environment to be exposed to that spectacle, it is a –

        "The Pharisees, who loved money, heard all this and laughed at him. He said to them, 'You are the very ones who pass yourselves off as virtuous in people's sight, but God knows your hearts. For what is thought highly of by men is loathsome in the sight of God."
        Luke 16: 14-15

        Neurophysiological impossibility.
        And – as a matter of fact and remember too, for any one individual who has actually spent a lifetime's worth of time, purposefully effectually forming a truly humanistic Omnidimensional refractive gem of a mind, and parallel functioning central nervous system, for their own selves to be in possession of, simply reading the words: actually simply "reading the words," would – at the very least, cause them to "feel" like this –

        "At Hiroshima: The common lot was random, indiscriminate and universal violence inflicting terrible pain, the physics of hydraulics and leverage and heat run riot...A junior-college girl: 'Ah, that instant! I felt as though I have been struck on the back with something like a big hammer, and thrown into boiling oil – I seem to have been blown a good way to the north and I felt as though the directions were all changed around."
        Richard Rhodes – The Making of The Atomic Bomb

        And/or as though somebody has – first, tied them down to the ground, and then taken chocolate and honey coated sugar cubes, with cinnamon, molasses and syrup, and forced them down their throat, and up their nostrils, while – and simultaneously, taking twelve-inch-long jagged-edged stilettos, and jamming them into their eyeballs and eardrums, and while – simultaneously, wrapping a plastic bag

327

around their face, and head, and while – and simultaneously, beginning to hit them in the face with a baseball bat, and/or "something like a big hammer," and while – also and simultaneously too, beginning to peel back all of their flesh: of their entire body, so that they then could proceed to pour salt into the open wounds, and then to simply "finish," by actually being –

"A Shock Grows in Brooklyn –

A fiery controversy over a museum's new show brings New York's Mayor out slugging: The mayor blew up three weeks ago over the controversial exhibition, 'Sensation: Young British Artists from the Saatchi Collection.' Giuliani threatened to cut all city funding to the museum – $7 million a year – unless the show was canceled...Are Ad Mogul (Charles) Saatchi – and auctioneers Christie's – the real winners?"

C. McGuigan, M. Malone, R. Sawhill, G. Beals – Newsweek

Laughed at: by all of the worldly psychopathic con-artists, who actually are raping the collective consciousness of mankind, and/or defecating upon our faces, and laughing all the way to their worldly banks too. And only: any individual human being would feel that way, if they had not experienced truly humanistic brain death for their own selves to be in possession of only, and their addiction to all things worldly only also.

And too and of course, which is exactly why they do have it: schizophrenia, hanging in all of their worldly art museum parks. And again, which is exactly where the "more than ordinary," is supposed to be, and/or the "what is beautiful," is supposed to be too. Which is exactly because, that: "schizophrenia," is exactly "what" is inside of their individually affected minds. And remember, they –

"Picasso and Einstein cross paths, and offer a mirthful night –

In the program for *Picasso at the Lapin Agile*, which opened Tuesday at the Arden Theater, the director, cast and staff pose 20 questions you might ponder after viewing the play. 'What is genius?' they ask. How does genius get recognized..."

Clifford A. Ridley – The Philadelphia Inquirer – Thursday March 8, 2001

Were simply conned into believing that it: schizophrenic, and/or paranoid delusional, and/or obsessive compulsive, and/or neurotic, and/or psychotic, and/or unbalanced, is the very definition of intelligence.

Because everything is exactly backwards: remember? And there is an exact because too, and an exact definition of truly humanistic intelligence: "Remember?" Wherein: a truly humanistic being's universally applicable, and simultaneously relative, "memory" – and/or intelligence, there will be no schizophrenic anything.

So here is that because: for the schizophrenic function within the majority of mankind's three-dimensional electrical potential mass minds, and within which there are contained no images of things. Remember what year Paul Cezanne made manifest his own personally affected space/time singularities, which was while actually functioning as the simple definition of truly humanistic brain death, and an actual regressing back to point time zero: of individually affected human being minds, and as a neurophysiological inability to even simply see past a single point of space/time, while at any one point within simultaneously relative space/time, and which was the year 1880: that Paul Cezanne did make manifest his space/time singularities, and while having actually occurred within the aristocratic elite's minds also. And – too remember, which was a 400-year time-evolutive effectuated degradation: actually occurring within their three-dimensional electrical potential mass minds, and because of their purposefully allowed exposure to a purely schizophrenic environment: and/or absolutely abstracted from exposure to harmoniously proportioned amounts of truly humanistic Reality only, and while simply not continuously practicing their scales of simultaneously relative Reality also. And up until this point in time: 1880, the common man masses simply could not afford the leisure time, to begin to become capable of experiencing truly humanistic brain death for their own selves. As they simply had no choice, but to be forced to be exposed to, only, harmoniously proportioned amounts, of truly humanistic Reality: while simultaneously actually forcing them to become capable of performing exactly proportional amounts of purposefully affected reuptake function – calcium production/induction, and serotonin production/induction, within their individually affected electrical potential mass minds, and parallel function central nervous systems. But then the industrial revolution did begin to become affected, and so that – then, at approximately this point in time: 1880 and exactly because of the industrial revolution, mankind was enabled to become capable of affecting –

"On a darkened screen, a small dot would appear. Slowly it opened and a beam of light revealed the action...Audiences then could relax much of their active rational minds and let the images penetrate deep into their subconscious. Mesmerized in the darkness and absorbed into the crowd, viewers shed the concerns of social life, and even relinquished their individuality, giving themselves up to the magnified, larger-than-life images that raced across the screen..."
Larry May – Movies and Mass Culture – Ed. John Belton

Absolutely abstracted: and purely schizophrenic, effectual stimulus, and/or "movies," for the common man masses to be exposed to. But – still, while only on a weekly basis, and, still, while not yet capable of causing very much permanently affected neurophysiological damage, within the common man masses' individually affected, electrical potential mass minds, and parallel functioning central nervous systems. And too, which: movies, was, of course, while *only* capable of functioning as a purely schizophrenic effectual stimulus, and as a diversion from truly humanistic simultaneously relative *a prior* Omnidimensional Reality, and/or the spectacle of entertainment.

But – remember, the industrial revolution did also, and simultaneously, enable the proliferation of many other industrialized conveniences, to enable mankind to become capable of simplifying their lives. And also, and simultaneously, begin to enable them to become capable of "living" like truly humanistic beings less, and while simultaneously practicing their scales of truly humanistic simultaneously relative Omnidimensional Reality less, also. And – again and as we can remember, which was beginning to become inversely affected: an individually affected human being's regression back to point time zero, and while actually occurring within the common man masses, while as through the proliferation of mass produced, and relatively accelerated, transportation methods: automobiles – trains and airplanes. And too then – and simultaneously, as through the proliferation of assembly line, and mechanized, industrial processes: for human beings to be performing. And also then and simultaneously, as through the proliferation of mass produced, and segregated, humanistic communities: suburban housing developments and shopping malls. And then – and simultaneously, as through the proliferation of the mass production of television screens, while positioned within the mass produced housing development's living rooms. And too then and simultaneously, as through the proliferation of computer monitor screens – the Internet – virtual reality and dot-coms, and as this too was positioned with the individual households. And, of course, which was while including all the other absolutely abstracted, and purely psychopathic, and/or schizophrenic, dopamine biochemical inducing stimulus, actually functioning as pure *pleasure* only, and all of it: absolutely abstracted schizophrenic effectual stimulus. And which was while actually –

"Bringing the Future Into Sharp Focus –
Visually, high-definition television is actually better than being there – Times change – Look at your current TV. The focus of each shot is pretty clear; the background is murky. Your mind fills in whatever details might interest it – No filling necessary with HDTV (the) HDTV camera presents its picture on a flat screen (On) HDTV, the foreground and background are on the same plane (and this is) an entire generation starting to reach adulthood that, literally, see things very differently from their elders..."
J. Storm/S. Seplow – The Philadelphia Inquirer – December 7, 1997

Enabling the common man masses, and/or the overwhelming vast majority of mankind, to actually: to;"This (is) an entire generation starting to reach adulthood that, literally, see things differently from their elders" – literally regress back to point time zero. It is actually a neurophysiological impossibility for these individually affected human beings, to consciously "see" past a single point: of truly humanistic simultaneously relative space/time, while at any one point within space/time. And it is also an absolute neurophysiological impossibility, for these individually affected human beings, to consciously cognize any truly humanistic simultaneously relative Time *made manifest*: and/or to purposefully cognize any patterns in space/time.

And which is the very definition of –

"One way to think about this view is to imagine spatial relationships as a kind of universal language that the brain uses no matter what specific language – social, moral, engineering, poetic – we are using at the moment...(George) Lakoff believes he can tie this mental language to the physical structure of the brain and its maps – 'When you think about dynamic structure, you begin to think there are a lot of things that are analogous with life. Life is more pattern(s) in space/time than it is a set of particular physical things."
Jim Jubak – In the Image of the Brain

"Life": they are brain dead. And which is exactly why everybody is going to die: soon. Because they love it, and they cannot even live without it.

And remember, the only thing they hate is; "Reality' reigns – If these 'reality' shows were *really* real, of course, nobody would watch" – universally applicable Reality, and/or their day-time jobs, or – rather, most of the common man masses do hate their day-time jobs. Simply because, they *are* absolutely abstracted from Reality. And – too remember, so that they then can become capable of producing absolutely no serotonin production/induction, within their individually affected minds, and parallel functioning central nervous systems, and while – simultaneously, they are functioning while as in an absolutely abstracted, and/or schizophrenic, manner, and that is extremely "painful": their day-time jobs that is, for the majority of the common man masses, and which was while beginning with the birth of the industrial revolution. As more and more individually affected human beings, did begin to function while as in an absolutely abstracted, and/or automatous, manner, and while capable of performing only the same absolutely abstracted, and automatous, function, day, after day, after day, which is relatively painful, and/or schizophrenic. So then – and at night and after their relatively painful daytime jobs: which enabled them to produce no proportional amounts of purposefully affected serotonin production/induction, more and more individually affected human beings did begin to spend more and more time, at night and after a relatively painful, and/or "frustrating," and/or "aggravating," and/or "anxiety causing," day, simply escaping the *pain* of facing-up to Reality, and/or simply consuming some absolutely abstracted dopamine biochemical inducing stimulus. And by simply watching television, and/or reading a novel, and/or going to the movies, and/or using a computer, and/or talking to someone: about their day, and while capable of inducing a purely pleasurable dopamine biochemical induction: within their individually affected minds, and parallel functioning central nervous systems. And while capable of functioning as pure *pleasure,* and a "quick fix," for the *pain* they had experienced during the day, and exactly instead of going outside, and practicing their scales of Reality. And –

"You are the salt of the earth. But if salt becomes tasteless, what can make it salty again? It is good for nothing, and can only be thrown out to be trampled underfoot by men.

You are the light of the world. A city built on a hilltop cannot be hidden. No one lights a lamp to put under a tub; they put it on the lampstand where it shines for everyone in the house. In the same way your light must shine in the sight of men, so that, seeing your good works, they may give the praise to your Father in heaven."
Matthew 5: 13-16

Purposefully affecting serotonin production/induction: within their individually affected minds, and parallel functioning central nervous systems. And –

"A Little Help From Serotonin –
Could a single brain chemical hold the key to happiness – as the 20th century winds down, we humans seem increasingly convinced that serotonin is the key to a good life – and it's easy to see why. This once obscure neurotransmitter is the secret behind Prozac, the drug that revolutionized the pursuit of happiness ten years ago this winter – serotonin pacifies neurons in the limbic system, the Brain's Department of Animal Instincts..."
Geoffery Cowley / Anne Underwood – Newsweek – December 29, 1997

Beginning to find the key to happiness. And/or: a well-balanced mind, and parallel functioning central nervous system.
But, instead, all the individually affected human beings did – exactly and while gradually and as through the passing of time, begin to become capable of; "the key to psychotic behavior (is) the unstable fluctuations in a chemical system – the key to schizophrenia is chaotic fluctuations in dopamine production" – creating unstable chemical fluctuations, in their own personally affected minds, and central nervous systems. And – too remember, which was also – and simultaneously, as they were – exactly, practicing their scales of truly humanistic simultaneously relative Reality less, and less, and less, and too while: exactly and simultaneously, they were beginning to function in a purely abstracted, and absolutely automatous, manner. And which was, while actually beginning to become capable of; "Joyce Kovelman and Arnold Scheibel of UCLA's Brain Research Institute spotted a weird cellular 'disarray' in the schizophrenic brains – The pyramid-shaped cells of the hippocampus, normally arranged in an orderly manner, were grossly misaligned – A schizophrenic's dopamine neurons would start to fire in two different rhythms and rapidly become uncoupled" – functioning in a purely schizophrenic manner.
And, of course, the more and more affected individual human beings did become, the more and more they did continue to only perpetuate the cycle, of personally affected neurophysiological dysfunction – addiction, and denial too. And which is only exactly because – remember, all effectual humanistic phenomena is inversely affected, and so the more and more individual human beings did begin to

332

become affected, the more they did only continue to perpetuate the cycle: of personally affected neurophysiological dysfunction. And – too remember, which was exactly because, all of the worldly psychopathic con-artists, had hijacked the name of Leonardo da Vinci, and his ability to "shape the invisible," and/or to make manifest an Omnidimensional space/time continuum, which was while actually functioning as a truly humanistic: multidimensional, effectual communicative apparatus, and while only, simply, conning mankind into believing that there actually is a "fine line between intelligence and insanity." And, exactly, instead of actually enabling them, to –

"Dr. David Pickar: Dealing with the cortex of a schizophrenic is an unbelievable thing. It's alien, yet there are these essential moments when you know a patient well and you can peek into that world. It's an abyss – empty..."
The 3-Pound Universe – Judith Hooper and Dick Teresi

Come to an understanding of the absolute scientific truth. And/or, actually encouraging them to face-up to *their* own neuroscientific Reality.

And remember too, as more and more individually affected human beings did actually begin to become capable of experiencing truly humanistic brain death for their own selves, they did – also and simultaneously, actually begin to become more, and more, addicted: to excessive amounts of absolutely abstracted, and purely psychopathic – and/or schizophrenic, dopamine biochemical inducing stimulus, actually functioning as pure *pleasure*. And – too and simultaneously and actually, more and more "unbalanced," and/or more and more "neurotic," and actually capable of becoming –

"Two simple experiments reveal the power of suggestion in different contexts. The first looks at an individual's response to someone who is in the position of authority. An experimenter repeatedly gives the subject the same suggestion: for example, she tells the subject his body is swaying. Soon his body will begin to sway. Not everyone is susceptible to this form of suggestibility – sometimes known as primary suggestibility, and neurotic people succumb more easily than 'well-balanced' individuals…the power of suggestion can sometimes override the evidence of our senses."
David Cohen – The Secret Language of The Mind

Victims of primary suggestibility: exactly "brainwashed." And – too and simultaneously, victims of the con: of *their* own personally affected, truly humanistic, and universally applicable, simultaneously relative Omnidimensional empirical self-consciousness, and/or their truly humanistic souls. And as was exactly explained by –

"Anyone who wants to win the broad masses must know the key that opens the door to their heart: propaganda tries to force a doctrine on the whole people – The whole art consists in doing this so skillfully that everyone will be convinced – Some idea of genius arises in the brain of a man who feels called upon to transmit his knowledge to the rest of humanity. He preaches his view and gradually wins a certain circle of adherents…In the place of committee decisions, the principle of absolute responsibility was introduced (to): Adolf Hitler."

Adolf Hitler: remember?

And too remember, as more and more individually affected human beings did actually begin to experience truly humanistic brain death, for their own selves to be in possession of only, they did also, and simultaneously, begin to regress back towards point time zero: of their own personally affected existence within truly humanistic simultaneously relative space/time. And which was while – beginning in 1880 and with the introduction of movies, they: all of the individually affected human beings, did – also and simultaneously, begin to become capable of actually confusing the map with the territory: and/or capable of confusing consciously cognizing the Mind of God made manifest, and/or consciously cognizing The Eternal Harmony – actually functioning as a truly humanistic simultaneously relative multidimensional communicative apparatus: and/or an orchestration, and/or capable of consciously cognizing any truly humanistic simultaneously relative Time *made manifest*: and/or capable of consciously cognizing any truly humanistic simultaneously relative patterns in space/time, and/or capable of employing the use of any truly humanistic universally applicable empirical self-consciousness, and/or simply capable of functioning as a "humanistic" being: they did become capable of confusing "it," with –

"Woods' Saga Is Just Beginning –
Probably we should have had enough of him for a while. Shouldn't we? But just about the time you think you would be Tigered out, he conjures up some new feat of daring and derring-do – Get enough? How can you get enough when every time out – every time – he's apt to do something you've never seen before…It looked like a concert. And, of course, in a way it was – Maestro Tiger Woods, using his 8-iron like a baton…The maestro walked the darkening 18th fair-way, trying to beat nightfall home, as the gallery flicked on cigarette lighters and waved them and swayed in time to its own cheers."
Bill Lyon – The Philadelphia Inquirer

Becoming capable of experiencing a simple absolutely abstracted, and purely psychopathic – and/or absolutely "animalistic," dopamine biochemical inducing stimulus, actually functioning as pure *pleasure* only, and/or simply consuming The Apple. And too, while actually allowing themselves to become –

"Jesus, then was brought before the governor, and the governor put to him this question, 'Are you the king of the Jews?' Jesus replied, 'It is you who say it.' But when he was accused by the chief priests and the elders he refused to answer at all. Pilate then said to him, 'Do you not hear how many charges they have brought against you?' But to the governor's complete amazement, he offered no reply to any of the charges.

At festival time it was the governor's practice to release a prisoner for the people, anyone they chose. Now there was at that time a notorious prisoner whose name was Barabbas. So when the crowd gathered, Pilate said to them, 'Which do you want me to release for you: Barabbas, or Jesus who is called Christ?' For Pilate knew it was out of jealousy that they had handed him over.

Now as he was seated in the chair of judgment, his wife sent to him a message, 'Have nothing to do with that man; I have been upset all day by a dream I had about him.'

The chief priests and elders, however, had persuaded the crowd to demand the release of Barabbas and the execution of Jesus. So when the governor spoke and asked them, 'Which of the two do you want me to release for you?' they said, 'Barabbas.' 'But in that case,' Pilate said to them, 'what am I to do with Jesus who is called Christ?' They all said, 'Let and be crucified!' 'Why?' he asked. 'What harm has he done?'"
Matthew 27: 11-23

A part of the In Crowd: which was being purposefully allowed exposure to the spectacle event, and of the purely schizophrenic dopamine biochemical inducing stimulus, functioning as pure discord, and chaos, and pain, and death, and suffering too. But *not* for the individually affected human beings, who were only allowed to become a part of the In Crowd, and while also: simultaneously, functioning as their allowing of their own selves to become victims of primary suggestibility, and exactly brainwashed too. As the Son of God/Son of Man/Collective Consciousness of Mankind, was betrayed by individually affected human beings. Who did: all of the individually affected human beings and within the entire history of mankind, simply sell their souls, to allow their own selves to become a part of the In Crowd. And too which was, that all of the individually affected victims of a con did allow their own selves to sell their souls, simply so that they would not be forced to –

"Jesus was going to Jerusalem, on the way he took the Twelve to one side and said to them, 'Now we are going up to Jerusalem, and the Son of Man is about to be handed over to the chief priests and scribes. They will condemn him to death and will hand him over to the pagans to be marked and scourged and crucified; and on the third day he will rise again."
Matthew 21: 17-19

Face-up to their own personally affected neurophysiological Reality. And too which is of their own personally affected truly humanistic brain death, and ability to function in a purely "paganish" manner: *only*.

Because – remember, He: The Son of God, had told them: all of the individually affected victims of the con, over, and over, and over again, to –

"He said, 'Imagine a sower going out to sow. As he sowed, some seeds fell on the edge of the path, and the birds came and ate them up. Others fell on patches of rock where they found little soil and sprang up straight away, because there was no depth of earth; but as soon as the sun came up they were scorched and, not having any roots, they withered away. Others fell among the thorns, and the thorns grew up and choked them. Others fell on rich soil and produced their crop, some a hundred fold, some sixty, some thirty. Listen, anyone who has ears!"
Matthew 13: 4-9

Pay attention: to nothing but universally applicable *a priori* Reality.
And to –

"Therefore, everyone who listens to these words of mine and acts on them will be like a sensible man who built his house on rock. Rain came down, floods rose, gales blew and hurled themselves against that house, and it did not fall: It was founded on rock. But everyone who listens to these words of mine and does not act on them will be like a stupid man who built his house on sand. Rain came down, floods rose, gales blew and struck that house, and it fell; and what a fall it had!"
Matthew 7: 24-27

Actually go out into truly humanistic Reality each and every day, and to actually practice your scales of truly humanistic simultaneously relative *a priori* Omnidimensional Reality, only. While actually causing permanently affected changes, within a truly humanistic being's own personally affected, simultaneously relative: quantum dynamically functioning, electrical potential mass of a mind, and parallel functioning central nervous system. And which would have been, while actually beginning to become capable of creating, a –

"Do not store up treasures for yourselves on earth, where moths and woodworms destroy them and thieves can break in and steal. But store up treasures for yourselves in heaven, were neither moth nor woodworms destroy them and thieves cannot break in and steal. For where your treasure is, there will your heart be also."
Matthew 6: 19-21

Truly humanistic Omnidimensional refractive gem of a mind, for their own selves to be in possession of, and *only*.
But – remember, they *exactly* –

"Then he said to his host, 'When you give a lunch or a dinner, do not ask your friends, brothers, relations or rich neighbors, for fear they repay your courtesy by inviting you in return. No; when you have a party, invite the poor, the crippled, the lame, the blind; that they cannot pay you back means that you are fortunate, because repayment will be made to you when the virtuous rise again,'

On hearing this, one of those gathered around the table said to him, 'Happy the man who will be at the feast in the kingdom of God!' But he said to him, 'There was a man who gave a great banquet, he sent his servant to say to those who had been invited, 'Come along: everything is ready now.' But all alike started to make excuses. The first said, 'I have bought a piece of land and must go and see it. Please accept my apologies.' Another said, 'I have bought five yoke of oxen and am on my way to try them out. Please accept my apologies.' Yet another said, 'I have just got married and so am unable to come.'

'The servant returned and reported this to his master. Then the householder, in a rage, said to his servant, 'Go out quickly into the streets and alleys of the town and bring in here the poor, the crippled, the blind and the lame.' 'Sir,' said the servant, 'your orders have been carried out and there is still room.' Then the master said to his servant, 'Go to the open roads and hedgerows and force people to come to make sure my house is full; because, I tell you, not one of those who were invited shall have a taste of my banquet."

Luke 14: 12-24

Did not: pay attention, nor practice their scales of truly humanistic simultaneously relative, and universally applicable, Omnidimensional *a priori* Reality. Nor build their truly humanistic, and simultaneously relative, Omnidimensional synaptic capabilities: within their individually affected truly humanistic, and simultaneously relative Omnidimensional: quantum electrodynamically functioning, minds, and parallel functioning central nervous systems. And – instead, they: all of the individually affected victims of the con and while as in the entire history of mankind too, did only begin to –

"At Enron, Lavish Excess Often Came Before Success –

For years, the Enron Corporation thrived on spending big, and even as late as October – with warnings ringing loudly about its rickety finances – no one at Enron saw any reason to change…And like many an Internet start-up in its heyday, Enron spent freely on image and luxury – At work, the attention to quotidian comfort was boundless – And many employees concluded that they deserved the perks, since joining Enron often meant 12-hour workdays and ceaseless travel...Like other former employees, Ms. B- and her friend Angela B- , who worked in the Broadband unit, remember Enron's excesses with a mix of amazement and wistfulness – 'We knew we weren't making money,' Ms B- said. 'But the extravagance, you know, is what made it great to work there."

N. Banerjee, D. Barboza, A. Warren, The New York Times, February 6, 2002

Become capable of regressing all the way back to point time zero. While actually becoming capable of experiencing truly humanistic brain death, for their own selves to be in possession of only, and a complete, and absolute, addiction to all things worldly only too. And too remember, a complete, and absolute, inability to understand anything, and – simultaneously while actually experiencing truly humanistic brain death for their own selves, while remaining only capable of believing only what they have been programmed to believe, by all of the worldly psychopathic con-artists. Who are actually supplying them: the victims, with allowed access to all of their absolutely abstracted, and purely psychopathic – and/or schizophrenic, effectual stimulus, actually functioning as pure *pleasure* only, and/or The Apple. And/or –

"When he returned to Capernaum some time later, word went around that he was back; and so many people collected that there was no room left, even in front of the door. He was preaching the word to them when some people came bringing him a paralytic carried by four men, but as the crowd made it impossible to get the man to him, they stripped the roof over the place where Jesus was; and when they had made an opening, they lowered the stretcher on which the paralytic lay. Seeing their faith Jesus said to the paralytic, 'My child, your sins are forgiven.' Now some scribes were sitting there, and they thought to themselves, 'How can this man talk like that? He is blaspheming. Who can forgive sins but God?' Jesus, inwardly aware that this was what they were thinking, said to them, 'Why have you these thoughts in your hearts? Which of these is easier: to say to the paralytic, 'Your sins are forgiven' or to say, 'Get up, pick up your stretcher and walk?' But to prove to you that the Son of Man has authority on earth to forgive sins,' – he said to the paralytic – 'I order you: get up, pick up your stretcher, and go off home.' And the man got up, picked up his stretcher at once and walked out in front of everyone, so that they were all astonished and praised God saying, 'We have never seen anything like this.'"
Mark 2: 1-12

The spectacle event: the perceivable performance of some "thing," and/or any thing, that they had never simply "seen" before. While they were, only, capable of functioning as young children are capable functioning, as they had regressed all the way back to point time zero. And had become capable of *only* experiencing –

"They were astounded and praised God, and were filled with awe, saying, 'We have seen strange things today.'"
Luke 5: 26

A sense of awe: within their childishly impressionable minds.
And, of course, which was while only capable of functioning as a simple dopamine biochemical inducing stimulus, actually functioning as pure *pleasure* only, and/or The Apple, and/or their –

"Now as he was speaking, a woman in the crowd raised her voice and said, 'Happy the womb that bore you and the breasts you sucked!' But he replied, 'Still happier those who hear the word of God and keep it."
Luke 11: 27-28

Mother's breasts.
And – remember, He: The Son of God/Son of Man/Collective Consciousness of Mankind, had simply told them: all of the individually affected victims of the con, over, and over, and over, again, to –

"Enter by the narrow gate, since the road that leads to perdition is wide and spacious, and many take it; but it is a narrow gate and a hard road that leads to life, and only a few find it."
Matthew 7: 13-14

Pay attention: to *a priori* Reality only.
And to –

"Then the disciples came up to him and asked, 'Why do you talk to them in parables? 'Because,' he replied, 'the mysteries of the kingdom of heaven are revealed to you, but they are not revealed to them. For anyone who has will be given more, and he will have more than enough; but from anyone who has not, even what he has will be taken away."
Matthew 13: 10-13

Practice your scales of truly humanistic simultaneously relative Omnidimensional Reality, only. And to begin to become capable of building your truly humanistic simultaneously relative Omnidimensional foundations: within your own personally affected mind, and parallel functioning central nervous system.
And while beginning to become capable of –

"Asked by the Pharisees when the kingdom of God was to come, he gave them this answer, 'The kingdom of God does not admit of observation and there will be no one to say, look here! Look there! For, you must know, the kingdom of God is within you."
Luke 17: 20-21

Effectually forming a truly humanistic simultaneously relative, and quantum electrodynamically functioning, Omnidimensional refractive gem of a mind, and parallel functioning central nervous system, for yourself to be in possession of only. But they exactly did not: pay attention, nor build their truly humanistic foundations, within their individually affected minds, and parallel functioning central nervous systems.

So they did exactly, and instead –

"Drugs are like sledgehammers' – 'They profoundly alter many pathways' –
the realization that dopamine may be a common endpoint of all those pathways
represents a signal advance. Provocative – the dopamine hypothesis provides a basic
framework for understanding (what does) cause a serious behavioral disorder..."
Addicted – J. Madeline Nash – Time – May 5, 1997

Begin to become exactly deviated: from purposefully affecting a truly
humanistic Omnidimensional refractive gem of a mind, and parallel functioning
central nervous system, for their own selves to be in possession of only. And a
purposefully affected understanding of a more divinely purposeful existence, for
their own selves to be in possession of only too: while beyond our excessively
simplistic, and animalistic, existence, upon this point-mass of Earth. And which is
while finding the entrance to The Garden and Our Innocence Lost too, and while
actually beginning to become capable of consciously cognizing The Mind of God
made manifest – The Eternal Harmony actually functioning as a truly humanistic,
and simultaneously relative, Omnidimensional space/time continuum, and the
function of *The Annunciation* too. And which is – also and simultaneously, The
Kingdom of God *and* The Kingdom of Heaven, which they did not do.
So, we can now know, and for an unequivocal scientific fact, the exact reason
"why" –

"The chief priests and elders, however, had persuaded the crowd to demand
the release of Barabbas and the execution of Jesus. So when the governor spoke and
asked them, 'Which of these two do you want me to release for you? They said,
'Barabbas.' 'But in that case,' Pilate said to them, 'what am I to do with Jesus who is
called Christ?' They all said, 'Let him be crucified!' Why?' he asked. 'What harm has
he done? But they shouted all the louder, 'Let him be crucified!' Then Pilate saw
that he was making no impression, that in fact a riot was imminent. So he took some
water, washed his hands in front of the crowd and said, 'I am innocent of this man's
blood. It is your concern. And the people to a man, shouted back, 'His blood be on
us and our children! Then he released Barabbas for them. He ordered Jesus to be
first scourged and then handed over to be crucified."
Matthew 27: 20-26

All of the individually affected victims of the con have sold their souls.
And exactly betrayed The Collective Consciousness of Mankind: condemned their
very own selves, and allowed their own selves to become; "The chief priests and
elders, however, had persuaded the crowd to demand the release of Barabbas and the
execution of Jesus" – victims of primary suggestibility: brainwashed, and consumed
by all of the worldly psychopathic con-artists. Who are supplying all of their victims
with their purposefully allowed exposure to the absolutely abstracted, and purely

340

psychopathic – and/or schizophrenic, dopamine biochemical inducing stimulus, actually functioning as pure *pleasure* only, and/or The Apple. And which is exactly because of –

"At a purely chemical level (just as the injection of) heroin triggers release of dopamine – every experience humans find enjoyable – amounts to little more than an explosion of dopamine in the nucleus accumbens, as exhilarating and ephemeral as a firecracker – dopamine can be elevated by a hug, a kiss, a word of praise..."
Addicted – J. Madeleine Nash – Time – May 5, 1997

DOPAMINE: The Apple.
And which is exactly because of the function of uniquely humanistic brainwashing, and/or primary suggestibility. And which: uniquely humanistic primary suggestibility, is while actually functioning as through –

"Candace Pert: we've measured opiate receptors in everything from fruit fly heads to human brains. Even uni-cellular organisms have peptides' – Even bacteria have a little hierarchy of primitive likes and dislikes. They're programmed to migrate toward or away from a chemotactic substance. They're little robots that go for sugar at all costs and away from salt – Behavior is controlled by the anticipation of pain or pleasure, punishment or reward..."
The 3-Pound Universe – Judith Hooper and Dick Teresi

The function of the two extremes, of the basic biological functioning capabilities which *are* encoded within the DNA of all living cells, of: *pleasure* – dopamine – sugar, and *pain* – serotonin – salt, and punishment and reward too. And the fact that, remember, all humanistic phenomena does actually occur while –

"One thing has become clear to scientists: memory is absolutely crucial to our consciousness – 'There's almost nothing you do, from perception to thinking, that doesn't draw continuously on your memory. (And) It can't be otherwise, since there really is no such thing as a present (while) memory provides a personal context, a sense of self and a sense of familiarity – past and present and a frame for the future' – But memory is not a single phenomenon. 'We don't have a memory system in the brain' – 'We have memory systems, each playing a different role' – When everything is going right, these different systems work together seamlessly. If you're taking a bicycle ride, for example, the memory of how to operate the bike comes from one set of neurons; the memory of how to get from here to the other side of town comes from another; the nervous feeling you have left over from taking a bad spill last time out comes from still another. Yet you are never aware that your mental experience has been assembled, bit by bit, like some invisible edifice inside your brain..."
Michael D. Lemonick – Smart Genes? – Time – September 13, 1999

On a subconscious level: while actually occurring within a human being's parallel functioning mind, and central nervous system. While as through the intermingling of the two extremes of the basic biological functioning capabilities, which are encoded within the DNA of all living cells. And, again, which actually is of: *pleasure* – sugar – dopamine, and *pain* – salt – serotonin, and – again, which is while; "Yet you are never aware that your mental experience has been assembled, bit by bit, like some invisible edifice inside your brain" – actually occurring on a subconscious level. And – too remember, which is while all effectual humanistic phenomena, is actually inversely affected.

So that, we can know, exactly the way primary suggestibility does function, is simply that if an individually affected human being: who is the "victim," does simply "go along with the In Crowd," they will become capable of receiving a simple dopamine biochemical induction, for their own selves to become capable of consuming, and while actually functioning as pure *pleasure* only: for their own selves. But – and simultaneously, if they do NOT simply go along with the In Crowd, they will NOT only exactly NOT receive a simple dopamine biochemical induction, for their own selves to consume, they will also – *and simultaneously*, receive a simple serotonin biochemical induction, for themselves to consume: and which is while actually functioning as *pain*. And so, we can now know, that the experienced humanistic phenomenon will be "twice as effectual": for the individual person who does not go along with the In Crowd. And – too, while not simply contradicting the perceivable reality: placed before their very own selves.

And – remember, the Son of God had told them, over, and over, and over again, that –

"Do not store up treasures for yourselves on earth, where moths and woodworms destroy them and thieves break in and steal. But store up treasures for yourselves in heaven, were neither moth nor woodworms destroy them and thieves cannot break in and steal. For where your treasure is, there will your heart be also."
Matthew 6: 19-21

You can NOT simply see it: it is exactly NOT any simple dopamine biochemical inducing stimulus of any kind, functioning as pure *pleasure* only, and/or a "sense of awe" – of any kind. And it is exactly NOT –

"Enter by the narrow gate, since the road that leads to perdition is wide and spacious, and many take it; but it is a narrow gate and a hard road that leads to life, and only a few find it."
Matthew 7: 13-14

Just that easy: it is exactly NOT apathy; it is exactly NOT complacency; it is exactly NOT spirituality. It is exactly NOT the security of an artificially effectuated Mother's womb environment – it is exactly NOT truly humanistic brain death:

342

delusion and/or becoming a part of the In Crowd, which is being purposefully allowed exposure to the absolutely abstracted dopamine biochemical inducing stimulus, functioning as pure pleasure only – and/or The Apple, it is "beyond belief," and it is *exactly* "Real."

But – remember, they had already –

"They were astounded and praised God, and were filled with awe, saying, 'We have seen strange things today."
Luke 5: 26

Allowed themselves to become a part of the In Crowd *only*: which was being purposefully allowed exposure to the spectacle event. While actually affecting a sense of awe, within their childishly impressionable minds, and parallel functioning central nervous systems, and while actually functioning as pure *pleasure* only, and as through purposefully affected dopamine biochemical inductions. While they did, also and simultaneously, exactly NOT practice their scales of truly humanistic, and simultaneously relative, Omnidimensional Reality: they did NOT affect proportional amounts of purposely affected reuptake function, of the dopamine biochemical induction, and/or calcium production/induction: within and while affecting their truly humanistic multidimensional synaptic capabilities, and they did NOT affect any proportional amounts of purposely affected serotonin production/induction, within their individually affected minds, and parallel functioning central nervous systems. And they did only –

"Dopamine, like most biologically important molecules, must be kept within strict bounds – too much causes the hallucinations, and bizarre thoughts, of schizophrenia – addicts' neurons assaulted by abnormally high levels of dopamine, have responded defensively and reduced the number of sites (or receptors) to which dopamine can bind – so while addicts begin by taking drugs to feel high, they end up taking them in order not to feel low."
Addicted – J. Madeleine Nash – Time – May 5, 1997

Become addicted: to the spectacle, to the dopamine biochemical inducing effectual stimulus functioning as pure *pleasure* only. And they exactly had not practiced their scales of truly humanistic simultaneously relative Omnidimensional Reality, and while as on a daily basis too. They exactly had not enabled their own selves to become capable of forming a truly humanistic Omnidimensional refractive gem of a mind for their own selves, and they had also – and simultaneously, only enabled their own selves to become capable of regressing back to point time zero, of their own personally affected existence within truly humanistic Reality. And they had actually enabled their own selves to begin to become capable of experiencing truly humanistic brain death for their own selves. And while they had – also and simultaneously, begun to become neurophysiologically incapable of understanding anything for their very own selves, and only capable of believing what they were simply being programmed to believe: by all of the worldly psychopathic con-artists. And: remember, all of the worldly psychopathic con-artists, were telling them: all of the individually affected victims of the con, that He: The Son of God/Son of Man/Collective Consciousness of Mankind, was –

"When day broke there was a meeting of the elders of the people, attended by the chief priests and scribes. He was brought before their council, and they said to him, 'If you are the Christ, tell us.' 'If I tell you,' he replied, 'you will not believe me, and If I question you, you will not answer. But from now on, the Son of Man will be *seated at the right hand* of the Power *of God*.' Then they all said, 'So you are the Son of God then?' He answered, 'It is you who say I am.' 'What need of witnesses have we now?' they asked. 'We have heard it for ourselves from his own lips.' The whole assembly then rose, and they brought him before Pilate.
They began their accusation by saying, 'We found this man inciting our people to revolt...'"
Luke 22: 66-71, 23: 1-2

Attempting to become capable of deviating exactly from the function of the Letter of the Law, and/or attempting to become capable of creating a diversion: from universally applicable, and simultaneously relative, Omnidimensional *a priori* Reality. And that He: The Son of God/Son of Man/Collective Consciousness of Mankind, was attempting to become capable of creating discord, and chaos, and pain, and death, and suffering too. And too, so that He: The Son of God – The Son of Man – The Collective Consciousness of Mankind made manifest, was attempting to enable Himself to become capable of –

"One thing has become clear to scientists: memory is absolutely crucial to our consciousness – 'There's almost nothing you do, from perception to thinking, that doesn't draw continuously on your memory. (And) It can't be otherwise, since there really is no such thing as a present (while) memory provides a personal context, a sense of self and a sense of familiarity – past and present and a frame for the future' – But memory is not a single phenomenon. 'We don't have a memory system in the brain' – 'We have memory systems, each playing a different role' – When everything is going right, these different systems work together seamlessly. If you're taking a bicycle ride, for example, the memory of how to operate the bike comes from one set of neurons; the memory of how to get from here to the other side of town comes from another; the nervous feeling you have left over from taking a bad spill last time out comes from still another. Yet you are never aware that your mental experience has been assembled, bit by bit, like some invisible edifice inside your brain..."
Michael D. Lemonick – Smart Genes? – Time – September 13, 1999

"Pushing them off of the bicycle": and/or attempting to become capable of taking control over them, and/or attempting to cause them to experience extreme pain for their own selves: while forcing them to be exposed to discord, or chaos, or death, or suffering. And/or attempting to become capable of empowering Himself, and while "Creating a diversion from Reality," and/or attempting to brainwash them, and/or attempting to enable them to become "victims of primary suggestibility." And, of course, **NO HE WAS NOT**, that was – of course, only –

"The chief priests and elders, however, had persuaded the crowd to demand the release of Barabbas and the execution of Jesus. So when the governor spoke and asked them, 'Which of the two do you want me to release for you?' they said, 'Barabbas.' 'But in that case,' Pilate said to them, 'what am I to do with Jesus who is called Christ?' They all said, 'Let him be crucified!' 'Why?' he asked. 'What harm has he done?'"
Matthew 27: 20-23

Exactly backwards. He was trying to –

"Drug's Effect On Brain Is Extensive, Study Finds –
Heavy users (of highly addictive stimulants) are doing more damage to their brains than scientists had thought, according to the first study that looked inside addicts' brains nearly a year after they stop using the drug – When the dopamine system goes seriously awry – people lose their excitement for life and can no longer move their limbs – The addicts (started out as) occasional users but over time the drug hijacked their natural dopamine systems..."
Sandra Blakeslee – The New York Times – Tuesday March 6, 2001

Enable them to become capable of taking back control over their very own selves. As he was attempting to help them, to become capable of forming a truly humanistic simultaneously relative Omnidimensional refractive gem of a mind, and parallel functioning central nervous system, for their own selves to be in possession of only. Which would have – then, enabled them to become capable of beginning to find their Innocence Lost – The Entrance to The Garden, and capable of cognizing the Mind of God made manifest, and while actually experiencing The Eternal Harmony – The Kingdom of Heaven, and the function which is *The Annunciation* also: for their own selves only. And while telling them: all of the individually affected victims of the con, to: "Get back up on that bike" – for your own self, and to: "Take back control over your own self, and your destiny too" – beyond your simplistic mortal existence, upon this point-mass of Earth.

But – remember, they had, exactly, not practiced their scales of Reality, and while on a daily basis too. And they had not performed any proportional amounts of purposefully affected reuptake function, of the individually affected dopamine biochemical inductions, and/or affected any proportional amounts of purposefully affected serotonin production/induction. And they had: simultaneously, actually

345

begun to regress back towards point time zero, of their purposefully affected existence within truly humanistic simultaneously relative Reality. And they had begun to experience truly humanistic being brain death, for their own selves to be in possession of only too. And they had – also and simultaneously, begun to become addicted: to their purposefully allowed exposure to excessive amounts of absolutely abstracted, and purely psychopathic – and/or schizophrenic, dopamine biochemical inducing stimulus, functioning as pure *pleasure* only. And they had also – and simultaneously, actually begun to become "neurotic," and/or "unbalanced," and too exactly –

"We're All Suffering From Anxiety, but Why? –
Our nation has developed an anxiety disorder. This anxiety effects the way we care for ourselves and our loved ones. It affects how we vote, shop, eat, sleep and even – how we think. Most of all, it affects how much we enjoy our lives – I don't know about you, but almost everyone I know suffers from anxiety. We have anxiety about our children, our future, our neighbors, and our intimate relationships...Doctors report that the majority of visits to their offices are anxiety related..."
Dan Gottlieb – The Philadelphia Inquirer – Tuesday December 12, 2000

Anxious, and/or nervous, and/or distressed, and/or apprehensive. And too, so that they were *actually* beginning to feel as though; "One thing has become clear to scientists: memory is absolutely crucial to our consciousness – 'There's almost nothing you do, from perception to thinking, that doesn't draw continuously on your memory (but) 'We don't have a memory system in the brain' – 'We have memory systems' (And) When everything is going right, these different systems work together seamlessly. If you're taking a bicycle ride, for example, the memory of how to operate the bike comes from one set of neurons; the memory of how to get from here to the other side of town comes from another; the nervous feeling you have left over from taking a bad spill last time out comes from still another. Yet you are never aware that your mental experience has been assembled, bit by bit, like some invisible edifice inside your brain" – somebody *was* trying to "Push them off the bicycle." And/or attempting to violate them, and/or attempting to take control over them, and/or attempting to brainwash them, too. Which was – remember, only exactly backwards: in truly humanistic neuroscientific Reality only of course. And which was, exactly, while He: The Son of God/Son of Man/Collective Consciousness of Mankind, was attempting to help them: all of the individually affected victims of the con, to begin to become capable of taking back control over their very own selves only. As he was saying: "Get back up on that bike," and overcome the nervous feeling you are beginning to experience for your own self, and as they are beginning to experience –

346

"A Painkiller's Double Life As an Illegal Street Drug –
In a scene of creepy voyeurism and joltingly effective reporting, a 22-year-old named Troy S-, who looks like any middle-class college student in a red sweatshirt and baseball cap, sits in his messy apartment in Maine and prepares to stick a needle in his arm as the cameras watch – Later (we observe) him in a hospital bed, sedated so he will not be aware of what we see: his body twitches as it goes through withdrawal..."
Carynn James – The New York Times – Wednesday December 12, 2001

Extreme withdrawal. And pain, for their own selves only too. As they *will* actually begin to experience withdrawal. And too – remember, which will be exactly because – also and while in addition to actually beginning to feel as though they are being "Pushed off the bicycle," they: all of the individually affected victims of the con, will begin to feel as though somebody has placed a plastic bag over their heads, if they are being denied allowed access to all of their absolutely abstracted, and purely psychopathic, and/or schizophrenic, dopamine biochemical inducing stimulus, actually functioning as pure *pleasure* only. And too so that they: all of the individually affected victims of the con and while as in the entire history of mankind too, will begin to feel as though they actually are "losing control," and exactly because they have, and of their very own selves. And, remember, they have *actually* regressed back to point time zero: of their own personally affected existence within truly humanistic Reality, and too they have – also and simultaneously, allowed their own selves to become *only* capable of functioning as a young child is capable of functioning, and/or neurophysiologically incapable of cognizing any Time *made manifest* whatsoever, and/or too any truly humanistic nothingness functioning as "0." So they can – also and simultaneously, only be affected by the perceivable tangible form mass stimulus, functioning as "1." And – remember, which is as they have actually –

"He said again to the crowds, 'When you see a cloud looming up in the west you say at once that rain is coming, and so it does. And when the wind is from the south you say it will be hot, and it is. Hypocrites! You know how to interpret the face of the earth and the sky. How is it that you do not know how to interpret these times."
Luke 13: 54-56

Begun to experience truly humanistic brain death, for their own selves. While they have become neurophysiologically incapable of understanding anything, for their own selves, and – simultaneously, only capable of believing that which they can simply see with their eyes alone. And/or that which they have been programmed to believe, by all the worldly psychopathic con-artists, who have been supplying them with allowed access to all of their dopamine biochemical inducing stimulus. Which is as they are – now, incapable of being affected by The Function of The

347

Letter of The Law, actually functioning as the increase of lawlessness. And too so that – now, they can, simply, actually contradict the Letter of the Law themselves: to simply feed to their addiction, and to all things worldly. Which is as they do: now, actually make manifest real discord, and chaos, and suffering. And too which is, exactly, as their cerebral cortices have become destroyed, and they have actually lost control over their very own selves. And remember too, which is also – and simultaneously, as their individually affected receptors: which are responsible for cognizing all perceivable effectual humanistic phenomena, have exactly become worn-out, and/or less sensitive, and to everything. And – remember, if you do actually feel as though somebody has placed a plastic bag over your head: and/or as though you simply cannot breathe, you will "do" absolutely anything, to enable your own self to become capable of breathing again: and/or to feed your addiction. And so, there is just one thing left to do. And that is to actually become capable of –

"It was now about the sixth hour and, with the sun eclipsed, a darkness came over the whole land until the ninth hour. The veil of the Temple was torn right down the middle; and when Jesus had cried out in a loud voice, he said, 'Father, *into your hands I commit my spirit*.' With these words he breathed his last.

When the centurion saw what had taken place, he gave praise to God and said, 'This was a great and good man.' And when all the people who had gathered for the spectacle saw what had happened, they went home beating their breasts. "
Luke 23: 44-48

Betraying the Collective Consciousness of Mankind, and to sell your very own soul too. And to become capable of feeding their addiction: they *will* make manifest death.

And: remember too, they will exactly–

"The passers-by jeered at him; they shook their heads and said, 'So you would destroy the Temple and rebuild it in three days! Then save yourself! If you are God's son, come down from the cross!' The chief priests with the scribes and elders mocked him in the same way. 'He saved others,' they said, 'he cannot save himself. He is the king of Israel; let him come down from the cross now, and we will believe in him. He puts his trust in God; now let God rescue him if he wants him. For he did say, 'I am the son of God."
Matthew 27: 39-44

Rationalize it: their own personally affected truly humanistic brain death, and/or their own personally affected regression back towards point time zero, and/or their own personally affected losing control over their very own selves, and/or their own personally affected betraying of the Collective Consciousness of Mankind, and/or their own personally affected selling of their souls. And too, their very own –

"Whoever believes in me
believes not in me
but in the one who sent me,
and whoever sees me,
sees the one who sent me.
I, the light, have come into the world,
so that whoever believes in me
need not stay in the dark anymore.
If anyone hears my words and does not keep them faithfully,
it is not I who shall condemn him,
since I have come not to condemn the world,
but to save the world;
he who rejects me and refuses my words
has his judge already:
the word itself that I have spoken
will be his judge on the last day.
For what I have spoken does not come from myself;
no, what I was to say, what I had to speak,
was commanded by the Father who sent me,
and I know that his commands mean eternal life.
And therefore what the Father has told me
is what I speak."
John 12: 44-50

Condemning of their very own selves: they will rationalize.

And – remember, which is as this word: rationalize, does mean: "to ascribe (one's acts, opinions, etc.) to causes that seem valid but actually are not true." And which is, also and simultaneously, as they will, exactly, project their own personally affected neurophysiological dysfunction, upon –

"If the world hates you,
remember that it hated me before you.
If you belonged to the world,
the world would love you as its own;
but because you do not belong to the world,
because my choice withdrew you from the world,
therefore the world hates you.
Remember the words I said to you:
A servant is not greater than his master.
If they persecuted me,
they will persecute you too;
if they kept my word,
they will keep yours as well.

But it will be on my account that they do all this,
because they do not know the one who sent me."
John 16: 18-21

The Collective Consciousness of Mankind: and/or any individual human being who does join this revolution. And any human being, who has not experienced truly humanistic brain death, for their own selves. And any human being, who has not betrayed the collective consciousness of mankind. And any human being, who has not simply betrayed their very own selves too: and sold their souls. And any human being, who has not simply handed over control of their very own selves, to all of the worldly psychopathic con-artists, to become capable of consuming. And any human being, who is –

"This is my commandant:
love one another,
as I have loved you.
A man can have no greater love
than to lay down his life for his friends.
You are my friends,
if you do what I command you.
I shall not call you servants any more,
because a servant does not know
his master's business;
I call you friends,
because I have made known to you
everything I have learned from my Father."
John 15: 12-15

Willing to die for their love of mankind.
And too which is as this word: projection, does mean, that –

"Projection: Distortion of a perception as a result of its repression, resulting in such a phenomenon as hating without cause one who has been dearly loved, or attributing to others one's own undesirable traits. Characteristics of the paranoid reaction."
Taber's Cyclopedic Medical Dictionary

They: any one individually affected human being who you do sincerely love, and not simply "lust" and who you are willing to die for, will – actually, become capable of –

"The passers-by jeered at him; they shook their heads and said, 'So you would destroy the Temple and rebuild it in three days! Then save yourself! If you are

350

God's son, come down from the cross!' The chief priests with the scribes and elders mocked him in the same way. 'He saved others,' they said, 'he cannot save himself. He is the king of Israel; let him come down from the cross now, and we will believe in him. He puts his trust in God; now let God rescue him if he wants him. For he did say, 'I am the son of God."
Matthew 27: 39-44

Killing you: DEAD, while exactly laughing as they do it too. Even after they have made a public proclamation that they do sincerely "love" you, and/or the collective consciousness of mankind. And/or, that they are capable of experiencing truly humanistic love at all, and exactly instead of self-lust, and for their continued allowed exposure to abstracted dopamine biochemical inducing stimulus, functioning as pure *pleasure* only. Which is while including truly humanistic apathy, and/or while simply existing in ignorance of Reality. And while being enabled to do so, because of any one other individual humanistic being, such as Man, or a Woman, and while as in this real Edenic tale too. And, too, which is exactly because: as they do simply exist while in ignorance of Reality, they: any one individually affected human being and whom you may sincerely love, will: remember, exactly begin to feel as though somebody has placed a plastic bag over their head, as they are simply having *a priori* Reality explained to them – and by you. And so, they are going to feel as though you are placing that bag over their heads: as you explain Reality to them. And/or, they are going to feel as though you have "Pushed them off of the bicycle": as you explain Reality to them. And/or, they are going to feel as though you are trying to take control over them: as you explain Reality to them. And/or, they are going to feel as though their entire worlds are beginning to collapse: as you explain Reality to them. And – remember too, if they had actually formed an Omnidimensional refractive gem of a mind, for their own selves to be in possession of, then they would have no need to have Reality explained to them. But we do now actually know, that –

"A Shock Grows in Brooklyn –
A fiery controversy over a museum's new show brings New York's Mayor out slugging: The mayor blew up three weeks ago over the controversial exhibition, 'Sensation: Young British artists from the Saatchi Collection' – The mayor was especially outraged by 'The Holy Virgin Mary,' a painting by Chris Ofili, who used, among other materials, elephant dung...polls showed that both New York residents and a nationwide sample were against shutting down the exhibit..."
C. McGuigan, M. Malone, R. Sawhill, G. Beals /Newsweek/ October 11, 1999

They did not, so they *will*: need to have Reality explained to them, and kill you dead too.
Because – remember, this is the single most contemptuous society while as in

the entire history of mankind, and which is as they have – exactly, effectually regressed back to point time zero, and beyond: as they have passed the point of no return. While actually becoming capable of contradicting the basic biological functioning capabilities: of *pleasure* and *pain*, which are encoded within the DNA of all living cells. And which is exactly because – remember, as individually affected human beings do actually regress all the way back to point time zero, they will become only capable of functioning as a young child is capable of functioning, and so, too, only capable of believing, and/or understanding, the perceivable Reality which is "immediately in front of them," and/or tangible form mass stimulus: "1." And which is exactly why –

"He then left to make his way as usual to the Mount of Olives, with the disciples following. When they reached the place he said to them, 'Pray not to be put to the test.'

Then he withdrew from them, about a stone's throw away, and knelt down and prayed. 'Father,' he said, 'if you are willing, take this cup away from me. Nevertheless, let your will be done, not mine.' Then an angel appeared to him coming from heaven to give him strength. In his anguish he prayed even more earnestly, and his sweat fell to the ground like great drops of blood.

When he rose from prayer he went to the disciples and found them sleeping for sheer grief. 'Why are you asleep?' he said to them. 'Get up and pray not to be put to the test."
    Luke 22: 39-46

He: The Son of God/Son of Man/Collective Consciousness of Mankind, did have to be betrayed: by all of the individually affected victims of the con. And too did – exactly, have to be "crucified." And which was, while –

"Cracking the Cosmic Code With A Little Help From Dr. Hawking –
...Dr. Hawking's first book for a wide audience, 'a Brief History of Time,' took readers on a tour through black holes, the gravitational traps from which not even light can emerge – quantum theory and relativity have taught us, science is about what can be observed and measured or it is about nothing at all. In science, as in democracy, there is no hidden secret knowledge, all that counts is on the table, observable and falsifiable. All else is metaphysics..."
    Dennis Overbye – The New York Times – Tuesday December 11, 2001

Making manifest a "perceivable proof," for all the world to simply see, with their eyes alone. BECAUSE: "All else is metaphysics."
    And – remember, He: The Son of God/Son of Man/Collective Consciousness of Mankind, had explained the function of universally applicable, simultaneously relative, *a priori* Omnidimensional Reality: actually effectually functioning as Omnidimensional Time *made manifest,* to them, OVER, and OVER, and OVER,

again. And He had said: in "words," that it: Finding Our Innocence Lost and Finding the entrance to The Garden too – Gaining access to The Mind of God made manifest and the Eternal Harmony also, and which is while actually functioning as The Kingdom of Heaven and the function which is *The Annunciation*, is exactly not "Just that easy." That it is exactly not purposefully allowed exposure to any amounts of dopamine biochemical inducing stimulus, actually functioning as pure *pleasure* only, and/or The Apple. That it is exactly not truly humanistic apathy, and/or truly humanistic brain death, and/or simply existing while in ignorance of Reality. And remember too, they: all of the individually affected victims of the con, had simply said: in words, that they *had* exactly followed the function of the letter of the Law. That they had, exactly, practiced their scales of truly humanistic simultaneously relative Omnidimensional Reality, and while as on a daily basis too. That they had, exactly, enabled their own selves to become capable of purposefully effectually forming an Omnidimensional refractive gem of a mind, and parallel functioning central nervous system, for their own selves to be in possession of only. That they had, exactly, enabled their own selves to become capable of functioning as truly virtuous human beings, and not as animals only. That they had, exactly, enabled their own selves to become capable of gaining access to the Mind of God made manifest, and the function which is *The Annunciation* too. That they had, exactly, enabled their own selves to become capable of "understanding Him," and as they had made a public proclamation that they did sincerely love Him: and/or anything, besides their very own selves only. But – in reality, they did not actually do anything, and except, of course, to simply exist while in ignorance of Reality, and to continue to consume excessive amounts of absolutely abstracted dopamine biochemical inducing effectual stimulus, actually functioning as pure *pleasure* only. And, so: "THEY" **WERE THE LIARS**. Which is exactly why they did project their own personally affected neurophysiological dysfunction upon Him: **BECAUSE THEY HAD NOT PAID ATTENTION, AND FACING-UP TO REALITY WAS TOO PAINFUL FOR THEM**. And – so, He was exactly forced to do something that he did not particularly want to do, and say: Alright; watch this, and with your eyes alone –

"It was now about the sixth hour and, with the sun eclipsed, a darkness came over the whole land until the ninth hour. The veil of the Temple was torn right down the middle; and when Jesus had cried out in a loud voice, he said, 'Father, *into your hands I commit my spirit*.' With these words he breathed his last.

When the centurion saw what had taken place, he gave praise to God and said, 'This was a great and good man.' And when all the people who had gathered for the spectacle saw what had happened, they went home beating their breasts."
Luke 23: 44-48

NOW – DO YOU "GET IT": UNDERSTAND JUST HOW DIFFICULT IT IS?

And they did. As they did – then and while after simply seeing the perceivable evidence: **OF THEIR OWN PERSONALLY AFFECTED NEUROPHYSIOLOGICAL DYSFUNCTION**, make a public proclamation, that they; "And when all the people who had gathered for the spectacle had saw what had happened, they went home beating their breasts" – had, finally, realized that they had "made a mistake." And too, that they had simply lost sight of Reality, and that they *had* simply–

"Day of wrath, that day
Will dissolve the earth in ashes
As David and the Sibyl bear witness.

What dread there will be
When the Judge shall come
To judge all things strictly.

A trumpet, spreading a wondrous sound
Through the graves of all lands,
Will drive mankind before the throne.

Death and Nature shall be astonished
When all creation rises again
To answer to the Judge.

A book, written in, will be brought forth
In which is contained everything that is,
Out of which the world shall be judged.

When therefore the Judge takes His seat
Whatever is hidden will reveal itself.
Nothing will remain unavenged.

What then shall I say, wretch that I am,
What advocate entreat to speak for me,
When even the righteous may hardly be secure?

King of awful majesty,
Who freely savest the redeemed,
Save me, O fount of goodness.

Remember, blessed Jesu,
That I am the cause of Thy pilgrimage,
Do not forsake me on that day.

Seeking me thou didst sit down weary,
Thou didst redeem me, suffering death on the cross.
Let not such toil be in vain.

Just and avenging Judge,
Grant remission
Before the day of reckoning.

I groan like a guilty man.
Guilt reddens my face.
Spare a suppliant, O God.

Thou who didst absolve Mary Magdalene
And didst hearken to the thief,
To me also hast Thou given hope.

My prayers are not worthy,
But Thou in Thy merciful goodness grant
That I burn not in everlasting fire.

Place me among Thy sheep
And separate me from the goats,
Setting me on Thy right hand.

When the accursed have been confounded
And given over to the bitter flames,
Call me with the blessed.

I pray in supplication on my knees.
My heart contrite as the dust,
Safeguard my fate.

Mournful that day
When from the dust shall rise
Guilty man to be judged.
Therefore spare him, O god.
Merciful Jesu, Lord
Grant them rest.

Lord Jesus Christ, King of glory,
deliver the souls of all the faithful
departed from the pains of hell and from the bottomless pit.
Deliver them from the lion's mouth.

Neither let them fall into darkness
nor the black abyss swallow them up.
And let St. Michael, Thy standard-bearer,
lead them into the holy light
which once Thou didst promise
to Abraham and his seed."

Begun to allow their very own selves to become victims of the con: of their very souls. And capable of being led directly towards the "bottomless pit," and all the way back to the very point of no return, and of point time zero: *of* their own personally affected existence within Reality.

But remember too, the aristocratic elite, who had already passed the point of no return, and/or all of the worldly psychopathic con-artists, did exactly not –

"I am the true vine,
you are the branches.
Whoever remains in me, with me in him,
bears fruit in plenty;
for cut off from me you can do nothing.
Anyone who does not remain in me
is like a branch that has been thrown away – he withers;
these branches are collected and thrown on the fire,
and they are burned.
If you remain in me
and my words remain in you
you may ask what you will
and you shall get it."
John 15: 5-7

Get it.

Because it is a neurophysiological impossibility: after an individually affected human being has actually passed the point of no return. And does become capable of actually falling into a black hole, and/or a bottomless pit, of personally affected neurophysiological dysfunction, for their own selves.

But too – remember, which: that all individually affected human beings did actually begin to regress back towards point time zero, and become capable of experiencing truly humanistic brain death for their own selves, and while actually passing the point of no return – *and* falling into the bottomless pit of the abyss: *of* their own personally affected neurophysiological dysfunction, was, actually, while beginning to enable all of the individually affected victims of the con, and while as in the entire history of mankind too, to become capable of –

"Psychopaths seem to know the dictionary meaning of words but fail(ed) to comprehend or appreciate their emotional value or significance (while functioning as if) 'He knows the words but not the music' – Recent laboratory research provides convincing support for these clinical observations. This research is based on evidence that, for normal people, neutral words generally convey less information than do emotional words: A word such as PAPER has dictionary meaning, whereas a word such as DEATH has dictionary meaning *plus* emotional meaning and unpleasant connotations. Emotional words have more 'punch' than do other words – Picture yourself sitting before a computer screen on which groups of letters are flashed for a fraction of a second. Electrodes for recording brain responses have been attached to your scalp and connected to an EEG machine, which draws a graph of the electrical activity of the brain – Emotional content of the word seems to give a sort of 'turbo-boost' to the decision-making process. At the same time, emotional words evoke larger brain responses than do neutral words – When we used this laboratory test with prison inmates, the non-psychopaths showed the normal pattern of response – but the psychopaths did not: *They responded to emotional words as if they were neutral words* – to a psychopath, a word is just a word."

Dr. Robert D. Hare – Without Conscience

Actually experiencing truly humanistic brain death.

And remember, as individually affected human beings do actually begin to experience truly humanistic brain death, and which is as they do actually effectually regress back towards point time zero: of their own personally affected existence within Reality, they will – and simultaneously, actually begin to become only capable of functioning as a young child is capable of functioning. And – too remember, who: a young human being child, can only physiologically respond to the two extremes of basic biological functioning capabilities, which are encoded within the DNA of all living cells, of: *pleasure* and *pain*, and who also, and simultaneously, can only: neurophysiologically, be in possession of zero universally applicable empirical sell-consciousness. So they: all children, can: neurophysiologically, "understand" absolutely nothing: they can not yet form an associated cognition "to" anything. And so – to them: all young children, a "word" can only be a "word": no word can "mean" anything to a young child, and/or any one individually affected adult human being either. And so, and simultaneously, they: all young children and/or individually affected adult human beings, can only "believe" only *exactly* what they are being "programmed to believe," by their worldly authoritative god figures: who are supplying them with allowed access to all of their absolutely abstracted dopamine biochemical inducing stimulus, functioning as pure *pleasure* only. As they are – simultaneously, neurophysiologically incapable of understanding, and/or being affected by, any of the universally applicable *a priori* Laws of truly humanistic simultaneously relative Omnidimensional Reality, and while actually functioning as Time *made manifest*: it simply is a neurophysiological impossibility. And which is – remember and again, as they: all of the individually affected victims of the con, will simply remain neurophysiologically incapable of consciously seeing, and/or consciously cognizing, past a single point of truly humanistic simultaneously relative space/time, while at any one point within truly humanistic simultaneously relative space/time. So to them: all of the individually affected victims of the con, and while as in the entire history of mankind too, a word can only be a word: it cannot possibly mean any thing, within all of their personal, and individually affected, minds: it is simply a neurophysiological impossibility. And remember, the Son of God had actually simply "told": in words, them: all of the individually affected victims of the con, to –

"Do not store up treasures for yourselves on earth, where moths and woodworms destroy the and thieves can break in and steal. But store up treasures for yourselves in heaven, where neither moth nor woodworms destroy them and thieves cannot break in and steal. For where your treasure is, there will your heart be also."
Matthew 6: 19-21

Actually practice your scales of *a priori* Omnidimensional Reality – each and every day, and for a lifetime also.
And which would have been while –

"Great crowds accompanied him on his way and turned and spoke to them. 'If any man comes to me without hating his father, mother, wife, children, brothers, sisters, yes and his own life too, he cannot be my disciple. Anyone who does not carry his cross and come after me cannot be my disciple."
Luke 14: 25-27

Actually "Carrying your cross, " each and every day, and for a lifetime also.
And too, He: The Son of God, did say: in "words," that there *are* –

"Then he said to his host, 'When you give a lunch or a dinner, do not ask your friends, brothers, relations or rich neighbors, for fear they repay your courtesy by inviting you in return. No; when you have a party, invite the poor, the crippled, the lame, the blind; that they cannot pay you back means that you are fortunate, because repayment will be made to you when the virtuous rise again.
On hearing this, one of those gathered around the table said to him, 'Happy the man who will be at the feast of the kingdom of God!' But he said to him, 'There was a man who gave a great banquet, and he invited a large number of people. When the time for the banquet came, he sent his servant to say to those who had been invited, 'Come along: everything is ready now.' But all alike started to make excuses...'"
Luke 14: 12-18

NO EXCUSES ACCEPTED: NONE.

So that, we can now know, and for a verified scientific fact, that what all truly humanistic beings were supposed to have actually done, was to have "heard" the "words": which The Son of God did communicate absolutely abstractly, and while as "in" a simple spoken language, as young children. And – then, to have actually gone out, each, and every, day, and practiced their scales of truly humanistic simultaneously relative Omnidimensional *a priori* Reality. And/or, to have actually "Carried their crosses," for their own selves, and each, and every, day, also. And which would have – then and simultaneously and for their own selves, enabled them to become capable of actually experiencing the "functions," and/or "verbs," of truly humanistic simultaneously relative Omnidimensional *a priori* Reality, and while actually functioning as The Common Law of Reality, and for their own selves only also. And: simultaneously, actually begin to become neurophysiologically capable of purposefully affecting truly humanistic, simultaneously relative, multidimensional synaptic capabilities, within all of their individually affected minds, and parallel functioning central nervous systems. Which would have – then and simultaneously, begun to enable them to become capable of, purposefully, effactually forming a truly humanistic simultaneously relative Omnidimensional refractive gem of a mind, and parallel functioning central nervous system, for their own selves to be in possession of only. And which would have – then and simultaneously, enabled them: all truly humanistic beings *who had actually done what they were supposed to have done*, to become –

> "Is it not written in your Law:
> *I said, you are gods?*
> So the Law uses the word gods
> of those to whom the word of God was addressed,
> and scripture cannot be rejected.
> Yet you say to someone the Father has concentrated and sent into the world'
> 'You are blaspheming,'
> because he says, 'I am the Son of God.'
> If I am not doing my Father's work,
> there is no need to believe me;
> but if I am doing it,
> then even if you refuse to believe in me,
> at least believe in the work I do;
> then you will know for sure
> that the Father is in me and I am in the Father."
> John 10: 34-38

"Sure": That Jesus of Nazareth *is* the Son of God.

And – remember, which is as this word: sure, does actually mean: "assured or certain beyond question," and too the word sure does actually mean: "free from doubt as to the reliability, character, action, etc., of something," *and for their own selves too.*

But, in Reality, nobody – NOBODY, had actually paid attention: to Reality. And nobody – NOBODY, had actually practiced their scales of truly humanistic simultaneously relative Omnidimensional Reality, and while as on a daily basis too. And nobody – NOBODY, had actually enabled their own selves, to become capable of affecting a truly humanistic, simultaneously relative, Omnidimensional refractive gem of a mind, and parallel functioning central nervous system, for their own selves to be in possession of. And everybody – EVERYBODY, had actually begun to regress back towards point time zero, of their own personally affected existence within Reality. And everybody – EVERYBODY, had actually begun to experience truly humanistic brain death, for their own selves. And nobody – NOBODY, was capable of understanding *any* of the truly humanistic simultaneously relative *a priori* functions, of simultaneously relative Reality. And because nobody – NOBODY, had actually Carried their crosses, while beginning to become capable of affecting a Cross of change, for their own selves to become capable of experiencing, and for their very own selves only. Which was while they did also, and simultaneously, begin to become capable of believing that a word is just a word in Reality, and that they don't really mean anything. And so, The Son of God was forced: "FORCED," to –

"Then they took charge of Jesus, and carrying his cross he went out of the city to the place of the skull or, as it was called in Hebrew, Golgotha, where they crucified him with two others, one on either side with Jesus in the middle. Pilate wrote out a notice and had it fixed to the cross; it ran: 'Jesus the Nazarene, King of the Jews.' The notice was read by many of the Jews, because the place where Jesus was crucified was not far from the city, and the writing was in Hebrew, Latin and Greek. So the Jewish chief priests said to Pilate, 'You should not write 'King of the Jews,' but 'This man said: I am King of the Jews.' Pilate answered, 'What I have written, I have written."
John 19: 17-22

Show them how to get it: A truly humanistic simultaneously relative Omnidimensional refractive gem of a mind, and parallel functioning central nervous system, for their own selves to be in possession of only: and/or a formed understanding of a more divinely purposeful existence, for them to be in possession of for their very own selves only also.

So that, and again, we can now know, what human beings were supposed to have actually done, was to hear the words: of The Letter of the Law, while as young children. And to – then, go out into truly humanistic simultaneously relative Omnidimensional Reality, and begin to practice their scales of truly humanistic simultaneously relative Omnidimensional Reality. And: "simultaneously," begin to, actually, become capable of causing permanently affected neurophysiological multidimensional synaptic capabilities, within their individually affected minds, and

360

parallel functioning central nervous systems: while *actually* effectually functioning as the "function" of the Law, and which can not be simply explained in words. Which would have been while – actually, Carrying their crosses, and experiencing relatively painful experienced humanistic phenomena for their own selves, and/or "*pain,*" and exactly instead of relatively pleasurable experienced humanistic phenomena, and/or "*pleasure.*" And which would have then – and simultaneously, enabled the individually affected human beings, to begin to become capable of effectually forming an understanding of the Function of The Letter of The Law: of universally applicable Omnidimensional *a priori* Reality. And while, actually, effectually functioning as Omnidimensional Time *made manifest*: The Mind of God made manifest – The Eternal Harmony – The Kingdom of Heaven – Finding Our Innocence Lost and The Entrance to the Garden too, and – too, which is the function of *The Annunciation* also. Which the Son of God was communicating an understanding of, and/or becoming capable of affecting for all the world to simply see, with their eyes alone. And – remember, which was as He: The Son of God/Son of Man/Collective Consciousness of Mankind, did have to make manifest a simple "perceivable proof" of –

"The passers-by jeered at him; they shook their heads and said, 'So you would destroy the Temple and rebuild it in three days! Then save yourself! If you are God's son, come down from the cross!' The chief priests with the scribes and elders mocked him in the same way. 'He saved others,' they said, 'he cannot save himself. He is the king of Israel; let him come down from the cross now, and we will believe in him. He puts his trust in God; now let God rescue him if he wants him. For he did say, 'I am the son of God.'"
Matthew 27: 39-44

Their: all of be individually affected victims of the con, own, individually affected, truly humanistic neurophysiological dysfunction, and for all the world to simply see with our eyes alone. And – too, which is as they have – exactly, effectually regressed back to point time zero, of their own personally affected existence within truly humanistic simultaneously relative Omnidimensional Reality. And have become – exactly, neurophysiologically incapable of understanding anything for their own selves, and too they have, and simultaneously, become only neurophysiologically capable of believing exactly only what they have been programmed to believe: by all of the worldly psychopathic con-artists. Who are supplying them with allowed access to all of their absolutely abstracted, and purely psychopathic, and/or schizophrenic, dopamine biochemical inducing stimulus, actually effectually functioning as pure *pleasure* only, and/or The Apple. And/or, the –

361

"At Wing Bowl X, the focus is on more than just chicken –

Bob M- was bleeding from cuts in his brow and hand. But he was a proud and happy man. Moments before, he had circled the floor of the First Union Center, high-fiving his fans – He had stepped up. He had done what he had to do. In less than two minutes, he had smashed and burst six full cans of beer against his head – M- was one of the featured attractions at the Wing Bowl X, which packed the house yesterday, drawing an estimated 23,000. This gift from WIP-AM (to) Philadelphia, has grown from a bizarre and uproarious promotional stunt into a bizarre and uproarious cultural rite – Why do we love it so – It's a celebration (and) if you think ill of that, the hell with you – It's an in-your-face repudiation (of) the dictatorship of virtue..."

Art Carey – The Philadelphia Inquirer – Saturday January 26, 2002

Spectacle.

And too: remember, which is as all of the worldly psychopathic con-artists have always – always, simply conned all of the individually affected victims, and while as in the entire history of mankind, into believing that, if –

"The police went back to the chief priests and Pharisees who said to them, 'Why havn't you brought him?' The policed replied, 'There has never been anybody who has spoken like him.' 'So,' the Pharisees answered, 'you have been led astray as well? Have any of the authorities believed in him? Any of the Pharisees? This rabble knows nothing about the Law – they are damned! One of them, Nicodemus – the same man who had come to Jesus earlier – said to them, 'But surely the Law does not allow us to pass judgment on a man without giving him a hearing and discovering what he is about?' To this they answered, 'Are you a Galilean too? Go into the matter, and see for yourself: prophets do not come out of Galilee."

John 7: 45-52

An individually affected human being, has not experienced truly humanistic brain death for their own selves, and become neurophysiologically incapable of understanding the function of the Letter of The Law, then they: any individual human being, who has not experienced truly humanistic brain death for their own selves to be in possession of only; any individual human being, who has not betrayed the Collective Consciousness of Mankind; any individual human being, who has not simply sold their soul: to allow themselves an opportunity to be a part of the In Crowd – which is being purposefully allowed exposure to the spectacle event of any, and/or all, kinds, and/or: abstracted dopamine biochemical inducing stimulus functioning as pure *pleasure* only; any individual human being, who can still actually begin to become capable of being affected by The Function of the Law: any individual human being, who does have The courage – The integrity – The constitution, to stand up to worldly tyranny: To oppose it – To confront it – To renounce it – To combat it – To annihilate it, is "damned." And which is, of course,

362

only exactly backwards: in self-evident Reality. And only, exactly –

"Men of passive tempers look somewhat lightly over the offenses (upon human nature): you are deceiving yourselves, and by your delay bringing ruin upon posterity. Your future connection – with society, whom you can neither love nor honour, will be forced and unnatural, and being formed only on the plan of present convenience, will in little time fall into a relapse more wretched than the first. But if you say, you can still pass the violations over, then I ask – Have you lost a parent or child by their hands, and yourself the ruined and wretched survivor? If you have not, then are you not a judge of those who have. But if you have, and you can still shake hands with the murderers, then you are unworthy the name of husband, father, friend, or lover, and whatever may be your rank or title in life, you have the heart of a coward, and the spirit of a sycophant...Thomas Paine: Common Sense."

Common Sense.
And – remember, the exact reason that everybody is going to die and soon too, is simply because the overwhelming vast majority of mankind, actually has been affected: by the con. And they have regressed back to point time zero, of their own personally affected existence within Reality. And they have passed the point of no return, while they are just about to lose control over their very own selves. And they have allowed their own selves to become capable of becoming addicted to excessive amounts of absolutely abstracted, and purely psychopathic – and/or schizophrenic, dopamine biochemical inducing stimulus, functioning as pure *pleasure* only, and too which they actually simply cannot live without. And they have become only capable of functioning, as the aristocratic elite have, always, allowed their own selves to become only neurophysiologically capable of functioning: which is brain dead, and actually neurophysiologically incapable of understanding, and/or being affected by, anything – any "thing," besides –

"(Napoleon) Bonaparte had two ruling passions: glory and war. He was never more happy than in the camp, and never more morose than in the idleness of peace. Plans for building public monuments also satisfied his imagination and helped fill the void – Bonaparte did not esteem mankind, whom he despised more and more in proportion as he became more acquainted with them – His manner was imposing rather than pleasant and those who did not know him experienced an involuntary feeling of awe in his presence – He (was) lacking any ear for harmony; he could never recite a verse without violating the meter – He had no idea of power except as direct force..."
Louis Bourrienne: Memoirs Of Napoleon Bonaparte, Roots of Western Civilization, Volume II – Wesley D. Camp

The spectacle: of any kind. And/or tangible form mass stimulus actually functioning as "1," and of any kind. And which is – only, allowed exposure to

363

any kind of purely psychopathic, and/or schizophrenic, dopamine biochemical inducing stimulus, functioning as pure *pleasure* only. And/or The Apple: the orgy, and/or; "Bonaparte had two ruling passions: glory and war. He was never more happy than in the camp, and never more morose than in the idleness of peace" – the chaos, and/or discord: the pain, and suffering, and death too: The Lawlessness. And they DO; "Why do we love it so" – love it: remember, because they are brain dead, and nothing else can affect them.

And which is exactly why, all of them: all of them and while as in the entire history of mankind too, were – are, and always will be –

"Napoleon never knew a generous feeling. That is what made him such boring company. He regarded men as base coin with which to gratify his whims and ambitions..."
Jean Chaptal: Recollections of Napoleon, Roots of Western Civilization, Volume II – Wesley D. Camp

Boring as sin: BORING – BORING – BORING: **ALL OF THEM**. And while as in the entire history of mankind too: what a bunch of bores. Making manifest their schizophrenic inarticulate cries for attention: and/or their discord, and chaos, and entertainment, and spectacle events, and aristocratic environments, and worldly power. And any, and/or all, tangible form mass stimulus functioning as "1" only: and/or truly humanistic brain death, and apathy, and complacency, and stupidity too. And all, simply because, their itty-bitty little; "Bonaparte had two ruling passions: glory and war. He was never more happy than in the camp, and never more morose than in the idleness of peace – He (was) lacking any ear for harmony – He had no idea of power except as direct force" – childishly impressionable minds, cannot cognize any Time *made manifest* whatsoever: because they are truly humanistic brain dead. And they have no truly humanistic talents of their own: to be in possession of. And too – remember, which is exactly as Thomas Jefferson did explain:

"Those which depend on ourselves, are the only pleasures a wise man will count on: for nothing is ours, which another may deprive us of. Hence the inestimable alum of intellectual pleasures. Ever in our power, always leading us to something new, never cloying, we ride serene and sublime above the concerns of this mortal world, contemplating truth and nature, matter and motion, the laws which bind up their existence, and that Eternal Being who made and bound them by those laws...Put into one scale the pleasures which any object may offer; but put fairly into the other, the pains which are to follow, and see which preponderates – Let this be our employ. Leave the bustle and the tumult of society to those who have not talents to occupy themselves without them..."
Thomas Jefferson: Letter to Mrs. Cosway

And they: all of the individually affected victims of the con who have experienced truly humanistic brain death for their own selves to be in possession of only, **CAN HAVE NO IDEA WHAT** –

"Pilate said, 'Take him yourselves and crucify him: I can find no case against him.' 'We have a Law,' the Jews replied, 'and according to that Law he ought to die, because he has claimed to be the Son of God.'
When Pilate heard them say this his fears increased. Re-entering the Praetorium, he said to Jesus, 'Where do you come from?' but Jesus made no answer. Pilate then said to him, 'Are you refusing to speak to me? Surely you know I have power to release you and I have power to crucify you?' 'You would have no power over me,' replied Jesus, 'if it had not been given to you from above; that is why the one who handed me over to you has the greater guilt."
John 19: 6-11

Power "is," in Reality.
And they are actually going to –

"The psychopath is like an infant, absorbed in his own needs, vehemently demanding satiation' – Psychopaths view people as little more than objects to be used for their own gratification – Psychopaths sometimes verbalize remorse but then contradict themselves in words or actions – Besides being impulsive – doing things on the spur of the moment – psychopaths are highly reactive to perceived insults or slights – psychopaths are short-tempered or hot-headed and tend to respond to frustration, failure, discipline, and criticism with sudden violence, threats, and verbal abuse. They take offense easily and become angry and aggressive over trivialities, and often in a context that seems inappropriate to others."
Dr. Robert D. Hare – Without Conscience

Bore us: the entire world, to death.
And, of course, the more boring they ever were, and/or are; the more simple they ever were, and/or are; the more childish they ever were, and/or are; the more brain dead they ever were, and/or are; the more mediocre they ever were and/or are, then the more –

"You know that among the pagans their rulers lord it over them, and their great men make their authority felt. This is not to happen among you. No; anyone who wants to be great among you must be your servant, and anyone who wants to be first among you must be your slave, just as the Son of Man came not to be served but to serve, and to give his life as ransom for many."
Matthew 21: 25-20

Of a spectacle they ever made of their own selves, and for everyone else to be forcibly exposed to also. While including any, and/or all, of their *ridiculous* worldly spectacle events.

     And too and of course, which does enable us to plainly understand the fact, that no truly virtuous, and/or intelligent, and/or compassionate, and/or non-brain dead, human being: while as in the entire history of mankind, has ever – EVER, purposefully affected chaos, and/or discord, and/or a diversion from Reality, and/or entertainment, and/or a spectacle event, and/or *pain* and death and suffering too, to simply enable their own selves to become capable of taking control over any other human beings, and/or over anything. And/or, to simply enable their own selves to become capable of –

     "When you fast do not put on a gloomy look as the hypocrites do: they pull long faces to let men know they are fasting. I tell you solemnly, they have had their reward. But when you fast, put oil on your head and wash your face, so that no one will know you are fasting except your Father who sees all that is done in secret; and your Father who sees all that is done in secret will reward you."
     Matthew 6: 16-18

     Making a spectacle of themselves: to enable their own selves to become capable of becoming the "center of attention," and while receiving a simple dopamine biochemical induction functioning as pure *pleasure,* for their own selves to consume. While at the expense of all of the non-brain dead human beings, who must be exposed to their psychopathic, and/or schizophrenic, inarticulate cries for attention.
     They: all truly intelligent human beings, did always simply, and only –

     "A Declaration by the Representatives of the United States of America:
     We hold these truths to be self-evident: that all men are created equal; that they are endowed by their creator with CERTAIN [*inherent and*] inalienable rights; that among these are life, liberty, and the pursuit of happiness..."

     Explain their "formed understanding of Reality" to them: any, and/or all, individually affected human beings, who have begun to experience truly humanistic brain death, for their own selves to be in possession of only. And their addiction to all things worldly only too, which is while including their need to actually become capable of controlling everything: to maintain their addiction. And remember, which does simply – then, cause them: all of the individually affected brain dead victims, to perceive it: their own personally affected dysfunction, as an; "Besides being impulsive – doing things on the spur of the moment – psychopaths are highly reactive to perceived insults or slights – psychopaths are short-tempered or hot-headed and tend to respond to frustration, failure, discipline, and criticism with sudden violence, threats, and verbal abuse. They take offense easily and become angry and aggressive" – insult. And – remember too, they do – and simultaneously,

366

actually begin to feel as though someone is placing a plastic bag over their heads, as they are beginning to be denied access to their "drugs": which is their acquired ability to control everything. And too and simultaneously, their cerebral cortices have become destroyed: exactly because of their continued allowed exposure to excessive amounts of absolutely abstracted, and purely psychopathic, dopamine biochemical inducing stimulus, functioning as pure *pleasure* only. And too, and simultaneously: as they have actually experienced truly humanistic brain death for their own selves, they can, only, be affected by their allowed exposure to all of their worldly spectacle events, and they are actually only capable of functioning as young children, and/or; "Lying, deceiving, and manipulation are natural talents for psychopaths. With their powers of imagination in gear and focused on themselves, psychopaths appear amazingly unfazed by the possibility – or even the certainty – of being found out. When caught in a lie or challenged with the truth, they are seldom perplexed or embarrassed – they simply change their stories or attempt to rework the facts so that they appear to be consistent with the lie" – master manipulating worldly psychopathic con-artists only also. And so, they: all of the master manipulating worldly psychopathic con-artists, and while as in the entire history of mankind too, do *then* –

"A Shock Grows in Brooklyn –

A fiery controversy over a museum's new show brings New York's Mayor out slugging: The mayor blew up three weeks ago over the controversial exhibition, 'Sensation: Young British Artists from the Saatchi Collection.' Giuliani threatened to cut all city funding to the museum – $7 million a year, about one third of its operating budget, unless the show was canceled. The Mayor was especially outraged by 'The Holy Virgin Mary,' a painting by Chris Ofili, who used, among other materials, elephant dung. 'This is sick stuff,' Giuliani said – A Roman Catholic, the Mayor says he has no problem making enemies – though it must have hurt when he was booed at the Metropolitan Opera last week...polls showed that both New York residents and a nationwide sample were against shutting down the exhibit."

Cathleen McGuigan, Maggie Malone, Ray Sawhill, Gregory Beals –
Newsweek – October 11, 1999

Initiate a confrontation, and/or; "though it must have hurt when he was booed at the Metropolitan Opera last week" – start a fight: *as* they *are* having "Reality" "explained to them." And/or, actually begin to make manifest even more discord, and even more chaos, and even more pain, and death and suffering too: to maintain their addiction. And which is while also – and simultaneously, simply projecting their own personally affected neurophysiological dysfunction upon mankind: while exactly "creating a diversion" – from Reality, and/or simply deviating exactly from the fact: of the perceivable Reality. Which is the perceivable evidence of their own personally affected neurophysiological dysfunction, that they are making manifest, for all the world to simply see with our eyes alone.

And remember too, the; "polls showed that both New York residents and a nationwide sample were against shutting down the exhibit" – majority has been affected. And they: The Majority, are the ones who are actually making manifest a perceivable proof, of their –

"In Crisis, Giuliani's Popularity Overflows City –
Perhaps it was yesterday, when the President of France proclaimed that the French had begun praising the 'Maire-heros' – which he called the French equivalent of 'Rudy the Rock.' Or maybe it was a few days before, when Barbara Walters promised the nation that she would reveal the Mayor of New York as he had never been seen before – While Mr. Giuliani's popularity has understandably swelled in New York City, it also appears to be expanding nationwide and even to the world – New York's Mayor has risen from the ashes of the tragedy as an unequivocal hero of the moment..."
Jennifer Steinhauer – The New York Times – Thursday September 20, 2001

Own personally affected neurophysiological dysfunction: The Majority.
Which is – exactly, as the majority has been affected by the con: of their truly humanistic universally applicable empirical self-consciousness, and/or their truly humanistic simultaneously relative conscious cognizant capabilities, and/or their truly humanistic ability to form formal abstract reasoning: of Reality, and/or their truly humanistic ability to function as an adult human being is capable of functioning. And which is as they have – actually and neurophysiologically, regressed back to point time zero, of their own personally affected existence within Reality. And they have, and simultaneously, become neurophysiologically capable of consciously cognizing, and/or "seeing," only the actual tangible form mass stimulus which is immediately "in front of them": which they can simply see, with their eyes alone, and be simply affected by also. While they actually have, and simultaneously: while as through a lifetime's worth of exposure to absolutely abstracted dopamine biochemical inducing stimulus functioning as pure *pleasure* only, become only capable of functioning as; "Psychopaths are very good at giving their undivided attention to things that interest them most and at ignoring other things. Some clinicians have likened this process to a narrow-beam search-light that focuses on only one thing at a (point in) time – Psychopaths seem to suffer a kind of emotional poverty that limits the depth of their feelings – Psychopaths are easily bored (and they) have an ongoing and excessive need for excitement – In some respects they are like the emotionless androids depicted in science fiction, unable to imagine what real humans experience" – psychopaths at best. And; "Joyce Kovelman and Arnold Scheibel of UCLA's Brain Research Institute spotted a weird cellular 'disarray' in the schizophrenic brains – The pyramid-shaped cells of the hippocampus, normally arranged in an orderly manner, were grossly misaligned – A schizophrenic's dopamine neurons would start to fire in two different rhythms and rapidly become uncoupled – 'in schizophrenia the brain fragments into active and

inactive clusters of neurons…" – schizophrenics at worst.

Because, remember, there simply are no images of things being projected all throughout, and within, our minds, and parallel functioning central nervous systems.

And when this –

"In Seconds, Confident N. Y. Is Shaken –

Life changed fast and forever yesterday morning, when an unseen terrorist hand guided two planes into the twin towers of the World Trade Center, collapsing the symbols of New York city's commercial and cultural greatness – Casualties were expected to be in the thousands…Strangers tried to find comfort and assurance. People in buildings far from the towers streamed onto the street, seeking a kind of solace among neighbors they normally ignored – Ultimately, many people were left seething with anger, feeling rage against an unknown enemy for an unconscionable act – 'I feel violated,' said Raymond S-, 'I feel raped. I feel humiliated. This is just shameful what they did."

Alfred Lubrano – The New York Times – Wednesday September 12, 2001

Did actually occur, it was, in fact, a "violation" of the basic universally applicable, and –

"A declaration by the representatives of the United States of America –

We hold these truths to be self-evident: that all men are created equal; that they are endowed by their Creator with CERTAIN [*inherent and*] inalienable rights; that among these are life, liberty, and the pursuit of happiness…"

Self-evident truths, of *a priori* Reality. While beginning with the basic biological functioning capabilities which are encoded within the DNA of all living cells, and while as from one end of the universe to the other. Of: *pleasure* – dopamine – sugar – harmony – 11111, and *pain* – serotonin – salt – chaos – 10010. And which was – exactly, as they: the brain dead individuals who were responsible for making manifest *that* schizophrenic inarticulate cry for attention, did simply become neurophysiologically incapable of caring about anything, and/or anyone, besides their very own selves. And while, then, becoming capable of simply projecting their own personally affected neurophysiological dysfunction upon mankind, and while – then, causing all of mankind to be forcibly exposed to their personally affected schizophrenic inarticulate cry for attention. While actually functioning as chaos, and/or discord: and/or 10010, and/or –

"A Shock Grows in Brooklyn –

A fiery controversy over a museum's new show brings New York's Mayor out slugging: The mayor blew up three weeks ago over the controversial exhibition, 'Sensation: Young British Artists from the Saatchi Collection' –The Mayor was especially outraged by 'The Holy Virgin Mary,' a painting by Chris Ofili, who used, among other materials, elephant dung. This is sick stuff,' Giuliani said – A Roman Catholic, the Mayor says he has no problem making enemies...polls showed that both New York residents and a nationwide sample were against shutting down the exhibit."

C. McGuigan, M. Malone, R. Sawhill, G. Beals – Newsweek

Elephant dung: "10010."

And remember, which was also while the "elephant dung" – 10010 – *pain* – serotonin – chaos – discord, was actually functioning as their: the aristocratic elite's, and while including the Majority as they did actually approve, and finance, it, own personally affected schizophrenic inarticulate cry for attention: made manifest by the people of The United States of America. Which was, as they did actually project their own personally affected neurophysiological dysfunction upon mankind, and as they: all of the individually affected victims of the con, did – then, simply; "I feel raped. I feel humiliated. This is just shameful what they did" – "rape," the –

"Near the cross of Jesus stood his mother and his mother's sister, Mary the wife of Clopas, and Mary of Magdala. Seeing his mother and the disciple he loved standing near her, Jesus said to his mother, 'Woman, this is your son.' Then to the disciple he said, 'This is your mother.' And from that moment the disciple made a place for her in his home."

John 19: 25-27

Mother of The Son of God/Son of Man/Collective Consciousness of Mankind, and assail the Collective Consciousness of Mankind, and violate the Collective Consciousness of Mankind. And –

"...Serrano is an urban artist of considerable political sophistication...in high art the word 'moral' is usually considered laughable..."

Andres Serrano – The Spirit and The Letter – Lucy Lippard, Art in America

Laugh as they did it too: remember?

And – remember, the; "Giuliani threatened to cut all city funding to the museum – unless the show was canceled. The Mayor was especially outraged by 'The Holy Virgin Mary,' a painting by Chris Ofili, who used, among other materials, elephant dung. This is sick stuff, Giuliani said" – Mayor had actually tried to explain Reality to them. But they did – remember, only; "though it must have hurt when he was booed at the Metropolitan Opera last week" – persecute him, and/or –

"Adolf Hitler: And this is not complicated, but very simple and all of a piece. It does not have multiple shadings; it has a positive and negative; love or hate..."

Hate him: as he was explaining Reality to them. And, of course, functioning as the Father: while forcing them to come to an understanding of Reality. And not simply allowing them to exist while in ignorance of Reality, and too, not; "In Crisis Giuliani's Popularity Overflows City – While Mr. Giuliani's popularity has understandably swelled in New York City it also appears to be expanding nationwide and even to the world – New York's Mayor has risen from the ashes of the tragedy as an unequivocal hero" – functioning as the Mother, while providing comfort for them. And again and remember, which is as they are only capable of; "Psychopaths – frequently change topics, go off on irrelevant tangents, and fail to connect phrases and sentences in a straightforward manner – Jack was a mile-a-minute talker, with the psychopath's characteristic ability to contradict himself from one sentence to the next" – functioning in a purely psychopathic manner – at best. As they did – simply, "change their minds," and their professed hatred for the Mayor, did turn to love.

And remember and again, which is as they: all of the individually affected victims of the con, and which is now the majority of our entire global society, have actually regressed back to point time zero, of their own personally affected existence within Reality. While they have, and simultaneously, actually experienced truly humanistic brain death for their own selves to be in possession of only, and their addiction to all things worldly. Which is – and simultaneously, as they have actually become neurophysiologically incapable of consciously cognizing, and/or "seeing," past a single point, of simultaneously relative space/time while at any one point within simultaneously relative space/time. And which is the single point of –

"Paul MacLean, for one, considers the frontal lobes the 'heart' of the cortex – Clinically, there is evidence that the prefrontal cortex by looking inward, so to speak, obtains the gut feeling for identifying with another individual. In other words: empathy – Through its centers for vision, hearing, and bodily sensations, we traffic with the external world..."
The 3-Pound Universe – Judith Hooper and Dick Teresi

Their very own selves: which they can not "see" beyond, it is simply a neurophysiological impossibility. And which is – remember, simply because –

"PET-scan images of the brains of recovering addicts – reveal other striking changes, including a dramatically impaired ability to process glucose, the primary energy source for working neurons. Moreover, this impairment – is greatest in the prefrontal cortex..."
Addicted – J. Madeleine Nash – Time – May 5, 1997

Their prefrontal cortices are destroyed.
And so it is a neurophysiological impossibility: it actually is a neurophysiological impossibility, for these individually affected people, and which is now the majority of our entire global society, to care about anything: TO "CARE" ABOUT ANY "THING," it is actually a neurophysiological impossibility for them.

Except for –

"At a purely chemical level (just as the injection of) heroin triggers release of dopamine – every experience humans find enjoyable – amounts to little more than an explosion of dopamine in the nucleus accumbens, as exhilarating and ephemeral as a firecracker – dopamine can be elevated by a hug, a kiss, a word of praise..."
Addicted – J. Madeleine Nash – Time – May 5, 1997

Their allowed access to their drugs. And which is, as –

"Drug's Effect On Brain Is Extensive, Study Finds –
Heavy users (of highly addictive stimulants) are doing more damage to their brains than scientists had thought, according to the first study that looked inside addicts' brains nearly a year after they stop using the drug – At least a quarter of a class of molecules that help people feel pleasure and reward were knocked out – The addicts (started out as) occasional users but over time the drug hijacked their natural dopamine systems..."
Sandra Blakeslee – The New York Times – Tuesday March 6, 2001

Their: The Majority, cerebral cortices have been hijacked. And We: the entire world, have been –

"Peace Of Mind Falls Victim To Mayhem –
Psychologically, yesterday's attacks were a watershed event likely to leave many Americans feeling afraid, unsure of their government and vengeful, trauma experts said…The victims of the multipronged onslaught were civilians working in big-city buildings that are the very symbols of American Commerce and military might. They were passengers on commercial jetliners that were hijacked and used as weapons – 'There will be enormous fear and uncertainty,' (Frank) F- said, precisely the goals of a terrorist attack – and they will be questioning whether 'we are losing control'..."
S. Burling, M. McCullough and M. Uhlman – The Philadelphia Inquirer
Sunday September 12, 2001

Led on a collision course with our very own destiny. And –

"A Creepin Horror –
Buildings Burn and Fall as Onlookers Search for Elusive Safety:
It kept getting worse – The horror arrived in episodic bursts of chilling disbelief, signified first by trembling floors, sharp eruptions, cracked windows. There was the actual unfathomable realization of a gaping, flaming hole in first one of the tall towers, and then the same thing all over again in its twin. There was the merciless site of bodies hopelessly tumbling out, some of them in flames – Finally,

the mighty towers themselves were reduced to nothing. Dense plums of smoke raced through the downtown avenues, coursing between the buildings, shaped like tornadoes on their sides – For several panic-stricken hours yesterday morning, people in Lower Manhattan witnessed the inexpressible, the incomprehensible, the unthinkable. 'I don't know what the gates of hell look like, but it's got to be like this,' said John M-, a security director for an Internet firm in the trade center. I'm a combat veteran, Vietnam, and I never saw anything like this – Brianne W-, a student at Pace University, was walking to class (and) she heard a blast and felt the ground shake. She ran to the bank, where people were banging on the glass, breaking it, trying to get inside. 'I saw a guy bleeding from the head right by the bank,' she said. People were getting stomped on under the crowd. It was horrible. I felt I was in a bad nightmare' – As emergency vehicles, sirens blaring, sped downtown, people stood and gaped at the towers with holes in them. Many people were steadily inching downtown, not imagining anything worse was to come – And then it got worse – Abruptly, there was an ear-splitting noise. The south tower shook, seemed to list in one direction and then began to come down, imploding upon itself – A plume of smoke reminiscent of an atomic bomb rose upward and then descended to street level and sped uptown. People began running, chased by the smoke – For several blocks, everything was black. People found their eyes burned. Many wondered if they were seeing the very face of death..."

N.R. Kleinfield – The New York Times – Wednesday September 12, 2001

Nobody – NO BODY, is going to wake up from this nightmare, and everybody is going to see the very face of death too: soon. And – yes too, it is going to; "Many people were steadily inching downtown, not imagining anything worse was to come" – get even worse: than simply dying that is. For The Majority, as they have become victims of the con: of their very own selves, and as they will; "I don't know what the gates of hell look like, but it's got to be like this" – see the very gates of hell. And – too, they are going to –

"Therapists Hear Survivors' Refrain: 'If Only' –
They are an uneasy current running beneath the stories of close calls, courageous acts and sudden losses: regrets shaped by hindsight, what-ifs and if-only's, wishes to undo what can not be undone...'There are concentric circles of survivor experience,' said Dr. Robert J. Lifto, a psychiatrist at Harvard, who has studied the survivors of Hiroshima, the Holocaust and other human-inflicted terrors – Dr. Lifton, in interviewing survivors of Hiroshima, said that 'what many come to as a kind of meaning was their having been the first to experience these dreadful weapons' – 'They could therefore know something about what the weapons do to people,' he said, 'and could warn the world about their dangers..."

Erica Goode – The New York Times – Tuesday September 25, 2001

Spend an eternity saying: "If only I had listened" – as they do see the very "gates of hell," and – exactly, trying to "undo what can not be undone," too.

And: remember, so says – only, The –

"I tell you solemnly,
I am the gate of the sheepfold.
All others who have come
are thieves and brigands;
but the sheep took no notice of them.
I am the gate.
Anyone who enters through me will be safe:
he will go freely in and out
and be sure of finding pasture.
The thief comes
only to steal and kill and destroy.
I have come
so that they may have life
and have it in full.
I am the good shepherd;
the good shepherd is one who lays down his life for his sheep.
The hired man, since he is not the shepherd
abandons the sheep and runs away
as soon as he sees a wolf coming,
and then the wolf attacks and scatters the sheep;
this is because he is only a hired man
and has no concern for the sheep.
John 10: 7-13

Son of God: only.

And, of course, which is as all of the worldly psychopathic con-artists, and while as in the entire history of mankind too, have always – ALWAYS, only "created a diversion" from Reality, and made manifest human-inflicted terrors, and/or worldly political empowerment, for their own selves to become capable of acquiring. As they: the psychopathic con-artists, did become capable of hijacking the collective consciousness of mankind, and/or simply creating a diversion from it.

And, of course, there are many who have simply said, that –

"Air Passengers Vow to Resist Any Hijackers –
Up at 30,000 feet, the rules have changed – 'You can't just sit there any more,' said Tony L-, (a) former high school linebacker who makes an average of four trips a week as a field support specialist for a medical device company based in Minneapolis – 'You've got to be prepared,' he said. If someone rushes that cockpit, absolutely, I'm up. I'd do anything I can to stop it' – Donald A-, (an) auto mechanic aboard a Delta Air Lines flight to Las Vegas on Tuesday night, said he felt the same

way – 'It's a sorry man that would sit still during a hijacking now,' said Mr. A-, 'It would be a bad idea for someone to try to hijack a plane while I'm on it, I'll tell you that. I think the American citizenry as a whole, especially males, are pretty pumped up about this now..."

Sam Howe Verhovek – The New York Times – Thursday October 11, 2001

They would not simply allow any worldly psychopathic con-artists, to become capable of hijacking the collective consciousness of mankind, and to become capable of leading us on a collision course with our very own destiny too.

And they did –

"Strong Support For Using Force Is Found In Poll –
As they move from shock to fury, Americans are bracing for the United States to go to war, and they overwhelmingly say the nation should take military action against those responsible for the terrorist attacks on New York and Washington, the latest New York Times/CBS News poll shows – Americans say they're ready to alter their lifestyles, and even sacrifice some of their own liberties, for safety considerations..."

R. L. Burke and J. Elder – The New York Times – September 16,   2001

Conduct a poll. Which did show that The Majority did say: in words, that they would be willing to "go to war," to combat –

"In Speech, Bush Says Terrorism Cannot Prevail –
Addressing the nation from the Oval Office, a somber President Bush vowed tonight that the United States would hunt down and punish those responsible for the 'evil, despicable acts of terror' which he said took thousands of American lives. He said the United States would make no distinction between those who carried out the hijackings and those who harbored and supported them – 'These acts of mass murder were intended to frighten our nation into chaos and retreat, but they have failed,' the president said. 'Our country is strong. Terrorist acts can shake the foundation of our largest buildings, but they cannot touch the foundation of America' – Mr. Bush asked the country to pray tonight, 'for the thousands who are dead, for the children whose worlds have been shattered, for all those whose sense of safety and security has been threatened.' He quoted from the 23rd Psalm, intoning 'Even though I walk through the valley of the shadow of death, I fear no evil, for You are with me."

E. Bumiller/D. E. Sanger – The New York Times – September 12,   2001

Anyone, and/or anything, that would attack the very foundation, which is the truly virtuous Child: The Truly Idealist Democratic Society. And too, specifically and exactly, not just – NOT JUST, the perceivable tangible form mass, and not just the buildings: not just the people places and things. But that we: The Truly Idealist Democratic society which is The United States Of America, would attack, and we would destroy, and we would annihilate, any one – and/or any thing, responsible for "evil despicable acts of terror" inflicted upon The Child. And while those responsible, for those "evil despicable acts of terror," were creating only: 'were intended to frighten our nation into chaos and retreat," a diversion from Reality: chaos – discord – a schizophrenic inarticulate cry for attention of any kind: 10010, and fear – complacency – insolence – indifference – disrespect, and lawlessness too, and so they did say in words.

And there were some who actually did –

"On Flight 93, Defiant Voices –
In cell-phone calls to loved ones, captives spoke of fighting back:
In the end, the passengers on Flight 93 had one thing in common with their hijackers: They knew they were going to die – But if the terrorists on board the United Airlines flight were bent on mass death and destruction, some of their captives were willing to die to save others – 'I know we're all going to die,' Thomas E. Burnett Jr., 38, the father of three, told his wife in San Ramon, Calif., by cellular phone, his relatives said. 'There's three of us who are going to do something about it' – 'Are you OK?' Burnett's wife, Deena asked him – 'No,' came the reply – Then she heard him say his plane had been hijacked…Another passenger, Mark Bingham, 31, a public-relations executive, called his mother before the crash to tell her that the 'plane has been taken over by three guys who say they have a bomb' – When he called his mother at 9:45 a.m., Bingham was so frustrated that he began his conversation with his mother by saying, 'Mom, this is Mark Bingham' – Minutes later, at 9:58 a.m., just twelve minutes before the crash, an unidentified man locked himself in the bathroom and called 911, connecting with a dispatcher in Westmoreland County – 'We are being hijacked!' the man desperately told the dispatcher – The caller implored the dispatcher to believe him. This was no prank, he said – As the call ended, the man said he heard an explosion and saw smoke. The plane, he said, was 'going down...'"
R. Ciotta/C. R. McCoy – The Philadelphia Inquirer – September 13, 2001

Come to an understanding of the fact of our 21st century Reality. And that we: the entire world, have been hijacked, and led him a collision course with our very own destiny too: THIS PLANE IS GOING DOWN, and; "In the end, the passengers on Flight 93 had one thing in common with their hijackers: They knew they were going to die" – everybody is going to die too: soon. And they: some truly virtuous human beings, did; "But if the terrorists on board the United Airlines flight were bent on mass death and destruction, some of their captives were willing to die to save others" – actually do something about it, and take back control of their very own destinies.

But – remember too, the majority has been affected: by the con, and they have actually regressed back to point time zero: of their own personally affected existence within Reality. And they have become capable of employing the use of zero universally applicable empirical self-consciousness. And they are – and simultaneously, only capable of functioning while as in a purely psychopathic manner: at best, and which is while to a psychopath, a word can; "Emotional content of a word seems to give a sort of 'turbo-boost' to the decision-making process. At the same time, emotional words evoke larger brain responses than do neutral words – When we used this laboratory test with prison inmates, the non-psychopaths showed the normal pattern of response – but the psychopaths did not: *They responded to emotional words as if they were neutral words* – to a psychopath, a word is just a word" – not possibly "mean" anything: they're just words. Words cannot actually mean anything to a psychopath, they are just words: it is actually an absolute neurophysiological impossibility for "words" to mean anything, to a psychopath. And which is exactly why they do use so many words, and so *frivolously* too, and words like: Virtue – Honor – Respect – Integrity – Courage – Peace – Justice – Compassion – Mercy – Good-faith – Truth – Commitment, and Love too. They use *this* word: LOVE, like they breathe: they actually use it everywhere, and "on" every one, they do use it too. And too remember, which is just; "The psychopath is like an infant, absorbed in his own needs, vehemently demanding satiation' – Psychopaths (do also) display a general lack of empathy. They are indifferent to the rights and suffering of family members and strangers alike. Psychopaths are very good at giving their undivided attention to things that interest them most and at ignoring other things. Some clinicians have likened this process to a narrow-beam search-light that focuses on only one thing at a (point in) time" – self-lust that they are capable of experiencing: for their very own selves only. Because, while they do become capable of employing the use of "words," they do – also and simultaneously, become capable of –

"...dopamine, can be elevated by a hug, a kiss, a word of praise..."
Addicted – J. Madeleine Nash – Time – May 5, 1997

Becoming the "center of attention." And receive the dose of dopamine biochemical induction, that they have developed a neurophysiological dependency upon, with their the ability to control even one other individually affected human being, with their simple spoken words.

And remember too, they: the majority of our entire society and while at this point in time while upon the threshold of the 21st century, have become so affected, that The Majority is –

"Drug Use, and Concern, On Rise –
In the movie version of madness, Psycho and Hannibal reign supreme. The terror of Norman Bates and Hannibal Lector lies in their mysterious strangeness and their abrupt lunges into violence – But in real life, most mentally ill people act...like you – Federal mental-health experts say that more than one in five Americans are afflicted with a diagnosable mental illness every year – although few are the

psychotic type that seems to interest moviegoers – Add drug addicts to that number, and nearly a third of the country is said to suffer from 'a mental or addictive disorder' each year – In the last few decades, more and more of them have begun to seek psychiatric care (and) medications – Sales of medications for psychiatric conditions dwarf the gross national products of some small countries. Last year, Americans and their insurers paid more than $8 billion for antidepressants, $3.9 billion for antipsychotics, and more than $1 billion for antianxiety medication. Doctors wrote more than 125 million prescriptions for mental disorders – up from 73 million in 1995..."

Shanker Vedantam – The Philadelphia Inquirer – Monday March 10, 2001

Beginning to become capable of suffering from a severe mental disorder, and while they have become addicted too. And – simultaneously, which is as they have actually been affected by the con: and have actually regressed back to point time zero, of their own personally affected existence within Reality. And remember too, become so severely confused, that they would actually continue to believe: within their individually affected minds, that God: The God, and any God, would bless them: as they actually were defecating upon The Mother of God, and the Collective Consciousness of Mankind. And too and just as; "He – Adolf Hitler, tried to bury his confusion under shouts of ultra-nationalism, but these only led to more rage" – Adolf Hitler did do, they do –

"Does Flag-waving Signal U. S. Chauvinism –
U.S. Flags are hanging from buildings, flapping from cars, and flapping on TV screens. They are pinned to lapels and painted on T-shirts – across the nation – ubiquitous flag-waving (has) started to discomfort some people unaccustomed or opposed to such graphic national pride. They fear the line is graying between patriotism and war-time-like support for any U.S. military action, they said...Pat Croce, an indefatigable civic booster in Philadelphia who launched a flag-themed charity drive called 'Raise a Million, Wave a Million,' said he had heard nobody express discomfort about waving the flag or criticism of those who do not – The intent ...was to be a unit together under the red, white and blue,' Croce said. 'If you don't want to wave it, don't wave it. That's why we're here. You can do anything you want in this country."

Thomas Ginsgerg – The Philadelphia Inquirer – Sunday October 7, 2001

Continue to only bury their confusion in shouts of ultra-nationalism.
And too as they have, now, simply hijacked the name of Thomas Jefferson: the function of The Truly Idealist Democratic Society – The Declaration of Independence – The American Mind, and The American Constitution. As they: all of the individually affected victims of the con, do sincerely believe: within all of their individually affected minds, that the "definition" of all these things: that the "function" of all these things, is to simply enable –

"A Shock Grows in Brooklyn –

A fiery controversy over a museum's new show brings New York's Mayor out slugging: The mayor blew up three weeks ago over the controversial exhibition, 'Sensation: Young British artists from the Saatchi Collection' – The mayor was especially outraged by 'The Holy Virgin Mary,' a painting by Chris Ofili, who used, among other materials, elephant dung...polls showed that both of New York residents and a nationwide sample were against shutting down the exhibit..."

C. McGuigan, M. Malone, R. Sawhill, G. Beals – Newsweek

Any one, and/or every one, to actually "do" whatever they want – whenever they want to do it, and to whomever they want to do it to, and with public funds also.

And – remember, which is only –

"A Declaration by the Representatives of the United States of America:

We hold these truths to be self-evident: that all men are created equal; that they are endowed by their Creator with CERTAIN [*inherent and*] inalienable rights; that among these are life, liberty, and the pursuit of happiness; that to secure these rights, governments are instituted among men, deriving their just powers from the consent of the governed..."

Exactly backwards, and exactly a self-evident truth also.

And: in Reality, and while according to The American Constitution too, which is the real applicable function *of* The Truly Idealist Democratic Society – The Declaration of Independence, and The American Mind, anybody – ANY BODY, who does forcibly expose The Child to –

"Police: Girl Chained To Bed For 5 Years –

Police in (a) Southern California town have discovered and freed a 6-year-old girl who they believe spent almost all her life – five years – chained to a bed in a filthy room filled with human waste, officials said yesterday – The girl, found in a fetal position and apparently unable to speak other than by grunts and moans, was found by police Tuesday after the county sheriff's department received an anonymous call believed to be from a neighbor – Her mother, and grandfather – were being held on suspicion of child endangerment..."

Reuters – Philadelphia Inquirer – Thursday September 9, 1999

The Reality of a schizophrenic environment: of any kind, does not become labeled a "genius," they go to jail: they are put inside a prison, and to protect – TO PROTECT, the sanctity of the innocence of The Child. While only the single most contemptuous society, as in the entire history of mankind, would actually simply place it: schizophrenia, inside an art museum park, and force the child to be exposed to it: and/or brainwash the child, into believing that it: schizophrenia – chaos – discord – pain and death and suffering too, is the very definition of intelligence. And too, continue to believe that God – The God, and any God, would bless them for what they did do to the Child. And, again and of course, no –

"He said to his disciples, 'obstacles are sure to come, but alas for the one who provides them! It would be better for him to be thrown into the sea with a millstone put around his neck than he should lead astray a single one of these little ones. Watch yourselves!"
Luke 17: 1-3

He does not.
And too remember, everything is exactly backwards, and so that not only does He: The God, not "bless" it, but He does –

"The Pharisees, who loved money, heard all this and laughed at him. He said to them, 'You are the very ones who pass yourselves off as virtuous in people's sight, but God knows your hearts. For what is thought highly of by men is loathsome in the sight of God."
Luke 16: 14-11

Actually "loathe" it: ALL OF IT. And – too, He: The God, does actually –

"For I tell you, if your virtue goes no deeper than that of the scribes and Pharisees, you will never get into the kingdom of heaven."
Matthew 5: 20

Condemn it: all of it.
And remember, which would include all escaping of Reality: ALL OF IT. While including: the lawlessness – the discord – the chaos – the spectacle – the entertainment – the television – the movies – the theatre – the novels – the spectator sporting events – the amusement parks – the art museum parks – the theme parks – the spectacle event parks – the grandiosely and deliberately styled automobiles – the trains and airplanes – the excessively simplistic, and histrionic and monochromatic and Romanticized, musical sounds, the worshiping of worldly gods: the television stars – the movie stars – the worldly god stars – the boy band stars – the girl band stars – the pop icon band stars – the composer stars, and the musician stars. The grandiosely and deliberately styled tangible form masses of any and/or all kinds: the parties and aristocratic environments – the money – the worldly power – the complacency – the apathy – the truly humanistic brain death: The Apple – the living in ignorance of Reality: The Mind of God made manifest. All of the allowed exposure to purely psychopathic, and/or schizophrenic, dopamine biochemical inducing stimulus, functioning as pure *pleasure* only: He does condemn all of it. And remember, so says –

"Enter by the narrow gate, since the road that leads to perdition is wide and spacious, and many take it; but it is a narrow gate and a hard road that leads to life, and only a few find it."
Matthew 7: 13-14

Only the Son of God: again. And –

"One of the scribes who had listened to them debating and had observed how well Jesus answered them, now came up and put a question to him, 'Which is the first of all the commandments?' Jesus replied, 'This is the first: *Listen, Israel, the Lord our God is the one Lord, and you must love the Lord your God with all your heart, with all your soul, with all your mind and with all your strength.* The second is this: You must love your neighbor as yourself. There is no greater commandment than these."
Mark 12: 28-32

Again. And –

"When the Son of Man comes in his glory, escorted by all the angels, then he will take his seat on his throne of glory. All the nations will be assembled before him and he will separate men one from another as the shepherd separates sheep from goats. He will place the sheep on his right hand and the goats on his left. Then the King will say to those on his right hand, 'Come, you whom my Father has blessed, take for your heritage the kingdom prepared for you since the foundation of the world. For I was hungry and you gave me food; I was thirsty and you gave me drink; I was a stranger and you made me welcome; naked and you clothed me, sick and you visited me, in prison and you came to see me.' Then the virtuous will say to him in reply, 'Lord, when did we see you hungry and feed you; or thirsty and give you drink? When did we see you a stranger and make you welcome; naked and clothe you; sick or in prison and go to see you?' And the King will answer, 'I tell you solemnly, in so far as you did this to one of the least of these brothers of mine, you did it to me.' Next he will say to those on his left hand, 'Go away from me, with your curse upon you, to the eternal fire prepared for the devil and his angels. For I was hungry and you never gave me food; I was thirsty and you never gave me anything to drink; I was a stranger and you never made me welcome, naked and you never clothed me, sick and in prison and you never visited me.' Then it will be their turn to ask, 'Lord, when did we see you hungry or thirsty, a stranger or naked, sick or in prison, and did not come to your help?' Then he will answer, 'I tell you solemnly, in so far as you neglected to do this to one of the least of these, you neglected to do it to me.' And they will go away to eternal punishment, and the virtuous to eternal life."
Matthew 25: 31-46

Again.

And, remember, 20th century scientific research says, that —

"Clinically, there is evidence that the prefrontal cortex by looking inward, so to speak, obtains the gut feeling for identifying with another individual. In other words: empathy — Through its centers for vision, hearing, and bodily sensations, we traffic with the external world."
The 3-Pound Universe — Judith Hooper and Dick Teresi

They: the majority which has been affected, could not care less. It is actually a neurophysiological impossibility for them to care about anything, except for their very own selves. And too remember, when this: "U. S. ATTACKED — Hijacked Planes Destroy Trade Towers, Hit Pentagon; Thousands Feared Dead," did actually occur, it did actually function as the overdose, for the majority. Which is, remember, while there simply are no images of things being projected all throughout, and within, our minds, and parallel functioning central nervous systems. But only simultaneously relative fundamental frequency modulations: A "linear code" of 1's and 0's, actually functioning as: harmony and/or 11111, or chaos and/or 10010, and biochemical inductions too. And so that, when this: "U. S. ATTACKED — Hijacked Planes Destroy Trade Towers, Hit Pentagon; Thousands Feared Dead," did occur, it was the absolute pinnacle of, and/or the ultimate "dose," of —

"There are two essential yet complementary aspects of this new vision of time which are as striking in contrast as heaven and hell. Heaven is ruled by dynamical equations that are reversible and 'timeless'; their simplicity ensures stability for eternity. Hell is more akin to the real world, where fluctuations, uncertainty, and chaos reign..."
The Arrow of Time — Peter Coveney and Roger Highfield

Chaos made manifest: actually functioning as 10010. And/or, the ultimate dose of escaping universally applicable, and harmoniously proportioned, Reality. Which is while actually effectually functioning as Omnidimensional Time *made manifest*, and/or The Eternal Harmony made manifest: The Mind of God made manifest, while actually functioning as; "Heaven is ruled by dynamical equations that are reversible and 'timeless'; their simplicity ensures stability for eternity" — The Kingdom of Heaven. Which — remember, cannot possibly affect any individually affected victim of the con: only chaos can, and/or 10010. And which this: "U. S. ATTACKED — Hijacked Planes Destroy Trade Towers, Hit Pentagon; Thousands Feared Dead," was the ultimate dose of, and/or the overdose of. Which is exactly why —

"United They Stood, for an Awfully Long Time —
...United We Stand signaled American entertainment's return to its old reflexes, ready to piggyback pop marketing atop altruistic or patriotic impulses.

Musicians plugged their new albums, whether or not songs were germane to the events of Sept. 11 – Many of the performers apparently decided to oppose terror with exhilaration and insolence. P. Diddy called for 30 seconds of pure noise instead of a moment of silence: 'A lot of noise, the American way.' He was onto something. In American culture, vulgarity and vitality can be exactly the same and everybody gets a chance to join in – James Brown segued 'Sex Machine' into 'God Bless America' – The most bellicose performer was P. Diddy, wearing military-chic camouflage fatigues with a nonregulation diamond earring. He added a new verse to 'Come With Me,' which is set to the behemoth tread of 'Kashmir' by led Zeppelin – 'Check this out, terrorists,' he shouted. 'I want to fight you, love to fight you, can't stand nobody like you' – Then he waved a flag..."

Jon Pareles – The New York Times – Tuesday October 23, 2001

They did actually "do" absolutely nothing, like they did not "say": in words, they were going to do. They did say, in words, that they did not like chaos, and discord, and noise, and pain and death and suffering too. And too so that: within any Truly Idealist Democratic Society, they did realize, that it: any deviation from *a priori* Reality, and/or the purposeful manifestation of any noise, and/or discord, and/or chaos, was only a necessary evil, and only as an absolute last resort. And, of course, they did only exactly contradict, what they did say in words. And – too remember, which is exactly simply because, to them: The Majority, words cannot possibly mean anything: "to" them. And they also – and simultaneously, cannot affect them. Because: remember, nothing can: "AFFECT" them, except for; "A lot of noise, the American way.' He was onto something. In American culture, vulgarity and vitality can be exactly the same" – the noise: the chaos – the discord – the spectacle – the orgy – the purely psychopathic, and schizophrenic, dopamine biochemical inducing stimulus, functioning as pure *pleasure* only, and/or The Apple, is the only thing that can cause an effect within them. Which is also exactly why –

"Harry Potter and the Box Office of Gold –
The fledging wizard with the zigzag scar rode his Quidditch broom to the biggest movie opening of all time this weekend as 'Harry Potter and the Sorcerer's Stone' earned an estimated $93.5 million in its first three days, making it all but assured of breaking the $100 million mark Monday afternoon – 'There aren't enough adjectives to describe how spectacular this opening weekend for Potter has been,' said Paul Dergarabedian, chairman of Exhibitor Relations – 'It's one of those few times when you don't have to add a lot of qualifiers. It's the biggest opening weekend of all time, bar none..."

Rick Lyman – The New York Times – Monday November 19, 2001

They are – NOW, consuming record amounts of it: absolutely abstracted romanticized escapism. Actually functioning as, pure; "It's one of those few times when you don't have to add a lot of qualifiers" – uncut schizophrenic dopamine biochemical inducing effectual stimulus, functioning as pure *pleasure* only, and/or The Apple.

And – too, which is even after they did plainly admit, that –

"Gossip Holds Its Tongue –

Two nights after the attack on the World Trade Center, Harrison Ford walked into Da Silvano, a favorite restaurant in Greenwhich Village, with a woman on each arm. Mr. Ford has been a constant source of celebrity gossip because of his separation from his wife of 18 years. But what would have turned heads two weeks ago went totally unremarked – New Yorkers, jaded by celebrity, seem thoroughly tired of it for now. They are also shrugging off the industry that both sustains celebrity and feeds off it: gossip, as natural a part of New York as designer martinis and trophy wives. In the days immediately after the attack, the city's professional tattletales fell appropriately silent – in a chastened statement, the eminent Liz Smith, whose syndicated column also appears in the Post and about 70 other newspapers, complained to readers of the trivial nature of her work at such a time. 'I want to go somewhere and volunteer,' she wrote. To hell with gossip and entertainment' – 'We all seem so superficial to have ever cared,' said a woman whose name often appears in gossip columns and asked that it not be used. 'It all seems shameful and stupid, that we had such tiny lives' – Gossip's significant position in New York culture stems from its ability to separate the insiders from the outsiders,' said Leo Braudy, a historian (and) author – 'Are you helping the world by passing on gossip and wondering who a better sexual partner for Anne Heche is?' he asked. 'No. But I don't think the events have changed celebrity and gossip forever. I can only hope it gives us a sense of proportion. This is the fall. A fall of innocence. A fall into a different kind of awareness."

Alex Kuczynski – The New York Times – Sunday September 23, 2001

They did fully realize that this *is* our Innocence Lost: purposefully allowed exposure to absolutely abstracted, and psychopathic – and/or schizophrenic, dopamine biochemical inducing stimulus, actually functioning as pure *pleasure* only. And they did say, that they fully realize, that "we": our entire global society, have passed the Point of no return: that we have fallen into a black hole of truly humanistic dysfunction, and which has – exactly, "consumed us," and led us on a collision course with our very own destiny. And too they did simply say in words, that they do: NOW, fully understand just how; "We all seem so superficial to have ever cared – It all seems shameful and stupid" – filled with remorse they are supposed to be feeling, for their very own selves. But, remember, they are only capable of functioning while as in a; "Psychopaths tend to live day-to-day and to change their plans frequently. They give little serious thought to the future and worry about it even less – psychopaths sometimes verbalize remorse but then contradict themselves in words or actions" – purely psychopathic manner: at best. And a; "Robert G. Heath: 'The primary symptom of schizophrenia isn't

384

hallucinations or delusions,' he tells us. It's a defect in the pleasure response –
schizophrenics are extremely insensitive to pain and (are) unreactive to other sensory
stimuli, as well" – purely schizophrenic manner: at worst, and as the majority has
been affected too: remember?

Which is exactly simply because: as they actually have been proportionally
affected as through the passing of time, right at about the time of the overdose, and
which was the; "U. S. ATTACKED – Hijacked Planes Destroy Trade Towers, Hit
Pentagon; Thousands Feared Dead" – attack, functioning as an actual schizophrenic
inarticulate cry for attention, the majority was – too and while as through a lifetime's
worth of allowed exposure to purely psychopathic dopamine biochemical inducing
stimulus, beginning to become capable of functioning while as in a –

"Narrowing Search on Schizophrenia –
Schizophrenia – is characterized by apathy, delusions, disorganized thinking,
and disconnected social interactions..."
Shanker Vendantum – The Philadelphia Inquirer – Friday April 28, 2000

Purely schizophrenic manner.
Which was, as their –

"As shock of Sept. 11 fades, subtle changes linger in U. S. –
Slightly more than a hundred days after terrorism shocked a complacent
America, fear has given way to quiet resolve – Americans are turning back to the
security of the familiar – the comforts of home..."
Stephen Thomma – Philadelphia Inquirer – Wednesday December 26, 2001

Complacency, and/or insolence, and/or indifference, and/or apathy, did give
way to "quiet resolve": and/or contempt, and/or disrespect, and/or complete and
utter brain death: schizophrenia – the lawlessness, the discord, the chaos, the pain,
and the death and suffering too. And to simply become capable of causing an affect
of any kind: within all of their individually affected minds, and parallel functioning
central nervous systems, and within which there are contained no images of things.
And – remember, which is exactly why –

"A Shock Grows in Brooklyn –
A fiery controversy over a museum's new show brings New York's Mayor
out slugging: The mayor blew up three weeks ago over the controversial exhibition,
'Sensation: Young British artists from the Saatchi Collection' – The mayor was
especially outraged by 'The Holy Virgin Mary,' a painting by Chris Ofili, who used,
among other materials, elephant dung..."
C. McGuigan, M. Malone, Ray Sawhill, G. Beals – Newsweek

They do actually have it: the purist of schizophrenia, hanging in their art museum parks. And which is: remember, exactly because that is – only exactly, what is "inside" all of their electrical potential mass minds, and parallel functioning central nervous systems, and within which there are contained no images of things, but only schizophrenic everything: within their minds. Which is exactly why, they do believe: within all of their individually affected minds, that "it": schizophrenia, is *the* "definition of intelligence," and which is, of course, only exactly backwards in neuroscientific Reality. And too, which is exactly why –

"An Artist Who's Grateful For Elephants –

For a decade Mya, Layang and Dilberta have been the unheralded contributors to Chris Ofili's rise to fame. The three Asian elephants, visited nearly every month by Mr. Ofili, the British-born painter, replenish the supply of dung that he uses in nearly all his paintings, including the one of the black Virgin Mary that enraged Mayor Rudolph W. Giuliani when it appeared in the 'Sensation' exhibition at the Brooklyn Museum of Art in 1999...In retrospect, Mr. Ofili said that it did not consider Mr. Giuliani's view reflective of local sentiment. 'New York didn't treat me badly,' he said. It was a certain New Yorker that treated the painting in a way he considered appropriate..."

Carol Vogel – The New York Times – Tuesday February 21, 2002

Everybody can relate to him: Mr. Ofili, the person who was actually given money: by the common man masses of the United States of America, to simply "throw some shit" upon the face of the Mother of God, and while making manifest his own personally affected schizophrenic inarticulate cry for attention, and theirs too. Which is as this word: relate, does mean: "to have reference or relation – to establish a social or sympathetic relationship with a person or thing."

Because, EVERYBODY wants to defecate upon the Mother of God, and EVERYBODY wants to rape the Collective Consciousness of Mankind, and EVERYBODY wants to simply project their own personally affected neurophysiological dysfunction upon the Collective Consciousness of Mankind too. And too, EVERYBODY wants to make manifest personally affected schizophrenic inarticulate cries for attention, and EVERYBODY wants to –

"The King Of PAIN: Jackass –

Johnny Knoxville Went From Cheerful Slacker To MTV's Hottest New Star When He Discovered A Simple Principle: It's Not Funny Until Someone Gets Hurt:

'Well, I guess I don't really intellectualize it,' he says thickly, and with that he's ambling out the door, moving toward a big Ford Van piled with today's props of self-destruction. Later on, he'll maybe end up in the emergency room, maybe in the courthouse, maybe in both. But you can be sure of one thing: By the time the day's over, there will have been very little deep thinking done by (P.J.) Clapp. As Clapp himself sometimes likes to say, 'F- that. Let's get some chili and beer, and then I'll go hump a cow' – 'We're working toward a common goal,' Clapp says, 'doing what most people wished they could do – Over soup, Clapp says he doesn't really enjoy talking about himself but is doing the best he can – 'I really beat myself up over things as a teenager,' he says. 'I was always pretty much smiling on the outside, but inside I was a little bit of a mess. I remember having dreams of being in a public place and my mother not recognizing me. I was really self-conscious about my looks and my personality. I mean, starting school each year, I felt I had the class on my side. But by the end of the year, I'd just worn everyone out, throwing insults and pulling pranks. I needed to tone it down, but I couldn't. I had to keep going. I don't know why…This is mind-pecking stuff, of course – the way Clapp has reconstructed his childhood in his adulthood. And it keeps right on coming – Maybe none of it means anything – Or maybe – calling Dr. Freud! – Bam's not the only one trying to topple a dad – Back in the van, everyone is yelling and screaming and laughing. Clapp is at the center of the hubbub. 'That reporter, God bless her, but what an idiot,' he shouts happily. A moment later, he's fumbling in his pocket. He pulls out his inhaler, inserts the white plastic barrel between his lips and puffs. If Clapp's mom were here, she'd be worried sick. But it's best not to think about that. The world is still laughing…"

Erik Hedgegarrd – Rolling Stone – February 1, 2001

Laugh all the way to their worldly graves too: rather than to face-up to Reality that it is. Because: remember, that: facing-up to their own personally affected neuroscientific Reality, is –

"A Painkiller's Double Life As an Illegal Street Drug –

In a scene of creepy voyerism and joltingly effective reporting, a 22-year-old named Troy S-, who looks like any middle-class college student in the red sweatshirt and baseball cap, sits in his messy apartment in Maine and prepares to stick a needle into his arm as the cameras watch – Later (we observe) him in a hospital bed, sedated so he will not be aware of what we see: his body twitchs as it goes through withdrawal..."

Carynn James – The New York Times – Wednesday December 12, 2001

Simply too painful, and which is, and simultaneously, as – remember, they do actually; "He pulls out his inhaler, inserts the white plastic barrel between his lips and puffs. If Clapp's mom were here, she'd be worried sick" – "need" it: escaping Reality, to simply enable them to breathe.

And remember, which is exactly as –

"Then the disciples went up to him and asked, 'Why do you talk to them in parables? 'Because,' he replied, 'the mysteries of the kingdom of heaven are revealed to you, but they are not revealed to them. For anyone who has will be given more, and he will have more than enough; but from anyone who has not, even what he has will be taken away. The reason I talk to them in parables is that they look without seeing and listen without hearing or understanding. So in their case this prophecy of Isaiah is being fulfilled:

You will listen and listen again, but not understand,
see and see again, but not perceive.
For the heart of this nation has grown course,
their ears are dull of hearing, and they have shut their eyes,
for fear they should see with their eyes,
hear with their ears,
understand with their heart,
and be converted
and be healed by me.

But happy are your eyes because they see, your ears because they hear! I tell you solemnly, many prophets and holy men longed to see what you see, and never saw it; to hear what you hear, and never heard it."
Matthew 13: 10-17

The Son of God did explain.

They: The Majority, have actually regressed back to point time zero, of their own personally affected existence within Reality. As they have become capable of experiencing truly humanistic brain death, for their own selves. And they have – and simultaneously, become capable of consciously cognizing zero Time *made manifest*, as they have actually become neurophysiologically incapable of maintaining a single cognizable point time zero, within their individually affected minds, and parallel functioning central nervous systems. And they have – and simultaneously, become only capable of functioning while as in a purely psychopathic, and/or schizophrenic, manner. And they have – and simultaneously, allowed their very own selves to become absolutely addicted to excessive amounts of absolutely abstracted, and purely psychopathic, and/or schizophrenic, dopamine biochemical inducing stimulus, actually functioning as pure *pleasure* only: which they simply can not live without. And so they have, and simultaneously, actually lost control over their very own selves, and as they have, too, actually Passed the point of no return, and fallen into a black hole of neurophysiological dysfunction. And so that for them: The Majority, facing-up to their own personally affected Reality, would simply be too painful. And which is exactly why –

"A Shock Grows in Brooklyn –
A fiery controversy over a museum's new show brings New York's Mayor out slugging: The mayor blew up three weeks ago over the controversial exhibition, 'Sensation: Young British artists from the Saatchi Collection' – The mayor was especially outraged by the Holy Virgin Mary, a painting by Chris Ofili, who used, among other materials, elephant dung...polls showed that both New York residents and a nationwide sample were against shutting down the exhibit..."
C. McGuigan, M. Malone, R. Sawhill, G. Beals – Newsweek

They: The Majority, did not just sit idly by, and allow another human being to actually "throw some shit" upon the face of the Mother of God. They did actually "finance it": the single most offensive assault upon the Collective Consciousness of Mankind, while as in the entire history of Mankind. Which was as they did finance the manifestation of the purest of chaos, and/or discord, and/or 10010, and/or pain and death and suffering too.

Which is simply because, if they did not allow it, then they just might – they just might, have to admit that they too do have a problem: within their own minds. And too – then, they just might – just might, have to face-up to their own reality also, and then they just might – just *might*, have to begin to take back control over their very own selves, and – *then*, they just might – just *might*, have to begin to deny their own selves allowed access to *their* drugs, and/or their chaos, and discord, and 10010. And which is exactly what watching television is: in scientific Reality, and too it is exactly what all of it "is." And while including the movies; the theatre; the novels; the entertainment; the spectacle events; the spectator sporting events; the art museum parks; the amusement parks; the theme parks; the spectator sporting event parks, and the spectacle event parks: all excessive tangible form mass stimulus of any and/or all kinds. The grandiosely, and deliberately, styled, automobiles, and trains, and airplanes – the excessively simplistic, and histrionic, and monochromatic, and romanticized, musical sounds – the worshiping worldly gods: the television stars; the movie stars; the worldly god stars; the boy band stars; the girl band stars; the pop icon band stars; the composer stars, and the musician stars. The grandiosely, and deliberately, styled, tangible form masses of any any/or all kinds: the fine fabrics; the excessive clothing; the diamonds; the gold; the silver; the fatty tasting foods and sweet tasting foods. The alcoholic and caffeine laced beverages. The computers; the Internet; the Virtual reality; the dot-coms; the cell phones, and video recorders. The parties and aristocratic environments: the money; the worldly power; the complacency; the apathy; the abstract knowledge; the truly humanistic being brain death; the living in ignorance of Reality; the orgy; the heroin; The Apple: all of the allowed exposure to absolutely abstracted, and purely psychopathic, and/or schizophrenic, dopamine biochemical inducing stimulus, actually functioning as pure *pleasure* only it is, and only 10010 too, and/or chaos, and/or "hell made manifest." And too remember, it is a –

"There are two essential yet complementary aspects of this new vision of time which are as striking in contrast as heaven and hell. Heaven is ruled by dynamical equations that are reversible and 'timeless'; their simplicity ensures stability for eternity. Hell is more akin to the real world, where fluctuations, uncertainty and chaos reign..."
The Arrow of Time – Peter Coveney and Roger Highfield

"Scientific fact."
And remember, the only thing that is exactly NOT simply functioning while

as in a purely psychopathic, and/or a purely schizophrenic, manner, is –

"One thing has become clear to scientists: memory is absolutely crucial to our consciousness – 'There's almost nothing you do, from perception to thinking, that doesn't draw continuously on your memory. (And) It can't be otherwise, since there really is no such thing as a present (while) memory provides a personal context, a sense of self and a sense of familiarity – past and present and a frame for the future' – But memory is not a single phenomenon. 'We don't have a memory system in the brain' – 'We have memory systems, each playing a different role' – All of these different systems of memory are ultimately stored in the brain's cortex – When everything is going right, these different systems work together seamlessly..."
Michael D. Lemonick – Smart Genes? – Time – September 13, 1999

Consciously employing the use of our truly humanistic, and universally applicable, simultaneously relative Omnidimensional empirical self-consciousness. Which is while actually simultaneously consciously cognizing truly humanistic simultaneously relative Omnidimensional Time *made manifest*. And too which is while *only* it: truly humanistic simultaneously relative Omnidimensional Time *made manifest*, *is* capable of functioning as "a" truly humanistic simultaneously relative, and simultaneously relative multidimensional, "effectual communicative apparatus." And which is while it: truly humanistic simultaneously relative Omnidimensional Time *made manifest*, is only capable of –

"The sensations which arise from muscle, joint and tendon are conveniently grouped under one heading not because of their anatomical source, but because they collaborate to provide the brain with a distinctive form of information – None of this information could be put to use unless it was firmly located against a fixed horizon; it would float about weightlessly in a vacuum. If you regard the body as an aircraft flying in a thick cloud, the proprioceptive system re-creates a scale-model of a machine on the instrument board..."
The Body in Question – Jonathan Miller

Effectually functioning as simultaneously relative to/from, and within, a truly humanistic – and simultaneously relative, single cognizable point time zero. Which is located simultaneously within truly humanistic simultaneously relative space/time, as it is within –

"Candace Pert: I see the brain in terms of quantum mechanics – the brain is just a receiver, an amplifier, a little wet minireceiver for collective reality. We make maps, but we should never confuse the map with the territory' (While) the ratio of frontal core may be one index of evolutionary advancement – What the frontal lobes 'control' is something like awareness, or self-awareness – Do these lobes govern some essential feature of humanness or even godliness, as some scientists have suggested? If God speaks to man, if man speaks to God,' neuroscientist Candace Pert tells us, 'it would be through the frontal lobes' – Stephen LaBarge: 'And it's capable of what look like miraculous things, so miraculous that we're tempted to say it's divine, that it's not natural."

The 3-Pound Universe – Judith Hooper and Dick Teresi

A truly humanistic being's simultaneously relative: quantum electrodynamically functioning, electrical potential mass of a mind, and parallel functioning central nervous system: as it is within truly humanistic simultaneously relative Omnidimensional Reality, which is while actually functioning "as" truly humanistic simultaneously relative Omnidimensional Time *made manifest*. And which is while actually –

"The equivalent of the machine language of the brain, in (Alan) Gevin's view, is very complex electromagnetic field configurations, with every fine modulation in amplitude, wave shape and spatial distribution – And after several years of painstaking mapping of these psychic never-never lands, discovered an extraordinary thing: The mind of man contains only so many visions – four basic, recurrent geometrical forms..."

The 3-Pound Universe – Judith Hooper and Dick Teresi

Effectually functioning as consciously cognizing truly humanistic simultaneously relative Omnidimensional patterns in space/time, and/or consciously cognizing Omnidimensional Time *made manifest*. And/or –

"One way to think about this new view is to imagine spatial relationships as a kind of universal language that the brain uses no matter what specific language – social, moral, engineering – we are using at the moment – (George) Lakoff believes he can tie this mental language to the physical structure of the brain and its maps – 'When you think about dynamic structure, you begin to think there are a lot of things that are analogous with life. Life is more pattern(s) in space/time than it is a set of particular physical things."

Jim Jubak – In The Image of the Brain

LIFE.
And, remember, as was exactly explained by –

"Enter by the narrow gate, since the road that leads to perdition is wide and spacious, and many take it; but it is a narrow gate and a hard road that leads to life, and only a few find it."

Matthew 7: 13-14

The Son of God.

But – remember too, there is only one way to only begin to become neurophysiologically capable of consciously cognizing simultaneously relative patterns in Omnidimensional space/time, and/or Life. And that is while actually going out into truly humanistic simultaneously relative Omnidimensional Reality each and every day, and for a lifetime too, and actually practicing our scales: of Reality. And which is while capable of –

"If humans are less robotlike than salamanders or ducks, it's not because we have no wired-in behaviors. In fact, we have quite a few. What makes the difference is the ratio of 'unwired' to wired-in gray matter, because neurons that are not committed at birth to a set function, are available for learning, for modification."
The 3-Pound Universe – Judith Hooper and Dick Teresi

Causing permanently affected changes, within all of the individually affected minds, and parallel functioning central nervous systems: only one way or the other.
And again remember, they: the majority, did exactly not go out each, and every, day, and Carry their crosses, and/or practice their scales of Reality. So they did not begin to become capable of causing permanently affected, and truly humanistic, simultaneously relative multidimensional synaptic capabilities: within their individually affected minds, and parallel functioning central nervous systems. And they did – and instead, simply continue to access excessive amounts of absolutely abstracted, and purely psychopathic – and/or purely schizophrenic, dopamine biochemical inducing stimulus, actually functioning as pure *pleasure* only. And they did begin to regress back to point time zero, of their own personally affected existence within Reality. And they did –

"For anyone who has will be given more, and he will have more than enough; but from anyone who has not, even what he has will be taken away."
Matthew 13: 12-13

Only experience truly humanistic brain death for their own selves to be in possession of *only*.
And they did simply –

"Each of us lives within the universe – the prison – of his own brain. Projecting from it are millions of fragile sensory nerve fibers, in groups, uniquely adapted to sample the energetic states of the world about us: heat, light, force, and chemical compositions. That is all we ever know directly; all else is logical inference..."
The 3-Pound Universe – Judith Hooper and Dick Teresi

Become a prisoner of their own personally affected electrical potential mass of a mind, and parallel functioning central nervous system. Within which, there cannot possibly be any Time *made manifest* whatsoever: it is a neurophysiological impossibility. And which is as they have been –

"What is a black hole? For astronomical purposes it behaves as a small, highly condensed dark 'body.' But it is not really a material body in the ordinary sense. It possesses no ponderable surface. A black hole is a region of empty space – What is known as a space/time singularity – a place where physical laws, as presently understood, must cease to apply..."
　　　Roger Penrose – Black Holes – The World Treasury of Physics, Astronomy and Mathematics

Consumed by the global dysfunction, which is our 21st century Reality. And they actually have allowed their very own selves to become capable of falling into a black hole of misery for their own selves to experience, while along with their truly humanistic brain death too of course.
　　　And remember, "Misery loves company," which is exactly why they did –

"Bewitched By a Book –
They're lining up for Harry Potter author for weeks: Keith (has) begged his mom to take him to the kid event of the season, even though it will mean waiting in line with hundreds, maybe thousands, of other young fans so they can meet their idol – for a few seconds...the three small bookstores that will host the celebrity author say they have been inundated with calls from parents – to handle the anticipated throngs, the stores have hired security guards, a first for a children's book signing..."
　　　Kathy Boccella – The Philadelphia Inquirer – Saturday October 9, 1999

Simply hand their children's souls over to their worldly gods: to be consumed by them also, while long with their very own selves. And which was as they did actually teach their children, and/or program their children, to worship, and/or to "idolize," their psychopathic worldly gods too.
　　　But – remember, that's not the only thing they did: to their very own children. Because: remember, they did actually –

"Media Fill Up the Children's Hours –
They aren't building tree houses. They aren't playing hopscotch. They aren't stringing tin cans together. So what are today's 2-to-18-year-olds doing? – If a study released yesterday by the Henry J. Kaiser Family Foundation holds true, there's a good chance Jane and Junior are holed up alone in their bedrooms watching TV for hours at a time – The study, found that children are consuming vast amounts of media – almost 40 hours a week..."
　　　Jennifer Weiner – The Philadelphia Inquirer – Thursday November 18, 1999

Give their children an unlimited supply of –

"At a purely chemical level (just as the injection of) heroin triggers release of dopamine – every experience humans find enjoyable – embracing a lover or savoring chocolate – amounts to little more than an explosion of dopamine in the nucleus accumbens, as exhilarating and ephemeral as a firecracker..."
Addicted – J. Madeleine Nash – Time – May 5, 1997

DOPAMINE: and/or heroin.
And which was while actually –

"Drugs are like sledgehammers,' observes Dr. Eric nestler of the Yale University School of Medicine. 'They profoundly alter many pathways' – the realization that dopamine may be a common endpoint of all those pathways represents a signal advance. Provocative – the dopamine hypothesis provides a basic framework for understanding (what does) cause a serious behavioral disorder..."
Addicted – J. Madeleine Nash – Time – May 5, 1997

Destroying their children's cerebral cortices: creating a "serious behavioral disorder," for their very own children.
But that's not the worst thing that they did do: to their very own children.
Because, remember how there are exactly –

"...Many of the provinces of the brain (are) topographical maps of projections of the sensory fields which they represent – the same geometrical decorum applies to all projections – physical events impinging on the sensory surface are transformed into the characteristic digital language of the brain – a linear code dictates the construction of the visible object."
Jonathan Miller – The Body in Question

No images of things being projected all throughout, and within, our truly humanistic simultaneously relative electrical potential mass minds, and parallel functioning central nervous systems, but only a "linear code" of the *a priori* information, while actually functioning as simultaneously relative to/from, and within, a single cognizable point time zero. And remember how we went out every day, and practiced our scales of simultaneously relative Reality, and how: *while* we actually were practicing our scales of Reality, we did begin to become capable of affecting all of those simultaneously relative functions, within our electrical potential mass minds, and parallel functioning central nervous systems. And how, and simultaneously, all of those individually completed functions, actually did effectually function as: *simply*, a variation of the same exact function. Which was – remember, simply a different variation of the base of the width: *of* individually completed geometrical formations, and/or individually completed non-tangible form pyramids, and while being projected all throughout, and within, our truly humanistic simultaneously relative electrical potential mass minds, and parallel function central

394

nervous systems: as simultaneously relative to/from, and within, a single cognizable point time zero. And how: as we were actually moving our bodies all throughout, and within, simultaneously relative space/time, and while practicing our scales of truly humanistic simultaneously relative Reality, we were capable of actually seeing everything: every "thing," only begin to become visible in the simultaneously relative distance, as a single cognizable point. And remember too, as Leonardo da Vinci did explain, while occurring within a human being's mind: nothing can "give rise" to that point. And remember how the apparent image of that point: of perceivable tangible form mass stimulus, and/or noun, did appear to "grow larger" *as* we "moved" in a purposefully affected direction, towards its position within simultaneously relative space/time, and how that apparent size, and growth proportional equivalency, does always in Reality – ALWAYS "IN" "REALITY," effectually occur while as "in" a "harmoniously proportioned manner." And which is while perceivable Reality, does always – ALWAYS, vary inversely by the square of the distance: while capable of causing an exactly harmoniously proportioned affect, within a human being's mind, and parallel functioning central nervous system. And which was while capable of –

"At birth, a baby's brain contains about 100 million neurons, the brain cells that cary electrical messages through the brain. Each one can produce up to 15,000 synapses, or connections, to the other cells. Those synapses are the key to healthy development and learning – At birth a baby is flooded with sensory experiences (and) These experiences cause the brain to create trillions of connections, essentially 'wiring' the brain for learning – Repeated early experiences determine how the brain is wired. Those synapses that have been activated frequently by virtue of repeated early experence tend to become permanent; the synapses that have not been used at all, or often enough, tend to become eliminated..."
Fertile Minds – J. Madeleine Nash – Time – February 3, 1997

Causing neurophysiological changes: within all of those individually affected children's electrical potential mass minds, and parallel functioning central nervous systems. And which is –

"It should be stressed that transmitters (and their regulators) are semantically as well as syntactically functional – As they synaptic signals, transmitters obviously alter communication and function. Consequently, transmitters are not simply indifferent or neutral storehouses of environmental information. Rather, environmental alteration of long-term transmitter function *ipso facto* alters function of the nervous system."
Ira Black – Molecular Memory Mechanisms, Synapses Circuits and the Beginnings of Memory – Gary Lynch

PERMANENTLY AFFECTED.

Now, go turn on your television set, and wait for approximately a second or two. And you will then "see": within your three-dimensional electrical potential mass of a mind and parallel functioning central nervous system, and wherein there are actually contained NO "images of things" – but only a linear code of information, the non-tangible form "image" OF a three-dimensional tangible form point-mass noun, appear: AND/OR "POP-UP," exactly "where" it should NOT be "within" truly humanistic simultaneously relative space/time. Which is exactly the manifestation, and the function, of a "shift of angle," and/or a "shift of scale," and/or a "shift of location," and/or a "shift of tone," and/or a "shift of matter," and/or a "shift of image," and/or a "shift of status," and/or –

"Joyce Kovelman and Arnold Scheibel of UCLA's Brain Research Institute spotted a weird cellular 'disarray' in the schizophrenic brains (and not in the matched controls) – A schizophrenic's dopamine neurons would start to fire in two different rhythms and rapidly become uncoupled – The key to schizophrenia is chaotic fluctuations in dopamine production..."
The 3-Pound Universe – Judith Hooper and Dick Teresi

Schizophrenia: the only thing that these people did give their children the key to, was schizophrenia. These: The Majority, people, did *actually*; "Many of the provinces of the brain are topographical maps of projections of the sensory fields which they represent – the same geometrical decorum applies to all projections – a linear code dictates the construction of the visible object" – "program" schizophrenia directly into their children's electrical potential mass minds, and parallel functioning central nervous systems: television is the very definition of schizophrenia.
And too and simultaneously, which was while they did give them only also –

"Hijacking the Brain Circuits With a Nickel Slot Machine –
Compulsive gambling, attendance at sporting events, vulnerability to telephone scams and exuberant investing in the stock market may not seem to have much in common. But neuroscientists have uncovered a common thread – Such behaviors, they say, rely on brain circuits that evolved to help animals assess rewards important to their survival, like food and sex – In navigating the world and deciding what is rewarding, humans are closer to zombies than sentient beings much of the time...the brain has evolved to shape itself, starting in infancy, according to what it encounters in the external world – As Dr. (P. Read) Montague explained, much of the world is predictable: buildings usually stay in one place, gravity makes objects fall – as children grow older their brains build internal models of everything they encounter, gradually learning to identify objects and to predict how they move through space and time – But if there is a surprise – a car suddenly runs a red light, the mismatch between what is expected and what is happening instantly shifts the brain into a new state (and) animals use these circuits to know what to attend to (while) The two circuits that have been studied most extensively involve how

396

animals and people assess rewards. Both involve a chemical called dopamine – The circuit was described in greater detail several years ago by Dr. Wolfram Schultz, a neuroscientist at Cambridge University in England, who tracked dopamine production in monkey's midbrains and experimented with various types of rewards, usually squirts of apple juice…"
Sandra Blakeslee – The New York Times – Tuesday February 19, 2002

The Apple, and which was while exactly creating unstable fluctuations in their chemical systems. And exactly because, each – and every, one of those functions: of a shift of angle, and/or a shift of scale, and/or a shift of location, and/or a shift of tone, and/or a shift the matter, and/or a shift of image, and/or a shift of status, and/or "shift" of any "thing," was – exactly, capable of; "But if there is a surprise – a car suddenly runs a red light – the mismatch between what is expected and what is happening instantly shifts the brain into a new state (and) animals use the circuits to know what to attend to" – causing a purposefully affected, and PURELY ANIMALISTIC, dopamine biochemical induction within all of those children's minds. And too, just as –

"The Musical Mind –
Music means nothing to Isabel Peretz's patients. The University of Montreal psychologist studies people who have suffered brain damage from a stroke or surgery and lost the ability to make sense of the simplest tune. To the most seriously affected, 'Happy Birthday To You' is a meaningless jumble of notes, and a Mozart sonata sounds no better or worse when it is played off key…As David Huron, a musicologist at Ohio State University, puts it, 'Music is weird' – The more scientists learn about it, the weirder it seems…Some evidence comes from scientists in Germany, who have found that even in people with no training in music, the brain is capable of sophisticated musical analysis. The faint magnetic signals emitted as neurons fire show that the brain gives a little start of surprise when a passage of music takes an unexpected turn…"
Tim Appenzeller – U.S. News & World Report

Atonality – polytonality – dissonance and discord is: capable of causing a purposefully affected dopamine biochemical induction, within a human being's parallel functioning mind and central nervous system, and unstable chemical fluctuations too. And/or too, so is the noise, and/or the chaos, and/or the television, and/or the movies, and/or the spectacle events, and/or the entertainment, and/or the spectator sporting events, and/or the art museum parks, and amusement parks, and theme parks, and spectator sporting event parks, and spectacle event parks. And/or the grandiosely, and deliberately styled, automobiles, trains and airplanes, and/or the excessively simplistic, and histrionic, and monochromatic, and romanticized, musical sounds, of any and/or all kinds. And/or the worshiping of worldly god stars: the boy band stars; the girl band stars; the pop icon band stars; the musician stars; the

397

movie stars, and the television stars. And/or, the grandiosely and deliberately styled tangible form masses of any and/or all kinds: the fine fabrics; the gold; the silver; the diamonds, and the alcoholic and caffeine laced beverages. And/or the –

"Teenage Overload, Or digital Dexterity?

When Colleen M- , a 17-year-old high school senior in Pearl River, N. Y., sits down at her home computer, her attention is not simply divided. It is generously and neatly distributed – While working recently on a paper for class on state drug laws, a project that involved not just writing but searching on the Web for information, Colleen checked e-mail on a running basis and kept up to eight Instant Messenger screens running, engaging in bursts of online conversation with friends about weekend plans. All this while listening to Faith Hill on her MP3 player and burning a CD – Colleen is an expert at multitasking, the human practice named for the computer term describing a machine's ability to run several programs at once..."
Katie Hafner – The New York Times – Thursday April 12, 2001

Purist of "schizophrenia": simultaneously allowed access to pure abstracted every "thing" – simultaneously, and/or "multitasking." And – too remember, which is the "orgy" only: of pure schizophrenic dopamine biochemical inducing stimulus, actually functioning as pure *pleasure* only, and/or The Apple.

And which is as they also –

"Learning That Goes Beyond Books –

New Yorker artist Baranby R-, clad in a paint-spattered apron, sounded distinctly like a football coach, even though he stood before a 12-foot canvas – 'Get aggressive! Bah! Bah! Bah!' R- Bellowed in a rat-a-tat rush, exhorting Ursinus College freshman Scott B-. Egged on, B- started to wield the brush boldly, almost punching at the canvas – The canvas under attack was a half-finished mish-mash of styles, an impressionistic rendition of Ralphael's 1511 fresco in the Vatican, *School of Athens*, which depicts sages from different epochs as colleagues in a timeless academy – beyond its function as a gathering place for intrigued students, R-'s modern rendition plays a larger role in an ambitious new experiment Ursinus has launched to create a shared academic experience for its freshmen – This fall, all 379 Ursinus freshmen are taking the same course, the 'Common Intellectual Experience.' In large groups of 16, the students are studying weighty texts – Genesis and Job, Buddhist scripture, works by Plato, Dante, Galileo – They're also studying the sea change in thinking during the Renaissance, when great thinkers rediscovered the valuable lessons of the ancient philosophers and scientists featured in Raphael's fresco – Ursinus faculty say they hope that by providing every freshman with a shared intellectual experience, academic discussions will spill over into the students non-class time – a real life re-creation of the fervent intellectual discourse depicted in Raphael's masterpiece – 'We wanted to expose all students to interdisciplinary types of thinking,' said program director Paul S-, – 'Basically, through these texts we try to explore questions like, 'What does it mean to be human?' and 'How should we live our lives? Said John V- , a creating writing professor – V's class tackled Buddhism last week. The religion's focus on disengaging from material desires was clearly a baffling concept for the students steeped in a culture of materialism and the American drive to achieve – 'If we have no desires, you won't be able to do anything,' said freshman Kimberly M-. 'If you have nothing to strive for, what is the reason to live?'..."

James M. O'Neill – The Philadelphia Inquirer – Tuesday October 10, 2000

Cannot even begin to understand, that there can exist anything besides the orgy, and/or The Apple, and/or pure schizophrenic dopamine biochemical inducing stimulus, functioning as pure *pleasure* only, it is actually a neurophysiological impossibility. And/or it is also too, a neurophysiological impossibility for the vast majority of this entire generation, to experience anything but unstable chemical fluctuations, within all of their individually affected minds, and parallel functioning central nervous systems. And/or it is also too, a neurophysiological impossibility for the vast majority of this entire generation, to consciously cognize any Time *made manifest*. And/or it is also too, a neurophysiological impossibility for the vast majority of this entire generation, to maintain a single simultaneously relative, and cognizable, point time zero: within all of their individually affected electrical potential mass minds, and parallel functioning central nervous systems. And/or it is also too, a neurophysiological impossibility for the vast majority of this entire generation, to function while as in a quantum dynamical manner: while as simultaneously relative to/from, and within, a truly humanistic, and universally applicable, single cognizable point time zero. And/or – and again, it is also too a neurophysiological impossibility for the vast majority of this entire generation, to function in any way, except for –

"Joyce Kovelman and Arnold Scheibel of UCLA's Brain Research Institute spotted a weird cellular disarray in the schizophrenic brains (and not in the matched controls). The pyramid-shaped cells of the hippocampus, normally arranged in an orderly manner, were grossly misaligned – A schizophrenic's dopamine neurons would start to fire in two different rhythms and rapidly become uncoupled – 'the key to schizophrenia is chaotic fluctuations in dopamine production' – 'What I saw was that people were fluctuating between opposites states,' – 'And a light bulb went off in my head. I saw that the key to psychotic behavior was not too much or too little of a specific neurotransmitter. It was the unstable fluctuations in a chemical system..."

The 3-Pound Universe – Judith Hooper and Dick Teresi

Schizophrenic, and/or psychotic, and which is as this word: psychosis, does mean: "any major, severe form of mental disorder – affecting the total personality."

Remember Adolf Hitler, and how –

399

"Kubizek tells of seeing a teenager in 'deep depression': Adolf was at odds with the world. Wherever he looked, he saw injustice, hate and enmity. Nothing was free from his criticism – He wallowed deeper and deeper in self-criticism. Yet it only needed the slightest touch – for his self-accusation to become an accusation against the times, against the whole world; choking with his catalog of hates, he would pour his fury over everything, against mankind in general who did not understand him, who did not appreciate him and by whom he was persecuted – In Hitler's youth, his schoolteachers flunked him and Kubizek found him strangely depressed and enraged. Yet Adolf and his family saw no problem with his loafing around the house for years, nursing huge aspirations. They explained his condition as an interest in the arts."
    Michael Nelken M. D. – Hitler Unmasked

Disgruntled, and/or "unbalanced," he was: as an adolescent.
And remember too, how –

"When he asked, she bought him a piano. He studied just a few months; actual playing at the piano did not interest mother or son. The purchase showed their attitudes: Adolf protested his isolation and entrapment with outrageous demands; his mother soothed him by granting them."
    Michael Nelken M. D. – Hitler Unmasked

Adolf Hitler never practiced his scales of truly humanistic simultaneously relative Omnidimensional *a priori* Reality, and while as on a daily basis too. But how – too, his Mother did actually "buy" him: The Child, a piano, and/or an excessive dopamine biochemical inducing stimulus, actually functioning as pure *pleasure* only, and which was only to ease her: The Mother's, conscience also. And which was exactly because –

"...he – Hitler, had a coddling but controlling mother and a distinguished but brutal father. Adolf became dedicated to evading control by anyone. However, he could not evade his memories...In admiration, Adolf himself learned endurance: 'I resolved not to make a sound the next time my father whipped me. And when the time came – I still can remember my frightened mother standing outside the door – I silently counted the blows. My mother thought I had gone crazy when I beamed proudly and said, 'Father hit me thirty-two times!' – In this account, Hitler's mother, Klara, participates as a voyeur of the sadism of the father. The outwardly meek and servile woman had her eldest surviving child, Adolf, fight her battles with her husband..."
    Michael Nelken M. D. – Hitler Unmasked

Adolf Hitler's Father, and/or The Man, was a tyrant, and she: Adolf Hitler's Mother and/or The Woman, allowed it: The abuse of The Child, and while as in an attempt to simply preserve her own complacency, and/or her own apathy, and/or her own truly humanistic neurophysiological dysfunction, and/or her own reluctance to FACE-UP TO HER OWN REALITY. And which was the fact, that she did simply "Betray the Child." And she did, in fact –

"Enter by the narrow gate, since the road that leads to perdition is wide and spacious, and many take it; but it is a narrow gate and a hard road that leads to life, and only a few find it."
Matthew 7: 13-14

Choose the path of least resistance: and the easy way out, for her own self only, and while simply ignoring the reality that was yet to come: *for* the entire world to be forcibly exposed to. And –

"Deeper Dissatisfaction Found in Teens Today –
Unlike their earlier counterparts, they feel powerless, and believe that nothing is worth saving, experts said. 'Today's group is full of gloom and doom, and nothing is worth saving' – (said) Wayne Wooden – Pollsters such as J. Walker Smith of Yankelovich Partners said that milder versions of this angst were widespread. Smith used the metaphor of the 1964 World's Fair. 'For young boomers, life was always going to be better,' he said. 'We might have to fix things up, but we'd be on the monorail. Kids today – don't even know if they'll make it beyond (the next year) – In a recent poll, more than half the teens surveyed said young people would make little difference to the country, or would make things worse, Jean Johnson, senior vice president of public agenda, said…"
Laura Session Stepp – Wa. Post/Ph. Inquirer – Saturday April 24, 1999

Just as this 21st century aristocracy has done too: TO THE CHILD.
And too which is exactly because, they are –

"Teen Convicted of Murders –
A teenager was convicted yesterday of shooting his parents to death with his brother's help – Prosecutors said Robert killed his parents because he was fed up with their strict rules and curfews – Jeffrey admitted shooting his parents first as they arrived home from work that afternoon, but said Robert planed the killings and finished off both parents, taunting each one first – Jeffrey said Robert also chafed under their parents rules, especially the recent refusal to let him buy a cellular telephone – When Robert said the night before the killings that he wanted to shoot their mother to see the look on her face, Jeffrey quipped, 'Why do you get all the fun..."
A.P. Dover New Hampshire – Bucks County Courier Times, May 29, 1997

Afraid to face-up to Reality. And/or –

"If the world hates you
remember that it hated me before you.
If you belonged to the world,
the world would love you as its own;
but because you do not belong to the world,
because my choice withdrew you from the world,
therefore the world hates you.
Remember the words I said to you:
A servant is not greater than his master.
If they persecuted me,
they will persecute you too;
if they kept my word,
they will keep yours as well.
But it will be on my account that they do all this,
because they do not know the one who sent me.
John 16: 18-21

Afraid of being told just how much they are being hated: by the Child, and of any age. And, for simply not giving them whatever they want, and whenever they want it, and while enabling them to "do" absolutely nothing for their very own selves also. And except, of course, to simply exist while in absolute ignorance of Reality, and/or the ability to –

"This is my commandment:
love one another,
as I have loved you.
A man can have no greater love
than to lay down his life for his friends.
You are my friends,
if you do what I command you.
I shall not call you servants and more,
because a servant does not know
his master's business;
I call you friends,
because I have made known to you
everything I have learned from my Father."
John 15: 12-15

Experience truly humanistic any thing: They are afraid of.
And too so that they: all of the individually affected victims of the con, are simply afraid of –

"It was now about the sixth hour and, with the sun eclipsed, a darkness came over the whole land until the ninth hour. The veil of the Temple was torn right down the middle; and when Jesus had cried out in a loud voice, he said, 'Father, *into your hands I commit my spirit*.' With these words he breathed his last.

When the centurion saw what had taken place, he gave praise to God and said, 'This was a great and good man.' And when all the people who had gathered for the spectacle saw what had happened, they went home beating their breasts."
Luke 23: 44-48

Being left out of the In Crowd: which is being purposefully allowed exposure to the purely psychopathic – and/or schizophrenic, dopamine biochemical inducing stimulus, functioning as pure *pleasure* only, and/or The Apple, and/or the worldly spectacle event of any kind.

And remember, which is the actual function of the "perceivable proof," of any human being's own individually affected truly humanistic brain death, for their own selves to be in possession of only, and their addictions to all things worldly too. Which is their ability to simply stand in awe in front of, and/or to "worship," their worldly gods, who are supplying them with allowed access to all of their purely psychopathic, dopamine biochemical inducing stimulus. But, unlike all of the previous aristocratic elite, while as throughout the entire history of mankind and as they did allow their very own selves to become victims of the con: who did have to "Buy a picture," this brand new 21st century aristocracy: *this* 21st century aristocratic elite – *this* 21st century victims of the con, can simply –

"Oscar's Home Is Smaller, but the Night Still Thrills Fans –
The nature of adulation demands extraordinary sacrifices. People who revere Hollywood stars will go to ends of the earth (to) catch a glimpse of the objects of their obsessions – 'We drove all the way from Miami,' said Elizabeth B-, 28, a physician's assistant who traveled with her friend Lori R-, 33, after applying for bleacher seats on the Academy Awards' Web site. We arranged our entire trip around this event. It's the American way...fans were issued photo identification cards and were promised food, refreshments and disposable cameras for the almost daylong wait until the stars were to arrive..."
Nick Madigan – The New York Times – Monday March 25, 2002

Take a picture of "it": the "proof" of their own personally affected truly humanistic brain death, and/or their ability to become capable of becoming a part of the In Crowd. Which is being purposefully allowed exposure to any, and/or all, purely psychopathic, and/or schizophrenic, dopamine biochemical inducing stimulus, actually functioning as pure *pleasure* only, and/or the Apple, and which is being supplied to them by their worldly god stars.

And too remember, which is as "we": this 21st century aristocracy – this 21st century America, has affected the single most contemptuous society while as in the entire history of mankind. And too, the single most paganish society while as in the entire history of mankind. And which is as this word: pagan, *does* mean: "One of a people or community professing a polytheistic religion – an irreligious or hedonistic person," and as this word: polytheistic, does mean: "The doctrine or belief in more than one god or in many gods," and this word: hedonistic, does mean: "The doctrine that pleasure (is) the highest good; devotion to pleasure as a way of life." And remember too, which is only in scientific reality of course, and *not* in the mind of any one individual, who has already become affected by the con, and/or any one individual, who has actually experienced truly humanistic brain death for their own selves. Because – remember, within there: all of their individually affected minds and which is now the majority, there can be no "understanding of Reality": it is simply a neurophysiological impossibility. And it: our "society," would seem to be something like that which is only capable of occurring, in some kind of –

"The Ravaged Minds From a Generation of War –

JALALABAD, Afghanistan – Check-in today for Patient No. 17 went like this: The patient – a 25-year-old vegetable vendor whose right leg had been severed at the knee in an American airstrike, was separated from his crutches and chained to a mulberry tree – With the nods of two male nurses, Mr. K- was determined to be sufficiently insane – The staff closed in. They pinned Mr K- down to a bed frame, yanked down his pants and used a syringe to the rump to inject him with Thorazine – soon Mr. K- grew blank-eyed and dreamy, and his blinks became slower (as) he blended right in – 'All of these people are mad, their minds have left them,' Mr Sabur said, pointing to his sedated charges, who huddled under blankets in the courtyard, squinting into the late morning light – Diagnosis here is simple. All patients are described as either nervous or mad. All receive the same drugs – Thorazine and trihexyphenidyl hydrochloride, which the staff says is useful because 'it makes their body soft'...The staff also noted that the authorities in Nangarhar province seem to have little interest in the hospital's future, having busied themselves in recent weeks with the sorting out which warlord will have more power and prestige, rather than trying to resume social services..."

C. J. Chivers – The New York Times – Wednesday January 9, 2002

Paganish land. But *not* –

"Drug Use, and Concern, On Rise –

In the movie version of madness, Psycho and Hannibal reign supreme. The terror of Norman Bates and Hannibal Lector lies in their mysterious strangeness and their abrupt lunges into violence – But in real life, most mentally ill people act...like you – Federal mental-health experts say that more than one in five Americans are afflicted with a diagnosable mental illness every year – Add drug addicts to that number, and nearly a third of the country is said to suffer from 'a mental or addictive disorder' each year – In the last few decades, more and more of them have begun to seek psychiatric care (and) medications – Sales of medications for psychiatric conditions dwarf the gross national products of some small countries. Last year, Americans and their insurers paid more than $8 billion for antidepressants, $3.9 billion for antipsychotics and more than $1 billion for antianxiety medications. Doctors wrote more than 125 million prescriptions for mental disorders – up from 73 million in 1995..."

Shanker Vendantum – The Philadelphia Inquirer – Monday March 10, 2001

Here: within the United States of America. And – certainly, not while; "The staff also noted that the authorities in Nangarhar province seem to have little interest in the hospital's future, having busied themselves in recent weeks with the sorting out which warlord will have more power and prestige" – the "government": "of" – "by," and "for," the people, is busy while attempting to empower themselves only, and/or while simply escaping Reality, and/or while indulging in excessive amounts of absolutely abstracted, and purely psychopathic, dopamine biochemical inducing stimulus, actually functioning as pure *pleasure* only. And just like –

"Not all VIPs paid $5,000 for Kimmel Center gala –
Many local politicians got free passes to Friday's inaugural concert. Most said they went out of civic duty.

Beautiful people from Philadelphia and beyond forked over $5000 per ticket to attend last Friday's inaugural fund-raising concert at the Kimmel Center featuring Elton John – Then there were the polls – They got in free – 'The city and state were major contributors to this project,' said Leslie Ann Miller, president of the nonprofit corporation that owns the Kimmel – Indeed, the city and state did make the $265 million project possible – city and state *taxpayers*, that is – to the tune of $100 million in grants. But Verizon Hall seats 2,543, not 12 million, so the politicians were invited to accept the Kimmel's gratitude on their constituents' behalf – Accept it they did..."

Ken Dilanian – The Philadelphia Inquirer – Wednesday December 19, 2001

In Reality: which is a neurophysiological impossibility for them – The Majority, to understand: remember? And which is our 21st century "Reality," and/or the fact of their own personally affected neurophysiological dysfunction, which they neurophysiologically can not understand: remember? And which is as they –

"...towards the middle of the fifth century B. C. – So it was that there arose in Greece a class that devoted itself to the teaching of rhetoric, or the art of persuasion, upon which worldly success so largely depended. The ministers of this new gospel of utility and 'Business first' were known as Sophists – They had themselves to be thoroughly conversant, not only with rhetoric in all its branches, such as grammar, diction, logical argument, an appeal to the emotions, but also with constitutional, civil, and criminal law, and parliamentary procedure. Furthermore,

405

they must keep their ear to the ground and know everything that was going on behind the scenes, if they were to give expert advice to their clients – Moreover, as his opinions change, so each man's truth will change. What appeared true yesterday looks false today. Very well, what was true for the individual *is* asserting that one man's truth is truer than another's, so in the same individual there is no possible means of measuring the truth of one against that of the next. Whatever it is that seems true is true so long as it seems so and no longer. All of my shifting opinions are equally true for me during the time that I hold them and equally false after I have discarded them – there is no 'Reality' that reason can know (for) the Sophists – Again, this habit turned the Sophists into servants of the rich, and allied them with the classes against the masses, since naturally they put themselves at the disposition of the highest bidder."

B.A.G. Fuller – The History of Philosophy

Have experienced truly humanistic brain death, for their own selves to be in possession of only. And too their purely psychopathic – and/or schizophrenic, function, within truly humanistic Reality: only, and which is as the Majority has been affected by the con: remember?

And too which is as *this* "21st century aristocracy" – *this* "21st century America," has – exactly, betrayed the sanctity of The Child: OF the once Truly Idealist Democratic Society. And simply while as in an attempt to preserve their very own truly humanistic complacency: their very own truly humanistic apathy; their very own truly humanistic creature comforts; their very own truly humanistic proprietorship; their very own truly humanistic brain death, and their very own truly humanistic anonymity too, and as they have allowed The Child to become a victim of the con also. And remember, which is as the government: of – by, and for the people, and the very same people which comprises the society, has allowed their very own selves to become so severely confused, and/or so severely dysfunctional, and/or so severely psychotic, and/or so severely psychopathic, and/or so severely schizophrenic, and/or so severely truly humanistic brain dead, and/or so severely afraid of our 21st century Reality, and/or so severely incapable of understanding Reality, that they did actually appropriate the use of public funds for –

"A Shock Grows in Brooklyn –
A fiery controversy over a museum's new show brings New York's Mayor out slugging: The mayor blew up three weeks ago over the controversial exhibition, 'Sensation: Young British artists from the Saatchi Collection' – The mayor was especially outraged by 'The Holy Virgin Mary,' a painting by Chris Ofili, who used, among other materials, elephant dung...polls showed that both New York residents and a nationwide sample were against shutting down the exhibit..."
C. McGuigan, M. Malone, R. Sawhill, G. Beals – Newsweek

The single most schizophrenic inarticulate cry for attention while as in the entire history of mankind. And while – exactly, projecting their own personally affected neurophysiological dysfunction upon the Collective Consciousness of Mankind, and while making manifest the single greatest offense upon the Collective Consciousness of Mankind, while as in the entire history of mankind also. And remember, which was while making manifest the purest of chaos: and /or discord, and/or lawlessness, and/or 10010. And too remember, which was while actually functioning as a direct contradiction towards: and assault upon, the universally applicable function of The Common Law: *of* all of simultaneously relative Reality, and/or The Mind of God made manifest. And which was, while simultaneously the exact same government: of – by, and for, the people: *and the people too*, was –

"Emotions run high on 10 Commandants ruling –
In what could become the Supreme Court's next chance to tackle the emotional debate over the Constitution's ban on government endorsement of religion, a federal judge yesterday ordered Chester County officials to remove a Ten Commandants plaque from a courthouse where it has hung since 1920..."
Joseph A. Slobodzian and Jonathan Gelb – The Philadelphia Inquirer – Thursday March 7, 2002

Making the function *of* The Common Law –

"Pharisees and scribes from Jerusalem then came to Jesus and said, 'Why do your disciples break away from the tradition of the elders? They do not wash their hands when they eat food.' 'And why do you,' he answered, 'break away from the commandment of God for the sake of your own tradition? For God said; *Do your duty to your father and mother* and : *Anyone who curses father or mother must be put to death.* But you say, 'If anyone says to his father or mother: Anything I have that I might have used to help you is dedicated to God,' he is rid of his duty to father or mother. In this way you have made God's word null and void by means of your tradition. Hypocrites!"
Matthew 15: 1-7

Null and void: within the once Truly Idealist Democratic Society, and which is exactly why everybody is going to die: soon.
Because, remember Thomas Paine simply explaining the universally applicable function of –

"Society is produced by our wants, and government by our wickedness; the former promotes our happiness positively by uniting our affections, the latter negatively by restraining our vices. The one encourages intercourse, the other creates distinction. The first is a patron, the last a punisher...There are injuries which nature cannot forgive; she would cease to be nature if she did – The Almighty hath implanted in us these indistinguishable feelings for good and wise purposes – They are the guardians of his image in our hearts. They distinguish us from the herd of common animals – I draw my idea of the form of government from a principle in nature, which no art can overturn, viz. that the more simple anything is, the less liable it is to be disordered..."

Truly humanistic universally applicable common-sense intelligence. And/or; truly humanistic universally applicable empirical self-conscious awareness, and/or; a truly humanistic being's universally applicable soul: that which *does* distinguish us from an animal. And/or – and as Thomas Jefferson did explain, a truly humanistic being's –

"...We have indeed an innate sense of what we call beautiful – nature hath implanted in our breasts a love of others, a sense of duty to them, a moral instinct, in short, which prompts us irresistibly to feel and to succor their distresses...I sincerely, then, believe – in the general existence of a moral instinct. I think it the brightest gem with which the human character is studded, and the want of it as more degrading than the most hideous of the bodily deformities."
Thomas Jefferson (to) Thomas Law

Omnidimensional refractive gem of a mind, and parallel functioning central nervous system, to be in possession of only. And/or, and as The Son of God did explain, truly humanistic universally applicable –

"Be compassionate as your Father is compassionate. Do not judge, and you will not be judged yourselves; do not condemn, and you will not be condemned yourselves; grant pardon, and you will be pardoned. Give, and there will be gifts for you: a full measure, pressed down, shaken together, and running over, will be poured into your lap; because the amount you measure out is the amount you will be given back."
Luke 6: 36-38

Unbridled compassion: and as directly opposed to self-lust only, and/or truly humanistic brain death, and/or an absolute addiction to all things worldly, and a neurophysiological inability to cognize any truly humanistic Time *made manifest* at all. And/or a neurophysiological inability to cognize any truly humanistic patterns in space/time: and/or a neurophysiological inability to maintain a single cognizable point time zero, within an individually affected human being's three-dimensional electrical potential mass of a mind, and parallel functioning central nervous system, and/or a neurophysiological inability to experience truly humanistic any "thing" whatsoever. And/or –

"Clinically, there is evidence that the prefrontal cortex by looking inward, so to speak, obtains the gut feeling for identifying with another individual. In other words: empathy – Through its centers for vision, hearing, and bodily sensations, we traffic with the external world."
The 3-Pound Universe – Judith Hooper and Dick Teresi

The function of a truly humanistic being's cerebral cortex.
Which: remember, are –

"PET-scan images of the brains of recovery – addicts reveal other striking changes, including a dramatically impaired ability to process glucose, the primary energy source for working neurons. Moreover, this impairment – which persists for up to 100 days after withdrawal, is greatest in the prefrontal cortex..."
Addicted – J. Madeleine Nash – Time – May 5, 1997

Destroyed: within the Majority.
And – remember too, which is: also and simultaneously and besides being the area of a human being's mind which *does* distinguish us from an animal, and/or the area of a human being's mind which is directly responsible for cognizing any Time *made manifest,* and/or the area of a human being's mind which affects the function of a human being's soul, the area of a human being's mind which *is* –

"Candace Pert: I see the brain in terms of quantum mechanics – the brain is just a receiver, an amplifier, a little wet minireceiver for collective reality (While) the ratio of frontal core may be one index of evolutionary advancement – what the frontal lobes 'control' is something like awareness, or self-awareness – Do these lobes govern some essential feature of humanness or even godliness, as some scientists have suggested? 'If God speaks to man, if man speaks to God,' neuroscientist Candace Pert tells us, 'it would be through the frontal lobes' – Stephen LaBarge: 'And it's capable of what look like miraculous things, so miraculous that we're tempted to say it's devine, that it's not natural."
The 3-Pound Universe – Judith Hooper and Dick Teresi

Capable of coming to an understanding of a more divinely purposeful existence, for their own selves to be in possession of only, and too which is while at its absolute best: or exactly not, and while at its absolute worst. And too remember, it is also, and simultaneously, the area of the human being's mind, which is directly responsible for cognizing –

"One way to think about this new view is to imagine spatial relationships as a kind of universal language that the brain uses no matter what specific language – social, moral, engineering – we are using at the moment...(George) Lakoff believes he can tie this mental language to the physical structure of the brain and its maps –

409

'When you think about dynamic structure, you begin to think there are a lot of things that are analogous with life. Life is more pattern(s) in space/time than it is a set of particular physical things."
Jim Jubak – In The Image of the Brain

Life: and/or harmony, and/or *a priori* Reality. And/or – and exactly as Thomas Jefferson did explain, the –

"...of although the doctrines which have ever been broached by the federal government, the novel one, of the common law being in force and cognizable as an existing law in their courts, is to me the most formidable..."
Thomas Jefferson, Monticello – August 18, 1799

Common Law: of all *of* simultaneously relative Omnidimensional *a priori* Reality, while actually functioning as pure harmony too.
And which, It: The Common Law, has now become "null and void," within the once Truly Idealist Democratic Society: which is the United States of America, and which *is* within the majority of the individually affected minds. Which does actually mean, that it is a neurophysiological impossibility for these individually affected human beings, to consciously cognize the Common Law: and/or be affected by it, and which is harmony. And which is as the Majority has been affected by the con, within the Democratic Society, which is governed of – by, and for, the "people," and which has been affected: The Majority; which is the "government" *of* the United States of America. And which has been affected, and can not consciously cognize, and/or be affected by, any "thing," except for –

"There are two essential yet complementary aspects of this new vision of time which are as striking in contrast as heaven and hell. Heaven is ruled by dynamical equations that are reversible and 'timeless'; their simplicity ensures stability for eternity. Hell is more akin to the real world, where fluctuations, uncertainty and chaos reign..."
The Arrow of Time – Peter Coveney and Roger Highfield

Hell made manifest. And/or –

"At Hiroshima: The common lot was random, indiscriminate and universal violence inflicting terrible pain, the physics of hydraulics and leverage and heat run riot...A junior-college girl: 'Ah, that instant! I felt as though I have been struck on the back with something like a big hammer – I seem to have been blown a good way to the north, and I felt as though the directions were all changed around...'"
Richard Rhodes – The Making of the Atomic Bomb

Chaos, and discord, and pain and death and suffering too.

And remember Thomas Jefferson explaining, *as* –

"...He proves also, that man, once surrendering his reason, has no remaining guard against absurdities the most monstrous, and like a ship without rudder, is the sport of every wind. With such persons, gullibility which they call faith, takes the helm from the hand of reason, and the mind becomes a wreck..."
Thomas Jefferson (To) James Smith – Monticello December 8, 1822

All of the individually affected human beings do become affected: by the con, so too does –

"...I hold (without appeal to revelation) that when we take a view of the universe, in its parts, general or particular, it is impossible for the human mind not to perceive and feel a conviction of design, consummate skill, and indefinite power in every atom of its composition. The movements of the heavenly bodies, so exactly held in their course by the balance of centrifugal and centripetal forces; the structure of the earth itself – We see, too, evident proofs of the necessity for a superintending power, to maintain the universe in its course and order. Stars, well known, have disappeared, new ones have come into view; comets, in their incalculable course, may run foul of suns and become extinct; and require renovation under other laws; certain races and animals are become extinct; and were there no restoring power, all existences might extinguish successively, one by one, until all should be reduced to a shapeless chaos..."

The Whole become affected: of a society, and/or The World.
And which is exactly because – and as Thomas Jefferson did plainly explain, as the United States of America flies: and/or becomes hijacked, so too does –

"...But would the honest patriot, in the full tide of successful experiment, abandon a government which has so far kept us free and firm, on the theoretic and visionary fear that this government, the world's best hope, may by possibility want energy to preserve itself? I trust not. I believe this, on the contrary, the strongest government on earth. I believe it is the only one where every man, at the call of the laws, would fly to the standard of the law, and would meet invasions of the public order as his own personal concern. Sometimes it is said that man cannot be trusted with the government of himself. Can he, then, be trusted with the government of others? Or have we found angels in the forms of kings to govern him? Let history answer this question..."
Thomas Jefferson: *Inauguration Address* – March 4, 1801

Fly the World: and/or become hijacked.
And – remember too, the Son of God did explain, that –

411

"Jesus left the Temple, and as he was going away his disciples came up to him to draw his attention to the Temple buildings. He said to them in reply, 'You see all these things? I tell you solemnly, not a single stone here will be left on another: everything will be destroyed.' And when he was sitting at the Mount of Olives the disciples came up and asked him privately, 'Tell us, when is this going to happen, and what will be the sign of your coming and the end of the world.

And Jesus answered them, 'Take care that no one deceives you; because many will come using my name and saying,'I am the Christ,' and they will deceive many. You will hear of wars and rumors of wars; do not be alarmed, for this is something that must happen, but the end will not be yet. For nation will fight against nation, and kingdom against kingdom. There will be famines and earthquakes here and there. All this is only the beginning of the birth pangs.

Then they will hand you over to be tortured and put to death; and you will be hated by all nations on account of my name. And then many will fall away; men will betray one another and hate one another. Many false profits will arise; they will deceive many, and with the increase of lawlessness, love in most men will grow cold; but the man who stands firm to the end will be saved.

This Good News of the kingdom will be proclaimed to the whole world as a witness to all the nations. And then the end will come."
Matthew 24: 1-14

The beginning of the end of time, will come at the point in time, when He has become revealed: and/or capable of being proven to be, most probably, the Son of God, and which is what we just did: for our very own selves. While along with the actual "increase of lawlessness," as the Majority has experienced truly humanistic brain death for their very own selves to be in possession of only: and "love" in them has grown cold too, and/or their cerebral cortices have become destroyed, and which they have. And too, which is while the revealing of The "Good news of the kingdom": of the applicable function of The Mind of God made manifest, actually functioning as The Kingdom of Heaven and Our Innocence Lost: The Entrance to The Garden and The Eternal Harmony too, can be proven to be an absolute fact: and for all the world to simply see with their eyes alone also, and which is as it can now. And which is while this function: of Omnidimensional Time *made manifest* actually functioning as the Mind of God made manifest, is capable of actually functioning as the function which is *The Annunciation* – which it is. Which is, the simultaneous applicable function, of the proving of the con: of the individually affected human beings, and of their individually affected three-dimensional electrical potential mass minds, and parallel functioning central nervous systems: as they have actually regressed back to point time zero, of their individually affected existence within simultaneously relative truly humanistic Omnidimensional Reality, and experienced truly humanistic brain death for their own selves to be in possession of only. And as they will have –

"Then to all he said, 'If anyone wants to be a follower of mine, let him renounce himself and take up his cross every day and follow me. For anyone who wants to save his life will lose it; but anyone who loses his life for my sake, that man will save it. What gain, then, is it for a man to have won the whole world and to have lost or ruined his very self? For if anyone is ashamed of me and of my words, of him the Son of Man will be ashamed when he comes in his own glory and in the glory of the Father and the holy angels."

Luke 9: 23-26

Lost control of their very own selves, while allowing their very own selves to become capable of betraying the Collective Consciousness of Mankind: for their very own selves only. And they will have allowed themselves to become capable of simply selling their souls: for their very own selves only, and too they will have allowed themselves to become capable of becoming the accursed and the confused: for their very own selves only, and they will have allowed themselves to become the victims of the con: for their very own selves only. And they *will* have allowed themselves to become –

"When the Son of Man comes in his glory, escorted by all the angels, then he will take his seat on his throne of glory. All the nations will be assembled before him and he will separate men one from another as the shepherd separates sheep from goats. He will place the sheep on his right hand and the goats on his left. Then the King will say to those on his right hand, 'Come, you whom my Father has blessed, take for your heritage the kingdom prepared for you since the foundation of the world."

Matthew 25: 31-34

The "goats," and which is as this word: goat, does mean: "a – victim."

So that, we can now know, and for a *verified* scientific fact, that there is only one thing that an individual can become capable of "doing," and which is to become capable of saving their very own selves. And that is to –

"Candace Pert: I see the brain in terms of quantum mechanics – the brain is just a receiver, an amplifier, a little wet minireceiver for collective reality. We make maps, but we should never confuse the map with the territory' (While) the ratio of frontal core may be one index of evolutionary advancement – What the frontal lobes 'control' is something like awareness, or self awareness..."

The 3- Pound Universe – Judith Hooper and Dick Teresi

Take it back: the "control" – *and over their very own selves too*.

And which will be while actually taking back control over their very own destinies also: and/or taking back control over their very own personally affected cerebral cortices also, and/or taking back control over their very own humanistic

413

being souls, and for their very own selves. And too and simultaneously, which will be while becoming capable of *actually* –

"Then to all he said, 'If anyone wants to be a follower of mine, let him renounce himself and take up his cross every day and follow me. For anyone who wants to save his life will lose it; but anyone who loses his life for my sake, that man will save it. What gain, then, is it for a man to have won the whole world and to have lost or ruined his very self? For if anyone is ashamed of me and of my words, of him the Son of Man will be ashamed when he comes in his own glory and in the glory of the Father and the holy angels."
Luke 9: 23-26

Joining the revolution, of the Collective Consciousness of Mankind, for their love of Mankind too. Which is as this word: renounce, does mean: "to give up or put aside voluntarily – to give up by formal declaration: *to renounce a claim* – to repudiate; to disown," and which is also as this word: repudiate, does mean: "to reject as having no authority or binding force – to cast off or disown – to reject with disapproval or condemnation," and too which is as this word: condemn, does mean: "to pronounce adverse judgment on; express strong disapproval of – to give grounds or reason for convicting – to pronounce guilty or to sentence to punishment – to judge or pronounce to be unfit for service – to declare incurable." But – remember, which is only in scientific Reality, and not in the mind of any one individual that has already become a victim of the con, and because – remember too, within there: their minds, words cannot possibly mean anything: it is actually a neurophysiological impossibility. And remember too, which: personally affected neurophysiological dysfunctions and for individually affected human beings to experience for their very own selves, and their very own personally affected inability to understand Reality and/or The Absolute Truth, was the *actual* –

"So Pilate went back into the Praetorium and called Jesus to him, 'Are you the king of the Jews? he asked. Jesus replied, 'Do you ask this of your own accord, or have others spoken to you about me?' Pilate answered, 'Am I a Jew? It is your own people and the chief priests who have handed you over to me: what have you done?' Jesus replied, 'Mine is not a kingdom of this world; if my kingdom were of this world, my men would have fought to prevent my being surrendered to the Jews. But my kingdom is not of this kind.' 'So you are a king then?' said Pilate. 'It is you who say it,' answered Jesus. 'Yes, I am a king. I was born for this, I came into this world for this: to bear witness to the truth; and all who are on the side of truth listen to my voice.' Truth?' said Pilate, 'What is that?'"
John 18: 33-38

Reason for His: The Son of God/Son of Man/Collective Consciousness of Mankind made manifest and perceivable, "coming into" this world, and the reason

414

for His birth: and for all the world to simply see with our eyes alone, and to simply explain truly humanistic universally applicable *a priori* Reality too, and while as in simple spoken words also. And – then and simultaneously, His own purposefully affected death, and the simultaneous purposefully affected function of the con, which is the function of truly humanistic brain death, and/or truly humanistic brainwashing, and/or truly humanistic primary suggestibility, and/or truly humanistic betraying of the Collective Consciousness of Mankind, and/or the truly humanistic preservation of their very own selves, and/or the truly humanistic Selling of their souls, *was* the exact reason for the –

"When Pilate heard them say this his fears increased. Re-entering the Praetorium, he said to Jesus, 'Where do you come from?' But Jesus made no answer. Pilate then said to him, 'Are you refusing to speak to me? Surely you know I have power to release you and I have power to crucify you?' 'You would have no power over me,' replied Jesus, 'if it had not been given to you from above; that is why the one who handed me over to you has the greater guilt."
John 19: 8-11

Perceivable proof: *of* individually affected human beings.
And so, there is only one thing at any one individual humanistic being can do: to become capable of joining this revolution and saving their very own selves too, and that is to actually –

"But anyone who is an obstacle to bring down one of these little ones who have faith, would be better thrown into the sea with a great millstone around his neck. And if your hand should cause you to sin, cut it off; it is better for you to enter into life crippled, than to have two hands and go to hell, into the fire that can not be put out. And if your foot should cause you to sin, cut it off; it is better for you to enter into life lame, than to have two feet and be thrown into hell. And if your eye should cause you to sin, tear it out; it is better for you to enter into the kingdom of God with one eye, than to have two eyes and be thrown into hell where *their worm does not die nor fire go out*. For everyone will be salted with fire. Salt is a good thing, but if the salt has become insipid, how can you season it again? Have salt in yourselves and be at peace with one another."
Mark 9: 42-50

Cut their losses: IMMEDIATELY.
And which is to actually "Let it go" too: all of the allowed exposure to absolutely abstracted, and purely psychopathic, and/or schizophrenic, dopamine biochemical inducing effectual stimulus, actually functioning as pure *pleasure* only, and/or The Apple. And again and as we can remember, we do now know that any simple spoken words are absolutely meaningless, so that we can now also know that they must actually do it, and immediately too. Not next week, and not tomorrow

either, but immediately: today – not just this very minute, but this very second. Which is, if there is a child in the household, to actually pick up the God "damned" television set, and throw it away. If there is an adult human being in the household, who cannot watch less than one hour of television a week, so too: pick up the God "damned" television set, and throw it away. Stop all purposefully allowed exposure to all worldly God "damned" spectacle events: the God "damned" movies – the God "damned" theatre – the God "damned" entertainment – the God "damned" novels. And stop all of the purposefully allowed exposure to the God "damned" amusement parks – the God "damned" art museum parks – the God "damned" theme parks – the God "damned" spectator sporting event parks, and the God "damned" spectacle event parks. And too, stop all of the purposefully allowed exposure to the God "damned" excessive tangible form mass stimulus of any and/or all kinds: the God "damned" grandiosely, and deliberately, styled, automobiles, trains and airplanes, and too drive only a minimalist of an automobile, and only a minimal amount of time. Stop the purposefully allowed exposure to the God "damned" excessively simplistic, and histrionic, and monochromatic, and romanticized, musical sounds: the God "damned" worshiping of worldly god stars – the God "damned" worshiping of worldly anything stars. And while including the television stars – the movie stars – the worldly god stars – the boy band stars – the girl band stars – the pop icon band stars – the composer stars, and musician stars. And too take off – TAKE OFF, the God "damned" excessively fine fabrics – the God "damned" diamonds – the God "damned" gold, and the God "damned" silver too, and throw it away. And too stop all of the purposefully allowed exposure to the God "damned" excessively fatty tasting foods, and the excessively sweet tasting foods. And too pick up the God "damned" computers, and Internet, and virtual reality, and dot-coms and cell phones and video recorders too, and throw them away. And renounce the God "damned" parties, and aristocratic environments: the God "damned" lawlessness – the God "damned" noise – the God "damned" chaos – the God "damned" discord – the God "damned" complacency – the God "damned" apathy – the God "damned" simple accessing of abstract knowledge – the God "damned" truly humanistic brain death – the God "damned" ignorance of the Mind of God made manifest, and the God "damned" ignorance of our Reality. And too, take all of the God "damned" money that would have been spent on all of *these* God "damned" worldly things: all of the allowed exposure to the absolutely abstracted, and purely psychopathic, and/or schizophrenic, dopamine biochemical inducing stimulus functioning as pure *pleasure* only: and/or The Apple, and feed the poor: Let no one go to sleep hungry – and/or alone – and/or afraid, tonight, and from this day forward, and on the entire face of this point-mass of Earth: God's "footstool."

While in addition, and of course, in order for an individual to even begin to actually become capable of taking back control of their very own selves: while *away* from all of the worldly psychopathic con-artists, and while as through purposefully allowed exposure to all worldly psychopathic, and/or schizophrenic, dopamine biochemical inducing stimulus actually functioning as pure *pleasure* only, and to even begin to become capable of taking back control of their very own destinies too, they must also –

"Enter by the narrow gate, since the road that leads to perdition is wide and spacious, and many take it; but it is a narrow gate and a hard road that leads to life, and only a few find it."
Matthew 7: 13-14

Start practicing their scales, of truly humanistic simultaneously relative Omnidimensional *a priori* Reality, and while as on a daily basis too. And/or, begin to experience all relatively painful experienced humanistic phenomena, and/or *pain*, and while as for their very own selves only: and The Child also. And which is while also enabling The Child to "do" nothing, except to –

"Tuning Up The Brain –
The 'Mozart effect' suggests that classical compositions can stimulate learning. But the jury is still out – What scientists do know is that keyboard instruction – making music, not just hearing it – seems to resonate within the brain. In one typical study, neuroscientists – tested 3- to 5-year-olds who received six months of piano lessons. The researchers found that the tiny pianists improved significantly in spatial-temporal reasoning – Such effects are even more pronounced in older kids. After a year of twice-a-week piano lessons, a recent study in California found, second graders from a poor district improved their math scores to those of fourth graders from an affluent one..."
Sharon Begley – Newsweek – Fall/Winter 2000

Learn Reality, and not simply experience truly humanistic brain death for their own selves, and while being simply betrayed by the Parent also.
And remember too, which is exactly as Thomas Jefferson did explain –

"...If ever you find yourself environed with difficulties and perplexing circumstances, out of which you are at a loss how to extricate yourself, do what is right, and be assured that that will extricate you the best of the worst situations. Though you cannot see, when you take one step, what will be the next, yet follow truth, justice, and plain dealing, and never fear their leading you out of the labyrinth, in the easiest manner possible – Make these, then, your first object. Give up money, give up fame, give up science, give up the earth itself and all it contains, rather than do an immoral act..."
Thomas Jefferson (to) Peter Carr – Paris, August 19, 1785

That rather than to actually do a single immoral act, we should be willing to give up, and/or let go of, everything: all worldly things, and while including, even, our excessively simplistic mortal existence. And while as in an attempt to even begin to; "certain races and animals are become extinct; and were there are no restoring power, all existences might extinguish successively, one by one, until all should be reduced to a shapeless chaos" – preserve our very own selves: to restore social harmony to the society, and to return the innocence back to The Child, of the once Truly Idealist Democratic Society, which was the United States of America. And which is as the entire world is now "looking at us," and – also and exactly as the Son of God did explain, so too is –

"Do not imagine that I have come to abolish the law of the Prophets. I have come not to abolish but to complete them. I tell you solemnly, till heaven and earth disappear, not one dot, not one little stroke, shall disappear from the law until its purpose is achieved. Therefore, the man who infringes even one of the least of these commandments and teaches others to do the same will be considered the least in the kingdom of heaven."
Matthew 5: 17-19

God: The God.
And this once Truly Idealist Democratic Society: *this* 21st century aristocracy, *this* 21st century America, has actually –

"A Shock Grows in Brooklyn –
A fiery controversy over a museum's new show brings New York's Mayor out slugging: The mayor blew up three weeks ago over the controversial exhibition, 'Sensation: Young British artists from the Saatchi Collection' – The mayor was especially outraged by 'The Holy Virgin Mary,' a painting by Chris Ofili, who used, among other materials, elephant dung...polls showed that both New York residents and a nationwide sample were against shutting down the exhibit..."
C. McGuigan, M. Malone, R. Sawhill, G. Beals – Newsweek

Done the *single* most immoral act while as in the entire history of mankind. And we: as a whole and as a society, have also – and simultaneously, made the Common Law null and void, and/or infringed upon The Commandment of God, and taught, and/or programmed, The Child to actually do so also. And so they: all of the individually affected victims of the con and who actually can *not* "let it go," *will be considered the least in the kingdom of heaven.* And: again, so says only –

"Enter by the narrow gate, since the road that leads to perdition is wide and spacious, and many take it; but it is a narrow gate and a hard road that leads to life, and only a few find it."
Matthew 7: 13-14

The Son of God.
And, remember too, the Son of God did plainly explain, that –

418

"I did not tell you this from the outset,
because I was with you;
but now I am going to the one who sent me.
Not one of you has asked, 'Where are you going?'
Yet you are sad at heart because I have told you this.
Still, I must tell you the truth:
it is for your own good that I am going
because unless I go
the Advocate will not come to you;
but if I do go,
I will send him to you.
And when he comes,
he will show the world how wrong it was,
about sin,
and about who was in the right,
and about judgment:
about sin:
proved by their refusal to believe in me;
about who was in the right:
proved by my going to the Father
and your seeing me no more;
about judgment:
proved by the prince of this world being already condemned.
I still have many things to say to you
but they would be too much for you now.
But when the Spirit of truth comes
he will lead you to the complete truth,
since he will not be speaking as from himself
but will say only what he has learned;
and he will tell you of the things to come.
He will glorify me,
since all he tells you
will be taken from what is mine.
Everything the Father has is mine;
that is why I said:
All he tells you
will be taken from what is mine."
John 16: 5-15

I am going to tell you what is *now* going to happen.
And so here that is.
Remember how: within a child's mind, everything does –

"One thing has become clear to scientists: memory is absolutely crucial to our consciousness – 'There's almost nothing you do, from perception to thinking, that doesn't draw continuously on your memory. (And) It can't be otherwise, since there really is no such thing as a present (while) memory provides a personal context, a sense of self and a sense of familiarity – past and present and a frame for the future' – But memory is not a single phenomenon. 'We don't have a memory system in the brain' – 'We have memory systems, each playing a different role'...When everything is going right, these different systems work together seamlessly. If you're taking a bicycle ride, for example, the memory of how to operate the bike comes from one set of neurons; the memory of how to get from here to the other side of town comes from another; the nervous feeling you have left over from taking a bad spill last time out comes from still another. Yet you are never aware that your mental experience has been assembled, bit by bit, like some invisible edifice inside your brain..."
Michael D, Lemonick – Smart Genes? – Time – September 13, 1999

Actually effectually occur while as on a purely subconscious level: it is actually a neurophysiological impossibility, for a young child to form formal abstract reasoning, and exactly because of their lack of exposure to experienced Reality. And so, they will remain only neurophysiologically capable of functioning, exactly as a young child is only neurophysiologically capable of functioning. And – remember, which is while a young child is only neurophysiologically capable of responding, to the two extremes of the basic biological functioning capabilities, which are encoded within the DNA of all living cells, and of: *pleasure* – harmony – dopamine, and *pain* – chaos – serotonin. So that The Child, actually "riding upon the bicycle," and exactly because of the relatively accelerated velocity of the bicycle and while upon this point-mass of Earth, does also – and simultaneously, become capable of inducing a dopamine biochemical induction within his, or her, own "self": truly humanistic three-dimensional electrical potential mass of a mind, and parallel functioning central nervous system. And too which is capable of being consciously cognized as a "relatively pleasurable experienced humanistic phenomenon," and/or *pleasure*, and exactly because of the purposefully affected dopamine biochemical induction. But exactly because the young child is personally, and physically, responsible for affecting his, or her, own personally affected relatively accelerated velocity, the young child will also, and simultaneously, become capable of affecting a proportional amount of purposefully affected reuptake function – serotonin production/induction, and too calcium production/induction, within his, or her, own personally affected three-dimensional electrical potential mass of a mind, and parallel functioning central nervous system. And which does also – and simultaneously, produce, and maintain, a "balanced" truly humanistic three-dimensional electrical potential mass of a mind, and parallel functioning central nervous system, and while enabling the child to practice his, or her, scales of truly humanistic simultaneously relative Omnidimensional Reality too, and while as on a daily basis also, and for his, or her, own self only.

Now, imagine that that exact same young child does – temporarily, "lose control" of his, or her, own personally affected simultaneously relative function, within truly humanistic simultaneously relative Reality, and while upon this truly humanistic simultaneously relative point-mass of Earth, and does – then and while at a relatively accelerated velocity and while upon the bicycle: *and while moving at a relatively accelerated velocity,* fall off of the bicycle, and "come in contact" with the ground. Who does then – and simultaneously, experience a relatively painful experienced humanistic phenomenon, and/or relatively chaotic experienced humanistic phenomenon, and which does then – *and simultaneously,* affect an elevated serotonin induction within the child's three-dimensional electrical potential mass of a mind, and parallel functioning central nervous system: and which can be consciously cognized within the child's mind as *pain* only, while simultaneously the young child will remain neurophysiologically incapable of forming formal abstract reasoning, and/or of understanding exactly why they did "fall off the bicycle." Now too imagine, that the young Childs' Mother, and/or Father, has simply seen: with their eyes alone, the young child fall down off of the bicycle, and come in contact with the ground while at a "relatively accelerated velocity": and experience a relatively painful experienced humanistic phenomenon for the child, and because of the induced elevated serotonin induction: occurring within the child's parallel functioning mind and central nervous system, which the Mother, and/or Father, can *not* simply see with their eyes alone. But because the Mother, and/or Father, *can* simply see the child's *pain,* they will, of course, attempt to ease the child's *pain,* and/or attempt to begin to balance the biochemical induced effect, which is actually simultaneously effectually occurring within the child's mind, and parallel functioning central nervous system. So that the Mother, and/or Father, would probably say: to the young Child, that the "bad ground" *did* cause their pain – and exactly instead of explaining Reality to them, and as well they should *while at that point in time.* Well, we: all truly intelligent, and adult, human beings, are "in contact with the ground" now: DO YOU FEEL ANY PAIN? And the answer is, of course, that NO you do not: now feel any pain, while being in contact with the ground. So that, we can simply understand, and for our very own selves only, that the exact "thing" which did cause the Child to experience *pain*, was His, or Her, inability to "control" His, or Her, very own "self," and/or the chaotic environment which The Child was capable of being forcibly exposed to, and by some other human being: for the Childs to experience.

And remember how the majority of our entire global society has actually become affected, by the con: *of* their own personally affected, and truly humanistic, universally applicable empirical self-consciousness, and as they have actually effectually regressed back to point time zero, of their own personally affected existence within simultaneously relative truly humanistic Omnidimensional Reality. And so they *will* remain only neurophysiologically capable of functioning as a young child is capable of functioning, *and* simultaneously addicted to their purposefully allowed exposure to absolutely abstracted, and purely psychopathic, and/or schizophrenic, dopamine biochemical inducing stimulus, actually functioning as pure *pleasure* only. And too remember, how when one individually affected human being does begin to become addicted: and/or unbalanced, and/or –

"Drug's Effect On Brain Is Extensive, Study Finds –

Heavy users (of highly addictive stimulants) are doing more damage to their brains than scientists had thought, according to the first study that looked inside addict's brains nearly a year after they stop using the drug – At least a quarter of a class of molecules that help people feel pleasure and reward were knocked out...Dopamine is a brain chemical that regulates movement, pleasure and motivation. When the dopamine system goes seriously awry – people lose their excitement for life and can no longer move their limbs – The addicts (started out as) occasional users but over time the drug hijacked their natural dopamine systems..."
Sandra Blakeslee – The New York Times – Tuesday March 6, 2001

Hijacked: and/or as though they have actually begun to "lose control" over their very own selves, and exactly because they will *have*, they will – remember, have begun also – and simultaneously, to; "If you're taking a bicycle ride, for example, the memory of how to operate the bike comes from one set of neurons; the memory of how to get from here to the other side of town comes from another; the nervous feeling you have left over from taking a bad spill last time out comes from still another" – *actually* "feel" nervous, and/or anxious, and/or as though somebody is actually attempting to push them off the bicycle, and/or as though somebody is actually attempting to "take control over them." And too remember, which is as any one other individual human being, does simply attempt to "explain Reality" to them.

And remember exactly what this book was. How it was, simply, a communication of an understanding of Reality, and/or The Absolute Truth of truly humanistic universally applicable, and simultaneously relative, *a priori* Reality, and which is while actually functioning as the Common Law of Reality. Which we did, enable our own selves to become capable of coming to an understanding of, while including truly humanistic neurophysiological dysfunctions too. But remember too, which does enable us: any one who is actually capable of joining this revolution, to simply understand, that –

"The psychopath is like an infant, absorbed in his needs, vehemently demanding satiation – Psychopaths (do also) display a general lack of empathy. They are indifferent to the rights and suffering of family members and strangers alike. Psychopaths are very good at giving their undivided attention to things that interest them most and at ignoring other things. Some clinicians have likened this process to a narrow-beam search-light that focuses on only one thing at a (point in) time...Besides being impulsive – doing things on the spur of the moment – psychopaths are highly reactive to perceived insults or slights – As a result, psychopaths are short-tempered, or hot-headed and tend to respond to frustration, failure, discipline, and criticism with sudden violence, threats, and verbal abuse. They take offense easily and become angry and aggressive over trivialities, and often in a context that seems inappropriate to others..."

Dr. Robert D. Hare – Without Conscience

They: any one individually affected human being, which does comprise The Majority, are not going to *even* look at Reality, and/or too, *any* "communicated understanding" *of* Reality, and such as that which is contained within this book. And so – too, they will also – and simultaneously, actually "do" *only* exactly what Adolf Hitler did do *too*. And which was to –

"...Manstein rages: 'Hitler was guilty of dire irresponsibility (and he) ignored all factual considerations – (once) I sent Hitler a detailed appraisal and it was ignored for five days...General Walter Warlimont: Hitler created complete confusion (while his Chief of Staff) reported to Hitler that his Army was in no way prepared – nevertheless within five hours improvised orders had to be got out – Warlimont offers details: 'I had brought a number of documents (but) Hitler dismissed them with a flood of objections and misgivings. And, when I refused it to budge, signaled for his aides to take away the maps and tables without looking at them...The more difficult the military situation became, the greater importance he attached to *'faith'* as a guarantee of victory."

Michael Nelkin M.D. – Hitler Unmasked

Simply ignore it: Reality, and hope it goes away: they *will* simply do. And too, while remaining confined to the delusions of their own, personally affected, truly humanistic brain death: their psychotic; and/or paranoid delusional; and/or psychopathic; and/or schizophrenic, behavior, as well: and/or blind faith.

And – too remember, which is exactly simply because, if they can not –

"The Pharisees, who loved money, heard all this and laughed at him. He said to them, 'You are the very ones who pass yourselves off as virtuous in people's sight, but God knows your hearts. For what is thought highly of by men is loathsome in the sight of God."

Luke 16: 14-11

Make any money "doing it," and/or have an orgasm doing it, and/or affirm their truly humanistic brain death: their own personally affected truly humanistic complacency; their own personally affected truly humanistic apathy; their own personally affected *exactly* betraying of the Collective Consciousness of Mankind, and too their own personally affected becoming a victim of primary suggestibility, doing it, THEN THEY ARE NOT GOING TO DO IT.

And they will only –

"It will be the same as it was in Lot's day: people were eating and drinking, buying and selling, planting and building, but the day Lot left Sodom, God rained fire and brimstone from heaven and it destroyed them all. It will be the same when the day comes for the Son of Man to be revealed.'

'When that day comes, anyone on the housetop, with his possessions in the house, must not come down to collect them, nor most anyone in the fields turn back either. Remember Lot's wife. Anyone who tries to preserve his life will lose it; and anyone who loses it will keep it safe. I tell you, on that night two will be in one bed: one will be taken, the other left; two women will be grinding corn together: one will be taken, the other left.' The disciples interrupted. 'Where, Lord' they asked. He said, 'Where the body is, there too will the vultures gather."

Luke 17: 28-37

Ignore Reality. And continue to move while as in a purposefully effectuated direction, to enable their own selves to become capable of becoming a part of the In Crowd: which is being purposefully allowed exposure to the absolutely abstracted, and purely psychopathic, and/or schizophrenic, dopamine biochemical inducing stimulus, *actually* functioning as pure *pleasure* only, and/or The Apple. And too, which is being supplied to them by the worldly authoritative god figures, and/or all of the worldly psychopathic con-artists. And – *too*, they will move: while as in a purposefully effectuated direction, towards the point of no return: of the black hole of truly humanistic neurophysiological dysfunction, and to become capable of consuming their very own selves, and while, exactly, because of their own personally affected addictions to all things worldly, and as they *have* lost control over their very own selves.

So, we can know, that your: anyone who does decide to join this revolution and because of your love for mankind, responsibility, and while as "to" any one individual who you may sincerely love, and/or all of mankind also, will be to –

"You are the salt of earth. But if salt becomes tasteless, what can make it salty again? It is good for nothing, and can only be thrown out to be trampled underfoot by men.

You are the light of the world. A city built on a hilltop cannot be hidden. No one lights a lamp to put under a tub; they put it on the lampstand where it shines for everyone in the house. In the same way your light must shine in the sight of men, so that, seeing your good works, they may give the praise to your Father in heaven."

Matthew 5: 13-16

Explain Reality to them.

And – remember and as you do simply explain Reality to them, they are *actually* going to "feel" real "pain," and as though you are attempting to place a plastic bag over their heads, and/or as though you are attempting to take control over them, and/or as though you are attempting to violate them, and/or as though you are

424

attempting to become capable of "pushing them off the bicycle." And too OVER, and OVER, and OVER, again: they will feel real *pain*, and for each, and every, function, that you do explain to them, and/or for each, and every, word, that you do speak to them: about Reality, and while simply explaining their own personally affected neurophysiological dysfunction. And too remember, they are only capable of functioning while as in a purely psychopathic manner: at best, and/or a purely schizophrenic manner: at worst, and which *is* "psychotic." And – remember, which is as this word: psychosis, does mean –

"A term formerly applied to any mental disorder, but now generally restricted to those disturbances of such magnitude that there is personality disintegration and loss of contact with reality. The disturbances (are) characterized by delusions and hallucinations."
Taber's Cyclopedic Medical Dictionary

That they simply cannot understand Reality, and/or what exactly is causing them to begin to experience anxiety. And/or; beginning to become capable of causing them to feel as though they have lost control of their very own selves, and as they *have,* and/or; beginning to become capable of causing them to feel as though somebody has placed a plastic bag over their heads, and/or; beginning to become capable of causing them to feel as though somebody is attempting to violate them, and/or; beginning to become capable of causing them to feel as though somebody is attempting to "push them off of the bicycle," over, and over, and over, again, and as you do simply explain Reality to them. And too – as you do attempt to explain Reality to them *and* as they do begin to experience real *pain* for their very own selves, they *will* begin to "obsess" about it, and which is as this word: obsession, does mean –

"The neurotic mental state of having an uncontrollable desire to dwell on an idea or an emotion."
Taber's Cyclopedic Medical Dictionary

That they *are* going to dwell upon it: the *pain*, which they will sincerely believe you did cause them to experience for their very own selves. And exactly as you do attempt to become capable of helping them to become capable of taking back control over their very own selves, and/or as you do attempt to become capable of encouraging them to become capable of facing-up to Reality.

And – remember, the Son of God did explain, that as you do explain Reality to them *and* as they do begin to experience pain for their very own selves, they *will* –

"Do not suppose that I have come to bring peace to the earth: it is not peace I have come to bring, but a sword. For I have come to set *a man against his father, a daughter against her mother, a daughter-in-law against her mother-in-law. A man's*

enemies will be those of his own household."
Matthew 10: 34-36

Perceive it: their own personally affected neurophysiological dysfunction, as an insult. And they will – and simultaneously, be experiencing real *pain* for their very own selves, and they will – and simultaneously, begin to become capable of simply obsessing about it, and they will – and simultaneously, have allowed themselves to become a part of the Majority, and a part of the In Crowd, which has become victims, and been affected by the con. And they will, and simultaneously, become capable of –

"He was still speaking when Judas, one of the Twelve, appeared, and with a large number of men armed with swords and clubs, sent by the chief priest and elders of the people. Now the traitor had arranged a sign with them. 'The one I kiss,' he had said, 'he is the man. Take him in charge.' So he went straight up to Jesus and said, 'Greetings, Rabbi,' and kissed him. Jesus said to him, 'My friend, do what you are here for.' Then they came forward, seized Jesus and took him in charge. At that, one of the followers of Jesus grasped his sword and drew it; he struck out at the high priest's servant, and cut off his ear. Jesus then said, 'Put your sword back, for all who draw the sword will die by the sword. Or do you think that I cannot appeal to my Father who would promptly send more than twelve legions of angels to my defense? But then, how would the scriptures be fulfilled that say this is the way it must be?' It was at this time that Jesus said to the crowds, 'Am I a brigand, that you had to set out to capture me with swords and clubs? I sat teaching in the Temple day after day and you never laid hands on me.' Now all this happened to fulfill the prophecies in scripture."
Matthew 26: 47-56

Conspiring with all of their friends: and/or with members of their family too, and who are also a part of the majority which has become affected and victims of the con, to come and assail you: *for what you did do to them*. And they *will* belittle you, and they *will* ridicule you, and they will mock you and they will taunt you *too*. And too they *will* –

"If the world hates you
remember that it hated me before you.
If you belonged to the world,
the world would love you as its own;
but because you do not belong to the world,
because my choice withdrew you from the world,
therefore the world hates you.
Remember the words I said to you:
A servant is not greater than his master.

If they persecuted me,
they will persecute you too;
if they kept my word,
they will keep yours as well.
But it will be on my account that they do all this,
because they do not know the one who sent me."
John 16: 18-21

Persecute you. And they are going to hate you too: with a "passion." And which is, as this word: passion, does mean: "any powerful or compelling emotion or feeling – the sufferings of Christ on the cross or His sufferings subsequent to the Last supper." Which will be exactly, as their; "Now the traitor had arranged a sign with them. 'The one I kiss,' he had said, 'he is the man. Take him in charge" – professed "love," *does* turn to hate: for *you* and as they do exactly betray you too, and the Collective Consciousness of Mankind also.

And too that will be the easy ones: the ones who are *only* addicted to abstracted dopamine biochemical inducing stimulus, functioning as pure *pleasure* only, and/or The Apple: and while including all things worldly too and/or simply escaping Reality, *for* entertainment, and NOT the difficult ones. Which are the ones, who have *actually* become capable of developing a neurophysiological dependency upon real drugs in Reality – *prescribed or not*, and too the ones who have *actually* been abused in Reality, and/or the ones who have actually been violated in reality, and/or the ones who have actually been "pushed off the bicycle" in reality, and, remember, that real number is huge in Reality. And they: anyone who has actually become addicted to real drugs and/or been abused in their lives, do need escaping reality, to simply enable them to become capable of surviving Reality, and while as on a daily basis too. And too which is while including dependencies upon Prozac, and/or Ritalin, and even for the children also, and – too, which is as they have become capable of experiencing *very* real conditions, such as "post traumatic stress disorder." Which is as this very real condition, *will* –

"STRESS – and your shrinking – BRAIN:
War, rape, sexual abuse, and other severe trauma – even a car accident – could make a part of your brain disappear –
Every now and then, someone with a medical problem needs a CT scan or MRI of the brain – If it's his or her first one, the patient will probably get the willies – Rookie med. students feel the same disquiet in anatomy class when they first hold a cadaver's brain in their hands. The same uneasiness makes neurosurgeons joke, 'There go the piano lessons,' when they cut into gray matter. The brain, after all, is the Seat of the Soul, the Big Enchilada of Consciousness, the organ of Me-ness. From this mass of tissue resembling marinated tofu emanates a person...(while) a brain region has attracted a lot of attention recently because it may atrophy in response to a certain type of serious stress – And in modern psychiatric parlance, the

427

long-lasting residue of horror is called post-traumatic stress disorder. It's not just restricted to combat trauma, either. Gang rape, childhood sexual abuse, the carnage of yet another choir-boy next door going postal with an automatic weapon – all are experiences that have produced the broken person labeled with the acronym PTSD – According to the American Psychiatric Association, patients with PTSD suffer from flashbacks, nightmares and other sleep problems, emotional numbness or outbursts, loss of pleasure, an inappropriate startle reflex, and problems with memory and concentration...Meanwhile, Thomas Freeman, a psychiatrist at the North Little Rock Veterans Administration Medical Center, is taking another approach to untangling the question of cause and effect. If the hippocampus shrinks after the trauma, especially if it does so as a function of the ongoing post-trauma period, the extent of atrophy should be more dramatic in survivors of older disasters than of recent ones..."

       Robert Sapolsky – Discover – March 1999

       Cause it to become just about impossible, to help these people: the ones who are actually suffering a real mental disorder and/or a real addiction, to begin to become capable of taking back control of their very own selves. And remember, that real number is –

"Drug Use, and Concern, On Rise –
       In the movie version of madness, Psycho and Hannibal reign supreme. The terror of Norman Bates and Hannibal Lector lies in their mysterious strangeness and their abrupt lunges into violence – But in real life, most mentally ill people act...like you – Federal mental-health experts say that more than one in five Americans are afflicted with a diagnosable mental illness every year – Add drug addicts to that number, and nearly a third of the country is said to suffer from 'a mental or addictive disorder' each year...Last year, Americans and their insurers paid more than $8 billion for antidepressants, $3.9 billion for antipsychotics, and more than $1 billion for antianxiety medication. Doctors wrote more than 125 million prescriptions for mental disorders – up from 73 million in 1995..."

       Shanker Vendantam – The Philadelphia Inquirer – Monday March 10, 2001

       HUGE.
       And all of these individually affected people, *are going to go nowhere near a bicycle*: and/or even begin to become capable of taking back control over their very own selves, and/or even begin to listen to another human being attempt to explain Reality to them. And – remember, which: if one individual does *even attempt* to help these people to begin to become capable of taking back control over their very own selves, will cause them to actually feel as though they are being violated, and/or being "pushed off the bicycle," over, and over, and over, again. And too remember, which will cause these individually affected human beings, to become capable of projecting their hatred upon *any* other one individual human being, who is

attempting to help them. And remember too, which is as this word: projection, does *actually* mean –

"Distortion of a perception as a result of its repression, resulting in such a phenomenon as hating without cause one who has been dearly loved, or attributing to others one's own undesirable traits. Characteristics of the paranoid reaction."
Taber's Cyclopedic Medical Dictionary

That they: *any* one individual humanistic being and/or all of Mankind too *and* who you do sincerely love *and may be attempting to help*, will become capable of –

"If I had not come,
if I had not spoken to them,
they would have been blameless;
but as it is they have no excuse for their sin.
Anyone who hates me hates my Father.
If I had not performed such works among themselves
as no one else has ever done
they would be blameless;
but as it is, they have seen all this,
and still they hate both me and my Father.
But all this was only to fulfill the words written in their Law:
They hated me for no reason.
When the Advocate comes,
whom I shall send to you from the Father,
the Spirit of truth who issues from the Father,
he will be my witness."
John 15; 22-26

Hating you for no reason.
And too *as* they do hate you, and persecute you, and belittle you, and mock you, and taunt you: *for attempting to become capable of helping them and because of your love for them*, you *must* –

"But I say this to you who were listening: Love your enemies, do good to those who hate you, bless those who curse you, pray for those who treat you badly. To the man who slaps you on one cheek, present the other cheek too; to the man who takes your cloak from you, do not refuse your tunic. Give to everyone who asks you, and do not ask for your property back from the man who robs you. Treat others as you would like them to treat you. If you love those who love you, what thanks can you expect? Even sinners love those who love them. And if you do good to those who do good to you, what thanks can you expect? For even sinners do that much.

And if you lend to those from whom you receive, what thanks can you expect? Even sinners lend to sinners to get back the same amount. Instead, love your enemies and do good, and lend without any hope of return. You will have a great reward, and you will be sons of the Most High, for he himself is kind to the ungrateful and the wicked."

      Luke 6: 27-35

      Not hate them back.
      And too you must not hate them back, even *as* –

      "And when they lead you away to hand you over, do not worry beforehand about what to say; no, say whatever is given to you when the time comes, because it is not you who will be speaking: it will be the Holy Spirit. Brother will betray brother to death, and the father his child; children will rise against their parents and have them put to death. You will be hated by all men on account of my name; but the man who stands firm to the end will be saved."

      Mark 13: 11-13

      They are betraying you: *and killing you too.*
      And remember, *this is exactly the point in time which we are now at*: when the Father, and/or Mother, *has* betrayed The Child, and so that the disgruntled Child *is,* now, *rising up against* The Parent, and/or The Rule Maker. And they *are* –

"Teen Convicted of Murders –
      A teenager was convicted yesterday of shooting his parents to death with his brother's help – Prosecutors said Robert killed his parents because he was fed up with their strict rules and curfews..."

      A.P. Dover New Hampshire – Bucks County Courier Times, May 29, 1997

      Having them put to death.
      And too remember, which is also while –

"U.S. ATTACKED –
Hijacked Planes Destroy Trade Towers, Hit Pentagon; Thousands Feared dead;
      A series of near-precision assaults shattered two symbols of America's military and financial power yesterday, killing untold numbers of people, halting Americans' daily routine, and forever destroying a nation's feeling that it can't happen here..."

      Ralph Vigado – The Philadelphia Inquirer – Wednesday September 12, 2001

      Becoming capable of making manifest their own personally affected schizophrenic inarticulate cries for attention, and/or simply projecting their own personally affected neurophysiological dysfunctions upon mankind. And, of course, which is simply because *all* little children, hate *the* Rule Maker, and/or The Father, while including the "World's Father," and/or the United States of America. And too remember, which is as the other applied method for brainwashing is; "a method for systematically changing attitudes or altering beliefs, esp. through the use of – drugs, or psychological-stress techniques" – while as through psychological-stress techniques, and as opposed to dopamine. And, of course, which *is* the *other* half of the world, *besides* –

"Gunshots, Blood and Chaos –
A bomb went off. The shooting began. What followed at Columbine High School was like a real-life horror movie – Chris D-, 15, a ninth grader at Columbine High School, was in the cafeteria when he saw the bomb going off in the parking lot – He crouched down in fear and started crawling toward the staircase. He heard gunshots and began to run...Still others said the gunmen giggled as they fired – For students, teachers and parents, the shootings at Columbine High were a horror movie brought to life..."
Gwen Florio – The Philadelphia Inquirer – Wednesday April 21, 1999

This half: *of* The World.
And again, which is simply because *all* little children, and/or any one individually affected person, who is only capable of functioning as a young child is capable of functioning: which is as they have actually regressed back to point time zero for their very own selves, and while becoming neurophysiologically capable of understanding absolutely nothing for their very own selves, do *exactly* "hate the rule maker." And/or any one individual person, who is capable of explaining Reality to them, and/or any one individual person, who may be forcing them to face-up to Reality, and while exactly not enabling them to simply exist while in ignorance of Reality: and/or *not* simply giving them whatever they want, and whenever they want it too. While including all of their allowed exposure to absolutely abstracted, and purely psychopathic, and/or schizophrenic, dopamine biochemical inducing stimulus, actually functioning as pure *pleasure* only: and/or The Apple. And, as exactly opposed to –

"You are the salt of the earth. But if salt becomes tasteless, what can make it salty again? It is good for nothing, and can only be thrown out to be trampled underfoot by men."
Matthew 5: 13

Serotonin. And/or forcing any other one individual person, to come to an understanding of universally applicable *a priori* Omnidimensional Reality. And too which is while actually effectually functioning as The Common Law, and while including forcing The Child to come to an understanding of Reality, and/or NOT

431

allowing their salt to become tasteless, and/or insipid, and/or ineffective, and/or unbalanced: their minds that is, and for The Child to become disgruntled because of the powerless Parent. And – remember, which is exactly as Thomas Jefferson did explain, because then –

"...Now, take any race of animals, confine them in idleness and inaction, whether in a sty, a stable or state-room, pamper them with high diet, gratify all their sexual appetites, immerse them in sensualities, nourish their passions, let everything bend before them, and banish whatever might lead them to think, and in a few generations they become all body and no mind; and this, too, by a law of nature, by that very law by which we are in constant practice of changing the characters and propensities of the animals we raise for our own purposes. Such is the regiment in raising Kings, and in this way they have gone on for centuries – In this state Bonaparte found Europe; and it was this state of its rulers which lost it without scarce a struggle. These animals had become without mind and powerless; and so will every hereditary monarch be after a few generations..."

The disgruntled adolescent can simply become capable of consuming an entire society.

And: remember, which is: that any one disgruntled adolescent, and/or group of disgruntled adolescents, does actually become capable of consuming an entire society, while actually becoming capable of making manifest REAL discord, and REAL chaos, and REAL noise, and REAL pain and suffering and death too. And too remember, which is as –

"Teen's Lust For Killing Emerged In Prose –
Eric Harris thought about war, fantasized about war and wrote about war. He was thrilled when he heard, one morning in philosophy class, that the United States was on the verge of bombing Yugoslavia...on Web pages (Harris) wrote: 'My belief is if I say something, it goes. I am the law, and if you don't like it, you die. If I don't like you or I don't like what you want me to do, you die...What's clear is that they liked war, war was a game, war was entertainment..."
Joel Achenbach, Dale Russakoff – Philadelphia Inquirer – April 29, 1999

They love it: remember, they do simply love it: the REAL chaos, and the REAL discord, and the REAL pain and suffering and death too.

And remember, which: that they do actually love it, is exactly because their cerebral cortices are destroyed, and so too are their receptors, contained within those individually affected three-dimensional electrical potential mass minds, and parallel functioning central nervous systems: remember? And remember, their receptors *are* destroyed, *exactly because of* –

432

"Dopamine, like most biologically important molecules, must be kept within strict bounds – Too much causes the hallucinations, and bizarre thoughts, of schizophrenia – addicts' neurons assaulted by abnormally high levels of the dopamine, have responded defensively and reduced the number of sites (or receptors) to which dopamine can bind..."
Addicted – J. Madeleine Nash – Time – May 5, 1997

Dopamine: remember? And remember, which is simply another name for –

"Media Fill Up Children's Hours –
They aren't building tree houses. They aren't playing hopscotch. They aren't stringing tin cans together. So what are today's 2-to-18-year-olds doing? – If a study released yesterday by the Henry J. Kaiser Family Foundation holds true, there's a good chance Jane and Junior are holed up alone in their bedrooms watching t.v. for hours..."
Jennifer Weiner – The Philadelphia Inquirer – Thursday November 18, 1999

The God "damned" television. And/or purposefully allowed exposure to absolutely abstracted, and purely psychopathic and/or schizophrenic, dopamine biochemical inducing stimulus actually effectually functioning as only pure *pleasure,* and/or The Apple: remember? And – remember, which is simply –

"...addicts' neurons assaulted by abnormally high levels of dopamine, have responded defensively and reduced the number of sites (or receptors) to which dopamine can bind – so while addicts begin by taking drugs to feel high, they end up taking them in order not to feel low..."
Addicted – J. Madeleine Nash – Time – May 5, 1997

To enable them to feel alive. And/or to enable them to breathe, and/or to enable them NOT to feel as though somebody has placed a plastic bag over their heads, and/or to enable them NOT to feel as though somebody is attempting to "push them off of the bicycle," and/or to enable them NOT to feel as though somebody is trying to take control over them: remember? And – REMEMBER, which is as –

"Drug's Effect On Brain Is Extensive, Study Finds –
Heavy users (of highly addictive stimulants) are doing more damage to their brains than scientists had thought, according to the first study that looked inside the addict's brains nearly a year after they stop using the drug – At least a quarter of a class of molecules that help people feel pleasure and reward were knocked out – This is the first study to show directly that brain damage (caused by the addiction) produces deficits in learning and memory – In the study, Dr. (Nora) Volkow used an imaging technique – to measure dopamine levels in the brains of 15 recovering addicts and 18 healthy volunteers. Dopamine is a brain chemical that regulates

movement, pleasure and motivation. When the dopamine system goes seriously awry, she said, people lose their excitement for life and can no longer move their limbs – The addicts (started out as) occasional users but over time the drug hijacked their natural dopamine systems..."

Sandra Blakeslee – The New York Times – Tuesday March 6, 2001

This is no joke, and it is exactly not a simple metaphorical analogy: WE HAVE BEEN "HIJACKED," and led on a collision course with our very own destiny, and: THIS PLANE IS GOING DOWN. And everybody is going to die: soon

And – again and for an absolute neuroscientific fact and for all the world to simply understand *and with our eyes alone too*, because –

"Drugs are like sledgehammers,' observes Dr. Eric Nestler of the Yale University School of Medicine. 'They profoundly alter many pathways' – the realization that dopamine may be a common endpoint of all those pathways represents a signal advance. Provocative – the dopamine hypothesis provides a basic framework for understanding (what does) cause a serious behavioral disorder..."

Addicted – J. Madeleine Nash – Time – May 5, 1997

It: the personally affected neurophysiological dysfunction of all of the individually affected human beings, *is* inversely affected. And which is while, as each single day goes by: EACH SINGLE DAY, they do become twice as affected, and twice as many individually affected people, do become affected too. And too, which: the purposefully allowed exposure to the absolutely abstracted, and purely psychopathic and/or schizophrenic, dopamine biochemical inducing stimulus, *and* while including the God "damned" television set, is while beginning to become capable of causing a "serious behavioral disorder": within each, and every, one of those individually affected minds, and parallel functioning central nervous systems. And which is as they are just about to lose control over their very own selves, and become capable of making manifest REAL chaos, and REAL discord, and REAL pain, and REAL suffering, and REAL death too: remember? And – too remember, which is as –

"Teen's Lust For Killing Emerged In Prose –
Eric Harris thought about war, fantasized about war and wrote about war. He was thrilled when he heard, one morning in philosophy class, that the United States was on the verge of bombing Yugoslavia...on Web pages (Harris) wrote: 'My belief is if I say something, it goes. I am the law, and if you don't like it, you die. If I don't like you or I don't like what you want me to do, you die – What's clear is that they liked war, war was a game, war was entertainment..."

"Portrait of madness –
Now that we can dissect DNA to identify a murderer or nail down

fatherhood, now that we can tiptoe through the human genome to predict who will be a candidate for colon cancer or Alzheimer's disease, probing the – tortured psyche of Vincent Van Gogh is a notion too tantalizing to resist – When you look at his work – the intensity with which he put paint on canvas – you feel so excited, stimulated and sometimes frightened. You not only see, but feel the mania – the loud color, the noise – you should relate to it from your own experiences..."

"91 Years After Dying, Mahler Hits His Stride –

Classical musicians sometimes apply what they call the hundred-year rule to composers. Only a century after music is composed, they say, can its quality and value truly be appraised – By that standard, the works of Gustav Mahler, who died in 1911, should now be reaching their largest audience – Today, after the 20th century's world wars and mass slaughters, Mahler's music touches many more souls than it did when it was written..."

"The Sopranos': Brutally Honest –

At the start of the season Tony Soprano, America's favorite mob boss, was becoming a little too lovable – Season 3 fixed all that. In the last few weeks as the show's season approached its end, Tony almost strangled his girlfriend when she threatened to reveal their affair. As he flung her body in the air, slammed it to the floor, then put his hands around her neck with rage, it was entirely plausible that he was going to kill her. And his violent reaction was not an isolated event...For the first time this season's 'Sopranos' relied heavily on violence directed against innocents, especially women – The 'Sopranos,' with its superb level of accomplishment, has used extreme violence to a profound artistic end..."

"Sorry spectacle –

How low can television go – Call it extreme television or even spectacle TV – shows that push the envelope until it is in shreds. In terms of graphic, shocking, explicit programs, television is breaking – maybe plumbing is a better word – new ground every day...'Has it ever been this bad – 'Has it ever been this explicit? The answer is no..."

"Thou shall not wallow in adultery –

We love to watch; always have. That impulse explains everything from the National Enquirer to its tamer stepchildren such as People and Us to the gossip columns in most newspapers...Sometimes, we're even a little jealous. We might tsk-tsk about Meg Ryan's running off with Russell Crow and leaving crooked-grinned Dennis Quaid and their 8-year-old son, Jack. But when the kids are crying and the house is a mess, a grin can lose its charm – at which point, you find yourself envying Meg and her rugged new guy...Because the affair nearly always has the pull of overwhelming romance – or at least, the best sex ever..."

"As Tourists Jam Yosemite, the Warnings Go Unheeded –

It's hard to be a wilderness in the long, hot days of summer – when people drive in by the thousands, bringing their big-city ways. Each day in high season here, cars crash on the narrow park roads. Car alarms blare. Traffic comes to a standstill. In crowded parking lots in Yosemite Valley, drivers circle, searching for

spaces..."
"The Horror, The Spectacle, Then Lunch –
With so much going on, an update on a few items of interest:
Ground zero, three months later: A visit last week was unsettling, at least to
this New Yorker – The site of the terrorist attack has many identities. It is hallowed
ground, a relentless work site, an international crime scene, a backdrop for memorial
services, a destination for celebrities and tourists – It has become a magnet...."

They do love it: THEY DO SIMPLY LOVE IT – LOVE IT – LOVE IT –
LOVE IT. And they do; "It has become a magnet" – actually feed off of it: all of
the; "Schizophrenics (have a) weird cellular 'disarray' (in their) brains – The
pyramid-shaped cells of the hippocampus, normally arranged in an orderly manner,
(are) grossly misaligned – A schizophrenic's dopamine neurons would start to fire in
two different rhythms and rapidly become uncoupled – 'I think that in schizophrenia
the brain fragments into active and inactive clusters of neurons and different parts of
the brain become disassociated' – Schizophrenics often feel that their minds and
bodies are split apart (and) find it difficult to distinguish between signal and noise
and to assign levels of importance to various classes of stimuli. Everything becomes
important; nothing is trivial – 'The primary symptom of schizophrenia – is a defect in
the pleasure response (while) schizophrenics are extremely insensitive to pain (and)
unreactive to other sensory stimuli, as well – schizophrenics (are) 'reducers,' (and)
their brains naturally reduce, or dampen, stimuli" – purely schizophrenic effectual
stimulus. They do actually "feed" off of it, AS IT DOES **ACTUALLY** CAUSE
THEM –

"What is a black hole? For astronomical purposes it behaves as a small
highly condensed dark 'body.' But it is not really a material in the ordinary sense. It
possesses no ponderable surface. A black hole is a region of empty space – which
acts as a center of gravitational attraction. At *one* time a material body *was* there.
But the body collapsed inwards under its own gravitational pull...Since the black
hole acts as a center of attraction it can draw new material towards it – which once
inside can never escape. The material thus swallowed contributes to the effective
mass of a black hole...What is known as a 'space/time singularity' – a place where
physical laws, as presently understood, must cease to apply."
Roger Penrose – Black Holes – The World Treasury of Physics, Astronomy
and Mathematics – Ed. Timothy Ferris

To become more powerful: while it does simultaneously cause them to
experience truly humanistic brain death, for their very own selves to be in possession
of only, and to be consumed by it: their inability to control their very own selves.
And – *again*, which is as –

"It will be the same as it was in Lot's day: people were eating and drinking, buying and selling, planting and building, but the day Lot left Sodom, God rained fire and brimstone from heaven and it destroyed them all. It will be the same when the day comes for the Son of Man to be revealed.

'When that day comes, anyone on the housetop, with his possessions in the house, must not come down to collect them, nor must anyone in the fields turn back either. Remember Lot's wife. Anyone who tries to preserve his life will lose it; and anyone who loses it will keep it safe. I tell you, on that night two will be in one bed: one will be taken, the other left; two women will be grinding corn together: one will be taken, the other left.' The disciples interrupted. 'Where, Lord,' they asked. He said, 'Where the body is, there too will the vultures gather."

Luke 17: 28-37

They have *already* lost control over their very own selves. And they do actually feed off of it: the schizophrenia, and/or spectacle, and/or chaos, and/or discord, and/or noise, and/or all of the pain and death and suffering too, as it is the only thing that can affect them, and they do actually love it. And so, as you begin to attempt to explain Reality to them, and/or do attempt to become capable of helping them to become capable of taking back control over their very own selves, and which is while including any, and/or every, one, who has been affected by the con, and which is now The Majority, there *is* going to be made manifest REAL chaos, and REAL discord, and REAL yelling and screaming and hollering too, and REAL pain, and REAL suffering, and REAL death, also. AS THEY ARE ACTUALLY GOING TO LOVE YOU TO DEATH: they are going to love –

"As they were leading him away they seized on a man, Simon from Cyrene, who was coming in from the country, and made him shoulder the cross and carry it behind Jesus. Large numbers of people followed him, and of women too, who mourned and lamented for him. But Jesus turned to them and said, 'Daughters of Jerusalem, do not weep for me; weep rather for yourselves and for your children. For the days will surely come when people will say, 'Happy are those who are barren, the wombs that have never borne, the breasts that have never suckled!' Then they will begin to *say to the mountains, 'Fall on us!'; to the hill, 'Cover us!'* For if men use the green wood like this, what will happen when it is dry?"

Luke 23: 26-32

Killing you.

And – remember, which is as you must – *now*, begin to help them to become capable of shouldering that cross of change for their very own selves, and which is as you must *actually* do it: become capable of helping them to take back control over their very own selves. And – too remember, which is as they must now be encouraged to renounce their worldly selves, and to not look back as they do it. And, which is as they must be encouraged to *actually* pick up the God "damned" television

437

set, and throw it away, and – too, to actually stop all purposefully allowed exposure to all worldly God "damned" spectacle events: to all of the God "damned" entertainment, the God "damned" movies – theater – novels – amusement parks – theme parks – spectator sporting event parks – art museum parks and spectacle event parks. To stop all of the purposefully allowed exposure to all worldly God "damned" excessive tangible form mass stimulus of any and/or all kinds, and while including the God "damned" excessive, and grandiosely styled, automobiles – trains and airplanes. And to stop all of the purposefully allowed exposure to all of the God "damned" excessively simplistic, *and* histrionic, *and* monochromatic, *and* romanticized, musical sounds, and if they listen to anything, then they should listen to only the Classical period: Bach – Tallis – Handel – Hayden – Taverner – Pergolesi – Vivaldi – Monteverdi – Scarletti – Mozart: *for* The Child to "Hear." And while actually eliminating all of the God "damned" worshiping of worldly gods, for The Child. And to take off the God "damned" diamonds – gold and silver too, and to throw it away: for The Child. And to stop all of the purposefully allowed exposure to the God "damned" excessively fatty tasting foods, and sweet tasting foods, and too for The Child. And to pick up the God "damned" computers – Internet – dot-coms – virtual reality – cell phones and video recorders, and throw them away – *and again* for The Child. And to actually eliminate the God "damned" parties and aristocratic environments, eliminate the God "damned" lawlessness: the God "damned" noise, the God "damned" chaos, the God "damned" discord, the God "damned" complacency, the God "damned" apathy, the God "damned" truly humanistic brain death – the God "damned" ignorance of Reality: for the Child, you must help them to actually become capable of doing.

And remember, they: The Parents, have *never* worked harder, than they have in the past 20 years, and they: The Majority, do "have" very little to actually show for it, and/or to be in possession of for their very own selves, and except, of course, for their frustration, and/or their anxiety, and because it was a con. But – remember too, it *was* a "con," and *now* –

"Americans, Gradually, Feel Grip of Recession –
The recession that started in March is gradually intruding on people's lives, forcing them to cut back in ways that contribute to the downturn – Young people just out of college find themselves unable to land jobs in their chosen careers, or to afford rent for their first homes. Retirees try to get by on suddenly shrunken incomes. Immigrants send less money to relatives back home, or cut their own expenses. And a growing number of middle-income people (are eliminating) luxury out of their lives..."
Louis Uchitelle – The New York Times – Monday January 7, 2002

It is beginning to collapse, and it is only going to get worse: because it *was* the con: remember? And – remember, which is as they were *exactly* –

"Pharisees and scribes from Jerusalem then came to Jesus and said, 'Why do your disciples break away from the tradition of the elders? They do not wash their hands when they eat food.' 'And why do you,' he answered, 'break away from the commandment of God for the sake of your own tradition? For God said: *Do your duty to your father and mother* and: *Anyone who curses father or mother must be put to death.* But you say, 'If anyone says to his father or mother: Anything I have that I might have used to help you is dedicated to God,' he is rid of his duty to father and mother. In this way you have made God's word null and void by means of your tradition. Hypocrites! It was you Isaiah meant when he so rightly prophesied:

'This people honors me only with lip service,
while their hearts are far from me.
The worship they offer me is worthless;
the doctrines they teach are only human regulations.'

He called the people to him and said, 'Listen, and understand. What goes into the mouth does not make a man unclean; it is what comes out of the mouth that makes him unclean.'

Then the disciples came to him said, 'Do you know that the Pharisees were shocked when they heard what you said?' He replied, 'Any plant my heavenly Father has not planted will be pulled up by the roots. Leave them alone. They are blind men leading blind men; and if one blind man leads another, both will fall into a pit."

Matthew 15: 1-14

Led by their blind guides: back to point time zero, of their own personally affected existence within truly humanistic simultaneously relative Omnidimensional Reality, *and* to become capable of experiencing truly humanistic brain death for their own selves to the possession of only. As they have never practiced their scales of truly humanistic simultaneously relative Omnidimensional Reality, and for their own selves, and while as on a daily basis too. And they *have* – and simultaneously, had their truly humanistic simultaneously relative multidimensional synaptic capabilities "Taken away from them" also: as they have experienced truly humanistic brain death, for their own selves to be in possession of and only.

And remember too, the absolute last thing in the world – the absolute last thing in the world, that anybody: one individually affected victim of the con, would want to do now, is to begin to attempt to take back control over their very own selves, because they are going to "need" it: "ESCAPING REALITY," now more than ever, and too which is while actually effactually functioning as "CHAOS" that "IS": "ESCAPING REALITY." And – REMEMBER, which is while only "Reality" does actually effactually function *as* the universally applicable Common Law: of truly humanistic simultaneously relative Omnidimensional *a priori* Reality, and as The Mind of God made manifest, and/or Pure HARMONY. And – remember, which is the *exact* definition, of –

"What is a black hole? For astronomical purposes it behaves as a small highly condensed dark 'body.' But it is not really a material body in the ordinary sense. It possesses no ponderable surface. A black hole is a region of empty space, which acts as a center of gravitational attraction...Since the black hole acts as a center of attraction it can draw new material towards it – which once inside can never escape. The material thus swallowed contributes to the effective mass of a black hole. And as its mass increases the black hole grows in size, its linear dimensions being proportional to its mass. Its attractive power likewise increases – a maelstrom in space which sweeps up all in its path...What is known as a 'space/time singularity' – a place where physical laws, as presently understood, must cease to apply."

> Roger Penrose – Black Holes The World Treasury of Physics, Astronomy and Mathematics, Ed. Timothy Ferris

The End of time.

And remember and again, everything *is* actually exactly backwards: within all of the individually affected minds, which does comprise the Majority of our entire global society, and while at this point in time while upon the threshold of the 21st century, and while as within this real Edenic tale too, which *is* our 21st century Reality. And they: the overwhelming vast majority of mankind and while upon this entire point-mass of Planet Earth, do actually know that they *have* –

"At Enron, Lavish Excess Often Came Before Success –

For years, the Enron Corporation thrived on spending big, and even as late as October – with warnings ringing loudly about its rickety finances, no one at Enron saw any reason to change – Everything Enron did had to be better and flashier – and no gesture seemed too lavish...the company's spending reflected a go-go corporate culture, former employees said, in which top executives cast traditional business controls by the wayside. And that figured heavily in Enron's collapse – 'The lack of risk controls was mind boggling,' said Gary C-, whose parent company has hired a number of energy traders and other employees from Enron...(But) At work the attention to quotidian comfort was boundless: free laptops and hand-held devices, the best ergonomic chairs money could buy – lunches at Houston's best restaurants (and) many employees concluded that they deserved the perks, since joining Enron often meant 12-hour workdays and ceaseless travel..."

> Neela Banerjee, David Barboza and Audry Warren – The New York Times – Tuesday February 26, 2002

Worked very hard: while as "at" their day-time jobs, and to enable them to become capable of making large amounts of money. Which was as they actually were being led by their blind guides also, and which was while actually effectually regressing back towards point time zero: for their very own selves, and as they are capable of understanding nothing, and only capable of believing exactly what they have been programmed to believe: by all of the worldly psychopathic con-artists. Who were supplying them with all of their allowed exposure to all of the absolutely abstracted, and purely psychopathic, and/or schizophrenic, dopamine biochemical inducing stimulus, actually functioning as pure *pleasure* only, and/or The Apple. So that they do actually believe, that they *have* enabled their own selves to become capable of Carrying their crosses: for their very own selves, and exactly instead of understanding that it *was* a con, and too that "that": applied very real time-evolutive function, was *only* –

"Then he said to his host, 'When you give a lunch or a dinner, do not ask your friends, brothers, relations or rich neighbors, for fear they repay your courtesy by inviting you in return. No; when you have a party, invite the pour, the crippled, the lame, the blind; that they cannot pay you back means that you are fortunate, because repayment will be made to you when the virtuous rise again.'

On hearing this, one of those gathered around the table said to him, 'Happy the man who will be at the feast in the kingdom of God!' But he said to him, 'There was a man who gave a great banquet, he sent his servant to say to those who had been invited, 'Come along: everything is ready now.' But all alike started to make excuses. The first said, 'I have bought a piece of land and must go and see it. Please accept my apologies.' Another said, 'I have bought five yoke of oxen and am on my way to try them out. Please accept my apologies.' Yet another said, 'I have just got married and so am unable to come.'

The servant returned and reported this to his master. Then the householder, in a rage, said to his servant, 'Go out quickly into the streets and alleys of the town and bring in here the poor, the crippled, the blind and the lame.' 'Sir,' said the servant, 'your orders have been carried out and there is still room.' Then the master said to his servant, 'Go to the open roads and hedgerows and force people to come to make sure my house is full; because, I tell you, not one of those who were invited shall have a taste of my banquet."

Luke 14: 12-24

Exactly backwards.

And remember, if they have begun to lose control over their very own selves, and become capable of being affected *only* by schizophrenic effectual stimulus of any and/or all kinds – and The Majority *has*, it is because their cerebral cortices will have begun to become destroyed. And remember too, which is exactly because, all of their individually affected receptors *too* will have become destroyed, and/or their ability to be affected by *any* thing will be severely diminished, and which is exactly why they do continue to move while in a purposefully effectuated direction, to enable their own selves to be exposed to it, instead of away from it: chaos of any, and/or all, kinds, and while including all of it. To the point, that they cannot even simply breathe, without their purposefully allowed exposure to it: chaos of any and/or all kinds, and/or noise, and/or discord, and/or pain and death and suffering.

While including, all allowed exposure to all absolutely abstracted, and purely psychopathic, and/or schizophrenic, dopamine biochemical inducing stimulus functioning as pure *pleasure* only, and/or The Apple. And which is *while* – and simultaneously and remember too, any one individual human being who has actually enabled their own selves to become capable of forming a truly humanistic simultaneously relative Omnidimensional refractive gem of a mind, and parallel functioning central nervous system: for their very own selves to be in possession of only, will have – *actually neurophysiologically and simultaneously*, enabled their own selves to become capable of effectually forming an "augmenter," of an –

"Candace Pert: 'I see the brain in terms of quantum mechanics – the brain is just a receiver, an amplifier, a little wet minireceiver for collective reality…'"
The 3-Pound Universe – Judith Hooper and Dick Teresi

Omnidimensional refractive gem of a mind, and/or an amplifier: to *every* thing. As this word: augment, does mean: "to increase or intensify, as in size, degree, or effect." Which is, actually and neurophysiologically, as that individually affected mind: and parallel functioning central nervous system, will have begun to become MORE, and MORE, and MORE, sensitive: TO EVERY "THING." And too while – simultaneously, those who have not: practiced their scales of Reality, and while as on a daily basis also, *will* have; "Schizophrenics (have a) weird cellular disarray (in their) brains – The pyramid-shaped cells of the hippocampus, normally arranged in an orderly manner, (are) grossly misaligned – Schizophrenics often feel that their minds and bodies are split apart (and) find it difficult to distinguish between signal and noise and to assign levels of importance to various classes of stimuli – schizophrenics (are) 'reducers' (as opposed to augmenters), (and) their brains naturally reduce, or dampen, stimuli" – begun to a become LESS, and LESS, and LESS, sensitive, to every thing: remember? And too remember, we do now know, that their simple spoken words, are –

"Make a tree sound and its fruit will be sound; make a tree rotten and its fruit will be rotten. For the tree can be told by its fruit. Brood of vipers, how can your speech be good when you are evil? For a man's words flow out of what fills his heart. A good man draws good things from his store of goodness; a bad man draws bad things from his store of badness. So I tell you this, that for every unfounded word men utter they will answer on Judgement day, since it is by your words you will be acquitted, and by your words condemned."
Matthew 12: 33-37

Absolutely meaningless: *except to condemn their very own selves.*
And which is the simple "perceivable proof" that we will be capable of simply seeing, and with our eyes alone too: of the lie, which they *are* the "manifestation of." And: remember, which was the *exact* reason for –

"When Pilate heard them say this his fears increased. Re-entering the Praetorium, he said to Jesus, 'Where do you come from?' But Jesus made no answer. Pilate then said to him, 'Are you refusing to speak to me? Surely you know I have power to release you and I have power to crucify you?' 'You would have no power over me,' replied Jesus, 'if it had not been given to you from above; that is why the one who handed me over to you has the greater guilt."

John 19: 8-11

His: The Son of God/Son of Man/Collective Consciousness of Mankind made manifest, being betrayed: by the victims of the con.

And – remember, which was – exactly, as the victims of the con, did allow their very own selves to become victims of primary suggestibility – exactly brainwashed, and capable of being controlled: to sell their souls, and to simply enable their own selves to remain a part of the In Crowd. Which is being purposefully allowed exposure to the absolutely abstracted, and purely psychopathic, and/or schizophrenic, dopamine biochemical inducing stimulus, actually functioning as pure *pleasure* only, and/or The Apple. And only rather than to face-up to their own neurophysiological Reality: to secure their truly humanistic apathy; their truly humanistic complacency; their truly humanistic anonymity; their truly humanistic brain death; their truly humanistic cowardice, and their truly humanistic addiction to all things worldly. And too, only while, exactly, betraying the Collective Consciousness of Mankind – Selling their souls, and becoming collaborators with all of the worldly psychopathic con-artists: who have hijacked the Collective Consciousness of Mankind, and led us on a collision course with our very own destiny.

So that, we can now exactly know, for a verified scientific fact, that any one individual human being, who has not become a victim of the con, will simply, and exactly, become capable of taking back control over their very own selves, and also capable of joining *this* revolution, and while: simultaneously, any one individual human being, who has become a victim of the con, will – exactly, not become capable of taking back control over their very own selves.

Because – remember, everything is –

"There are two essential yet complementary aspects of this new vision of time which are as striking in contrast as heaven and hell. Heaven is ruled by dynamical equations that are reversible and 'timeless'; their simplicity ensures stability for eternity. Hell is more akin to the real world, where fluctuations, uncertainty and chaos reign."

The Arrow of Time – Peter Coveny and Roger Highfield

Chaos: except for Time *made manifest*.
And – simultaneously, for anyone who has –

443

"Do not store up treasures for yourselves on earth, where moths and woodworms destroy them and thieves can break in and steal. But store up treasures for yourselves in heaven, where neither moth nor woodworms destroy them and thieves cannot break in and steal. For where your treasure is, there will your heart be also."
Matthew 6: 19-21

Begun to allow their very own selves to become capable of effectually forming an Omnidimensional refractive gem of a mind, and parallel functioning central nervous system: to be in possession of only, it will be –

" Candance Pert: 'I see the brain in terms of quantum mechanics – the brain is just a receiver, an amplifier, a little wet minireceiver for collective reality...'"
The 3-Pound Universe – Judith Hooper and Dick Teresi

A neurophysiological impossibility for them to purposefully expose their truly humanistic Omnidimensional refractive gem of a mind, and parallel functioning central nervous system, to any absolutely abstracted, and purely psychopathic, and/or schizophrenic, dopamine biochemical inducing effectual stimulus, of any and/or all kinds. It does cause a severe neurophysiological disturbance within the mind, and parallel functioning central nervous system, of any one individual human being, who has actually enabled themselves to become capable of forming an Omnidimensional refractive gem of a mind, and parallel functioning central nervous system, to actually be "in possession of": only. And which is while – and simultaneously, for anyone who has not, and who has allowed themselves to become a victim of the con, it *will* –

"The prefrontal cortex (is) a dopamine-rich area of the brain that controls impulsive and irrational behavior. Addicts, in fact, display many of the symptoms shown by patients who have suffered strokes or injuries to the prefrontal cortex. Damage to this region – destroys the emotional compass that controls behaviors that the patient (should) know are unacceptable."
Addicted – J. Madeleine Nash – Time – May 5, 1997

Remain a neurophysiological impossibility for them to actually take back control over their very own selves. And/or, to actually renounce their: all of the worldly psychopathic con-artists, acquired control over them: all of the victims of the con. And – remember, which is as this word: renounce, does mean: "to give up or put aside voluntarily – to give up by formal declaration – to repudiate," and this word: repudiate, does mean: "to reject as having no authority or binding force." And – remember too, which is as the prefrontal cortex is the area of a human being's mind, responsible for –

444

"Paul MacLean, for one, considers the frontal lobes the 'heart' of the cortex – Clinically, there is evidence that the prefrontal cortex by looking inward, so to speak, obtains the gut feeling for identifying with another individual. In other words: empathy – Through its centers for vision, hearing, and bodily sensations, we traffic with the external world."

The 3-Pound Universe – Judith Hooper and Dick Teresi

Empathy, and which is as this word: empathy, does mean: "intellectual identification with or vicarious experiencing of the feelings, thoughts, or attitudes of another person," and this word: vicarious, does mean: "performed, exercised, received, or suffered in place of another – taking the place of another person or thing."

So that, we can now know and for a verified scientific fact, that any one individually affected victim of the con, will, simply, remain neurophysiologically incapable of caring about any thing else: except for their very own selves, and their continued purposefully allowed exposure to all of their absolutely abstracted, and purely psychopathic – and/or schizophrenic, dopamine biochemical inducing effectual stimulus, actually functioning as pure *pleasure* only, and/or The Apple. And which is as they will actually remain incapable of; "to reject as having no binding force" – breaking free of the attractive force of the black hole, of their own personally affected neurophysiological dysfunction. And which is, as they will remain incapable of *actually* picking up the God "damned" television set, and throwing it away. And/or, they will remain incapable of stopping their purposefully allowed exposure to all worldly God "damned" spectacle events of any and/or all kinds: the God "damned" movies – the God "damned" theatre – the God "damned" entertainment – the God "damned" novels, and the God "damned" patronizing of amusement parks – theme parks – spectator sporting event parks – art museum parks and spectacle event parks. And the God "damned" excessive tangible form mass stimulus of any and/or all kinds: the God "damned" grandiosely, and deliberately, styled, buildings – automobiles – trains and airplanes, and the God "damned" excessively simplistic, and histrionic, and monochromatic, and romanticized, musical sounds. And too the God "damned" worshiping of any worldly god stars: the television stars – movie stars – spectator sporting event stars – boy band stars – girl band stars – pop icon band stars – composer stars, and musician stars. And the God "damned" excessively fine fabrics, the God "damned" diamonds, gold and silver, and too the God "damned" excessively fatty tasting foods and sweet tasting foods, the God "damned" computers – Internet – virtual reality – dot-coms – cell phones, and video recorders. And the God "damned" parties and aristocratic environments, and too the God "damned" simple accessing of abstract knowledge, the God "damned" worldly power and money, and the God "damned" apathy – the God "damned" complacency – the God "damned" ignorance of Reality: The Mind of God made manifest, and too all of the God "damned" absolutely abstracted, and purely psychopathic and/or schizophrenic, dopamine biochemical inducing effectual

445

stimulus: actually effectually functioning as pure *pleasure* only and/or The Apple, they: all of the individually affected victims of the con, will remain absolutely neurophysiologically incapable of renouncing. And/or absolutely incapable of breaking free of its: Truly humanistic brain death and the black hole of dysfunction, attractive force. And they will only become capable of making manifest a simple perceivable proof, of their own personally affected dysfunction – their betraying of the Collective Consciousness of Mankind, and their Selling of their souls too. And again, which is simply because, if an individual has actually enabled their own selves to become capable of forming an Omnidimensional refractive gem of a mind, and parallel functioning central nervous system, to be in possession of only, all of these things will actually cause a severe neurophysiological disturbance within them, and while: simultaneously, anyone who has not, will remain incapable of caring about anything, *except* for their purposefully allowed exposure to them. And which is while they are actually killing The Child: which they could not care less about, and/or have empathy for, and/or "suffer in the place of."

And – too and simultaneously, which will be as the person who *has* enabled their own selves to become capable of forming an Omnidimensional refractive gem of a mind, will – exactly, have become capable of experiencing truly humanistic empathy: and/or capable of vicariously experiencing another human being's personally experienced emotions, and/or *pain* and suffering too. And as that one individually affected: and truly virtuous human being and which will be *you*, does begin to help *any* other one individually affected human being: of the con, to begin to become capable of taking back control over their very own selves, there *is* going to be made manifest a tremendous amount of REAL chaos, and/or REAL yelling, and REAL screaming, and REAL hollering, and REAL hatred too, and all of it will be directed at you. So that, you will become capable of experiencing, at least, twice as much *pain*: as any other individual human being and/or all of Mankind, who you are attempting to help. And – remember, which is as they are actually going to feel as though somebody is attempting to violate them, and/or as though somebody is attempting to "push them off the bicycle," and/or as though somebody is attempting to take control over them, as you attempt to help them, and that *pain* is going to be real. And: as you are capable of experiencing their emotions and/or having empathy for them, you too will be experiencing *that* "pain." But – too and simultaneously and as you will have formed an augmenter of a mind, you will be experiencing the very real *pain* made manifest: within you, as from the noise, and chaos, and screaming, and yelling and hollering too, and – remember, which is as they will not be affected hardly at all by that exact same chaos made manifest. And – remember too, which is as they *will* actually begin to enjoy it, and feed off of it, and that: the chaos and yelling and screaming and hollering, is not why they are going to feel any *pain*: they are going to be feeling *pain* for their own selves, because they are not being allowed access to their drugs, and/or their inability to control their very own selves. But they will remain incapable of understanding that, so they will hate you for that: *their* inability to control their own selves, too, and that is some more *pain* that you are going to feel.

And – too remember, the majority actually has become affected, and the majority cannot even begin to understand what it is that you will be talking about. And simultaneously, the majority will need to be allowed exposure to the absolutely abstracted dopamine biochemical inducing effectual stimulus, actually functioning as pure *pleasure*, and – simultaneously, the majority will remain neurophysiologically incapable of understanding Reality: and/or their own personally affected neurophysiological dysfunctions, and – *simultaneously*, the majority is going to blame you – and/or us, FOR EVERYTHING: EVERY "THING." And while including the chaos, and the noise, and the screaming and yelling and hollering too. And too they are going to blame you for *their* anxiety: and/or their own personally affected neurophysiological dysfunction, and/or their own personally affected feeling as though they have lost control over their very own selves, and/or their own personally affected feeling as though somebody has placed a plastic bag over their heads, and/or their own personally affected feeling as though somebody is attempting to push them off the bicycle, and/or their own personally affected feeling as though their entire worlds are beginning to crumble: BECAUSE THEY ARE, AND IT IS. And they are even go to blame you – and/or us, for the collapse of the global socioeconomic structure: YOU WILL BE BLAMED FOR EVERYTHING, AND YOU WILL BE CREDITED FOR ABSOLUTELY NOTHING: **FOR ABSOLUTELY NOTHING THEY WILL CREDIT YOU**. Or – rather, here on Earth, you will be –

"And when they lead you away to hand you over, do not worry beforehand about what to say; no, say whatever is given to you when the time comes, because it is not you who will be speaking: it will be the Holy Spirit. Brother will betray brother to death, and the father his child; children will rise against their parents and have them put to death. You will be hated by all men on account of my name; but the man who stands firm to the end will be saved."
Mark 13: 11-13

Credited for nothing.

And – remember too, it: their own personally affected neurophysiological dysfunctions, and/or their own personally affected becoming a victim of the con, and/or their own personally affected psychosis, and/or their own personally affected inability to understand truly humanistic universally applicable, and simultaneously relative, Omnidimensional Reality: actually functioning as Omnidimensional Time *made manifest,* and/or The Common Law, is inversely affected, and proportionally applicable: for The Majority. And because they have never practiced their scales of truly humanistic simultaneously relative Omnidimensional Reality, and while as on a daily basis too, and/or enabled themselves to become capable of effectually forming truly humanistic simultaneously relative multidimensional synaptic capabilities, for their own selves to be in possession of: and/or used their talents, and so they *were* taken away from them. And as they: The Majority, have become the 21st century aristocratic elite, and have become only capable of functioning, as the Monarch was only capable of functioning, and have experienced truly humanistic brain death for themselves to be in possession of *only*. And their tangible form mass stuff: their addiction to all things worldly, and while including their purposefully allowed exposure to all absolutely abstracted, and purely psychopathic and/or schizophrenic, dopamine biochemical inducing stimulus, actually functioning as pure *pleasure* only, and/or The Apple. And remember when Christopher Columbus went selling off into uncharted territories, and – then, how he did become capable of acquiring the Holy Grail of understanding for his own self to be in possession of – *only*, but how the Monarch did get truly humanistic brain death, for her own self to be in possession of only: Her addiction to all things worldly, and while including Her truly humanistic delusion: as everybody was telling Her only exactly what She wanted to hear. And too remember, which was only exactly because, everybody was afraid of being left out of the In Crowd, and/or, too, they: everybody, was afraid *of* Reality: remember? But – too remember and while as in this real Edenic tale, a personally affected truly humanistic Omnidimensional refractive gem of a mind, and/or truly humanistic simultaneously, and universally applicable, empirical self-consciousness, and/or a truly humanistic being's purposefully affected ability to come to an understanding of Reality, and/or a human being's soul, and/or The Holy Grail of understanding, is the only thing which CAN NOT –

"$1 million for science to discover God's plan –
Can science divine the hand of God in the universe? – Investment tycoon Sir John Templeton wants to know, and he's paying a total of $1 million to 15 scientists to look for a purpose in the cosmos – The scientists, many with international reputations, have spent their careers studying the Big Bang, the origin of stars and galaxies, the fundamental physical constants, and the origin of life – But the money gives the opportunity to focus on the question that intrigues Templeton, as it has philosophers and astronomers for centuries: Is the universe a product of design or accident? – Templeton, 88, two years ago faxed his request for the meaning of it all from his home in the Bahamas to Radnor, home of his Templeton foundation...The foundation's executive director, Charles Harper, who is trained in physics and theology, crafted the grant program based on the question, 'Is there a fundamental purpose in the cosmos..."
Faye Flam – The Philadelphia Inquirer – Saturday April 6, 2002

Be simply bought: with *any* amount of God "damned" Money, remember? And remember too, the –

"Then Jesus said to his disciples, 'I tell you solemnly, it will be hard for a rich man to enter the kingdom of heaven. Yes, I tell you again, it is easier for a camel to pass through the eye of a needle than for a rich man to enter the kingdom of heaven.'

When the disciples heard this they were astonished. 'Who can be saved, then? they said. Jesus gazed at them. 'For men, he told them, 'this is impossible; for God everything is possible."
Matthew 19: 23-26

More truly humanistic brain dead an individual human being has become, the less they will be capable of understanding truly humanistic universally applicable, and simultaneously relative, Omnidimensional Reality. And/or, have begun to become capable of purposefully affecting a truly humanistic, simultaneously relative, Omnidimensional refractive gem of a mind, and parallel functioning central nervous system, for their own selves to be in possession of: ONLY. And – too and of course and *simultaneously*, the more offended they will become by "it," the –

"And indeed, everybody who does wrong
hates the light and avoids it,
for fear his actions should be exposed;
but the man who lives by the truth
comes out into the light
so that it may be plainly seen that what he does is done in God."
John 3: 20-21

Absolute truth that is.
And/or the –

"Cracking the Cosmic Code With a Little Help From Dr. Hawking –
...Dr. Hawking's first book for a wide audience, 'A Brief History of Time,' took readers on a tour through black holes, the gravitational traps from which not even light can emerge, and imaginary time as he described the quest for the vaunted 'theory of everything' that would enable us to 'know the mind of God'...quantum theory and relativity have taught us, science is about what can be observed and measured or it is about nothing at all. In science, as in democracy, there is no hidden secret knowledge, all that counts is on the table, observable and falsifiable. All else is metaphysics."
Dennis Overbye – The New York Times – Tuesday December 11, 2001

Observable facts: which we can simply see with our eyes alone. As in science, *and* democracy too – *only*.
And too remember, how as in the purposeful formation of the world's first Truly Idealist Democratic Society, that they: the aristocratic elite, and/or worldly psychopathic con-artists, and/or entertainers, were not going to let them: *any* of the truly virtuous common man masses, begin to become capable of taking back control over their very own selves, *without* a war being waged, for that control. And which is simply because, without that control, they have –

"And he went on to tell the people this parable: 'A man planted a vineyard and leased it to tenants, and went abroad for a long while. When the time came, he sent a servant to the tenants to get his share of the produce of the vineyard from them. But the tenants thrashed him, and sent him away empty-handed. But he persevered and sent a second servant; they thrashed him too and treated him shamefully and sent him away empty-handed. He still persevered and sent a third; they wounded this one also, and threw him out. Then the owner of the vineyard said, 'What am I to do? I will send them my dear son. Perhaps they will respect him.' But when the tenants saw him they put their heads together. 'This is the heir,' they said, 'let us kill him so that the inheritance will be ours.' So they threw him out of the vineyard and killed him.

'Now what will the owner of the vineyard do to them? He will come and make an end of these tenants and give the vineyard to others.' Hearing this they said, 'God forbid!' But he looked hard at them and said, 'Then what does this text in the scriptures mean:

It was the stone rejected by the builders
that became the keystone?

Anyone who falls on that stone will be dashed to pieces; anyone it falls on will be crushed.'

But for their fear of the people, the scribes and the chief priests would have liked to lay hands on him that very moment, because they realized that this parable was aimed at them."

Luke 20: 9-19

Less than nothing. Because they do have *absolutely* nothing to be in possession of, for their very own selves. And except, of course, for their own personally affected regression back to point time zero, of their own personally affected existence within truly humanistic simultaneously relative Omnidimensional Reality: their own personally affected truly humanistic brain death, and their own personally affected addiction to all things worldly, which they did get by maintaining their control over other human beings – *all of it*. And while – simultaneously, they did place their entire existence upon it: the facade of the absolutely abstracted, and purely psychopathic and/or schizophrenic, dopamine biochemical inducing stimulus, actually functioning as pure *pleasure* only, and/or The Apple, and which has just been torn in half.

And – remember too, *these* are –

"Lying, deceiving, and manipulation are natural talents for psychopaths. With their powers of imagination in gear and focused on themselves, psychopaths appear amazingly unfazed by the possibility – or even the certainty, of being found out. When caught in a lie or challenged with the truth, they are seldom perplexed or embarrassed – they simply change their stories or attempt to rework the facts so that they appear to be consistent with the lie – Psychopaths have what it takes to defraud

450

and bilk others: They are fast-talking, charming, self-assured, at ease in social situations, cool under pressure, unfazed by the possibility of being found out, and totally ruthless. And even when exposed, they can carry on as if nothing has happened, often leaving their accusers bewildered and uncertain about their own positions – Psychopaths (are) experts at distorting the truth to suit their purposes – psychopaths are very good at putting on a good impression when it suits them, and they often paint their victims as the real culprits..."

Dr. Robert D. Hare – Without Conscience

Master manipulating psychopathic con-artists. Who are incapable of experiencing what real humans experience, and/or of coming to an understanding of truly humanistic simultaneously relative Omnidimensional Reality, and/or incapable of consciously cognizing any Time *made manifest* at all, and/or simply incapable of experiencing truly humanistic *any* thing for their own selves. And – simultaneously, only capable of functioning while as in an absolutely abstracted – purely automatous, and fragmented, manner, and: only, capable of experiencing a simple dopamine biochemical induction, actually functioning as pure *pleasure*. While as through their purposefully allowed exposure to the absolutely abstracted, and purely psychopathic and/or schizophrenic, dopamine biochemical inducing stimulus, actually functioning as pure *pleasure* only, and which actually is truly humanistic brain dead that they are: remember!

And – remember too, they: the psychopathic con-artists, were so extremely proficient, at; "Lying, deceiving, and manipulation are natural talents for psychopaths. With their powers of imagination in gear and focused on themselves, psychopaths appear amazingly unfazed by the possibility – or even the certainty, of being found out" – lying deceiving *and* manipulation, that they did actually become capable *of* –

"Picasso and Einstein cross paths, and offer a mirthful night –

In the program for *Picasso at the Lapin Agile*, which opened Tuesday at the Arden Theater, the director, cast and staff pose 20 questions you might ponder after viewing the play. 'What is genius?' they ask. How does genius get recognized..."

Clifford A. Ridley – The Philadelphia Inquirer – Thursday March 8, 2001

Conning the entire world into believing that the very definition of psychosis *is* the definition of intelligence, and/or that the very definition of chaos *is* harmony, and/or that the very definition of a lie *is* the truth, and/or that the very definition of Death *is* Life too, remember? And remember, the overwhelming majority of the entire world does now actually believe that it: psychotic, and/or neurotic, and/or psychopathic, and/or schizophrenic, and/or paranoid delusional, and/or obsessive compulsive, and/or unbalanced, and/or addicted, and/or simply incapable of understanding any of *a priori* Reality, is the definition of intelligence, and/or the definition of being normal. And – remember too, which is simply because, The

Majority of the world has actually become affected: by the con.

So that, we can simply understand and for our very own selves, as you do only even begin to become capable of encouraging any one other individual human being: who you may sincerely love and/or all of Mankind too, to actually begin to become capable of –

"When day broke there was a meeting of the elders of the people, attended by the chief priests and scribes. He was brought before their counsel, and they said to him, 'If you are the Christ, tell us.' 'If I tell you,' he replied, 'you will not believe me, and if I question you, you will not answer. But from now on, the Son of Man will be *seated at the right hand* of the Power of God.' Then they all said, 'So you are the Son of God then?' He answered, 'It is you who say I am.' 'What need of witnesses have we now?' they asked. 'We have heard it for ourselves from his own lips.' The whole assembly then rose, and they brought him before Pilate.

They began their accusation by saying, 'We found this man inciting our people to revolt...''

Luke 22: 66-71, 23: 1-2

Joining *this* Revolution: which is simply our Return to Innocence and an adherence to The Common Law, they–

"The police went back to the chief priests and Pharisees who said to them, 'Why haven't you brought him?' The police replied, 'There has never been anybody who has spoken like him.' 'So,' the Pharisees answered,' you have been led astray as well? Have any of the authorities believed in him? Any of the Pharisees? This rabble knows nothing about the Law – they are damned.' One of them, Nicodemus – the same man who had come to Jesus earlier – said to them, 'But surely the Law does not allow us to pass judgment on a man without giving him a hearing and discovering what he is about?' To this they answered, 'Are you a Galilean too? Go into the matter, and see for yourself: prophets do not come out of Galilee.''

John 7: 45-52

All of the worldly psychopathic con-artists, who are responsible for supplying all of their victims with all of their purposefully allowed exposure to all of their absolutely abstracted, and purely psychopathic – and/or schizophrenic, dopamine biochemical inducing stimulus, actually functioning as pure *pleasure* only and/or The Apple, will be telling all of their victims: of the con and which is now The Majority, that you: any one individual who does join this revolution, *are* attempting to become capable of "creating chaos." And/or that you are attempting to disturb the peace, and/or that you are attempting to violate them, and/or that you are attempting to cause them pain, and/or that you are attempting to take control over them, and/or that you are attempting to cause them to become victims of primary suggestibility, and/or that you are attempting to brainwash them, and exactly as you

452

do begin to become capable of "explaining reality to them." Which is, as they, must, actually become capable of taking back control of their very selves, while as from all of the worldly psychopathic con-artists. And which will be: *actually occurring*, as the worldly psychopathic con-artists *will* be telling them: any, and/or every, one, to "Pay no attention" *to* Reality – as you do actually attempt to explain it: Reality, to them: any one who has begun to become a victim of the con, and who you may sincerely love, and/or all of Mankind also. So that they: all of the worldly psychopathic con-artists, will be telling all of their victims, to simply pay no attention to "you": as you attempt to explain Reality to *them* – and/or to actually "RENOUNCE" ONLY **YOU**, as you do only attempt to become capable of encouraging them to become capable of joining this revolution. And become capable of taking back control over their very own selves, and/or as you do *only* attempt to become capable of encouraging them, to become capable of understanding their own selves.

And remember, which is as all of those things: all of *those* aforementioned absolutely abstracted, and purely psychopathic and/or schizophrenic, dopamine biochemical inducing stimuli actually functioning as pure *pleasure* only, are nothing more than –

"There are two essential yet complementary aspects of this new vision of time which are as striking in contrast as heaven and hell. Heaven is ruled by dynamical equations that are reversible and 'timeless'; their simplicity ensures stability for eternity. Hell is more akin to the real world, where fluctuations, uncertainty and chaos reign..."
The Arrow of Time – Peter Coveny and Roger Highfield

Hell made manifest.
So that, we can now know, for a verified scientific fact, that the purely identifiable function, *is* exactly backwards. And that any one individual human being, who does decide to join this revolution, is – in fact, rebelling against worldly tyranny, and remaining obedient to God, and for their love of Mankind only.
But – remember, the majority has already become affected, and they will remain incapable of understanding Reality, and/or you, as you do attempt to explain it to them. And they will also – and simultaneously, simply remain incapable of understanding exactly why they are beginning to feel extremely anxious, and as they exactly are, and as each day does go by they will become proportionally affected, and "suffer" more. So, as the Majority has become affected: as they have actually regressed back to point time zero and become only capable of functioning as young children are capable of functioning, they will – and simultaneously, remain incapable of understanding complex neurophysiological cause and effect: and/or that which they cannot simply see with their eyes alone. And they will – and simultaneously, become capable of "seeing" other individual human beings being encouraged, by truly virtuous human beings, to become capable of joining this revolution, and/or to

become capable of taking back control over their very own selves. And which will be, as those individual human beings: the ones who are attempting to take back control over their very own selves, will be experiencing very real *pain,* and it will be proportionally applicable: *as* to the amount that they have been affected, and while including those who actually have become addicted to larger amounts of drugs, and/or been abused at some point in their lives. And the majority has already become affected: so they will remain only capable of seeing the *pain* that other individual human beings are beginning to experience for their own selves, and incapable of understanding exactly why, they *are* experiencing that *pain.* So that, the majority, too, will simply say: to any one individual, who you may be attempting to help, that: "You don't need that: *pain*, come join us." And – remember, which is only exactly because: "Misery loves company." And the absolute last thing in the world, that any one individually affected victim of the con, and which is now the majority, would ever want to simply "see," and with their eyes alone, is one other individual, begin to become capable of taking back control over their very own selves: and while as with the assistance of one other truly virtuous human being. Who *is* capable of experiencing Truly humanistic love, and who will be sharing that love with the person they are attempting to help, and/or all of mankind too.

And remember too, which is as any other one individually affected human being, who is only capable of functioning while as in a purely psychopathic manner, will need to become capable of "controlling" the individual who you may be attempting to help. And they will be telling that person: who you are attempting to help, that *you* are attempting to become capable of taking control over them: while *they* are actually the ones who are attempting to take control of them. While – *and* simultaneously, the person who you are attempting to help, will be experiencing real *pain,* because of you: and your explaining of Reality to them, and while – too and simultaneously, the person who is actually attempting to take control of them, will be telling them *only* exactly what they want to hear, and giving them only exactly what they want: an escape from Reality, and too while enabling them to experience *pleasure* – instead of *pain.* Which: *pain*, is what you will be causing them to experience, but only within their minds alone of course, and – too, which is *exactly* what they will remain incapable of understanding, and while – simultaneously, the actual *pain* they will be experiencing, is only going to be actually becoming *worse* and *worse*: with each passing day, and as our Reality begins to affect our entire global community, and as it is inversely affected.

So that: in Reality, as each single day does go by, twice as many people will become twice as affected, as they will be reaching the Point of no return, and *lose control over their very own selves.* And remember, which is as the psychopathic con-artists: who are responsible for supplying all of their victims with all of their purposefully allowed exposure to all of the absolutely abstracted, and purely psychopathic and/or schizophrenic, dopamine biochemical inducing stimulus, functioning as pure *pleasure* only, will actually never – NEVER, willfully relinquish their control: which they have acquired over other individual human beings, and/or simply admit that they did make a mistake. And while they: all of the worldly psychopathic con-artists, will only continue, to –

"He had just finished speaking when a Pharisee invited him to dine at his house. He went in and sat down at the table. The Pharisee saw this and was surprised that he had not first washed before the meal. But the Lord said to him, 'Oh, you Pharisees! You clean the outside of the cup and plate, while inside yourselves you are filled with extortion and wickedness. Fools! Did not he who made the outside make the inside too? Instead, give alms from what you have and then indeed everything will be clean for you. But alas for you Pharisees! You who pay your tithe of mint and rue and all sorts of garden herbs and overlook justice and the love of God! These you should have practiced, without leaving the others undone. Alas for you Pharisees who like taking the seats of honor in the synagogues and being greeted obsequiously in the market squares! Alas for you, because you are like the unmarked tombs that men walk on without knowing it!'

A lawyer then spoke up. 'Master,' he said, 'when you speak like this you insult us too.' 'Alas for you lawyers also,' he replied, 'because you load on men burdens that are unendurable, burdens that you yourselves do not move a finger to lift.'

'Alas for you who build the tombs of the prophets, the men your ancestors killed! In this way you both witness what your ancestors did and approve it; they did the killing, you do the building.'

'And that is why the Wisdom of God said, 'I will send them prophets and apostles; some they will slaughter and persecute, so that this generation will have to answer for every prophet's blood that has been shed since the foundation of the world, from the blood of Abel to the blood of Zechariah, who was murdered between the altar and the sanctuary.' Yes, I tell you, this generation will have to answer for it all.'

'Alas for you lawyers who have taken away the key of knowledge! You have not gone in yourselves, and have prevented others going in who wanted to.'

When he left the house, the scribes and the Pharisees began a furious attack on him and tried to force answers from him on innumerable questions, setting traps to catch him out in something he might say."
Luke 11: 37-54

Purposefully make manifest chaos, and/or enable people to become capable of experiencing neurophysiological dysfunctions for their own selves, and/or teach people how to become capable of only functioning while as in an absolutely abstracted, and/or automatous, and unidirectionally successive, manner, and/or simply enable people to experience truly humanistic being brain death for their own selves, so that they can become capable of benefiting from it: the chaos and/or lack of harmony, and/or lack of understanding of truly humanistic Reality. And which is while – simultaneously, the more chaos becomes made manifest, and/or affected truly humanistic brain death, the more they do promote it: the chaos and/or lack of harmony, and/or personally affected truly humanistic brain death, for individually affected human beings to be in possession of only. And the more they do love it, feed off of it: consume it, and profit from it.

And which is as it: their own personally affected inability to understand Reality, *is* proportionally applicable, to their own personally affected brain death, as they are only capable of functioning while as in a purely psychopathic manner. And remember, which is simply because, the more the absolute truth is beginning to become revealed – and for all the world to simple see with our eyes alone, the less powerful they will become: because they actually are in possession of absolutely nothing, except for their own personally affected brain death, and their personally affected addictions to all things worldly. And – too remember, which they do maintain: their own personally affected truly humanistic brain death, and their addictions to all things worldly, by maintaining their control over other human beings. So that: exactly because they are in possession of absolutely nothing for their very own selves, and exactly because they have not practiced their scales of Reality: and/or built their foundations *of* truly humanistic simultaneously relative Reality, they do have no truly humanistic talents, for their own selves to be in possession of. So, they do need to have: they do need to control – they do need to consume, and they do need to take hold of, EVERYTHING: EVERYTHING, they do need to control, because they can not control their very own selves, and their own destines too. And – remember, which is simply because, they do have NO single simultaneously relative, and cognizable, point time zero located anywhere within their own selves: THEY HAVE NO "POINT OF REST." So they cannot possibly consciously control "anything": so they must become capable of controlling "everything." And which is exactly why, they do believe: within their minds alone, that nobody can "understand" them: BECAUSE THEY SIMPLY CAN NOT UNDERSTAND THEIR VERY OWN SELVES. And – remember, which is exactly because, there can be NO –

"Ernst Hanfstaengl, describes the shapelessness at the root of Hitler's mesmerizing oratorical power: 'His brain was a sort of primeval jelly or ectoplasm which quivered in response to every impulse from its surroundings – You could never pin him down, say that he was this thing or that thing, it was all floating, without roots, intangible and mediumistic...Momentum had driven him into an extreme position from which there was no escape...'"
Michael Nelken M. D. – Hitler Unmasked

Simultaneously relative anything, within their minds.
And too remember and again, all effectual humanistic phenomena is inversely affected: and proportionally applicable, as to their own personally affected brain death, which they have experienced for their own selves to be in possession of only, and their addictions to all things worldly only. So that – remember too, the

more truly humanistic brain death they have experienced: the more mediocre they are; the more simplistic they are; the more childish they are; the more materialistic they are; the more only capable of functioning as animals they are: the *less* they will be capable of understanding *any* of truly humanistic universally applicable Reality, and too the more offended they will become by their own personally affected dysfunction: remember? And – remember too, which is as they are – now, only capable of experiencing psychosis for their own selves.

Which is as they will be only capable of functioning while as in a purely psychotic manner: and/or only capable of remaining confined to their own personally affected delusions, and incapable of understanding any of *a priori* Reality: IT IS A NEUROPHYSIOLOGICAL IMPOSSIBILITY. While they will only, and simultaneously too, remain confined to their own personally affected neurophysiological dysfunctions: their own personally affected psychosis, and/or their own personally affected neurosis, and/or their own personally affected psychopathic – schizophrenic – obsessive compulsive, and paranoid delusional, minds. And – too and simultaneously and remember, which is as they will need to maintain their addictions to all things worldly, while including their control over other human beings, which they have simply acquired. Again, which is as it: truly humanistic brain death and purely psychopathic behavior, does always function while being proportionally applicable.

To enable our own selves to simply see this observable fact, and with our eyes alone too, we can simply reference this –

"Piss Christ 1987 – Cibachrome – 60by 40 inches – Andres serrano"

Personally affected schizophrenic inarticulate cry for attention. And too remember, which was made manifest while as through the conspired appropriation of public funds too, and while as within The United States of America: with taxed dollars.

So that, we can simply understand, that this worldly psychopathic con-artist, and his conspiring collaborators, did actually become capable of appropriating the use of public funds, to make manifest his own personally affected schizophrenic inarticulate cry for attention, and/or a projected abstraction of his own personally affected –

"Andres Serrano was raised by his grandmother and his African-Cuban mother (who) never learned English and was frequently hospitalized for psychosis..."
Andres Serrano – The Spirit of The Letter – Lucy Lippard, Art In America

Psychosis: it was a very small part of the con. But, as it: personally affected truly humanistic brain death and/or psychosis, is exactly proportionally applicable, and which was as they did actually become capable of conning the world into believing that the very definition of schizophrenia and/or psychosis is intelligence, they did also – and simultaneously and exactly, allow their very own selves to begin to become capable of "believing": within all of their individually affected minds, that they *are* "intelligent" – instead of "understanding," that they *have* experienced truly humanistic brain death for their own selves to be in possession of only, and their addictions to all things worldly only too of course. And which: their own personally affected truly humanistic brain death, and their addictions to all things worldly, they do need to maintain: while they do also, and simultaneously too, sincerely believe, that they have –

"Napoleon Bonaparte: Power is my mistress. I have done too much to capture her to let her be snatched away. Although some will say that power came to me naturally, I know what work it took, what sleepless nights, what scheming – My power comes from my reputation and my reputation from my victories. It would collapse if I did not bolster it with even more victories and more glories. Conquest has made me what I am and so it also sustains me...Friendship is only a word. I love nobody: no, not even my brothers – I know perfectly well I have no real friends (But) for appearances sake, I will have as many as I need..."
Napoleon Speaks – Diaries, Letters, Proclamations, etc.
Roots of Western Civilization, Volume II – Wesley D. Camp

Earned the right to take control over everything, and/or to simply have acquired it: truly humanistic brain death and their addictions to all things worldly. And too and simultaneously, their ability to make manifest: only, their own personally affected schizophrenic inarticulate cries for attention, and/or chaos, and pain and death and suffering too of course. And – too and simultaneously and of course, while becoming capable of offending, and/or violating, and/or assailing, and/or attacking, any one – and/or every one: to actually become capable of acquiring that which they have developed a neurophysiological dependency upon. And – too, which is as they are – now, only capable of functioning while as in a neurotic, and/or obsessive compulsive, manner, and while – simultaneously, needing to become capable of maintaining their addiction: which is to actually control everything: remember? And so that they will –

"Fitting Out a Triplex Cloister –
On a dazzling spring afternoon, Andres Serrano sat in the dark, still living room of his East Village apartment waiting for his visitors eyes to adjust to the light. A wrought-iron chandelier hung ineffectually from the 16-foot-high vaulted ceiling, its dimmer switch on the fritz he explained – With just a hint of apology, he turned up the room's one working light, a spot trained on the center of a broad maroon brick wall. There, suspended by heavy steel chain, hung a nearly life-size 16th-century statue of Jesus. It was an arresting sight, arms missing, a carved figure of quiet torment – Asked about the religious significance of the figure, Mr. Serrano shrugged. He'd never been particularly religious, he said: 'I just like the way it looks. And it

goes with the furniture'...As he settled into a boxy bishop's chair from the 16th-century, Mr Serrano turned to the question of transgression. Some outrages, he said, simply would not stand – 'I've had parties where people spill drinks on the furniture and don't think to pick it up,' he said, clearly galled by the effrontery..."
John Leland – The New York Times – Thursday May 10, 2001

Lose their minds: if they lose control – over every thing else. Because they have nothing to be in possession of for their very own selves, except for their truly humanistic addictions to all things worldly, remember? And which is as it: their own personally affected brain death, *is* – exactly, proportionally applicable: remember?

And, as it is proportionally applicable, we can simply understand, that *this* person: Mr Serrano, did become capable of acquiring hundreds of thousands of dollars, while including public taxed dollars, while allowing himself to become a collaborator in the con: while creating a diversion from Reality, and becoming capable of making manifest his own personally affected schizophrenic inarticulate cry for attention, and/or chaos, and/or discord, and/or 10010. And too while projecting his own personally affected psychosis upon mankind: to be forcibly exposed to it also, and while assailing Mankind too, and/or simply violating MANKIND, and to enable him to maintain his addiction. And – then, he did actually "feel" violated, and real *pain* too, when somebody did "touch his stuff," which he did "illicitly acquire," while as through the con. And – of course and as I did actually read this article *over* and *over* again, I kept waiting for the punch line, and then, I did –

"...Serrano is an urban artist of considerable political sophistication – in high art (the) word 'moral' is usually considered laughable..."
Andres Serrano – The Spirit and The Letter – Lucy Lippard – Art in America

Remember that the joke was on Mankind.
And – again and remember too, this is simply their own –

"Psychopaths have what it takes to defraud and bilk others: They are fast-talking, charming, self-assured, at ease in social situations, cool under pressure, unfazed by the possibility of being found out, and totally ruthless. And even when exposed, they can carry on as if nothing has happened, often leaving their accusers bewildered and uncertain about their own positions – Psychopaths view people as little more than objects to be used for their own gratification – The psychopath is a rebel, a religious disobeyer of prevailing codes and standards – a rebel without a cause, an agitator without a slogan, a revolutionary without a program; in other words, his rebelliousness is aimed to achieve goals satisfactory to him alone..."
Dr. Robert D. Hare – Without Conscience

Personally affected psychopathic behavior: AT BEST.

And remember, The Majority: of the entire world, has actually become affected: by the con, and they will actually remain only capable of functioning while as in a purely psychopathic manner: at best. And – too remember, which is exactly because, they have actually regressed back to point time zero: of their own personally affected existence within Reality. While they have actually – and simultaneously, experienced truly humanistic brain death for their own selves to be in possession of only, and their personally affected psychosis, and/or their inability to understand Reality. And they have – and simultaneously, allowed their own selves to become addicted to absolutely abstracted, psychopathic dopamine biochemical inducing stimulus: to simply enable their own selves to become capable of breathing – remember? So that, we can simply understand, and for a scientific fact, it will be – in Reality, either you or them: who will be consumed. And too so that, we can simply understand and for a scientific fact also, that they: the majority of the entire world, will actually need to become capable of convincing *you*, that "you" must be mad: that you must be psychotic – that you must be delusional – that you must be out of your mind – that you must be evil, and that you must be institutionalized: to protect them, and/or *their* delusion.

And remember, this is no joke: we have actually passed the point of no return, and everybody is going to die: soon. And remember too, we will function only as scientists while as in our pursuit of the truth, and become capable of understanding only that which we can simply prove, for our very own selves too. And, so: Go ahead, and start explaining Reality to anybody that you do know, and/or do sincerely love. Then watch: with your eyes alone, how quickly their professed love does turn to hate, and for you too. And – too, you will simply see, there become made manifest a tremendous amount of chaos: and/or discord, and/or screaming, and/or yelling and hollering too, and *pain* and death and suffering also, and all of it will be directed at you. And remember too, if they did understand Reality, then they would have no need to have it explained to them, and there would be made manifest NO chaos, and screaming and yelling and hollering too. But the majority does not, and so they do continue to consume it, and be proportionally affected by it: purposefully allowed access to absolutely abstracted, and purely psychopathic and/or schizophrenic, dopamine biochemical inducing stimulus, actually functioning as pure *pleasure* only, and/or The Apple. And as they are beginning to become capable of experiencing truly humanistic brain death, exactly because of it: AND WHICH THEY DO FEED OFF OF – REMEMBER, AND WHICH IS AS THEY DO LOVE IT ALSO: REMEMBER? And so that we can now know, and for a scientific fact and as the majority has already become affected, as we do begin to explain Reality to them: anyone who does not understand it and for their very own selves and which is The Majority, they are going to kill us, and/or simply consume us, and because they will love it, and they will feed off of it: the chaos and discord and *pain* and death and suffering. And – *then*, they *will* be left to their own devices, and everybody will die: as they simply consume each other. Or, you could simply wait, *and –*

460

"Rat-a-tat-tat. Rat-a-tat-tat. Rat-a-tat-tat – If scientists could eavesdrop on the brain of a human embryo 10, maybe 12 weeks after conception, they would hear an astonishing racket. Inside the womb, long before light first strikes the retina of the eye or the earliest dreamy images flicker through the cortex, nerve cells in the developing brain crackle with purposeful activity – the same processes that wire the brain before birth, neuroscientists are finding, also drives the explosion of learning that occurs immediately afterward...(And) evidence is growing that the Staccato bursts of electricity that form these distinctive rat-a-tat-tats arise from coordinated waves of neural activity, and that those pulsing waves, like currents shifting sand on the ocean floor, actually change the shape of the brain...If parents and policy makers don't pay attention to the conditions under which this delicate process takes place, we will all suffer the consequences – starting around the year 2010."

Fertile Minds – J. Madeleine Nash – Time – February 3, 1997

It: the individually and personally affected truly humanistic brain death, the dysfunction and the chaos: the REAL discord, and the REAL pain and death and suffering too, would come to you, and everybody would; "If parents and policy makers don't pay attention to the conditions under which this delicate process takes place, we will all suffer the consequences" – die then too: soon. Either way, it is simply a matter of time.

And – too remember and again, which is as this *is* –

"Drug's effect On Brain Is Extensive, Study Finds –
Heavy users (of highly addictive stimulants) are doing more damage to their brains than scientists had thought, according to the first study that looked inside addicts' brains nearly a year after they stop using the drug – At least a quarter of a class of molecules that help people feel pleasure and reward were knocked out – The addicts (started out as) occasional users but over time the drug hijacked their natural dopamine systems..."

Sandra Blakeslee – The New York Times – Tuesday March 6, 2001

No joke, and it is not a simple metaphorical analogy, we have been hijacked, and led on collision course with our very own destiny. So that, we can simply understand and as a matter of scientific fact, if they: The Majority, were left to their own devices, just how long do you think it is before they would actually come waltzing into your Living Room, to defecate all over *your* face too: just as they did do to the Mother of God. And to violate you and your family too, and/or to simply do whatever they want, whenever they want to do it, and to whomever they want to do it to too, and while making manifest their personally affected schizophrenic inarticulate cries for attention also.

And which is simple to understand, by understanding that they had it all: The entertainment – the televisions – the movies – the theatre – the novels – the spectacle events of any, and/or, all kinds. The entertainment parks: the theme parks – the spectator sporting event parks – the amusement parks – the art museum parks. The excessive tangible form mass stimulus of any, and/or all, kinds: the grandiosely, and deliberately, styled, buildings – automobiles – trains and airplanes, the fine fabrics – diamonds – gold, and silver. The excessively simplistic, and histrionic, and monochromatic, and romanticized, musical sounds. The worshiping of worldly god stars: the television stars – movie stars – spectator sporting event stars – boy band stars – girl band stars – pop icon band stars – musicians stars, and composer stars. The excessively fatty tasting foods, and sweet tasting foods – the alcoholic laced beverages, and caffeine laced beverages. The parties and aristocratic environments. And the computers: Internet – virtual reality – dot-coms – cell phones and video recorders. And also, all of the worldly power – the money and all of the stuff: all of the absolutely abstracted dopamine biochemical inducing stimulus, actually functioning as pure *pleasure* only, and/or The Apple: REMEMBER – BUT THEY STILL DIDN'T "GET IT": REMEMBER? Which was as they: all of the individually affected victims of the con and while as in this real Edenic tale too, were simply programmed, and/or conned, into believing that they *could* simply acquire it: remember?

And which is as we do now know, and for an absolute verified scientific fact, that –

"One thing has become clear to scientists: memory is absolutely crucial to our consciousness – 'There's almost nothing you do, from perception to thinking, that doesn't draw continuously on your memory. (And) It can't be otherwise, since there really is no such thing as a present (while) memory provides a personal context, a sense of self and a sense of familiarity – past and present and a frame for the future' – But memory is not a single phenomenon. 'We don't have a memory system in the brain' – 'We have memory systems, each playing a different role' – All of these different systems of memory are ultimately stored in the brain's cortex – what's happening when the brain forms memory (is that) it's the connections between nerve cells – and particularly the strength of those connections, that are altered by experience (as) the cells are firing simultaneously (and) coordinating different sets of information – when everything is going right, these different systems work together seamlessly..."
Michael D. Lemonick – Smart Genes? – Time – September 13, 1999

NO YOU CAN NOT: simply acquire a truly humanistic being's universally applicable, and simultaneously relative, empirical self-consciousness, and to actually become capable of being in possession of *only*. And/or, a truly humanistic being's soul, and/or control over their very own selves: which cannot be simply acquired. But, remember, it: a human being's soul, can be willfully relinquished, and to simply enable their own selves to remain a part the In Crowd, which is being purposefully allowed exposure to the absolutely abstracted, and purely psychopathic and/or schizophrenic, dopamine biochemical inducing stimulus, actually functioning as pure

462

pleasure only and/or The Apple, and which is while as in this real Edenic tale also.

And so we can now know, and for an absolutely verified, and unequivocal, scientific fact, that any one individual human being who can not join this revolution, IS A TRAITOR: THEY HAVE ACTUALLY ALLOWED THEMSELVES TO BECOME A VICTIM OF THE CON – THEY HAVE LOST CONTROL OVER THEIR VERY OWN SELVES, AND THEY HAVE BETRAYED: GOD – COUNTRY – FAMILY – MANKIND – HUMANITY – THEIR OWN SELVES, AND THE COLLECTIVE CONSCIOUSNESS OF MANKIND: **THEY HAVE SOLD THEIR SOULS**. And only to simply enable their own selves to become capable of preserving their own personally affected truly humanistic complacency: their truly humanistic apathy; their truly humanistic cowardice; their truly humanistic proprietorship, and their truly humanistic anonymity also. But – also of course and now only because of 20th century scientific research, the entire world will know *their* names, and too there will be *no* place for them to hide.

And they still won't get it, as they will –

"Whoever believes in me
believes not in me
but in the one who sent me,
and whoever sees me,
sees the one who sent me.
I, the light, have come into the world,
so that whoever believes in me,
need not stay in the dark any more.
If anyone hears my words and does not keep them faithfully,
it is not I who shall condemn him,
since I have come not to condemn the world
but to save the world;
he who rejects me and refuses my words
has his judge already:
the word itself that I have spoken
will be his judge on the last day.
For what I have spoken does not come from myself;
no, what I was to say, what I had to speak,
was commanded by the Father who sent me,
and I know that his commands mean eternal life.
And therefore what the Father has told me
is what I speak."
John 12: 44-50

Be condemning their very own selves.
And *they still won't get it*, because: REMEMBER, it is –

"Psychopaths seem to know the dictionary meaning of words but fail(ed) to comprehend or appreciate their emotional value or significance (while functioning as if) 'He knows the words but not the music' – Recent laboratory research provides convincing support for these clinical observations...Emotional content of a word seems to give a sort of 'turbo-boost' to the decision-making process. At the same time, emotional words evoke larger brain responses than do neutral words – When we used this laboratory test with prison inmates, the non-psychopaths showed the normal pattern of response – but the psychopaths did not: *They responded to emotional words as if they were neutral words* – to a psychopath, a word is just a word..."

　　　Dr. Robert D. Hare – Without Conscience

　　　A neurophysiological impossibility: THEY ARE BRAIN DEAD. They can neurophysiologically understand, and/or be affected by, absolutely nothing for their own selves: which they cannot simply see, with their eyes alone. And so, words can mean absolutely nothing to them: they cannot understand Reality, and the Reality is, that: EVERYBODY – IS – GOING – TO – DIE: soon.

　　　AND THEY STILL WON'T GET IT. This *is* the end of time, and –

　　　"When you see *the disastrous abomination* set up where it ought not to be (let the reader understand), then those in Judea must escape to the mountains; if a man is on the housetop, he must not come down to go into the house to collect any of his belongings; if a man is in the fields, he must not turn back to fetch his cloak. Alas for those with child, or with babies at the breast, when those days come! Pray that this may not be in winter. For in those days there will be *such distress as, until now, has not been seen* equaled since the beginning when God created the world, nor ever will be again. And if the Lord had not shortened that time, no one would have survived; but he did shorten the time, for the sake of the elect whom he chose.

　　　And if anyone says to you then, 'Look, here is the Christ' or, 'Look, he is there,' do not believe it; for false Christs and false prophets will arise and produce signs and portents to deceive the elect, if that were possible. You therefore must be on your guard. I have forewarned you of everything.

　　　But in those days, after that time of distress, the sun will be darkened, the moon will lose its brightness, the stars will come falling from heaven and the powers in the heavens will be shaken. And then they will see the Son of Man coming in the clouds with great power and glory; then too he will send the angels to gather his chosen from the four winds, from the ends of the world to the ends of heaven.

　　　Take the fig tree as a parable: as soon as its twigs grow supple and its leaves come out, you know that summer is near. So with you when you see these things happening: know that he is near, at the very gates. I tell you solemnly, before this generation has passed away all these things will have taken place. Heaven and earth will pass away, but my words will not pass away.

　　　But as for that day or hour, nobody knows it, neither the angels of heaven, nor the Son; no one but the Father.

Be on your guard, stay awake, because you never know when the time will come. It is like a man traveling abroad: he has gone from home, and left his servants in charge, each with his own task; and he has told the doorkeeper to stay awake. So stay awake, because you do not know when the master of the house is coming, evening, midnight, cockcrow, dawn; if he comes unexpectedly he must not find you asleep. And what I say to you I say to all: Stay awake!"

Mark 13: 14-37

He is on His way: they *have* been warned.

And, of course, it is inevitable that somebody is going to have to allow their own selves to become the conductor on *the* Express train to hell, while continuing to lead the blind farther still: past the point of no return, and into the abyss of truly humanistic brain death. And while allowing their own selves to be accompanied by some of the stupidest human beings while as in the entire history of mankind, and, of course, which will be while allowing their own selves to become capable of saying some of the stupidest things while as in the entire history of mankind also. Such as, that I: the person responsible for communicating this formed understanding of Reality, am probably just plain jealous, and/or envious, of *some* thing, and/or some body, and/or *any* thing, and/or any body, and which is as this word: jealous, does mean: "resentful and envious, as of someone's attainments or of a person because of his attainments, advantages," and too as this word: envy, does mean: "a sense of discontent or jealousy with regard to another's advantages, success, possessions," and which is, of course, exactly impossible, and here's why.

Remember what this communicated understanding, and/or real Edenic tale, was all about: the function which is The Annunciation *and/or* The Mind of God made manifest, actually functioning as Omnidimensional Time *made manifest*: The Eternal Harmony actually functioning as The Kingdom of Heaven, Finding our Innocence Lost and while actually Finding The Entrance to The Garden also, and too which is while actually functioning as the universally applicable Common Law: of simultaneously relative Omnidimensional Time *made manifest*. And too remember, which is while actually functioning as a "real communicable language": as the universally applicable common language of Omnidimensional Time *made manifest*, and The Holy Grail of understanding. And remember also, which was the language that Leonardo da Vinci did learn how to harness – abstract from within Reality, and then reapply. While functioning as the "universally applicable common language" of simultaneously relative Omnidimensional Reality, and as The Holy Grail of understanding, and as the function which is *The Annunciation* also. And – remember too, how as in defining that function, we did use their own words to actually define it: the function which is The Mind of God made manifest and *The Annunciation* also. But remember also, how there was only one single representation of that actual function, while as in the entire history of mankind, and which is *The Annunciation* actually functioning as Omnidimensional Time *made manifest*. Well, now there are three more, and they belong to me. While they are, exactly, what they are, and which is –

"...As we found with quantum mechanics, the full structure of the world is richer than our language can express and our brains comprehend – it is not possible for us to visualize the geometries of dimensions higher than three...There are two essential yet complementary aspects of this new vision of time which are as striking in contrast as heaven and hell. Heaven is ruled by dynamical equations that are reversible and 'timeless'; their simplicity ensures stability for eternity. Hell is more akin to the real world, where fluctuations, uncertainty, and chaos reign..."
The Arrow of Time – Peter Coveny and Roger Highfield

The Eternal Harmony: The Kingdom of Heaven made manifest – The Mind of God made manifest – The Entrance to The Garden – Finding Our Innocence Lost and The Holy Grail of Understanding also, and these are their words: *not mine*. And they are –

"What the frontal lobes 'control' is something like awareness, or self-awareness – Do these lobes govern some essential feature of humanness, or even godliness, as some scientists have suggested? 'If God speaks to man, if man speaks to God,' neuroscientist Candace Pert tells us, 'it would be through the frontal lobes, which is the part of the brain that has undergone the most evolutionary expansion' – Stephen LaBarge: 'And it's capable of what look like miraculous things, so miraculous that we're tempted to say it's devine, that it's not natural."
The 3-Pound Universe – Judith Hooper and Dick Teresi

"God talking back." And the perceivable proof of coming to an understanding of a more divinely purposeful existence, and/or of a more divinely purposeful existence: for human beings to be "in possession of," beyond our excessively simplistic mortal existence, while upon this point-mass of Earth. And they are the function of some thing: "perceivable proof," that would seem to be "not natural," and beyond belief, and almost "miraculous" too. And they actually are, doing –

"Computing One Atom At a Time –
The only hint that anything extraordinary is happening inside – is a small metal sign posted in front: 'Warning! Magnetic Field in Use...The machine at Los Alamos has been enlisted on a recent morning (to) carry out an experiment in Quantum computing – The goal, still but a distant glimmer, is to harness thousands of atoms, resulting in a machine so powerful that it would easily break codes now considered impenetrable and solve other problems that are impossible for even the fastest supercomputer..."
George Johnson – The New York Times – Tuesday March 27, 2001

Exactly what is supposed to be impossible to do, and for even the world's fastest supercomputer. Which *is* becoming capable of actually doing some real time quantum computing, and while – and simultaneously, becoming capable of making manifest the perceivable proof of real Omnidimensional space/time continuums, and which is while seeing, and/or coming to an understanding of, "geometries," which are supposed to be impossible to see, and/or come to an understanding of, also. And they *are* –

"1 million for science to discover God's plan –
Can science divine the hand of God in the universe? – Investment tycoon Sir John Templeton wants to know, and he's paying a total of $1 million to 15 scientists to look for a purpose in the cosmos – The scientists, many with international reputations, have spent their careers studying the Big Bang, the origin of stars and galaxies, the fundamental physical constants, and the origin of life – But the money gives the opportunity to focus on the question that intrigues Templeton, as it has philosophers and astronomers for centuries: Is the universe a product of design or accident..."
Faye Flam – The Philadelphia Inquirer – Saturday April 6, 2002

Exactly what they said they were looking for.
But – remember, their words cannot actually mean anything in Reality. Because it is a neurophysiological impossibility for them to understand anything, while including that which they can not simply see, with their eyes alone. Which is the applicable function of Omnidimensional Time *made manifest,* and/or The Mind of God made manifest, and The Eternal Harmony too. And which: The Mind of God made manifest and/or The Eternal Harmony made manifest, and/or The function which is *The Annunciation* made manifest, and/or Omnidimensional Time *made manifest*, can not be simply seen and with our eyes alone – it can only be understood, and within our truly humanistic, and simultaneously relative Omnidimensional: quantum electrodynamically functioning, minds, and parallel functioning central nervous systems. While actually functioning as simultaneously relative to/from, and within, a single cognizable point time zero: the point of the Big Bang. And, remember, within which: a truly humanistic being's quantum electrodynamically functioning mind, and parallel functioning central nervous system, there are actually contained no projected images of things, but only simultaneously relative differential equations, expanded into simultaneously relative geometrical formations: and/or Time *made manifest,* and while actually functioning as simultaneously relative to/from, and within, a single cognizable point time zero.
So that, we can understand, "what" our truly humanistic, simultaneously relative, three-dimensional electrical potential mass minds, do actually "do": in truly humanistic simultaneously relative Reality, is to perform real time differential equation analysis: as simultaneously relative to/from, and within, an identifiable single cognizable point time zero, and which is a single ten degree point

467

approximately the size of The Apple: while located at a distance of approximately 20 feet within identifiable truly humanistic simultaneously relative space/time, and **NOT** SIMPLY "WITHIN" SPACE. Wherein: the real time differential equation analysis *and* within our three-dimensional electrical potential mass minds, and as simultaneously relative to/from and within a single cognizable point time zero, the first derivative – of the function, identifies the maximum, and minimum, point of the curve, defined by the function, while – simultaneously, the second derivative identifies the point of the greatest change, within the function: as it tends from its maximum to its minimum with respect to *t*, and/or Time. And too which is also while: and exactly "simultaneously," a truly humanistic being's three-dimensional, and quantum electrodynamic potential, mass of a mind, will be performing simultaneously relative sinusoidal – integral – geometrical equation, and trigonometric function analysis, and/or cognizing Time *made manifest*. And – again, only while actually effectually functioning as simultaneously relative "to," " from," and "within," a single cognizable point time zero. And – remember, which is while everything – EVERY "THING," in "simultaneously relative Reality," is –

"There are two essential yet complementary aspects of this new vision of time which are as striking in contrast as heaven and hell. Heaven is ruled by dynamical equations that are reversible and 'timeless'; their simplicity ensures stability for eternity. Hell is more akin to the real world, where fluctuations, uncertainty and chaos reign..."
The Arrow of Time – Peter Coveny and Roger Highfield

The manifestation of chaos, and except for the "thing" that they said they were looking for: Omnidimensional Time *made manifest*, while actually effectually functioning as simultaneously relative to/from, and within, a single cognizable point time zero. And, of course, which: Omnidimensional Time *made manifest*, simply can not exist "upon" a two-dimensional plane, it can only exist within truly humanistic simultaneously relative Omnidimensional Reality: and/or within a truly humanistic being's simultaneously relative Omnidimensional refractive gem of a mind, and parallel functioning central nervous system. And which can then be communicated as a formed understanding of Reality, which is while being projected upon a two-dimensional plane, and which is while functioning as the perceivable proof: of Reality and its formed understanding. And only if an individual human being can –

"Candace Pert: 'I see the brain in terms of quantum mechanics – the brain is just a receiver, an amplifier, a little wet minireceiver for collective reality. We make maps but we should never confuse the map with the territory...'"
The 3-Pound Universe – Judith Hooper and Dick Teresi

Not actually confuse the map with the territory. And/or, only if an individual human being, has not actually regressed back to point time zero, of their own personally affected existence within Reality. And too only if an individual human being, has not experienced truly humanistic brain death for their own selves to be in possession of only, and only if an individual human being has not actually passed the point of no return, and fallen into a black hole of truly humanistic neurophysiological dysfunction, for their own selves to experience, and for eternity too. And/or, only if any individual human being is not –

"Make a tree sound and its fruit will be sound; make a tree rotten and its fruit will be rotten. For the tree can be told by its fruit. Brood of vipers, how can your speech be good when you are evil? For a man's words flow out of what fills his heart. A good man draws good things from his store of goodness; a bad man draws bad things from his store of badness. So I tell you this, that for every unfounded word men utter they will answer on Judgement day, since it is by your words you will be acquitted, and by your words condemned."
Matthew 12: 33-37

Lying.
And because I did simply place it: the "perceivable proof" of The Mind of God made manifest, and The Eternal Harmony, right in front of their very own faces, and which was time, after time, after time, again, and too only after they did, first, claim that they understood the language: of Reality, and/or anything besides their very own selves: and/or their own personally affected truly humanistic brain death, and/or their own worldly political opportunism. And, of course, which did, only, cause me to feel as though I must have been simply transported to some kind of foreign point-mass. Which could only be: in Reality, a fairy tale escape land, where the philosophers rule, and there is *no* rule – except for one rule, the "Rule of the day," but which changes from day to day, and while depending, only, on whose day that day it is only "it" to be. And too, which did seem to be, like no place that was like any place that *could* ever be. And/or – it did seem to be and only to me, a place where up *is* down – in *is* out – left *is* right and right *is* wrong too, but only for a second or two too. And – too it did seem to be but again *only* to me, a place where there is no simultaneously relative *any* thing in Reality, and/or any Reality at all in Reality. So and of course, I did begin to wonder whether, or not, I would ever find any one here: on planet Earth, who could actually see, what I do actually see: in Reality. And too and simultaneously and of course also, time, after time, after time again, they did simply tell me, that I *must* be psychotic: only because they could *not* understand me, and/or Reality. Then I did actually see *The Annunciation*, and so I did – *then*, know that, at least, one other human being, had seen it: Omnidimensional Time *made manifest* and The Mind of God, too. And I did then know, that they had hijacked the name of Leonardo da Vinci, and of The Mind of God made manifest also.
And exactly because if they had *not*: experienced truly humanistic brain

death for their own selves to be in possession of only, and which is while actually effectually regressing back to point time zero, of their own personally affected existence within truly humanistic simultaneously relative Omnidimensional space/time, they could exactly understand, that: While actually effectually occurring within simultaneously relative Omnidimensional space/time, and while as pertinent to cognizing the applicable function of a perceivable Omnidimensional space/time continuum, the perceivable – and simultaneously effectual, applied function of *scales,* actually functions as simultaneously relative, and effectuated harmoniously proportioned, three-dimensional displacements *of* three-dimensional humanistic nothingness, and which is while actually effectually functioning as a simultaneously effectuated quantized succession of *steps* – and/or *degrees*, which are specifically applied to form a simultaneously relative gradated series: of quantized individually completed movements, and/or differentials, and/or notes/atoms/superstrings. Which are capable of effectually functioning, as an effectuated succession of simultaneously relative, and perceivable, three-dimensional tones: made manifest and effectually functioning, as simultaneously relative – individually completed, and harmoniously proportioned, fundamental frequency modulations. Which is: effectually occurring within simultaneously relative Omnidimensional space/time, while – simultaneously, the individually completed – and effectually projected, simultaneously relative, and harmoniously proportioned, fundamental frequency modulations, will be effectually ascending – or descending, *only* while as simultaneously relative to our identifiable humanistic single cognizable point time zero, and while actually positioned within simultaneously relative Omnidimensional space/time. And – remember, which is an actual single cognizable point approximately the size of an Apple, and while located within simultaneously relative space/time, and which: the individually completed fundamental frequency modulations effectually functioning within a quantized gradient, will be effectually occurring "in" exactly harmoniously proportioned intervals: while actually effectually functioning as individually completed continuous quantities. Which will be effectually occurring while the "rate" – of the perceivable change, is only capable of being identified with respect to the distance of the variable quantity, and which does effectually effectuate the formation of a differential operator, and while capable of operating upon a function of the variable. Which results in the effectuation of a "simultaneously relative" wave/radiant function, and which is while effectuated as through the identifiable amount of displacement of three-dimensional nothingness – and/or "0," and while actually effectually functioning as the identifiable amplitude function. Which is capable of being identified by the universally applicable vector function, and – remember, which is while capable of actually effectually functioning within a perceivable, and identifiable, truly humanistic simultaneously relative three-dimensional field, and of: $x - y$ and z, and – too remember, which is while actually affecting our coordinate point system, and/or beginning to identify the simultaneously relative "function" of the "territory," and while *not* confusing the "map" with it: the territory. And which: while actually effectually functioning as a "real" perceivable and identifiable

470

simultaneously relative function, is actually effectually functioning while – simultaneously, the "coordinators" *are* the "identifiable partial derivatives": *of* the effectuated function. And which – while actually effectually functioning as an applicable, and perceivable, function, will be effectually occurring, while the identifiable derivatives exist *as* the ratio of the increment *of* the function *to* the increment of the variable, as it tends "to" – and "from," point time zero. Which will be effectually occurring, while simultaneously identifying the instantaneous change of one effectuated quantity with respect to another, and/or – and especially while effectuated as through a visual musical equivalency, "as" simultaneously relative to all others. Which is the effectuated perceivable change: within an "identifiable field," with respect to Time – and/or *t*, and while effectually functioning as simultaneously with respect to, and from, an identifiable single cognizable *point time zero*: while effectually functioning simultaneously as the Omnidimensional applied function of Time beginning to become "made manifest," and which is while actually effectually preceding, and too as a fundamental prerequisite for, the purposeful formation of a purposefully effectuated Omnidimensional space/time continuum. And while actually effectually functioning as Omnidimensional Time *made manifest* also, and a literal visual musical equivalency AND/OR The Eternal Harmony – The Kingdom of Heaven and The Mind of God made manifest too, and – too, the function which is *The Annunciation*.

Which: while actually effectually functioning as an Omnidimensional space/time continuum and while actually making Time *made manifest*, is the effectuated formation *of* purposefully projected, and/or directed, non tangible form pyramids of rays, and/or vectors, and while actually effectually functioning as projected magnitudes. And too and as we can remember, which is while simultaneously possessing both direction and quantity, and – too and as we can remember, while simultaneously effectually being reduced to a single point, as they are effectually functioning as through their purposefully effectuated, and/or projected, non-tangible form tetrahedrally arranged, and octahedrally formed, dihedral angles. And while – simultaneously, being expanded into simultaneously relative, and harmoniously proportioned, individually completed basic non-tangible form geometrical movements: and/or differential equations, while actually effectually functioning as completed harmoniously proportioned volumes, of truly humanistic, simultaneously relative three-dimensional nothingness, and/or cognizable volumes of space, made manifest as through the applied function of Time. Which: the individually completed geometrical formations, are then – and simultaneously, capable of being simultaneously expanded into a simultaneously relative – geometrically effectuated, and harmoniously proportioned, sub-structure, and/or melodic movement. Which is then also – and simultaneously, capable of being expanded into a simultaneously relative, and geometrically effectuated, harmoniously proportioned whole, and/or Central Keynote Theme, and – remember, as was exactly explained by –

"Wolfgang Amadeus Mozart: The work grows; I keep expanding it, conceiving it more and more clearly until I have the entire composition finished in my head though it may be long. Then my mind seizes it as a glance of my eye a beautiful picture or a handsome youth. It does not come to me successively, with various parts worked out in detail, as they will later on, but in its entirety that my imagination let's me hear it."

Wolfgang Amadeus Mozart, *and* –

"Leonardo da Vinci: Do you not know that our soul is composed of harmony, and that harmony cannot be generated other than when the proportions of the (non-tangible) form are seen and heard instantaneously – The harmonic proportionality (of the whole) is composed simultaneously from various components, the sweetness of which may be judged instantaneously, both in its general and particular affects – in general according to the dictates of the composition; in particular according to the dictates of the component parts from which the totality is composed (and as it) can generate a proportional harmony in the time equivalent to a single glance."

Leonardo da Vinci, *and* –

"Space Mach argued, is not a thing, but an expression of interrelationships among events. '*All* masses and *all* velocities, and consequently *all* forces, are relative,' he wrote. Einstein agreed, and was encouraged to attempt to write a theory that built space and time out of events alone – He never entirely succeeded in satisfying Mach's criteria – but the effort helped propel him toward relativity – Einstein had replaced Newton's space with a network of light beams; *theirs* was the absolute grid, within which space itself became..."
Timothy Ferris – Coming of Age in the Milky Way

Albert Einstein too.
So, what does this mean in simple English? Well, what they: the purposefully affected manifestation *of* identifiable space/time continuums: while functioning as real time quantum computing and while also actually functioning as a representation of The Mind of God made manifest and The Eternal Harmony too, *do* "prove," is that there must be a "purposefully affected cause" for the actual "point time zero": preceding the purposefully affected function of simultaneously relative Omnidimensional space/time, and/or Reality. This does prove that there must have been, and must be, a purposefully affected cause, for the purposefully affected function *of* the point time zero: The Big Bang. And which was, and is, while actually preceding the beginning of Time *made manifest*, and/or *a priori* Omnidimensional Reality: actually functioning as Omnidimensional Time *made manifest*, and while actually functioning as The Mind of God made manifest, and

472

which is while actually functioning as The Eternal Harmony also: and/or The Kingdom of Heaven, and the function which is *The Annunciation*, and – too, while actually finding Our Innocence Lost and The Entrance to The Garden. This: perceivable and identifiable evidence, does prove that there must be a God, and for all the world to simply see with their eyes alone too. But they still won't get it, because this is what else it does mean.

It does mean, that if any individual, can not begin to become capable of –

"Candace Pert: 'I see the brain in terms of quantum mechanics – the brain is just a receiver, an amplifier, a little wet minireceiver for collective reality. We make maps but we should never confuse the map with the territory...'"
The 3-Pound Universe – Judith Hooper and Dick Teresi

Functioning Quantum electrodynamically, and while –

"The sensations which arise from muscle, joint and tendon are conveniently grouped under one heading not because of their anatomical source, but because they collaborate to provide the brain with a distinctive form of information – None of this information could be put to use unless it was firmly located against a fixed horizon; it would float about weightlessly in a vacuum..."
The Body in Question – Jonathan Miller

As simultaneously relative to/from, and within, a single truly humanistic, simultaneously relative and universally applicable, cognizable point time zero, and while actually beginning to become capable of cognizing –

"One way to think about this new view is to imagine spatial relationships as a kind of universal language that the brain uses no matter what specific language, we are using at the moment – (George) Lakoff believes he can tie this mental language to the physical structure of the brain and its maps – 'When you think about dynamic structure, you begin to think there are a lot of things that are analogous with life. Life is more pattern(s) in space/time than it is a set of particular physical things."
Jim Jubak – In The Image of the Brain

Truly humanistic, and purposefully affected, simultaneously relative patterns in space/time, and/or –

"Enter by the narrow gate, since the road that leads to perdition is wide and spacious, and many take it; but it is a narrow gate and a hard road that leads to life, and only a few find it."
Matthew 7: 13-14

Life: they have experienced truly humanistic brain death for their own selves to be in possession of only, if an individually affected human being cannot actually perform this function, for their own selves.

And – *too* and again and remember, which is: if an individually affected human being has actually become incapable of purposefully affecting this simultaneously relative function: of consciously cognizing Time *made manifest*, as they will – actually and neurophysiologically, have allowed their own selves to become capable of being –

"What is a black hole? For astronomical purposes it behaves as a small, highly condensed dark 'body.' But it is not really material body in the ordinary sense. It possesses no ponderable surface. A black hole is a region of empty space – What is known as a space/time singularity – a place where physical laws, as presently understood, must cease to apply..."
Roger Penrose – Black Holes – The World Treasury of Physics, Ed. T. Ferris

Led back to point time zero: *of* their own personally affected existence within truly humanistic simultaneously relative Reality. And they will have allowed their very own selves, to become capable of only –

"Ernst Hanfstaengl, describes the shapelessness at the root of Hitler's mesmerizing oratorical power: 'His brain was a sort of primeval jelly or ectoplasm which quivered in response to every impulse from its surroundings – You could never pin him down, say that he was of this thing or that thing, it was all floating, without roots, intangible and mediumistic...Momentum had driven him into an extreme position from which there was no escape – He was like an airman in a fog, who loses all contact with the earth...'"
Michael Nelken M. D. – Hitler Unmasked

Functioning as Adolf Hitler had allowed his own self to become only neurophysiologically capable of functioning. And – too and of course, which was as Adolf Hitler did –

"Hitler – spent much of the war at his headquarters in the East Prussian forest. To dignify hiding out, he called it Wolf's Lair and had himself called 'Wolf.' Seen from there, Jews were not a huge range of complex creatures – but a single, abstract entity to be erased (and) Hitler never saw a camp; in the abstract, death was simply a by-product of policy – The horrors Hitler brought to the world reenacted the tensions and events of his early life – Adolf became dedicated to evading control by anyone – Robbed of his childhood, Adolf became a grim and severe person...Hitler insists that war is normal, not peace..."
Michael Nelken M. D. – Hitler Unmasked

Never actually "kill" anybody. He did only simply exist while in absolute ignorance of, and/or absolutely abstracted from, Reality. And which was while, enabling his own self to become capable of projecting his own personally affected neurophysiological dysfunction upon mankind, and/or becoming capable of making manifest his own personally affected schizophrenic inarticulate cry for attention, and/or: chaos, and discord, and pain and death and suffering too. And too and of course, which was also while actually believing: within his own personally affected random and amorphous agglomeration of individual nerve cells and/or mind, that it: chaos, and/or discord, and/or pain and death and suffering too and/or his mind, was normal, and which was – of course, only exactly backwards: IN REALITY ONLY, **BUT NOT IN HIS MIND**. And/or also not –

"Hitler – was a tremendous salesman of ideas, an extraordinary orator who could pivot with the mood of an audience and mold it (while) Hitler mocked Germany's moral qualms – and his own: 'To find internal peace – rid the race of the consciousness of its own guilt – Freeing men from (the) dirty and degrading (ideas of) conscience and morality, is my work'...death meant little to Hitler, because neither did life (And) (Guido) Knopp (explained) 'The average German had little idea what was happening to the Jews at the time' – ' Germans knew that something was going on (but) they knew enough to know that they didn't want to know more than they knew."
Michael Nelken M. D. – Hitler Unmasked

Within the mind of any other one individually affected human being, who had also enabled their own selves to become capable of believing him. And/or, to actually become capable of being simply led back to point time zero, and while experiencing truly humanistic brain death for their own selves to be in possession of only. And – too and simultaneously, while actually allowing their very own selves, to become victims of the con: of their truly humanistic, and simultaneously relative, universally applicable empirical self-consciousness, and while simply existing while in absolute ignorance of reality. Exactly as the majority has allowed their own selves to become capable of actually doing, while at this point in time, upon the threshold of the 21st century. And, which will be exactly instead of –

"Lord Jesus Christ, King of glory,
deliver the souls of all the faithful
departed from the pains of hell and from the bottomless pit.
Deliver them from the lion's mouth.
Neither let them fall into darkness
nor the black abyss swallow them up.
And let St. Michael, Thy standard-bearer,
lead them into the holy light
which once Thou didst promise
to Abraham and his seed."

Joining this revolution: and beginning to take back control over their very own selves, and their destinies too.

And exactly because I do know that I am not deluded, I do also know that there are very few people: upon this entire point-mass of Earth and while at this point in time, while upon the threshold of the 21st century, who are actually neurophysiologically capable of performing this function: OF consciously cognizing simultaneously relative Omnidimensional space/time continuums, while actually functioning as the Mind of God made manifest, and/or The Eternal Harmony too. And/or, even neurophysiologically capable of maintaining a single truly humanistic, and simultaneously relative, cognizable point time zero, within their individually affected three-dimensional electrical potential mass minds, and parallel functioning central nervous systems: which is while actually becoming capable of functioning quantum electrodynamically. While they: The Majority, will actually remain neurophysiologically incapable of differentiating between the map and the territory, IT IS SIMPLY A NEUROPHYSIOLOGICAL IMPOSSIBILITY, so they will – and simultaneously, remain incapable of understanding Reality, and/or the fact that they *are* incapable of understanding Reality. And so they will have sealed their very own fate, and –

"Make a tree sound and its fruit will be sound; make a tree rotten and its fruit will be rotten. For the tree can be told by its fruit. Brood of vipers, how can your speech be good when you are evil? For a man's words flow out of what fills his heart. A good man draws good things from his store of goodness; a bad man draws bad things from his store of badness. So I tell you this, that for every unfounded word that men utter they will answer on Judgement day, since it is by your words you will be acquitted, and by your words condemned."
Matthew 12: 33-37

Condemned their very own selves.

Unless, of course, they do *actually* pick up the God "damned" television set, and throw it away. And too they do *actually* stop all of their purposefully allowed exposure to all worldly God "damned" spectacle events, of any and/or all kinds: the God "damned" movies – theater – novels and entertainment, and/or "escaping" of Reality, of any and/or all kinds, and especially for the children: DO NOT GIVE A CHILD A SINGLE PENNY FOR ANY THING – EXCEPT FOR FOOD. And too, *actually* stop all of the purposefully allowed exposure to all of the God "damned" amusement parks – theme parks – spectator sporting event parks – art museum parks and spectacle event parks, of any and/or all kinds. And *actually* stop all of the purposefully allowed exposure to all of the God "damned" excessively simplistic, and histrionic, and monochromatic, and romanticized, musical sounds. And too, *actually* stop all of the God "damned" worshiping of worldly god stars: the movie stars – television stars – spectator sporting event stars – boy band stars – girl band stars – pop icon band stars – composer stars, and musician stars. And *actually* stop

476

all of the purposefully allowed exposure to the God "damned" computers – Internet – virtual reality – dot-coms – cell phones, and video recorders. And too, *actually* stop all of the purposefully allowed exposure to all of the God "damned" parties and aristocratic environments of any and/or all kinds, and *actually* DO NOT EVEN LOOK AT A GRANDIOSLEY STYLED AUTOMOBILE OF ANY AND/OR ALL KINDS – LITERALLY: IF YOU SEE ONE, LOOK THE OTHER WAY. And too drive only a minimalist of an automobile, and a minimal amount of time, and only after you have actually practiced your scales of simultaneously relative Reality, and while as on a daily basis also. And too, *actually* stop all of the purposefully allowed exposure to the all of the God "damned" grandiosely styled trains and airplanes. And too, exactly because –

"...Hitler insisted on quoting for the hundredth time the figures of men and material used in construction on the Siegfried Line' Jodl dryly records: 'There were 4,000 concrete mixers' – In a meeting at the end of August 1943: (Hitler tried) to ramble off into all sorts of technical details – The stenographic notes show Hitler makes no direct references to the trapped men...Sustained by daily injections of amphetamines, Hitler in no way alters his program. Warlimont is beside himself, remembering Hitler's astonishing rigidity, and his ability to draw Germany on: 'The determination of one man possessed of the devil governed everything (and) the German soldier, and civilian, followed this lead..."
Michael Nelken M. D. – Hitler Unmasked

Adolf Hitler never did actually watch any television. He did simply remain incapable of consciously seeing pass a single point, of simultaneously relative space/time, while at any one point within simultaneously relative space/time. Adolf Hitler did, simply, remain addicted to absolutely abstracted, and purely psychopathic and/or schizophrenic, dopamine biochemical inducing stimulus, actually functioning as pure *pleasure* only, and/or the need to become capable of controlling *everything,* and/or to become capable of consuming The Apple, and/or to suckle his Mother's breast: because Adolf Hitler's Mother did actually betray The Child. And so, Adolf Hitler did spend an eternity searching for his Mother's Womb, and/or a single point of rest for his own self to be in possession of, and which he did never find, and as did neither his victims.

And too so, we can know, that you must actually pick up all of your worldly God "damned" stuff: *any thing* that you do own and which does serve no necessary function, and/or which did cost more than a couple of dollars, and while including *all* "decorative" items of any and/or all kinds, and throw it away, and which would be while actually renouncing your worldly self. And which will be as you do actually take off the God "damned" excessively fine fabrics – the God "damned" diamonds – gold and silver, and throw it away. And too, *actually* stop all the God "damned" purposeful consumption of excessively fatty tasting foods, and sweet tasting foods – the *excessive* consumption of alcoholic and caffeine laced beverages. And *actually* stop all of the God "damned" simple accessing of abstract knowledge, and too *actually* stop all of the purposeful accessing of the God "damned" worldly power and money, and which is only but a necessary evil at its absolute best. And *actually* eliminate all of the worldly God "damned" apathy, the God "damned" complacency, the God "damned" ignorance of Reality: The Mind of God made manifest, and too *actually* stop all of the purposefully allowed exposure to *any* amounts of absolutely abstracted, and purely psychopathic and/or schizophrenic, dopamine biochemical inducing stimulus, functioning as pure *pleasure* only and/or The Apple. And to *actually* take all of the money, that would have been spent on all of these worldly things – and while including at least "some" of your real liquid assets, and: FEED THE POOR, of the entire world.

And – in actually so doing, an individual person can become capable of taking back control over their very own self, and while actually becoming capable of breaking free of the attractive force of The Apple: and/or to actually become capable of consciously seeing past its single point, and/or the single point of their very own self, within truly humanistic simultaneously relative Reality. And while actually beginning to become capable of Finding their Innocence Lost: The Entrance to The Garden – The Kingdom of Heaven: The Holy Grail of Understanding *and* The Mind of God made manifest also, and – too, which is while actually effectually functioning as The Eternal Harmony and the function which is *The* Annunciation also. And which is while actually –

> "If anyone loves me he will keep my word,
> and the Father will love him,
> and we shall come to him
> and make our home with him.
> Those who do not love me do not keep my words.
> And my word is not my own:
> it is the word of the one who sent me.
> I have said these things to you
> while still with you;
> but the Advocate, the Holy Spirit,
> whom the Father will send in my name,
> will teach you everything
> and remind you of all I have said to you.
> Peace I bequeath to you,
> my own peace I give to you,
> a peace the world cannot give, this is my gift to you.
> Do not let your hearts be troubled or afraid.
> You heard me say:
> I am going away, and shall return.
> If you loved me you would have been glad to know that I am going to the
> Father,

for the Father is greater than I.
I have told you this now before it happens,
so that when it does happen you may believe.
I shall not talk with you any longer,
because the prince of this world is on his way.
He has no power over me,
but the world must be brought to know that I love the Father
and that I am doing exactly what the Father told me.
Come now, let us go.
John 14: 23-31

Becoming capable of joining this revolution.

And too remember, which is as we can now know, and for a verified scientific fact, that any one individual human being who can not join this revolution, has allowed their own selves to become a victim of the con, and it is a scientific fact. Which is as they have actually allowed their own selves to become capable of regressing back to point time zero: of their own personally affected existence within truly humanistic simultaneously relative Omnidimensional space/time. And actually become neurophysiologically incapable of consciously cognizing past a single point, while at any one point within simultaneously relative Omnidimensional space/time, and/or only capable of consuming The Apple. They have actually allowed their very own selves to become capable of functioning only as an animal *is* capable of functioning, and/or a mindless automaton: they have actually lost control over their very own selves; they have betrayed the Collective Consciousness of Mankind, and they HAVE Sold their souls too.

And which is how we can know, that it is impossible that I: the person who actually was responsible for communicating this formed understanding of universally applicable *a priori* Omnidimensional Reality, actually functioning as the Common Law, could be jealous, and/or envious, of some thing, and/or some body, and/or any thing, and/or any body, and too remember, which is as this word: jealous, does mean: "resentful and envious, as of someone's attainments or of a person because of his attainments." Because remember, this IS *The Annunciation*, and remember too, *The Annunciation*: and/or the abstracted and projected pictorial representation entitled *The Annunciation*, is exactly what started it all, and/or did actually begin the formation for the foundation for the greatest collective con in the entire history of mankind. And – exactly, only because it: *The Annunciation,* is the actual only thing, in the entire history of mankind, which is actually the manifestation of the collective consciousness of mankind, and/or The Mind of God made manifest: The Holy Grail of Understanding – The Eternal Harmony actually functioning as The Kingdom of Heaven and actually Finding our Innocence Lost too: and/or The actual Entrance to the Garden, and/or too, universally applicable Omnidimensional intelligence made manifest, *and while as from one end of the universe to the other*. And – too it is and simultaneously, doing exactly what is supposed to be impossible to do, and/or doing so real time quantum computing also. And it: doing some real time quantum computing and/or making manifest a demonstration of the actual Grand Unification Theory, and/or the Theory of Everything, functioning as an actual representation of The Mind of God made manifest and the Holy Grail of understanding too, is the single thing which Albert Einstein did plainly admit, does actually make everything else – EVERY THING ELSE, seem like "Child's play." And which is while actually becoming capable of reading, and/or being inside, people's minds: which is also a fundamental prerequisite to doing some real time quantum computing, and demonstrating it too. Which I did actually do, and do actually have: representations of the Mind of God made manifest, and the Holy Grail of understanding: The Eternal Harmony actually functioning as The Kingdom of Heaven, and Finding our Innocence Lost – The Entrance to the Garden, and doing some real time quantum computing also. So if *any* "thing" should be worth *any* thing: money, it should be "these," and, remember, according to *them* –

"Grounded by an Income Gap –
For 30 years the gap between the richest Americans and everyone else has been growing so much that the level of inequality is higher than in any other industrialized nation – Why there has been increasing inequality in this country has been one of the big puzzles in our field and has absorbed a lot of intellectual effort, said M-, a professor of economics – 'But if you ask me whether we should worry about the fact that some people on Wall Street and basketball players are making a lot of money, I say no'..."
Alexander Stille – The New York Times – Saturday December 15, 2001

The only thing worth any thing is intelligence: and/or skills, and/or abilities, and/or talents. Which does exactly mean, and while according to their math, that the more difficult, and/or complex, and/or unique, and/or rare, and/or incredible, and/or beyond belief, some thing is, the more money the person who is in possession of it, and/or actually responsible for making it manifest, perceivable and effectual, should actually become capable of acquiring because of it: the thing which they may be in possession of, and/or responsible for making manifest – perceivable *and* effectual. And I've got three of them: the single most valuable things while as in the entire history of mankind: according to *their* math. And only, of course, if I were actually attempting to empower my very own self, and to sell my soul too, which I am not.
And, of course, I am attempting *only* to –

"My teaching is not from myself:
it comes from the one who sent me;
and if anyone is prepared to do his will,
he will know whether my teaching is from God
or whether my doctrine is my own.
When a man's doctrine is his own

he is hoping to get honor for himself;
but when he is working for the honor of the one who sent him, he is sincere
and by no means an impostor.
Did not Moses give you the Law?
And not one of you keeps the Law!"
John 7: 16-19

Glorify God, and His Son too.
So they can take their God "damned" Money, and –

"Hunger is everywhere –
Unprecedented prosperity is the cliché. Millions of hungry Americans are
the reality. Who – and where – are they? You may be surprised – Nationally, 31
million Americans – one in nine, are hungry or at risk of hunger – 'With all of the
talk about the unprecedented economic prosperity, how can you possibly imagine
that people are going hungry?' (Joan) Ulmer said. 'Look at the cost of a box of
cereal. It's amazing."
Lini S. Kadaba – The Philadelphia Inquirer – Sunday January 14, 2001

Feed the poor: To save their very own selves too.
And too and of course, which is as this –

"The kingdom of heaven is like treasure hidden in a field which someone has
found; he hides it again, goes off happy, sells off everything he owns and buys the
field."
Matthew 13: 44

Was *not* a simple metaphorical analogy: It was a Reality.
In Reality, I did actually have to become capable of losing everything I did
ever own, and which wasn't very much, to enable myself to become capable of
making manifest perceivable – effectual, and real, truly humanistic simultaneously
relative Omnidimensional space/time continuums, while actually functioning as truly
humanistic visual musical equivalencies, and as the actual manifestations of real
Eternal Harmonies too. Which was while actually becoming capable of knowing
The Mind of God made manifest – experiencing The Kingdom of Heaven, and
proving it too, and while actually Finding The Entrance to The Garden also. And
which actually is an experience that is like no experience mankind can ever simply
experience: I'VE SEEN IT – IT IS BEYOND BELIEF, and I can prove it too: for
all the world to simply see, and with their eyes alone also. And so that, I do know
how it feels to be hungry, and – too, that: actually losing everything I did own, and
most people that I did know too, and to become capable of actually proving my
formed understanding of Reality, was another lifetime ago: before the constraint of
communicating this formed understanding of Reality, and/or writing this book, was

put on my mind.

But – too, in so doing: actually losing all of my worldly stuff, and exactly because of the worldly psychopathic con-artists and/or worldly vultures, who do actually only pay 10 cents on the dollar *after* they do purposefully create the dysfunction, and/or inflationary processes, was exactly not because I had lost touch with Reality, and/or had exceeded my limits, and/or had failed. But – exactly, because *they* had hijacked the name of Leonardo da Vinci, and intelligence too: I knew exactly what I had done, and was attempting to communicate. And remember, which was because I had spent a lifetime's worth of time, practicing my scales of truly humanistic simultaneously relative Omnidimensional Reality, and while purposefully affecting truly humanistic simultaneously relative multidimensional synaptic capabilities: I had come to understand the Mind of God, and I knew it too. And – too remember, which was exactly simply because I had read the Book, and/or The Letter of The Law, as a young child, and exactly as I was "told to do" – BY THEM: REMEMBER? And which is, as they are the exact ones who have told the world that they are capable of understanding Reality, and/or capable of being intelligent, and actually capable of proving it while as with *their* two-dimensional planes also: and/or their pictures hanging in their Art Museum Parks, and/or exactly where the intelligence is supposed to be: within their minds – remember? Which is exactly why, I did expect to see them: truly humanistic Omnidimensional space/time continuums, EVERYWHERE, and exactly – *only*, instead of truly humanistic brain death: EVERYWHERE, and within their victims too, and remember, which is now The Majority. And which did enable me to experience the single most bizarre experience: of personally affected psychopathic, and/or schizophrenic, behavior, and as The Majority has been affected too, and for my own self to personally witness also.

Which is, that I did actually hear them say, and right to my very face too, and time, after time, after time again also: "Well, you can do what you do to 'relax' – (ESCAPE REALITY), and I'll do what I do to 'relax.'" And too which was even after time, after time, after time again, I did simply explain to them: "NO: THAT IS ONLY EXACTLY BACKWARDS – THAT WAS THE 'CON.'" Within all of their individually affected minds, they do actually sincerely believe, that the function *of* escaping Reality IS EXACTLY THE SAME, as Learning Reality: that the definition of escaping Reality, is the definition of Learning Reality, and that *pain* is *pleasure*. And/or, that purposefully enabling your own self to come to an understanding of The Mind of God made manifest: actually functioning as finding The Kingdom of Heaven, and The Entrance to The Garden too, and/or actually finding your Innocence Lost while experiencing the function of *The Annunciation* also, is simply enabling your own self to become capable of consuming some absolutely abstracted, and purely psychopathic and/or schizophrenic, dopamine biochemical inducing stimulus: actually functioning as pure *pleasure* only, and/or consuming The Apple. And/or, that their *pain* will be *pleasurable*, and which is, of course, *only* –

"Then to all he said, 'If anyone wants to be a follower of mine, let him renounce himself and take up his cross every day and follow me. For anyone who wants to save his life will lose it; but anyone who loses his life for my sake, that man will save it. What gain, then, is it for a man to have won the whole world and to have lost or ruined his very self? For if anyone is ashamed of me and of my words, of him the Son of Man will be ashamed when he comes in his own glory and in the glory of the Father and the holy angels."

Luke 9: 23-26

Exactly backwards.

Which does enable us to simply understand, that I am – exactly, not attempting to empower my very own self, but only individual human beings: for their very own selves, and while at the expense of my very own self: I am going to be leading the way in this revolution.

And, of course, if I were doing that: attempting to empower only my own self and as it is simple to understand, I could have, simply, communicated my formed understanding of the function of "art," and/or intelligence. While continuing to perpetuate the lie, and/or the function of the con, that human beings are supposed to stand in awe in front of something, and/or anything, and/or someone, and/or anyone, and/or even simply enable their own selves to become capable of experiencing a sense of awe, because of something, and/or anything, and/or someone, and/or anyone. And to become capable of "paying a fee" *because* of that experience, and/or relinquish a part of their empirical self-consciousness, to some kind of worldly god: who is providing allowed exposure to an absolutely abstracted, and biochemical inducing, effectual stimulus, of any and/or all kinds. And while continuing to perpetuate the con, and/or the lie, that it: gaining access to any "thing," is Just that easy. And: remember, NO –

"It is like a man on his way abroad who summoned his servants and entrusted his property to them. To one he gave five talents, to another two, to a third one; each in proportion to his ability. Then he set out. The man who had received the five talents promptly went and traded with them and made five more. The man who had received two made two more in the same way. But the man who had received one went off and dug a hole in the ground and hid his master's money. Now a long time after, the master of those servants came back and went through his accounts with them. The man who had received the five talents came forward bringing five more. 'Sir,' he said, 'you entrusted me with five talents; here are five more that I have made.' His master said to him, 'Well done, good and faithful servant; come and join in your master's happiness.' Next the man with the two talents came forward. 'Sir,' he said, 'you entrusted me with two talents; here are two more that I have made.' His master said to him, 'Well done, good and faithful servant; you have shown you can be faithful in small things, I will trust you with greater; come and join in your master's happiness.' Last came forward the man who had the one talent. 'Sir,' he

483

said, 'I heard you were a hard man, reaping where you have not sown and gathering where you have not scattered; so I was afraid, and I went off and hid your talent in the ground. Here it is; it is yours, you have it back.' But his master answered him, 'You wicked and lazy servant! So you knew that I reap where I have not sown and gathered where I have not scattered? Well then, you should have deposited my money with the bankers, and on my return I would have recovered my capital with interest. So now, take the talent from him and give it to the man who has the ten talents. For to everyone who has will more be given, and he will have more than enough; but from a man who has not, even what he has will be taken away. As for this good-for-nothing servant, throw him out into the dark, where there will be weeping and grinding of teeth."

    Matthew 25: 14-30

    It is not.

    And which does enables us to plainly understand, that we: all human beings, are all only "servants": TO GOD, and no human being was ever – EVER, supposed to actually stand in awe in front of any other human being.

    And again and remember, what truly humanistic beings were supposed to actually have done, was to have –

    "One of the scribes who had listened to them debating and had observed how well Jesus answered them, now came up and put a question to him, 'Which is the first of all the commandments?' Jesus replied, 'This is the first: *Listen, Israel, the Lord our God is the one Lord, and you must love the Lord your God with all your heart, with all your soul, with all your mind and with all your strength.* The second is this: You must love your neighbor as yourself. There is no greater commandment than these."

    Mark 12: 28-32

    Actually Carried their crosses each and every day: to have actually gone out each and every day, and practiced their scales of *a priori* Reality. To have enabled their own selves, to become capable of purposefully affecting truly humanistic, and simultaneously relative, multidimensional synaptic capabilities, within their own individually affected minds, and parallel functioning central nervous system. And to have actually enabled their own selves, to become capable of purposefully affecting a truly humanistic, and simultaneously relative, Omnidimensional refractive gem of a mind, and parallel functioning central nervous system, for their own selves to be in possession of only. And which would have *then* – and simultaneously, actually enabled their own selves, to become capable of –

    "If God were your Father, you would love me
    since I have come from God; yes, I have come from him;
    not that I came because I chose,

no, I was sent, and by him.
Do you know why you cannot take in what I say?
It is because you are unable to understand my language."
John 8: 42-43

Speaking the language: of Omnidimensional Time *made manifest,* and of
The Eternal Harmony too. And – too, of The Mind of God made manifest, and while
actually finding our Innocence Lost: finding The Entrance to The Garden, and while
actually gaining access to The Kingdom of Heaven, and the function which is *The
Annunciation*. And, remember, it is a –

"There are two essential yet complementary aspects of this new vision of
time which are as striking in contrast as heaven and hell. Heaven is ruled by
dynamical equations that are reversible and 'timeless'; their simplicity ensures
stability for eternity. Hell is more akin to the real world, where fluctuations,
uncertainty and chaos reign..."
The Arrow of Time – Peter Coveny and Roger Highfield

Scientific fact. And: their words too, not mine.
And –

"Candance Pert: 'I see the brain in terms of quantum mechanics – the brain is
just a receiver, an amplifier, a little wet minireceiver for collective reality…'If God
speaks to man, if man speaks to God,' neuroscientist Candace Pert tells us, 'it would
be through the frontal lobes, which is the part of the brain that has undergone the
most evolutionary expansion' – Stephen LaBarege: 'And it's capable of what look
like miraculous things, so miraculous that we're tempted to say it's divine, that it's
not natural."
The 3-Pound Universe – Judith Hooper and Dick Teresi

Again: *their words – not mine.*
And, again, which is simply because, I did actually spend a lifetime's worth
of time, actually practicing my scales: and/or actually Carrying my cross, and while
enabling myself to become capable of speaking the language. While actually coming
to an understanding of simultaneously relative Omnidimensional *a priori* Reality,
and/or The Mind of God made manifest, and The Eternal Harmony too: the actual
Kingdom of Heaven, and the function which is *The Annunciation* also. And – again,
which does enable us to prove, that It: The Mind of God made manifest and/or the
actual existence of a God, is – exactly, not a belief: IT IS A SCIENTIFIC FACT, for
all the world to simply see, with their eyes alone too. And, I'll even translate them,
and/or the language: of truly humanistic simultaneously relative Omnidimensional
Time *made manifest*, and/or The Mind of God made manifest, and while as into
simple English, and/or a simple spoken language: for all the world to simply see,

and with their eyes alone also *again*.

But remember, that: making manifest a simple perceivable proof for all the world to simply see with their eyes alone, will not enable any one individual person: who has actually not practiced his, or her, scales of Reality and for a lifetime's worth of time, to become capable of experiencing the actual function, which is The Mind of God made manifest and The Eternal Harmony. And/or, the function which is The Kingdom of Heaven and *The Annunciation* also, and while actually finding The Entrance to The Garden too. It will only enable them to become capable of knowing that it does, possibly, exist.

But too remember, if an individual has enabled their own selves to become capable of purposefully affecting an Omnidimensional refractive gem of a mind, and parallel functioning central nervous system: for their own selves to be in possession of only – and NO THINGS WORLDY, they will have also – and simultaneously, actually enabled their own selves to become capable of purposefully affecting a truly humanistic augmenter of a mind, and parallel functioning central nervous system: for their own selves to be in possession of. And/or, a truly humanistic soul to be in possession of, and within which: a truly humanistic being's augmenter of a mind and parallel functioning central nervous system and/or soul, everything will actually be magnified. Which is, while including: The Mind of God made manifest, and/or The Eternal Harmony, and/or The kingdom of Heaven and Finding our Innocence Lost: and/or The Entrance to The Garden, and The function which is *The Annunciation*.

Which I did actually do, and I can prove it too, for all the world to simply see and with their eyes alone. But – too and remember, which was only exactly because I had actually read the Letter of The Law as a young child, and did, then, actually become capable of, willfully, choosing a lifetime's worth of exposure to all relatively painful experienced humanistic phenomena – and/or *pain*, instead of all relatively pleasurable experienced humanistic phenomena – and/or *pleasure*. And while I did not, simply, allow myself to become a part of the In Crowd, and/or simply allow myself to *simply* escape Reality *only* too.

Because I did go in search of the Absolute Truth, and/or: sailing off into uncharted territories, but – too, which actually was a rather arduous journey, and for a lifetime's worth of time. Which, I do admit, I did not particularly want to do, and/or be forced to simply communicate: absolutely abstractly, and while as within this book: my own personally formed understanding of Reality. And/or, to actually have to be subjected to *their* projection too: and/or their personally affected truly humanistic brain death. Who: the majority, will – and simultaneously too, remain *only* capable of projecting their own personally affected neurophysiological dysfunction upon any one other individual human being, who can explain Reality to them, and/or, who will remain only capable of experiencing hatred: for their own selves. Which is as we can now know, that *this* –

"This is my commandment:
love one another,

486

as I have loved you.
A man can have no greater love
than to lay down his life for his friends.
You are my friends,
if you do what I command you.
I shall not call you servants any more,
because a servant does not know
his master's business;
I call you friends,
because I have made known to you
everything I have learned from my Father."
John 15: 12-15

Is not a simple metaphorical analogy only: I'VE DONE THIS FOR YOU, and so that you can experience it also: I am actually going to be leading the way in this revolution, and I will, willfully, be the first to actually die too.

And which was, exactly as –

"The passers-by jeered at him; they shook their heads and said, 'So you would destroy the Temple and rebuild it in three days! Then save yourself! If you are God's son, come down from the cross!' The chief priests with the scribes and elders mocked him in the same way. 'He saved others,' they said, 'he cannot save himself. He is the king of Israel; let him come down from the cross now, and we will believe in him. He puts his trust in God; now let God rescue him if he wants him. For he did say,'I am the son of God."
Matthew 27: 39-44

The Son of God did do *for you* too: remember?

And, remember, which was exactly as He: The Son of God/Son of Man/Collective Consciousness of Mankind made manifest, was forced – actually "FORCED": because of human stupidity and ignorance too, to show Mankind exactly how to get it, and for their own selves to be in possession of only. And, I'm sorry, but ingrates – *exactly*, do not go to heaven.

And all of the Sophists – worldly political opportunists, and psychopathic con-artists too? Well, they: all of the Sophists – worldly political opportunists and psychopathic con-artists, and while as in the entire history of mankind *too*, actually told Mankind, that they could, simply, teach Mankind what power actually is. And so, they said: "Simply allow yourself to become a part of the In Crowd: look at the pretty colors before you – and/or dopamine biochemical inducing effectual stimulus, actually functioning as pure *pleasure* only, and/or simply 'consume' The Apple, experience an orgasm – and/or reach climax, disassociate yourself from the Reality before you, and, then: reapply your childish 'imagination." Perhaps they should look again: It is Time – it *is*...

The Annunciation:

My soul doth magnify the Lord.
And my spirit hath rejoiced in God my Saviour.
For He hath regarded the low estate of His handmaiden:
for, behold, from henceforth (all generations) shall call me blessed.
All generations.
For He that is mighty hath done to me great things;
and holy is His Name.
And His mercy is on them that fear Him from generation unto generation.
He hath showed strength with His arm;
He hath scattered the proud in the imagination of their hearts.
He hath put down the mighty from their seats,
and exalted them of low degree.
He hath filled the hungry with good things;
and the rich He hath sent empty away.
He hath holpen His servant Israel,
in remembrance of His mercy;
As He spake to our fathers,
to Abraham, and to his seed for ever.
Glory be to the Father, and to the Son,
and to the Holy Ghost.
As it was in the beginning, is now, and ever shall be: world without end.
Amen.

Everybody *is* going to die: soon.

And remember, you can be absolutely assured, that any one individual, who can actually do absolutely nothing: to enable their own selves to become capable of joining this revolution, and/or any one individual, who does actually ridicule, and/or belittle, and/or mock, and/or assail, you: *as you do attempt to help them and as you do join this revolution,* is going –

"Whatever town or village you go into, ask for someone trustworthy and stay with him until you leave. As you enter his house, salute it, and if the house deserves it, let your peace descend upon it; if it does not, let your peace come back to you. And if anyone does not welcome you or listen to what you have to say, as you walk out of the house or town shake the dust from your feet. I tell you solemnly, on the day of Judgment it will not go as hard with the land of Sodom and Gomorrah as with that town. Remember, I am sending you out like sheep among wolves; so be cunning as serpents and yet as harmless as doves."
Matthew 10: 11-16

To get exactly what they do deserve. And they are not going to love it.

Printed in the United States
By Bookmasters